Finland

Lapland
p227

Oulu, Kainuu &
Koillismaa
p208

West
Coast
p187

The Lakeland
p144

Karelia
p166

Åland
Archipelago
p108

Tampere
& Häme
p124

Turku & the
South Coast
p74

Helsinki
p42

THIS EDITION WRITTEN AND RESEARCHED BY

Andy Symington, Catherine Le Nevez

BENGTSKÄR LIGHTHOUSE
P91

PYHÄ-LUOSTO NATIONAL
PARK P246

Contents

Welcome to Finland

Finland is deep north: vast horizons of forests and lakes with revitalising crisp air plus cutting-edge urbanity. Choose summer's endless light or winter's eerie frozen magic.

Call of the Wild

The Finland you encounter will depend on the season of your visit, but whatever the month, the call of the wilderness is a siren song not to be resisted. There's something pure in the Finnish air and spirit that's really vital and exciting; it's an invitation to get out and active year-round. With vast tracts of forest, speckled by picture-perfect lakes as if an artist had flicked a blue paintbrush at the map, Suomi offers some of Europe's best hiking, kayaking and canoeing. A fabulous network of national parks has well-marked routes and regularly spaced huts for overnighting. Bears and elk deep in the forests can be observed on nature-watching trips.

Summer Days

Finland's short but reliable sunny season sees the country burst into life. Finns seem to want to suck every last golden drop out of the summer in the hope that it will last them through the long dark winter months, and there's an explosion of good cheer and optimism. It's a time for music festivals, art exhibitions, lake cruises, midnight sunshine on convivial beer terraces, lazy days at remote waterside cottages and mouth-watering market produce.

After the Snowfall

Winter, too, has a special charm as snow blankets the pines and lakes freeze over. The best way to banish those frosty subzero temperatures is to get out and active. For starters, there's great skiing until May. But how about chartering a team of dogs, a posse of reindeer, or a snowmobile for a trek across snowy solitudes, lit by a beautiful, pale winter sun? Catch the aurora borealis (Northern Lights) after your wood-fired sauna and you'll feel blessed by the universe. Need to cool down? A night in an ice hotel or a session of ice-fishing – drill your own hole – should do the trick.

City Lights

Don't get the idea that the country's just a backwoods emptiness, though. Vibrant cities stock the southern parts, headed by the capital, Helsinki, a cutting-edge urban space with world-famous design and music scenes. Embraced by the Baltic, it's an enticing ensemble of modern and stately architecture, island restaurants, and stylish and quirky bars. And complaints about Finnish food are so last century: the 'new Suomi' restaurant scene is kicking, with locally foraged flavours to the fore.

Why I Love Finland

By Andy Symington, Author

My first impression of Finland was a winter one, when snow-hushed forests and Christmastime conviviality made an instant impact. You must come back in summer, everyone said, so I did, for midnight daytime saunas by impossibly picturesque lakes and melt-in-the-mouth fresh berries and potatoes. Fresh air, the Lapland wilderness, the hiking, the wildlife: it's a natural wonderland within an impressively technological modern nation. The real bonus? The Finns, who do their own thing and are much the better for it. Independent, loyal and welcoming – memorable people in an inspirational country. Make it your business to get to know some.

For more about our authors, see page 312

Above: Sámi man with reindeer

Finland

0 ——— 100 km
0 ——— 50 miles

ELEVATION

800m
600m
400m
200m
0

Northern Finland
Hike the north's stunning national parks (p227)

Inari
Learn about Finnish Sámi culture (p255)

Lapland
Explore the area, pulled by a team of huskies (p230)

Kemi
Spend the night in an ice hotel (p237)

RUSSIA

NORWAY

SWEDEN

Barents Sea

White Sea

Arctic Circle

ARCTIC OCEAN

Murmansk
Kirkenes
Nikel
Neiden
Nuorgam
Utsjoki
Lakselv
Karasjok
Kautokeino
Alta
Tromsø
Kilpisjärvi
Kaaresuvanto
Karesuando
Kiruna
Övre
Överkalix
Övertorneå
Pajala
Lappea
Kolari
Muonio
Hetta (Enontekiö)
Pallas-Yllästunturi
Kaamanen
Karigasniemi
Sevettijärvi
Näätämö
Inari
Nellim
Ivalo
Raja-Jooseppi
Lemmenjoki
Saariselkä
Tankavaara
Urho Kekkonen
Tulppio
Kovdor
Alakurtti
Salla
Savukoski
Tanhua
Pelkosenniemi
Oulanka
Riisitunturi
Kandalaksha
Kuusamo
Posio
Syöte
Pudasjärvi
Ranua
Kemijärvi
Pyhä-Luosto
Sodankylä
Unari
Napapiiri
Rovaniemi
Sinettä
Tornio
Kemi
Haparanda
Boden
Luleå
Perämeri
Kittilä
Köngäs
Ylläsjärvi
Pello
Kongas

69°N
68°N
66°N

14°E 15°E 16°E 17°E 18°E
31°E 34°E 35°E 36°E 37°E

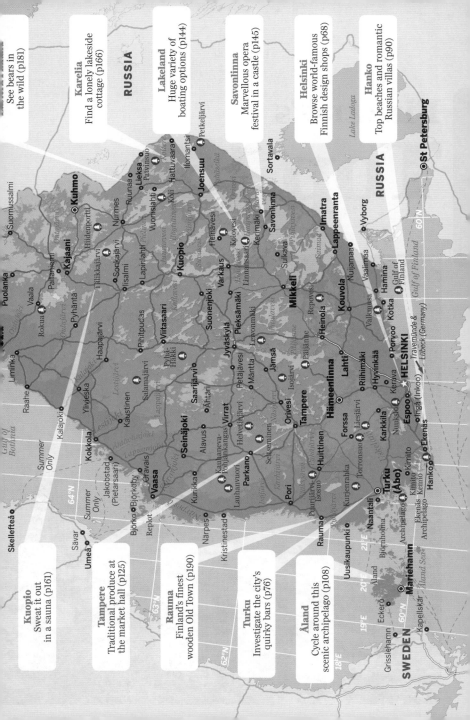

See bears in the wild (p181)

Karelia
Find a lonely lakeside cottage (p166)

RUSSIA

Lakeland
Huge variety of boating options (p144)

Savonlinna
Marvellous opera festival in a castle (p145)

Helsinki
Browse world-famous Finnish design shops (p68)

Hanko
Top beaches and romantic Russian villas (p90)

Kuopio
Sweat it out in a sauna (p161)

Tampere
Traditional produce at the market hall (p125)

Rauma
Finland's finest wooden Old Town (p190)

Turku
Investigate the city's quirky bars (p76)

Åland
Cycle around this scenic archipelago (p108)

Finland's
Top 15

1

National Park Hiking, Northern Finland

1 Finland's great swathes of protected forests and fells make it one of Europe's prime hiking destinations. Head to the Karhunkierros (p223) near Kuusamo for a striking terrain of hills and sharp ravines, never prettier than in autumn. The Urho Kekkonen National Park (p253) in Lapland is one of Europe's great wildernesses; the spectacular gorge of the Kevo Strict Nature Reserve (p260) and the fell scenery of Pallas-Yllästunturi National Park (p243) are other great northern options. A network of camping huts makes planning easy and are good spots to meet Finns. Hiking the Karhunkierros (Bear's Ring) Trek (p223)

Sledding & Snowmobiling, Lapland

2 Fizzing over the snow behind a team of huskies under the low winter sun is tough to beat. Short jaunts are great, but overnight safaris give you time to feed and bond with your lovable dogs and try out a wood-fired sauna in the middle of the winter wilderness. It's no fairy-tale ride though; expect to eat some snow before you learn to control your team. If you're more of a cat person, you can enjoy similar trips on a snowmobile or behind reindeer. Dog-sledding near Umnas, Lapland

Design Shopping, Helsinki

3 Functional, elegant, outrageous or wacky: the choice is yours. The capital's decidedly nonmainstream chic is best explored by browsing the vast variety of design shops that spatter its centre. Whether examining iconic 20th-century Finnish forms in the flagship emporia of brands such as Iittala, Marimekko and Artek, or tracking down the cutting-edge and just plain weird in the bohemian Punavuori district, you're sure to find something you didn't know you needed but just can't do without. Candleholders by designer Alfredo Haberli, Iittala (p68) Helsinki

Music Festivals

4 Are you a chamber-music aficionado? Or do you like rock so raucous it makes your ears bleed? Whatever your pleasure, Finland has a music festival to suit. Savonlinna's castle is the dramatic setting for a month-long opera festival (p147); fiddlers gather at Kaustinen for full-scale folk; Pori, Espoo and Tampere attract thousands of jazz fans; Seinäjoki flashes sequins and high heels during its five-day tango festival; Turku's Ruisrock is one of several kicking rock festivals; and the Sibelius Festival in Lahti ushers in autumn with classical grace. Savonlinna Opera Festival (p147)

Bear-Watching, Eastern Finland

5 Old Honeypaws, the brown bear (*Ursus arctos*), is the national animal of Finland. Around a thousand of these creatures live in the northeast, coming and going with impunity across the Finnish–Russian border. Several operators run bear hides where you can sit a night's vigil as bruins snuffle out elk carcasses and hidden chunks of salmon. The best time to see them is between mid-April and August – with a gap in July when the bears have mating rather than meals in mind.

Summer Cottages

6 The symbol of the Finnish summer is a cottage perched on a placid blue lake, with a little rowboat, a fishing pier and its own swimming beach. The simplest rustic cabins have outside loos and water drawn from a well, while the most modern designer bungalows have every comfort, from state-of-the-art coffee machines to infrared saunas. Whether you're looking for a wilderness escape – picturesque Karelia offers some of Finland's most deeply forested corners – or somewhere for a big family party, you're bound to find the perfect place.

Food Markets, Tampere

7 Counters selling local cheeses, rough rye breads, handmade chocolates, Finnish sausages and smoked fish fill each town's indoor kauppahalli (covered market). Tampere's (p125) is typical – try traditional *mustamakkara* (blood sausage). In summer the kauppatori (market square) bursts with straight-from-the-garden vegetables: tiny new potatoes, mouthfuls of juicy red strawberries, or peas popped fresh from the pod. Autumn brings piles of peppery chanterelles and glowing Lapland cloudberries. Kauppahalli in Tampere (p131)

Sámi Culture, Inari

8 Finland's indigenous northerners have used technology to ease the arduous side of reindeer herding while maintaining an intimate knowledge of Lapland's natural world. Their capital, Inari, and the nearby Lemmenjoki National Park are the best places to begin to learn about Sámi culture and traditions, starting at the marvellous Siida (p255) museum. Arrange wilderness excursions with Sámi guides, meet reindeer and browse high-quality handicrafts and music. Sámi man and reindeer, Lapland

MARLEEN / GETTY IMAGES ©

OLIVER GOUJON / ROBERT HARDING ©

Traditional Sauna, Kuopio

9 These days most Finns have saunas at home, but there are still a few of the old public ones left. They smell of old pine, tar shampoo and long tradition, with birch whisks and no-nonsense scrubdowns available as extras. Weathered Finnish faces cool down on the street outside, loins wrapped in a towel and hand wrapped around a cold beer. Helsinki and Tampere are the best places for this, while Kuopio's old-style smoke sauna (p161) takes a day to prepare and offers a more rural experience, with a lake to jump into right alongside.

On the Water, The Lakeland

10 This part of Finland seems to have more water than land, so it'd be a crime not to get out on it. You can take three days to paddle the family-friendly Oravareitti (Squirrel Route) or head out into Kolovesi and Linnansaari National Parks (p151) to meet freshwater seals. Tired arms? Historic lake boats still ply what were once important transport arteries; head out from any town on short cruises, or make a day of it and head from Savonlinna right up to Kuopio or across Finland's largest lake, Saimaa, to Lappeenranta. Lake Saimaa (p168)

Barlife

11 Rumours about Finnish beer prices are a little exaggerated, and there's a big social drinking scene here that's great to take part in. Finns lose that famous reserve after a *tuoppi* (half-litre glass) or three of beer and are keen to chat to foreigners; it's the best way to meet local people. The main cities are full of original and offbeat bars, and you'll soon find a favourite Suomi tipple, whether it's the Finnish ciders, microbrewed beers, sweet-and-sour *lonkero* (ready-made mix of gin and fruity soft drink), or unusual shots such as salty liquorice vodka or cloudberry liqueur. Boat bars, Turku (p82)

MOORAK GAEL / GETTY IMAGES ©

Seaside Hanko

12 Offering some of Finland's finest beaches, genteel Hanko(p90), the country's southernmost town, has a history intimately connected with Russia. The St Petersburg gentry for whom it was a favoured summering place have left a noble legacy of achingly lovely wooden villas, while the area saw heavy fighting in WWII when it was occupied by Russia and locals forced to evacuate. Today the long sandy peninsula is all about yachts and sandcastles rather than gunboats and trenches and makes a great place to relax.

Cycling, Åland Archipelago

13 Charming Åland is best explored by bicycle (p116): you'll appreciate its understated attractions all the more if you've used pedal power to reach them. Bridges and ferries link many of its 6000 islands, and well-signposted routes take you off 'main roads' down winding lanes and forestry tracks. Set aside your bicycle whenever the mood takes you, to pick wild strawberries, wander castle ruins, sunbathe on a slab of red granite, visit a medieval church, quench your thirst at a cider orchard, or climb a lookout tower to gaze at the glittering sea.

Snow Hotels, Kemi

14 Just the words 'snow hotel' can shoot a shiver up your spine, but spending a night in one of these ethereally beautiful, artistic icy buildings is a marvellous, though expensive, experience. There are several to choose from in Lapland, including Lumihotelli (p237) in Kemi; heavy-duty sleeping bags ensure a cosy slumber, and a morning sauna banishes any lingering chills. Even if you don't fancy spending the night, you can visit the complexes, maybe pausing for a well-chilled vodka cocktail in the bar.

Rauma Old Town

15 The largest wooden Old Town in the Nordic countries, Vanha Rauma (p190) deserves its Unesco World Heritage status. Its 600 houses might be museum pieces, but they also form a living centre: residents tend their flower boxes and chat to neighbours, while visitors meander in and out of the low-key cafes, shops, museums and artisans' workshops. Rauman giäl, an old sailors' lingo that mixes up a host of languages, is still spoken here, and the town's medieval lace-making heritage is celebrated during Pitsiviikko (Rauma Lace Week).

CHRISTOPHE BOISVIEUX / GETTY IMAGES ©

Need to Know

For more information, see Survival Guide (p287)

Currency
Euro (€)

Language
Finnish
Swedish
Sámi languages
English is widely spoken

Visas
Generally not required for stays of up to 90 days; some nationalities will need a Schengen visa.

Money
ATMs are widespread. Credit/debit cards are accepted for most transactions.

Mobile Phones
Local SIMs, including data, are cheap and easy if you have an unlocked phone. Roaming rates apply, but are low or zero for EU phones.

Time
East European Time (GMT/UTC plus two hours).

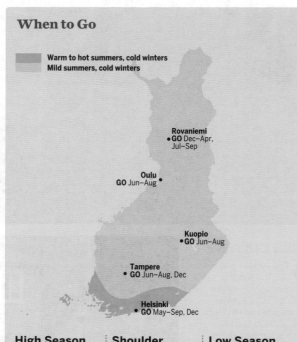

When to Go

Warm to hot summers, cold winters
Mild summers, cold winters

Rovaniemi
• GO Dec–Apr, Jul–Sep

Oulu
GO Jun–Aug •

Kuopio
• GO Jun–Aug

Tampere
• GO Jun–Aug, Dec

Helsinki
• GO May–Sep, Dec

High Season
(Jul)

➡ Attractions and lodgings open, including summer budget accommodation.

➡ Hotels outside Helsinki are often substantially cheaper.

➡ Boat cruises running.

➡ Festivals across the country.

Shoulder Season
(Jun & Aug)

➡ Long days, decent temperatures.

➡ Most attractions are open.

➡ Not as crowded as July.

➡ Fewer insects up north.

➡ Country shuts down Midsummer weekend.

Low Season
(Sep–May)

➡ Outside cities, many attractions are closed.

➡ Hotels charge top rates except on weekends.

➡ December to April is busy for winter sports.

➡ Short, cool or cold days.

Useful Websites

Metsähallitus (www.outdoors.fi) Truly excellent resource, with detailed information on all Finland's national parks and protected areas.

Finnish Tourist Board (www.visitfinland.com) Excellent official site.

Helsinki Times (www.helsinki times.fi) English-language newspaper.

This is Finland (finland.fi) Maintained by the Ministry of Foreign Affairs, excellent, informative and entertaining.

Lonely Planet (www.lonely planet.com/finland) Destination information, bookings, travel forum and more.

Important Numbers

Eliminate the initial zero from area/mobile codes if dialling from abroad.

Finland's country code	☏358
International access code	☏00
General emergency	☏112

Exchange Rates

Australia	A$1	€0.65
Canada	C$1	€0.69
Japan	¥100	€0.68
New Zealand	NZ$1	€0.62
Norway	NKr10	€1.06
Russia	R100	€1.17
Sweden	Skr10	€1.05
UK	UK£1	€1.26
USA	US$1	€0.80

For current exchange rates, see www.xe.com.

Daily Costs

Budget: Less than €120

➡ Dorm bed: €25–€35 – HI membership gets you 10% off many hostels

➡ Bike hire per day: €10–€20

➡ Lunch specials: €8–€16

➡ Two-hour bus/train to next town: €25–€40

Midrange: €120–€250

➡ Standard hotel double room: €80–€130

➡ Two-course meal for two with wine: €100–€160

➡ Week-long car hire: €40–€50 per day

Top end: Over €250

➡ Room in boutique hotel: €150–€300

➡ Upmarket degustation menu for two with wine: €200–€300

➡ Taxi across town: €20–€30

➡ Two-hour husky sled ride: €90–€140

Opening Hours

Many attractions in Finland only open for a short summer season, typically mid-June to late August. Opening hours tend to shorten in winter in general.

Alko (state alcohol store) 9am–8pm Monday to Friday, to 6pm Saturday

Banks 9am–4.15pm Monday to Friday

Businesses & shops 9am–6pm Monday to Friday, to 3pm Saturday

Nightclubs 10pm–4am Wednesday to Saturday

Pubs 11am–1am (often later on Friday and Saturday)

Restaurants 11am–10pm, lunch 11am–3pm. Last orders generally an hour before closing.

Arriving in Finland

Helsinki-Vantaa airport (p70) Local buses and faster Finnair buses run into the city from 5am to 1am (30 to 45 minutes). Taxis cost €45 to €55 to the city centre (30 minutes). Cheaper shared airport taxis cost from €29. The airport to city rail link will open in 2015 (30 minutes).

Tampere-Pirkkala airport (p134) Buses meet all arriving flights (30 to 40 minutes to the city centre). Shared taxis cost €19, standard taxis €35 (20 minutes to the city centre).

Getting Around

You can set your watch by Finnish transport. For bus timetables, head to www.matkahuolto.fi, for trains it's www.vr.fi.

Train Generally modern and comfortable, with good coverage. Book busy routes in advance.

Car Hire widely available, week or weekend deals booked in advance much better than sky-high day rates. Drive on the right.

Bus Around the same price as trains but slower. Cover the whole country. Rarely need booking.

Flights Generally expensive but you can get some good deals on Lapland routes, saving time and money over the train.

For much more on **getting around**, see p293

If You Like...

Wildlife

Bears Observe these magnificent carnivores through the long summer evenings from the comfort of a hide in Kuusamo, among several other places. (p220)

Elk These large beasts are widespread over Finland but harder to see now that increased fencing tends to keep them off the roads. Try an elk-watching safari out of Kuhmo for your best chance. (p217)

Reindeer These domesticated animals are ubiquitous in Lapland, so much so that they are a real hazard on the roads. There are numerous places where you can meet and feed them, or take a sled safari with them in winter.

Wolverines With luck, you'll spot this elusive predator on a trip out of Lieksa. (p181)

Seals The rare Saimaa ringed seal is a freshwater variety, best seen by grabbing a canoe and exploring the lakes of the Kolovesi and Linnansaari national parks. (p151)

Music Festivals

Finland's passion for music of all varieties is reflected in its summer program of festivals: a continuous wall of sound across the nation.

Tangomarkkinat The Pohjanmaa town of Seinäjoki packs out with four days of tango singing and dancing. (p199)

Air Guitar World Championships Imaginary instruments are the order of the day as the highlight of a music video festival in Oulu. (p211)

Ruisrock Finland's oldest and biggest rock festival descends upon Turku's Ruissalo island in July. (p80)

Kuhmon Kamarimusiikki Excellent chamber music festival in the remote northeastern forests. (p218)

Savonlinna Opera Festival Finland's prettiest town hosts excellent opera in the incomparable setting of its majestic island castle. (p147)

Sibelius Festival Lahti's famous orchestra tackles Finland's most famous composer. (p142)

Pori Jazz Festival Finland's biggest jazz festival livens up the west coast port of Pori. (p196)

Kaustinen Folk Music Festival This famous festival is one of Finland's summer highlights. (p205)

Offbeat Accommodation

Are people suckers for paying top dollar to sleep in subzero temperatures or is a night in the icy splendour of a snow hotel a passport to frosty paradise? You decide.

Lumihotelli On the Lapland coast, a romantic snow castle offers stylish chateau sleeping in what is the most spectacular of Finland's snow hotels. (p237)

Lainio Snow Village Down vodkas from icy glasses in the igloo bar, then snuggle up atop your icy mattress here in western Lapland. (p240)

Arctic Snow Hotel In easy reach of Lapland's capital, this friendly place also boasts an ice restaurant. (p234)

Kylmäpihlajan Majakka Have an away-from-it-all experience in this lighthouse hotel on a west coast island. (p192)

Art

Helsinki Several worthwhile galleries, headed up by the Ateneum – a real 'who's who' of Finnish art – and the contemporary Kiasma gallery. (p49)

Espoo Adds two more to the picture: the Gallen-Kallelan Museo and its impressive Espoo Museum of Modern Art (EMMA). (p71)

Mänttä This small town has a great gallery, Gösta, with a striking modern annexe for contemporary works. (p136)

Tampere Stunning frescoes by Hugo Simberg adorn the interior of the cathedral. (p126)

Visavuori Visit the lakeside studio of sculptor Emil Wickström. (p136)

Vaasa This west-coast city has several small galleries and styles itself as an art capital. (p199)

Traditional Architecture

Once upon a time, all towns in Finland were picturesque rows of painted wooden houses. Wars and a succession of great fires started by some unwary baker or smoker put paid to most of them, but some classic examples remain.

Porvoo Classic wooden warehouses and a noble Old Town less than an hour from Helsinki. (p98)

Rauma Vanha Rauma, the Old Town, is the most extensive and intriguing wooden district left in Finland. (p190)

Jakobstad An area of unspoiled wooden homes stretches north of the centre. (p203)

Turku Luostarinmäki is a historic quarter of the city that has been preserved in situ as a museum. (p76)

Naantali The quaint old cobbled streets here make for a very picturesque stroll. (p83)

Hanko Opulent wooden villas built for Russian aristocracy line the streets of this coastal town. (p90)

Kerimäki Enormous church planned by a churchman who overestimated the willingness of his congregation to attend his services. (p151)

Top: Wolverine, Lieksa (p181)
Bottom: Pori Jazz Festival (p196)

Saunas

The sauna is where Finns go to sweat away their troubles, to socialise, or to contemplate the mysteries of life. While you'll come across electric saunas in hotels and apartments, it's worth seeking out some of the more traditional varieties.

Kuopio The sociable Jätkänkämppä smoke sauna is fired up here twice a week, a great chance to try this traditional type with its softer steam. (p161)

Tampere Over a century old, the venerable Rajaportin Sauna is a classic of its kind. (p129)

Helsinki There are several offbeat saunas in bars and cafes, but the Kotiharjun Sauna in working-class Kallio is a winner for its traditional atmosphere and optional scrub down. (p55)

Cabin rentals The best sauna of them all is a wood-burning one that you've managed to light yourself. Rent a cabin by a lake somewhere and try it out. Add beer and sausages afterwards for the most classic Finnish experience. (p289)

Island-Hopping

Finland has tens of thousands of islands, ranging from suburbs of Helsinki to rocky islets in the middle of nowhere.

Ukko In Lapland's enormous Lake Inari, this island has traditionally been a Sámi sacred spot and can be visited on a boat trip. (p256)

Åland This archipelago between Finland and Sweden is ripe for exploration using local ferries or a sea kayak. (p108)

Island dining Head out to one of the island restaurants in Helsinki harbour for a seafood dinner with great views. (p62)

Kvarken This intriguing landscape of islands west of Vaasa is constantly changing. (p203)

Hailuoto Grab the ferry out to this island near Oulu for a peaceful northerly beach break. (p214)

Bengtskär Finland's southernmost inhabited island is famous for its staunch Baltic lighthouse. (p91)

Turku archipelago Freewheel around this complex of islands south of Turku by bike. (p86)

National parks There are five maritime national parks dotted along Finland's coast, and it's great to hire a boat and potter around the islands. One of these is near Ekenäs. (p28)

Traditional Dishes

Smoked fish Head to any market in the country for a huge array of salmon and other fish; such as Hakaniemi in Helsinki. (p64)

Lemin särä Majestic mutton roast, cooked on a birch tray, is a gastronomic highlight. (p171)

Ålandspannkaka Hit the Åland archipelago for semolina pudding with stewed prunes. (p108)

Kalakukko Tasty rye loaf stuffed with *muikku* (vendace, or whitefish, a small lake fish), a speciality of Kuopio. (p161)

Game Dine on bear, elk or grouse by the Ruka ski slopes. (p220)

Comfort food Finnish staples like herring, meatballs and liver in the unchanged '30s atmosphere of Sea Horse in Helsinki. (p64)

Mustamakkara This black sausage is a Tampere speciality and best eaten with a dollop of lingonberry jam. (p131)

Karjalanpiirakka Rice-filled pastry that has its origins in Karelia and is best tried with traditional egg butter topping. (p166)

Reindeer Staple meat of Lapland that's found right across the region, including Rovaniemi. (p231)

Modern Architecture

Jyväskylä University town central to Alvar Aalto's work; you can also visit his experimental summer house nearby. (p156)

Musiikkitalo This cool, crisp music centre is the latest addition to Helsinki's stable of elegant buildings. (p66)

Tampere Tampere's striking concert hall, built in 1990, glistens like a glacier. (p133)

Temppeliaukion Kirkko Helsinki's most striking church is bored into a hill of solid rock. (p50)

Seinäjoki Aalto was given licence to experiment as he redesigned the centre of this western Finnish town. (p198)

Sibeliustalo By the waterside in Lahti, this spectacular wood and glass auditorium is the home of the city's garlanded symphony orchestra. (p141)

Month by Month

January

It's cold. Very cold and very dark. But this is the beginning of the active winter; there's enough snow for the ice hotels, and sledding, snowmobiling and skiing are reliable.

☆ Skábmagovat

In the third week of January, this is a film festival (www.skabmagovat.fi) with an indigenous theme held in the Sámi capital of Inari.

🛏 Ice Hotels

It's a memorable experience to spend a night in one of these ethereally beautiful places.

February

Skiing really kicks off in northern Finland, with a peak holiday season around the middle of the month.

🎉 Runeberg Day

This day, on 5 February, commemorates Finland's national poet. Flags are flown at half mast and people eat 'Runeberg tarts'.

March

Hours of light dramatically increase and temperatures begin to rise: an excellent time to take advantage of the hefty snow cover and indulge in some winter activities.

🏃 Sled Safaris & Skiing

Whizzing across the snow pulled by a team of huskies or reindeer is a pretty spectacular way to see the northern wildernesses. Add snowmobiling or skiing to the mix and it's a top time to be at high latitude.

🏃 Tervahiihto, Oulu

In the March snow of Oulu, Tervahiihto (Tar Ski Race; www.tervahiihto.fi) is a historic skiing race that's been running for over a century.

🎉 Reindeer Racing

Held over the last weekend of March or first of April, the King's Cup in Inari is the grand finale of Finnish Lapland's reindeer-racing (www.paliskunnat.fi) season and a great spectacle.

April

Easter is celebrated in a traditional fashion. Spring begins in southern Finland, but there's still solid snow cover in the northern reaches. It's a great month for outdoor activities in Lapland.

🎉 Pääsiäinen (Easter)

On Easter Sunday people go to church, paint eggs and eat *mämmi* (pudding of rye and malt). The Sunday before, kids dress as witches and bless neighbouring houses in exchange for treats.

☆ Tampere Biennale

Festival featuring new Finnish music, held in even-numbered years only (www.tamperemusicfestivals.fi).

☆ April Jazz

Held in Espoo on the outskirts of Helsinki, this has jazz with big-name artists and big crowds (www.apriljazz.fi).

May

A transitional month in the north, with snow beginning to disappear and signs of life emerging after the long winter. In the south, spring's in full flow. This is a quiet but rewarding time to visit.

☆ Vappu

Traditionally a festival of students and workers, this also marks the beginning of summer, and is celebrated with plenty of alcohol and merrymaking. Held 1 May.

June

Midsummer weekend in late June is celebrated with great gusto, but it's typically a family-and-friends event. Lapland's a little muddy, but the rest is warm and welcoming.

☆ Praasniekka

These Orthodox celebrations are day-long religious and folk festivals held in North Karelia and other eastern provinces between May and September, most notably around the end of June.

☆ Juhannus (Midsummer)

The most important annual event for Finns. The country completely shuts down as people head to summer cottages to celebrate the longest day of the year with bonfires, dancing and copious drinking. Ornate poles are decorated and raised in Åland. Seurasaari sees the best celebration around Helsinki. Held the weekend closest to 22 June.

☆ Music Festivals

The glut of summer music festivals in Finland begins. Provinssirock (www.provinssirock.fi) is a big three-day rock fiesta in Seinäjoki; Kuopio Tanssii ja Soi is a major dance extravaganza in Kuopio (www.kuopiodancefestival.fi); and Mikkeli Music Festival (www.mikkelinmusiikkijuhlat.fi) serenades that city with classical pieces.

☆ Midnight Sun Film Festival

Round-the-clock screenings in Sodankylä (www.msff.fi) while the never-setting sun circles around the sky outside. Great atmosphere in this small Lapland town.

☆ Helsinki Päivä

Celebrations (www.helsinkipaiva.fi) of the capital's anniversary are a busy time to be in town, with lots of events and activities around Esplanadin Puisto (Esplanade Park) on 12 June.

July

Peak season sees long, long days and sunshine.

Finland really comes to life, with festivals throughout, boat trips, activities, cheaper hotels and a celebratory feel. Insects in Lapland are a nuisance.

☆ Savonlinna Opera Festival

A month of excellent performances in the romantic location of one of Europe's most picturesquely situated castles makes this Finland's biggest summer drawcard for casual and devoted lovers of opera (www.operafestival.fi).

☆ Ruisrock

Finland's oldest and possibly best rock festival (www.ruisrock.fi) takes place in early July on an island just outside the southwestern city of Turku. Top Finnish and international acts take part.

☆ Wife-Carrying World Championships

Finland's, nay, the world's premier wife-carrying event (www.eukonkanto.fi) is held in the village of Sonkajärvi in early July. Winning couples (marriage not required) win the woman's weight in beer as well as significant kudos.

☆ Tangomarkkinat

Finnish tango is an institution, and the older generations converge on Seinäjoki in this massive celebration of singing and dancing (www.tangomarkkinat.fi) in early July.

☆ Sulkavan Suursoudut

This massive rowing festival (www.suursoudut.fi) in the Lakeland is all about participation...and downing lager in what turns into one of Finland's biggest parties. Second Sunday in July.

☆ Pori Jazz Festival

The nation's biggest jazz event (www.porijazz.fi) packs out the port city of Pori on the west coast over a week in mid-July. More than a hundred concerts, free jam sessions, and dancing in the street make this hugely enjoyable.

☆ Kaustinen Folk Music Festival

This tiny cereal-belt settlement hosts a massive folk music and dance knees-up in the third week of July. It's so emblematic that in Peanuts cartoons in Finland, Woodstock is called Kaustinen (www.kaustinen.net).

☆ Kuhmon Kamarimusiikki

In remote Kuhmo, this is an excellent fortnight of chamber music (www.kuhmofestival.fi), with concerts featuring a large bunch of young and talented performers from around Europe.

☆ Other Music Festivals

There are numerous others. Imatra draws international big bands (www.ibbf.fi); Tammerfest (www.tammerfest.fi) rocks Tampere; and the Hamina Tattoo (www.visithamina.fi) has military music in even years.

⭐ Jyväskylän Kesä

This multifaceted festival (www.jyvaskylankesa.fi) makes sure the university town of Jyväskylä stays

lively in summer. It's one of Finland's oldest and most important arts festivals.

⭐ Pitsiviikko, Rauma

A week in late July sees the old wooden centre of Rauma come alive with music and cultural events, as well as lace-making demonstrations and a carnival (www.pitsiviikko.fi).

⭐ Kotkan Meripäivät

The port of Kotka celebrates this maritime festival (www.meripaivat.com) at the end of the month. It features music, sailing races and cruises.

⭐ Unikeonpäivä

In Naantali, the 'laziest person' (usually actually the mayor or someone important) is thrown into the sea in the morning, sparking a day of festivities (www.naantali.fi).

August

Most Finns are back at work, so it's quieter than July but still with decent weather across most of the region. It's a great time for hiking in Lapland or biking in Åland.

☆ Air Guitar World Championships

Tune your imaginary instrument and get involved in this crazy rockstravaganza (www.airguitarworldchampionships.com) held in Oulu in late August as part of a music video festival. This surfeit of cheesy guitar classics and seemingly end-

less beer is all in the name of world peace.

☆ Neste Oil Rally Finland

Rallying is huge in Finland, and the local leg of the world championship, held around Jyväskylä, is a massive event (www.nesteoilrallyfinland.fi) that draws half a million spectators, normally in early August. The town packs out for a huge party.

⭐ Siirrettävien Saunojen

Kind of like Wacky Races but with saunas, these mobile building championships (www.sauna-ajot.com) near Närpes offer a solid portion of offbeat Finnish humour and frivolity.

☆ Ijahis Idja

Over a weekend usually in August in Inari, Lapland, is this excellent music festival (www.ijahisidja.fi) that features groups from all spectra of Sámi music.

☆ Helsingin Juhlaviikot

Held over two weeks and three weekends from late August to early September, the all-arts Helsinki Festival (www.helsinginjuhlaviikot.fi) keeps the capital pumping with loads of events, including plenty for kids.

September

The winter is fast approaching: pack something warm. Autumn colours are spectacular in northern forests, making it a great hiking month. Many attractions and activities close.

 Ruska Hiking

Ruska is the Finnish word for the autumn colours, and there's a mini high season in Kainuu, Koillismaa and Lapland as hikers take to the trails to enjoy nature's brief, spectacular artistic flourish.

☆ Sibelius Festival

Performances by the famous Lahti Symphony Orchestra, honouring composer Jean Sibelius, in the city's spectacular waterside auditorium (www.sinfoni alahti.fi).

October

Snow is already beginning to carpet the north. It's generally a quiet time in Finland, as locals face the realities of yet another long winter approaching.

✕ Baltic Herring Fair

Traditional outdoor herring market (www.portof helsinki.fi), held since 1743 in Helsinki in the first week of October.

November

Once the clocks change in late October, there's no denying the winter. November's bad for winter sports, as there's little light and not enough snow. It can be a good month to see the aurora borealis (Northern Lights), though.

 Aurora-Watching

Whether or not you are blessed with seeing the aurora borealis is largely a matter of luck, but the further north you are, the better the chances. Dark, cloudless nights, patience, and a viewing spot away from city lights are the other key factors.

December

The Christmas period is celebrated enthusiastically with cinnamon smells, warming mulled drinks, and festive traditions putting the meaning back into the event.

 Itsenäisyyspäivä

Finland celebrates its independence day on 6 December with torchlight processions, fireworks and concerts.

Joulu (Christmas)

Pikkujoulu (little Christmas) parties, with plenty of *glögi* (hot punch) consumed, dot the lead-up to the main event, which features a family meal on Christmas Eve. Lapland sees Santas galore, reindeer, and plenty of kitschy but fun Christmas spirit.

Itineraries

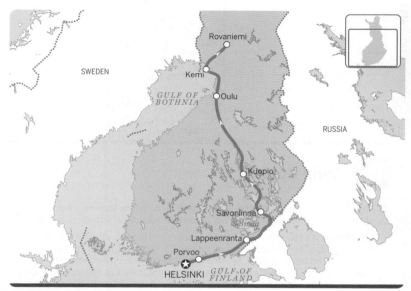

 **Essential Suomi**

This highlights tour of Finland covers some of the best places the country has to offer, with cities, castles, lakes, saunas and Santa on the menu.

Kick-off in capital **Helsinki**, prowling the buzzing design district and unwinding in excellent restaurants and bars. Hit Suomenlinna or an island restaurant to get a feel for the archipelago, and day trip to historic **Porvoo's** enchanting wooden buildings. Next head to **Lappeenranta** on the shores of Finland's largest lake. Then – go by boat in summer – it's gorgeous **Savonlinna**, where the stunning castle hosts an opera festival. It's a memorable place with plenty to do in the surrounding area: take your time.

Then to the heart of the Lakeland, **Kuopio**, another segment you can do on a lake boat. Try to time your visit to coincide with the convivial smoke sauna. The high latitudes are in evidence once you get to **Oulu** – depending on the season, the sun barely sets or barely rises. It's one of Finland's liveliest towns, with a great summer marketplace.

In winter stop in **Kemi** to see the snow castle and take an ice-breaker cruise. Finally, head to **Rovaniemi**, capital of Lapland and a great base for any number of activities. From there, explore the north or get the sleeper train back to Helsinki.

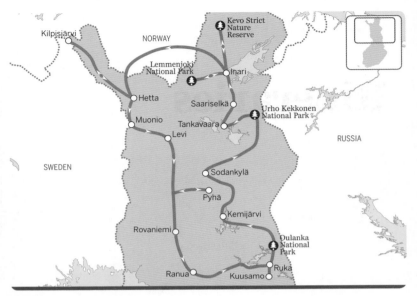

Lapp Gold

10 DAYS

Lapland's unique charms deserve plenty of time. This can be done in a week, but take two if you can, giving yourself time for some of the numerous activities on offer.

Rovaniemi is Lapland's capital and a logical place to start. It's also a good spot to hire a car. Santa Claus is the big crowd-puller here, but the real don't-miss attraction is the excellent Arktikum museum to learn about these northern latitudes. Further south in **Ranua**, you can see some of the region's fauna at its zoo. Cut eastward to **Ruka**, a lively winter ski resort and activity base. Here, there's walking to be done in **Oulanka National Park**, including the Karhunkierros, one of Finland's best treks. You can also canoe some great river routes and go bear-watching from nearby **Kuusamo**.

From Ruka, head north via **Kemijärvi** to **Sodankylä**. Don't miss the wonderful old wooden church. Continue north through ever-more-sparsely populated territory; when you reach **Urho Kekkonen National Park**, you're in one of Europe's great wildernesses. Take some time out for a hike across the fells, or try gold-panning at **Tankavaara**. **Saariselkä** is the best base to organise all sorts of summer and winter activities.

Inari, one of Lapland's most intriguing towns, is the capital of Finland's Sámi, a handicrafts centre and home to the memorable Siida museum. Next it's nearby **Lemmenjoki National Park**, where treks, river trips, gold-panning and more Sámi culture await. With time, head up to **Kevo Strict Nature Reserve** for a great three-to-four day trek.

Continue the loop towards northwest Finland, perhaps cutting through Norway, ending up at **Hetta**, another Sámi town, and trailhead for more excellent walking. If you have time, take a detour up the 'arm' of Finland to remote **Kilpisjärvi**, in the shadow of fearsome Norwegian mountains and the smaller bulk of Saana Fell, a rewarding climb with some memorable views over three nations.

Then **Muonio**. In winter you should go husky-sledding, but even in summer it's worth meeting the lovable dogs. Finally, return to Rovaniemi, stopping to ski or rent a summer cottage at built-up **Levi** or peaceful **Pyhä**.

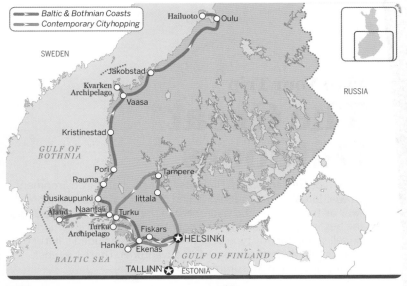

 ## Contemporary Cityhopping

10 DAYS

Finland's thriving design and music industries mean that its cities, though small, pack plenty of contemporary punch.

Take a few days to get to know **Helsinki**. Check out the Design Museum, then Punavuori's small studios and shops. See what's on at Kaapelitehdas and Korjaamo cultural centres, and pay Kiasma a visit. Fine-dining restaurants and stylish, quirky or just plain weird bars make the evenings fly by.

Ferryboat across to **Tallinn**, Estonia's capital. The traditional architecture of the Old Town meets post-Soviet creative energy in an intriguing mix. Back in Helsinki, aim for **Tampere**, a model of post-industrial regeneration. Take in the bohemian vibe and stunning lakescapes, and head for a halfday trip down to **Iittala** to see the home of one of Finland's iconic design brands.

Cut southwest down to **Turku**. The country's stateliest city has plenty going on, whether it's the Ruisrock festival or the latest exhibition in Ars Nova, the contemporary art centre that hosts the Turku Biennaali. Head back to Helsinki along the coast. Thirsty for more? Sort out your visa and St Petersburg is just a train ride away.

 ## Baltic & Bothnian Coasts

10 DAYS

This trip takes you through Swedish- and Finnish-speaking communities and gives the chance to see picture-perfect wooden towns and sparkling blue water.

Heading west from Helsinki, stop at the pretty ironworks village of **Fiskars**, near family-friendly seaside **Ekenäs**. Then on to the noble wooden villas of **Hanko**, where St Petersburg society once summered. **Turku** has many drawcards, as does the surrounding **archipelago** and picturesque **Naantali**. Further offshore, **Åland** offers cycling and maritime history.

Uusikaupunki's museum deserves a prize for ironic humour, while **Rauma** features charming wooden buildings. **Pori** hosts a pumping jazz festival. The next coastline is 'Parallel Sweden': first stop **Kristinestad** with its Swedish-speaking majority. **Vaasa** has an excellent museum. West of here, **Kvarken archipelago** is an ever-changing landscape.

Jakobstad's Old Town rivals Rauma's for beauty. Beautiful coastline runs north to **Oulu**. Stop off at **Hailuoto** island for a relaxing stay by the sandy beach; it's not often you can have a dip this far north.

Plan Your Trip

The Great Outdoors

Finland's beauty and appeal lie in its fantastic natural environment, with vast forests, long waterways and numerous lakes to explore, as well as the harsh Arctic wilderness in the north. Getting outdoors is the best way to experience the country and Finland is remarkably well set up for any type of activity, from all-included safari-style packages to map-and-compass DIY adventures. There's almost unlimited scope in both summer and winter.

Hiking Essentials

When to Hike

June to September is the main hiking season in Finland.

Where to Hike

There's a wide range of national parks with marked trails offering anything from short strolls to multiday treks.

What to Take

Insect repellent! There are literally clouds of biting insects, especially in July, and especially in Lapland. You'll have to bring and carry all food when you walk in wilderness areas. Though there are plenty of huts to overnight in (sleeping bag and sleeping mat required), your own tent gives more flexibility and protection from mosquitoes.

How to Plan a Hike

Finland's protected areas are comprehensively covered in English by the website www.outdoors.fi. It details walking routes, including all camping and other accommodation possibilities.

National Parks

Finland's excellent network of national parks and other protected areas is maintained by **Metsähallitus** (Finnish Forest & Park Service; www.outdoors.fi). At last count, there were 38 national parks that made up a total area of over 8000 sq km. A similar amount of territory is protected under other categories, while further swathes of land are designated wilderness reserves. In total, over 30,000 sq km – some 9% of the total area – is in some way protected land.

The Metsähallitus website provides wonderful information on all these spots; the organisation also publishes individual leaflets on each park.

The largest and most pristine national parks are in northern Finland, particularly Lapland, where vast swathes of wilderness invite trekking, cross-country skiing, fishing and canoeing.

Many of the national parks have excellent networks of wilderness huts that provide cosy free places to overnight on hiking routes.

Finland's National Parks

0 ——— 100 km
0 ——— 50 miles

Hiking

The superb system of national parks offers memorable trekking throughout Finland in the summer months. The routes are backed up by resources for camping and overnighting in huts, so it's easy to organise a multiday wilderness adventure.

National parks offer excellent marked trails, and most forest and wilderness areas are criss-crossed by locally used walking paths. Nights are short or nonexistent in summer, so you can walk for as long as your heart desires or your feet permit.

It's important to remember what the Finnish landscape does and doesn't offer. You will get scented pine and birch forest, low hills, jewel-like lakes and brisk, powerful rivers. Don't expect epic mountainscapes and fjords; that's not Finland.

The trekking season runs from late May to September in most parts of the country. In Lapland the ground is not dry enough for comfortable hiking until mid-June, and mosquitoes and horseflies are an irritation during July. The first half of September is the *ruska* (autumn hiking) season, when the forests are alive with a glorious palette of autumn colours; it's a very popular time to take to the trails. The insects have long since disappeared, and if there's a bit of a chill in the air in Lapland, all the better for ruddy-faced treks through the forests.

If heading off trekking on your own, always advise someone of your route and intended arrival time/date, or note these details in trekkers' books in huts and hostels.

Right of Public Access

The *jokamiehenoikeus* (literally 'everyman's right') is an ancient Finnish code that gives people the right to walk, ski or cycle anywhere they like in forests and other wilderness areas – even across private land – as long as they behave responsibly. Canoeing, rowing and kayaking on lakes and rivers is also unrestricted. You can rest and swim anywhere in the Finnish countryside, and camp for one night *almost* anywhere. Travel by motorboat or snowmobile, though, is heavily restricted.

Watch out for stricter regulations regarding access in nature reserves and national parks where access might be confined to marked paths.

Camping

Everyman's right allows you to rest and camp temporarily in the countryside without permission, even on private property as long as you don't do so near homes. Try to camp on already-used sites to preserve the environment. Camping is not permitted in town parks or on beaches, and in national parks and reserves it may be restricted to certain designated areas.

Under the right of public access, you cannot make a campfire on private land unless you have the owner's permission. In

GREAT NATIONAL PARKS

NATIONAL PARK	FEATURES	ACTIVITIES	WHEN TO GO
Lemmenjoki	Broad rivers and old-growth forests; golden eagles, reindeer	Trekking, boating, gold-panning	Aug-Sep
Linnansaari & Kolovesi	Luscious lakes and freshwater seals	Canoeing	May-Sep
Oulanka	Pine forests and river valleys; elk, white-tailed eagles; calypso flowers	Trekking the Bear's Ring, canoeing, rafting	late Jun-Sep
Urho Kekkonen	Fells, mires and old Sámi settlements; reindeer, flying squirrels	Trekking, cross-country skiing, fishing	Jul-Sep & Nov-Apr
Archipelago & Ekenäs Archipelago	Strings of islets and skerries; seals, eider ducks, greylag geese	Boating, fishing	May-Sep
Nuuksio	Forest within striking distance of Helsinki; woodpeckers, elk, divers	Nature trails	May-Oct
Patvinsuo	Broad boglands and old forest; bears, beavers, cranes	Hiking	Jun-Oct
Pallas-Yllästunturi	Undulating fells; bears, snow buntings, ptarmigans	Hiking, trekking, skiing	Jul-Sep & Nov-Apr

national parks, look for a designated campfire area *(nuotiopaikka)*, and watch for fire warning signs – *metsäpalovaroitus* means the fire risk is very high. Felling trees or cutting brush to make a campfire is forbidden; use fallen wood instead.

Huts & Shelters

Metsähallitus operates a huge network of free, properly maintained wilderness huts across its swathe of national parks and protected areas. Huts typically have sleeping platforms, cooking facilities, a pile of dry firewood and a compost toilet. You are required to leave the hut as it was – ie replenish the firewood from the woodshed and carry away your rubbish. The Finns' 'wilderness rule' states that the last person to arrive will be given the best place to sleep, but, on busy treks in peak season, it's good to have a tent, because someone usually ends up sleeping outside. You may also sleep sounder in a tent, as the huts tend to fill with mosquitoes as the evening goes on.

Some huts require advance booking, or have a separate, lockable section with sleep-mats that must be booked ahead (usually €11 per bed). This is called a *varaustupa*.

Various other structures, including day huts and tepee-style *kotas* (Sámi huts) in Lapland, are designed for cooking and for temporary or emergency shelter from the weather. In a *laavu* (simple log shelter), you can pitch your tent inside or just roll out your sleeping bag.

It's a sociable scene in wilderness huts – take a bottle of something to join in the sharing culture.

The website www.outdoors.fi has invaluable information on huts and hiking routes; a 1:50,000 trekking map is recommended for finding wilderness huts. These are published by **Karttakeskus** (www.karttakauppa.fi) and cost €19.90 from tourist offices, national park visitor centres or online.

Where to Trek

You can hike anywhere in Finland, but national parks and reserves have marked routes, designated campfire places, well-maintained wilderness huts and boardwalks over the boggy bits.

NORDIC WALKING

Finland is proud of having invented the burgeoning sport of Nordic Walking, which was originally devised as a training method for cross-country skiers during the summer months. Basically, it involves using two specially designed hand-held poles while briskly walking; it may look a little weird at first, but involves the upper body in the activity and results in a 20% to 45% increase in energy consumption, and an increase in heart rate, substantially adding to the exercise value of the walk. Nordic Blading is a speedier version, using poles while on in-line skates, while Nordic skating is the on-ice equivalent.

Lapland is the main trekking region, with huge national parks that have well-equipped huts and good, long hiking routes. There are other classic trekking areas in the Kainuu and Koillismaa regions, and in North Karelia, which has several long-distance forest trails.

Excellent trekking maps are available in Finland for most of the recommended routes.

Hetta–Pallastunturi One of western Lapland's best walks heads through light forest and up and down fells offering spectacular views for 55km through national park.

Karhunkierros (Bear's Ring) The most famous of all Finnish trekking routes, this trail in northern Finland covers 80km of rugged cliffs, gorges and forest.

Karhunpolku (Bear's Trail) This 133km marked hiking trail of medium difficulty leads north from Lieksa through a string of stunning national parks and nature reserves.

Kevo Route A fabulous point-to-point or loop walk of 64km to 78km through a memorable gorge in far-north Lapland.

UKK Route The nation's longest trekking route is this 240km route through northern Finland. It starts at Koli Hill, continues along the western side of Lake Pielinen and ends at Syöte. Further east, there are more sections.

FOREST FOOD

Except in strict nature reserves, it's permissible to pick berries and mushrooms – but not other kinds of plants – under Finland's right of public access. Finns do so with gusto, filling pails with blueberries, which come into season in late July, and delicious little wild strawberries. But there are more. Bearberries, cowberries (lingonberries), crowberries, cranberries, whortleberries and more are there to look out for. But the prize is the cloudberry, so appreciated by Finns that you may not have a chance to sample this orange, slightly sour, creamy berry in the wild. Edible mushrooms are numerous in Finnish forests, as are poisonous ones; make sure you have a mushroom guide or know your stuff.

Seasonal Planning

The big swing between the seasons in Finland means that preparing for a trip depends greatly on when you want to go. Pack decent thermals and a warm top layer for winter visits, when temperatures can easily be 20ºC below, or less. A cosy hat and proper gloves, and eyewear if you're going out on the snow, are also essential.

In summer you can shed the long johns, but plan on protection of a different nature. The insect season is a short one, but the clouds of mosquitoes, gnats, black flies and horseflies make the most of it. This isn't the kind of blood donor you want to be so, especially in July, especially in Lapland, and especially if you're hiking or camping, a heavy-duty insect repellent will be your best friend.

Cycling

Riding a bike in Finland is one of the best ways to explore parts of the country in summer. The country is flat, main roads are in good condition and traffic is generally light. Bicycle tours are further facilitated by the liberal camping regulations, excellent cabin accommodation at camp-grounds, and the long hours of daylight in June and July.

The drawback is this: distances in Finland are vast. It's best to look at planning shorter explorations in particular areas, and combining cycling with bus and train trips – Finnish buses and trains are very bike-friendly.

Even if your time is limited, don't skip a few quick jaunts in the countryside. There are very good networks of cycling paths in and around most major cities and holiday destinations (for instance, the networks around Oulu and Turku).

In most towns bicycles can be hired from sports shops, tourist offices, campgrounds or hostels for €15 to €25 per day, or €50 to €90 a week.

Bikes on Buses & Trains

Bikes can be carried on long-distance buses for €3 to €12 (often free in practice) if there is space available (and there usually is).

Bikes can accompany passengers on most normal train journeys, with a surcharge of up to €5. Inter-City (IC) trains have spaces for bikes, which should be booked in advance; take your bike to the appropriate space in the double-decker wagon – you can lock it in with a 50-cent coin, You can take your bike on regional trains that have a suitcase symbol on the timetable; put it in the luggage van.

Where to Cycle

You can cycle on all public roads except motorways. Many public roads in southern Finland have a dedicated cycling track running alongside.

Åland

The Åland islands are the most bicycle-friendly region in Finland, and the most popular region for bicycle tours. The flat, scenic terrain, manageable distances, network of ferries and general absence of traffic make the archipelago ideal.

Southern Finland

Southern Finland has more traffic than other parts of the country, but with careful planning you can find quiet roads that offer pleasant scenery. Around Turku, the Archipelago route offers excellent coastal scenery and island-hopping.

Karelia & Northeastern Finland

Two themed routes cover the whole eastern frontier, from the south to Kuusamo in the north. Runon ja Rajan tie (Poem and Border Rte) consists of secondary sealed roads, and passes several typical Karelian villages before ending in Lieksa. Some of the smallest and most remote villages along the easternmost roads have been lumped together to create the *Korpikylien tie* (Road of Wilderness Villages). This route starts at Saramo village in northern Nurmes and ends at Hossa in the northeastern Kainuu region.

A recommended loop takes you around Lake Pielinen, and may include a ferry trip across the lake. Another good loop is around Viinijärvi, west of Joensuu.

Western Finland

This flat region, known as Pohjanmaa, is generally good for cycling, except that distances are long. The scenery is mostly agricultural, with picturesque wooden barns amid fields of grain in this breadbasket of Finland. The 'Swedish Coast' around Vaasa and north to Kokkola is the most scenic part of this area.

Winter Sports

Winter's a wonderful time to get active in Finland. For most activities, the best time is in March and April; you get a decent amount of light, and temperatures are more acceptable.

Sled Safaris & Snowmobiling

Whether you head out for an hour, or on an epic week-long adventure, being whisked across the snow by an enthusiastic team of huskies or reindeer is an experience like no other. Lapland is the best place to do this, but it's also available further south in places like Nurmes and Lieksa. Driving a sled takes a bit of practice, so expect sore arms and a few tumbles at first.

Similar excursions can be made on snowmobiles (skidoos). Operators are in the same locations offer these trips. You'll need a valid driving licence to use one.

Prices for both sled safaris and snowmobiling are normally based on two sharing, taking it in turns to drive. If you want one to yourself, expect a hefty supplement.

Downhill Skiing & Snowboarding

Finnish slopes are generally quite low and so are well suited to beginners and families. The best resorts are in Lapland, where the fells allow for longer runs. In central and southern Finland, ski runs are much shorter, averaging about 1km in length.

The ski season in Finland runs from late November to early May and slightly longer in the north, where it's possible to ski from October to May. Beware of the busy Christmas, mid-February (or early March) and Easter holiday periods – they can get very crowded, and accommodation prices go through the roof.

You can hire all skiing or snowboarding equipment at major ski resorts for about €35/120 a day/week. A lift pass costs around €40/200 a day/week (slightly less in the shoulder and off-peak seasons), although it is possible to pay separately for each ride. Skiing lessons are also available and start at around €60 for an hour's lesson for two.

The best resorts are Levi, Ruka, Pyhä-Luosto and Ylläs, but Syöte, Koli, Pallas, Ounasvaara and Saariselkä are also good.

Cross-Country Skiing

Cross-country skiing is one of the simplest and most pleasant things to do outdoors in winter in Finland. It's the ideal way to explore the beautiful, silent winter countryside of lakes, fells, fields and forests, and is widely used by Finns for fitness and as a means of transport.

Practically every town and village has a network of ski tracks *(latu or ladut)* around the urban centre, in many cases illuminated *(valaistu)*. The one drawback to using these tracks is that you'll need to bring your own equipment (or purchase some), as rentals often aren't possible.

Cross-country skiing at one of Finland's many ski resorts is an easier option. Tracks are much longer and also usually better maintained. Ski resorts offer excellent instruction and hire out equipment. The best cross-country skiing is in Lapland, where resorts offer hundreds of kilometres of trails. Keep in mind that there are few hours of daylight in northern Lapland during winter – if you're planning on a longer trek, spring is the best time. Cross-country skiing is best during January and February in southern Finland, and from December to April in the north.

Water Sports

Rowing, Canoeing & Rafting

With 10% water coverage, Finland has always been a boating country, and until relatively recently boats were an important form of transport on the lakes and rivers. Every waterside town has a place (most frequently the campground) where you can hire a canoe, kayak or rowboat by the hour or day. Rental cottages often come with rowboat included that you can use free of charge to investigate the local lake and its islands.

Canoes and kayaks are suitable for longer adventures lasting several days or weeks. Route maps and guides may be purchased at local or regional tourist offices and at Karttakeskus (p31), which takes orders via its website. Canoe and kayak rentals cost €25 to €45 per day, and €90 to €200 per week, more if you need overland transport to the start or end point of your trip.

Where to Row & Paddle

The sheltered bays and islands around the Turku archipelago and Åland in southwest Finland are good for canoeing in summer.

Finland's system of rivers, canals and linked waterways means there are some extensive canoeing routes. In the Lakeland, the Kolovesi and Linnansaari national parks are excellent waters for canoeing, and offer plenty of exploration opportunities. North Karelia, particularly around Lieksa and Ruunaa, also offers good paddling. Rivers further north are fast-flowing, with tricky rapids, making many of them suitable for experienced paddlers only.

Ivalojoki Route (easy) A 70km route along the Ivalojoki, in northeast Lapland, that starts at the village of Kuttura and finishes in Ivalo, crossing 30 rapids along the way.

Lakeland Trail (easy to medium) This 350km route travels through the heart of the lake district (Kangaslampi, Enonkoski, Savonranta, Kerimäki, Punkaharju, Savonlinna and Rantasalmi) and takes 14 to 18 days.

Oravareitti (easy to medium) In the heart of the Lakeland, the 'Squirrel Route' is a well-marked two- or three-day trip from Juva to Sulkava.

Oulankajoki and Kitkajoki (easy to difficult) A variety of choices on these neighbouring rivers in a spectacular wilderness area of northeast Finland.

Savonselkä Circuit (easy to difficult) The circuit, near Lahti, has three trails that are 360km, 220km and 180km in length. There are many sections that can be done as day trips and that are suitable for novice paddlers.

Seal Trail (easy) Explore the watery national parks of Kolovesi and Linnansaari, maybe spotting a rare ringed seal from your canoe.

Plenty of operators offer whitewater rafting expeditions in canoes or rubber rafts. The Ruunaa area is one of the best of many choices for this adrenalin-packed activity.

Fishing

Finnish waters are teeming with fish, and with people trying to catch them; Finns must be among the Earth's most enthusiastic anglers. Commonly caught fish include salmon, trout, grayling, perch, pike, zander (pike-perch), whitefish and Arctic char.

With so many bodies of water there is no shortage of places to cast a line, and not even the lakes freezing over stops the Finns. Lapland has the greatest concentration of quality fishing spots, but the number of designated places in southern

---

ICE-FISHING

Nothing stops a Finn on a mission for fish. Not even when the winter closes in, the lakes freeze over, and the finny tribes below grow sluggish and hope for a breather from those pesky hooks.

No, the intrepid locals just walk or drive out to a likely spot on the ice, carve a hole using a hand drill, unfold the campstool, and drop in a line. And wait, even if the temperature is around -30°C. Seriously warm clothes and your choice of a flask of coffee or a bottle of Koskenkorva complete the picture.

Many tour operators offering winter activities organise ice-fishing excursions.

Finland is also increasing. Some of the most popular fishing areas are the spectacular salmon-rich Tenojoki in the furthest north, the Tornionjoki, the Kainuu region around Kajaani, Ruovesi, Hossa, Ruunaa, Lake Saimaa around Mikkeli, Lake Inari, and the Kymijoki near Kotka, where the tsar used to catch his dinner.

Tourist offices can direct you to the best fishing spots in the area, and usually can provide some sort of regional fishing map and put you in touch with local guides. Fishing equipment of varying quality is widely available for hire from campgrounds and other accommodation providers in fishy areas.

The websites www.fishinginfinland.fi and www.fishing.fi have plenty of useful information in English on fishing throughout the country.

Permits

Several permits are required of foreigners (between the ages of 18 and 64) who wish to go fishing in Finland, but they are very easy to arrange. The website www.mmm.fi has all the details. Simple angling with hook and line requires no permit; neither does ice-fishing, unless you are doing these at rapids or other salmon waterways.

For other types of fishing, first you will need a national fishing permit, known as the 'fisheries management fee'. A permit is €7/24 per week/year; they're payable online or at any bank or post office. Second, fishing with a lure requires a regional permit (€7/31), also available online or at banks and post offices. In addition to this a local permit may be required. There are often automatic permit machines; tourist offices, sports shops and campgrounds can also supply permits. The waters in Åland are regulated separately and require a separate regional permit.

The Metsähallitus website (www.outdoors.fi) details fishing restrictions in protected areas.

Birdwatching

Birdwatching is increasingly popular in Finland, in no small part because many bird species migrate to northern Finland in summer to take advantage of the almost continuous daylight for breeding and rearing their young. The best months for watching birds are May to June or mid-July, and late August to September or early October.

Limanganlahti (Liminka Bay), near Oulu, is a wetlands bird sanctuary and probably the best birdwatching spot in Finland. Other good areas include Puurijärvi-Isosuo National Park in Western Finland, Siikalahti in the Lakeland, Oulanka National Park near Kuusamo, the Porvoo area east of Helsinki and the Kemiö islands. Dave Gosney's *Finding Birds in South Finland* and *Finding Birds in Lapland* are field handbooks on birding sites with many practical tips. You can order them online at www.easybirder.co.uk.

Check out www.birdlife.fi for a good introduction and a few links for birdwatching in Finland.

Plan Your Trip
Travel with Children

Finland is incredibly child friendly, and is a terrific place to holiday with kids. Domestic tourism is largely dictated by children's needs, and child-friendly attractions abound in the height of summer, while winter brings its own snowy delights, including Santa.

Best Regions for Kids

Helsinki
Many attractions, with trams, boats, zoo, Linnan-mäki amusement park, and Serena waterpark at Espoo. Most museums have child-friendly exhibits.

Åland Archipelago
Flat archipelago perfect for family cycling and gentle beaches; also has forts and castles both stone and bouncy.

The Lakeland
The castle at Savonlinna and scope for watery activities make this region one of the best for children.

West Coast
Theme parks at Vaasa, sandy beaches at Yyteri and Kalajoki, and tranquil shores.

Turku & the South Coast
Moominworld at Naantali is a magnet for the young. Turku itself offers rope courses, skiing and karting, while the Sirius Sport Resort in the southeast has flying, surfing and more.

Lapland
Winter wonderland with Kemi's snow castle, sled trips and children's ski runs. In summer there's gold-panning, meeting reindeer or huskies, and national parks. The region's most famous resident, Santa, is at Napapiiri year-round.

Finland for Kids

Planning a trip for kids could include splashing about on lakes and rivers, hikes in national parks, and cycling. In winter the snow opens up a world of outdoor possibilities, and there's also the Santa Claus angle in Lapland. There are several standout theme parks across the country, and even potentially stuffy museums make the effort to engage kids, with simplified child-height information, hands-on activities, interactive displays. Boat trips, canoeing and fishing are available almost everywhere, and large towns all have a swimming complex that includes water slides and Jacuzzis.; excellent for all ages year-round.

Children's Highlights

Castles
➡ Raseborg, perch near Ekenäs (p96).

➡ Savonlinna, an island castle that is Finland's most impressive (p146).

➡ Turun Linna, lording it over the medieval city of Turku (p76).

Animals
➡ Boat it over to the zoo in Helsinki (p53), or learn about Arctic fauna at Ranua in Lapland (p236).

➡ Meet the dogs at a Lapland husky kennel or feed the reindeer at a farm.

➡ See the tame orphaned bears near Kuusamo (p220).

Winter

➡ Strap the skates on at Helsinki's outdoor rink, Jääpuisto (p55).

➡ Tackle the family-friendly slopes at ski resorts like Levi (p240), Pyhä-Luosto (p246) or Jyväskylä (p155).

➡ Get into the Christmas spirit around Rovaniemi, where Santa can be visited year-round (p231).

➡ Visit the snow castles at Kemi (p237) or Hetta (p242), or the snow village at Ylläs (p239).

➡ Take a sledge ride pulled by huskies or reindeer in Lapland, or rev up a snowmobile and go for a spin.

➡ Soak in the atmosphere of an ice hockey game in Helsinki (p67).

Theme Parks

➡ Linnanmäki, Helsinki (p53).

➡ Särkänniemi, Tampere (p128).

➡ Muumimaailma, Naantali (p84).

➡ Wasalandia and Tropiclandia, Vaasa (p200).

On the Water

➡ Paddle your way around the Linnansaari and Kolovesi national parks (p152).

➡ Tackle the Oravareitti (Squirrel Route; p153), a multiday canoeing adventure.

➡ Shoot the rapids at Ruunaa (p183), or on the Kitkajoki near Kuusamo (p221).

Beaches

➡ The Hanko area (p90) has numerous beaches, ranging from paddleable to windsurfable.

➡ Check out the amazing Hiekkalinna sandcastle in Lappeenranta (p169).

➡ Yyteri (p194) near Pori has a great variety.

Museums

Outdoor museums exhibit traditional buildings and have activities in summer. There are good ones in Helsinki, Turku, and at Turkansaari near Oulu.

➡ Heureka, Vantaa (p50).

➡ Tietomaa, Oulu (p210).

➡ Kierikkikeskus, near Oulu (p215).

➡ Vakoilumuseo, Tampere (p127).

Planning

When to Go

Many child-oriented activities are closed outside of mid-June to early August. This is when campgrounds are buzzing with Finnish families and temperatures are usually reliably warm.

Winter is also a great time to take the family to Finland. December sees Christmassy things spring up in Lapland, with Santas, elves and reindeer. If your kids are older and want to get active in the snow, March or April are the months to go: there's plenty of daylight, better snow, and not such extreme negative temperatures.

Accommodation

Self-catering is huge in Finland; the wide network of rental cabins, apartments and cottages – ranging from simple huts to luxurious bungalows – make excellent family bases. Campgrounds are also good, with cabins, rowboats and bikes available for hire, and often a lake beach. There are always other children in these places, and larger ones offer activity programs.

Most Finnish hotels and hostels will put an extra bed in a room for little extra cost – and kids under 12 often sleep free. Many hotel rooms have sofas that can fold out into beds or family suites, and hostels often have connecting rooms. The **Holiday Club** (www.holidayclub.fi) and **Rantasipi** chains of spa hotels are especially child-friendly. These and other resort hotels always have family-friendly restaurants with a menu for the kids, or deals where children eat free if accompanied by adults.

Other Practicalities

➡ Local tourist information booklets and websites highlight attractions with family appeal.

➡ Car-hire firms have children's safety seats for hire, but it is essential that you book them in advance.

➡ Highchairs and cots (cribs) are standard in many restaurants and hotels, but numbers may be limited.

➡ Entrance fees and transport tickets for children are around 60% of the adult charge.

➡ Most museums in Helsinki are free for kids.

➡ Nappies and baby food are widely available.

➡ Public breast-feeding is normal practice.

Regions at a Glance

Helsinki

Design
Museums & Galleries
Food & Drink

Showrooms & Studios

Finnish design is a byword for quality, but it's not just the reliable excellence of the big-name brands that impresses. Wander through Helsinki's back streets to discover numerous small ateliers and shops displaying the quirky, the innovative, the oh-dear and the brilliant.

See the Sights

Finns are fond of museums, and Helsinki has an enviable selection. You'll have to rigorously prune most of them, but there are enough must-see galleries and exhibitions to keep you busy for several days.

New Suomi Cuisine

Finnish food unfairly had a bad rap for years, but Helsinki's fine-dining restaurants are turning heads. Ally that with traditional places serving heart-warming wintry fare and an array of offbeat drinking options, and you've got quite a package.

p42

Turku & the South Coast

Architecture
Islands
Beaches

Castles & Churches

This region holds the lion's share of Finland's historic buildings. Turku's castle and cathedral, old ironworks, Porvoo's wooden warehouses, Hanko's posh tsarist villas, and various fortresses and churches make this prime territory to explore the past.

Archipelago Exploration

Prepare to be astounded by the quantity of small islands speckling Finland's Baltic coastline. Some you can explore by bike, others will need boat hire.

Beaches

The sea might be a little chilly but there's plenty of sand and sun. The area around Hanko has many choices, but you can find decent strands right across the region.

p74

Åland Archipelago

Cycling
Islands
Historic Sights

Two Wheels

Flat, comparatively sunny, light traffic: these islands are a cycling paradise. Campsites, farmstays and bike-friendly inter-island ferries make touring here a breeze.

Baltic Islands

If you love islands you'll love Åland. The main ones are already tranquil, but get out to the eastern archipelago and you'll virtually have a rock in the Baltic to yourself. Grab a kayak and you literally will.

Ships & Redoubts

As an important strategic point in the Baltic, Åland has a couple of major fortresses to explore, plus a grand post office. In the capital, Mariehamn, the museum-ship *Pommern* speaks of the islands' maritime heritage.

p108

Tampere & Häme

Galleries
Beer
Boat Trips

Hidden Sights

Finland's art has traditionally been linked with its nature, so it should be no surprise to find studios and galleries in small towns or by some lake in the middle of nowhere. The three main cities of the region back these up with a fistful of excellent museums.

Microbreweries

Finland downs a lot of the stuff, but most Suomi beer is generic mass-produced lager. Small breweries and bars in this region buck the trend; sampling their ales and ciders is one of the area's highlights.

On the Water

Getting out on the water, whether for a short jaunt or town-to-town lake cruise, is one of the region's great summer pleasures.

p124

The Lakeland

Canoeing
Festivals
Cruises

Paddling

There's no better way to appreciate the lakes and rivers that form this watery land than by grabbing a canoe or kayak. Explore national parks hoping to spot an inland seal, or canoe the family-friendly Squirrel Route.

Sublime to Ridiculous

Finland's festivals are a diverse bunch, and never more so than in the Lakeland, where glorious castle opera takes the stage alongside rowboat regattas, car rallies, wife-carrying and mobile-phone throwing.

Lake Transport

Why jump on a bus to get to the next town when you can make the journey on the deck of a historic lake boat and appreciate the scenery at a stately pace?

p144

Karelia

Hiking
Festivals
Food

Forest Treks

Karelia has some excellent long-distance hiking routes winding through some of Finland's deepest and most remote forests. There are hundreds of kilometres of marked trails to keep you busy.

Celebrations

Karelia is the best place to explore Finnish Orthodox customs. Onion-domed churches and traditional festivals give the place a different feel from the predominantly Lutheran rest of the country.

Pies & Roasts

The savoury 'Karelian pie' is a rice-filled staple eaten widely across the country, but you'll find several intriguing variants here. Better yet is Lemi's speciality, birch-roasted mutton, a Finnish culinary highlight.

p166

West Coast

Festivals
Architecture
Coastline

Fiesta Time

Normally tranquil Seinäjoki kicks its heels up for contrasting tango and rock festivals, while Kaustinen becomes a folk-music mecca. Add Pori's jazz do and Rauma's bustling lace week and it's a busy season.

Wonderful Wood

Rauma, Jakobstad and Kokkola bring Finnish history alive with their rows of charming wooden buildings, some of the few to have survived the years and the fires.

Coastal Pleasures

The Gulf of Bothnia isn't the likeliest of sun-and-sand destinations, but there are some great family beaches here. The weird rising landscapes of the Kvarken archipelago are another highlight.

p187

Oulu, Kainuu & Koillismaa

Activities
Wildlife
Festivals

Out & About

The area around Kuusamo and Ruka is fantastic for getting active. In summer great hiking, canoeing and rafting is the draw; winter sees skiing, sled safaris and snowmobiling.

Bears & More

Around Kuhmo and Kuusamo there are all sorts of impressive beasts to see if you creep out into the forest with a guide. Elk, flying squirrels, wolverines and bears are all viewable from the comfort and safety of a hide.

Imaginary Instruments

Oulu raises the weirdness stakes with its ice-fishing marathon, garlic ice cream and air-guitar championships. A statelier counterpoint is Kuhmo's chamber music festival.

p208

Lapland

Hiking
Activities
Sámi Culture

Northern Walking

Big skies, clear air, splendid landscapes and enormous national parks make Lapland one of Europe's best hiking destinations. Networks of wilderness huts and campsites mean planning a walk is easy.

Deep Winter

Winter doesn't get much more wintry than Lapland, but that's no invitation to huddle indoors: there's a fistful of things to do, like skiing, safaris with huskies or reindeer, ice-fishing and snowmobiling.

Indigenous Northerners

The northern part of Lapland is the homeland of various indigenous Sámi groups. Learning a little about their culture, art and reindeer-herding is a highlight of any visit.

p227

On the Road

Helsinki

📱 09 / POP 1.09 MILLION TOTAL URBAN AREA

Best Places to Eat

➜ Olo (p62)

➜ Savoy (p62)

➜ Demo (p62)

➜ Kuu (p63)

➜ Hietalahden Kauppahalli (p64)

Best Places to Stay

➜ Hotel Fabian (p58)

➜ Hotel Haven (p58)

➜ Hotelli Helka (p57)

➜ Klaus K (p58)

➜ Hotel Katajanokka (p60)

Why Go?

It's fitting that harbourside Helsinki, capital of a country with such watery geography, melds so graciously into the Baltic. Half the city seems liquid, and the writhings of the complex coastline include any number of bays, inlets and islands.

Though Helsinki can seem a younger sibling to other Scandinavian capitals, it's the one that went to art school, scorns pop music and works in a cutting-edge studio. The design scene here is legendary, whether you're browsing showroom brands or taking the backstreet hipster trail. The city's gourmet side is also flourishing, with new gastro eateries offering locally sourced tasting menus popping up at dizzying speed.

Nevertheless, much of what iws lovable in Helsinki is older. Its understated yet glorious art-nouveau buildings, the spacious elegance of its centenarian cafes, dozens of museums carefully preserving Finnish heritage, restaurants that have changed neither menu nor furnishings since the 1930s: all part of the city's quirky charm.

When to Go
Helsinki

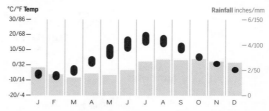

Jun Terraces are sprouting outside every cafe and the nights never seem to end.

Aug The city is functioning again after the July lull, but all of the summer activities are still on.

Dec Ice skate and absorb the Christmassy atmosphere before temperatures get too extreme.

Helsinki Highlights

1 Descending into the weekend maelstrom of Helsinki's excellent variety of **pubs** and **bars** (p65)

2 Grabbing a picnic and exploring the fortress island of **Suomenlinna** (p44) that guarded Helsinki harbour

3 Browsing the design district of **Punavuori** (p68)

4 Selecting from the huge range of **museums** (p50) and **galleries** (p49)

5 Buying fresh produce in **market halls** (p64)

6 Sweating in atmospheric **Kotiharjun Sauna** (p55)

7 Tripping across to **Tallinn** to admire its Old Town (p56)

8 Strolling among traditional wooden buildings on **Seurasaari** (p53)

9 **Dining** (p62) on avant-garde forage-based tasting menus or traditional food such as meatballs or liver

10 Absorbing the atmosphere inside **Temppeliaukion Kirkko** (p50)

History

Helsinki was founded in 1550 by King Gustav Vasa to rival the Hansa trading town of Tallinn. Earlier trials at Ekenäs were fruitless, so traders from there and a few other towns were shanghaied to newly founded Helsingfors (the Swedish name).

For over 200 years it remained a backwater, though it was razed in 1713 to prevent the Russians occupying it. The inhabitants fled or were captured, and only returned after the Peace of Nystad in 1721. Later the Swedes built the Sveaborg (Suomenlinna) fortress to protect this eastern part of their empire against further Russian attack. Following the war of 1808, however, the Russians succeeded in taking the fortress and a year later Russia annexed Finland as an autonomous grand duchy. A capital nearer Russia than Sweden was required and Helsinki was chosen in 1812: Turku lost its longstanding status as Finland's capital and premier town.

In the 19th and early 20th centuries, Helsinki grew rapidly and German architect CL Engel was called on to dignify the city centre. The city suffered heavy Russian bombing during WWII, but postwar Helsinki recovered and hosted the 1952 Summer Olympics. These days the capital is so much the centre of everything that goes on in Finland that its obscure market-town past is totally forgotten.

◉ Sights

Helsinki has over 50 museums and galleries but some are too obscure to interest any but enthusiasts. For a full list, pick up the *Museums* booklet (free) from the tourist office.

A day trip to Porvoo (p98) is a popular and worthwhile excursion.

ⓘ HELSINKI CARD

The **Helsinki Card** (www.helsinkiexpert. com; adult per 24/48/72hr €36/46/56, child €15/18/21) gives you free travel, entry to more than 50 attractions in and around Helsinki, and discounts on day tours to Porvoo and Tallinn. It's cheaper online; otherwise, get it at the tourist office, hotels, R-kioskis or transport terminals. To make it worthwhile, you'd need to pack lots of sightseeing into a short time.

◉ Suomenlinna

Just a 15-minute ferry ride from the kauppatori (market square), a visit to **Suomenlinna** (Sveaborg; www.suomenlinna.fi), the 'fortress of Finland', is a Helsinki must-do. Set on a tight cluster of islands connected by bridges, the UNESCO World Heritage site was originally built by the Swedes as Sveaborg in the mid-18th century.

At the main quay, the pink Rantakasarmi (Jetty Barracks) is one of the best-preserved of the Russian era. It holds a small exhibition and helpful multilingual **tourist office** (✆0295-338 410; ⊙10am-6pm May-Sep, 10am-4pm Oct-Apr), with downloadable content for smartphones. Near here are the hostel (p59), supermarket and distinctive **church** (⊙noon-4pm Wed-Sun, plus Tue Jun-Aug), the only one in the world to double as a lighthouse.

A blue-signposted walking path connects the main attractions. By the bridge that connects Iso Mustasaari and the main island, Susisaari-Kustaanmiekka, is **Suomenlinna-museo** (adult/child €6.50/free; ⊙10.30am-4.30pm Oct-Apr, 10am-6pm May-Sep), a two-level museum covering the history of the fortress. It's very information heavy, but the first part gives good background. There's also an audiovisual display. Guided walks from here (adult/child €10/4) run in English three times daily from June to August, and 1.30pm Saturday and Sunday the rest of the year.

Suomenlinna's most atmospheric part is on Kustaanmiekka at the end of the blue trail. Exploring the old bunkers, crumbling fortress walls and cannons lets you appreciate the fortress, and there are plenty of grassy picnic spots. Monumental **King's Gate** was built in 1753–54. In summer you can get the JT-Line waterbus back to Helsinki from here, saving you the walk back to the main quay.

Several other museums dot the islands. Perhaps the most interesting is **Ehrensvärd-museo** (adult/child €3/1; ⊙11am-4pm May & Sep, 11am-6pm Jun-Aug), once home to the man responsible for designing and running the fortress. An attractive 18th-century house, it holds numerous portraits, prints and models giving an insight into daily life on the island. Ehrensvärd's elaborately martial tomb sits outside, and opposite is Viaporin Telakka, a picturesque **shipyard** where sailmakers and other workers have been building since the 1750s. The dry dock holds up to two dozen boats; these days it's used for the maintenance of wooden vessels.

SUOMENLINNA: THE LION THAT SQUEAKED

In the mid-18th century, Sweden was twitchy about a potential Russian invasion, and decided to build a state-of-the-art offshore fortress near the eastern limits of its declining empire. At the time, Helsinki wasn't a major town, and the bastion itself, Sveaborg, became one of Finland's largest settlements and a thriving community.

Despite Suomenlinna's meticulous planning and impressive military hardware, its history in war has been rather less than glorious. When the Russians finally came calling in 1808, the besieged commander, alarmed by Russian threats to bombard every last civilian to smithereens, tamely surrendered the fortress to spare the soldiers' families.

Once Finland was under Russian rule, the capital was moved from Turku to Helsinki, but the fortress was allowed to deteriorate. A wake-up call came with the Crimean War and rapid improvements were made. Or so they said. As it turned out, British ships pounded the islands with 21,000 shots in a two-day bombardment, but Suomenlinna's guns were so out of condition that they couldn't even reach the attacking ships.

The fortress nevertheless remained in Russian hands until independence. During the Finnish Civil War it served as a prison for communist prisoners; these days there's still an open prison on the islands.

Nearby is another fish out of water. The **Vesikko** (adult/child €5/free; ⏲11am-6pm May-Sep) is the only WWII-era submarine remaining in Finland. It saw action against the Russians. It's fascinating to climb inside and see how it all worked. Needless to say, there's not much room to move.

Back on Iso Mustasaari is **Sotamuseo Maneesi** (adult/child €5/free; ⏲11am-6pm early May-Sep), with a comprehensive overview of Finnish military hardware from bronze cannon to WWII artillery. Quite a contrast is nearby **Lelumuseo** (Toy Museum; www.lelumuseo.fi; adult/child €6/3; ⏲10am or 11am to 5pm or 6pm mid-May–mid-Sep), a delightful collection of hundreds of dolls and teddy bears. The cafe serves delicious home-baked cakes under a line of samovars.

There are several other eating places, largely mediocre. Best for a beer or bite is **Suomenlinnan Panimo** (☏09-228-5030; www.panimoravintola.fi; mains €19-30; ⏲noon-10pm Mon-Sat, noon-6pm Sun May-Aug, shorter hours winter), by the quay. It brews some excellent beers including a hefty porter and offers good food to accompany it. Taking a picnic is a great way to make the most of Suomenlinna's grass and views. Around 5.15pm find a spot to watch the enormous Baltic ferries pass through the narrow gap between islands.

Ferries head from Helsinki's kauppatori to Suomenlinna's main quay. Tickets (one way/return €2.50/5, 15 minutes, three times hourly, less frequent in winter, 6.20am to 2.20am) are available at the pier. In addition, **JT-Line** (Map p46; www.jt-line.fi) runs a waterbus at least hourly from the kauppatori, making three stops on Suomenlinna (one way/return €4.50/7, 20 minutes, 8am to 7pm May to mid-September).

◉ Central Helsinki

The heart of central Helsinki is the harbourside **kauppatori** (Map p46), where cruises and ferries leave for archipelago islands. It's completely touristy these days, with reindeer souvenir stands having replaced most market stalls, but there are still some berries and flowers for sale, and adequate cheap food options.

★**Tuomiokirkko** CHURCH
(Lutheran Cathedral; Map p46; www.helsinginseurakunnat.fi; Unioninkatu 29; ⏲9am-6pm, to midnight Jun-Aug) FREE One of CL Engel's finest creations, the chalk-white neoclassical Lutheran cathedral presides over Senaatintori. Created to serve as a reminder of God's supremacy, its high flight of stairs is now a meeting place for canoodling couples. The spartan, almost mausoleum-like interior has little ornamentation under the lofty dome apart from an altar painting and three stern statues of Reformation heroes Luther, Melanchthon and Mikael Agricola, looking like they've just marked your theology exam and taken a dim view of your prospects.

Uspenskin Katedraali CHURCH
(Uspenski Cathedral; Map p52; http://hos.fi/uspenskin-katedraali; Kanavakatu 1; ⏲9.30am-4pm Tue-Fri, 10am-3pm Sat, noon-3pm Sun) FREE Facing the Lutheran cathedral, the eye-catching red-brick Uspenski Cathedral stands on

Central Helsinki

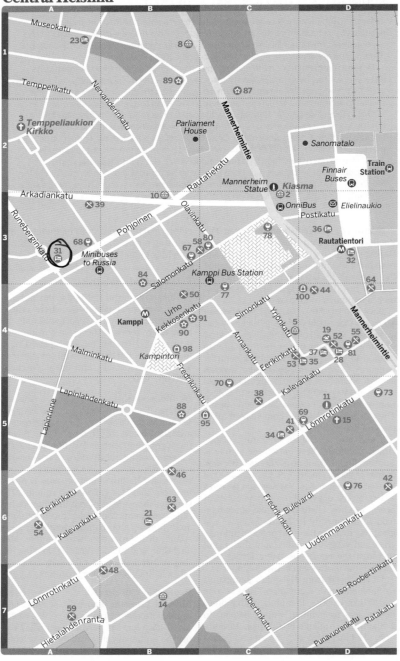

Museokatu

23

8

89

87

Temppelikatu

Nervanderinkatu

Mannerheimintie

3 Temppeliaukion Kirkko

Parliament House

Sanomatalo

Finnair Buses

Train Station

Arkadiankatu

Rautatiekatu

Mannerheim Statue

Kiasma 2

39

Olavinkatu

Pohjoinen

OnniBus

Elielinaukio

Postikatu

Runeberginkatu

36

68

31

58 80

67

78

Rautatientori

32

Minibuses to Russia

84

Salomonkatu

Kamppi Bus Station

64

50

77

100 44

Kamppi

Urho Kekkosenkatu

91

Simonkatu

Yrjönkatu

5

19

52 55

90

Annankatu

Eerikinkatu

37

81

Malminkatu

98

53 35

28

Kampintori

Fredrikinkatu

70

Kalevankatu

11

73

Lapinlahdenkatu

38

69

15

88

41

34

Lönnrotinkatu

95

Lapinrinne

Mannerheimintie

46

42

76

Eerikinkatu

63

54

Kalevankatu

21

Fredrikinkatu

Fredrik Bulevardi

Uudenmaankatu

48

Iso Roobertinkatu

Lönnrotinkatu

59

14

Hietalahdenranta

Albertinkatu

Punavuorenkatu

Ratakatu

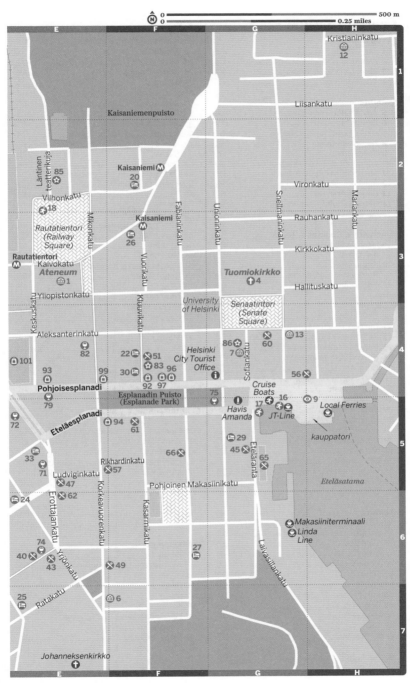

HELSINKI

Central Helsinki

Top Sights
1 Ateneum E3
2 Kiasma.................................... C3
3 Temppeliaukion Kirkko A2
4 Tuomiokirkko G3

Sights
5 Amos Andersonin Taidemuseo C4
6 Design Museum F7
7 Helsingin Kaupunginmuseo G4
8 Kansallismuseo................................B1
9 Kauppatori H5
10 Luonnontieteellinen Museo B3
11 Memorial to Elias Lönnrot D5
12 Ruiskumestarin talo H1
13 Sederholmin talo.............................. G4
14 Sinebrychoffin Taidemuseo B7
15 Vanha Kirkko D5

Activities, Courses & Tours
16 Helsinki Sightseeing G5
17 IHA Lines.................................... G5
18 Jääpuisto....................................E2
   Royal Line ....(see 16)
19 Yrjönkadun Uimahalli D4

Sleeping
20 City Apartments................................F2
21 GLO Hotel Art B6
22 GLO Hotel Kluuvi F4
23 Hellsten Helsinki Parliament A1
24 Hostel Erottajanpuisto E6
25 Hotel Anna E7
26 Hotel Carlton F3
27 Hotel Fabian F6
28 Hotel Finn....................................D4
29 Hotel Haven G5
30 Hotel Kämp....................................F4
31 Hotelli Helka A3
32 Hotelli Seurahuone D3
33 Klaus K E5
34 Omenahotelli Lönnrotinkatu C5
35 Omenahotelli Yrjönkatu D4
36 Sokos....................................D3
37 Sokos Hotel Torni D4

Eating
38 A21 Dining C5
39 Ateljé Finne A3
40 Café Balzac E6
   Café Bar 9 ....(see 42)
41 Cholo C5
42 Demo D6
43 Fafa's E6
44 Forum....................................D4
45 Goodwin G5
46 Gran Delicato..............................B6
47 Grotesk E5
48 Hietalahden Kauppahalli B7
49 Juuri....................................F6
50 Kamppi B4

51 Karl Fazer Café F4
52 KarlJohan D4
53 Kitch C4
54 Konstan Möljä A6
55 Kosmos....................................D5
56 Olo H4
57 Rikhards.................................... E5
58 Ruohonjuuri..............................C3
59 Salve....................................A7
60 Savotta.................................... G4
61 Savoy F5
62 Skiffer....................................E6
63 Thai Orchid..............................B6
64 UniCafe....................................D4
65 Vanha Kauppahalli G5
66 Zucchini F5

Drinking & Nightlife
   A21 Cocktail Lounge ....(see 69)
67 Aussie Bar B3
68 Bäkkäri....................................A3
69 Bar Loose D5
70 Corona Baari & Kafe Mockba C5
71 Cuba! Cafe E5
72 DTM E5
73 Hercules.................................... D5
74 Hugo's Room E6
75 Kappeli G5
76 Los Cojones..............................D6
77 Maxine....................................C4
78 Mbar....................................C3
79 Teatteri E4
80 Teerenpeli.................................... C3
81 U Kaleva.................................... D4
82 Wanha Kauppakuja E4

Entertainment
83 FinnKino Maxim F4
84 FinnKino Tennispalatsi B3
85 Kansallisteatteri.................................E2
86 Kino Engel.................................... G4
   Lippupalvelu..............................(see 101)
87 Musiikkitalo.................................... C1
88 Orion Theatre................................B5
   Semifinal.................................(see 90)
89 Storyville B1
90 Tavastia B4
91 Tiketti B4

Shopping
92 Aarikka.................................... F4
93 Akateeminen Kirjakauppa E4
94 Artek E5
95 Fennica Records..............................C5
96 Iittala F4
97 Kalevala Koru F4
98 Levykauppa Äx B4
99 Marimekko.................................... E4
100 Moomin Shop..............................D4
101 Stockmann E4

nearby Katajanokka island. The two buildings face off high above the city like two queens on a theological chessboard. Built as a Russian Orthodox church in 1868, it features classic onion-topped domes and now serves the Finnish Orthodox congregation. The high, square interior has a lavish iconostasis with the Evangelists flanking panels depicting the Last Supper and the Ascension. Orthodox services held at 6pm on Saturday and 10am Sunday are worth attending for the fabulous chorals and candlelit atmosphere.

★**Ateneum** GALLERY
(Map p46; www.ateneum.fi; Kaivokatu 2; adult/child €12/free; ☺10am-6pm Tue & Fri, 9am-8pm Wed & Thu, 10am-5pm Sat & Sun) The top floor of Finland's premier art gallery is an ideal crash course in the nation's art. It houses Finnish paintings and sculptures from the 'golden age' of the late 19th century through to the 1950s, including works by Albert Edelfelt, Hugo Simberg, Helene Schjerfbeck, the Von Wright brothers and Pekka Halonen. Pride of place goes to the prolific Akseli Gallen-Kallela's triptych from the *Kalevala* depicting Väinämöinen's pursuit of the maiden Aino. There's also a small but interesting collection of 19th- and early-20th-century foreign art. Downstairs is a cafe, good bookshop and reading room. The building itself dates from 1887.

★**Kiasma** GALLERY
(Map p46; www.kiasma.fi; Mannerheiminaukio 2; adult/child €10/free; ☺10am-5pm Sun & Tue, 10am-8.30pm Wed-Fri, 10am-6pm Sat) Now just one of a series of elegant contemporary buildings in this part of town, curvaceous and quirky metallic Kiasma, designed by Steven Holl and finished in 1998, is still a symbol of the city's modernisation. It exhibits an eclectic collection of Finnish and international modern art and keeps people on their toes with its striking contemporary exhibitions. The interior, with its unexpected curves and perspectives, is as invigorating as the outside. Kiasma's outstanding success is that it's been embraced by the people of Helsinki. Its sleek, glass-sided cafe and terrace are hugely popular, locals sunbathe on the grassy fringes and skateboarders perform aerobatics under the stern gaze of Mannerheim's statue outside.

Kansallismuseo MUSEUM
(Map p46; www.kansallismuseo.fi; Mannerheimintie 34; adult/child €8/free; ☺11am-6pm Tue-Sun) The impressive National Museum, built

THE ART ISLAND

The upmarket island of Kuusisaari has two excellent private galleries, **Didrichsen Taidemuseo** (www.didrichsenmuseum.fi; Kuusilahdenkuja 1, Kuusisaari; admission from €5; ☺11am-5pm Tue-Sun) and **Villa Gyllenberg** (www.gyllenbergs.fi; Kuusisaarenpolku 11, Kuusisaari; adult/child €10/free; ☺4-8pm Wed, noon-4pm Sun Aug–late-Jun), both set in elaborate villas and showing the collections of their one-time owners. Both have a good permanent collection of Finnish art of the golden age as well as local and international 20th-century art, supplemented by changing exhibitions. Bus 194 or 195 will get you to the island; the galleries are under five minutes' stroll apart. It's also an easy walk from Seurasaari, so there's plenty out here for a day trip.

in National Romantic style in 1916, looks a bit like a Gothic church with its heavy stonework and tall square tower. This is Finland's premier historical museum and is divided into rooms covering different periods of Finnish history, including prehistory and archaeological finds, church relics, ethnography and changing cultural exhibitions. It's a very thorough, old-style museum – you might have trouble selling this one to the kids – but provides a comprehensive overview. Look for the imperial throne of Tsar Alexander I dating from 1809, and the basement treasury, gleaming with coins, medals, pewter and swords. From the 1st-floor balcony, crane your head up to see the superb frescoes on the ceiling arches, depicting scenes from the epic *Kalevala,* painted by Akseli Gallen-Kallela.

Katajanokka ISLAND
(Map p52) Just east of the kauppatori, this island is divided from the mainland by a narrow canal and makes for an enjoyable stroll. It's a paradise of upmarket Jugendstil (art nouveau) residential buildings with extravagant turrets and curious carvings galore.

While the south side of the island has a major ferry terminal, the other side is more peaceful, with the Engel-designed Foreign Ministry looking out over the impressively functional **ice-breaker fleet** (Map p52). At the western end of the island, the Orthodox

WORTH A TRIP

HEUREKA!

Essentially, Vantaa (Swedish: Vanda) is a satellite suburb of Helsinki best known as the location of the airport. However it's also home to **Heureka** (www.heureka.fi; adult/child exhibitions only €19/13.50, with planetarium film €23.50/16.50; ⊙10am-5pm Mon-Wed & Fri, 10am-6pm Sat & Sun, 10am-8pm Thu), a fantastic hands-on science centre, IMAX theatre and planetarium, by Tikkurila train station (15 minutes from Helsinki on a commuter train). In high summer it opens until 7pm weeknights.

cathedral looks over a leisure harbour and a series of warehouses attractively converted into enticing restaurants and bars.

Luonnontieteellinen Museo　　　MUSEUM
(Natural History Museum; Map p46; www.luomus.fi; Pohjoinen Rautatiekatu 13; adult/child €10/5; ⊙10am-5pm Tue-Sun Jun-Aug, 9am-4pm Tue-Fri, to 6pm Thu, 10am-4pm Sat & Sun Sep-May) The city's natural history museum is known for its controversial weathervane of a sperm impregnating an ovum. Modern exhibitions such as *Story of the Bones,* which puts skeletons in an evolutionary context, bring new life to the University of Helsinki's extensive collection of mammals, birds and other creatures, including all Finnish species.

Design Museum　　　MUSEUM
(Map p46; www.designmuseum.fi; Korkeavuorenkatu 23; adult/child €10/free; ⊙11am-8pm Tue, 11am-6pm Wed-Sun Sep-May, 11am-6pm daily Jun-Aug) The Design Museum has a permanent collection that looks at the roots of Finnish design in the nation's traditions and nature. Changing exhibitions focus on contemporary design – everything from clothing to household furniture.

Helsingin Kaupunginmuseo　　　MUSEUM
(Helsinki City Museum; Map p46; www.helsinkicitymuseum.fi; Sofiankatu 4; ⊙9am-5pm Mon-Fri, to 7pm Thu, 11am-5pm Sat & Sun) **FREE** A group of small museums scattered around the city centre constitute this city museum: all have free entry and focus on an aspect of the city's past or present through permanent and temporary exhibitions. The mustsee of the bunch is the main museum, just off Senaatintori. Its excellent collection of historical artefacts and photos is backed up

by entertaining information on the history of the city, piecing together Helsinki's transition from Swedish to Russian hands and into independence.

The museum is due to extend into nearby **Sederholmin talo** (Map p46; Aleksanterinkatu 18) **FREE**, Helsinki's oldest central building (dating from 1757 and built by a wealthy merchant), which will reopen in 2016. Other museums include delightful **Ratikkamuseo** (Tram Museum; Map p52; ☎09-3103-6630; www.hel.fi; Töölönkatu 51A; ⊙11am-5pm) **FREE**, which displays vintage trams and depicts daily life in Helsinki's streets in past decades; mustard-coloured **Ruiskumestarin talo** (Burgher's House; Map p46; Kristianinkatu 12; ⊙11am-5pm Wed-Sun Jun-Aug & Nov & Dec), central Helsinki's oldest wooden town house, built in 1818; and the **Työväenasuntomuseo** (Museum of Worker Housing; Map p52; Kirstinkuja 4; ⊙11am-5pm Wed-Sun early May–late Oct) **FREE**, showing how industrial workers lived in the early 20th century.

Vanha Kirkko　　　CHURCH
(Map p46; Lönnrotinkatu; ⊙noon-3pm Mon-Fri, to 9pm Thu) Helsinki's most venerable church is this white wood beauty, designed by CL Engel. Opposite is a **memorial to Elias Lönnrot**, compiler of the *Kalevala* epic, depicting the author flanked by his most famous character, 'steady old Väinämöinen'.

Amos Andersonin Taidemuseo　　　GALLERY
(Map p46; www.amosanderson.fi; Yrjönkatu 27; adult/child €10/free; ⊙10am-6pm Mon, Thu & Fri, 10am-8pm Wed, 11am-5pm Sat & Sun) This gallery houses the collection of publishing magnate Amos Anderson, one of the wealthiest Finns of his time. Temporary exhibitions mix the old and cutting-edge contemporary, while the permanent exhibition includes a chapel, Empire-style interiors and lots of Magnus Enckell works among other Finnish artists, including works by 20th-century Finnish female artists.

◎ Greater Helsinki

★**Temppeliaukion Kirkko**　　　CHURCH
(Map p46; ☎09-2340-6320; www.helsinginseurakunnat.fi; Lutherinkatu 3; ⊙10am-5.45pm Mon-Sat, 11.45am-5.45pm Sun Jun-Aug, to 5pm Sep-May) The Temppeliaukio church, designed by Timo and Tuomo Suomalainen in 1969, remains one of Helsinki's foremost attractions. Hewn into solid stone, it feels close to a Finnish ideal of spirituality in nature –

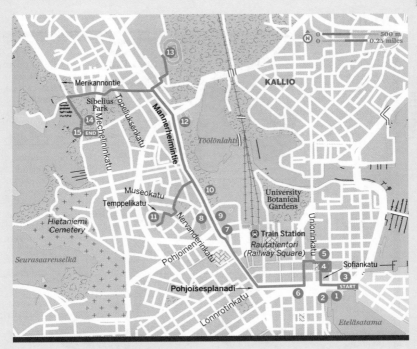

City Walk
Iconic Buildings and Monuments

START KAUPPATORI
END CAFE REGATTA
LENGTH 3.5KM; THREE HOURS

The bustling ① **kauppatori** (market square) is flanked by 19th-century buildings. The eagle-topped obelisk is the Keisarinnankivi (Empress' Stone), Helsinki's oldest monument, unveiled in 1835 in honour of Tsar Nicholas I and Tsarina Alexandra. ② **Havis Amanda**, the female nude statue in a fountain just west of the market, is regarded as the symbol of Helsinki. Across from the kauppatori is the guarded ③ **Presidential Palace**.

Head up Sofiankatu to ④ **Senaatintori** (Senate Sq). Engel's stately ⑤ **Tuomiokirkko** (Lutheran Cathedral; p45) is the most prominent feature. The main University of Helsinki building is on the west side and the magnificent National Library a little further north along Unioninkatu. Walking back to Pohjoisesplanadi, stroll through ⑥ **Esplanadin Puisto** (Esplanade Park), or browse the design shops along the pavement. Turn right onto

Mannerheimintie, the main thoroughfare. An equestrian ⑦ **statue of Marshal Mannerheim**, Finland's most revered military leader, dominates the square alongside Kiasma. Continue northwest. ⑧ **Parliament House** (1931) dominates this stretch. Opposite it is striking modern ⑨ **Musiikkitalo** (p66), with concert halls and studios. Further up on the right is one of Alvar Aalto's most famous works, ⑩ **Finlandia-Talo**, a concert hall built in 1967–72. You can detour west through backstreets to ⑪ **Temppeliaukion Kirkko** (p50), a modern church hewn from solid rock.

A few blocks north, on Mannerheimintie, is the 1993 ⑫ **Oopperatalo** (p67), home of the Finnish National Opera. Continue to the 1952 ⑬ **Olympic Stadium** (p54), with great city views from the tower. Finally, extend this walk westward to take in the ⑭ **Sibelius monument** (p53). This striking sculpture was created by artist Eila Hiltunen in 1967 to honour Finland's most famous composer. Kick back at waterside **Cafe Regatta** (p63), then bus 24 takes you back to the centre from Mechelininkatu.

Helsinki

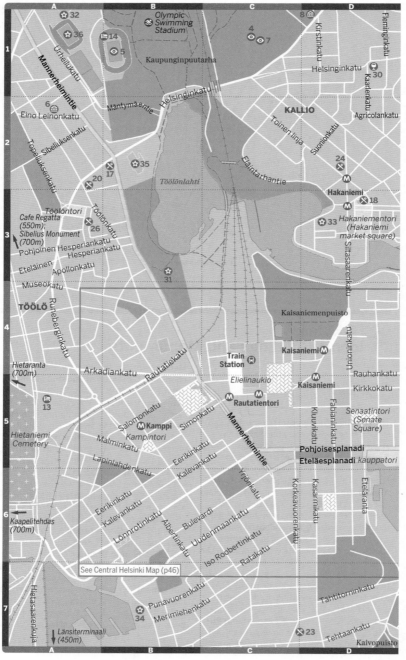

A **B** **C** **D**

32
36
Olympic Swimming Stadium
14
5
4
7
8
Kirstinkatu
Flemininkatu
Kaupunginpuutarha
Helsinginkatu
Urheilukatu
Mannerheimintie
Helsing015gainkatu
30
Kaarlenkatu
6
Eino Leinonkatu
Mäntymäentie
KALLIO
Toinen linja
Agricolankatu
Topeliuksenkatu
Sibeliuksenkatu
Suonionkatu
35
Töölönlahti
24
17
20
Hakaniemi
18
Töölöntori
Cafe Regatta (550m);
Sibelius Monument (700m)
26
Töölönkatu
33
Hakaniementori (Hakaniemi market square)
Pohjoinen Hesperiankatu
Hesperiankatu
Siltasaarenkatu
Eteläinen
Apollonkatu
Museokatu
31
TÖÖLÖ
Runeberginkatu
Kaisaniemenpuisto
Hietaranta (700m)
Arkadiankatu
Rautatiekatu
Kaisaniemi
Train Station
Kaisaniemi
Unionikatu
Rauhankatu
13
Elielinaukio
Kaisaniemi
Kirkkokatu
Hietaniemi Cemetery
Salomonkatu
Simonkatu
Rautatientori
Senaatintori (Senate Square)
Kamppi
Kampintori
Mannerheimintie
Kluuvikatu
Fabianinkatu
Malminkatu
Eerikinkatu
Kalevankatu
Pohjoisesplanadi
Lapinlahdenkatu
Yrjönkatu
Eteläesplanadi kauppatori
Kaapelitehdas (700m)
Eerikinkatu
Kalevankatu
Bulevardi
Uudenmaankatu
Korkeavuorenkatu
Kasarmikatu
Etelärantaa
Lönnrotinkatu
Albertinkatu
Iso Roobertinkatu
Ratakatu
See Central Helsinki Map (p46)
Hietasaarenkuja
Punavuorenkatu
Merimiehenkatu
Tähtitorninkatu
34
Länsiterminaali (450m)
23
Tehtaankatu
Kaivopuisto

A **B** **C** **D**

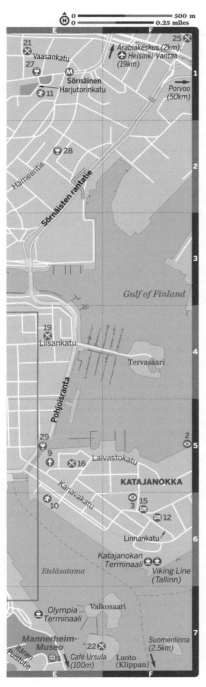

you could be in a rocky glade were it not for the stunning 24m-diameter roof covered in 22km of copper stripping. There are regular concerts, with great acoustics. Opening times vary depending on events, so phone or search for its Facebook page updates. There are fewer groups midweek.

Sibelius Monument MONUMENT

This famous, striking sculpture was created by artist Eila Hiltunen in 1967 to honour Finland's most famous composer. Bus 24 takes you there, but it's a pleasant walk or cycle.

Linnanmäki & Sea Life AMUSEMENT PARK, AQUARIUM

(Map p52; www.linnanmaki.fi; Tivolikuja 1; admission free, single ride/day pass €8/39; ⊙ roughly 11am-9pm mid-May–Aug plus some weekends Apr-May & Sep-Oct) 🕊 Famous Linnanmäki is a real kid-pleaser with rides, rollercoaster, 75m freefall and nightly fireworks. Its profits are donated to child-welfare organisations. There are various day passes, some of which discount admission to nearby **Sea Life** (Map p52; ☎09-565 8200; www.visitsealife.com; Tivolitie 10; adult/child €16/12; ⊙10am-7pm May-Sep, to 8pm Jun-Jul, 10am-5pm Oct-Apr, to 7pm Wed Oct-Apr), an aquarium complex with walk-through tunnels that let you spot sharks, rays, octopuses and myriad fish up close.

Discounted tickets are available online. Bus 23 and trams 3 and 8 take you there.

Helsinki Zoo ZOO

(www.korkeasaari.fi; Korkeasaari; adult/child €12/6, incl ferry ride €18/9; ⊙10am-8pm May-Aug, 10am-4pm Oct-Mar, 10am-6pm Sep & Apr) This spacious island zoo is located on Korkeasaari, best reached by ferry from the kauppatori. Established in 1889, it has animals and birds from Finland and around the world housed in large natural enclosures, as well as a tropical house, a small farm, and a good cafe and terrace. Ferries leave from the kauppatori (eastern end) and from Hakaniemi every 40 minutes or so during May to September, and bus 16 goes from the train station daily year-round.

★Seurasaaren Ulkomuseo MUSEUM

(Seurasaari Open-Air Museum; www.seurasaari. fi; adult/child €8/2.50; ⊙11am-5pm Jun-Aug, 9am-3pm Mon-Fri, 11am-5pm Sat & Sun late May & early Sep) West of the city centre, this excellent island museum has a collection of historic wooden buildings transferred here from around Finland. There's everything from haylofts to a mansion, parsonage and

Helsinki

church, as well as the beautiful giant rowboats used to transport churchgoing communities. Prices and hours refer to entering the buildings themselves, where guides in traditional costume demonstrate folk dancing and crafts. Otherwise, you're free to roam the picturesque wooded island, where there are several cafes.

There are guided tours in English at 3pm in summer. The island is also the venue for Helsinki's biggest Midsummer bonfires and a popular area for picnicking. From central Helsinki, take bus 24.

★ Mannerheim-Museo   MUSEUM
(Map p52; ☑09-635443; www.mannerheim-museo.fi; Kalliolinnantie 14; adult/child €10/free; ⊙11am-4pm Fri-Sun) This fascinating museum by Kaivopuisto (park) was the home of Baron Gustav Mannerheim, former president, commander in chief of the Finnish army and Finnish Civil War victor. The great field marshal never owned the building; he rented it from chocolate magnate Karl Fazer until his death. The house tells of Mannerheim's intrepid life with hundreds of military medals and photographs from his Asian expedition. Entry includes an informative one-hour multilingual guided tour, plus plastic booties to keep the hallowed floor clean.

Suomen Urheilumuseo   MUSEUM, TOWER
(Finnish Sports Museum; Map p52; www.urheilu museo.fi; Olympiastadion; adult/child €5.50/free, tower adult/child €5/2; ⊙11am-5pm Mon-Fri, noon-4pm Sat & Sun, tower 9am-8pm Mon-Fri, 9am-6pm Sat & Sun) This museum, in the 1952 Olympic Stadium, houses Finland's sporting hall of fame including the triumphs of runner Paavo Nurmi and ski-jumper Matti Nykänen. Good simulations let you compete in the 200m against champions and there's an exhibition about pesäpallo, Finland's baseball-like game. HI members get discounted admission. The stadium's tower has a 72m-high viewing platform with top city vistas. Admission lets you into the still-handsome stadium to look at the running track and gives €2 discount to the sports museum (€3 vice versa).

Kaapelitehdas   CULTURAL CENTRE
(Cable Factory; www.kaapelitehdas.fi; Tallberginka-tu; ⊙museums 11am-6pm Tue-Sun) This sprawling site once manufactured sea cable and later became Nokia's main factory until the 1980s. It's now a cultural complex with design studios, galleries, expositions and regular music, theatre and dance performances. There's also a photography museum, theatre museum and a hotel-and-restaurant museum. Tram 8 stops here, or take the metro to Ruoholahti and walk five minutes.

Sinebrychoffin Taidemuseo GALLERY
(Map p46; www.sinebrychoffintaidemuseo.fi; Bulevardi 40; adult/child €7/free; ☉10am-6pm Tue & Fri, 10am-8pm Wed-Thu, 10am-5pm Sat & Sun) The largest collection of classic European paintings in Finland is in this former brewery. The main collection is Italian, Flemish and Swedish in origin. The Empire room is an impressive re-creation that drips with chandeliers and opulence. Entrance rises to €10 if you want to visit all the temporary exhibitions.

🏃 Activities

Finnair Sky Wheel FERRIS WHEEL
(Map p52; www.finnair-skywheel.com; Katajanokanlaituri 2; adult/child €12/9; ☉10am-10pm Mon-Thu, 10am-11pm Fri & Sat, 10am-8pm Sun) Rising over the harbour, this ferris wheel gives good perspectives over the comings and goings of central Helsinki. If you fancy forking out €195, you get the VIP gondola, with glass floors below, leather seats and a bottle of champagne.

★ **Kotiharjun Sauna** SAUNA
(Map p52; www.kotiharjunsauna.fi; Harjutorinkatu 1; adult/child €12/6; ☉2-8pm Tue-Sun, sauna to 9.30pm) This traditional public wood-fired sauna in Kallio dates back to 1928. This type of place largely disappeared with the advent of shared saunas in apartment buildings, but it's a classic experience, where you can also get a scrub down and massage. There are separate saunas for men and women; bring your own towel or rent one (€3). It's a short stroll from Sörnäin-

en metro station. Closes Sundays June to mid-August.

Yrjönkadun Uimahalli SWIMMING
(Map p46; www.hel.fi; Yrjönkatu 21; swimming €5-5.40, swimming plus saunas €14; ☉open Sep-May, men 6.30am-8pm Tue & Thu, 8am-8pm Sat, women noon-8pm Sun & Mon, 6.30am-8pm Wed & Fri) For a sauna and swim, these art deco baths are a Helsinki institution – a fusion of soaring Nordic elegance and Roman tradition. There are separate hours for men and women. Nudity is compulsory in the saunas; bathing suits are optional in the pool.

Jääpuisto SKATING
(Ice Park; Map p46; ☏09-3108-7934; www.jaapuisto.fi; adult/child €6/4, skate rental €5; ☉noon-9pm Mon-Fri, 10am-9pm Sat, 10am-7pm Sun Nov–Mar) In winter Rautatientori (Railway Sq) becomes this outdoor ice-skating area where you can hire skates and get involved.

Hietaranta BEACH
Helsinki has several city beaches and this is the best. It's a likeable stretch of sand just west of the city centre, and ideal in summer for either swimming or enjoying the terrace. The nicest way to get here is to stroll from Mechelininkatu west through the Hietaniemi cemetery.

Cruises
When strolling through the kauppatori in summer, you won't have to look for cruises – the boat companies will find you. One-and-a-half hour cruises cost €20 to €25, while

---

GAY & LESBIAN HELSINKI

Helsinki has an active scene with several dedicated venues and a host of gay-friendly spots. There's a list of gay-friendly places at www.visithelsinki.fi, and the tourist office stocks a couple of brochures on gay Helsinki. Every June **Helsinki Pride** (www.helsinkipride.fi) includes balls, karaoke and picnics.

Bars & Clubs

DTM (Map p46; www.dtm.fi; Mannerheimintie 6; ☉9pm-4am; 🏳️) Finland's most famous gay venue (Don't Tell Mama) now occupies smart premises in a very out-of-the-closet location on the city's main street. There are various club nights with variable entry fees.

Hercules (Map p46; www.herculesgayclub.com; Lönnrotinkatu 4; ☉9pm-4am) A busy disco, aimed at men aged 30-plus, but dance-floor classics and campy karaoke attract everyone.

Hugo's Room (Map p46; www.hugosroom.fi; Iso Roobertinkatu 3; ☉2pm-2am; 🏳️) This popular lounge bar is elegant but doesn't take itself too seriously. It's got a great streetside terrace on this always-intriguing pedestrian thoroughfare.

Fairytale (Map p52; www.fairytale.fi; Helsinginkatu 7; ☉4pm-2am Mon-Fri, 2pm-2am Sat & Sun) One of Kallio's dark drinking dens, this is frequented by both men and women. The front terrace is a prime streetside spot.

DON'T MISS

TRIPPING TO TALLINN

The short ferry trip to Tallinn, capital of Estonia, offers so much more than the booze cruise that many Finns use it for. The city's charming **Vanalinn** (Old Town) is one of Europe's most evocative medieval districts, best enjoyed with an afternoon of ambling, particularly around **Raekoja plats** (Town Hall Sq), dominated by its Gothic town hall complete with minaret-like tower that you can climb to see the lie of the land. Wander a little further to **Saiakang** (White Bread Passage) with the 14th-century **Püha Vaimu Kirik** (Holy Spirit Church) at one end.

If you've worked up an appetite by now, head to **Ö** (☎372-661 6150; www.restoran-o. ee; Mere pst 6e; 4-/6-/8-course menu €46/59/76; ☺6-11pm Mon-Sat), an ethereal dining room that highlights Estonian produce. For heartier fare in a medieval atmosphere, **Olde Hansa** (☎627 9020; www.oldehansa.ee; Vana turg 1; mains €10-40; ☺10am-midnight) is fun. There are plenty of good places to wet your whistle, such as comfy purveyor of local brews **Hell Hunt** (www.hellhunt.ee; Pikk 39; ☺noon-2am; 📶). Don't worry about the name; it actually means 'gentle wolf'.

Check out **Tallinn Tourist Information Centre** (☎372-645 7777; www.tourism.tallinn. ee; Kullassepa 4; ☺9am-7pm Mon-Fri, to 5pm Sat & Sun May-Aug, 9am-6pm Mon-Fri, to 3pm Sat & Sun Sep-Apr) for a range of accommodation options.

Handily, euros are the currency here, and Estonia is a Schengen country so there are no entry requirements to visit from Finland.

For more info on Tallinn and Estonia, head to shop.lonelyplanet.com for a downloadable PDF of the chapter from Lonely Planet's *Estonia, Latvia & Lithuania* guide.

dinner cruises, bus-boat combinations and sunset cruises are also available. Most go past Suomenlinna and weave between other islands. A visit to the zoo or Suomenlinna is a good way to combine a scenic boat ride with other sightseeing. There are also longer day cruises by ferry and steamer from Helsinki to the Finnish town of Porvoo and beyond.

IHA Lines   CRUISE
(Map p46; ☎09-6874-5050; www.ihalines.fi; adult/child €19/10) Two archipelago routes plus a sunset cruise and lunch/dinner cruises.

Royal Line   CRUISE
(Map p46; ☎020-711-8333; www.royalline.fi; adult/child €22/free) Offers bus-and-boat combinations, and also has a 45-minute express cruise (€14).

Helsinki Sightseeing   CRUISE
(Gray Line; Map p46; ☎09-2288-1600; www. stromma.fi; adult/child €22/10) Offers a standard islands-and-canal cruise plus jazz cruises, dinners, and bus-and-boat combinations.

☞ Tours

There are a couple of the standard hop-on hop-off bus tours running; expect to pay around €25 to €30 for a ticket. An excellent budget alternative is to do a circuit of town on **Tram 2** then **Tram 3** or vice versa; pick up the free *Sightseeing on Tram 2/3* bro-

chure as your guide around the city centre and out to Kallio.

Helsinki Cityride   WALKING, CYCLING
(☎044-955-8720; www.helsinkicityride.com) This outfit offers a variety of walking (or Nordic walking) tours around various parts of the capital, year-round. Prices cost €30 to €50 but you get two people for the price of one. It also does a three-hour grand cycling tour that passes most of the major sights (€45 per person including bike rental). Book in advance.

Natura Viva   KAYAKING
(☎010-292-4030; www.naturaviva.fi; Ramsinniementie 14; ☺Jun-Aug) Located at the Rantapuisto hotel on Vuosaari, east of the city centre, these guys run daily three-hour paddling excursions around the Helsinki archipelago. It's beginner-friendly and they'll pick you up from the centre of town. You can rent kayaks at the paddling centre here, which is also open in May and most of September.

Happy Guide Helsinki   WALKING, CYCLING
(☎0445-020066; www.happyguidehelsinki.com) Runs a range of original, light-hearted but informative bike and walking tours around the city. There are a lot of options, so study its website.

✨ Festivals & Events

Vappu STUDENT
(May Day) This student graduation festival is celebrated by gathering around the Havis Amanda statue, which receives a white graduation cap, at 6pm on 30 April. The following day, May Day, is celebrated with plenty of sparkling wine, preferably outdoors.

Helsinki Päivä CITY
(Helsinki Day; www.helsinkipaiva.fi) Celebrating the city's anniversary, Helsinki Day brings many free events to Esplanadi on 12 June.

Tuska Festival MUSIC
(www.tuska-festival.fi) A big metal festival in late June or early July.

Helsingin Juhlaviikot PERFORMING ARTS
(Helsinki Festival; www.helsinginjuhlaviikot.fi) From late August to early September, this arts festival features chamber music, jazz, theatre, opera and more.

Flow Festival MUSIC
(www.flowfestival.com) An August weekend festival that sees indie, hip-hop, electronic and experimental music rock the suburb of Suvilahti.

Baltic Herring Fair FOOD
(www.portofhelsinki.fi) In the first week of October fisherfolk and chefs gather at the kauppatori to sell delicious salted and marinated herring. It's been going since 1743.

🛏 Sleeping

There's a dearth of cheap accommodation in Helsinki. From mid-May to mid-August bookings are strongly advisable, although July's a quieter time for midrange and top-end hotels. The Sokos (p289) and Scandic (p289) chains have several business hotels in the city centre, and other multinationals are present.

🛏 Central Helsinki

Hostel Erottajanpuisto HOSTEL €
(Map p46; ☑ 09-642169; www.erottajanpuisto. com; Uudenmaankatu 9; dm/s/d €30/60/75; @ 🛜) Helsinki's most characterful and laid-back hostel occupies the top floor of a building in a lively street of bars and restaurants. Forget curfews, lockouts, school kids and bringing your own sleeping sheet – this is more like a guesthouse with (crowded) dormitories. Shared bathrooms are new; private rooms offer more peace and there's a great

lounge and friendly folk. HI members get 10% off; breakfast is extra.

★ Hotelli Helka HOTEL €€
(Map p46; ☑ 09-613580; www.helka.fi; Pohjoinen Rautatiekatu 23; s €110-132, d €142-162; P @ 🛜) One of the centre's best midrange hotels, the Helka has competent, friendly staff and excellent facilities, including free parking if you can bag one of the limited spots. Best are the rooms, which seem to smell of pine with their Artek furniture, ice-block bedside lights and print of a rural Suomi scene over the bed, backlit to give rooms a moody glow. Premium rooms are €20 extra and somewhat larger. There's a good restaurant, and bike hire is available for guests in summer.

Hotel Finn HOTEL €€
(Map p46; ☑ 09-684-4360; www.hotellifinn. fi; Kalevankatu 3B; s €59-119, d €109-199; P 🛜) High in a central-city building, this friendly two-floor hotel is upbeat with helpful service and corridors darkly done out in sexy chocolate and red, with art from young Finnish photographers on the walls. Rooms all differ but are bright, with modish wallpaper and tiny bathrooms. Some are furnished with recycled materials. Rates vary widely – it can be a real bargain.

Browse its website well ahead for the best deals. Breakfast, in a nearby cafe, is extra.

Hotel Carlton HOTEL €€
(Map p46; ☑ 09-684-1320; www.carlton.fi; Kaisaniemenkatu 3; s/d €139/165; @ 🛜) On a busy street near the train station, and very handy for trams and metro, this friendly small hotel has rooms in several shapes and sizes, all with decent-sized bathrooms and not too much street noise. It represents value by central Helsinki standards and has a bit of soul. Prices are often lower than the maximum we list here. It can be difficult to spot from the street: enter via Roberts Coffee.

Hotel Anna HOTEL €€
(Map p46; ☑ 09-616621; www.hotelanna.fi; Annankatu 1; s/d €135/170; P @ 🛜) Owned by the Finnish Free Church, this smallish hotel is good for family or business visitors looking for a bit of quiet. Rates are usually quite a bit lower than the rack rates we list here.

Omenahotelli HOTEL €€
(☑ 0600-18018; www.omenahotels.com; r €70-130; 🛜) This good-value staffless hotel chain has two handy Helsinki locations: **Lönnrotinkatu** (Map p46; Lönnrotinkatu 13); **Yrjönkatu**

(Map p46; Yrjönkatu 30). As well as a double bed, rooms have fold-out chairs that can sleep two more, plus there's a microwave and mini-fridge. Book online or via a terminal in the lobby. Windows don't open, so rooms can be stuffy on hot days.

★**Hotel Fabian** HOTEL €€€
(Map p46; ☎ 09-6128-2000; www.hotelfabian.fi; Fabianinkatu 7; r €200-270; @ ☎) Central, but in a quiet part without the bustle of the other designer hotels, this place gets everything right. Elegant standard rooms with whimsical lighting and restrained modern design are extremely comfortable; they vary substantially in size. Higher-grade rooms add extra features and a kitchenette. Staff are super-helpful and seem very happy to be here. There's no restaurant, but breakfast is cooked in front of you by the chef

★**Hotel Haven** HOTEL €€€
(Map p46; ☎ 09-681930; www.hotelhaven.fi; Unioninkatu 17; s/d from €189/220; P @ ☎) The closest hotel to the kauppatori is elegant, welcoming and scores high on all levels. All room grades feature excellent beds and linen, soft colour combinations, classy toiletries and thoughtful extras such as sockets in the safes. 'Comfort' rooms face the street and are very spacious; higher grades give add-ons – such as a Nespresso machine in 'Lux' category – and some offer a magnificent harbour view. There's good on-site eating, expensive parking and a range of excellent facilities. Service is great.

★**Klaus K** HOTEL €€€
(Map p46; ☎ 020-770-4700; www.klauskhotel.com; Bulevardi 2; d €175-315; @ ☎) ✐ Boasting excellent service and extremely comfortable beds, this central, independent design hotel has a theme of *Kalevala* quotes throughout, and easy-on-the-eye space-conscious architecture. A range of slick new 'Sky Loft' rooms offer a more modern feel; some come with balconies. A host of amenities ease the stay, but the best bit is the fabulous breakfasts.

The morning spread features all sorts of original and tasty morsels sourced from small Finnish producers.

GLO Hotel Kluuvi HOTEL €€€
(Map p46; ☎ 010-344-4400; www.glohotels.fi; Kluuvikatu 4; s €234-269, d €249-284; @ ☎) There are no starched suits at reception at this laid-back designer joint, and the relaxed atmosphere continues through the comfortably modish public areas to the rooms. Beds:

exceptionally inviting. Facilities: top notch and mostly free. Location: on a pedestrian street in the heart of town. Cute extra: a stuffed tiger toy atop the covers.

Online prices are best; if there's not much difference between the standard and the standard XL, go for the latter as you get quite a bit more space.

Hotel Kämp HOTEL €€€
(Map p46; ☎ 09-576111; www.hotelkamp.fi; Pohjoisesplanadi 29; r from €351; P @ ☎) This grand, stylish hotel is a Helsinki emblem, whose history includes long, animated piss-ups as the likes of Sibelius and Gallen-Kallela thrashed out their ideas. Its romantic marble lobby seduces you back to historic inward-facing rooms furnished with antiques and then surprises in the marble bathrooms with their trademark rubber duck. Facilities include a plush day spa, saunas and restaurants.

Sokos Hotel Torni HOTEL €€€
(Map p46; ☎ 020-123-4604; www.sokoshotels.fi; Yrjönkatu 26; s €134-209, d €149-219; P @ ☎) In 1931 this building became Finland's Empire State Building and although no longer the country's tallest edifice, it still boasts excellent views, especially from its Ateljee Bar. Today rooms have been stylishly renovated in keeping with the historic feel in art deco and art nouveau styles, though modern rooms in rich red and black have hip decor.

You pay a little extra for rooms with views, but they're worth it. Still a great Helsinki address.

Hotelli Seurahuone HOTEL €€€
(Map p46; ☎ 09-69141; www.hotelliseurahuone.fi; Kaivokatu 12; s/d €219/239; P @ ☎) This *seurahuone* (literally, 'club room') was a meeting place for high society, where visiting officers, gentlemen and ladies came to stay, and a venue for concerts and ballroom dances. The building remains a classic, with stately rooms in black and gold, and period fittings including the smoking cabinet and ballroom. Sadly there's no sauna, but Rautatientori views provide succour.

⊨ Greater Helsinki

Hostel Academica HOSTEL €
(Map p52; ☎ 09-1311-4334; www.hostelacademica.fi; Hietaniemenkatu 14; dm/s/d €28.50/63/75; ☉ Jun-Aug; P @ ☎ 🏊) ✐ Finnish students live well, so in summer take advantage of this residence, a clean busy spot packed

HOME IN HELSINKI

Ideal for families, apartment-rental options range from one-room studios to expansive multi-room affairs. Often you'll get use of a sauna, parking area and other facilities. The longer you stay the cheaper rates get, with deals for weekly and monthly stays. Apartments are located throughout the city. Recommended agents include the following:

City Apartments (Map p46; ☎09-612-6990; www.cityapartments.fi; Vuorikatu 18; s/d from €122/142; P 📶) Variety of apartments in a handy central location near railway and metro.

Kotihotelli (☎010-420-4700; www.kotihotelli.fi; studios from €74, 1-/2-bedroom apt from €109/125; P 📶) Good agent with excellent modern apartments in several locations around central Helsinki.

SATO Hotelhome (☎020-134-4344; www.satohotellikoti.fi; per wk €600-950; P 📶) Offers excellent modern apartments for stays of a week or longer, though you can find shorter rentals online. There are two locations, one on Lapinlahdenkatu near Kamppi bus station, the other in the quiet but central Kruununhaka district

with features (pool and sauna) and cheery staff. The modern rooms are great, and all come with bar fridges and their own bathrooms. Dorms have only two or three berths so there's no crowding. It's also environmentally sound. Breakfast available. HI discount.

Wi-fi doesn't reach all rooms, but you can get a cable for laptops.

Eurohostel HOSTEL €
(Map p52; ☎09-622-0470; www.eurohostel.eu; Linnankatu 9; dm €31, s €54-60, d €60-70; @ 📶) On Katajanokka island close to the Viking Line ferry and easily reached on tram 4, this hostel is busy and convenient, if a little impersonal. Two grades of room are similar and both come with share bathrooms; the 'Eurohostel' rooms are more modern with TV and parquet floors. Dorm rates mean sharing a twin – a good deal. The cafe-bar serves breakfast and other meals, and there's a morning sauna included. HI and online-booking discount. Rates vary widely.

Hostel Suomenlinna HOSTEL €
(☎09-684-7471; www.snk.fi; Suomenlinna C9; dm/s/d/tr €30/62/76/111; ⏰reception 8am-3.30pm Mon-Sat, 8am-noon Sun; @ 📶) This excellent alternative to staying in central Helsinki is near the ferry pier on Suomenlinna. Once a Russian primary school then a barracks, it's understandably got an institutional feel. Dormitories are bright high-ceilinged classrooms, while private rooms upstairs have cosy sloping ceilings. There's a kitchen (supermarket nearby) and laundry. Inconveniently, you must check in during reception hours and get the keycode. HI discount.

Breakfast is available. The place is quite often booked out by groups in term time.

Hostel Stadion HOSTEL €
(Map p52; ☎09-477-8480; www.stadionhostel.fi; Pohjoinen Stadiontie 3; dm/d/q €24/60/104; P @ 📶) An easy tram ride from town, this well-equipped hostel is actually part of the Olympic Stadium. There are no views though, and it feels old-style, with big dorms and heavy decor. Nonetheless, it's a cheap bed and there are good facilities, including laundry, kitchen, bike hire, a cafe and free parking. Linen and towels included; HI discount.

Rastila Camping CAMPGROUND, COTTAGES €
(☎09-3107-8517; www.rastilacamping.fi; Karavaanikatu 4; campsites €14, plus per adult/child €5/1, 2-to 4-person cabins €79, cottages €107-213; P @ 📶) Only 20 minutes on the metro from the city centre (Rastila station), this year-round campground makes a good budget option. Though scarcely rural, it's green and well equipped, with a supermarket nearby. As well as grassy tent and plenty of van sites, there are wooden cabins and more-upmarket log cottages, plus a gentle beach and facilities, including good showers, fast wi-fi, saunas and bike hire.

There's also a summer hostel (dm/s/d €21/36/62 from mid-June to July)

Hellsten Helsinki Parliament APARTMENT €€
(Map p46; ☎09-251-1050; www.hellstenhotels.fi; Museokatu 18; apt €120-190; ⏰reception 7am-10pm Mon-Fri; @ 📶) A step up in style and comfort from many hotels, the apartments here have sleek modern furnishings, kitchenette, internet connections and cable TV. Prices vary seasonally and there are discounts for longer stays. It's in a great location. You will receive a keycode if you arrive outside hours.

GLO Hotel Art HOTEL €€
(Map p46; ☑ 010-344-4100; www.glohotels.fi; Lönnrotinkatu 29; r €120-180; P @ 🛜) Built in 1903 as the student clubhouse for the technical university opposite, this turreted art nouveau castle-like building features a dark but atmospheric vaulted lobby. Rooms have been given a makeover and are modern, with designer furniture and excellent amenities; there's a range of different sizes. Easy on-site parking makes this a good choice for drivers.

★ **Hotel Katajanokka** HOTEL €€€
(Map p52; ☑ 09-686450; www.bwkatajanokka. fi; Merikasarminkatu 1A; d €150-250; P @ 🛜) Set in a refurbished prison, this place offers character in spades on Katajanokka island. Rooms stretch over two to three ex-cells, so they're anything but pokey, and boast not slop buckets but sleek modern bathrooms. Penitentiary jokes – handcuffs for sale at reception – aside, there's plenty of luxury and a sumptuous sauna. Tram 4 stops right outside. This jailhouse rocks.

🛏 Airport Hotels

GLO Airport HOTEL €€€
(☑ 010-344-4600; www.glohotels.fi; d €154-200; @ 🛜) The most convenient spot for the airport is this hotel in Terminal 2 itself. The windowless rooms (no planespotting, folks) are small and a little claustrophobic, but feature attractive design; some have saunas. Singles are €15 cheaper and no-breakfast rates are available. The day rate (€89 from 9am to 6pm) is decent value.

✖ Eating

Helsinki has by far the nation's best range of restaurants, whether for Finnish classics, modern Suomi cuisine or international dishes. Good budget options are in shorter supply: cafes offer lunch choices and there are plenty of self-catering opportunities.

> **🛈 EAT.FI**
>
> A good resource is the website www.eat. fi, which plots restaurants on a map of town: even if you can't read the reviews (though there are usually some in English), you'll soon spot what are the latest favourites and what's open.

✖ Central Helsinki

Zucchini VEGETARIAN €
(Map p46; Fabianinkatu 4; lunch €8-12; ☉ 11am-4pm Mon-Fri; ✓) One of the city's few vegetarian cafes, this is a top-notch lunchtime spot; queues out the door are not unusual. Piping-hot soups banish winter chills, and fresh-baked quiche on the sunny terrace out the back is a summer treat. For lunch, you can choose soup or salad/hot dish or both.

Café Balzac CAFE €
(Map p46; www.cafebalzac.fi; Iso Roobertinkatu 3-5; lunches €10-12; ☉ 11am-3pm Mon-Tue, 11am-9pm Wed-Fri, noon-9pm Sat; 🛜) A reader put us on to this little cafe hidden in a courtyard off this pedestrian street. It's an atmospheric spot with just a handful of crowded tables. There are great daily lunch specials – pasta, elaborate salads, all colourful and tasty, and a helpful owner.

Karl Fazer Café CAFE €
(Map p46; www.fazer.fi; Kluuvikatu 3; light meals €6-11; ☉ 7.30am-10pm Mon-Fri, 9am-10pm Sat, 10am-6pm Sun; 🛜) This classic cafe can feel a little cavernous, but it's the flagship for the mighty chocolate empire of the same name. The cupola famously reflects sound, so locals say it's a bad place to gossip. It is ideal, however, for buying Fazer confectionery, fresh bread, salmon or shrimp sandwiches or enjoying the towering sundaes or slabs of cake. Good special-diets options.

Café Bar 9 CAFE €
(Map p46; www.bar9.net; Uudenmaankatu 9; mains €10-16; ☉ food 11am-11pm Mon-Fri, noon-11pm Sat & Sun; 🛜) It's tough to find low-priced food at dinnertime in Helsinki that's not shaved off a spinning stick, so this place stands out. It would anyway, with its retro red formica tables and unpretentious artsy air. Plates vary, with some solid Finnish fare backed up by big sandwiches, Thai-inspired stir-fries and pastas. Portions are generous so don't overdo it: you can always come back.

Skiffer PIZZA €
(Map p46; www.skiffer.fi; Erottajankatu 11; pizzas €12-17; ☉ 11am-9.30pm Mon-Thu, 11am-11pm Fri, 2-11pm Sat, 2-8pm Sun; 🛜) Crusty goodness and great-tasting fresh ingredients combine to excellent effect in this popular, out-of-the-ordinary pizza joint. Nautical-themed art exhibitions brighten the darkish interior; it's a popular meeting spot, so be prepared to wait a wee bit for a table.

Cholo

MEXICAN €

(Map p46; www.cholo.fi; Lönnrotinkatu 9; meals €9.80; ⊙11am-8pm Tue-Fri, noon-9pm Sat) This pint-sized place packs out with a young hipster crowd who are prepared to queue for the really tasty burritos and tacos that come bursting with colour and flavour. It gets a bit cramped, so head out and eat in the park opposite on a nice day.

UniCafe

CAFETERIA €

(Map p46; www.hyyravintolat.fi; Mannerheimintie 3B; lunch €7-9; ⊙11am-7pm Mon-Fri, 11am-6pm Sat; 🕏🖉) Not just for students, these university cafeterias – there are several branches around town – offer a good range of solid daily meals, with special diets catered for, at a budget-friendly price. This one, entered next to the Zetor restaurant, has the longest hours, which are restricted during summer break. Check the website for the daily menu.

Fafa's

TAKEAWAY €

(Map p46; www.fafas.fi; Iso Roobertinkatu 2; meals €7-11; ⊙11am-9pm Mon-Wed, 11am-4am Thu-Fri, noon-4am Sat) A cut above the usual kebab places, this serves delicious falafel until late. Opening hours are a bit variable depending on how much has been sold.

Salve

FINNISH €€

(Map p46; ☑010-766-4280; www.ravintolasalve. fi; Hietalahdenranta 11; mains €19-27; ⊙10am-midnight Mon-Sat, 10am-11pm Sun) Down by the water in the west of town, this centenarian establishment has long been a favourite of nautical types, and has appropriately high-seas decor, with paintings of noble ships on the walls. It serves great Finnish comfort food such as meatballs, fried Baltic herring and steaks in substantial quantities. The atmosphere is warm and the service kindly.

Kosmos

FINNISH €€

(Map p46; ☑09-647255; www.kosmos.fi; Kalevankatu 3; mains €20-34; ⊙11.30am-1am Mon-Fri, 4pm-1am Sat) Designed by Alvar Aalto, and with a bohemian history, this nonagenarian place is a Helsinki classic. It combines a staid, very traditionally Finnish atmosphere with tasty not-very-modern dishes, including reindeer, sweetbreads, kidneys and succulent fish options. Service can be no-nonsense but straight from the days when waiting tables was a career.

Rikhards

GASTROPUB €€

(Map p46; ☑010-423-3256; www.rikhards.fi; Rikhardinkatu 4; mains €19-29; ⊙food 4-10pm Tue-

BRUNSSI

Finns like a lie-in on the weekend, after the debauches of Friday and Saturday nights, so *brunssi* (brunch) was sure to catch on. Usually served as a buffet with everything from fruit and pastries to canapes, salads and pasta, it's so popular that you'll often have to book or wait. Expect to pay around €15 to €25 for this meal, which is served around 10.30am to 3.30pm, weekends only. The blog brunssipartio.fi keeps tabs on the scene; there's an English section.

Fri, 2-10pm Sat, 1-6pm Sun; 🕏) The latest venture of top Finnish chef Hans Välimäki, this gastropub blends the stylish and the casual with notable success. Some intriguing creations – try the 'popcorn' – back up classic bistro fare – sausage and mash, succulent pork chop, fish 'n' chips – all of which reach great taste levels. A classy meal at a decent price.

Bellevue

RUSSIAN €€

(Map p52; ☑09-179560; www.restaurant-bellevue.com; Rahapajankatu 3; mains €20-33; ⊙11am-midnight Tue-Fri, 5pm-midnight Sat Aug-Jun) Helsinki's best Russian restaurant, complete with pot-roasted bear (€70). More standard choices include *zakuska* (mixed starters) and a range of blini choices. The atmosphere is elegant and old-fashioned. Closes Saturday lunch in summer.

Grotesk

MEDITERRANEAN €€

(Map p46; ☑010-470-2100; www.grotesk.fi; Ludviginkatu 10; mains €20-30; ⊙11.30am-2pm & 5-10pm Tue-Fri, 5-10pm Sat; 🕏) Elegant but reasonably informal, this has a Finnish-baroque dining room where cured meat starters precede excellent grilled meats. There's also a worthwhile tasting menu, featuring smaller, inventive portions. The wine list is especially good, and priced fairly. The wine-cocktail bar is very worthwhile too, particularly in summer when it migrates into the courtyard space.

KarlJohan

FINNISH €€

(Map p46; ☑09-612-1121; www.ravintolakarl-johan.fi; Yrjönkatu 21; mains €17-32; ⊙11am-3pm Mon, 11am-3pm & 5-11pm Tue-Fri, 2-11pm Sat; 🖉) Welcoming service and an elegant but relaxed atmosphere provide a fitting backdrop for carefully prepared Finnish cuisine that's strong on both local fish dishes, vegetarian choices and rich, delicious meat options. The central location is another plus point. Wines are rather pricey.

Thai Orchid
THAI €€
(Map p46; www.thaimaalainenravintola.fi; Lönnrotinkatu 27; mains €18-25; ⊙11am-2pm Mon, 11am-2pm & 5pm-midnight Tue-Thu, 11am-midnight Fri & Sat; ⚐) With a much more intriguing menu than most of the capital's southeast Asian restaurants, this offers high-quality Thai cuisine using excellent ingredients and authentic spices. There are various tasting menus that showcase the best on offer. The ambience is modern, soothing and classy.

Goodwin
STEAK €€
(Map p46; ☎050-419-8000; www.steak. fi; Eteläranta 14; mains €25-30; ⊙11am-11pm) There's a lot to be said for doing one thing well, and Goodwin achieves it, with very tasty tenderised steaks cooked carefully to order. Sauces and sides are extra, salads are tasty and there's a long wine list with some decent reds on offer.

Kitch
CAFE €€
(Map p46; www.kitch.fi; Yrjönkatu 30; mains €15-23; ⊙11am-2pm & 4-10pm, to 11pm Wed-Fri, noon-11pm Sat; ⚐⚐) ⚐ Handily located in a central area, this is great for watching the world go by. Simply furnished, it offers good-value lunches as well as generous tapas portions, original salads and fat burg-

---

ISLAND DINING

There's no better way to appreciate Helsinki's seaside location than by heading out to one of the many island restaurants. Most are served by small boats ferrying to and from quays on the mainland opposite. Most famous is stylish, spired **Saaristo** (Map p52; ☎09-7425-5505; www.asrestaurants.com; Luoto; mains €21-33; ⊙noon-11pm Mon-Fri May-Jun, 5-11pm daily Jul-Sep), on Luoto island and famous for society weddings and crayfish parties. There are several others; quality of food and service tends to vary each summer, so ask around about where's good that year. Even if you're not dining, the islands can make a refreshing break and give a new perspective on the city. The boats cost around €5 to €8 return for non-diners and run every 10 to 20 minutes during eating hours.

---

ers with slabs of goat cheese. Plenty of the produce is sustainably sourced.

Savotta
FINNISH €€
(Map p46; ☎09-7425-5588; www.asrestaurants. com; Aleksanterinkatu 22; mains €22-30; ⊙noon-11pm Mon-Sat, 1-10pm Sun) Theme-y but good quality and light-hearted, this representation of a logger's mess hall fits a lot of specialities from around Finland into its short but tasty menu. Serving staff in peasant tops are happy to explain the dishes, which include excellent fishy mixed starters and quality mains that might include succulent slow-roasted lamb or Arctic char. Summer dining is a pleasure on the courtyard terrace.

★Olo
MODERN FINNISH €€€
(Map p46; ☎010-320-6250; olo-ravintola.fi; Pohjoisesplanadi 5; lunch €53, degustations €89-137, with drinks €224-292; ⊙11.30am-3pm Mon, 11.30am-3pm & 6pm-midnight Tue-Fri, 6pm-midnight Sat) Thought of by many as Helsinki's best restaurant, Olo occupies smart new premises in a handsome 19th-century harbourside mansion. It's at the forefront of modern-Suomi cuisine, and its memorable degustation menus incorporate both the forage ethos and a little molecular gastronomy. The shorter 'journey' turns out to be quite a long one, with numerous small culinary jewels. Book a few weeks ahead.

★Savoy
FINNISH €€€
(Map p46; ☎09-6128-5300; www.savoy.fi; Eteläesplanadi 14; mains €44-47; ⊙11.30am-2.30pm & 6pm-midnight Mon-Fri, 6pm-midnight Sat) Originally designed by Alvar and Aino Aalto, this is definitely a standout dining room, with some of the city's best views. The food is a modern Nordic tour de force, with the 'forage' ethos strewing flowers and berries across plates that bear the finest Finnish game, fish and meat.

★Demo
MODERN FINNISH €€€
(Map p46; ☎09-2289-0840; www.restaurant demo.fi; Uudenmaankatu 9; 4-/5-/6-/7-course menu €62/75/92/102; ⊙4-11pm Tue-Sat) Book a table at this chic spot, where young chefs wow a designer crowd with modern Finnish cuisine. The quality is excellent, the combinations innovative, the presentation top notch and the slick contemporary decor appropriate. A place to be seen, not for quiet contemplation.

★A21 Dining
MODERN FINNISH €€€
(Map p46; ☎040-171-1117; www.a21.fi; Kalevankatu 17; 5-/7-course menu €65/79, cocktail flight

€49-63; ⊘5pm-midnight Tue-Sat) A very out-of-the-ordinary experience is to be had here, with a blinding white interior and innovative degustation menu accompanied by a mood-setting intro to each course. The idea is to transport you into Finland's natural world, and it works, with stunning flavour combinations accompanied by unusual cocktails.

Juuri MODERN FINNISH €€€
(Map p46; ☑09-635732; www.juuri.fi; Korkeavuorenkatu 27; mains €28-30; ⊘11am-2.30pm & 4-10pm Mon-Fri, 4-10pm Sat & Sun) Creative takes on classic Finnish ingredients draw the crowds to this stylish modern restaurant, but the best way to eat is to sample the 'sapas', which are tapas with a Suomi twist (€4.70 per plate). You might graze on marinated fish, smoked beef or homemade sausages. There are good lunches too, but they're not as interesting.

Greater Helsinki

Tin Tin Tango CAFE €
(Map p52; www.tintintango.info; Töölöntorinkatu 7; light meals €7-10; ⊘7am-midnight Mon-Fri, 9am-midnight Sat, 10am-midnight Sun; 🤶) This buzzy neighbourhood cafe decorated with prints from the quiffed Belgian's adventures has a bit of everything. There's a laundry and a sauna, as well as lunches, brunches, and cosy tables where you can sip a drink or get to grips with delicious rolls absolutely stuffed full. The welcoming, low-key bohemian vibe is the real draw, though.

Konstan Mölja FINNISH €
(Map p46; ☑09-694-7504; www.konstanmolja.fi; Hietalahdenkatu 14; buffet €18; ⊘5-10pm Tue-Fri, 4-10pm Sat) The maritime interior of this old sailors' eatery hosts an impressive husband-and-wife team who turn out a great-value Finnish buffet for dinner. Though these days it sees plenty of tourists, it serves solid traditional fare, with salmon, soup, reindeer and friendly explanations of what goes with what. There's also limited à la carte available.

Cafe Regatta CAFE €
(Merikannontie 10; pastries €1.50-3; ⊘10am-11pm) Near the Sibelius monument in a marvellous waterside location, this historic cottage is scarcely bigger than a sauna, but has great outdoor seating on the bay. You can hire a canoe or paddleboards alongside, buy sausages and grill them over the open fire, or just kick back with a drink or cinnamon pastry. Expect to queue on sunny weekends.

WORTH A TRIP

SLAUGHTERHOUSE SNACKS

Teurastamo (Map p52; www.teurastamo.com; Työpajankatu 2) This former abattoir area between Sörnäinen and Kalasatama metro stations is an in place to be these days, with a range of locally sourcing eateries opening up in this casual post-industrial precinct. Choose to snack on dim sum, smokehouse fare, fresh pasta and more, or bring your own meat to grill and graze the kitchen garden for herbs and vegetables.

Café Ursula CAFE €
(www.ursula.fi; Ehrenströmintie 3; lunches €10-16; ⊘9am-9pm Sun-Thu, 9am-10pm Wed-Sat; 🤶) Offering majestic sea views, this cafe looks over the Helsinki archipelago and has marvellous outside seating. In winter you can sit in the modern interior and watch the ice on the sea. It's a posh lunch stop with good if pricey daily specials, elaborate open sandwiches, tasty cakes and glasses of fizz. It opens until midnight in summer, when Sunday brunch (€22) is a great option.

Pelmenit EASTERN EUROPEAN €
(Map p52; Kustaankatu 7; dishes €7-14; ⊘11am-5pm Mon-Thu, 11am-10pm Fri & Sat) A real change from all the designer places in central Helsinki, this simple Kallio eatery serves cheap, tasty authentic home cooking, including the excellent dumplings it's named after.

Silvoplee VEGETARIAN €
(Map p52; www.silvoplee.com; Toinen linja 7; food per kg €20; ⊘11am-8pm Mon-Fri, 11am-6pm Sat; 🤶) This large eatery serves decent vegan food, much of it organic. Near Hakaniemi market, it's a buffet and you pay by weight (the food's). Soups are cheaper and it opens earlier in the morning for tasty smoothies.

Gran Delicato CAFE €
(Map p46; www.grandelicato.fi; Kalevankatu 34; light meals €7-11; ⊘8am-8pm Mon-Fri, 10am-6pm Sat; 🤶) With a range of tasty fillings, this deli makes an ideal ciabatta grab, and also offers panini, salads, authentic strong coffee plus a selection of slices. The sultry aroma of the beans alone makes it worth hanging around.

⭐**Kuu** FINNISH €€
(Map p52; ☑09-2709-0973; www.ravintolakuu.fi; Töölönkatu 27; mains €19-30;

DON'T MISS

HELSINKI'S MARKET HALLS

While food stalls, fresh produce and berries can be found at the kauppatori, the real centre of Finnish market produce is the kauppahalli (market hall). There are three in central Helsinki, and they are fabulous places, with butchers, bakers, fishmongers and delis selling a brilliant range of traditional food. Apart from wandering around photographing the succulent range of smoked fish, they're great for self-catering, picnics and takeaway food, and all have cafes and other casual eateries where you can eat in.

Vanha Kauppahalli (Map p46; www.vanhakauppahalli.fi; Eteläranta 1; ⊙8am-6pm Mon-Sat; 🖊) Alongside the harbour, this is Helsinki's classic market hall. Built in 1889 and recently renovated, some of it is touristy these days (reindeer kebabs?), but it's still a traditional Finnish market.

Hietalahden Kauppahalli (Map p46; www.hietalahdenkauppahalli.fi; Lönnrotinkatu 34; ⊙8am-6pm Mon-Fri, to 5pm Sat, plus 10am-4pm Sun Jun-Aug; 🖊) This renovated market at Hietalahti has a fabulous range of food stalls and eateries, including enticing cafes with upstairs seating at each end. Take tram 6.

Hakaniemen Kauppahalli (Map p52; www.hakaniemenkauppahalli.fi; Hämeentie; ⊙8am-6pm Mon-Fri, to 4pm Sat; 🖊) This traditional-style Finnish food market is near the Hakaniemi metro. It's got a good range of produce and a cafe, and textile outlets upstairs. There's a summer market on the square outside.

Soppakeittiö (www.sopakeittio.fi; soups €8-10; ⊙11am-3.30pm Mon-Fri, 11am-3pm Sat) A great place to warm the cockles in winter; its bouillabaisse is famous. There's a branch at each kauppahalli.

⊙11.30am-midnight Mon-Fri, 2pm-midnight Sat, 2-10pm Sun) Tucked away on a corner behind the Crowne Plaza hotel on Mannerheimintie, this is an excellent choice for both traditional and modern Finnish fare. The short menu is divided between the two; innovation and classy presentation drive the contemporary dishes, while quality ingredients and exceptional flavour are keys to success throughout. Wines are very pricey, but at least there are some interesting choices.

Don't confuse with another (good) place, Kuu Kuu, not far away.

Sea Horse   FINNISH €€
(Map p52; ☎010-837-5700; www.seahorse.fi; Kapteeninkatu 11; mains €18-27; ⊙10.30am-midnight, to 1am Fri & Sat) Sea Horse dates back to the 1930s and is as traditional a Finnish restaurant as you'll find anywhere. Locals gather in the gloriously unchanged interior to meet and drink over hefty dishes of Baltic herring, Finnish meatballs, liver and cabbage rolls.

Carelia   BISTRO €€
(Map p52; ☎09-2709-0976; www.carelia. info; Mannerheimintie 56; mains €24-30; ⊙4pm-midnight Mon-Sat) Opposite the Oopperatalo, this is a striking spot set in a former pharmacy for a pre- or post-show drink or meal. Glamorously decorated in period style, it of-

fers smart bistro fare and plenty of intriguing wines by the glass.

Kolme Kruunua   FINNISH €€
(Map p52; ☎09-135-4172; www.kolmekruunua. fi; Liisankatu 5; mains €15-23; ⊙food 4pm-midnight Mon-Sat, 2-11pm Sun) This unpretentious Finnish local in the suburb of Kruununhaka offers tasty no-frills Finnish dishes such as fried vendace or sausages and mash in a fabulously retro dining area that hasn't changed since the 1950s. It's all very tasty, and you might want to try a couple of the other bars hereabouts, very traditional in feel and off the tourist trail.

Ateljé Finne   MODERN FINNISH €€€
(Map p46; ☎010-281-8242; www.ateljefinne.fi; Arkadiankatu 14; 2/3 courses €39/45; ⊙5-10pm Tue-Sat) Good-value modern cuisine at this elegant but relaxed spot. The menu changes regularly but the daily fish dish is always great.

Self-Catering

There are seven-day supermarkets and food courts in **Kamppi** (Map p46; www.kamppi. fi; Urho Kekkosenkatu 1; ⊙supermarket 7am-10pm Mon-Sat, 10am-10pm Sun) and **Forum** (Map p46; Mannerheimintie 20; ⊙7am-9pm Mon-Fri, 7am-6pm Sat, 10am-6pm Sun) shopping centres.

If you're after specialised supplies, **Ruohon-juuri** (Map p46; www.ruohonjuuri.fi; Salomonka-tu 5; ⏱9am-9pm Mon-Fri, 9am-6pm Sat, noon-6pm Sun) 🍴 stocks food that's ethically sound, organic and often catering to special dietary needs.

🍷 Drinking & Nightlife

Finns don't mind a drink and Helsinki has some of Scandinavia's most diverse nightlife. In winter locals gather in cosy bars, while in summer early-opening beer terraces sprout all over town. Some club nights have a minimum age of 20 or older, so check event details on websites before you arrive.

★Teerenpeli   PUB
(Map p46; www.teerenpeli.com; Olavinkatu 2; ⏱noon-2am Mon-Thu, noon-3am Fri & Sat, 3pm-midnight Sun; 📶) Get away from the Finnish lager mainstream with this excellent pub right by Kamppi bus station. It serves very tasty ales, stouts and berry ciders from its microbrewery in Lahti, in a long, split-level place with romantic low lighting, intimate tables and an indoor smokers' patio. The highish prices keep it fairly genteel for this zone.

Bar Loose   CLUB
(Map p46; www.barloose.com; Annankatu 21; ⏱4pm-2am Tue, 4pm-4am Wed-Sat, 6pm-4am Sun; 📶) The opulent blood-red interior and comfortably cosy seating seem too stylish for a rock bar, but this is what this is, with portraits of guitar heroes lining one wall and an eclectic mix of people filling the upstairs, served by two bars. Downstairs is a club area, with live music more nights than not and DJs spinning everything from metal to mod/retro classics.

U Kaleva   PUB
(Map p46; www.ukaleva.fi; Kalevankatu 3A; ⏱2pm-2am) Part of a knot of bars on this street just off Mannerheimintie in the heart of town, this unpretentious place stands out for its old-time Finnish atmosphere, cordial owners, eclectic local crowd and heated terrace.

A21 Cocktail Lounge   COCKTAIL BAR
(Map p46; www.a21.fi; Annankatu 21; ⏱6pm-midnight Wed, 6pm-1am Thu, 6pm-2am Fri & Sat) You'll need to ring the doorbell to get into this chic club but it's worth the intrigue to swing with Helsinki's arty set. The interior is sumptuous in gold, but the real lushness is in the cocktails, particularly the Finnish blends that toss cloudberry liqueur and rhubarb to create the city's most innovative tipples.

Bäkkäri   BAR, CLUB
(Map p46; www.bakkari.fi; Pohjoinen Rautatieka-tu 21; ⏱4pm-4am) Central and atmospheric, this bar is devoted to the heavier end of the spectrum, with lots of airplay for Finnish legends such as Nightwish, HIM, Children of Bodom and Apocalyptica. Outdoor tables are where the socialisng goes on, while upstairs is a club space. Beer's cheap until 8pm.

Corona Baari & Kafe Mockba   BAR
(Map p46; www.andorra.fi; Eerikinkatu 11-15; ⏱Corona 11am-2am Mon-Thu, 11am-3am Fri & Sat, noon-2am Sun, Kafe Mockba 6pm-2am Mon-Thu, 6pm-3am Fri & Sat; 📶) Those offbeat film-making Kaurismäki brothers are up to their old tricks with this pair of conjoined drinking dens. Corona plays the relative straight man with pool tables, no doorperson, an island bar and a relaxed mix of people. Mockba is back in the USSR with a bubbling samovar and Soviet vinyl. At closing they clear the place out by playing Brezhnev speeches.

Downstairs in Corona Dubrovnik is open for events: cinema screenings and album launches.

Mbar   BAR
(Map p46; www.mbar.fi; Mannerheimintie 22; ⏱9am-midnight Mon-Tue, 9am-2am Wed-Thu, 9am-4am Fri & Sat, noon-midnight Sun; 📶) Not just a geek haunt with internet terminals, this cafe-bar in the Lasipalatsi complex has a great terrace to soak up the sun, accompanied by DJs on most summer nights. It's one of Helsinki's most enjoyable spots, with great atmosphere.

Maxine   BAR, CLUB
(Map p46; www.maxine.fi; 6th fl, Kamppi; admission €3.50; ⏱4pm-4am Tue-Sat, shorter hours winter; 📶) On the top of Kamppi shopping centre, this refurbished venue makes the most of the inspiring city views from this high perch. It's divided into three sections, with a bar area – a great spot for a sundowner – and two dancefloors, one of which (the name, Kirjasto, or Library, gives it away) is quieter and aimed at an older crowd.

Enter down the side of the Kamppi building or from Urho Kekkosenkatu. Another club, The Tiger, on the floor below, has surly bouncers and a brasher scene.

THE CALL OF KALLIO
....

For Helsinki's cheapest beer (around €3 to €4 a pint), hit working-class Kallio (near Sörnäinen metro station), north of the city centre. Here, there's a string of dive bars along Helsinginkatu, but on this street as well as on the parallel Vaasankatu and crossing Fleminginkatu you'll find several more characterful bohemian places: go for a wander and you'll soon find one you like.

Majakkalaiva Relandersgrund BAR
(Map p52; www.majakkalaiva.fi; Pohjoisranta; ⊙noon-10pm or later May–mid-Oct) The deck of this elegant old lightship provides a fabulous and unusual venue for a coffee, beer or cider on a sunny afternoon.

Los Cojones BAR
(Map p46; Annankatu 15; ⊙6pm-1am Tue, 6pm-3am Wed-Sat; 🛜) A lighthearted Spanish theme here is backed up by hanging hams, wine barrels, guitars and bullfight posters. It's an atmospheric spot for a glass of wine or shot of oaky Jerez brandy and gets very lively later. You can soak it up with a range of Basque-style *pintxos* (canapes).

Aussie Bar BAR
(Map p46; www.aussiebar.net; Salomonkatu 5; ⊙2pm-2am Mon-Tue, noon-3am Wed-Sat, noon-2am Sun; 🛜) Run by descendants of convicts with plenty of 'G'days', this laid-back pub doesn't miss a cliché. Beneath the corrugated iron and faux-colonial fittings it makes for a good watering hole that's popular with locals. There's a good range of Down-Under beers and wines. It gets very upbeat and raucous on weekends, when there's a €3 admission charge.

Cuba! Cafe BAR, CLUB
(Map p46; www.cubacafe.fi; Erottajankatu 4; ⊙5pm-midnight Tue, to 2am Wed-Thu, to 4am Fri & Sat) Certainly one of Helsinki's brighter bars, this place doesn't take itself too seriously. Beers, cocktails and dancing – on the tables once the mojitos start flowing – are the order of the night in this party place; it packs out, but you'll hear more Suomi pop than salsa. There's no admission charge except the cloakroom fee.

Roskapankki PUB
(Map p52; Helsinginkatu 20; ⊙9am-2am) A Kallio classic with cheap beer and ragged character.

Kappeli BAR
(Map p46; www.kappeli.fi; Eteläesplanadi 1; ⊙10am-midnight; 🛜) This pleasant bar and outdoor terrace has regular music in the nearby bandstand. It's touristy but it's a great place to be on a sunny day.

Kuudes Linja CLUB
(Map p52; www.kuudeslinja.com; Hämeentie 13; entry from €8; ⊙7pm-1am Sun-Thu, 10pm-4am Fri & Sat) Between Hakaniemi and Sörnäinen metros, this is the place to find Helsinki's more experimental beats from top visiting DJs playing techno, industrial, post-rock and electro. There are also live gigs.

Teatteri BAR, CLUB
(Map p46; www.teatteri.fi; Pohjoisesplanadi 2; ⊙9am-2am Mon-Tue, 9am-4am Wed-Fri, 11am-4am Sat) This stylish central spot has three floors of fun, from the sophisticated Long bar, with its modernist paintings and web-spun light fixtures, to the summer-swelling terraces. It's got an older, more relaxed crowd and can be packed on weekends.

Wanha Kauppakuja BAR
(Map p46; www.center-inn.fi) This covered laneway off Aleksanterinkatu has a boisterous, meat-markety summer scene once the restaurant terraces are done with serving food for the night. There's usually a €5 admission charge.

☆ Entertainment

Live music is big in Helsinki, from metal to opera. The latest events are publicised in *Helsinki This Week*. Tickets for big events can be purchased from **Lippupalvelu** (Map p46; ✆0600-10800; www.lippupalvelu.fi), **Lippupiste** (✆0600-900-900; www.lippu.fi), **Tiketti** (Map p46; ✆0600-11616; www.tiketti.fi; Urho Kekkosenkatu 4; ⊙11am-7pm Mon-Fri) and **LiveNation** (www.livenation.fi).

Live Music
Major touring bands gig at Hartwall Areena (p67), though Kaapelitehdas (p54) and other places also attract big names.

★**Musiikkitalo** CONCERT VENUE
(Map p46; www.musiikkitalo.fi; Mannerheimintie 13) As cool and crisp as a gin and tonic on a glacier, this striking modern building is a

great addition to central Helsinki. The interior doesn't disappoint either – the main auditorium, visible from the foyer, has stunning acoustics. There are regular classical concerts, and prices are kept low, normally around €20. The bar is a nice place to hang out for a drink.

Tavastia
LIVE MUSIC

(Map p46; www.tavastiaklubi.fi; Urho Kekkosenkatu 4; ⊗8pm-1am Sun-Thu, 8pm-3am Fri, 8pm-4am Sat) One of Helsinki's legendary rock venues, this attracts both up-and-coming local acts and bigger international groups. There's a band every night of the week. Also check out what's on at Semifinal, the venue next door.

Semifinal
LIVE MUSIC

(Map p46; www.semifinal.fi; Urho Kekkosenkatu 6; ⊗8pm-1am Sun-Thu, 9pm-3am Fri, 9pm-4am Sat) Next to Tavastia, this smaller sibling has live music almost nightly, with a focus on up-and-coming Finnish bands.

Storyville
JAZZ

(Map p46; www.storyville.fi; Museokatu 8; ⊗6pm-2am Tue, 6pm-3am Wed-Thu, 6pm-4am Fri & Sat) Helsinki's number-one jazz club attracts a refined older crowd swinging to boogie woogie, trad jazz, Dixieland and New Orleans most nights. As well as the club section (from 8pm Wednesday to Saturday), there's a stylish bar that has a cool outside summer terrace in the park opposite.

Juttutupa
JAZZ, FUSION

(Map p52; www.juttutupa.com; Säästöpankinranta 6; ⊗10.30am-midnight Mon-Tue, 10.30am-1am Wed-Thu, 10.30am-3am Fri, 11am-3am Sat, noon-11pm Sun) A block from Hakaniemi metro station in an enormous granite building, Juttutupa is one of Helsinki's better music bars, focusing on contemporary jazz and rock fusion. Great beer terrace.

Nosturi
MUSIC

(Map p52; www.elmu.fi; Telakkakatu 8) This atmospheric harbourside warehouse hosts regular mid-size concerts with known Finnish and international performers.

Theatre

Oopperatalo
OPERA, BALLET

(Opera House; Map p52; ☑09-4030-2211; www.opera.fi; Helsinginkatu 58; tickets from €14) Opera, ballet and classical concerts are held here, though not during summer. Performances of the Finnish National Opera are surtitled in Finnish.

Kansallisteatteri
THEATRE

(Map p46; ☑010-733-1331; www.kansallisteatteri.fi; Läntinen teatterikuja 1) The Finnish National Theatre occupies a beautiful building by the train station. Performances (usually in Finnish) are always spectacular at this venue.

Cinemas

Cinemas show original-version films with Finnish and Swedish subtitles.

Kino Engel
CINEMA

(Map p46; ☑020-155-5801; www.cinemamondo.fi; Sofiankatu 4; adult €9.50-12.50) As well as the *kesäkino* (summer cinema) in the courtyard of Café Engel, in the warmer months this independent theatre shows arthouse and Finnish indie films.

Orion Theatre
CINEMA

(Map p46; ☑09-6154-0201; www.kavi.fi; Eerikinkatu 15; tickets €6.50; ⊗screenings Tue-Sun) This art-house cinema shows classics from the Finnish Film Archive.

FinnKino
CINEMA

(☑0600-007-007; www.finnkino.fi; adult €7-16) Several Helsinki cinemas screening big-name films; prices vary by day and session time. Branches include **Tennispalatsi** (Map p46; Salomonkatu 15) and **Maxim** (Map p46; Kluuvikatu 1).

Sport

Between September and April, ice hockey reigns supreme; going to a game is a good Helsinki experience. World championships in May are avidly watched on big screens.

Hartwall Areena
SPECTATOR SPORT

(www.hartwall-areena.com; Areenakuja 1) The best place to see top-level hockey matches, this arena is about 4km north of the city centre (take bus 23 or 69, or tram 7A or 7B). It's the home of Jokerit Helsinki, who now play in the international Kontinental Hockey League.

Helsingin Jäähalli
ICE HOCKEY

(Map p52; ☑09-477-7110; www.helsinginjaahalli.fi; Nordenskiöldinkatu 13) Helsinki's second venue for ice hockey is this arena in the Olympic Stadium complex.

Sonera Stadium
FOOTBALL

(Map p52; www.sonerastadium.fi; tickets €12-15) Next to the Olympic Stadium, this is HJK Helsinki's home ground. The team's closest thing Finland has to a Real Madrid or Manchester United, having won 26 league titles at last count.

HELSINKI APP

Hit the Helsinki App Store at apps.hel.fi on your smartphone or tablet for a range of helpful programs. Tourist info is also downloadable at www.visithelsinki.fi.

Shopping

Helsinki is a design epicentre, from fashion to the latest furniture and homewares. Central but touristy Esplanadi has the chic boutiques of Finnish classics. The most intriguing area to browse is nearby Punavuori, with a great retro-hipster vibe and numerous boutiques, studios and galleries to explore. A couple of hundred of these are part of **Design District Helsinki** (www.designdistrict.fi), whose invaluable map you can find at the tourist office.

Stockmann   DEPARTMENT STORE
(Map p46; 📞09-1211; www.stockmann.com; Aleksanterinkatu 52; ⊙9am-9pm Mon-Fri, 9am-6pm Sat, noon-6pm Sun; 🛜) Helsinki's 'everything store' does a good line of Finnish souvenirs and Sámi handicrafts, as well as textiles, jewellery, clothes and lots more. Export service.

Akateeminen Kirjakauppa   BOOKS
(Map p46; www.akateeminen.com; Pohjoisesplanadi 39; ⊙9am-9pm Mon-Fri, 9am-6pm Sat, noon-6pm Sun; 🛜) Finland's biggest bookshop, with a huge travel section, maps, Finnish literature and an impressively large English section including magazines and newspapers.

Aarikka   DESIGN
(Map p46; www.aarikka.fi; Pohjoisesplanadi 27; ⊙10am-7pm Mon-Fri, 10am-5pm Sat, noon-5pm Sun) Specialising in wood, Aarikka is known for its distinctly Finnish jewellery.

Artek   DESIGN
(Map p46; www.artek.fi; Eteläesplanadi 18; ⊙10am-7pm Mon-Fri, 10am-4pm Oct) Originally founded by Alvar Aalto and his wife Aino, this homewares, glassware and furniture store maintains the simple design principle of its founders.

Arabiakeskus   GLASS, CERAMICS
(www.arabiahelsinki.fi; Hämeentie 135; ⊙10am-8pm Mon-Fri, 10am-4pm Sat & Sun) Arabia refers to a whole district where the legendary Finnish ceramics company has manufactured its products since 1873. The complex includes an upmarket design mall, with several intriguing shops, including a large

Arabia/Iittala/Fiskars outlet. On the top floor the Arabian Museo tells of the brand's history. Take tram 6 or 8 to the Arabiankatu stop or one of several buses.

Iittala   GLASS
(Map p46; www.iittala.com; Pohjoisesplanadi 25; ⊙10am-7pm Mon-Fri, 10am-5pm Sat, noon-5pm Sun) Central outlet of Finland's famous glass manufacturer.

Marimekko   CLOTHING
(Map p46; www.marimekko.fi; Pohjoisesplanadi 33; ⊙10am-8pm Mon-Fri, 10am-5pm Sat, noon-5pm Sun) Finland's most celebrated designer fabrics, including warm florals and new designs, are available here as shirts, dresses, bags, sheets and almost every other possible application.

Kalevala Koru   JEWELLERY
(Map p46; www.kalevalakoru.fi; Pohjoisesplanadi 25-27; ⊙10am-7pm Mon-Fri, 10am-5pm Sat, noon-5pm Sun) Gold, silver and bronze jewellery with motifs based on Finnish history and legend.

Fennica Records   MUSIC
(Map p46; 📞09-685-1433; www.fennicakeskus.fi; Fredrikinkatu 38; ⊙10am-6pm Mon-Fri, 10am-3pm Sat) Secondhand and new CDs and vinyl from Suomi pop to jazz.

Moomin Shop   TOYS
(Map p46; www.moominshop.fi; Forum, Mannerheimintie 20; ⊙9am-9pm Mon-Fri, 9am-6pm Sat, noon-6pm Sun) All things Moomin, including books in English and Finnish. There's also a branch at the airport.

Levykauppa Äx   MUSIC
(Map p46; www.levykauppax.fi; Fredrikinkatu 59; ⊙11am-7pm Mon-Fri, 11am-5pm Sat) Record shop with a good attitude.

Information

EMERGENCY
General Emergency (📞112)

INTERNET ACCESS
Internet access at public libraries is free. Large parts of the city centre have free wi-fi, as do many bars and cafes.

MEDICAL SERVICES
Haartman Hospital (📞09-3106-3231; www.hel.fi; Haartmaninkatu 4; ⊙24hr) For emergency medical assistance.
Töölön Terveysasema (Töölö Health Station; 📞09-3104-5588; www.hel.fi; Sibeliuksenkatu

14; ⊙8am-4pm Mon-Fri, 8am-6pm Wed) A medical centre for non-emergencies.

Yliopiston Apteekki (www.yliopistonapteekki. fi) Branches at the city centre (Mannerheimintie 5; ⊙7am-midnight) and Mannerheimintie (Mannerheimintie 96; ⊙24hr). The central branch is more convenient.

MONEY

There are currency-exchange counters at all transport terminals.

Forex (www.forex.fi; Train station; ⊙8am-8pm Mon-Fri, 9am-7pm Sat, 9.30am-5pm Sun) One of several branches. Hours change through the year.

POST

Main Post Office (Map p46; www.posti.fi; Elielinaukio; ⊙8am-8pm Mon-Fri, 10am-4pm Sat, noon-4pm Sun) Across from the train station; enter via the supermarket.

TELEPHONE

Public telephones are nonexistent.

TOURIST INFORMATION

In summer you'll probably see 'Helsinki Helpers' wandering around in their green jackets – collar these useful multilinguals for any tourist information.

Free publications include *Helsinki This Week* (published monthly), available at tourist offices, bookshops and other points around the city.

Helsinki City Tourist Office (Map p46; ☑09-3101-3300; www.visithelsinki.fi; Pohjoisesplanadi 19; ⊙9am-8pm Mon-Fri, 9am-6pm Sat & Sun mid-May–mid-Sep, 9am-6pm Mon-Fri, 10am-4pm Sat & Sun mid-Sep–mid-May) Busy multilingual office with a great quantity of information on the city. Also has an office at the airport (www.visithelsinki.fi; Terminal 2, Helsinki-Vantaa airport; ⊙10am-8pm May-Sep, 10am-6pm Oct-Apr).

Helsinki Expert (www.helsinkiexpert.fi; Pohjoisesplanadi 19; ⊙9am-4pm Mon-Fri, 10am-4pm Sat) Books hotel rooms (with commission) and sells tickets for train, bus and ferry travel around Finland and for travel to Tallinn and St Petersburg; also sells the Helsinki Card. It's located in the tourist office, with another branch at the train station (Kaivokatu 1).

WEBSITES

City of Helsinki (www.hel.fi) Helsinki City website, with links to copious information.

HSL/HRT (www.hsl.fi) Public-transport information and journey planner.

Visit Helsinki (www.visithelsinki.fi) Excellent tourist board website full of information.

ⓘ RUSSIAN VISAS

One of Russia's most beautiful cities feels tantalisingly close to Helsinki, but for most visits, including on the fast trains, you'll need a Russian visa. At the time of writing, the exception to this was the overnight Helsinki–St Petersburg ferry run by St Peter Line, which allowed you a 72-hour visa-free stay in the city.

Applying in your home country for a Russian visa is the easiest option. If you want to apply in Finland, it's simpler to do it via a travel agent such as **Russian Expert** (☑09-321-2009; www.russianexpert.fi; Töölönkatu 7; ⊙9.30am-5pm Mon-Fri), **Rustravel** (☑050-585-0955; www.rustravel.fi; Tehtaankatu 12; ⊙9am-5pm Mon-Fri) – which is also helpful with visas for other former Soviet states – or **Venäjän Viisumikeskus** (☑045-679-6298; www.venajanviisumikeskus.fi; Urho Kekkosenkatu 2C; ⊙9am-5pm Mon-Fri). Depending on nationality, it'll cost €60 to €100 for the normal seven to eight working days processing time, plus a hefty fee for express processing (three to four working days).

If you want to do it yourself, applications in Helsinki should be submitted in person to the **Russian Visa Application Centre** (☑010-320-4858; www.vfsglobal.com; Urho Kekkosenkatu 7B; ⊙9am-4pm Mon-Fri, applications until 3pm). Save time by completing the form online first (visa.kdmid.ru) and printing it out.

In all cases, you'll need a passport with more than six months' validity, two free pages, a couple of photos, and 'visa support', namely an invitation document, typically either issued by accommodation you've booked in Russia (even hostels), or by an authorised tour agent. Travel agencies can also organise this for you, and there are reliable set-ups that arrange visa support documents online, such as **Way to Russia** (www.waytorussia.net) or **Visa to Russia** (www.visatorussia.com). These cost about US$30.

Thankfully, once you've got the paperwork sorted, it's easy to jump on a train, bus or boat and head east.

🛈 Getting There & Away

There are lockers at the bus and train stations and lockers or left-luggage counters at ferry terminals.

AIR

There are direct flights to **Helsinki-Vantaa airport** (www.helsinki-vantaa.fi), Finland's main air terminus, from many major European cities and several intercontinental ones. The airport is at Vantaa, 19km north of Helsinki.

Between them, **Finnair** (🖉 0600-140140; www.finnair.fi) and cheaper **FlyBe** (www.flybe.com) cover 18 Finnish cities, usually at least once per day.

BOAT

International ferries travel to Stockholm, Tallinn, St Petersburg and German destinations. There is also regular fast-boat service to Tallinn.

There are five main terminals, three close to the kauppatori: Katajanokan Terminaali is served by tram 4T, Makasiiniterminaali by tram 1A and 2, and Olympia Terminaali by trams 1A, 2 and 3. Länsiterminaali (West Terminal) is served by trams 6T and 9, while further-afield Hansaterminaali (Vuosaari) can be reached on bus 90A or 78 from Vuosaari metro.

Purchase tickets at the terminal, ferry company offices, online or (in some cases) the tourist office. Book well in advance during high season (late June to mid-August), and on weekends.

BUS

Kamppi bus station (Map p46; www.matkahuolto.fi) has a terminal for local buses to Espoo in one wing, while longer-distance buses also depart from here to all of Finland. OnniBus (p295) runs budget routes to several Finnish cities from a stop outside Kiasma: book online in advance for the best prices. Some destinations with several daily departures:

Jyväskylä €50.20, 4½ hours

Kuopio €66.30, 6½ hours

Lappeenranta €40.80, 3½ to 4½ hours

Oulu €98.30, nine to 12 hours

Savonlinna €53.50, 5½ hours

Tampere €27, 2¾ hours

Turku €31.50, 2½ hours

🛈 BUSES TO RUSSIA

There are two to four daily services from Helsinki's Kamppi bus station to St Petersburg (€35, nine hours). Speedier but not necessarily safer are the minibuses that leave at 3pm daily from the corner of Fredrikinkatu and Pohjoinen Rautatiekatu. These cost €30 to €35.

TRAIN

Helsinki's **train station** (Rautatieasema; www.vr.fi) is central, linked to the metro (Rautatientori stop) and a short walk from Kamppi bus station.

The train is the fastest and cheapest way to get from Helsinki to major centres: express trains run daily to Turku, Tampere, Kuopio and Lappeenranta among others, and there's a choice of day and overnight trains to Oulu, Rovaniemi and Joensuu. There are also daily trains (buy tickets from the international counter) to the Russian cities of Vyborg, St Petersburg and Moscow.

🛈 Getting Around

TO/FROM THE AIRPORT

Bus 615/620 (€5, 30 to 45 minutes, 5am to midnight) shuttles between Helsinki-Vantaa airport (platform 21) and platform 3 at Rautatientori next to Helsinki's train station. Regional transport tickets are valid. Faster Finnair buses depart from Elielinaukio platform 30 on the other side of Helsinki's train station (€6.30, 30 minutes, every 20 minutes, 5am to midnight). The last service leaves the airport at 1.10am. Bus 415 departs from the adjacent stand but it's slower than the other two options.

Door-to-door **airport taxis** (🖉 0600-555-555; www.airporttaxi.fi; 2/4passengers €29.50/39.50) need to be booked the previous day before 6pm if you're leaving Helsinki. A normal cab should cost €45 to €55.

There's a new airport–city rail link due to open in late 2015. It will be a 30-minute journey from the central train station and also means that, if you're coming by train from the north or east, you can change at Tikkurila and head to the airport (eight minutes) without going into the city centre.

There are direct bus services to/from the airport to nearby cities like Tampere and Lahti.

BICYCLE

With a flat inner city and well-marked cycling paths, Helsinki is ideal for cycling. Get a copy of the Helsinki cycling map at the tourist office.

Greenbike (🖉 050-404-0400; www.greenbike.fi; Bulevardi 32; per day €20-35, per week €75-105; ⊙10am-6pm early May–Aug) Offers a range of good-quality road and mountain bikes to hire. The entrance is actually around the corner on Albertinkatu. Call for low-season hiring.

CAR

Parking meters in the city centre cost up to €4 per hour, but are free on Sundays. There are several well-indicated underground car parks.

Car-hire companies have offices in the city as well as at the airport:

FERRIES TO TALLINN & ST PETERSBURG

Several companies cross the Gulf of Finland to Tallinn, capital of Estonia. You can also get to St Petersburg, Russia, by ferry.

Eckerö Line (✆0600-4300; www.eckeroline.fi) Sails twice daily to Tallinn year-round (adult €19 to €30, day return €25 to €40, car €19 to €39, two to 2½ hours) from Länsiterminaali (West Terminal).

Linda Line (Map p46; ✆0600-066-8970; www.lindaline.fi; Makasiiniterminaali; ◷Apr-Oct) The fastest to Tallinn. Small passenger-only hydrofoil company heading from handy Makasiiniterminaali (€35 to €48, return 25% off, day trips 40% off, 1½ hours) seven times daily.

St Peter Line (✆09-6187-2000; www.stpeterline.com; Makasiiniterminaali) Runs three to four times a week to St Petersburg (summer prices: bunks €55, private cabins from €182, cars €45, 14 hours). Visa-free stay of up to 72 hours allowed. From Makasiini terminal. There's a mandatory shuttle bus (for visa-free requirements) from the harbour to the centre in St Petersburg. This costs an extra €25.

Tallink/Silja (Tallinn) (✆0600-15700; www.tallinksilja.com) Runs at least seven Tallinn services (one-way adult €28 to €47, vehicle from €25, two hours), from Länsiterminaali.

Viking Line (Tallinn) (Map p52; ✆0600-41577; www.vikingline.fi; Katajanokan Terminaali) Operates car ferry to Tallinn (adult €21 to €39, vehicle plus two passengers €60 to €100, 2½ hours, two to three daily) from their terminal on Katajanokka island.

Budget (✆010-436-2233; www.budget.fi; Malminkatu 24)

Europcar (✆040-306-2803; www.europcar.fi; Elielinaukio 5) By the train station.

Lacara (✆09-719062; www.lacara.net; Hämeentie 12) A budget local option.

Sixt (✆0200-111222; www.sixt.com; Työpajankatu 2)

PUBLIC TRANSPORT

The city's public-transport system **HSL** (www.hsl.fi) operates buses, metro and local trains, trams and a ferry to Suomenlinna. A one-hour flat-fare ticket for any HSL transport costs €3 when purchased on board or €2.50 when purchased in advance. The ticket allows unlimited transfers but must be validated at the machine on board on first use. A single tram ticket is €2.20 advance purchase. Order any of these tickets for €2.40 using your Finnish SIM card: send an SMS to ✆16355 texting A1. Day or multiday tickets (per 24/48/72 hours €8/12/16, tickets up to seven days available) are worthwhile. The Helsinki Card gives you free travel anywhere within Helsinki.

Sales points at Kamppi bus station and the Rautatientori and Hakaniemi metro stations sell tickets and passes, as do many R-kioskis and the tourist office. The Helsinki Route Map, available at the tourist office, maps bus, metro and tram routes. Online, www.reittiopas.fi is a useful route planner.

For Vantaa or Espoo, you'll need a more expensive regional ticket.

TAXI

Grab cabs off the street or at taxi stands, or phone ✆0100-0700.

AROUND HELSINKI

Espoo

✆09 / POP 260,750

Officially Finland's second-largest city, Espoo (Swedish: Esbo) is part of greater Helsinki, with a commuter flood between the two. The city is known for its 'campus feel', with plenty of green space and spread-out environs. There are five distinct centres and many suburbs.

◉ Sights & Activities

Espoo Museum of Modern Art　　GALLERY
(EMMA; www.emma.museum; Ahertajantie 5, Tapiola; adult/child €12/free; ◷11am-6pm Tue, Thu, Fri, 11am-8pm Wed, 11am-5pm Sat & Sun) This has a huge collection of mostly Finnish modern art, ranging from the early 20th century to the present. It's definitely worth the trip from Helsinki. Sharing the same address and opening hours, and visitable with the same ticket, are four other museums that can round out a day trip. Several buses from Kamppi pass by here.

Around Helsinki

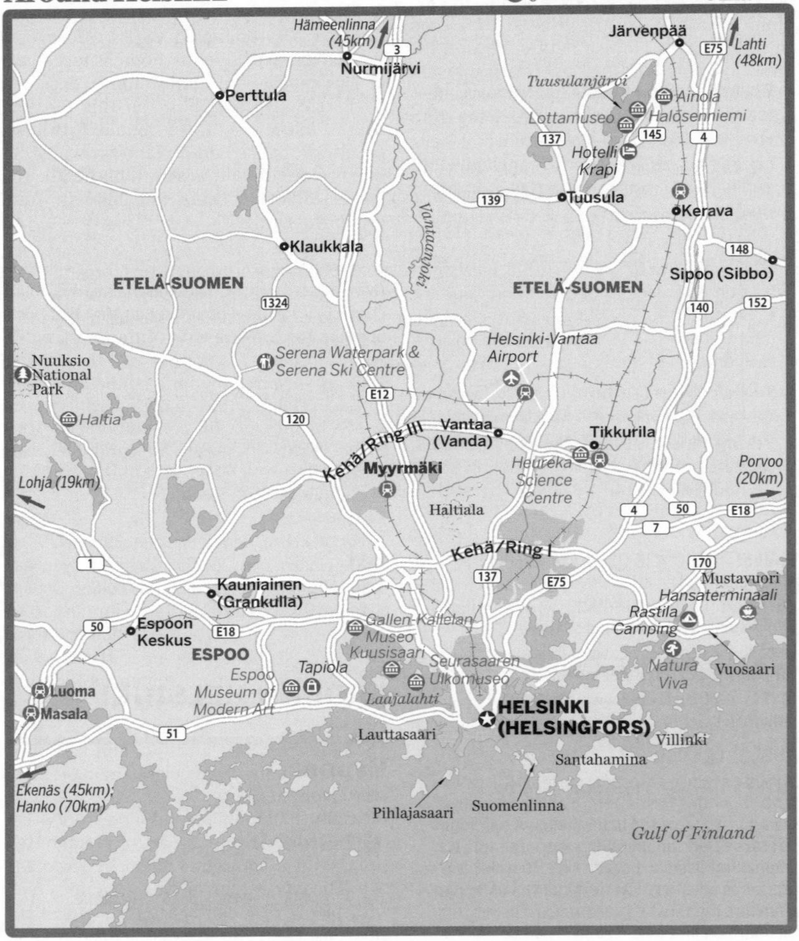

Map labels:
Hämeenlinna (45km), Nurmijärvi, 3, Perttula, Järvenpää, E75, Lahti (48km), Tuusulanjärvi, Lottamuseo, 137, Ainola, Haldsenniemi, 145, 4, Hotelli Krapi, Klaukkala, 139, Tuusula, Kerava, ETELÄ-SUOMEN, 1324, ETELÄ-SUOMEN, 148, Sipoo (Sibbo), 140, 152, Nuuksio National Park, Serena Waterpark & Serena Ski Centre, Helsinki-Vantaa Airport, Haltia, 120, E12, Vantaa (Vanda), Tikkurila, Porvoo (20km), Lohja (19km), Kehä/Ring III, Myyrmäki, Heureka Science Centre, Haltiala, 4, 50, E18, 7, Kehä/Ring I, 1, Kauniainen (Grankulla), 137, E75, 170, Mustavuori, Hansaterminaali, 50, Espoon Keskus, E18, ESPOO, Gallen-Kallelan Museo Kuusisaari, Rastila Camping, Tapiola, Seurasaaren Ulkomuseo, Natura Viva, Vuosaari, Luoma, Espoo Museum of Modern Art, Laajalahti, HELSINKI (HELSINGFORS), Masala, 51, Lauttasaari, Villinki, Ekenäs (45km); Hanko (70km), Santahamina, Pihlajasaari, Suomenlinna, Gulf of Finland, Vantaanjoki

10 km
5 miles

Gallen-Kallelan Museo GALLERY
(www.gallen-kallela.fi; Gallen-Kallelantie 27; adult/child €8/free; ⊙11am-6pm daily mid-May–Aug, 11am-4pm Tue-Sat, 11am-5pm Sun Sep–mid-May) Part castle, part studio, this was the home of Akseli Gallen-Kallela, one of Finland's most significant artists. Many of his works are displayed here including his famed *Kalevala* illustrations. The peace of the lakeside location is a little disturbed these days by the whoosh of the nearby Helsinki–Turku motorway but it remains a worthwhile visit. From Helsinki take tram 4 to its terminus then walk 2km.

Haltia NATURE CENTRE
(www.haltia.com; Nuuksiontie 84; adult/child €7/2.50; ⊙9.30am-7pm mid-Feb–Sep, 9.30am-5pm Oct–mid-Feb) Nuuksio National Park's gateway is Haltia, an atmospheric modern visitor centre in the shape of a nesting duck. Inside, the exhibitions bring you the sights and sounds of the Finnish landscape and are backed up by interactive information screens. At its heart is an offbeat installation of two swans playing DNA chess. There's an upstairs restaurant and pricey bike hire.

Nuuksio National Park   HIKING
(www.outdoors.fi) **FREE** Close enough to Helsinki for a half-day trip, this gives a good
introduction to Finnish nature. Beyond the
gateway centre, Haltia, are two trailheads,
Haukkalampi and Kattila (3km apart), offering easy walking or cross-country ski trails
through wooded Ice-Age-chiselled valleys,
a habitat for elk and nocturnal flying squirrels. There are campsites, cottages and huts
available.

Bus 85 from Espoo Central goes via Haltia
to a stop 2km from Haukkalampi. In summer from early Jun to mid-August, when
there's also a direct bus from Helsinki's Kiasma museum (one way €6), it continues to
Kattila.

Serena   WATERPARK
(www.serena.fi; Tornimäentie 10; admission €24.50;
⊙11am-8pm Jun–mid-Aug, plus noon-8pm most
weekends mid-Oct–May) Lots of fun, this waterpark is the largest in the Nordic countries,
with a cavalcade of pools, Jacuzzis and wa-
terslides. There's also a ski centre here in
winter that makes for a good day's skiing,
close to Helsinki. There are buses from
Kamppi or Espoo Central, or turn-off at the
1324 road at the Hotel Korpilampi sign.

✯ Festivals & Events

April Jazz Festival   MUSIC
(www.apriljazz.fi) Draws big crowds with international artists.

❶ Getting There & Away

You can catch buses to various parts of Espoo
from the dedicated Espoo wing in Kamppi bus
station in Helsinki. Local trains from Helsinki will
drop you off at several stations, including Espoo
Central.

Tuusulan Rantatie

Just a 30-minute drive from Helsinki, the
views from the narrow stretch of tar running
along Tuusulanjärvi (Tuusula Lake) have
inspired some of Finland's greatest artists.
Tuusulan Rantatie (www.tuusulanrantatie.com)
was home to many heroes of the National
Romantic movement, including Sibelius, Nobel Prize–winning novelist FE Sillanpää and
painter Pekka Halonen. Along the 9km road
between Tuusula and Järvenpää – after the
Hotelli Krapi detour down the smaller diver-
sion labelled 'Museotie' – are several attractions connected with them.

◉ Sights

Ainola   MUSEUM
(www.ainola.fi; adult/child €8/2; ⊙10am-5pm
Tue-Sun May-Sep) Sibelius' home is just south
of Järvenpää. The family home, designed
by Lars Sonck and built on this forested
site in 1904, contains original furniture,
paintings, books and a piano on which Sibelius plotted out tunes until his death. The
graves of Jean Sibelius and his wife Aino
are in the garden.

Halosenniemi   MUSEUM
(www.halosenniemi.fi; Halosenniemientie 4-6; adult/
child €6/2; ⊙11am-6pm Tue-Sun May-Aug, noon-
5pm Tue-Sun Sep-Apr) One of the most significant museums along this road; the sizeable
Karelian-inspired log-built studio and home
of Pekka Halonen has changing exhibition of
works by him and his contemporaries. It's a
lovely place with great views and a lakeside
garden.

Lottamuseo   MUSEUM
(www.lottamuseo.com; Rantatie 39; adult/child
€5/1; ⊙11am-6pm Tue-Sun, 11am-7pm Wed May-
Sep, 11am-7pm Wed, 11am-5pm Thu-Sun Oct-Apr)
This striking blue building commemorates
the Lotta women's voluntary defence force.
Named for a character in a JL Runeberg
poem, these unarmed women took on military service during WWII to become one of
the world's largest auxiliaries. Look out for
the blue-and-white swastika and rose medals, which many Lottas wore among the military paraphernalia.

🛌 Sleeping

Hotelli Krapi   HOTEL €€
(☑09-274841; www.krapi.fi; Rantatie 2; s/d
€128/155; Ⓟ🛜) 🅿 Belying its name, this
historic red wooden estate, 2km north of
Tuusula, features an excellent independent
hotel in a former cowshed. It has great modern rooms, three restaurants, a traditional
smoke sauna, golf course, summer theatre
and a ghost. Various activity packages are
available; it's a lot cheaper in summer and
on weekends.

❶ Getting There & Away

Tuusulanjärvi is 35km north of Helsinki. Buses
running between Helsinki and Järvenpää drop off
at or near most of the museums; you could also
make a bike tour of it, getting the train to Kerava
and back from Järvenpää.

Turku & the South Coast

Best Places to Eat

➡ Smor (p82)

➡ På Kroken (p93)

➡ Vausti (p105)

➡ Uusi Kilta (p85)

➡ Restaurant Kuparipaja (p97)

Best Places to Stay

➡ Sea Hotel Mäntyniemi (p103)

➡ Hotel Bridget Inn (p85)

➡ Hotelli Onni (p99)

➡ Villa Maija (p92)

➡ Ruissalo Camping (p80)

Why Go?

Anchoring the country's southwest is Finland's former capital, Turku. This striking seafaring city stretches along a broad river from the Gothic cathedral to a medieval castle and vibrant harbour, and challenges Helsinki's cultural cred with excellent galleries, museums, restaurants and rocking music festivals that electrify the summer air. Just northwest, charming Naantali makes an easy side trip or atmospheric alternative base.

Throughout the south, the coastline is strung with characterful little towns. The Swedish and Russian empires fought for centuries over the area's ports and today they're commandeered by castles and fortresses that seem at odds with the sunshine and sailing boats. Inland, charming *bruk* (ironworks precinct) villages offer an insight into the area's industrial past. Scattered offshore, islands provide yachting opportunities, sea-salt retreats and a sea full of stepping stones across to Åland and Sweden.

When to Go
Turku

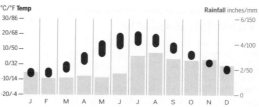

Jun Turku turns back to the Middle Ages during its lively Medieval Market.

Jul Boats race in the Hanko Regatta, famous for its carnival atmosphere.

Aug Marching and military music take place at the week-long Hamina Tattoo.

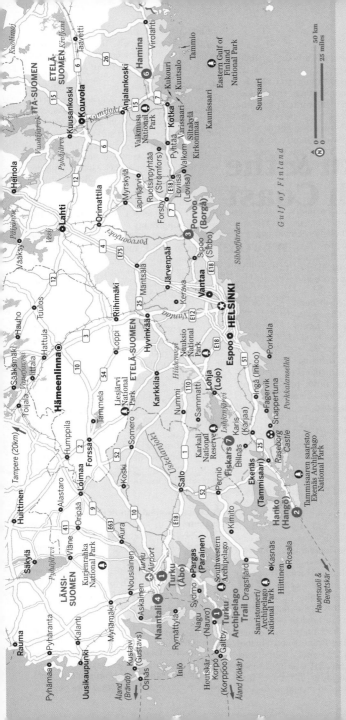

Turku & the South Coast Highlights

1 Unearthing Turku's medieval history along the crooked underground streets of **Aboa Vetus** (p77) and inside its mighty 13th-century **castle** (p76)

2 Cruising from Russian villa-crowned **Hanko** (p90) to see seals, rock carvings or visit a lighthouse island

3 Strolling cobbled lanes lined with colourful wooden warehouses in the picturesque Old Town of **Porvoo** (p98)

4 Meeting Finland's famous cartoon characters at Naantali's **Muumimaailma** (Moominworld; p84)

5 Picking wild strawberries, watching Arctic terns and swimming in an inlet on the **Turku Archipelago Trail**

6 Pelting downhill on a mountain bike, skis or a snowboard at **Uuperinrinteet** (p106), near Hamina

7 Browsing Finnish **designs** (p97) in the pretty former ironworks village of Fiskars

TURKU

📋 02 / POP 182,500

The historic castle and cathedral point to the city's rich cultural history when it was the capital, and contemporary Turku is a hotbed of experimental art and vibrant festivals, thanks in part to its spirited population from its university (the country's second largest), who make Turku's nightlife young and fun. As the first city many visitors encounter arriving by ferry from Sweden and Åland, it's a splendid introduction to the Finnish mainland.

History

Archaeological findings in the Turku area date back to the Stone Age, but the city was founded when Catholic settlement began at Koroinen, near the present centre of Turku, in 1229. The consecration of a new church in 1300 and the construction of Turku Castle created an administrative and spiritual base for rulership.

The original Swedish name, Åbo, comes from a settlement (*bo*) on a river (*å*). The town was the second largest in Sweden, though much of it was levelled by fires, including the Great Fire of 1827. When the Russians took over, the long Swedish connection led them to make their new capital Helsinki, leaving Turku to concentrate on commerce. The Finnish name, Turku, is an archaic Russian word for 'marketplace'. Today Turku's centre is still its kauppatori (market square), situated 3km northeast of the harbour.

🅾 Sights

Turun Linna   CASTLE
(Turku Castle; 📋 02-262-0300; www.turunlinna.fi; Linnankatu 80; adult/child €9/5, guided tours €2; ⊙10am-6pm daily Jun-Aug, 10am-6pm Tue-Sun Sep-May) Founded in 1280 at the mouth of the Aurajoki, mammoth Turku Castle is easily Finland's largest. Highlights include two dungeons and sumptuous banqueting halls, as well as a fascinating **historical museum** of medieval Turku in the castle's old bailey. Models depict the castle's growth from a simple island fortress to a Renaissance palace. Guided tours in English run several times daily from June to August.

Swedish Count Per Brahe ruled Finland from here in the 17th century, while Sweden's deposed King Eric XIV was imprisoned in the castle's round tower in the late 16th century. He was moved to several prisons including Åland's Kastelholms Slott to prevent his discovery by rebels. Today most Finns recognise its distinctive architecture as the logo for Turun Sinappi (Turku Mustard).

★ Turun Tuomiokirkko   CATHEDRAL
(Turku Cathedral; 📋 02-261-7100; www.turun seurakunnat.fi; cathedral free, museum adult/child €2/1; ⊙cathedral & museum 9am-8pm mid-Apr-mid-Sep, 9am-7pm mid-Sep–mid-Apr) The 'mother church' of Finland's Lutheran faith, Turku Cathedral towers over the town. Consecrated in 1300, the colossal brick Gothic building was rebuilt many times over the centuries after damaging fires.

The cathedral's pulpit was designed by German architect CL Engel (who in the spirit of impartiality also built the Orthodox church on the market square). Romantic frescoes by RW Ekman depict the baptism of Finland's first bishop, and Gustav Wasa presenting the nation with the first Finnish New Testament. Its most famous tomb belongs to Karin Månsdotter (d 1613), Queen of Sweden and wife of the unfortunate Erik XIV.

Listen out for the distinctive hourly bell, broadcast across the country at noon via the radio station YLE1 – a patriotic reminder of the Continuation War, when Finns were urged to pray together for victory at this designated hour.

Upstairs, a small **museum** traces the stages of the cathedral's construction, and contains medieval sculptures and religious paraphernalia.

Free **summer organ concerts** take place at 8pm Tuesday and 2pm Wednesday. English-language services are held at 4pm every Sunday except the last of the month year-round.

★ Luostarinmäki Handicrafts Museum   MUSEUM
(📋02-262-0350; www.turunmuseokeskus.fi; Vartiovuorenkatu 2; adult/child €6/4, guided tours €2.50; ⊙10am-6pm daily Jun-Aug, 10am-6pm Tue-Sun May & early Sep–mid-Sep, 10am-4pm Tue-Sun Dec–mid-Jan) When the savage Great Fire of 1827 swept through Turku, the lower-class quarter of Luostarinmäki escaped the flames. Set along tiny lanes and around grassy yards, the 19th-century wooden workshops and houses now form the outdoor handicrafts museum, a national treasure since 1940.

All of the buildings are in their original locations and include 30 workshops (such as a silversmith, watchmaker, bakery, pottery, shoemaker, printer and cigar shop), where artisans in period costume practise their trades in summer.

Guided tours in English are available five times daily from June to August. The gift shop sells goods produced in the museum's workshops.

Forum Marinum   MUSEUM, SHIPS
(www.forum-marinum.fi; Linnankatu 72; adult/child €8/5, incl museum ships €16/10, museum ships each €6/4; ⊙11am-7pm May-Sep, 11am-6pm Tue-Sun Oct-Apr, museum ships 11am-7pm Jun-Aug) Partly housed in an old granary, this excellent maritime museum offers a comprehensive look at ships and shipping, from scale models to full-sized vessels. Anchored outside is a small fleet of **museum ships**, which you can climb aboard. The mine-layer *Keihässalmi* and the corvette *Karjala* take you back to WWII, while the full-rigger *Suomen Joutsen* recalls more-carefree prewar days. The beautiful three-masted barque *Sigyn* (moored 500m upstream) was originally launched from Göteborg in 1887 and has well-preserved cabins.

Other highlights include the museum's hydrocopter, WWII torpedoes and multimedia displays, plus a cabin from a luxury cruise-liner (many of which were built in Turku). At the museum's cafe-restaurant, you'll find its namesake *Daphne,* a cute little boat that was home to author Göran Schild.

★**Aboa Vetus & Ars Nova**   MUSEUM, GALLERY
(☑020-718-1640; www.aboavetusarsnova.fi; Itäinen Rantakatu 4-6; adult/child €8/5.50; ⊙11am-7pm) Art and archaeology unite here under one roof. **Aboa Vetus** (Old Turku) draws you underground to Turku's medieval streets, showcasing some of the 37,000 artefacts unearthed from the site (digs still continue). Back in the present, **Ars Nova** presents contemporary art exhibitions. The themed Turku Biennaali (www.turkubiennaali.fi) takes place here in summer of odd-numbered years.

Opening to a grassy courtyard, the museums' cafe, Aula, hosts Sunday jazz brunches and Thursday night DJ sessions from June to August.

Turun Taidemuseo   GALLERY
(www.turuntaidemuseo.fi; Aurakatu 26; adult/child €8/free, admission free 4-7pm Fri; ⊙11am-7pm Tue-Fri, 11am-5pm Sat & Sun) FREE Turku Art Museum is housed in a striking granite

building with elaborately carved pilasters and conical turrets. Much of the art is modern, though the Victor Westerholm room offers traditional Finnish landscapes. Gunnar Berndtson's *Kesä* (Summer) is an idyllic depiction of sunny Suomi, while Akseli Gallen-Kallela's depictions of the epic *Kalevala* are compelling – look out for his *Akka ja kissa* (Old Woman and Cat).

Sibelius Museum   MUSEUM
(☑02-215-4494; www.sibeliusmuseum.fi; Piispankatu 17; adult/child €3/free; ⊙11am-4pm Tue-Sun, plus 6-8pm Wed) Finland's most extensive musical museum displays some 350 instruments from accordions to Zimbabwean drums. A separate section is devoted to Finnish composer and bohemian carouser Jean Sibelius, with manuscripts and personal memorabilia. You can listen to Sibelius' music on scratchy records, or hear live jazz, folk and chamber music at Wednesday-evening concerts (€4) held from autumn to spring.

Wäino Aaltonen Museum   GALLERY
(WAM; ☑02-262-0850; www.wam.fi; Itäinen Rantakatu 38; adult/child €6/4; ⊙10am-6pm Tue-Sun) Naturalistic and cubist-tinged sculptures donated by artist Wäino Aaltonen himself are a highlight of this gallery, along with temporary exhibitions of contemporary and experimental art.

Ett Hem Museum   MUSEUM
(☑020-786-1470; www.abo.fi; Piispankatu 14; adult/child €4/2; ⊙11am-4pm Tue & Fri, noon-3pm Wed, Thu, Sat & Sun May-Sep, noon-3pm Tue-Sun Dec) Designed by CL Engel, this gold-coloured turn-of-the-20th-century residence houses furniture of various styles, and works by painters Albert Edelfelt and Helene Schjerfbeck.

Turku

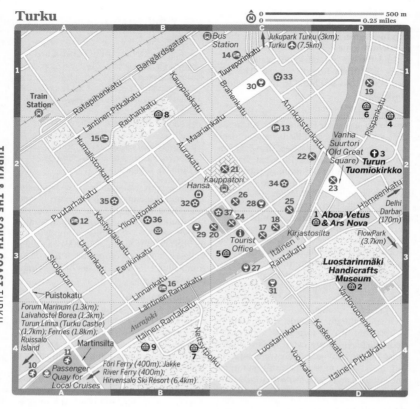

Qwensel House & Pharmacy Museum
MUSEUM

(☎02-262-0280; www.museumcentreturku. fi; Läntinen Rantakatu 13; adult/child €4.50/3; ⊙10am-6pm Tue-Sun May-Aug, 10am-4pm Tue-Sun Dec–mid-Jan) On the riverfront, **Qwensel House** is Turku's oldest, built around 1700. It contains the small **Pharmacy Museum** with an old laboratorium featuring medicinal herbs, 18th-century 'Gustavian' (Swedish) furnishings, and an exhibition of bottles and other pharmacy supplies.

Turku Biological Museum
MUSEUM

(☎02-262-0340; www.museumcentreturku.fi; Neitsytpolku 1; adult/child €4.50/3; ⊙9am-5pm Tue-Sun) In a beautiful 1907 building, the Turku Biological Museum features much of Finland's fauna and flora represented in 13 realistic dioramas, including Lapland's fjelds (barren, rocky plateaus).

🏃 Activities

Archipelago cruises are popular in summer; most departures are from the quay at Martinsilta bridge.

S/S Ukkopekka
CRUISE

(www.ukkopekka.fi; one way/return adult €24/29, child €12/14.50, Moomin package adult/child return €49/36) The historic steamship S/S *Ukkopekka* cruises to Naantali at 10am and 2pm Tuesday to Saturday mid-June to mid-August, docking next to Muumimaailma (Moomin World; p84). The trip takes 1¾ hours.

Evening dinner cruises (€43 to €49), with dancing on the pier of the island of Loistokari run from May to August.

M/S Rudolfina
CRUISE

(☎040-846-3000; www.rudolfina.fi) Harbour cruises include a 90-minute lunch cruise (1pm and 3pm; €29) and dinner cruises

Turku

(two-hour cruise 5pm; €29, three-hour cruise 7pm; €37) Monday to Saturday, as well as a leisurely two-hour Sunday lunch cruise (2pm; €33) from June to August.

Rosita CRUISE
(☑02-213-1500; www.rosita.fi) *Rosita* runs a one-hour cruise out to Vepsä island (€15 return) at 11am, 2pm and 5pm daily June to August, and occasional day-long adventures (€70) to the lighthouse island of Bengtskär (p91).

Jukupark Turku WATERPARK
(www.jukupark.fi; Kurrapolku 1; admission €21, evening ticket from 4pm €15; ◎11am-5pm or 7pm early Jun–mid-Aug) Finland's biggest waterpark has 16 slides, plastic pirates and over-excited nippers. It's 3km north of the town centre – take bus 2, 2A or 13.

Hirvensalo Ski Resort SNOW SPORTS
(☑02-258-0221; www.hirvensalo.fi; Kaks[?]errantie 111; lift tickets 3hr/day/evening only €22/28/23, ski/snowboard rental €15/22, boot rental €10; ◎3-9pm Mon-Fri, 10am-8pm Sat, 10am-7pm Sun Nov-Apr) On the island of Hirvensalo, 6.4km south of Turku (reached by buses buses 14, 15, 55 and 56), you can ski and snowboard in winter. OK, so it's not a serious mountain (more like a big hill), but there are five slopes, the

highest of which is 60m high and 300m long. Summertime **go-karting** (☑044-516-7390; www.mcc.action.com/turku; Kaks_errantie 111, Hirvensalo; per 20min Mon-Fri €15, Sat & Sun €20; ◎3-8pm Mon-Fri, noon-8pm Sat mid-May–Jun & mid-Aug–Sep, noon-8pm Mon-Sat, noon-6pm Sun Jul–mid-Aug) takes place here.

Jakke River Ferry CRUISE
(adult/child €5/2; ◎9am-5pm Mon-Sat late Jun-Aug) Floating through the centre of town, this laid-back river ferry with an on-board bar makes five stops but it's also possible to hail it from the bank if there's room for it to dock. Tickets include travel on the little **Jokke tourist train** on the river's northern bank so you can complete a circuit (around an hour all up).

FlowPark ADVENTURE SPORTS
(☑040-086-4862; www.flowpark.fi; Skanssinkatu 10; admission per day/evening only €22/15; ◎3-8pm Wed-Fri, noon-8pm Sat, noon-6pm Sun May, Sep & Oct, noon-8pm Mon-Sat, noon-6pm Sun Jun & Jul) Swaying bridges, swings, jumps and cable slides reach heights of up to 20m at this state-of-the-art ropes course; there's also a low-ropes course for little would-be Tarzans and Janes. It's 4km southeast of the town centre; take bus 7, 7A and 12.

✦ Festivals & Events

Medieval Market · CULTURAL
(www.keskiaikaisetmarkkinat.fi) Held over a variable long weekend in summer (usually late June), this lively event brings a Middle Ages market back to the Vanha Suurtori (Old Great Sq) near Turku Cathedral.

Paavo Nurmi Marathon · SPORTS
(http://paavonurmimarathon.fi) Named for legendary Finnish distance runner Paavo Nurmi (aka the Flying Finn), this international marathon in late June/early July loops through the town centre and Ruissalo island.

★ Ruisrock · MUSIC
(www.ruisrock.fi; 1-/3-day ticket €78/128) For three days in July, Finland's oldest and largest annual rock festival – held since 1969 and attracting 100,000-strong crowds – takes over Ruissalo island.

Down by the Laituri · MUSIC
(DBTL; ☑ 040-086 0446; www.dbtl.fi; tickets €22.50-79) By the river, this rock festival in late July/early August attracts mainly Finnish bands.

Turku Jazz · MUSIC
(☑ 040-582-9366; www.turkujazz.fi; tickets free-€32.50) Hot bebop and smoking sax hits the city from early to mid-August.

Turku Music Festival · MUSIC
(www.tmj.fi; tickets free-€148.50) From early August, this two-week extravaganza offers an eclectic mix of classical and contemporary music and opera in amazing venues including Turku Cathedral.

🛏 Sleeping

Turku has scads of chain hotels such as Sokos and Scandic, but some unique places too.

★ Ruissalo Camping · CAMPGROUND €
(☑ 02-262-5100; www.turkutouring.fi; tent sites €17 plus per person €5, 2-/4-/6-person cabin €68/125/165; ☺May-Sep; ℗) On idyllic Ruissalo island, 10km west of the city centre, this sprawling campground has gently sloping grassy sites and a great choice of cabins, along with saunas, a cafe and Turku's closest beaches (including a naturist beach). Book way, *way* ahead for the Ruisrock festival and Midsummer. Bus 8 runs from the kauppatori.

Laivahostel Borea · HOSTEL €
(☑ 040-843-6611; www.msborea.fi; Linnankatu 72; s €49, d €78-105.50, tr €102, q €124; 🎇) Built in Sweden in 1960, the enormous passenger ship S/S *Bore* is docked outside the Forum Marinum museum, just 500m northeast of the ferry terminal. It now contains an award-winning HI-affiliated hostel with vintage ensuite cabins. Most are squishy but if you want room to spread out, higher-priced doubles have a lounge area. Rates include a morning sauna.

Bridgettine Sisters' Guesthouse · GUESTHOUSE €
(☑ 02-250-1910; www.kolumbus.fi/birgitta.turku; Ursininkatu 15A; s/d €45/65; ℗) Glowing white and run by nuns, this Catholic convent's guest wing is a haven of peace: public areas are silent after 10pm, and the place has a general air of respectful hush. Its small rooms are austere, but cleanliness clearly goes with the godliness. Cash only.

★ Park Hotel · BOUTIQUE HOTEL €€
(☑ 02-273-2555; www.parkhotelturku.fi; Rauhankatu 1; s €89-124, d €115-162; @🎇) Overlooking a hilly park, this art nouveau building is a genuine character, with a resident squawking parrot, Jaakko, and classical music playing in the lift (elevator). Rooms are decorated in a lovably chintzy style and equipped with minibars. Family owners and facilities such as a lounge with pool table make it the antithesis of a chain hotel.

Hotelli Helmi · HOTEL €€
(☑020-786-2770; www.hotellihelmi.fi; Tuureporinkatu 11; s/d/tr/f €85/110/120/170; 🎇) Next door to the bus station, the family-owned Helmi (literally, 'pearl') has 34 autumnal-hued soundproofed rooms with minifridges, comfy mattresses and good-sized bathrooms. If you're catching an overnight ferry or late-night flight, day rooms (€55) are available.

Centro Hotel · HOTEL €€
(☑ 02-211-8100; www.centrohotel.com; Yliopistonkatu 12; s/d €111/119; @🎇) The 62-room Centro Hotel is (as its name implies) central, but its courtyard location cuts out street noise. Service is friendly and the blonde-wood rooms are a good compromise between size and price. The breakfast buffet is worth getting out of bed for. Arrive early to nab one of the 14 parking spaces.

Radisson Blu Marina
Palace Hotel HOTEL €€
(☑ 020-123-4710; www.radissonblu.com; Linnankatu 32; s €110-120, d €135-150, ste from €410; @ 🛜) It's worth paying extra for a river view at this sleek business hotel with streamlined Scandinavian-style dark-wood rooms. Couples weary of sleeping in pushed-together twin beds will be delighted by real doubles on the 7th floor. Suites have in-room espresso machines and saunas.

🍴 Eating

Turku is the home town of the ubiquitous Hesburger chain, Finland's answer to McDonald's, but the city has a sophisticated dining scene.

Delhi Darbar INDIAN €
(☑02-233-3988; http://delhidarbar.fi; Hämeenkatu 8; lunch platters €7.50-10.50, mains €9.50-18; ⊘10.30am-10pm Mon-Thu, 10.30am-11pm Fri, noon-11pm Sat, noon-10pm Sun) Turku's best Indian restaurant (and no, not its only Indian restaurant) fills with locals tucking into heaping portions of spicy curries, sizzling tikka dishes and other Subcontinent classics, accompanied by salad, rice and pillowy naan bread included in the price. Fantastic value.

CaféArt CAFE €
(www.cafeart.fi; Läntinen Rantakatu 5; dishes €2.20-4.80; ⊘10am-7pm Mon-Fri, 10am-5pm Sat, 11am-5pm Sun) With freshly ground coffee, prize-winning baristas, a beautifully elegant interior and artistic sensibility, there's no better place to get your caffeine-and-cake fix. In summer, the terrace spills onto the riverbank, shaded by linden trees.

Kauppahalli MARKET €
(www.kauppahalli.fi; Eerikinkatu 16; ⊘8am-6pm Mon-Fri, 8am-4pm Sat; 🍴) 🍴 Filled with speciality products, this historic covered market also contains the converted train carriage **Sininen Juna Aschan Café** (kauppahalli; pastries & sandwiches €2.50-6; ⊘8am-6pm Mon-Fri, 8am-4pm Sun), run by top-quality Turku bakery chain Aschan.

Kauppatori MARKET €
(⊘8am-4pm Mon-Sat May-Sep) The kauppatori hosts a fruit and vegetable market during the warmer months.

Tintå GASTROPUB €€
(☑02-230-7023; www.tinta.fi; Läntinen Rantakatu 9; lunch €8.50-13.50, pizza €12-16, mains €25-30; ⊘11am-midnight Mon, 11am-1am Tue-Thu, 11am-

2am Fri, noon-2am Sat, noon-10pm Sun) With a cosy exposed-brick interior, this riverside wine bar also offers weekday lunches, gourmet pizzas such as asparagus and smoked feta or prosciutto and fig, and classy mains such asorganic beef skewers with horseradish aioli. Grab a glass of wine and watch the world walking along the shore from the summer terrace.

Hus Lindman FINNISH €€
(☑0400-446-100; www.huli.fi; Piispankatu 15; lunch buffet €15, mains €22-28; ⊘11am-9pm Mon-Sat, noon-7pm Sun Jun-Aug, 11am-3pm Mon-Fri Sep-May) Hidden at the bottom of a garden, this gold-coloured wooden building opening to a riverside terrace is a charmer. Local seafood is a staple of the menu, along with steaks; lunch includes a daily vegetarian option. Live jazz plays from 6pm to 9pm on Thursday in July and August.

Mami BISTRO €€
(☑02-231-1111; www.mami.fi; Linnankatu 3; lunch €9-10, mains €20-25; ⊘11am-10pm Tue-Fri, 1-10pm Sat) 🍴 Mami's riverside summer terrace is perfect for people-watching, though its abiding popularity means you'll have to fight for a table with half of Turku. The seasonal ingredients from local, small-scale suppliers – chanterelles, perch, salmon, cockerel – are prepared with care.

Pinella INTERNATIONAL €€
(☑02-445-6500; www.pinella.fi; Vanha Suurtori 2; lunch mains €9-22, dinner mains €16-27; ⊘11am-11pm Mon-Fri, noon-11pm Sat, noon-10pm Sun) Founded in 1848, this is one of Finland's oldest restaurants but its menu is up to the minute: burgers in brioche buns with chilli mayo and fries, pan-fried salmon with crayfish sauce, blueberry mousse with crème fraîche and raspberries. The three-course lunch for €27 is a great deal. Upstairs, the bar stays open to 1am on Friday and Saturday.

Blanko BISTRO, BAR €€
(☑02-233-3966; www.blanko.net; Aurakatu 1; lunch €8-10, mains €15-30, Sun brunch €18; ⊘11am-11pm Mon-Tue, 11am-midnight Wed-Thu, 11am-3am Fri, noon-3am Sat, noon-6pm Sun) Look for the low-key black-tile signage to find this hip venue. Inside it's all Scandi chic with regular DJs, but the dining area is separate enough for you to concentrate on the food: stir fries, salads such as haloumi, avocado and strawberries with fig dressing, great lunch specials and the best Sunday brunch in town.

★**Smor** MODERN FINNISH €€€
(02-536-9444; www.smor.fi; Läntinen Rantakatu 3; mains €29, 3-/6-course tasting menu €47/65, incl wine €81/130; ⊙11am-2pm & 4.30-10pm Mon-Fri, 4-10pm Sat) A vaulted cellar lit by flickering candles makes a romantic backdrop for stunning, often organic Modern Finnish cuisine: spinach waffle with quail egg and air-dried pork, roast Åland lamb with cauliflower purée and nettle sauce, or whitefish with bronze fennel. Desserts such as almond pastry with yoghurt pudding and lemon-and-thyme sorbet are equally inspired.

Viikinkiravintola Harald SCANDINAVIAN €€€
(044-766-8204; www.ravintolaharald.fi; Aurakatu 3; lunch €9.50, set menus €34-52, mains €18-38.50; ⊙noon-11pm Mon, noon-midnight Tue-Thu, noon-1am Fri & Sat, 3-10pm Sun) Subtlety is run through with a berserker's broadsword at this over-the-top Viking restaurant, which serves dishes such as roast ox on a plank, 'witch of the north' reindeer or tar ice cream with cognac. Set menus (or Voyages as they're called here) are filling three-course samplers. It's not exactly gourmet, but it is great fun.

🍷 Drinking

Turku's drinking crowds surge towards the river in summer. Evenings kick off on one of the half-a-dozen-or-so **boat bars** lining the south bank; popular ones include the upmarket *Donna,* down-to-earth *Papa Joe* and *Cindy,* and good-time *Katarina* (the latter two open year-round).

★**Panimoravintola Koulu** BREWPUB
(www.panimoravintolakoulu.fi; Eerikinkatu 18; ⊙11am-2am) In a former school complete with inkwells, desks and a playground-turned-summer beer garden, this fantastic brewpub only serves its own brews – around five lager-style beers that change with the seasons, and a couple of interesting ciders flavoured with tart cranberries and blackcurrants. The exception is the whisky collection, with 75 or so to sample.

Upstairs, there's an excellent, kid-friendly restaurant.

Cosmic Comic Café BAR
(www.cosmic.fi; Kauppiaskatu 4; ⊙3pm-2am Mon-Thu, 3pm-3am Fri & Sat, 4pm-2am Sun) This fab late-night haunt is a fanboy's dream – comics paper the walls and you can browse its huge (mostly English-language) collection. Over 70 different kinds of beer and 25 ciders rotate on the eclectic menu. Occasional live music.

Uusi Apteekki PUB
(www.uusiapteekki.fi; Kaskenkatu 1; ⊙10am-2am) Lovely old fittings in this historic pharmacy include wooden dispensing drawers fashioned into tables where you can rest your pint.

The Waterloo PUB
(Puutori; ⊙noon-midnight Mon-Thu, noon-2am Fri, 10am-2am Sat, 10am-10pm Sun) The name is the giveaway: this quirky little cylindrical art deco building is a 1933-built former public lavatory (look up to see the lights made from original brass S-bends). It's now a British-style pub screening sports events, with tables on the concourse outside in summer. Cash only.

☆ Entertainment

Turku has a strong reputation for its music and cultural events.

Concert Hall CONCERT VENUE
(02-262-0804; www.tfo.fi; Aninkaistenkatu 9; tickets €8-43.50; ⊙Sep-May) The Turku Philharmonic Orchestra, with a history stretching back to 1790, when the Musical Society of Turku was founded, is the resident orchestra of this purpose-built 1952-built hall.

Dynamo LIVE MUSIC
(02-250-4904; www.dynamoklubi.com; Linnankatu 7; ⊙9pm-4am Mon-Sat Jun-Aug, 9pm-4am Tue-Sat Sep-May) Local DJs vie with national bands for a spot on the bill of this central wooden venue. Great outdoor terrace.

Klubi LIVE MUSIC
(www.klubi.net; Humalistonkatu 8A; ⊙8pm-4am Wed & Thu, 10pm-4am Fri & Sat, midnight-4am Sun) Part owned by a local record label, this massive complex has several speeds, from casual drinking at Kolo to the DJ-fuelled nightclub Ilta and big-name Finnish bands at Live.

Venus LIVE MUSIC
(www.venusnightlife.fi; Aurakatu 6; ⊙10pm-4am Tue-Sat) Catch Finnish pop acts at Venus Live; danceable grooves at the Schlager Disco Bar; and, for those who love the limelight, karaoke at Venus Bar.

Åbo Svenska Teater THEATRE
(02-277-7377; www.abosvenskateater.fi; Aurakatu 10; tickets €17.50-38.50) Founded in 1839, Finland's oldest theatre hosts performances in Swedish.

Monk   JAZZ
(📱 02-251-2444; www.monk.fi; Humalistonkatu 3; ⏱9pm-4am Fri & Sat year-round, plus 9pm-1am Mon spring & autumn) Intimate venue for live jazz, funk and Latin.

ℹ Information

Tourist Office (📱 02-262-7444; www.visit turku.fi; Aurakatu 4; ⏱ 8.30am-6pm Mon-Fri, 9am-4pm Sat & Sun) Busy but helpful office with information on the entire region.

ℹ Getting There & Away

The train station and ferry terminals have left-luggage lockers (€3 to €5).

AIR

Finnair (www.finnair.com) flies daily to Turku's tiny airport from Helsinki; SAS has flights to Stockholm-Arlanda. Business airline **Turku Air** (www.turkuair.fi) flies to Mariehamn on weekdays. Airport facilities are minimal and there are no ATMs – bring euros for the bus.

BOAT

Turku is a major gateway to Sweden and Åland. The harbour, about 3km southwest of the city centre, has terminals for **Silja Line** (www.tallinksilja.fi) and **Viking Line** (www.vikingline.fi). Both companies sail to Stockholm (11 hours) and Mariehamn (six hours). Prices vary widely according to season and class, with deck-class one-way tickets starting from €20. **Finnlink** (www.finnlines.com) sails to Sweden from nearby Naantali, though this service doesn't take foot passengers.

Tickets are available at the harbour, from Viking Line in the Hansa shopping centre, or Silja Lines at Aurakatu 5. Book ahead during high season if you plan to take a car or if you're travelling over a weekend.

It's also possible to travel to Sweden and Åland via the Turku archipelago.

BUS

Long-distance buses use the bus station at Aninkaistenkatu 20, while regional buses (including for Naantali) depart from the kauppatori.

Major intercity services:
Helsinki (€31.50, 2½ hours, hourly)
Pori (€28.80, 2¼ hours)
Rauma (€22, 1½ hours)
Tampere (€25.60, 2½ hours)

TRAIN

Turku's train station is 400m northwest of the city centre; trains also stop at the ferry harbour.
Destinations include the following:
Helsinki (€34, two hours, at least hourly)

Oulu (€85.40, eight hours, hourly, usually with a change in Tampere)
Rovaniemi (€91.40, 12 hours, four daily, usually with a change in Tampere)
Tampere (€28.20, 1¾ hours, two hourly)

ℹ Getting Around

TO/FROM THE AIRPORT

Bus 1 runs between the kauppatori and the airport, 8km north of the city, every 15 minutes from 5.20am to 11.15pm (€3, 25 minutes). The same bus continues from the kauppatori to the harbour.

A taxi costs around €30; there's a free hotline to order one at the entrance to Terminal 1.

BICYCLE

Turku's tourist office (p83) rents seven-gear bikes (per half-/full day €15/20) and publishes an excellent free *pyörätiekartta* (bike-route map) of the city and surrounding towns.

BUS

Frequent city and regional buses cost €3 for a two-hour ticket or €6.50 for a 24-hour ticket. The Turku Card (p77) includes bus travel.

Timetables are available from the tourist office, bus station and train station.

CAR

Major car-rental companies have offices at the airport, city centre, harbour and/or train station.

FERRY

Föri Ferry (⏱ 6.15am-9pm Sep-Apr, 6.15am-11pm May-Aug) Dating from 1904, this small, orange passenger and bicycle ferry yo-yos across the river a few blocks downstream of the last bridge.

NAANTALI
📱 02 / POP 18,840

Most visitors to charming Naantali (Swedish: Nådendal) are summer day-trippers from Turku, 18km to the east, who come to the adorable Muumimaailma (Moominworld) theme park or to wander the quaint Old Town, and even the Finnish president spends his summer holidays here.

Out of season Muumimaailma closes its gates, and the Old Town acquires the melancholic air of an abandoned film set. But Naantali continues to work hard behind the scenes, with Finland's third most-trafficked port, an oil refinery and an electricity power plant.

◉ Sights & Activities

Surrounding the harbour, Naantali's photogenic Old Town is made up of old narrow cobbled streets and wooden houses – many of which now house handicraft shops, art galleries, antiques shops and cafes.

Muumimaailma AMUSEMENT PARK
(Moomin World; ☑ 02-511-1111; www.muumimaa ilma.fi; 1-/2-day pass €26/36, winter magic 1-day pass €18; ⊙ summer season 10am-6pm early Jun–mid-Aug, noon-6pm late Aug, winter magic 10am-4pm mid-Feb–late Feb) Crossing the bridge from the Old Town to Kailo island takes you into the delightful world of the Moomins. The focus is on hands-on activities and exploration, not rides; littlies love the costumed characters wandering through the Moominhouse, Snork's Workshop (where they can help with inventions) and other places from the books and cartoons.

Older adventure seekers can rock climb and track down buccaneer relics at nearby pirate island **Väski** (☑ 02-511-1111; www.vaski. fi; over 3yr €22, 2-day ticket incl Moominworld entry €41; ⊙ 11am-7pm early Jun–mid-Aug), reached by boats (included in admission) departing regularly from Naantali.

Other Muumimaailma highlights include a swimming beach and Emma's Theatre (with some mimed performances, so language isn't an issue).

Convent Church CHURCH
(www.naantalinseurakunta.fi; organ concerts €5-10; ⊙ 10am-4pm Wed-Sun mid-May–end May, 10am-4pm Tue-Sun Jun–mid-Aug, noon-2pm Wed, 9am-noon Sun mid-Aug–mid-May) FREE Medieval Naantali grew up around the Catholic Convent of the Order of Saint Birgitta, which was dissolved after the 1527 Reformation. Towering above the harbour, the massive Convent Church, completed in 1462, is all that remains; its baroque stone tower dates from 1797. Archaeological digs have unearthed some 2000 pieces of jewellery, coins and relics now in the Naantali Museum.

At 8pm on summer evenings a trumpeter plays vespers (evensong) from the belfry; there are also regular organ concerts.

Naantali Museum MUSEUM
(Katinhäntä 1; adult/child €4/2; ⊙ 11am-6pm Tue-Sun mid-May–Aug) Housed in three Old Town wooden buildings dating from the 18th century, Naantali's museum casts a light on disappearing trades such as needlemaking and goldsmithing, and looks at how the town prospered from sock knitting.

Kultaranta HISTORIC BUILDING
The Finnish president's summer residence is an elaborate stone castle on Luonnonmaa island, its tower visible from Naantali harbour. Designed by Lars Sonck, it was built in 1916 and is surrounded by beautiful, extensive rose gardens. Although the castle's interior is closed to the public, the **grounds** (☑ 02-435-9800; tours from gate adult/child €11/5, from Naantali €16/7; ⊙ Tue-Sun mid-Jun–late Aug) can be visited by guided tours departing

---

THE MOOMINS

Beloved throughout Finland and beyond, the Moomins are an eccentric family of nature-loving, white-snouted, hippo-like trolls. Moominpappa, Moominmamma and their timid child Moomintroll are based closely on creator Tove Jansson's own bohemian family. Other characters include the eternal wanderer Snufkin; brutally honest Little My; the eerie Hattifatteners, who grow from seeds and are drawn to electrical storms; and the icy Groke, who leaves a frozen trail wherever she drifts.

Jansson's first published Moomin drawing appeared as a signature on her political cartoons. She wrote the first of her nine children's books, *Småtrollen och den stora översvämningen* (The Moomins and the Great Flood) during WWII, followed by several cartoon books based on her characters. Her comic strips debuted in the *London Evening News* in 1954, before being syndicated around the world: Canadian publisher Drawn & Quarterly recently republished them in six hardback editions. Adaptations have included a Japanese cartoon series, a film and an album; Moomintroll has even starred on the side of Finnair planes.

Moomin merchandise is everywhere in Finland but the real deal is the **Moomin Shop**, which was set up by Jansson's heirs; branches include Naantali's Old Town (p86). For an up-close encounter, visit Tampere's **Muumilaakso** (Moomin Valley Museum; p129) or Muumimaailma (Moomin World).

from the front gate (at 2pm in English) or by bus from Maariankatu, near Naantali's tourist office, at 1.40pm.

Naantalin Kylpylä SPA
(☑ 02-445-5100; www.naantalispa.fi; Matkailijantie 2; pool entry per 3hr adult/child Sun-Fri €20/8, Sat €24/12, day spa packages from €92; ☺ nonguests 8am-8pm Mon-Sat, to 7pm Sun) Naantali's spa traditions date from 1723 with the discovery of the health-giving properties of the Viluluoto spring waters and peaked in the 19th century. Today the town's top-class spa hotel allows nonguests to access its impressive facilities, including several pools and a Turkish bath. Its massage and beauty treatments are popular – book ahead in summer.

Minijuna Aikataulu TOURIST TRAIN
(adult/child return €7/5; ☺ hourly 9.30am-6.30pm Mon-Sat, 9.30am-4.30pm Sun early Jun-early Aug) In summer this cute little tourist train does a handy circuit between Naantalin Kylpylä and Muumimaailma via the Old Town.

Suosittu Iltaristeily CRUISE
(www.rosita.fi; adult/child €15/5; ☺ mid-Jun–early Aug) Evening harbour cruises aboard the 1947-built schooner M/S *Rosita* sail from the Old Town pier from 7pm to 8.30pm Monday to Saturday during summer.

★ Festivals & Events

Naantali Music Festival MUSIC
(☑ 02-434-5363; www.naantalinmusiikkijuhlat.fi; tickets €28-51) For over 30 years, this event featuring first-rate classical music has been held over two weeks from early June. Events in the Convent Church are a real highlight and performers come from around the globe.

Sleepyhead Day CULTURAL
On 27 July Naantali eccentrically elects a 'Sleepyhead of the Year', who is woken early by being tossed into the sea. A carnival with music, dancing and games ensues.

🛏 Sleeping

Naantali Camping CAMPGROUND €
(☑ 02-435-0855; http://naantalicamping.sportum. info; Kuparivuori; tent sites €15 plus per person €6, 2-/4-/6-person cottages €70/90/160; ☺ Sat & Sun only May, daily Jun-Aug) Good facilities at this campground 400m south of the harbour include a beachside sauna. Cabins range from basic accomodation to private saunas, bathrooms and kitchens.

★ Hotel Bridget Inn GUESTHOUSE €€
(☑ 02-533-4026; www.bridgetinn.fi; Kaivokatu 18; d €120-140, f €160, apt €220; 🛜) Steeped in history, this dove-white 1880-built wooden inn (a one-time cafe frequented by former Finnish president PE 'Ukko-Pekka' Svinhufvud) has gorgeous period-furnished rooms in champagne and chocolate hues, some with patios or balconies. Double-storey apartments include full kitchens. Parents can watch the kids romp in the playground from the umbrella-shaded terrace.

Hotel Palo GUESTHOUSE €€
(☑ 02-438-4017; www.palo.fi; Luostarinkatu 12; d €120-140, f €180; 🛜) Furnished with wrought-iron beds and countrified fabrics, all 14 of the rooms in this cosy wooden building have ensuite bathrooms and the family room has its own fridge and microwave (otherwise there's a shared fridge and microwave in the hallway leading to communal garden-view balconies). The family owners take pride in preparing excellent breakfasts.

Naantalin Kylpylä SPA HOTEL €€€
(☑ 02-445-5100; www.naantalispa.fi; Matkailijantie 2; spa hotel d €168-188, ste hotel d €188-248; @ 🛜 ≋) Indulge at this large, upmarket spa (p85) complex and its first-rate restaurants Le Soleil and Thai Garden. Rooms in the Spa Hotel and Suite Hotel are spacious (the latter has Moomin-themed rooms!), and spiffing Spa Residence apartments (double from €218) come with balconies. The spa also owns the neighbouring budget family hotel Naantalin Kylpylä Perhehotelli (2-/3-bedroom apartment €120/180).

🍴 Eating

Naantali has a cluster of eating options around the harbour and at Muumimaailma.

Merisali FINNISH €
(www.merisali.fi; Nunnakatu 1; breakfast/lunch/dinner buffet Mon-Sat €8.50/14.50/19, Sun €22; ☺ breakfast 9am-10.30 daily, lunch 11am-4pm Mon-Sat, dinner 4-10pm Mon-Sat May-Sep) In a restored spa pavilion, Merisali offers buffets with plentiful hot and cold choices. The pierside terrace often has live music.

★ Uusi Kilta INTERNATIONAL €€
(☑ 02-435-1066; www.uusikilta.fi; Mannerheiminkatu 1; mains €18-33; ☺ kitchen 10am-10pm May-Sep) Naantali's best restaurant has a sundrenched terrace overlooking the pier and a superb, mostly seafood-oriented

menu of whitefish with warm apple and fennel salad, fried perch with crayfish and potato gratin, and aromatic salmon soup with homemade bread; land-based dishes include lamb rump with garlic mash and brandy sauce.

Trappi FINNISH €€
(📞 02-435-2477; www.ravintolatrappi.fi; Nunnakatu 3; mains €18-26.50; ☺11am-9pm Mon & Tue, to 10pm Wed & Thu, to 11pm Fri, noon-11pm Sat, noon-8pm Sun) Finnish staples – whitefish, reindeer – are used inventively in international dishes such as pastas and curries. Save room for the expertly chosen cheeses including deep-fried camembert with *lakka* (cloudberries).

🛍 Shopping

Wanha Naantali Kauppa SWEETS
(Mannerheiminkatu 13; ☺11am-4pm daily Jun-Aug, Sat & Sun rest of yr) Nostalgic Wanha Naantali Kauppa sells old-fashioned Finnish sweets – brace yourself for the liquorice and tar drops.

Moomin Shop TOYS, CLOTHING
(www.moomin.com; Mannerheiminkatu 3; ☺11am-5pm mid-May–early Jun, 10am-7pm early Jun-early Aug, 11.30am-6.30pm early-Aug-late Aug) Moomin merchandise galore.

ℹ Information

Naantalin Matkailu (📞 02-435-9800; www.naantalinmatkailu.fi; Kaivotori 2; ☺9am-6pm Mon-Fri, 10am-4pm Sat & Sun Jun-Aug, 9am-4.30pm Mon-Fri Sep-May) By the harbour.

ℹ Getting There & Away

Naantali's bus station is 1km east of the harbour. Buses 6, 7 and 7A run to/from Turku's kauppatori (€3, 20 minutes, four per hour).

S/S Ukkopekka (p78) sails between Turku and Naantali in summer, arriving at the passenger quay on the south side of the harbour.

Finnlink (www.finnlines.com) offers a fast service to Kapellskär (passenger/car €47/from €36, nine hours, up to three daily), 90km north of Stockholm in Sweden. Tickets include two meals; berths are available. All passengers must board with a vehicle, or bicycle (free). Finnlink also has a ferry to Långnäs in Åland (passenger/car €19/29, 3½ hours, up to two daily).

TURKU ARCHIPELAGO
📞02

Twenty-thousand islands and skerries make up the Turku archipelago. The five largest inhabited islands – from east to west, Pargas, Nagu, Korpo, Houtskär and Iniö – are clustered in a tight crescent, and are known collectively as Väståboland (Länsi-Turunmaan). There are no big-ticket sights, just quiet settlements, abundant birdlife, and ever-changing views of sea and land.

The Turku archipelago – like much of Finland's south coast and west coast and all of Åland – is primarily Swedish speaking (see p191).

🛏 Sleeping

Tourist offices can help with accommodation bookings including private cottages and B&Bs.

ℹ Information

Turku's tourist office (p83) has useful information on the archipelago.

Archipelago Booking (📞02-410-6600; www.archipelagobooking.fi) Particularly useful for booking cottages.

Turun Saaristo (📞040-011-7123; www.saaristo.org) The best all-round source of information.

ℹ Getting There & Away

Out as far as Houtskär, the islands almost join. From mid-May to September, you can complete the 250km circular **Archipelago Trail** from Turku by hopping between the main islands and islets, which are linked by eight ferries and a dozen bridges. The further you travel, the more forward planning is required, particularly if you're using public transport – ferry timetable service **Ferry.fi** (http://lautta.net) has indispensable information.

Frequent, free ferries run continually between Pargas, Nagu and Korpo, with less frequent crossings from Korpo to Houtskär, and summer-only private ferries from Houtskär to Iniö. For details and timetables, consult **FinFerries** (www.finferries.fi).

It's possible to island-hop all the way to Åland with Åland's archipelago ferries (p115), either from Galtby in Korpo via Kökar and Föglö, or from Osnäs near Kustavi via Brändö and Kumlinge.

Pargas

Once a Hansa League port, Pargas (Finnish: Parainen) is the de facto 'capital' of the archipelago. It still has a substantial port and its limestone quarry – Finland's largest – is a major employer. There's a lack of good sleeping or eating options but a handful of interesting sights make it worth a quick stop before heading further into the archipelago.

◉ Sights & Activities

Pargas Hembygdsmuseum   MUSEUM
(Local History Museum; ☑ 02-458-1452; www.pargashembygdsmuseum.fi; Storgårdsgatan 13; adult/child €3/free; ☉ 11am-4pm Tue-Sun Jun-Aug) When Lenin was on the lam from Russia to Stockholm in 1907, he stayed in Pargas under the pseudonym Mr Mueller. The outdoor local history museum contains the house where he hid, along with cottages, crofts and a restored schoolhouse; enthusiastic guides show visitors around.

Pargas Church   CHURCH
(Kyrkoesplanaden 4; ☉ 10am-5pm Jun-Aug) The Old Town of wooden houses is tucked behind Pargas Church, a beautiful early-14th-century building with whitewashed walls, medieval murals and brick-Gothic supports.

Sattmark   CULTURAL CENTRE
(☑ 044-970-2599; ☉ 10am-7pm Jun-Aug) Situated 10km southwest of Pargas along the road to Nagu, Sattmark is a charming 18th-century red wooden sailor's cottage with a cafe and rustic handicrafts, plus nature trails and ski tracks.

🛏 Sleeping

Solliden Camping   CAMPGROUND €
(☑ 040-540-9884; www.solliden.fi; Solstrand 7, Norrby; tent sites €14 plus per person €4, 4-/8-person cottages €60/135) Pargas' seaside campground, 1.5km north of the town centre, has a range of cottages (cheaper from October to April), saunas, a laundry and bike rental (per day €15).

❶ Information

Tourist Office (☑ 040-011-7123; www.saaristo.org; Rantatie 28; ☉ 9am-5pm Mon-Fri, 10am-2pm Sat Jul–mid-Aug, 9am-4pm Mon-Thu, 9am-3pm Fri mid-Aug–Jun) Inside Pargas' library, the archipelago's main tourist office has information on all the islands.

❶ Getting There & Away

Regular buses run to/from Turku (€6.10, 40 minutes, half-hourly or more frequent).

To explore some of the more obscure islands south of Pargas, free **Rosita** (☑ 02-213-1500; www.rosita.fi) ferries hop to 14 islands including Nötö Aspö and Utö.

Nagu

The archipelago scenery really picks up once you reach Nagu (Finnish: Nauvo) – an idyllic island nestled between Pargas and Korpo. Its lively Swedish-style guest harbour has a string of shoreside huts selling souvenirs and designer sailor-wear, and attracts yachties and cruise ships. Pleasant little walking trails fan out around the harbour.

◉ Sights

Nagu Church   CHURCH
(☉ 10am-5pm Jun-Aug) Lovely Nagu church dates from the 14th century and contains the oldest Bible in Finland.

🛏 Sleeping & Eating

Hotel Strandbo   HOTEL €€
(☑ 02-460-6200; www.strandbo.fi; Strandvägen 3; s/d from €95/125; @ 🛜) Three light and airy bedrooms in a stately wooden seafront building, with balconies looking over the waves, are the pick of the rooms in the four buildings housing this sophisticated guest harbour hotel. Its restaurant offers a great lunch buffet and à la carte evening meals.

Västergård   B&B €€
(☑ 040-586-1317; www.nagu.net/vastergard; Gyttjavägen 29, Gyttja; s €70-90, d €90-110; ℗) In a blissful spot 10km east of Nagu, this B&B has cosy rooms with private bathrooms, based in a beautifully converted barn, with dinner (€35) by arrangement. Bicycles (per day seven-speed/24-speed/electric €15/25/40) and kayaks (€30 per day) are available (including for nonguests).

Hotel Stallbacken &
Grännäs B&B   HOTEL, B&B €€
(☑ 040-486-6822; www.grannasgard.fi; Grännäsintie 14, Grännäs; B&B s/d €90/100, hotel s/d €100/135; 🛜) The forested hamlet of Grännäs is tucked just off the main road 3km south of Nagu. B&B guests get to share the adjoining hotel's facilities – a private beach, summer evening restaurant, tennis court, sauna and boat, bike and canoe rental.

Najaden   PIZZERIA €
(☑ 040-879-3630; www.najaden.fi; opposite Nauvon Ranta 4; pizzas €9-12; ☉ noon-10pm) Moored at the guest harbour, this stubby steamboat is now a 'sail-in' pizzeria. Dock alongside it to pick up piping-hot, crispy-crust pizzas such as shrimp, feta and garlic, or chicken, fiery jalapenos and salsa (you can also walk here and/or dine aboard), or just drop by for a drink on the upper deck (the bar opens until late). Cash only.

L'Escale   INTERNATIONAL €€
(☑ 040-744-1744; www.lescale.fi; Nauvon Ranta 4; lunch buffet €12.50, mains €19-32, bar dishes €15-16; ☉ 11.30am-10pm Mon-Thu, 11.30am-11pm Fri, noon-11pm Sat, noon-8pm Sun) The name might be French, but this two-storey spot at the guest harbour – with fine dining upstairs, a casual bar downstairs and terraces on both levels that are heated in winter – incorporates influences from further afield: goatweed-pesto pasta, smoked salmon with chive cream and smashed dill potatoes, lamb liver with onion and mash, and rhubarb pannacotta.

❶ Getting There & Around

Buses run to/from Turku (€11.80, 1¼ hours, 10 daily).

At the guest harbour, the **Marina Cafe** (☑ 045-321-3400; ☉ 8am-9pm Jun-Aug) rents bikes (per day €12).

Korpo

Korpo (Finnish: Korppoo) is the gateway for shipping out to Kökar on the Åland archipelago's southern route but it's remote enough to be an enjoyable stop in its own right. The main harbour is Galtby, 3km east of Korpo village.

◉ Sights

Korpo Church   CHURCH
(www.korpo.net; Korppoontie 1; ☉ 10am-5pm Jun-Aug) A highlight of Korpo is its medieval church. Built in the late 13th century, it features naïve paintings on the ceiling and a statue of St George fighting a dragon.

🍴 Sleeping & Eating

Faffas B&B   B&B €€
(☑ 040-522-4306; www.faffas.fi; Österretaisvägen 23; s/d €45/70) A dignified old farmhouse, complete with corner stove in the downstairs bedroom, contains this four-roomed

B&B looking out onto fields and has its own serene bathing pier a short walk away. In summer there are also three simple cabins for rent (from €40). Payment is by cash only. It's 7.2km east of Korpo village.

Hjalmars   FINNISH, INTERNATIONAL €€
(☑ 02-463-1202; www.hjalmars.fi; Handelsmansvägen 1; mains €9.50-19.50; ☉ kitchen 10am-10pm Mon-Thu, 10am-midnight Fri & Sat, noon-9pm Sun Jun-Aug, 11am-9pm Mon-Thu, 11am-midnight Fri & Sat, noon-9pm Sun Sep-May) Regional delicacies at this local linchpin include fried herring with lingonberries, and fresh and cold-smoked whitefish soup with dark archipelago bread, while innovative twists on international favourites include a black Angus 'smuggler's burger'. The bar stays open until 2am on Friday and Saturday nights.

Buffalo Ravintola   STEAK €€
(☑ 02-463-1600; www.ravintolabuffalo.com; Verkan guest harbour; lunch buffet €8.50, mains €16-30; ☉ kitchen 11am-10pm Mon-Sat, 11am-9pm Sun late Jun–mid-Aug) You guessed it, Buffalo specialises in steaks, but there are also fish dishes (though few vegetarian options). Its waterside terrace is a prime spot for long lingering with a cold beer; the bar kicks on after the kitchen closes.

❶ Information

The friendly staff at Hjalmars have tourist information in English.

❶ Getting There & Away

Regular buses link Korpo with Turku (€15.50, two hours, eight daily).

Ferries run from Galtby harbour to Houtskär (free, 30 minutes, eight daily) and Kökar (passenger/bicycle/car free/€6/32, 2¼ hours, up to three daily).

Free passenger ferries depart at least once daily in summer from Verkan guest harbour, 3.2km southwest of Galtby, to outlying islands like Berghamn, Storpensar, Lillpensar, Kälderso and Elvsö. Check timetables at Ferry.fi (http://lautta.net).

Houtskär & Iniö

Houtskär and its tiny neighbour Iniö are delightfully tranquil, if short on sights. Both islands have Swedish-speaking populations. There are no ATMs.

Houtskär's two ports are Mossala in the north and Kittius in the south. You can pitch camp or rent a cabin at Mossala's **Skärgårdens Fritidscenter** (☑ 02-463-3322; www.saaristo.com; tent sites €20, cabins €65-170), which also has a restaurant and rents boats. The modest **Houtskär Archipelago Museum** (admission €2; ☺ noon-4pm Sat-Mon, 1-7pm Tue-Fri early Jun-early Aug) in Näsby includes a small windmill, restored dairy shed and period home, and can help with tourist information.

Iniö's sweet stone **Church of Sofia Wilhelmina** (☺ 10am-5pm Jun-Aug) was built in the 18th century. The area is good for nature strolls.

The *Antonia* ferry links Houtskär (Mossala) and Iniö (passenger/bicycle/car €8/15/35, one hour, four daily Monday to Saturday, three on Sunday) from June to August. FinFerries (p86) has timetables.

Kustavi

The island village of Kustavi (Swedish: Gustavs) represents the final piece of the Archipelago Trail puzzle, offering scenic seascapes and a jumping-off point for the Åland islands.

Kustavi's wooden **church** (☺ 10am-5pm mid-May–mid-Aug), built in 1783, features the cruciform shape and votive miniature ships common in coastal churches. It's possible to charter a boat from Kustavi to **Isokari lighthouse** and to **Katanpää Fort Island** – ask at the **tourist office** (☑ 02-842-6620; www.visitkustavi.fi; Keskustie 7; ☺ 8.30am-4pm Mon-Sat Jun-Aug). The best place to eat is **Peterzéns** (☑ 050-350-8346; www.peterzens.fi; buffet €23; ☺ 10am-6pm Mon-Fri, 10am-10pm Sat & Sun Jun, 8am-10pm Jul & Aug), with a bountiful buffet (no à la carte) and tables on a picturesque wooden deck.

ⓘ Getting There & Away

A free ferry, the M/S *Aurora*, runs from Iniö to Kustavi (25 minutes, up to three daily); check timetables at Ferry.fi (http://lautta.net). To complete the circle back to Turku, there are four direct buses (€13.70, 1½ hours).

If you're hopping across to the Åland archipelago, head for the port of Osnäs (Finnish: Vuosnainen) on the island's western tip. From here, regular passenger ferries run to Långö on northern Brändö; book through **Ålandstrafiken** (☑ 018-525 100; www.alandstrafiken.ax; passenger/bicycle/car free/€6/32).

KIMITO ISLAND & ARCHIPELAGO NATIONAL PARK

☑ 02

Kimito is the jumping-off point for the Archipelago National Park, a scattering of islands that stretches south of Korpo.

Kasnäs, the harbour on the southern extreme of Kimito island, is the best place from which to explore the park. It's worth breaking your journey at central Kimito village and Dragsfjärd, a quiet, rural settlement in the island's southwest.

◉ Sights

Sagalund   MUSEUM
(☑ 02-421-738; www.sagalund.fi; Museotie 7; adult/child €6/1; ☺ 11am-6pm Jun-Aug) Near Kimito village, Sagalund is an open-air museum with more than 20 old buildings including a traditional sauna and blacksmith. There are 90-minute guided tours (included in admission and available in English) hourly from 11am to 3pm.

Dragsfjärd Church   CHURCH
(Kappelimäentie 6; ☺ 10am-5pm Jun-Aug) Dragsfjärd's charming wooden church (gold-coloured on the outside, marine-blue inside) dates back to 1755.

Söderlångvik   HISTORIC BUILDING
(☑ 02-424-662; www.soderlangvik.fi; Amos Andersonvägen 2; adult/child €3.50/free; ☺ 11am-6pm mid-May–Aug) The beautiful manor house Söderlångvik belonged to local newspaper magnate and art collector Amos Anderson. There are paintings, furniture and special exhibitions, as well as extensive gardens and a cafe. It's signposted 6.3km southwest of Dragsfjärd.

⭆ Tours

Viking Islands   CRUISE
(☑ 02-466-7227; www.vikingislands.com) In summer Viking Islands organises a great one-day round trip (adult/child €36/18; 11am June to August) to Bengtskär's lighthouse (p91), calling at the **Rosala Viking Centre** (www.rosala.fi; ☺ 10am-6pm Jun-Aug, 10am-3pm mid–late May & early–mid-Sep), which looks at Viking ships and daily life.

Blåmusslan   BOAT TOUR
(Blue Mussel Visitor Centre; ☑ 020-564-4620; www.outdoors.fi; Meripuistontie; ☺ 10am-5pm daily mid-Jun–mid-Aug, 10am-3pm Tue-Fri, to 4pm Sat

mid-Feb–late Apr & Oct–mid-Nov, 10am-4pm Mon-Sat late Apr–mid-Jun & mid-Aug–Sep) In Kasnäs, near the pier, the Blåmusslan visitor centre organises tours to some Archipelago National Park islands between June and August, depending on demand, and has info on nature trails in the area. There are also several films in English (most around 10 minutes' long).

🛌 Sleeping

Hostel Panget   HOSTEL €€
(🗷 02-424-553; www.panget.fi; Täysihoitolantie 6, Kulla; s/d/tr/f €58/93/98/110) At the turn-off to Dragsfjärd, Hostel Panget was built in 1930 as a summer boarding house and retains art deco detailing. Its comfortable, old-fashioned rooms all have a private toilet; the four-person family rooms also have a private shower. Sociable common areas include a pub and lounge with board games.

Hotel Kasnäs   SPA HOTEL €€
(🗷 02-521-0100; www.kasnas.com; Käsnäsintie 1294; s/d/ste €90/130/214; @ 🌊) Literally at the end of the road, on the island's southern tip, this modern complex sprawling over several buildings is perfect for a spot of pampering, with facilities including a 25m pool, various saunas, massages and an excellent restaurant.

ℹ Information

Tourist Office (🗷 02-426-0170; www.visit-kimitoon.fi; Luckan, Villa Lande; ⊙ noon-5pm Mon-Fri) In Kimito village.

ℹ Getting There & Around

Buses run from Taalintehdas and, five minutes' later, Dragsfjärd to Turku (€17.30, two hours, 12 daily) and Helsinki (€32.80, three to four hours, six daily).

From Taalintehdas, free ferries serve the southern archipelago islands in summer, such as Hitis (Hiittinen). Check timetables at Ferry.fi (p86), which also has details of taxi boats.

SOUTH COAST

Finland's south coast is a boaties' paradise, with numerous islets forming chains of archipelagos. Most of the charming, history-steeped coastal towns offer summer cruises, guest harbour facilities, and charter boats to discover your own island.

In the hinterland you'll find intriguing *bruk* (ironworks) precincts and lakes.

West of Helsinki

From Kimito island to the western fringes of Finland's capital are a scattering of pretty lakeside and coastal towns and villages.

Hanko

🗷 019 / POP 9270
On a long sandy peninsula, Hanko (Swedish: Hangö) recalls the past grandeur of its heyday as a well-to-do Russian spa town in the late 19th century, and its opulent seaside villas from the era remain a star attraction. Visitors still flock here for the sun, sand and party atmosphere of the huge Hanko Regatta.

History

As the southernmost town in Finland, Hanko was a strategic anchorage well before its foundation in 1874. It was also a point of emigration: between 1881 and 1931 about 250,000 Finns left for the USA, Canada and Australia via its docks.

At the end of the Winter War, the March 1940 peace treaty with Russia required the ceding of Hanko as a naval base. Its inhabitants evacuated as the Russians moved in with a garrison of 30,000 and constructed a huge network of fortifications. Hanko was isolated from the Russian front lines and eventually abandoned in December 1941. Citizens returned to see their damaged town the following spring.

⊙ Sights

Finland's biggest guest harbour, Hanko's East Harbour (Itäsatama), is the centre of the town's activity in summer; the West Harbour (Ulkosatama) handles only commercial traffic. The Russian villas are on Appelgrenintie, east of East Harbour.

Neljän Tuulen Tupa   HISTORIC BUILDING
(⊙ 10am-7pm daily mid-May–mid-Aug, 10am-7pm Sat & Sun Sep) On Little Pine Island, 1.5km east of the town centre (now connected by a bridge), is the House of the Four Winds, where locals snuck swigs of 'hard tea' (alcohol) during the Finnish prohibition (1919–32). Disturbed by the merrymaking, Field Marshal CGE Mannerheim, who had his summer cottage nearby, bought it in 1927, imported teasets from France and personally ran the place until 1931. There's a beautiful cafe and summer terrace, with granite tables carved from the surrounding rocks.

Water Tower   TOWER
(Kirkkopuisto Park; admission €1; ☺ 1-4pm Sat May, 1-4pm daily Jun & Aug, 1-6pm daily Jul) Zip up the lift (elevator) to the top of the 50m-high water tower on Vartiovuori Hill for sweeping views across town and out to sea.

Hanko Church   CHURCH
(Kirkkopuisto Park; ☺ 1-3pm mid-Jun–late Jun & early Aug–mid-Aug, noon-6pm late Jun-early Aug) 🌿 Hanko's neo-Gothic church, built in 1892, was damaged in WWII but has been thoroughly renovated.

Monument of Liberty   MONUMENT
Where Bulevardi meets the beach is the Monument of Liberty, commemorating the landing of liberating German forces in 1918. The monument was taken down after WWII, but re-erected in 1960 with new text simply stating 'For our liberty'.

Front Museum   MUSEUM
(📞 019-244-3068; www.frontmuseum.fi; Rd 25, Lappohja; adult/child €5/2; ☺ 11.30am-6.30pm mid-May–early Sep) Original trenches, bunkers and artillery guns remain at the site of some of the worst Winter War fighting, 19km northeast of Hanko. Also here is a poignant indoor museum – the knowledgeable guide can answer any questions (including in English).

Bengtskär Lighthouse   LIGHTHOUSE
(📞 02-466-7227; www.bengtskar.fi; adult/child €8/4; ☺ 10am-7pm Jun-Aug) Towering 52m above the waves 25km offshore from Hanko, the Nordic countries' tallest lighthouse was built in 1906 to protect ships from the perilous archipelago waters. It was damaged extensively during the Continuation War by the departing Red Army, but has been refurbished. There are historical exhibits and simple but panoramic guest rooms (single/double/family €120/188/280).

Day cruises (p91) leave from Hanko and Kimito island (📞 0400-320-092; www.finferries.fi) in summer, or you can charter boats from Surfclub Hanko (p91).

Hauensuoli   HARBOUR
(Pike's Gut) This narrow strait between Tullisaari and Kobben is a protected natural harbour where sailing ships from countries around the Baltic Sea once waited out storms. The sailors killed time by carving their initials or tales of bravery on the rocks, earning the area the nickname 'Guest Book of the Archipelago'. Some 600 rock carvings

dating back to the 17th century remain. Hauensuoli can be reached by charter taxi boat or on a cruise (p91) from Hanko.

🏃 Activities

With over 30km of beaches, swimming and sunbathing are two of the town's chief attractions. Tennisranta beach (Plagen) includes some cute wooden changing boxes and a fantastic free water merry-go-round (move aside, kids!).

Some of Finland's best windsurfing is southwest of the guest harbour at Tulliniemi, and 3km northeast of town at Silversand.

You can also zoom around the harbour on a jet ski (€275 per hour) or motor boat (from €200 per four hours). SunFun (p91) has rentals available.

Marine Lines   CRUISE
(📞 040-053-6930; www.marinelines.fi; East Harbour; ☺ mid-Jun–mid-Aug) Two great options: a 5½-hour cruise (including lunch adult/child €58/25) to the lighthouse island of Bengtskär (p91), departing at 11am; and a 3½-hour cruise (adult/child €35/20 return) to/from Russaro, a former military base recently reopened to the public, leaving Hanko at 12.30pm each Tuesday during July and Saturday during August.

Surfclub Hanko   WATER SPORTS
(📞 040-552-2822; www.surfclubhanko.com; Lähteentie 17; ☺ 10am-6pm Jun–mid-Aug, 10am-6pm Sat & Sun mid-Aug–late Aug) Based at Silversand, Surfclub Hanko has windsurfing equipment (per hour €30), small-group four-hour lessons (per person €149), SUPs (stand-up paddleboards; per hour €25), canoes and kayaks (per hour €25), and snorkelling gear (per three hours €10).

Hanko Diving   DIVING
(📞 040-562-4241; www.hankodiving.com; Sillikuja 4, East Harbour; dives incl gear from €70) Offers dives exploring Hanko's many wrecks.

👣 Tours

SunFun   CRUISE
(📞 cruises 040-044-0802, rentals 040-414-5681; www.sunfun.fi; East Harbour) Two-hour seal safaris (adult/child €35/15) depart 11am Thursday and Sunday in July. At 11am on Saturday in July, there are two-hour tours (adult/child €25/10) to the rock carvings in Hauensuoli (Pike's Gut) strait.

Hanko

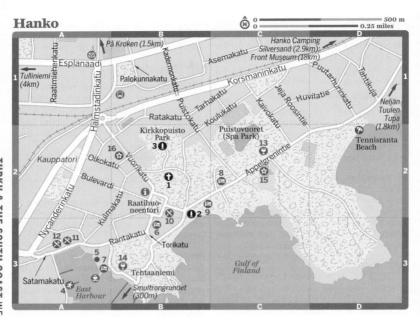

🎊 Festivals & Events

Hanko Theatre Days THEATRE
(☑ 050-584-9883; www.hangoteatertraff.org)
June brings Finland's biggest festival of
Swedish-language theatre.

Hanko Regatta SAILING
(www.hangoregattan.fi) More than 200 boats
compete in the Hanko Regatta. It usually
takes place on the first (sometimes second) weekend of July, attracting thousands
of spectators and a high-spirited carnival
atmosphere.

🛏 Sleeping

Several of Hanko's Empire-era Russian-style
villas operate as B&Bs. Don't expect luxury, but do come with open mind and lively
appreciation of history! You can book private accommodation (sometimes in villas)
through the tourist office.

Hanko Camping Silversand CAMPGROUND €
(☑ 019-248-5500; www.silversand.fi; Källvägen
27; tent sites €19 plus per person €5.40, huts Mon-
Thu/Fri-Sun €79/150, cottages Mon-Thu €84-129,
Fri-Sun €160-240; 🛜) Situated 4km northeast
of the town centre, this well-shaded campground stretches along a private beach. Its
simple six-person huts are supplemented by
newer, swisher four-person cottages. Hop on

a bike (per four/24 hours €7/20) for a spin
into and around town.

★ Villa Maija RUSSIAN VILLA €€
(☑ 050-505-2013; www.villamaija.fi; Appelgrenintie 7; s/d €135/175, without bathroom €100/130,
f €200; P) Built in 1888, this is Hanko's best
villa accommodation. Flawlessly restored
rooms are so cosy and packed with character that it's difficult to prise yourself away.
Prices vary according to the size of the room,
and whether it has a private bathroom and
balcony facing the sea. Breakfast is excellent.

Out the back, Villa Janne and Villa Anke
are as light-filled and pleasant as the main
building.

Hotelboat Hanko HOTEL €€
(☑ 044-514-1141; www.hotellilaivahanko.fi; East
Harbour; d €49-120; 🕙 Jun-Aug; 🛜) Left your
yacht in another harbour? This purpose-
built hotel boat gives you an ocean sleep
with 22 snug ensuite double rooms kitted
out with flatscreen TV and porthole views.
The best room aboard features its own 'balcony' on the bow.

Villa Tellina RUSSIAN VILLA €€
(☑ 019-248-6356; www.tellina.com; Appelgrenintie
2; d from €120, s/d without bathroom €70/100; P)
Right by the beach, Tellina is a rambling,

Hanko

paint-peeling, pistachio-coloured villa that looks as though it's seen its share of hidden treasure and wild adventure. TVs are banished from its basic but light-filled rooms. The same family owns two other villas that may have space if it's full. Phone reservations only.

Hotel Regatta BOUTIQUE HOTEL €€€
(☑019-248-6491; www.hotelregatta.fi; Torikatu 2; s €120, d €150-185; 🛜) Dating from 1898, this landmark art nouveau hotel designed by Finnish architect Lars Sonck reopened in 2012 after head-to-toe renovations. In an unbeatable beachfront location, its 49 rooms are uniquely decorated and come in a variety of sizes; the best have stunning sea views. Rates drop dramatically outside high season.

✗ Eating

Alan's Café CAFE €
(Raatihuoneentori 4; dishes €1.20-3; ⊙10am-7pm Mon-Sat, to 4pm Sun May-Aug) Set in an old villa, Alan's has hand-baked treats to eat in the courtyard, shaded by a huge tree. Afterwards, browse the attached craft shop.

Makasiini SEAFOOD €€
(☑019-248-4060; www.makasiini.fi; Satamakatu 9; buffet €25, mains €18-32; ⊙5-9pm Wed-Sat early Apr–Jun, 11am-10pm Mon-Sat, 11am-9pm Sun Jul & Aug) Makasiini's decor of rough timber, snow-white napkins and flickering candles is complemented by simple cooking that allows the high-quality regional ingredients to shine. Seafood such as crayfish, fish roe, shrimp and perch features in its archipelago buffet and tapas plates; there's a catch of the day, homemade ice cream and a lengthy wine list.

Hangon Portti SEAFOOD €€
(☑040-176-6284; www.hangonportti.fi; Smultrongrundet; tapas €13.30, mains €15-30; ⊙11am-10pm mid-Jun–early Aug, 1-9pm Wed-Sat mid-Aug–late Aug) You'll need to take a two-minute ferry journey from the East Harbour pier to this little whitewashed cottage perched on a rugged granite island. Baltic cod with vegetables roasted in lime butter, a smoked-cheese 'captain's burger' with potato salad, and archipelago tapas are among the dishes served in a wicker-furnished interior.

★ På Kroken SEAFOOD €€€
(☑040-358-1815; www.pakroken.fi; Tegelbruksvägen 12; cafe buffet €8, mains €10, restaurant buffet €26, mains €24-42; ⊙cafe 9am-8pm May-Sep, restaurant 11am-10pm Jun-Aug, 11am-10pm Fri & Sat, 11am-5pm Sun Sep-May) With its own smokehouse and boat-fresh lobster and shellfish (it sells to Helsinki's Hakaniemi market), På Kroken's yacht-shaped buffet teems with choices. If the restaurant's beyond your budget, its adjoining cafe serves cheaper dishes including fabulous salmon soup with dark archipelago bread, or you can stock up on picnic fare at its fish shop.

Origo ORGANIC €€€
(☑019-248-5023; www.restaurant-origo.com; Satamakatu 7; lunch buffet €29.80, mains €22-30; ⊙11am-10pm) 🍃 At the eatery-clad East Harbour, Origo distinguishes itself with geothermal heating, local, organic ingredients and a seasonal gourmet menu. Braised pork cheek cooked overnight is a treat, as is its salmon soup with dark bread. Vegetarians are treated to unusual dishes, such as black salsify pie.

♟ Drinking & Nightlife

Park Café
BAR

(www.restaurangpark.fi; Appelgrenintie 11; ☺4pm-midnight Mon-Fri, noon-1am Sat, noon-10pm Sun May-Sep) Barbecues, live bands and a great range of international beers make for a brilliant evening's boozing at this converted gymnastics hall.

Roxx
BAR

(☑019-248-4393; www.roxx.fi; East Harbour; ☺11am-midnight Sun-Thu, 11am-1am Fri & Sat) This harbourside summertime beer terrace attracts a young crowd.

☆ Entertainment

Casino
CASINO

(www.hangoncasino.fi; Appelgrenintie 9; ☺noon-10pm Sun-Tue, noon-4am Wed-Sat) An art nouveau beauty, Hanko's twin-turreted, mint-green-and-white casino is an atmospheric setting for roulette, terrace drinking, live music and dancing.

Kino Olympia
CINEMA

(☑019-248-1811; www.kino-olympia.fi; Vuorikatu 11) A local treasure, the Olympia has been an independent cinema since 1919.

❶ Information

Tourist Office (☑019-220-3411; www.hanko.fi; Raatihuoneentori 5; ☺9am-4pm Mon-Fri Sep-May, 9am-6pm Mon-Fri, 10am-4pm Sat & Sun Jun-Aug) Helpful office with a large list of private accommodation.

❶ Getting There & Around

Buses run to/from Helsinki (€25.20, 2¼ hours, 10 daily) via Ekenäs (€8.20, 35 minutes, nine daily).

Direct trains serve Helsinki (€25.60, 1¼ hours, hourly). Trains for Turku (€29, two hours, four daily) meet connecting trains or buses in Karis (Finnish: Karjaa).

SunFun (p91) has the biggest selection of bicycles for hire (per two hours/day €8/14).

For a taxi, call ☑019-106-910.

Ekenäs

☑019

Midway between Turku and Helsinki, the seaside resort of Ekenäs (Finnish: Tammisaari) is a magnet for summer holidaymakers. Ekenäs is one of Finland's oldest towns – in 1546 King Gustav Vasa envisioned it as a trading port to rival Tallinn in Estonia. Its fortunes failed and many of its artisans were

❶ EKENÄS OR RASEBORG?

Tourism and transport information for Ekenäs is often labelled 'Raseborg': the town combined with neighbours Karis and Pojo to collectively become Raseborg in 2009. Many (but by no means all) local establishments, however, still use the original name.

moved to Helsinki. Today the avenues of wooden buildings in its well-preserved Old Town are charming, and it's an ideal base for exploring the Ekenäs Archipelago National Park.

◉ Sights

Filled with 18th-century wooden buildings named after types of fish – a legacy of the area's fishing-village origins – Ekenäs' enchanting Old Town (Gamla Stan) is the result of the Swedish movement to create artisan centres for trade. Its narrow streets still bear their industries' names, such as Hattmakaregatan (Hatters' St) and Linvävaregatan (Linen Weavers' St). Today most of the Old Town is residential, giving it an untouristy air.

Gamla Stan Church
CHURCH

(Stora Kyrkogatan; ☺11am-5pm late Jun–Aug) The Old Town's stone church has a tower that can be seen from anywhere in town. It was constructed between 1651 and 1680, destroyed in the fire of 1821, and rebuilt in 1841 in the new classical style.

Ekenäs Museum
MUSEUM

(☑019-289-2512; Gustav Wasasgatan 11; admission €5; ☺11am-5pm Tue-Sun) Ekenäs' museum traces the town's history back to the Stone Age using illuminating models and audio. The Lindblad building re-creates a 1950s photographer's studio, and a small row of 19th-century red-painted outbuildings contain agricultural implements.

🏃 Activities

The small family beach has a **diving board** where you swim just metres away from preening swans.

Paddlingsfabriken
KAYAKING

(☑0400-411-992; www.paddlingsfabriken.fi) Paddlingsfabriken offers lessons and guided paddles, including an awesome one-day safari (€69) from Snappertuna's Raseborg Castle (p96) to Ekenäs – check the website for trip dates. In addition to summer kayaking trips (one- /two-day tours from €57/140), there are winter kayaking tours (€69) and Nordic ice skating (with poles; per day €10).

Saariston Laivaristeilyt CRUISE
(☑ 019-241-1850; www.surfnet.fi/saaristoristeilyt; ☺ Fri-Sun Jun & Aug, Wed-Sun Jul) Archipelago cruises aboard the 100-year-old former steamship M/S *Sunnan II* depart from the passenger harbour and last from two to four hours depending on the destination. Cruises cost €20 to €30 – timetables are online.

🛌 Sleeping

The tourist office has details of homestays and cottage and apartment rentals.

Ormnäs Camping CAMPGROUND €
(☑ 019-0241-4434; www.ek-camping.com; Ormnäsintie 1, Tammisaari; tent sites €12 plus per person €4, 2-/4-person cottages from €40/55; ☺ May-Sep) A 1.4km stroll southeast of the town centre, this easygoing campground has its own slice of beach (and a beach sauna), and rents bikes (€15 per day) and rowing boats (€25 per 24 hours). Right next door, the excellent cafe Bossa Nova has a terrace stepping down to the water.

Hotel Sea Front HOTEL €€
(☑ 019-246-1500; www.hotelseafront.fi; Pojogatan 2; s/d from €85/105; 🛜) Set some 400m north of the main harbour, this secluded 20-room family-run place feels like your own intimate retreat, with a private pier if you need to park your yacht. Higher-priced bayside rooms have great little balconies. Scrumptious local ice cream is available from its ice-cream bar on summer afternoons.

Ekenäs Stadshotell HOTEL €€
(☑ 019-241-3131; www.kaupunginhotelli.fi; Norra Strandgatan 1; s/d/f from €90/100/150; 🅿) In a bullseye location between the main square and the sea, this tiered concrete building has 20 sparingly furnished but comfortable neutral-toned rooms. Balcony rooms, with views over the park to the water, cost a smidge extra. It also rents boats and fishing gear.

🍴 Eating

Café Gamla Stan CAFE €
(☑ 050-556-1665; www.cafegamlastan.fi; Bastugatan 5; dishes €4.50-8; ☺ 11am-7pm mid-Apr–early Sep) 🍃 Tables sit beneath a shady apple orchard producing fresh juices at this family-

WORTH A TRIP

EKENÄS ARCHIPELAGO NATIONAL PARK

Almost 90% of the 5200-hectare Ekenäs Archipelago National Park is water, so to explore the 1300 islands you'll need to take a tour from Ekenäs harbour, such as with Saariston Laivaristeilyt or charter your own boat – the tourist office has a list of charter craft. For information on the park and campground bookings, visit Ekenäs' **Naturum Visitor Centre** (☑ 020-564-4613; www.outdoors.fi; Strandallén; ☺ 10am-8pm Jul, to 3pm Mar-May, to 6pm Jun & Aug).

The most popular island is **Älgö**, which has a 2km nature trail that takes in the island's observation tower. There's an old fisherman's home that's been converted to include a sauna and campsite facilities. There are also campgrounds on the islands of **Fladalandet** and **Modermagan**, but many other islands are off-limits to visitors, particularly the ecologically fragile outer islands.

run cafe, which is filled with the aromas of home baking (quiches, pies, cakes and other sweet treats). Also here is a craft shop; regular live music plays in the garden.

Guest Harbour Café CAFE €
(☑ 019-241-1790; Norra Strandgatan 6; pizzas €10-12.50; ☺ 8.30am-10pm Mon-Sat, 10am-10pm Jun-Aug) Inventive pizzas at this marina-side spot include Sea Battle (salami, mushrooms, pineapple and feisty jalapeno peppers), May Day (pepperoni, ham, blue cheese and red onion) and Baywatch (air-dried ham, rocket and parmesan).

Bossa Nova INTERNATIONAL €€
(☑ 019-239-5000; www.bossanova.fi; Ormnäsvägen 1; lunch €9.50, pizzas €11.50-13.50, mains €18-27; ☺ 11am-2pm Mon & Tue, 11am-9pm Wed & Thu, 11am-11pm Fri, noon-11pm Sat, noon-6pm Sun Jun-Aug) A spacious wooden terrace steps down towards the water, so you can watch the boats and jet-skiers while you're waiting for cartwheel-sized pizzas, grilled tuna and pan-seared whitefish or a tomahawk steak (weighing in at 2kg and serving two to three people). It's 1.4km south of town, next door to Ormnäs Camping.

WORTH A TRIP

MEDIEVAL RASEBORG CASTLE RUINS

Raseborg Castle (Raasepori; ☑019-234-015; www.raseborg.org; adult/child €5/free; ☺10am-5pm daily May–mid-Aug, 10am-5pm Sat & Sun mid-Aug–Sep) Looming on a high rock overlooking a grassy sward, the late 14th-century Raseborg Castle was strategically crucial in the 15th century, when it protected the trading town of Tuna, and Karl Knutsson Bonde, the exiled king of Sweden, held his court here. By the mid-16th century, Raseborg's importance had declined, and it was deserted for more than 300 years. It's 18km east of Ekenäs via Rd 25 in Snappertuna. Buses are limited to nonexistent so you'll need your own transport.

Albatross   SEAFOOD €€
(☑019-241-2848; www.albatross.fi; Norra Strandgatan 7; mains €16.50-39; ☺kitchen 11am-midnight Apr-Aug) Sea views stream through Albatross' huge windows to its cool, calm interior. Seafood, particularly fish, is a speciality, such as salmon soup and pan-fried archipelago pike-perch; turf-based dishes include lamb shanks with mash or pepper steak with wedges.

Knipan   FINNISH €€
(☑019-241-1169; www.knipan.fi; Strandallén; lunch buffet €12, mains €18-29; ☺noon-10pm Mon-Sat, noon-8pm Sun Jun-late Aug) In an 1867 building on the pier, this venerable summer restaurant has the best views in town. Its brief menu of Finnish favourites focuses on meat (beef fillet with crayfish and red wine sauce, slow-cooked boar neck with parsnip purée), with one vegetarian and one seafood dish daily.

ℹ Information

Tourist Office (☑019-289-2010; www.visit raseborg.com; Rådhustorget; ☺8.30am-6pm Mon-Fri, 10am-2pm Sat Jun-Aug, 8.30am-4pm Mon-Fri Sep-May) Info on the entire southwest region.

ℹ Getting There & Around

Ekenäs is served by buses (not always direct), but trains are invariably quicker and cheaper. Trains from Helsinki and Turku go via Karis (Finnish: Karjaa), where a change is required (some connections from Ekenäs to Karis involve a railbus).

Train services include the following:
Hanko (€5.40, 30 minutes, two hourly)
Helsinki (€19.80, 1½ hours, eight daily)
Turku (€23.10, 1½ hours, five daily)

The town is spread out and reasonably hilly: if you're puffed, get a **taxi** (☑019-106-9191) from the market square.

Bicycles (per day €10) can be hired at the marina from the Guest Harbour Café (p95).

Fiskars

☑019 / POP 450

Renowned for its cutting-edge Finnish design, Fiskars is a charming *bruk* village with a green river sidling between beautiful old brick buildings.

Fiskars' ironworks began in 1649 with a single furnace and went on to make millions of horse ploughs. In 1822 Turku apothecary Johan Jacob Julin bought Fiskars ironworks and the Fiskars company boomed, producing a huge range of farming and household items including its iconic orange-handled scissors in 1967, which are still made by the company (although not here).

Today over 100 artisans, designers and artists live and/or work here, and craft shops, studios and galleries fill its neoclassical buildings.

⊙ Sights

Strolling through the picturesque village and shopping for Finnish designs are the twin draws here – pick up a free town map from the tourist office, which details Fiskars' historic buildings.

Fiskars Museum   MUSEUM
(☑019-237-013; www.fiskarsmuseum.fi; Peltorivi 9; adult/child €5/free; ☺11am-5pm Jun-Aug, 11am-4pm Sep-May) Near the lake, Fiskars Museum details the ironworks' evolution and the village that grew around it, with a different display of art and craft each season.

🛏 Sleeping & Eating

Fiskars Wärdshus   INN €€
(☑019-276-6510; www.wardshus.fi; Fiskarsintie 14; s/d from €132/152; @🤍) The neoclassical exterior of this refined inn built in 1836 is a stark contrast to the 15 Scandi-chic rooms incorporating local timbers. Its restaurant (open 11am to 10pm Monday to Friday, to 10pm Saturday, to 4pm Sunday) serves up

local game (mains €23 to €30) and three-course lunches (€37) on the scenic terrace.

Café Antique   CAFE €

(☑019-237-275; www.cafeantique.fi; dishes €3-9; ⊙10am-6pm May-Sep) Inside Fiskars' red-brick clocktower building (originally a school, designed by CL Engel), heavenly, hand-baked cinnamon buns are among this family-run cafe's treats, along with sweet and savoury pies, soups, sandwiches and cakes.

★Restaurant Kuparipaja   FINNISH €€

(☑019-237-045; www.kuparipaja.fi; lunch buffet €19, dinner mains €13-29.50; ⊙11am-10pm Mon-Fri, noon-10pm Sat & Sun) The terrace overhanging the river at the old copper forge is a mesmerising setting for a foray into Finnish gastronomy. Starters such as cured whitefish with Jerusalem artichoke crème, pickled cucumber and malt bread are followed by mains like Åland lamb sausages with celeriac purée, and topped off by desserts such as rhubarb crème brulée.

🛍 Shopping

Onoma   CRAFT, HOMEWARES

(☑019-277-7500; www.onoma.org; Fiskarsintie; ⊙10am-6pm) 🖋 Sharp, stylish arts, crafts and homewares at this design shop in the distinctive clocktower building are produced by members of the Fiskars' Cooperative of Artisans, Designers and Artists.

Rekolan Panimo   DRINK

(www.rekolanpanimo.fi; Peltorivi 7; ⊙11am-5pm) Fiskars' former knife factory now houses this wonderful independent brewery (you can view its beer being brewed through the shop window). Currently its unique varieties like Katajn Kuiske (juniper rye), Metsän Henki (spruce ale), Kaksi Kotia (seabuckthorn berry) and Kesäkolli (ginger wheat beer) are take away only but plans are underway for a bar here.

Fiskars Shop   HOMEWARES

(⊙10am-6pm mid-May–Aug, 11am-5pm Sep–mid-May) You can buy distinctive Fiskars scissors at its shop in the clocktower building, which has a small exhibition on the company's storied history.

ℹ Information

Tourist Office (☑ 019-277-7504; www.fiskars-village.fi; ⊙8am-4pm Mon-Fri) Located in the workers' tenement buildings, near the clocktower building.

ℹ Getting There & Away

Bus services include the following:

Ekenäs (€7.40, 50 minutes, 12 daily)

Hanko (€15.50, 1½ hours, one daily)

Helsinki (€18.70, 1¾ hours, five daily, change in Karjaa)

Lohja

☑019 / POP 39,750

Lohjanjärvi is the biggest lake in these parts, and most of Helsinki's residents seem to have a summer cottage here. The town of Lohja (Swedish: Lojo) keeps the lake houses in beer and supplies. There are no stand-out places to sleep (or, for that matter, eat) but it's an easy day trip from Helsinki.

◉ Sights

★Tytyrin Kaivosmuseo   MINE

(Tytyri Mine Museum; www.tytyrinkaivos.fi; adult/child €14/8; ⊙tours 2pm Sat & Sun mid-May–early Jun & Sep, noon & 2pm Sat & Sun early Jun–mid-Jun, noon & 2pm daily mid-Jun–early Jul, noon, 2pm & 4pm daily early Jul-early Aug, 2pm daily early Aug-late Aug) A funicular takes you 80m down into the earth at this authentic working limestone mine 500m north of the town centre. Visits culminates in a sound-and-light presentation looking into an awesomely large quarried cavern. Book tours (available in English) through the tourist office.

Pyhän Laurin Kirkko   CHURCH

(St Lawrence Church; ⊙9am-4pm Jun-Sep, noon-3pm Oct-May) Lohja's church Pyhän Laurin Kirkko has a great wooden bell tower and is renowned for its medieval murals. Rustic and naive in style, they depicted biblical stories for the illiterate population of the early 16th century.

Lohja Museum   MUSEUM

(☑019-369-4204; Iso-Pappila; admission €5; ⊙11am-4pm Tue, Thu & Fri, 11-7pm Wed, noon-4pm Sat & Sun Jun–mid Aug, noon-4pm Tue & Thu-Sun, noon-7pm Wed mid-Aug–May) Lohja Museum re-creates a schoolhouse and a cowherd's cottage with an impressive range of horse-drawn carriages, including an old-style hearse. The main building is the former vicarage, and has special exhibitions in summer.

🍷 Drinking

Opus K   PUB

(☑0500-476-632; www.opusk.fi; Kauppakatu 6; ⊙3-11pm Tue-Thu, 2pm-2am Fri, noon-2am Sat)

Wonderfully cosy Opus K is lined floor to ceiling with books and new discoveries from obscure Finnish microbreweries.

ℹ Information

Tourist Office (☑ 044-369-1309; www.visit lohja.fi; Hossanmäentie 1; ☺ 9am-4pm Mon-Fri) Information on cottages around the lake, as well as summer canoeing and fishing and winter cross-country skiing.

ℹ Getting There & Away

Bus services include the following:

Ekenäs (€12, one hour, six daily)
Hanko (€17, 1½ hours, four daily)
Helsinki (€12, one hour, hourly)
Turku (€26, 2½ hours, half-hourly); most require a change at Salo.

Around Lohja

Lohja's wooded environs were the stomping ground of Elias Lönnrot, compiler of the *Kalevala*. The limestone-rich soil around the lake is ideal for growing apples, with orchards gracing the shores. You'll need your own wheels to explore.

☉ Sights

Paikkari Cottage   HISTORIC BUILDING
(☑ 019-356-659; Torpantie 20; adult/child €3/2; ☺ 11am-5pm Wed-Sun early Jun-early Aug) Twenty-three kilometres northwest of Lohja, and 5km north of the village of Sammatti, just off Rd 104, is Paikkari Cottage, the birthplace of Elias Lönnrot, compiler of the *Kalevala*. It's an endearing cottage set amid summer-flowering meadows that would have motivated Lönnrot's Arcadian vision but today inspire picnics. Inside there's a small museum that includes Lönnrot's *kantele* (Karelian stringed instrument).

🍺 Drinking

Kaljaasi   BAR
(☑ 040-522-6612; www.kaljaasi.com; ☺ 3-9pm Thu & Sun, noon-midnight Fri & Sat late May–mid-Jun, noon-11pm Sun-Thu, to midnight Fri & Sat mid-Jun–mid-Aug) You can dock your boat right next to this serene summer bar floating on a platform in the middle of the lake. If you don't have your own boat, staff can collect you from Virkkala, 7km south of Lohja (€10 return).

East of Helsinki

Finland's fascinating past comes to life in the towns east of Helsinki, with intact ironworks, defensive fortifications and museums exploring the country's seafaring history.

Porvoo

☑ 019 / POP 49,500

Finland's second-oldest town is an ever-popular day trip or weekender from Helsinki. Porvoo (Swedish: Borgå) officially became a town in 1380, but even before that it was an important trading post. The town's fabulous historic centre includes the famous brick-red former warehouses along the river that once stored goods bound for destinations across Europe. During the day, Old Town craft shops are bustling with visitors, but staying on a weeknight will mean you could have the place more or less to yourself. The old painted buildings are spectacular in the setting sun.

☉ Sights

★**Vanha Porvoo**   HISTORIC SITE
(Old Town) One of Finland's most enticing old quarters, this tangle of cobbled alleys and wooden warehouses is still entrancing. Once a vibrant port and market, Porvoo now has craft boutiques, art galleries, souvenir stores and antique shops jostling for attention on the main roads, Välikatu and Kirkkokatu. The rows of **rust-red storehouses** along the Porvoonjoki are a local icon: cross the old bridge for the best photos. The relatively less-touristed area is east of the cathedral; Itäinen Pitkäkatu is one of the nicest streets.

★**Tuomiokirkko**   CATHEDRAL
(www.porvoonseurakunnat.fi; ☺ 10am-2pm Tue-Sat, 2-4pm Sun Oct-Apr, 10am-6pm Mon-Fri, 10am-2pm Sat, 2-5pm Sun May-Sep) Porvoo's historic stone-and-timber cathedral sits atop a hill looking over the quaint Old Town. This is where the first Diet of Finland assembled in 1809, convened by Tsar Alexander I, giving Finland religious freedom. Damaged by fire in 2006, the church has been completely restored, so you can admire the ornate pulpit and tiered galleries. The magnificent exterior, with free-standing bell tower, remains the highlight.

Porvoon Museo

MUSEUM

(www.porvoonmuseo.fi; Vanha Raatihuoneentori; adult/child €6/3; ☺10am-4pm Mon-Sat, 11am-4pm Sun May-Aug, noon-4pm Wed-Sun Sep-Apr) Porvoo's town museum occupies two buildings on the beautiful cobbled square at the heart of the Old Town. The town-hall building houses most of the collection, with artefacts relating to the town's history, including work by painter Albert Edelfelt and sculptor Ville Vallgren, two of Porvoo's celebrated artists. The other building re-creates an 18th-century merchant's home.

Runebergin Koti

MUSEUM

(Runeberg House; www.runeberg.net; Aleksanterinkatu 3; adult/child €6/3; ☺10am-4pm May-Sep, 10am-4pm Wed-Sun Oct-Apr) National poet JL Runeberg's former home has become a museum, with a period interior including stuffed foxes and muskets portraying the poet's love of hunting. Across the road, the **Walter Runeberg Sculpture Collection** (Aleksanterinkatu 5) has 150 sculptures by Walter Runeberg, the poet's son. It's only open May to September; admission is included.

Porvoon Nukke- ja Lelumuseo

MUSEUM

(www.lelumuseo.com; Jokikatu 14; adult/child €3/2; ☺10am-3pm Jun–mid-Aug) Houses over a thousand dolls, tin toys and other childhood curiosities, making it Finland's largest toy museum.

🏃 Activities

Summer cruises leave from Porvoo's passenger quays for the archipelago and elsewhere; cruising here by boat from Helsinki is the nicest way to arrive. Departure times vary, so check websites.

Saaristolinja Ky

CRUISE

(☎019-523-1350; www.saaristolinja.com; Rantakatu; ☺mid-Jun–mid-Aug) 🚢 Runs 45-minute river jaunts past the Old Town hourly in summer from the passenger harbour (adult/child €10/5, hourly noon to 5pm, Tuesday to Sunday).

JL Runeberg

CRUISE

(☎019-524-3331; www.msjlruneberg.fi; ☺Tue, Wed, Fri, Sat mid-May–early Sep, plus Sun Jun-Aug & Mon Jul) This noble old steamship cruises from Helsinki's kauppatori to Porvoo (adult one way/return €27/39, daily except Thursday) in summer and makes an excellent day trip, with various lunch options available. The trip takes 3½ hours each way, so you may prefer to return by bus.

Royal Line

CRUISE

(☎020-711-8333; www.royalline.fi) The *Royal Cat* zips across to Porvoo from Helsinki's kauppatori in just over three hours (return €39, Tuesday, Thursday and Saturday late June to mid-August). It does a price for a boat-bus combination too.

🛌 Sleeping

Porvoo offers plenty of choice, plus there are several good options in the surrounding area, ranging from B&Bs to luxurious manor houses. Have a look online at www.visit porvoo.fi

Gasthaus Werneri

GUESTHOUSE €

(☎0400-494-876; www.werneri.net; Adlercreutzinkatu 29; s/d/tr €50/65/90; P🖂) This cosy family-run guesthouse in an apartment block, 10-minutes' walk from the Old Town (head east along the main road, then right down Adlercreutzinkatu), is decent value for Finland with five rooms (with shared bathrooms and kitchen) and a self-contained apartment.

Porvoon Retkeilymaja

HOSTEL €

(☎019-523-0012; www.porvoohostel.fi; Linnankoskenkatu 1-3; dm/s/d €22/37/52; P🖂) Four blocks south and two east of the kauppatori, this historic wooden house holds a well-kept hostel in a grassy garden. It caters for groups, so you'll need to book ahead to ensure a spot, and linen is extra, so be prepared. There's a great indoor pool and sauna complex over the road. Check-in is from 4pm. HI discount.

Ida-Maria

B&B €€

(☎045-851-2345; http://ida-maria.fi; Välikatu 10A; s/d/f €65/85/125; 🖂) Right on the square in the heart of old Porvoo, this can't be beaten for location, and the hospitable owner does her utmost to make you feel welcome. Historic character is the order of the day in this wooden building – the rooms share one bathroom – but the ambience, sauna and appetizing breakfast make it a winner.

★ Hotelli Onni

BOUTIQUE HOTEL €€€

(☎044-534-8110; www.hotelonni.fi; Kirkkotori 3; r/ste €182/292; P🖂) Right opposite the cathedral, this gold-coloured wooden building couldn't be better placed. There's a real range here, from the four-poster bed and slick design of the Funkishuone to the rustic single Talonpoikaishuone. Top of the line is the honeymoon suite, a small self-contained

Porvoo

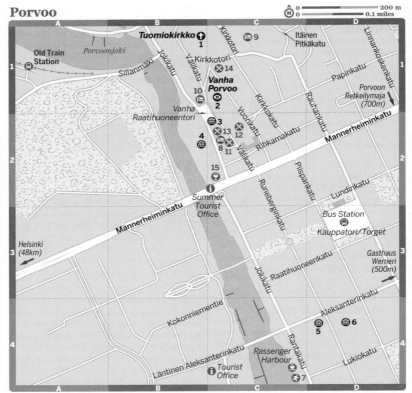

apartment with bathtub and complimentary champagne. Breakfast is downstairs where there's a terraced cafe and upmarket restaurant space.

Hotelli Pariisin Ville　BOUTIQUE HOTEL €€€
(019-580-131; www.pariisinville.fi; Jokikatu 43; r/superior r/ste €172/232/290; P) This plush place in the heart of the Old Town combines modern luxury and heritage feel. Rooms named for former residents are tastefully decorated, with 2nd-floor rooms boasting their own mini-saunas and views over the courtyard.

✗ Eating & Drinking

Porvoo's most atmospheric cafes, restaurants and bars are in the Old Town and along the riverfront. For cheaper eats, hit the area around the kauppatori.

Porvoo is famous for its sweets; **Brunberg** (www.brunberg.fi; Välikatu 4; 6 truffles €6.90;

10am-6pm Mon-Fri, 9am-4pm Sat, 10am-4pm Sun) does legendary chocolate and liquorice, while the delicious Runeberg cake, a dense rum-and-almond-flavoured cylinder crowned with white icing and raspberry jam, is ubiquitous.

Café Helmi　CAFE €
(www.porvoonhelmet.net; Välikatu 7; cakes €3-7; 10am-6pm Mon-Sat, 11am-5pm Sun) A kindly Russian grandmother would happily take tea from the distinctive lilac-and-white cups in the courtyard of this Tsarist teahouse. It does one of the best Runeberg tarts, but regular cakes and chocolates will also have you loosening your belt. Closed Mondays and Tuesdays in winter.

Wanha Laamanni　FINNISH €€
(020-752-8355; www.wanhalaamanni.fi; Vuorikatu 17; mains €20-29; 11am-11pm Mon-Sat, noon-8pm Sun) Top of the town in both geographic

Porvoo

and culinary terms, this old judges' chambers serves up a short menu of classy Finnish favourites and a rather tasty six-course surprise menu (€60). The building itself is a rambling late-18th-century conversion with a roaring fireplace and sprawling terrace that's ideal for people-watching.

Timbaali   FINNISH €€
(☑019-523-1020; www.timbaali.com; Jokikatu 43; mains €20-27; ☺11am-11pm Jun-Aug, 11am-10pm Mon-Sat, noon-6pm Sun) In the heart of the Old Town, this well-loved restaurant specialises in slow food: locally farmed snails (€18 for a dozen) prepared with garlic or cheese. There's also other tasty Finnish cuisine, served in quaint dining rooms or the inner courtyard. In summer a fish buffet (€26) is served at lunchtimes.

★ **Porvoon Paahtimo**   CAFE, PUB
(www.porvoonpaahtimo.fi; Mannerheiminkatu 2; ☺10am-midnight Sun-Thu, 9am-3am Fri & Sat) On the main bridge, this atmospheric red-brick former storehouse is a cosy, romantic spot for drinks of any kind: it roasts its own coffee and has tap beer and several wines. There's a terrace and boat deck, which come with blankets on cooler evenings.

① Information

Summer Tourist Kiosk (www.visitporvoo.fi; Jokikatu 35B; ☺10am-6pm Mon-Fri, 10am-4pm Sat & Sun May-Aug; 🖳) Under the bridge near the entrance to the Old Town. Rent bikes for €7.50/20 per one/four hours.

Tourist Office (☑040-489-9801; www.visit porvoo.fi; Läntinen Aleksanterinkatu 1; ☺9am-6pm Mon-Fri, 11am-4pm Sat; 🖳) Offers maps and local information in the Taidetehdas (Art Factory) building across the river. This former tractor factory is now an exhibition space, cinema and shopping mall.

① Getting There & Away

BUS

Buses depart for Porvoo from Helsinki's Kamppi bus station every 30 minutes or so (€11.80, one hour) and there are frequent buses to/from towns further east.

Loviisa
☑ 019

Named for Swedish Queen Lovisa Ulrika in 1752, Loviisa (Swedish: Lovisa) had its glory days as a Russian spa town in the 19th century. Like many of the coastal towns, it was a pawn in Russo-Swede conflicts, most devastatingly in 1855 when much of it burnt down – only a small vestige of the Old Town survives. Today it's a sweet, sleepy summer resort that positively hiberanates out of season when little is open.

◉ Sights & Activities

Most summertime activity is at **Laivasilta Marina**, 500m southeast of the town centre. A little cluster of old rust-coloured wooden storehouses now contains craft shops and cafes.

Svartholma Sea Fortress   FORTRESS
Situated 10km offshore from Loviisa, this four-bastion sea fortress was built in 1748 to protect against further Russian invasion after Swedish losses in eastern Finland. It lasted until the Crimean War (1853–6) when the British largely destroyed it, but it has been reconstructed. A free museum details the fort's history; there's a cafe here.

A **waterbus** (☑0500-102-111; adult/child return €15/7.50; ☺11am, 1pm & 3pm Tue-Sun mid-Jun–mid-Aug, 11am, 1pm & 3pm Sat & Sun mid-Aug–late Aug), taking 35 minutes (cash only), runs from Laivasilta Marina. Alternatively, the beautiful 19th-century replica yacht

WORTH A TRIP

HYDROPOWERED ORGANIC BREWS

Malmgård (http://malmgard.fi; Malmgård 47, Forsby; ⊙bar & shop 10am-4pm Tue-Thu, 10am-6pm Fri, 11-4pm Sat & Sun) Situated 23km northwest of Loviisa, this 500-hectare estate has been owned by the Creutz family since 1614 (current owner Count Johan Creutz is the 12th generation). Its brewery's all-organic beers and ciders are produced using local spring water and the estate's own hydropower; you can see the brewing process in action through the viewing window in the bar.

Adjacent to the bar, the shop sells bread made from organic flour hand-milled on site, plus hand-milled oils, homemade jam, vinegars, honey and, of course, Malmgård's mighty brews.

Österstjernan (☑040-012-0929; www.osterstjernan.fi; return trip €35) makes occasional trips.

Loviisa Church   CHURCH
(⊙11am-4pm Mon-Sat early May-early Aug) Dominating the market square is the red-brick neo-Gothic Loviisa Church, built in 1865.

Loviisa Town Museum   MUSEUM
(☑019-555-357; Puistokatu 2; ⊙11am-4pm Tue-Sun Jun-Aug, noon-4pm Tue-Fri & Sun Sep-May) FREE About 200m north of the town square, Loviisa Town Museum is set in an old manor house with three floors of interesting historical exhibits, particularly the exhibition on Jean Sibelius, who spent his childhood summer holidays at Sibeliuksenkatu 10.

★★ Festivals & Events

Sibelius Festival   MUSIC
(☑019-555-499; www.loviisansibeliuspaivat.fi; tickets €20-25) Loviisa's biggest annual event is the Sibelius Festival around early September, which features a weekend of Sibelius performances.

🛏 Sleeping & Eating

Accommodation in Loviisa is limited but the wonderful Sea Hotel Mäntyniemi is less than half-an-hour's drive southwest.

Tamminiemi   CAMPGROUND €
(☑040-041-4265; www.tamminiemi.net; Kapteenintie 1; tent sites €17 plus per person €6, d €77-89, 4-person apt €155; ⊙camping early Jun-late Aug, other accommodation year-round) About 2km south of town, Tamminiemi is a peaceful campground right by the sea (water's edge tent sites cost €23). Simple rooms (most with private bathroom) in two renovated wooden houses have access to a self-catering kitchen. Call ahead to confirm your arrival time.

Bistro Cantor   BISTRO €€
(☑040-135-5003; www.bistrocantor.fi; Mariankatu 1; lunch buffet €9.20, mains €18-25, 3-course menu €39; ⊙11am-2pm & 5-9pm Mon-Thu, 11am-2pm & 5-10pm Fri, noon-10pm Sat, noon-4pm Sun) Just across from the marina, this art nouveau building is a classy backdrop for contemporary dishes such as gourmet burgers (pulled-pork, salmon), sage-stuffed chicken breast wrapped in air-dried ham, and New York cheesecake with rhubarb coulis.

Cafe-Restaurant Saltbodan   FINNISH €€
(http://saltbodan.fi; Laivasilta 4; lunch mains €12-16, dinner mains €12-28; ⊙kitchen 10am-10pm May-Sep) Laivasilta Marina is a wonderful spot to while away a summer evening, particularly at this smart cafe-restaurant serving Finnish favourites (Baltic herring, salmon soup) in an atmospheric old storehouse. The bar stays open until 1am on Friday and Saturday.

ℹ Information

Tourist Office (☑019-555-234; www.visitloviisa.fi; Karlskronabulevardi 8; ⊙10am-4pm Mon-Fri, to 2pm Sat & Sun mid-Jun–Aug, 10am-4pm Mon-Fri Sep–mid-Jun)

ℹ Getting There & Around

Bus services include the following:
Helsinki (€22, 1½ hours, up to four hourly)
Kotka (€13.50, 50 minutes, up to four hourly)
Porvoo (€11.80, 40 minutes, up to four hourly)
You can hire bicycles at the marina for €5/20 per hour/day.

Ruotsinpyhtää & Around

There are several stand-out attractions located in and around the tiny village of Ruotsinpyhtää.

◉ Sights & Activities

Strömfors Ironworks HISTORIC BUILDINGS
(☺11am-5pm Sat & Sun mid-May–late May, daily
Jun–mid-Aug, Wed-Sun mid-Aug–late Aug) **FREE**
On the edge of Ruotsinpyhtää village,
Strömfors Ironworks is one of Finland's oldest *bruks,* dating back to 1698. Today its red-
stained buildings are an open-air museum
amid a patchwork of forest, rivers and bridges. The **Forge Museum** has two sections: an
old smith's workshop and the working mill-
wheel. One ironworks building serves as an
art gallery; you can also browse the little
craft shops.

Ruotsinpyhtää Church CHURCH
(☺11am-5pm Jun-Aug) Ruotsinpyhtää's
18th-century octagonal wooden church,
built after the old one was lost across yet
another Sweden–Russia border change, has
a fabulous altarpiece painted in 1898 by the
young Helene Schjerfbeck.

Sirius Sport Resort ADVENTURE SPORTS
(☏044-479-7100; www.siriussport.fi; Kotitie 10, Pyhtää; flying per 3 1-min sessions/10 1-min sessions
€85/235, surfing per hour €25, ropes course €25;
☺10am-8pm Tue-Thu, 10am-10pm Fri, 9am-10pm
Sat, 9am-7pm Sun) If you've ever fantasised
about flying, superhero-style, you can get
pretty close at this sport centre in Pyhtää,
soaring above a vertical wind tunnel (over-
alls, helmet and goggles provided; minimum
age limit five years). Also here is a FlowRid-
er surfable indoor wave, and ropes course.
Book online for deals and combo packages.

❶ Getting There & Away

Buses link Loviisa with Ruotsinpyhtää (€5.50,
15 minutes, two daily), and Pyhtää (€5.50, 20
minutes, up to two per hour).

Kotka & Around

☏05 / POP 54,850
Kotka is Finland's only city set on an island
and its fortunes have long been tied to the
sea. The Vikings used the archipelago to
launch themselves eastward into Russia,
and the Kymijoki was once an important
transport route for logging. Today it's a major industrial port, with some superb sea-
focused attractions.

◉ Sights

★**Maritime Centre Vellamo** MUSEUM
(☏040-350-0497; www.merikeskusvellamo.fi;
Tornatorintie 99; adult/child €8/free, Tarmo extra

€4; ☺11am-6pm Tue & Thu-Sat, to 8pm Wed) In a
tanker-sized, wave-like building with walls
of metal and printed glass and a rooftop
stage, this state-of-the-art dockside museum
recounts Finland's seafaring life. The star
exhibit is the *Tarmo,* the world's oldest
ice-breaker (1908), which ploughed Finnish
waters until it was retired in 1970. There are
also exhibitions on shipwrecks, navigation,
fishing and logging, and a boat hall containing an Olympic-winning 49er and a boat
that belonged to the Moomins' creator, Tove
Jansson.

Maretarium AQUARIUM
(☏040-311-0330; www.maretarium.fi; Sapokankatu 2; adult/child €12.50/7.50; ☺10am-7pm Jun-
Aug, 10am-5pm Mon & Tue & Thu-Sun, noon-7pm
Wed Sep-May) Kotka's modern Maretarium
has over 20 giant fish tanks representing
various bodies of water. The Baltic tank is
the largest, with local sea life fed regularly
by a diver (check the online calendar for
weekly feeding times). Water is piped in
from the sea to maintain the natural life cycle of fish, so salmon spawn in autumn and
in winter freakish eelpout give birth.

**Langinkoski Imperial
Fishing Lodge** MUSEUM
(☏05-211-1600; www.langinkoskimuseo.com; Keis-
arinmajantie 118; adult/child €6/free, nature reserve
free; ☺10am-4pm May & Sep, to 6pm Jun-Aug) Situated 5km north of Kotka amid the salmon-
rich Kymijoki's rapids, this simple wooden
lodge was built in 1889 for Tsar Alexander
III. Most of the furniture is original and
rooms look much as they did when he was a
frequent visitor. The riverside forest setting

WORTH A TRIP

HIDDEN HAVEN

Sea Hotel Mäntyniemi (☏05-353-
3100; www.hotelmantyniemi.fi; Mäntynie-
mentie 268, Siltakylä; s €79, d €89-118,
f €136; ☂☀) A little piece of Finnish
paradise, this family-run haven sits on
a secluded forested island (linked by
bridges) between Loviisa (35km) and
Kotka (32km). Of its 28 rooms, the
most idyllic have balconies overlooking
the islet-strewn sea. Fantastic facilities
include a traditional smoke sauna, excellent restaurant, and free use of boats,
bikes and fishing equipment. You won't
want to leave.

TURKU & THE SOUTH COAST EAST OF HELSINKI

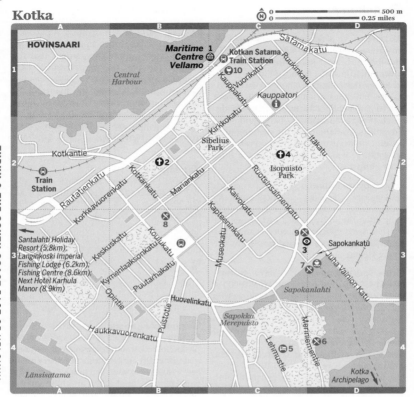

Kotka

◉ **Top Sights**

◉ **Sights**

🛌 **Sleeping**

🍴 **Eating**

🍷 **Drinking & Nightlife**

(now a 28-hectare nature reserve with walking trails) is beautiful. Frequent buses (€3.30, 10 minutes, up to five per hour) stop at Langinkoski church, from where it's a 1.2km walk.

St Nicholas Orthodox Church   CHURCH
(⊙noon-3pm Tue-Fri, to 6pm Sat & Sun Jun-Aug) Towering above Isopuisto Park, St Nicholas Orthodox Church was completed in 1801 and is Kotka's only building to survive the Crimean War. It's believed to be the work of architect Yakov Perrini, who designed the St Petersburg Admiralty.

Kotka Church   CHURCH
(📞05-225-9250; ⊙noon-6pm Jun-Aug) Kotka Church's distinctive steeple is visible throughout town. Inside the neo-Gothic church there's artful woodcarving, a resounding baroque-style organ and a beautiful altarpiece painted by Pekka Halonen.

🏃 Activities

The Kymijoki is one of Finland's best fishing rivers – for detailed information, visit www.lohikeskuskotka.fi. Fly-fishing is still allowed at Langinkoski Imperial Fishing Lodge (p103). The **Fishing Centre** (☑05-281-288; www.fishingcentre.fi; Kymijoentie 55; fishing gear rental per day from €15; ⊘11am-6.30pm Mon-Fri, to 3pm Sat) sells permits (prices depend on where you plan to fish and what you plan to catch) and can also organise fishing trips (from €350 for up to four people).

Archipelago cruises of all types depart from Sapokka Harbour (Sapokanlahti) in summer to the islands around Kotka, along with scheduled ferries to the outlying islands. Check seasonal options and timetables at the tourist office.

🎉 Festivals & Events

Kotkan Meripäivät SAILING

(Kotka Maritime Festival; ☑040-635-1764; www.meripaivat.com) Kotka's seafaring heritage is celebrated in late July with a regatta, concerts, markets and a huge wooden boat show.

🛏 Sleeping

Kotka's chain hotels include Sokos and Cumulus.

Santalahti Holiday Resort RESORT €

(☑05-260-5055; www.santalahti.fi; tent sites €19, cottages from €79, without bathroom from €64, d €85-100; 🌐) On the island of Mussalo, 5km west of central Kotka, Santalahti has a huge range of cottages (many with private bathrooms and wi-fi), ensuite hotel rooms (some with sea views and most with balconies) and conifer-shaded campsites. Shoreline and forest nature trails (each 2.5km long) weave through the property.

Kesähotelli Katarina UNIVERSITY ACCOMMODATION €

(☑050-913-5763; www.kesahotellikatarina.net; Lehmustie 4; s/tw/f €50/70/80; ⊘early Jun-early Aug) The hilltop location can be a tough walk with a lot of baggage but rooms here are clean and bright with a desk and TV, and they connect with a large shared kitchen and bathroom (two of the family apartments have private kitchens and bathrooms). Prices include breakfast.

Next Hotel Karhula Manor HISTORIC HOTEL €€

(☑010-234-6710; www.nexthotels.fi; Ahströmintie 26; d €140, without bathroom €102, tr €160; 🌐) Surrounded by sprawling gardens that run down to the river, this magnificent French-style manor completed in 1891 has just 20 rooms split between the main period-furnished manor house, the guest house and smaller garden cottage. It's 9km north of Kotka (2.2km east of the Kotka turn-off from the E18 motorway).

🍴 Eating

Tulikukko CAFE €

(www.tulikukko.fi; Sapokankatu 3; dishes €3-7.50; ⊘8.30am-10pm Mon-Sat, 9am-9pm Sun) Pies, pastries, salads and sandwiches are all excellent at this waterside cafe but the highlight is the dazzling array of cakes.

★ Vausti FINNISH €€

(www.kotkanravintolat.fi; Keskuskatu 33; mains €19-34; ⊘3-10pm Wed & Thu, 3-11pm Fri, 4-11pm Sat) Attached to Kotka's concert hall, charcoal-hued Vausti offers Kotka's finest dining. The seasonal menu is mostly traditional Finnish: butter-fried perch, cider-braised pork cheek with crispy pork neck, reindeer and cranberry. Vegetarians are well catered for, with dishes such as cabbage rolls filled with stewed lentils and artichoke cooked two ways.

Meriniemi MODERN FINNISH €€€

(☑045-341-9185; www.meriniemi.com; Meriniementie; lunch buffet €13, mains €22-34; ⊘11am-9.30pm Mon-Fri, noon-9.30pm Sat, noon-4pm Sun Jun-Aug) With the prettiest setting in Kotka, overlooking the boat-filled marina, this beautiful turret-topped wooden summer pavilion (a former yacht club) contrasts with its Modern Finnish menu (horse tenderloin with green pepper sauce, spinach strudel et al).

Wanha Fiskari SEAFOOD €€€

(☑05-218-6585; www.wanhafiskari.fi; Ruotsinsalmenkatu 1; mains €22-33; ⊘11am-10pm Mon-Fri, 2-8pm Sat) You might not expect much from the tacky Captain Haddock nautical decor but this seafood specialist by the Maretarium smokes its own salmon and pan fries a mean Baltic herring.

🍸 Drinking

Päätepysäkki   BAR
(www.viihdykotkassa.fi; Tornatorintie 96; ⊙noon-
8pm May-Sep) In an unlikely car-park location, Kotka's quirkiest bar is this 1950s
vintage railway carriage attached to a steam
locomotive, with great cocktails and beer
on tap. Terrace tables overlook the metallic
wave of the Maritime Centre Vellamo, but
the cosiest seats are on board.

Kairo   PUB
(www.ravintolakairo.fi; Satamakatu 7; ⊙5-10pm
Tue-Thu, 5pm-4am Fri & Sat) A legendary old
sailors' boozer right down to the ships' flags
and saucy paintings, with live music and a
great terrace. Ties are banned, and the rules
state that if someone asks you to dance, you
can't turn them down!

ℹ️ Information

Tourist Office (☏ 040-135-6588; www.south-
east135.fi; Keskuskatu 6; ⊙10am-5pm Mon-Fri
year-round, plus 10am-3pm Sat Jun-late Aug)
Has a useful board of weekly events.

ℹ️ Getting There & Away

Buses services include the following:
Hamina (€6.80, 45 minutes, up to three
hourly)
Helsinki (€29, 2½ hours, up to six hourly)
Loviisa (€13.50, 50 minutes, up to four hourly)
Porvoo (€20.50, 1½ hours)

Trains stop at both Kotka train station, 400m
northwest of the city centre, and Kotkan Satama, at the handier main harbour. Trains run to
Kouvola (€8, 45 minutes, six daily), which has
connecting trains to all major Finnish cities.

Hamina

🗓 05 / POP 21,250

Just 40km from the Russian border, Hamina (Swedish: Fredrikshamn) has long been
a military town. Founded in 1653 as a Swedish outpost, its fortifications were begun in
1722 after Vyborg fell to Russia but they were
unable to prevent Hamina's capture in 1743
and were never completed. Today there's a
modern military base in town and the whole
town is on parade for the annual Hamina
Tattoo.

👁 Sights & Activities

Wandering the restored 19th-century town's
streets, laid out like an octagonal wheel,
takes you past many of Hamina's sights.
The centre of the web is dominated by the
18th-century **town hall**, with a distinctive
church on either side.

Hamina Church   CHURCH
(Raatihuoneentori 10; ⊙11am-4pm Jun–mid-Aug)
On the northwestern side of the town hall,
neoclassical Hamina Church, designed by
CL Engel, was built in 1843.

**Orthodox Church of Saints
Peter & Paul**   CHURCH
(Raatihuoneentori 2; ⊙noon-4pm Tue-Sun Jun-
Aug) Topped by a classic onion dome, the
1837 Orthodox Church of Saints Peter &
Paul, on the southeastern side of the town
hall, is the work of architect Louis Visconti,
who designed Napoleon's mausoleum.

Kaupunginmuseo   MUSEUM
(Town Museum; ☏ 040-199-1201; Kadettikoulunka-
tu 2; admission €2; ⊙noon-4pm Wed-Sat, to 5pm
Sun Sep-May, 10am-4pm Tue-Sun Jun-Aug) Learn
about Hamina's history at the town museum, housed in Hamina's oldest building.
King Gustav III of Sweden and Catherine II
(the Great) of Russia held negotiations here
in 1783.

Hamina Bastion   RUIN
The ruins of the 18th-century Hamina Bastion include 3km of crumbling stone walls
that would have made a star-shaped fortress. The bastion comes alive for the annual Hamina Tattoo; otherwise pick up a free
copy of *Walking in Old Hamina* from the
tourist office.

Uuperinrinteet   MOUNTAIN BIKING, SKIING
(☏ 010-666-6120; www.uuperinrinteet.fi; Viirankan-
kaantie 237, Reitkalli; lift tickets per day summer/
winter €20/25, mountain bike/ski/snowboard/
boot rental €50/14/17/10; ⊙mountain biking
4-8pm Wed, 10am-5pm Sat & Sun May-Sep, skiing
3-8pm Tue-Fri, 10am-6pm Sat & Sun Nov-Apr) The
longest slope on this mountain at Reitkalli,
12km northwest of Hamina, is 80m high and
800m long, with nine runs in total. In summer you can pelt downhill on a mountain
bike, while in winter you can do it on skis or
a snowboard. You'll need your own wheels
to get here.

Meriset   CRUISE
(☏040-090-2494; www.meriset.fi; ⊙mid-May–
late Aug) Cruises run up to three times
weekly from Tervasaari guest harbour to the
old fishing village on the island of Tammio

(adult/child €20/10, three to four hours). Island cruises also run up to five times weekly further south to Ulko-Tammio (adult/child €25/10, five hours), within the boundaries of the Eastern Gulf of Finland National Park.

★ Festivals & Events

Hamina Tattoo MUSIC
(✆ 05-749-2633; www.visithamina.fi; tickets €11.50-53.50) Every even-numbered year in late July or early August, Hamina celebrates military music during the week-long Hamina Tattoo, featuring not only Finnish and Russian military marching bands, but rock, jazz and dance music.

⌂ Sleeping

**Hamina Camping
Pitkät Hiekat** CAMPGROUND €
(✆ 05-345-9183; Vilniementie 375; tent sites €12 plus per person €4, 4-/6-person cottages €50/80; ⊙May-Sep) In Vilniemi, 5km east of Hamina, this beachside spot surrounded by quiet forest offers free rowing boats, sauna and laundry.

Spa Hotel Hamina HOTEL €€
(✆ 05-353-5555; www.spahotelhamina.fi; Sibeliuskatu 32; s/d €118/138; @ 🛜 🏊) Ideally located between the bus station and Old Town, this hotel's recently renovated spa facilities are included in the price. Many of its hardwood-floored rooms have air-con – ask when you book. Rates drop on weekends.

✗ Eating

Eateries are thin on the ground in Hamina: in summer try your luck down at Tervasaari harbour.

Konditoria A Huovila CAFE €
(✆ 05-344-0930; www.elisanet.fi/konditoria.huovila.oy; Fredrikinkatu 1; dishes €2-4.50; ⊙8am-5pm Mon-Fri, 8am-1pm Sat) Fêted for its berry pies, this traditional cafe dating from 1966 is within the town's octagon of streets.

Kamu! INTERNATIONAL €€
(www.ravintolakamu.fi; Sibeliuskatu 32; mains €13.50-22.50, breakfast buffet €9, lunch buffet Mon-Fri/Sat & Sun €9.50/10.50; ⊙7am-10pm Sun-Thu, 7am-11pm Fri & Sat) 🍴 Beginning life as a pop-up restaurant at the Hamina Tattoo and now based at the Spa Hotel Hamina, effusive Kamu! serves out-of-the-ordinary combinations such as salmon baked in vanilla with crushed vegetables, barbecued pork with pear and raisin chutney, and horse steak served with pepper sauce. Adventurous kids' menu too.

ℹ Information

Tourist Office (✆ 040-199-1330; www.southeast135.fi; Raatihuoneentori 16; ⊙9am-5pm Mon-Fri year-round plus 10am-3pm Sat & Sun early Jun-late Aug)

ℹ Getting There & Away

Buses link Hamina with Kotka (€6.80, 45 minutes, up to three hourly) and Helsinki (€31.40, 2¾ hours, up to four hourly). If you have a Russian visa, you can catch a bus to Vyborg (€18, 3¾ hours, one daily) and St Petersburg (€23, 6½ hours).

Åland Archipelago

Best Places to Eat

➡ Smakbyn (p118)
➡ Nautical (p114)
➡ Bodegan (p123)
➡ Café Kvarnen (p120)
➡ Bagarstugan (p114)

Best Places to Stay

➡ Degersands Resort (p122)
➡ Kvarnbo Gästhem (p119)
➡ Hotell Arkipelag (p113)
➡ Sandösunds Camping (p119)
➡ Eckerö Hotell & Restaurang (p123)

Why Go?

The glorious Åland archipelago is a geopolitical anomaly: the islands belong to Finland, speak Swedish, but have their own parliament, fly their own blue-gold-and-red flag, issue their own stamps and have their own web suffix: 'dot ax'. Their 'special relationship' with the EU means they can sell duty free and make their own gambling laws.

Åland is the sunniest spot in northern Europe and its sweeping white-sand beaches and flat, scenic cycling routes attract crowds of holidaymakers during summer. Yet outside the lively capital, Mariehamn, a sleepy haze hangs over the islands' tiny villages and finding your own remote beach among the 6500 skerries and islets is surprisingly easy. A lattice of bridges and free cable ferries connect the central islands, while larger car ferries run to the archipelago's outer reaches.

When to Go

Aland Archipelago

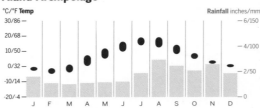

Feb & Mar Skate the islands' frozen seas.

Jun See decorated poles being raised around the islands during Midsummer.

Jul Celebrate Åland's viking heritage at Saltvik's Viking Market.

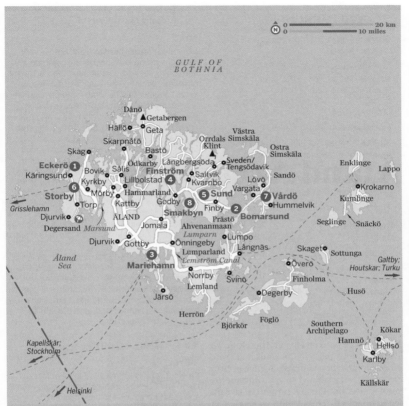

Åland Archipelago Highlights

1 Starting or ending in Eckerö, **cycle** the archipelago's fantastically flat, well-marked routes alongside green fields, red granite and sparkling seascapes (p116)

2 Running the ramparts of the cannonball-scarred ruins at **Bomarsund** (p117)

3 Climbing aboard the four-masted barque **Pommern** (p111) outside

Mariehamn's state-of-the-art maritime museum

4 Sipping blueberry beer on the terrace of Finström's **Stallhagen Brewery** (p117) after a behind-the-scenes tour

5 Touring Sund's 14th-century castle **Kastelholms Slott** (p117) on a picturesque inlet

6 Imagining the empire that constructed Storby's

majestically over-the-top post office **Post och Tullhuset** (p122) while browsing its artisan galleries and shops

7 Kayaking (p119) around Vårdö's islets of rustling silver birches and rippling bays

8 Cooking with local Åland produce at 'taste village' **Smakbyn** (p118) on a culinary course

History

More than a hundred Bronze and Iron Age *fornminne* (burial sites) have been discovered across the Åland archipelago, attesting to over 6000 years of human habitation. Though all are clearly signposted, most are in fairly nondescript fields. The discovery of fortress ruins confirm the archipelago was an important harbour and trading centre during the Viking era.

During the Great Northern War of 1700–21 (dubbed the 'Great Wrath'), most

ℹ NEED TO KNOW

Currency Euro; most places accept Swedish krona.

Emergencies The general EU-wide emergency number is ☑ 112 for ambulance, fire and police. For local police call ☑ 018-527-100, for medical services ☑ 018-538-500.

Language Swedish (see p191)

Mobile Phones Åland uses the Finnish mobile phone network but it can be sketchy, especially in the outer islands.

Post Mail sent in Åland must have (highly collectable) Åland postage stamps.

Time Åland shares Finland's time zone, one hour ahead of Sweden.

Tourist information The website www.visitaland.com has tourist info; www.alandsresor.fi lets you book accommodation online. There's a wealth of cottages for rent across the islands; **Destination Åland** (☑ 0400-108-800; www.destinationaland.com; Östra Esplanadgatan 7, Mariehamn) has a comprehensive list.

Ålanders fled to Sweden. Further Russian incursions took place in the 1740s and 1809. When Finland gained independence in 1917, many Ålanders lobbied to be incorporated into Sweden, but Finland refused to give up the archipelago. The dispute concluded in 1921, when Åland was given its status as an autonomous, demilitarised and neutral municipality within Finland by a decision of the League of Nations. Åland joined the EU in 1995, but was granted a number of exemptions, including duty-free tax laws that allow ferry services to mainland Finland and Sweden to operate profitably.

Today peaceful Åland is divided into 16 municipalities, 10 on 'Fasta Åland' (the main group of larger islands). The other six municipalities cover the far-flung archipelago and its multitudes of tiny islands.

ℹ Getting There & Away

AIR

Åland's airport is 4km northwest of Mariehamn, served by **NextJet** (www.nextjet.se; Turku and Stockholm-Arlanda, Sweden; both from €55 one way), and **FlyBe** (www.flybe.com; Helsinki; from €29) and business airline **Turku Air** (☑ 020-721-8800; www.turkuair.fi; Turku; from €222). There

are no regular buses: a **taxi** (☑ 018-10066) to the city centre costs about €15.

BOAT

Several car ferries head to Åland. Prices vary with season and web specials are common; cars and cabins cost extra. From Naantali, northwest of Turku, **Finnlink** (www.finnlines.com) ferries serve Långnäs, Lumparland. Alternatively, consider using the archipelago ferries (p115).

Eckerö Linjen (☑ 018-28000; www.eckerolinjen.ax) Mariehamn (☑ 018-28000; Torggatan 2) Eckerö (☑ 018-28300; Berghamn) Sails from Eckerö to Grisslehamn, Sweden (adult/adult and car €4/18, two hours).

Tallink/Silja Lines (☑ 018-16711; www.tallinksilja.com; Torggatan 14, Mariehamn) Runs direct services to Mariehamn from Turku (adult/adult and car €12/32, five hours), Helsinki (€33/80, 12 hours) and Stockholm (€12/32, six hours). Ferries also run to Långnäs, Lumparland, from Stockholm (€18/59, 5½ hours) and Turku (€12/44, five hours).

Viking Line (☑ 018-26211; www.vikingline.fi; Storagatan 3, Mariehamn) Ferries to Mariehamn from Turku (adult/adult and car €14/32, five hours), Helsinki (€30/66, 11 hours) and Stockholm (€11/32, 5½ hours). Ferries also link Långnäs, Lumparland, with Stockholm (€42/66, 5½ hours).

ℹ Getting Around

BICYCLE

Ro-No Rent has bicycles available at Mariehamn and Eckerö harbours. Many campgrounds and guest harbours also have bike hire.

Green-and-white signs trace cycling routes through the islands. Bicycle routes generally follow smaller, less busy roads; dedicated bicycle paths run parallel to some main roads.

BOAT

Three kinds of interisland ferry serve the islands. For short trips, free vehicle ferries sail nonstop. There are also two private summer bicycle ferries, Hammarland–Geta and Vårdö–Saltvik. For longer routes, ferries run to a schedule, taking cars, bicycles and foot passengers.

Timetables are available at Mariehamn's tourist office and **online** (www.alandstrafiken.ax).

BUS

Five main bus lines depart from Mariehamn's regional bus station on Styrmansgatan, in front of the police station. Route 1 goes to Hammarland and Eckerö; route 2 to Godby and Geta; route 3 to Godby and Saltvik; route 4 to Godby, Sund and Vårdö (Hummelvik); and route 5 to Lemland and Lumparland (Långnäs). Tickets from Mariehamn to the ferry ports cost around €4.50. Bicycles can be carried (space permitting) for €8.

MARIEHAMN

📍 018 / POP 11,400

Two out of every five Ålanders live in the village-like capital Mariehamn and the *lagting* (parliament) and *landskapsstyrelse* (Åland's government) are located here. The town was christened by Alexander II after the Empress Maria, and its broad streets lined with linden trees recall its Russian heritage.

Mariehamn's ports welcome crowds of summer visitors arriving on ferries from Finland and Sweden, but outside high season you may have the place to yourself.

👁 Sights

⭐ Sjöfartsmuseum   MUSEUM
(Maritime Museum; www.sjofartsmuseum.ax; Hamngatan 2; adult/child incl Museum Ship Pommern €10/6; ⊘10am-5pm Jun-Aug, 11am-4pm Sep-May) Centred on a re-creation of a ship with mast, saloon, galley and cabins, preserved boats make up most of the exhibitions at this state-of-the-art museum exploring Åland's marine heritage. It's a great place to discover your inner pirate with plenty of ships in bottles, sea chests and accoutrements. Anchored outside is the beautiful 1903-built four-masted merchant barque, the **Pommern** (📍018-531-423; Sjopromenaden; adult/child incl Sjöfartsmuseum €10/6; ⊘10am-5pm Jun-Aug, 11am-4pm May & Sep), which plied the trade route between Australia and England. Also here is Mariehamn's best restaurant, Nautical (p114).

Ålands Museum & Ålands Konstmuseum   MUSEUM, GALLERY
(www.museum.ax; Stadshusparken; adult/child €4/3; ⊘10am-5pm Jun-Aug, 10am-8pm Tue & Thu, 10am-4pm Wed & Fri, noon-4pm Sat & Sun Sep-May) Åland's museum offers an insight into the islands' history, with exhibits including a replica of a Stone Age boat made of sealskin and a large illustration of Bomarsund in all its glory. The adjoining art gallery has changing exhibitions and paintings by local artists. Both are expected to reopen after renovations for summer 2015.

Sjökvarteret   BOATYARD, MUSEUM
(📍018-16033; www.sjokvarteret.com; Österleden 110; museum adult/child €4/free; ⊘museum 11am-5pm Jun–mid-Aug, by arrangement mid-Aug–May) At the northern end of Österhamn, Sjökvarteret has long been devoted to boat-building. You can stroll along the quay, lined with traditional schooners, and

perhaps see boats under construction. The **museum**, with exhibitions on ship-building (no English information), is located in a small timber boatshed. Also here is a **reconstructed seafarers' chapel** as well as galleries, unique jewellery (p115) and an excellent craft shop (p115).

Sankt Göran's Kyrka   CHURCH
(⊘10am-6pm Mon-Fri, 10am-3pm Sat mid-Jun-Aug) The copper-roofed Sankt Göran's Kyrka, built in 1927, is one of the few modern churches on the islands. Its art nouveau style was conceived by Lars Sonck, who grew up in Åland. The glittering mosaic altarpiece is a real highlight.

Självstyrelsegården   BUILDING
(📍018-25000; cnr Österleden & Storagatan; ⊘tours 10am Fri Jun-Aug) **FREE** Åland parliament's free 90-minute guided tours (available in English) explain the autonomous nature of Åland and the election of the Lantråd, Åland's premier.

🏃 Activities

Ro-No Rent   OUTDOORS
(📍018-12820; www.rono.ax; ⊘9am-6pm Jun-mid-Aug, by arrangement Sep-May) Ro-No rents out a variety of bicycles (per day/week €10/50), kayaks (€80/150), small boats (that

---

SUNKEN TREASURE

Divers exploring an 1840s shipwreck off the coast of Föglö in 2010 raised 162 bottles of Champagne, the world's oldest. Two bottles were auctioned in 2011 for the princely sum of €54,000; you can see a couple in the Ålands Museum. Studies at the University of Reims, in Champagne, France, are now investigating the merits of seabed storage.

The divers also retrieved five bottles of 19th-century corked beer. It was analysed by the Technical Research Centre of Finland (VTT), and Mats Ekholm, master brewer at Åland's Stallhagen Brewery (p117) re-created the original recipe. Stallhagen's Shipwreck Beer is now on sale aboard Viking Line ferries, costing €113 per bottle.

The ship's identity, origin, destination and the cause of the wreck are still shrouded in mystery; part of the profits from Shipwreck Beer sales are being used to fund further research.

don't require a licence; per four hours/day €100/200) and mopeds (which do; per day/week €60/180) from its outlet at Österhamn. The smaller outlet at **Västerhamn** just has bicycles.

Mariebad   WATERPARK
(☑018-531-650; www.mariehamn.ax/mariebad; Österleden; adult/child €8.50/5.20; ☻noon-10pm Mon, 6-8am & 10am-10pm Tue-Fri, 10am-6pm Sat & Sun) This large waterpark is excellent for the whole family, with slides, saunas, indoor and outdoor pools with water jets, waterfalls etc, and a free sandy **beach**.

Ålandia Dive & Adventure   DIVING
(☑0407-068-045; www.divealand.com; Fiskehamnsvägen 2; 2-day dive incl gear, accommodation & meals from €280; ☻May-Aug) Ålandia can take qualified divers to some 20 wrecks off the Åland coast.

Midnight Sun Sailing   SAILING
(☑018-57500; www.midnightsunsailing.fi; Östra Hamnen) Rents yachts per week from €750; drop-off fees for mainland Finland or Sweden are €150. Skippers can be arranged if you don't want to go it alone.

🎉 Festivals & Events

Along with the decorating and raising of the **Midsummer poles** (p118), Mariehamn hosts plenty of lively summer events.

Ålands Sjödagar   CULTURAL
(www.alandssjodagar.ax) Åland's maritime history is celebrated in mid-July with boat races, folk music and short sailing tours on the schooner *Albanus*.

Rockoff   MUSIC
(www.rockoff.nu; 1-/9-day pass €30/90) Nine days of Swedish pop and rock bands kicking off in mid-July.

ÅLAND ARCHIPELAGO MARIEHAMN

Mariehamn

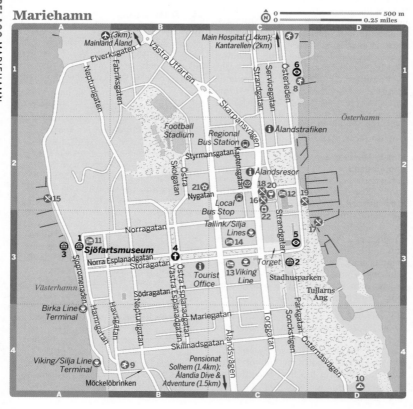

🛏 Sleeping

Mariehamn's hotel rates are highest between mid-June and the end of August. Booking ahead is recommended, especially on weekends. Mariehamn has no hostels.

Gröna Udden Camping   CAMPGROUND €
(☑018-528-700;   www.gronaudden.com; Östernäsvägen; tent site €10 plus per adult €10, d €80, 2-/4-/6-person cabins €95/115/160; ☺early May-early Sep; 🏊) By the seaside, 15 minutes' stroll south of the city centre, this campground is a family favourite so you'll need to book its fully equipped spruce cabins ahead in summer. Outdoor fun includes a safe swimming beach, minigolf course (admission €5) and bike hire (€15). Linen costs €8.50 per person.

Hotell Esplanad   HOTEL €
(☑018-16444;   www.cikada.aland.fi; Storagatan 5; s/d €65/76; 🛜) Mariehamn's best-value central accommodation is old style – basketweave wallpaper and huge retro TVs – but it's fine for a cheap sleep. Rooms contain minifridges; wi-fi's available in public areas. Its sister property Hotel Cikada is handy for the ferry terminals.

Park Alandia Hotel   HOTEL €€
(☑018-14130; www.parkalandiahotel.com; Norra Esplanadgatan 3; s/d €98/116; @🛜🏊) Spacious, modern rooms at this sophisticated spot on the main boulevard are done out in sandy hues and hardwood floors, and guests can borrow bikes for free. On sunny days its restaurant terrace packs in the crowds.

Pensionat Solhem   GUESTHOUSE €€
(☑018-16322; www.visitaland.com/solhem; Lökskärsvägen 18; s/d without bathroom €45/75; ☺May-Oct) Situated 3km south of the city centre, this seaside spot feels like your own villa. Simple rooms share bathrooms but you can use rowing boats and the sauna and cheerful staff keep the place running like clockwork. Local buses stop nearby.

Hotel Cikada   HOTEL €€
(☑018-16333; www.cikada.aland.fi; Hamngätan 1; s €74, d €91-103; ☺Mar-Oct; 🛜🏊) Just 700m from the ferry terminals, this basic 90-room hotel has dated decor but decent facilities including two saunas and a swimming pool. It's definitely worth paying for one of the 30 slightly pricier balcony rooms, with sweeping views over the sea. Three rooms are equipped for travellers with disabilities.

Hotell Arkipelag   HOTEL €€€
(☑018-24020; www.hotellarkipelag.com; Strandgatan 35; s/d €134/164, with sea view €158/188, ste €280; @🛜🏊) High-class Arkipelag is popular with business visitors, though water views from the balconies are tempting for anyone. Rooms are large, with minimalist decoration and bathrooms contain both baths and showers. Super facilities include indoor and outdoor pools, a freshly refurbished sauna, nightclub, casino, three restaurants and several bars.

ÅLAND ARCHIPELAGO MARIEHAMN

Mariehamn

✖️ Eating

Mariehamn's cafes serve the local speciality, *Ålandspannkaka* (Åland pancakes): the real deal is a fluffy semolina square served with stewed prunes (not strawberry jam). Look out in local markets for *Ålands svartbröd* (Åland dark bread), a malt fruit loaf that takes four days to make and complements *sill* (pickled herring) and light local cheeses. Some outer islands have limited general stores: Mariehamn may be your best chance to stock up.

Bagarstugan   CAFE €
(Ekonomiegatan 2; dishes €6-12.50; ⏱10am-5pm Mon-Fri, 11am-4pm Sat) 🍴 Wood-panelled walls, scrubbed pine floors, and pink geraniums on the windowsills provide a charming backdrop for homemade soups, salads, quiches, pies and cakes (scattered with flower petals and far too pretty to eat!) made from local, often organic produce. Nothing is too much trouble for the friendly staff.

Pub Niska   PIZZA €
(📋018-19151; www.mickesmat.ax; Sjökvarteret; pizza €11.50-12.50; ⏱11am-7pm Mon-Sat, 3-9pm Sun May & Sep, 11am-9pm Jun-Aug) 🍴 Star chef Michael 'Micke' Björklund, the mastermind behind Åland's sublime 'taste village' Smakbyn (p118), recently shifted his smuggler-named *plåtbröd* (Åland-style pizza) restaurant from the west harbour here to Mariehamn's maritime quarter. Condiments are homemade, cheese is from Åland's dairy, and toppings include cold smoked salmon and horseradish cream. There are also meal-sized baked potatoes and salads.

Kantarellen   SUPERMARKET €
(www.kantarellen.ax; Nya Godbyvägen; ⏱9am-9pm Mon-Fri, 9am-7pm Sat, 10am-7pm Sun) Åland's biggest supermarket, Kantarellen, is 2km north of town on the road to Godby.

FP von Knorring   INTERNATIONAL €€
(📋018-16500; www.fpvonknorring.com; Ångbåtsbron; restaurant mains €14-30, pub mains €13.50-22.50; ⏱11am-10pm Apr-Sep) Now permanently moored, the grand old 1928 steam ship M/S *Jan-Nieveen* retains gleaming brass fittings. Food is upmarket pub grub; from around late July, don't miss its local crayfish. Live music plays several times a week in summer.

Seapoint Restaurant & Bar   REGIONAL CUISINE €€
(📋018-15501; www.taste.ax; Österhamn; lunch mains €10.50-16, dinner mains €22-28; ⏱kitchen 11am-10pm Mon-Fri, 1-10pm Sat & Sun May–mid-Aug) Local ingredients are used to intriguing effect at this smart harbour pavilion: grilled fennel with roasted root vegetables, perch with wild garlic, smoked whitefish roe, and crème brûlée with seabuckthorn and strawberries. Tapas-style platters (€15) offer a taste of three seafood, meat or vegetable dishes.

Indigo   REGIONAL CUISINE €€
(📋018-16550; www.indigo.ax; Nygatan 1; lunch mains €12-13, dinner mains €20-32.50; ⏱kitchen 11am-3pm & 5-10pm Mon-Sat year-round plus 2-10pm Sun mid-May–early Sep) The building might be historic brick and timber but the menu is contemporary, with expertly cooked dishes like grilled Åland beef with béarnaise sauce and homemade fries. There's a buzzing summer courtyard and beautiful upstairs loft space. It's a stylish spot for a drink; the bar stays open to midnight Monday to Thursday and 3am on Friday and Saturday.

★ Nautical   REGIONAL CUISINE €€€
(📋018-19931; www.nautical.ax; Hamngätan 2; lunch mains €13-24, dinner mains €30-36, 6-course tasting menu €75; ⏱11am-10pm Jun-Aug, 5-10pm Sep-May; 🎟) Taking its cue from its maritime museum location, this spiffing marine-blue restaurant overlooking the western harbour and *Pommern* is decked out with a ship's wheel and has a splendid umbrella-shaded summer terrace. Sea-inspired dishes span salmon tartare with horseradish and fennel to pan-fried Åland perch with caraway foam; land-based options include red-wine-braised ox tail with forest mushrooms.

ÅSS Paviljongen   REGIONAL CUISINE €€€
(📋018-19141; www.paviljongen.ax; Västerhamn; lunch buffet €13, mains €28-32; ⏱11am-10pm Mon-Fri, noon-10pm Sat & Sun May-Aug) Listen to boat masts clinking in Åland's yacht club marina while dining on creatively prepared local produce: grilled rack of lamb with beetroot, caper and balsamic, and smoked-ham-and-goats-cheese potato cake; fried perch with split-pea and parsnip mash; or crayfish with rainbow trout.

🍸 Drinking & Nightlife

Most restaurant bars stay open late in summer and many have live music.

Dino's Bar & Grill   BAR
(www.dinosbar.com; Strandgatan 12; ⏱bar 10.30am-10pm Mon & Tue, to midnight Wed & Thu, to 2am Fri, noon-4am Sat, 2-10pm Sun) In summer Dino's

outdoor tables and balcony overflow with revellers. Live music performs most nights in summer and on weekends in winter.

Arken CLUB
(admission up to midnight/2am/closing, €5/10/20; 10pm-4am Jun–mid-Aug, 10pm-3am Wed-Sat mid-Aug–May) Inside the Hotell Arkipelag (p113), Arken (aka 'the Ark') has chart-conscious DJs.

☆ Entertainment

Casino Paf CASINO
(www.casinopaf.com; Strandgatan 35; 10am-midnight Sun-Thu, to 3am Fri & Sat) Punters can take advantage of Åland's autonomous gambling laws in this casino inside Hotell Arkipelag (p113).

Bio Savoy Cinema CINEMA
(018-19647; Nygatan 14; tickets €10-12) State-of-the-art cinema.

🛍 Shopping

Åland inspires plenty of local artists.

Salt CRAFTS
(www.salt.ax; Sjökvarteret; 10am-6pm Mon-Fri, to 3pm Sat, 11am-3pm Sun Jun-early Aug) In a red-brown timber shed in the maritime quarter, you can browse the work of 19 local artists and craftspeople's textiles, ceramics, silverware and other jewellery. It also sells local delicacies such as seabuckthorn jam.

Guldviva JEWELLERY
(www.guldviva.com; Sjökvarteret; 10am-5pm Mon-Fri, to 2pm Sat late Jun–mid-Aug) Brooches, cufflinks and necklaces based on the islands' flora and fauna. Some incorporate Åland's red rapakivi granite.

Jussis Keramik GLASS, CERAMICS
(www.jussiskeramik.fi; Nygatan 1; 10am-5pm Mon-Fri, to 4pm Sat) Watch the glass-blowers at work in this workshop turning out ceramics and glassware in a wide variety of bright colours.

❶ Information

Ålandsresor (018-28040; www.alandsresor.fi; Torggatan 2; 8.30am-5pm Mon-Fri year-round, plus 9am-2pm Sat Jun & Jul) Handles hotel, guesthouse and cottage bookings for the entire archipelago.

Ålandstrafiken (018-525-100; www.alandstrafiken.ax; Strandgatan 25; 9am-5pm Mon-Wed & Fri, 11am-5pm Thu) Information on buses and ferries around Åland, and Archipelago Ticket bookings. Can store luggage (per day €1).

Main Hospital (018-5355; Sjukhusvägen) Has an emergency ward.

Tourist Office (Ålands Turistinformation; 018-24000; www.visitaland.com; Storagatan 8; 9am-6pm early Jun-early Aug, 9am-5pm Mon-Fri, to 4pm Sat & Sun early Jun & mid-Aug–late Aug, 9am-4pm Mon-Fri, 10am-3pm Sat & Sun Apr, May & Sep, 9am-4pm Mon-Fri Oct-Mar; ☎) Helpful office with region-wide info.

❶ Getting There & Away

There are 24-hour coin-operated luggage lockers (€3 to €5) at the ferry terminal.

The **airport** is 4km northwest of the city centre.

Viking (p110) and Tallink/Silja (p110) ferries dock at the ferry terminal at Västerhamn (West Harbour). The guest harbour for small boats is at Österhamn (East Harbour). The harbours are linked by the long, tree-lined Storagatan.

---

❶ VIA THE ARCHIPELAGO FERRIES

Most visitors travel with the major ferry companies directly to Åland's mainland but it's possible to use the scheduled interisland ferries between Åland and mainland Finland via the **northern and southern archipelagos**. The **northern route** from Osnäs harbour, near Kustavi, 68km northwest of Turku, is via Brändö and Kumlinge. The **southern route** from Galtby harbour, Korpo, in the Turku Archipelago, is via the islands of Kökar and Föglö.

From mid-June to early August, the only viable way to travel is with an **Archipelago Ticket**, which requires you to break your journey overnight on the northern or southern routes en route to mainland Åland (you'll need to book the complete journey in one go). You *could* just turn up and take a chance on space being available for each leg but Archipelago Ticket bookings have priority and you could well find yourself stranded on the islands when ferries fill to capacity and sail without you. Outside summer, pricier 'transit' fares that don't require an overnight stay are available.

Book tickets online or by phone with Ålandstrafiken (p110).

Regional buses depart from the bus station opposite the post office; the tourist office has timetables.

ⓘ Getting Around

Local bus routes (€2) depart from Nygatan, outside the post office.

Hire cars from the friendly **RBS Biluthyrning** (☑ 018-525-505; www.rundbergs.com; Strandgatan 1) at the St1 garage petrol station opposite Mariebad. Rates for small cars start at around €65 per day. Delivery within Mariehamn is free. Book well in advance during summer.

Ro-No Rent (p111) hires out bicycles, mopeds and other recreation gear.

For a taxi, call ☑ 018-26000.

MAINLAND ÅLAND & AROUND

Several large islands form Åland's core. Some of Finland's oldest historical landmarks are in this region, particularly around Saltvik and Sund. Eckerö in the west is serviced by regular ferries to/from Grisslehamn, Sweden.

Jomala

☑ 018 / POP 4430

You'll see Jomala's coat of arms, which features an enthroned St Olaf, Åland's patron saint, around its two main centres: Kyrkby and smaller Gottby. Two kilometres west of Gottby and 4km off the main road, the peaceful hamlet of Djurvik overlooks a gentle bay.

CYCLING THE MAIL ROAD

A good taster for cycling in the archipelago is the Mail Rd, a former **postal route** (www.aland.com; admission €3; ⊙10am-3pm early Jun–mid-Aug) that crossed Åland between Stockholm and Turku. Today it has been transformed into a 65km cycling route, marked by red poles, that takes you from Eckerö to Värdö via some of the island's biggest sights including Kastelholms Slott and Bomarsund.

Allow a gentle two days – three if cycling with kids. There are accommodation and eating options along the way; pick up a free copy of *Mail Road Across Åland* from the tourist office.

◉ Sights

Museum   MUSEUM
(☑ 018-33710; Önningebyvägen 31; adult/child €4/3; ⊙noon-3pm Thu-Sat early Apr–May, 11am-4pm daily Jun–Aug) In 1886 landscape painter Victor Westerholm invited fellow artists to his summer house in Önningeby, a tiny village in eastern Jomala. For almost 30 years artists gathered here at 'Önningeby Colony'. This interesting museum showcases their work (although there are none by Westerholm himself) alongside memorabilia from the era. Other exhibits follow the work of contemporary artists.

Sankt Olof's Kyrka   CHURCH
(www.jomala.evl.ax; ⊙9.30am-3.30pm Tue-Fri, 1-3.30pm Sun Jun-Aug) Jomala's Sankt Olaf's Kyrka dates back to the 12th century. It's still possible to make out a lion's jaw with a human head inside in the worn stonework, which was originally worked on by Italian stonemasons.

🛏 Sleeping

Djurviks Gästgård   GUESTHOUSE €
(☑ 018-32433; www.djurvik.ax; s/d €40/50, 2-/4-person cabins €66/80; ⊙May-Oct; 🛜) Right by the water, Djurviks Gästgård offers a choice of cabins or simple rooms, and also has an endearing garden, and rowing boats and kayaks for guest use.

ⓘ Getting There & Away

From Mariehamn, catch bus 5 to Önningeby (€2.10, 15 minutes, up to 10 daily Monday to Friday, four on Saturday and Sunday).

Finström

☑ 018 / POP 2520

Åland's central municipality fans out around Godby, the island's second-biggest 'town' – though with 800 people, it's scarcely a metropolis. There are, however, some real highlights in this area, not least the wonderful Stallhagen Brewery.

◉ Sights & Activities

Sankt Mikael Kyrka   CHURCH
(⊙10am-4pm Mon-Fri May-Sep) In Pålsböle, a small village just 5km north of Godby, Sankt Mikael Kyrka features a well-preserved interior including a wealth of medieval frescoes and sculptures.

Observation Tower   TOWER

(adult/child €1.50/1; ☺10am-8pm Jun-Aug, 10am-6pm May, 10am-6pm Sat & Sun Sep) Above the tunnel before you cross the bridge to Sund, the 30m-high observation tower at Café Uffe på Berget (p117) affords superb views of the archipelago and is a popular photo stop. Across the road is **Godby Arboretum**, a small nature park with native and exotic trees along a short, marked nature trail.

🛏 Sleeping & Eating

Godby Vandrarhem   HOSTEL €

(☑018-41555; www.idrottscenter.com; Skolvägen 2, Godby; dm/s/d €22/39/59; 🕸🍴) Attached to Godby's sports centre and swimming pool, this hostel is often used by visiting youth sports teams and has that institutional vibe. But it can organise activities such as winter ice-skating tours, breakfast and linen are included, and there's free laundry, as well as a self-catering kitchen. There's a supermarket 800m north at the main crossroads.

Café Uffe på Berget   CAFE €

(dishes €2.50-7.50; ☺10am-8pm Jun-Aug, 10am-6pm May, 10am-6pm Sat & Sun Sep) If the creaking wooden observation tower causes trepidation, the views from the adjoining cafe alone are gorgeous. The espresso machine is busy and the pancakes are superb (skip the rest of the menu).

❶ Getting There & Away

Rd 2 from Mariehamn takes you to Godby. Buses 2, 3 and 4 from Mariehamn all go via Godby (€2.80).

Sund

☑018 / POP 1030

Situated 30km from Mariehamn just east of the main island group and connected to Saltvik by bridge, Sund is Åland's action hero, with a muscular medieval castle, mighty open-air museum, and battle scars in the ruins of a Russian stronghold.

Finby is the largest town, with all services.

◉ Sights & Activities

Kastelholms Slott   CASTLE

(☑018-432-150; www.kastelholm.ax; adult/child €6/4.50; ☺10am-5pm mid-May–Jun & Aug–mid-Sep, to 6pm Jul) One of Åland's premier sights is this breathtaking 14th-century castle on a picturesque little inlet (signposted off Rd 2). The keep towers are 15m high in parts, with

ÅLAND'S ARTISAN BREWERY

Stallhagen Brewery (☑018-48500; www.stallhagen.com; Getavägen 196; lunch mains €10, dinner mains €12.50-15.50; ☺bar 10.30am-8pm Mon-Thu, 10.30am-11pm Fri, noon-11pm Sat, noon-8pm Sun, kitchen 10.30am-2pm Mon-Thu, 10.30am-9pm Fri, noon-9pm Sat, noon-8pm Sun) Prebook a behind-the-scenes **tour** (€28 incl 4 samples; ☺90min tour 5pm Mon-Fri) of this fabulous brewery at the forest's edge overlooking a lake and horse paddocks, or just stop by to sample its unique brews such as blueberry or honey. Scandinavian folk music jam sessions often strike up on the terrace; limited-but-luscious gastropub fare includes a fish and meat option per day.

walls of 3m-thick red granite: it's easy to see how it would once have ruled over Åland. Exhibits showcase the castle's evolution and archaeological finds including a medieval silver-coin hoard. English-language tours (included in admission) depart at 2pm Saturday and Sunday from June to early August, lasting around 45 minutes.

Several extensions followed the castle's initial construction, most notably by Gustav Wasa. Mad king Eric XIV, deposed by an uprising in 1569, was moved from prison to prison around the Swedish kingdom. He spent three months here, shut up (according to tradition at least) in a tiny chamber in the Kuretorn keep. A fire in 1745 reduced the castle to ruins: only the northern wing survived.

Bomarsund   RUINS, FORTRESS

(www.bomarsund.ax) Following the war of 1808–09, Russia began building this major military structure as its westernmost defence against the Swedes. In 1854 the fortress was still incomplete when the Crimean War began and a French-British naval force bombarded it heavily from the sea. Within two days the Russians were forced to surrender it.

The ruins stretch for a couple of kilometres, on both sides of the road. Across the water on Prästö, the small **Bomarsund museum** (☑018-44032; admission by donation; ☺10am-5pm Mon-Fri Jun-Aug, plus 10am-5pm Sat & Sun Jul) displays excavated artefacts.

At the complex's core was a huge fortress, built from brick and strengthened with distinctive octagonal blocks, containing a garrison town, and protected by ramparts and a planned 15 fortified towers. Prästö became Bomarsund's island of the dead, with a military hospital and separate Greek Orthodox, Jewish, Muslim and Christian graveyards. The construction drew masons, craftsmen and soldiers from across the Russian Empire.

Only three of the defensive towers were completed and today, along with the Huvudfästet (Main Fort), they make the most impressive sights, particularly Brännklint tower, its walls scarred by cannon- and rifleballs. The overgrown foundations of the garrison town Nya Skarpans, populated only by ants and butterflies, are also atmospheric.

Jan Karlsgårdens Friluftsmuseum   MUSEUM
(☑018-432-150; www.kastelholm.ax; ⊙10am-5pm May–mid-Sep) FREE At this sprawling open-air museum next to Kastelholms Slott, you can stroll around traditional 18th- and 19th-century Ålandic buildings, including windmills and a smoke sauna. The museum shop's guidebook (€2) is invaluable for background on each building. By the entrance, the small **Fängelsemuseet Vita Björn** (admission €2; ⊙10am-5pm May–mid-Sep), a jail until 1975, demonstrates how cells and conditions evolved over the two centuries it was in use.

Sankt Johannes Kyrka   CHURCH
(⊙9am-4pm Mon-Fri, noon-4pm Sun Jun-Aug) FREE North of Kastelholm is the biggest church in Åland. The altarpiece is decorated with a dazzling triptych and a stone cross with the text 'Wenni E'. According to researchers, it was erected in memory of the Hamburg bishop Wenni, who died here while on a crusade in 936.

Ålands Golfklubb   GOLF
(☑018-41500; www.agk.ax; green fees Sun-Thu/Fri & Sat €50/63; ⊙May-Oct) Åland's finest golf club incorporates two 18-hole courses; you can see Kastelholms Slott from several of the fairways.

🛏 Sleeping & Eating

Puttes Camping   CAMPGROUND €
(☑018-44016; www.visitaland.com/puttescamping; Bryggvägen 2, Bomarsund; tent sites €12 plus per person €4, cabins from €35; ⊙May-Aug) Right on Bomarsund's doorstep, Puttes has plenty of grassy sites and simple four-bed cabins, plus a beach sauna, bike hire, rowing boats and a canoe jetty. Its cafe does delicious pancakes.

Kastelholms Gästhem   B&B €€
(☑018-43841; Tosarbyvägen 47; s/d €85/90, without bathroom €60/80; ⊙May–mid-Oct) The closest accommodation to Kastelholms Slott is this pleasant little guesthouse. Most of its spotless, floral rooms have private bathrooms, and there's access to a self-catering kitchen and laundry. The patios are perfect for evening lazing.

★**Smakbyn**   REGIONAL CUISINE €€
(www.smakbyn.ax; Slottsvägen 134, Kastelholm; lunch/dinner mains €10/29, 2-/3-course evening menus €39/49; ⊙kitchen 11am-7pm Mon-Fri, 1-8pm Sat & Sun) 🍴 The brainchild of award-winning chef Michael 'Micke' Björklund, this 'taste village' incorporates a farm shop, cookery courses (with/without drinks €90/120), distillery making spirits like Ålvados (Åland-apple calvados; tours and tastings available), bar, and an open-kitchen restaurant using seasonal organic produce in dishes like parsnip cheesecake with air-dried ham and pickled chanterelles, and butter-fried perch in shellfish sauce with crayfish compote.

MIDSUMMER POLES

Åland's Midsummer poles are a fixture on the landscape in summer. Up to 25m tall, the whitewashed spruce poles are a cross between a mast and a totem pole. Each village usually has at least one, decorated in a public gathering the day before Midsummer with leaves, ribbons, tissue paper, miniature flags and various trinkets, the nature and symbolism of which differs from place to place. Atop the poles is the Fäktagubbe, a figure representing toil and diligence. Other motifs include sailing boats, ears of corn representing the harvest, a wreath symbolising love, a sun facing east and other icons of community togetherness. Once raised, the pole then stands until the following Midsummer.

When the Midsummer pole came to Åland remains a mystery. Although some theorists believe that the pole is a manifestation of an ancient fertility rite, its origins on Åland itself are probably more recent. Others point to the resemblance to ships' masts, with cross-spars and cords, which suggests an appeal to a higher power for safe seas.

ℹ️ Getting There & Away

Rd 2 and bus 4 from Mariehamn to Vårdö serve Sund. The bus goes via Kastelholm (€2.90, 30 minutes), Bomarsund (€3.40, 40 minutes) and Prästö (€3.80, 45 minutes).

Vårdö

📍 018 / POP 440

Vårdö's cluster of isles, connected by bridges and ferries, stretches up to the two islands of **Simskäla** (Västra and Östra; West and East, respectively), with rustling silver birches, views over the archipelago's numerous islets, and remote beaches to discover.

Vårdö is a handy stop if you're travelling to the outer islands on the northern archipelago route, with ferries departing from Hummelvik.

Sandösunds Camping rents kayaks (from €28 per day) for exploring the rippling bays.

🛏️ Sleeping

Sandösunds Camping　　　CAMPGROUND €
(📞 018-47750; www.sandocamping.aland.fi; Trollvägen 40; tent sites €2 plus per person €4, s/d incl breakfast €90/110, 2-/4-person cabins €44/52; ☺ May-Aug) Just across the bridge from Vårdö, this idyllically positioned campground has remarkably peaceful sites, spiffy new townhouse rooms and well-kept beachside log cabins. Its facilities are the real bonus, and include a range of kayaks and bicycles, plus a 'floating sauna' that lets you hop straight into the water on the picture-perfect sound.

Bomans Gästhem　　　HOSTEL, B&B €
(📞 044-211-8475; www.bomansgasthem.info; Vårdöby; dm/s/d €30/50/75; ☺ May-Aug; 🅿) This HI-affiliated hostel is signposted 500m off the road between Vargata and Lövö. The cheapest rooms are in the main building, with slightly larger ones inside a row of little bungalows. There's a guest kitchen, sauna, bike hire and a driving range in the field out the front.

ℹ️ Getting There & Away

Vårdö is connected to the island of Prästö by a network of ferries. Bus 4 travels to Vårdö from Mariehamn (€3.80, one hour), crossing on the short, free car ferry from Prästö.

Ferries on the northern archipelago route (p115) depart from Hummelvik; the bus meets them.

Saltvik

📍 018 / POP 1820

Vikings sharpened their swords here for centuries: Saltvik's central village, Kvarnbo, is thought to have been their capital on Åland. Many relics have been unearthed around the municipality, though few signs of longhouses remain.

👁️ Sights & Activities

Southeast of Kvarnbo some stone outcroppings remain of the Iron Age fortress of **Borgboda**, built in the mid- to late 1st millennium.

Sankta Maria Kyrka　　　CHURCH
(☺ 10am-4pm Mon-Fri Jun-Aug) Kvarnbo's red-granite Sankta Maria Kyrka dates from the 13th century and contains a fine clover-shaped baptismal font and fragmentary frescoes of the period.

Orrdals Klint　　　MOUNTAIN
At 129m above sea level, Åland's highest 'mountain' Orrdals Klint has two short, well-marked walking tracks (1km and 2.5km long) leading to the top, where there's a viewing tower.

🎉 Festivals & Events

Viking Market　　　CULTURAL
(www.fibula.ax) The best chance to see Åland's Viking heritage is at the annual Viking Market, a three-day festival of feasting, drinking and costumed merrymaking in late July.

🛏️ Sleeping

⭐ **Kvarnbo Gästhem**　　　GUESTHOUSE €€
(📞 018-44015; www.kvarnbogasthem.com; Kvarnbo; d/tr/q €92/105/120) In a beautiful 19th-century building, Kvarnbo Gästhem has eight top-notch period-furnished rooms and does brilliant breakfasts – co-host Ella Grüssner Cromwell-Morgan is a Swedish TV chef and also runs wine tastings (€25).

ℹ️ Getting There & Away

Bus 3 runs from Mariehamn to Kvarnbo (€3.20, 35 minutes) and other villages in Saltvik.

A private bicycle ferry, **Kajo** (📞 040-078-3086; www.alandstrafiken.ax; adult/child €10/5; ☺ departs Västra Simskäla 11am & Tengsödavik 11.30am late Jun–mid-Aug by request), travels between Tengsödavik, Saltvik, and Västra Simskäla, Vårdö, once daily each way; call ahead to confirm.

Geta

📍 018 / POP 500

The main attraction of Åland's 'apple basket', Geta, is **Getabergen**, a formidable peak of 98m, with a nature trail (2km) aimed at kids, and a longer trail (5.5km) leading to Djupviksgrottan, a spacious natural grotto.

Bus 2 runs from Mariehamn to Geta (€3.80, 45 minutes) Monday to Friday via Godby.

The bicycle ferry **Silvana** (📞 040-022 9149; adult/child €10/5; ⊙ departs Skarpnåtö 11am, Hällö 11.30am late Jun–late Aug) makes one daily trip between Skarpnåtö, Hammarland, and Hällö, Geta.

NORTHERN & SOUTHERN ARCHIPELAGOS

Åland's tiny granite outer islets are strewn with silver birches, and offer great walking, cycling and kayaking and winter ice skating. Bring cash as none of the islands have ATMs. Fuel is limited, so fill up before travelling here.

The northern and southern archipelagos are served by the archipelago ferries (p115).

Northern Archipelago

Little-visited **Kumlinge** (www.kumlinge.ax), population 343, is a haven of peace. Its biggest attraction is a **walking path** from the Remmarina guest harbour to the beautiful church **Sankta Anna Kyrka** (📞040-031-1805; ⊙10am–noon & 2-6pm Mon-Sat early Jun–early Aug), 2km north of Kumlinge village, with astonishing 500-year-old Franciscan-style paintings. The best place to stay is **Hasslebo Gästhem** (📞0457-570-0834; www.hasslebo.com; tent sites €8 plus per person €4, s/d/f €50/60/100; ⊙Jun-Aug; @) 🍴, 3km outside Kumlinge village. It has a green emphasis including bio-toilets, solar power and organic breakfasts (with homemade jam; €9), as well as relaxing massages (€40) and bike hire (€9).

Ferries on the route between Hummelvik (Värdö) and Torsholma (Brändö) stop at Kumlinge (foot passenger/bicycle/car free/€4/27, 80 minutes).

Brändö (www.brando.ax) municipality, population 478, is composed of over 1180 islands. The core group of Brändö, Torsholma, Åva and Jurmo are connected by free ferries and bridges, with a signposted **bike route** running from Torsholma harbour north across the main island to Åva. Brändö's landmark church, **Sankt Jakobs Kyrka** (⊙10am-9pm May-Aug), is an example of the whitewashed style. On Jurmo, a 10-minute ferry from Långö, you can ride Icelandic horses at **Talli Perla** (📞050-465-4742; www.talliperla.com; 2-day packages €240), which does a two-day ride-and-accommodation package.

Campground **Brändö Stugby** (📞018-56221; http://home.aland.net/lameta; tent sites €9 plus per person €3, cabins €50-80; ⊙May–mid-Oct; 🛜) has log cabins, a shop-cafe with wi-fi and an extensive range of beer, barbecues and rowing boats for hire. Modest **Hotell Gullivan** (📞018-56350; www.gullivan.ax; s/d €70/104, cabins €88-104; 🛜) sits on Björnholma island, with a restaurant and minigolf as well as hire boats and fishing gear. Modern four-person ensuite cabins have kitchenettes.

Organic steaks from Jurmo's long-haired highland cattle, seasoned with island herbs, are the speciality of the wonderful **Café Kvarnen** (📞040-506-4777; www.jurmo.ax; mains €13-27; ⊙10am-10pm mid-Jun–mid-Aug, 10am-9pm mid-Aug–late Aug) 🍴 near the pier, along with homemade sausauges, burgers, locally caught fish, and fantastic Åland pancakes and cakes.

The **tourist office** (📞040-631-7878; www.brando.ax; Limslättsväg; ⊙1-5pm mid-Jun–mid-Aug, 2-4pm Mon-Fri mid-Aug–late Aug) is in a yellow wooden house on the island of Brändö, with free berry cordial and cake.

Coming from Kustavi (foot passenger/bicycle/car free/€6/21, 40 minutes) on the Finnish mainland, you'll arrive at Långö in the north of Brändö. Ferries from Hummelvik, Vårdö (foot passenger/bicycle/car free/€6/6/32, 2½ hours), dock at Torsholma.

Southern Archipelago

KÖKAR

Most of the 251 inhabitants of Kökar (www.kokar.ax) live in the quaint little town of Karlby. The islands' appealingly barren landscape attracted Bronze Age seal hunters and Hanseatic

Hammarland

 018 / POP 1540

◉ Sights

Quiet Hammarland in Åland's northwest is one of the archipelago's oldest inhabited areas. Kattby is the main village.

Sankta Catharina Kyrka   CHURCH
(◷9am-4pm Mon-Fri Jun-early Aug) Sankta Catharina Kyrka in Kattby was built in the 13th century, though a fire in the beginning of the 15th century led it to be rebuilt with fresh wall paintings. To the west of the church are more than 30 Iron Age burial sites.

traders. **Sankta Anne Kyrka** (◷9am-9pm May-Sep), with its unusual votive Turkish pirate ship, was built on top of a medieval Franciscan monastery – the monks' chapel and ruined walls make for a pensive evening stroll.

Nearby, Otterböte, where seal hunters set up camp 3000 years ago, is one of the archipelago's most important archaeological sites. Little remains, but a tangle of atmospheric walking trails criss-cross the area. **Kökar Homestead Museum** (☎0457-524-4077; admission €2; ◷11am-6pm late Jun–mid-Aug) is a sweet little collection of local history in the village of Hellsö.

Situated 3.5km southwest of Karlby, fabulous campground **Sandvik Gästhamn & Camping** (☎018-55911; www.sandvik.ax; tent sites €10 plus per person €2.50, 2-/4-person cabins €40/70; ◷May-Sep) has sheltered sites, kitchen facilities, a laundry, sauna, barbecue, shop, plenty of bikes for hire and a good swimming beach. By the visitor marina, **Hotell Brudhäll** (☎018-55955; www.brudhall.com; Karlby; s/d €113/139; ◷May-Aug; 🛜) is Kökar's only hotel, with basic rooms.

Up to three ferries daily (foot passenger/bicycle/car free/€6/32, 2¼ hours) come to Kökar from Galtby harbour, Korpo, in the Turku Archipelago. From Långnäs in Lumparland, Åland, there are up to five ferry connections (foot passenger/bicycle/car free/€6/32, 2¼ hours).

FÖGLÖ

Föglö (www.foglo.ax; population 572) island group is a short, easy hop from mainland Åland. Tiny **Degerby**, with art nouveau and empire-style architecture (many locals were civil servants rather than farmers), is the main town. There's a summer **tourist information kiosk** (☎045-7342-7274; www.foglo.ax/turism; ◷9.45am-5.30pm Mon-Sat, 1-4.30pm Sun mid-Jun–mid-Aug) and funny little local **museum** (admission by donation; ◷9.45am-5.30pm Mon-Sat, 1-4.30pm Sun mid-Jun–mid-Aug), containing the islanders' personal collections of biros, bottle tops and biscuit cutters.

A signposted **bike route** runs from Degerby to **Överö**; or you could pedal to the 14th-century **Sankta Maria Magdalena Kyrka** (◷11am-4pm Mon-Sat mid-Jun–mid-Aug), on an island south from Degerby, connected by a bridge and a scenic road. The conservation island of **Björkör** is close to Degerby harbour – **Coja Fishing** (☎040-094-7502; www.coja.nu; trips per hour from €80, boat rental per day from €75; ◷Jun-Aug) can take you across.

The two-day **Föglö Blues & Jazz Festival** (www.foglo.ax; ◷tickets €25) takes place in early August.

Enighetens Gästhem (☎018-50310; www.enighetens.ax; tent sites €10 plus per person €3, s/d €57/85; ◷May-Sep; 🛜), a rustic former courthouse, is the best place to stay in Degerby. Creaky-floored rooms (with shared bathrooms) contain old stoves and period furniture, and a harmonium graces the sitting room. There's a cafe and swimming pier. Bike hire per hour/day costs €4/15.

A dozen ferries make the one-hour trip between Svinö, Lumparland, and Degerby (foot passenger/bicycle/car free/€6/21), but only a couple link up with bus 5 from Mariehamn. Other ferries run from Långnäs to Överö (foot passenger/bicycle/car free/€6/21), some continuing to Kumlinge, and others to Kökar.

🛌 Sleeping

Kattnäs Camping CAMPGROUND €
(☑018-37687; www.kattnas.ax; Kattnäsvägen 285; tent sites €4 plus per person €4, cabins €50-60; ☺May-Sep) Set in 3.2 hectares of grassy meadows, it has a TV lounge and cafe in case you're missing civilisation. From the Eckerö–Mariehamn Rd, it's 3km south by the water's edge.

ℹ️ Getting There & Away

Bus 1 from Mariehamn to Eckerö runs through Hammarland (€3.10, 35 minutes). The bicycle ferry Silvana (p120) runs between Hammarland and Geta.

Eckerö

☑018 / POP 950
Just a two-hour ferry ride from mainland Sweden, Eckerö is a picturesque spot with rusty red boatsheds and granite rocks looming from the water.

⦿ Sights & Activities

There are plenty of little sandy beaches; **Degersand**, about 9km south of Storby ('Big Village') beyond the village of Torp, is good for swimming and sunning. **Käringsund harbour**, about 2km north of Storby, is a peaceful little cove with old wooden boathouses reflecting on the water. A nature trail here leads to a small beach; Käringsund resort rents canoes and rowboats.

Post och Tullhuset HISTORIC BUILDING
(Post & Customs House; Storby; ☺10am-5pm May-Aug, individual business hours vary) Designed by German architect CL Engel, today the Post & Customs House is a hub for local artists, with exhibitions, artisan shops and a terrific cafe (p123). The building was completed in 1828, during the era of Tsar Alexander I of Russia as a show of might to Sweden (as Åland was the Russian Empire's westernmost extremity). It was a crucial point on the Sweden–Finland Mail Rd, detailed at the one-roomed mailboat museum (p116). Between 1638 and 1895, local farmers were called to transport thousands of letters each week across the Åland sea. The most treacherous time was early spring when the sea ice broke. During the years the Mail Rd operated, 200 men from Eckerö died doing their postal duties.

Ålands Jakt och Fiskemuseum MUSEUM
(Åland Hunting & Fishing Museum; ☑018-38299; adult/child €5/2.50; ☺10am-6pm mid-Jun–Jul, 10am-5pm Mon-Sat early May-early Jun & Aug) By the harbour is Ålands Jakt och Fiskemuseum, with ghoulish stuffed wildlife and gun-toting photographs. If you prefer your animals alive, just outside the museum is **Viltsafari** (☑018-38103; tours adult/child €9/5.50; ☺up to 5 tours daily mid-Jun–early Aug, up to 3 tours Mon-Sat early-Jun–mid-Jun & early-Aug–mid Aug), a fenced-in nature park where you can get up close to Finnish fauna such as red and fallow deer, swans and wild boar (plus the odd ostrich) on a 45-minute tour aboard a safari 'train'.

Nimix KAYAKING
(☑0506-6716; www.nimix.ax; s kayak per 2hr/day €20/40, tandem per 2hr/day €35/75) Rents out single and tandem kayaks.

Stall Rosenqvist HORSE RIDING
(☑0457-522-1617; www.rosenqvist.ax; Ollasgätan 35; 45-/90-min lesson or tour €22/44) Offers lessons and forest tours on Icelandic horses and shetland ponies. Cash only.

Leklandet PLAY CENTRE
(☑040-550-0166; www.leklandet.ax; Käringsundsvägen 85; adult/child free/€12; ☺11am-6pm Fri-Sun mid-May–mid-Jun & mid-Aug-early Sep, 11am-6pm daily mid-Jun–mid-Aug) The 17 giant bouncing-castle-style inflatable attractions such as pirate ships at this indoor play centre will brighten kids' rainy days.

🛌 Sleeping & Eating

Eckerö has more cabin and cottage rentals than any other Åland municipality – book through Ålandsresor (p115).

Many accommodation options have good licensed restaurants.

★Degersands Resort CAMPGROUND €€
(☑018-38004; www.degersand.nu; Degersandsvägen 311; tent sites €8 plus per person €6, 1-2 person/3-4 person cabins €140/165; ☎) Bang on Åland's most beautiful beach, this haven has stunning cottages in sleek Scandinavian blonde wood with full kitchens, indoor and outdoor showers, and wraparound timber decks with barbecues. Awesome facilities include a traditional smoke sauna on the beach, an excellent **restaurant** (mains €10-23; ☺11.30am-8pm mid-Jun–early Aug, to 7pm early to mid-Aug) using local, organic produce, and rowboat, kayak, fishing gear and bike hire – even wintertime curling.

Käringsund RESORT €€
(☑018-38000; www.karingsund.ax; tent sites €16, cabins €93-162, bungalows €132-244; ☺mid-Mar–

Nov) A whistles-and-bells family resort set in green fields by the seashore, this place offers cabins and bungalows sleeping up to 10 people. Child-friendly entertainment ranges from air-football to minigolf, boules, pedal boats; there's a pizzeria, tennis court, sauna, and kayak, rowboat, bike and moped hire.

Eckerö Hotell & Restaurang
HOTEL €€

(☑018-38447; www.eckerohotell.ax; Käringsundsvägen 53, Eckerö; s/d/f €90/99/150; ⊘hotel Mar-Nov; @중) Elegant and welcoming, this family-run hotel has spacious, mostly ground-floor rooms with anti-allergen bedding and an excellent restaurant (pizzas €11-14, mains €19-32; ⊘4-10pm Mar-Nov). Owner/chef Ronald Karlsson also famously moonlights as Elvis during summer Saturday-night tribute shows.

Hotel Elvira
HOTEL €€

(☑018-38200; www.elvira.ax; Sandmovägen 85, Storby; s/d/tr €90/110/160; 중) Several of the 20 individually decorated rooms at this quirky retro hotel have sea views that, unusually, don't come with a higher price tag. Upstairs is a brand-new sauna, and there's a good à la carte summer restaurant (mains €22-32; ⊘6-9pm Mon-Sat mid-Jun–early Aug).

★Bodegan
CAFE €

(www.karingsundsgasthamn.ax; Käringsund harbour; mains €12-18; ⊘11am-7pm mid-Jun–late Jun, 8am-10pm late Jun–mid-Aug; 중) Right on the pier, this atmospheric little place is perfect for a drink while watching the sun set over the red creaking boathouses. But above all it's worth a visit for its food: marinated salmon with mustard sauce and potatoes, grilled black Angus steak, and an 'archipelago plate' of smoked salmon, herring, *skägen* (prawn toast), local cheese and black bread.

Tsarevna
CAFE €

(http://tsarevna.ax; dishes €3.50-7.50; ⊘11am-5pm Tue-Sun May, 10am-6pm Jun-Aug) ✐ With tables spilling into the courtyard of the historic Post och Tullhuset, Tsarevna is a much-loved venue for spectacular homemade cakes, pulled-pork sandwiches and bountiful organic salads with homebaked bread. From June, brunch (€17) on Saturdays and Sundays from 11am to 3pm is a local institution. Cash only.

🛒 Shopping

Mercedes Chocolaterie
FOOD

(www.amorina.ax; ⊘11am-5pm Fri-Sun May-Jun, 11am-5pm daily Jul-Aug) ✐ Inside the Post och Tullhuset, Venezuela native Mercedes makes exquisite chocolates using beans from her homeland and Åland cream. Unique varieties include seabuckthorn, orange and Åland nettle, and dried juniper berry.

❶ Information

Tourist Information Desk (☑018-39462; www.eckero.ax; ⊘10am-6pm Jun-Aug, 10am-5pm Sep-May) At Eckerö's ferry terminal.

❶ Getting There & Away

Rd 2 and bus 1 (€4.50, 50 minutes) run from Mariehamn to Eckerö.

Ferry passengers descend on the **Ro-No Rent** (☑018-12820; www.rono.ax; per day/week €12/60; ⊘9am-noon & 1-6pm Jun–mid-Aug) bike-hire hut at Eckerö harbour: book ahead to avoid disappointment. Bicycles can be dropped off at either of the Ro-No Rent outlets in Mariehamn.

Lemland

☑018 / POP 1930

When the occupying Russians needed a shipping route in the late 19th century, their prisoners of war dug the **Lemström Canal**. Today it remains one of Lemland's defining sights. Lemland lies between Lumparland and the canal, 5km east of Mariehamn on Rd 3, with **Norrby** village at its centre.

In Norrby, **Sankta Birgitta Kyrka** (⊘noon-6pm Mon-Fri Jun-early Aug) has 13th- and 14th-century wall paintings that tell the story of St Nicholas, the patron saint of seafarers.

Near the bridge to Lumparland, **Skeppargården Pellas** (☑018-34420; adult/child €4/free; ⊘11am-4pm mid-Jun–late Aug) is the rustic homestead museum of a local shipmaster.

Lumparland

☑018 / POP 415

Lumparland is home to Åland's oldest surviving wooden church. **Sankt Andreas Kyrka** (⊘10am-4pm early Jun–mid-Aug) was built in 1720; its curious cross is actually a weathervane that was once attached to the steeple. The large altarpiece was painted by Victor Westerholm of the Önningeby colony.

From Mariehamn take bus 5 to the ferry harbours Svinö (€3.80, 30 minutes) and Långnäs (€4.30, 40 minutes). From Långnäs, Finnlink (www.finnlines.com) ferries serve Naantali (adult/car €19/29, 3½ hours, up to two daily), and Tallink/Silja Lines (p110) runs to Turku (adult/car €12/32, five hours, up to three daily).

Tampere & Häme

Best Places to Eat

➡ Hella & Huone (p132)

➡ Tuulensuu (p131)

➡ Piparkakkutalo (p140)

➡ Ravintola Roux (p143)

➡ Neljä Vuodenaikaa (p131)

Best Places to Stay

➡ Dream Hostel (p130)

➡ Ylä-Tuuhosen Maatila (p134)

➡ Messilä (p143)

➡ Scandic Tampere Station (p130)

Why Go?

Modern cities and traditional settlements exist side by side in this historic region, where you can explore Finland's rural past at ancient wooden churches, its unsettled history at Hämeenlinna's castle, and its industrial heritage at Tampere's textile factories. Lahti excels in two major 21st-century Finnish exports: technology and classical music.

A gateway to Finland for many travellers thanks to its budget flight connections, Tampere is Finland's second city. Its imposing red-brick factories, left derelict in the hangover of industrial decline, now hold a spicy mixture of restaurants and museums, and the infectious energy of the people makes this a favourite Suomi stop.

Every town in the region sits on a magical stretch of water. Boats were once the main form of transport; one of Finland's essential summer experiences is bringing those slower-paced days back with a day-long lake cruise between towns.

When to Go

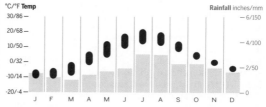

Tampere

Jul Lake cruises and long evenings on summer terraces.

Sep Great hiking in national parks, and the Sibelius festival in Lahti.

Dec Christmas atmosphere and spectacular lights in Tampere.

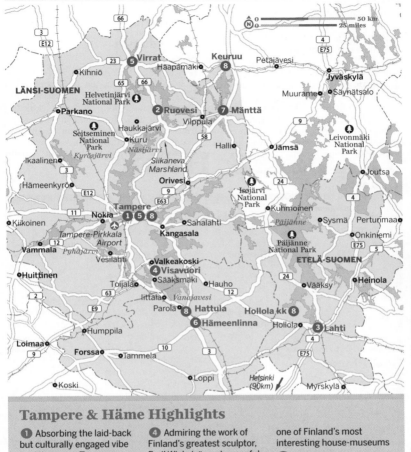

Tampere & Häme Highlights

❶ Absorbing the laid-back but culturally engaged vibe in picturesque **Tampere**

❷ Getting your kicks on Finland's Route 66, staying in peaceful **Ruovesi** (p134)

❸ Luxuriating in the acoustics of a Sibelius performance at Lahti's **Sibeliustalo** (p141)

❹ Admiring the work of Finland's greatest sculptor, Emil Wickström, at peaceful **Visavuori** (p136)

❺ Cruising the **Poet's Way** (p130) from Tampere to Virrat, a relaxing visual feast of Finnish lakescapes

❻ Snooping from room to room in Hämeenlinna's **Palanderin Talo** (p138),

one of Finland's most interesting house-museums

❼ Browsing top-quality Finnish art in Mänttä's **Gösta** (p136) gallery

❽ Contrast the venerable ancient artwork in the churches at **Hattula** (p137), **Keuruu** (p135) and **Hollola** (p143), with Tampere's memorable 20th-century **cathedral** (p126)

TAMPERE

🎵 03 / POP 217,400

Scenic Tampere, set between two vast lakes, has a down-to-earth vitality that makes it a favourite for many visitors. Through its centre churns the Tammerkoski rapids, whose grassy banks contrast with the red brick of the imposing fabric mills that once drove the city's economy. Regenerated industrial buildings now house quirky museums, enticing shops, pubs, cinemas and cafes.

TAMPERE & HÄME TAMPERE

History

In the Middle Ages the area was inhabited by the Pirkka, a devil-may-care guild of hunters, trappers and vigilante tax collectors. Modern Tampere was founded in 1779; during the 19th century its Tammerkoski rapids, which today supply abundant hydroelectric power, were a magnet for textile industries.

The 1917 Russian Revolution struck a chord with Tampere's large working-class population; the city became capital of the 'Reds' during the Finnish civil war and the scene of their biggest defeat.

As the textile industry dwindled, the city was forced to reinvent itself; its urban renewal is one of Finland's success stories.

◉ Sights

★ **Tuomiokirkko**　　　　　CHURCH
(www.tampereenseurakunnat.fi; Tuomiokirkonkatu 3; ⊙10am-5pm May-Aug, 11am-3pm Sep-Apr) **FREE** An iconic example of National Romantic architecture, Tampere's cathedral dates from 1907. Hugo Simberg created the frescoes and stained glass; you'll appreciate that they were controversial. A procession of ghostly childlike apostles holds the 'garland

Tampere

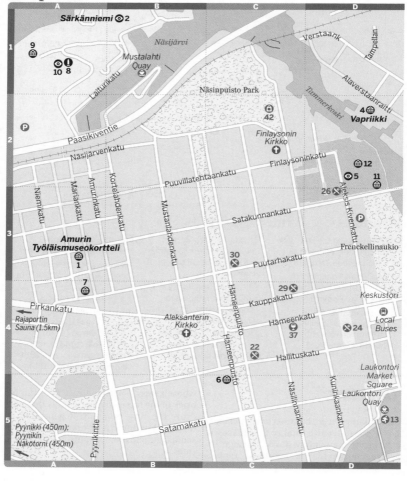

of life', graves and plants are tended by skeletal figures, and a wounded angel is stretchered off by two children. There's a solemn, almost mournful feel; the altarpiece, by Magnus Enckell, is a dreamlike Resurrection in similar style.

The symbolist stonework and disturbing colours of the stained glass add to the haunting ambience.

Finlayson Centre
CULTURAL CENTRE

(Satakunnankatu 18) Tampere's industrial era began with Scot James Finlayson, who established a cotton mill by the Tammerkoski in the 1820s. Later it grew massively and

was the first building in the Nordic countries to have electric lighting, which started operating in 1882. It has now been sensitively converted into a mall of cafes and shops; you'll also find a cinema here, as well as a great brewery pub and a couple of intriguing museums.

Vakoilumuseo
MUSEUM

(Spy Museum; www.vakoilumuseo.fi; Satakunnankatu 18, Finlayson Centre; adult/child €8/6; ⊙10am-6pm Mon-Sat, 11am-5pm Sun Jun-Aug, noon-6pm Mon-Sat, 11am-5pm Sun Sep-May) The offbeat spy museum under the Finlayson Centre offers a small but well-assembled display of

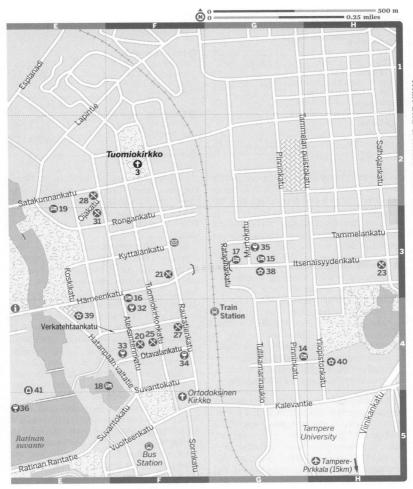

Tampere

devices of international espionage, mainly from the Cold War era. As well as histories of famous Finnish and foreign spies, it has numerous Bond-style gadgets and some interactive displays. English translations are slightly unsatisfying. For €5 extra, kids can take a suitability test for KGB cadet school.

★ **Amurin Työläismuseokortteli** MUSEUM (Amuri Museum of Workers' Housing; www.tampere.fi/amuri; Satakunnankatu 49; adult/child €7/3; ⊙10am-6pm Tue-Sun mid-May–mid-Sep) An entire block of 19th-century wooden houses, including 32 apartments, a bakery, a shoemaker, two general shops and a cafe, is preserved here. It's one of the most realistic house-museums in Finland and entertaining backstories (English translation available) give plenty of historical information.

★ Särkänniemi AMUSEMENT PARK (www.sarkanniemi.fi; day pass adult/child €37/31; ⊙rides roughly 10am-7pm mid-May–Aug) This promontory amusement park complex has numerous attractions, including dozens of rides, an observation tower, art gallery, aquarium, farm zoo, planetarium and dolphinarium. Buy all-inclusive entry or pay

per attraction (€10/5 per adult/child). Opening times are complex; check the website, where you can also get discounted entry. Indoor attractions stay open year-round. Take bus 20 from the train station or central square.

Rides include the Tornado roller coaster, super-fast High Voltage, speedboat rides on the lake and an Angry Birds area for younger kids. The **aquarium** (www.sarkanniemi.fi; adult/child day pass up to €29/€18; ⊙noon-7pm mid-May–Aug, 11am-9pm Sep–mid-May) is mediocre, with Finnish fish more interesting than the hobby-tank favourites. The planetarium is in the same complex, above which soars 168m **Näsinneula Observation Tower** (www.sarkanniemi.fi; adult/child €10/5; ⊙11am-11.30pm), the tallest in these northern lands. It's overpriced but gives spectacular city and lake views. There's a revolving restaurant.

Sara Hildénin taidemuseo (☎03-5654-3500; www.tampere.fi/sarahilden; adult/child €8/4; ⊙10am-6pm Tue-Sun Sep–mid-May, noon-7pm daily mid-May–Aug) has a collection of international and Finnish modern art and sculpture; the space is normally devoted to excellent exhibitions showcasing particular artists.

Werstas MUSEUM
(www.tyovaenmuseo.fi; Väinö Linnanaukio 8; admission charge for special exhibitions; ⊙11am-6pm Tue-Sun) FREE This worthwhile labour museum has a variety of changing exhibitions covering social history and labour industries. The permanent exhibition consists of three parts: a reconstruction of various historically typical Finnish workplaces – a shop, a printing press; an in-depth focus on textiles; and a hall holding the enormous steam engine and wheel that powered the Finlayson factory in the 19th century.

★**Vapriikki** MUSEUM
(www.vapriikki.fi; Veturiaukio 4; adult/child €10/4; ⊙10am-6pm Tue-Sun) A bright, modern glass-and-steel exhibition space in the renovated Tampella textile mill. As well as regularly changing exhibitions on anything from bicycles to Buddhism, there's a permanent display on Tampere's history, a beautiful **mineral museum**, a **natural history museum** and a small but cluttered **ice-hockey museum**, with memorabilia of star players and teams from Finland's sporting passion. There's also a **museum of shoes** – Tampere was known for its footwear industry – and a pleasant cafe.

Lenin-Museo MUSEUM
(www.lenin.fi; Hämeenpuisto 28; adult/child €5/free; ⊙11am-4pm Sep-May, 11am-6pm Jun-Aug) Admirers of bearded revolutionaries won't want to miss this small museum in the Workers' Hall where Lenin and Stalin first met in 1905. Lenin's life is documented with photos and papers; it's a little dry but it's fascinating to see, for example, his old school report (Vladimir was a straight-A student) or a threadbare couch that he slept on. The gift shop stocks Lenin pens, badges, T-shirts and other Soviet-era souvenirs.

Muumilaakso MUSEUM
(Moomin Valley; www.tampere.fi/muumi; Puutarhakatu 34; adult/child €7/3, incl Tampereen taidemuseo €10/4; ⊙9am-5pm Tue-Fri, 10am-6pm Sat & Sun) Explore the creation of Tove Jansson's enduringly popular Moomins in this atmospheric museum in the basement of the art gallery, Tampereen taidemuseo. It contains original drawings and beautiful dioramas depicting scenes from these quirky stories (English explanations available). It's scheduled to move to a new home in the Tampere-talo building in 2016.

HIKING NORTH OF TAMPERE

The **Pirkan Taival** is a loose network of hiking trails totalling 330km in an area that stretches from Helvetinjärvi National Park westward to Seitseminen National Park and beyond. It's easy to work out your own route here; it's well marked, and regular signboards show distances. Scenery ranges from peaceful Finnish farmland to marshes, forests and gravel ridges. Huts and camping areas offer overnighting options. Trailheads reachable by bus from Tampere are Virrat, Ruovesi and Kuru. Buy a map at Tampere bookshops or the Seitseminen park visitor centre.

🏃 Activities

The www.visittampere.fi website has plenty more ideas for getting active in and around Tampere, including fishing information.

Pyynikki PARK
Rising between Tampere's two lakes, this forested ridge has fine views plus walking and cycling trails. It soars 85m above the lakeshores – an Everest by southern Finnish standards – and claims to be the world's highest gravel ridge. A stone **observation tower** (www.munkkikahvila.net; adult/child €2/1; ⊙9am-8pm Sep-May, 9am-9pm Jun-Aug) holds a cafe serving brilliant doughnuts (€1.90).

From the city centre, head west along Satamakatu, bear left at a small park, then right up the hill.

Rajaportin Sauna SAUNA
(www.rajaportinsauna.fi; Pispalan Valtatie 9; adult/child €8/2, midweek €5; ⊙6-10pm Mon & Wed, 3-9pm Fri, 2-10pm Sat) This traditional place is Finland's oldest operating public sauna. It's a great chance to experience the softer steam from a traditionally heated sauna rather than the harsher electric ones. It's a couple of kilometres west of the city centre; buses 8, 11 and 13 among others head out there. There's a cafe on-site, and massages can be arranged. Take a towel or rent one there.

Cruises

There are plenty of summer options on Tampere's two magnificent lakes. Trips on Näsijärvi leave from Mustalahti Quay, while Laukontori Quay serves Pyhäjärvi. All cruises can be booked at the tourist office.

Suomen Hopealinja CRUISE

(Finnish Silverline; ☑010-422-5600; www.hopealinja. fi) From Laukontori Quay, short cruises run on Pyhäjärvi from June to August, as well as a shuttle service (adult/child return €12/6) to nearby **Viikinsaari**, a pleasant picnic island. There are various lunch- and dinner-cruise options, and pirate cruises for kids.

It also runs a Poet's Way cruise as well as another spectacular trip to Visavuori (one way/return €52/78, 4½ hours, 9.30am, Thursday to Saturday early June to mid-August), and on to Hämeenlinna (one way/ return €58/87, 8½ hours).

★Poet's Way CRUISE

(☑010-422-5600; www.runoilijantie.fi; ☺early Jun–mid-Aug) From Mustalahti Quay, the glorious steamship S/S *Tarjanne* operates one of Finland's finest lake cruises, departing on Wednesdays and Fridays and returning from Virrat on Thursdays and Saturdays. One way to Ruovesi (4¾ hours) costs €50 and to Virrat (8¼ hours) is €58.

For €50/25 per adult/child, you can overnight in this venerable vessel before or afterwards. Bike transport is €8. You can also book a day trip to Virrat (€78) or Ruovesi (€68), travelling one leg by bus.

✯✯ Festivals & Events

Tampere Film Festival FILM

(www.tamperefilmfestival.fi) A respected international festival of short films, usually held in early March.

Tampere Biennale MUSIC

(www.tamperemusicfestivals.fi) A festival of new Finnish music, held in April of even-numbered years.

Tammerfest ROCK

(www.tammerfest.fi) The city's premier rock-music festival, held over four days in mid-July with concerts at various stages around town.

Tampere International Theatre Festival THEATRE

(www.teatterikesa.fi) Held in early August, this is a showcase of international and Finnish theatre. **Off-Tampere** is a fringe festival held at the same time.

Tampere Illuminations LIGHTS

(www.valoviikot.fi) City streets are brightened by 40,000 coloured lights between late October and early January. The central square becomes a Christmas market in December.

🛏 Sleeping

★Dream Hostel HOSTEL €

(☑045-236-0517; www.dreamhostel.fi; Åkerlundinkatu 2; dm €24-29, tw/q €79/108; P@🖥) ✔ Sparky, stylish and spacious, this is Finland's best hostel. Helpful staff, super-comfortable wide-berth dorms (unisex and female) in various sizes, a heap of facilities including bike hire, original decor and the right attitude about everything make it a real winner. It's a short walk from the train station in a quiet area. Upstairs are compact ensuite rooms for those that want hostel atmosphere without sharing a shower

Camping Härmälä CAMPGROUND €

(☑020-719-9777; www.suomicamping.fi/harmala; Leirintäkatu 8; campsites €16 plus per person €5, one-person tent €16, 2-/4-person cabin €54/72; ☺early May-late Sep; P🖥) Four-and-a-half kilometres south of the city centre (take bus 1 or 11), this is a spacious campground on the Pyhäjärvi lakeshore. There's a cafe, saunas and rowboats, as well as bike hire.

★Scandic Tampere Station HOTEL €€

(☑03-339-8000; www.scandichotels.com; Ratapihankatu 37; s/d €139/159; P@🖥) ✔ As the name suggests, this is right by the train station. It's a sleek, beautifully designed place with a minimalist feel to the decor, based on soothing pink and mauve lighting breaking up the chic whites and blacks. Superior-plus rooms are particularly enticing, with dark-wood sauna and balcony, and don't cost a whole lot more. Facilities are modern, service excellent and prices competitive.

There are also several accessible rooms, with motorised beds.

Hotelli Victoria HOTEL €€

(☑03-242-5111; www.hotellivictoria.fi; Itsenäisydenkatu 1; s/d €139/172; P@🖥🏊) Just on the other side of the train station from the city centre, this friendly hotel offers sound summer value with its spruce rooms, free internet and commendable breakfast spread. Rooms are light and quiet despite the busy road and there's a good sauna (included), 20m pool and free parking. It's usually cheaper than these maximum rates. Closed most of December. Bike hire available.

Sokos Hotel Tammer HOTEL €€

(☑020-123-4632; www.sokoshotels.fi; Satakunnankatu 13; s/d €138/158; P@🖥) ✔ Constructed in 1929, this is one of Finland's oldest hotels and enjoys a fine rapids-side location. After the gloriously old-fashioned elegance of the public areas, the rooms, behind ornate doors, are a little disappointing, though they have the expected facilities and Nordic comfort levels. Parking is very limited; a good breakfast buffet and sauna are included.

Omenahotelli
HOTEL €€

(☑ 0600-18018; www.omenahotels.com; Hämeenkatu 7; r €60-96; 🛜) On the main drag and very handy for the train station, this receptionless hotel offers the usual comfortable rooms with twin beds, a microwave, a kettle and a fold-out couch. Rooms are great value for a family of four, for example. Book online or via the terminal at the entrance.

Sokos Hotel Ilves
HOTEL €€€

(☑ 020-123-4631; www.sokoshotels.fi; Hatanpään valtatie 1; s/d €165/185; 🅿 @ 🛜 🎿) This tower hotel was big news when it opened in the 1980s, and still keeps standards high. Very high: the view from upper-floor rooms is memorable, so ask for as lofty a chamber as you can get. Rooms are attractively furnished with Finnish design classics; superiors are the same size but with even better views. Impressive facilities include an excellent restaurant, chain eateries and an attractive nightclub with dedicated karaoke chamber.

✖ Eating

Tampere's speciality, *mustamakkara,* is a mild, rather tasty sausage made with cow's blood, normally eaten with lingonberry jam. Try it at the kauppahalli (covered market) or Laukontori Market.

★ Neljä Vuodenaikaa
BISTRO €

(4 Saisons; www.4vuodenaikaa.fi; Kauppahalli; dishes €10-25; ⊙ 11am-3.45pm Mon-Fri, 11am-2.30pm Sat) Tucked into a corner of the kauppahalli, this recommended spot brings Gallic flair to the Finnish lunch hour with delicious plates such as bouillabaisse and French country salad augmented by excellent daily specials and wines by the glass.

Runo
CAFE €

(www.kahvilaruno.fi; Ojakatu 3; sandwiches €4-6; ⊙ 9am-8pm Mon-Sat, 10am-8pm Sun) With an arty crowd and bohemian feel, Runo (Poem) is an elegant, almost baroque cafe with books, paintings, decent coffee and huge windows that allow you to keep tabs on the weather. It's a top hang-out for either a light lunch or a spot of quiet contemplation.

Kauppahalli
MARKET €

(Hämeenkatu 19; ⊙ 8am-6pm Mon-Fri, 8am-3pm Sat; 🖊) 🍴 This intriguing indoor market is one of Finland's best, with picturesque wooden stalls serving a dazzling array of wonderful meat, fruit, baked goodies and fish. There are good places to eat here too; this is the best place to try cheap *mustamakkara* with berry jam.

Panimoravintola Plevna
BREWPUB €

(www.plevna.fi; Itäinenkatu 8; mains €11-23; ⊙ food 11am-10pm; 🛜) Inside the Finlayson Centre, this barn of a place offers a wide range of delicious beer, cider and perry brewed here, including an excellent strong stout. Meals are large and designed to soak it all up: massive sausage platters and enormous slabs of pork in classic beer-hall style. Vegetables here mean potatoes and onions, preferably fried, but it's all tasty, and service is fast.

Vohvelikahvila
CAFE €

(www.vohvelikahvila.com; Ojakatu 2; waffles €5-8; ⊙ 10am-8pm Mon-Fri, 10am-7pm Sat, 11am-6pm Sun) This quaint little place does a range of sweet delights, but specialises in fresh waffles, which come laden with cream and chocolate. There's also a range of unusual savoury waffles, with chicken, roast beef and more. Another branch on **Tuomiokirkonkatu** (www.kuparitalonvohvelikahvila. fi; Tuomiokirkonkatu 34; waffles €6-9; ⊙ 10am-8pm Mon-Fri, 11am-7pm Sat, noon-6pm Sun) also does salads.

★ Tuulensuu
GASTROPUB €€

(www.gastropub.net/tuulensuu; Hämeenpuisto 23; mains €17-26; ⊙ 11am-midnight Mon-Fri, noon-midnight Sat, 3pm-midnight Sun; 🛜) The best of several Tampere gastropubs, this has a superb range of Belgian beers, good wines and a lengthy port menu. Food is lovingly prepared and features staples such as liver or schnitzel, as well as more elaborate plates such as duck confit and other bistro fare inspired by Belgium and northeastern France. Even the bar snacks are gourmet: fresh-roasted almonds. Closed Sundays in summer.

Frankly
BISTRO €€

(☑03-212-0235; www.ravintolafrankly.fi; Hallituskatu 22; mains €22-30; ☺11am-midnight Mon-Thu, 11am-1am Fri, noon-1am Sat, 2-11pm Sun; ☑) This eatery offers a comfortable neighbourhood feel and some pretty good food. The menu has meaty Finnish classics like pepper steak alongside more delicate dishes like breast of woodpigeon, plus some decent, cheaper vegetarian options, all in a cosy atmosphere with solicitous service.

2h+k
BISTRO €€

(www.2hk.fi; Aleksanterinkatu 33; mains €12-25; ☺noon-10pm Mon, noon-11pm Tue-Thu, noon-midnight Fri & Sat, 1-10pm Sun; ☎) Divided into a drinking side and an eating side, this attractive brick space offers tempting, well-priced fare from its open kitchen. A selection of huge toasted sandwiches, tasty salads as well as snails, antipasti and garlicky mains make for good bistro dining.

★Hella & Huone
FRENCH, FINNISH €€€

(☑03-253-2440; www.hellajahuone.fi; Salhojankatu 48; 1/2/3/7 courses €26/40/52/76; ☺6-11pm Tue-Sat) This smart spot serves exquisite French-influenced gourmet creations. There's a menu of seven courses: choose how many you want to have and pay accordingly. Leave room for the fine Finnish cheeses and fresh berries. There are wines matched to every course.

Ravintola C
MODERN FINNISH €€€

(☑010-617-9760; www.ravintola-c.fi; Rautatienkatu 20; mains €25-29; ☺5pm-midnight Tue-Sat) ☑ In a pristine dining room near the train station, this top Tampere restaurant creates innovative, beautifully presented modern dishes from a short menu with a focus on local ingredients and traditions. Meat tends to be slow-cooked and treated with respect, and there's always a non-dull vegetarian option.

Tiiliholvi
FINNISH €€€

(☑020-766-9061; www.tiiliholvi.fi; Kauppakatu 10; mains €29-36; ☺11am-3pm & 5-11pm Mon-Thu, 11am-3pm & 5pm-midnight Fri, 3pm-midnight Sat) Set in the brick vaulted cellar of a Jugendstil (art nouveau) building, Tiiliholvi is into its fifth decade. It's still old-fashioned in feel, but the food isn't, and there are some excellent flavour combinations, along with beautiful presentation and personal explanations by the chef if the restaurant's not too busy.

Bertha
MODERN FINNISH €€€

(☑0400-355-477; www.bertha.fi; Rautatienkatu 14; 2/3 courses €37/43; ☺4.30-9pm Tue-Fri, 1-9pm Sat) Cheerful rather than formal, this restaurant presents high-class fare with modern principles and avant-garde flavour combinations without too much frippery. Inventive fish dishes are reliably excellent, and beware of filling up on the delicious home-baked organic bread. A couple of glitches – charging for tap water? – let it down. Book; it doesn't like walk-ins.

🍷 Drinking & Nightlife

Panimoravintola Plevna (p131) and Tuulensuu (p131) are fine places for a beer or two.

★Café Europa
BAR

(www.ravintola.fi/europa; Aleksanterinkatu 29; ☺noon-midnight Mon-Tue, noon-2am Wed-Thu, noon-3am Fri & Sat, 1pm-midnight Sun; ☎) Lavishly furnished with horsehair couches, armchairs, mirrors, chandeliers and paintings, this successfully fuses a re-creation of a 1930s-style old-Europe cafe, and is a popular meeting spot for students and anyone else who appreciates comfort, board games, Belgian and German beers, and generously proportioned sandwiches and salads. There's good summer seating out the front.

Teerenpeli
PUB

(www.teerenpeli.com; Hämeenkatu 25; ☺noon-2am Sun-Thu, noon-3am Fri & Sat) On the main street, this is a good place with excellent microbrewery beer and cider. There's a relaxing, candlelit interior, heated terrace and heaps of choice at the taps. There's a huge downstairs space too, with comfy seating.

O'Connell's
PUB

(www.oconnells.fi; Rautatienkatu 24; ☺4pm-1am Sun-Mon, 4pm-2am Tue-Fri, 2pm-2am Sat) Popular with both Finns and expats, this rambling Irish pub is handy for the train station and has plenty of time-worn, comfortable seating and an air of bonhomie. Its best feature is the range of interesting beers on tap and carefully selected bottled imports. There's regular free live music.

Nordic Gastropub
PUB

(www.gastropub.net/nordic; Otavalankatu 3; ☺3pm-2am Sun-Fri, noon-2am Sat) The range of perfectly poured microbrewed Finnish beers on tap, backed up by guest ales from around the Nordic lands, would tempt anybody in for a pint. There's a small selection of good-value, original Nordic-based dishes to back it up.

Suvi   BAR
(www.laivaravintolasuvi.fi; Laukontori; ⊘10am-2am Jun-Sep) Moored alongside Laukontori Quay, this is a typical Finnish boat bar offering no-nonsense deck-top drinking. Prepare a boarding party and lap up the afternoon sun.

Ruma   CLUB, BAR
(www.ruma.fi; Murtokatu 1; ⊘6pm-4am Wed-Sat) A cool spot with offbeat decor, quirky lighting, friendly staff, and a mixture of Finnish and European pop and alternative rock. There's a cover of €3 to €6 on weekends. Opens 8pm in summer.

☆ Entertainment

Tampere is a thriving performing-arts centre. There are several theatres; a program of what's on is available from the tourist office.

Live Music

Tampere-Talo   CONCERT VENUE
(Tampere Hall; ☑03-243-4111; www.tampere-talo. fi; Yliopistonkatu 55) Classical concerts are held in this spectacular modern hall. Performances by Tampere Filharmonia (www. tampere.fi/filharmonia) are on Fridays from September to May. In addition to this it puts on regular chamber-music concerts, and visiting opera and ballet performances.

Klubi   LIVE MUSIC
(www.klubi.net; Tullikamarinaukio 2; ⊘11am-10pm Mon-Tue, 11am-4am Wed-Sat) This cavernous place, near the train station, is Tampere's main indoor live-music venue; there are usually several bands playing every week, and big Finnish names regularly swing by for concerts.

Paapan Kapakka   JAZZ
(☑03-211-0037; www.paapankapakka.fi; Koskikatu 9; ⊘noon-midnight Sun-Mon, noon-2am Tue-Thu, noon-3am Fri & Sat) A bit of a Tampere institution, it offers live jazz, blues or swing every evening. The crowd is mostly 30-plus and really gets into it; this can be a special place on a good night.

Cinema

Niagara   CINEMA
(www.elokuvakeskus.fi/niagara; Kehräsaari B-talo; tickets €6-9) In the Kehräsaari complex, this shows original-version art-house films daily.

Sport

Ilves & Tappara   ICE HOCKEY
(www.ilves.com) Tampere's two ice-hockey teams – Ilves and Tappara – are among Fin-

land's best; the city is generally regarded as the Finnish home of the sport. Hakametsä Ice Stadium, 2km east of the train station, has matches from September to March. Buy tickets (around €15 to €35) here or from www.lippupalvelu.fi (Tappara) or www. lippu.fi (Ilves). Eastbound bus 5, 20 or 24 gets you there.

🛍 Shopping

Kehräsaari   CRAFTS
(⊘10am-6pm Mon-Fri, 10am-4pm Sat) Just east of Laukontori Market Sq, this attractive converted brick factory has Finnish craft boutiques.

Tallipiha   CRAFTS
(www.tallipiha.fi; Kuninkaankatu 4; ⊘10am-6pm Mon-Fri, 10am-5pm Sat, 11am-5pm Sun Jun-Aug) This restored collection of 19th-century stableyards and staff cottages houses artists and craftworkers who make handicrafts, chocolates, ceramics and shoes. The cafe and a shop or two open outside summer, but there's not much going on, except at Christmastime.

ℹ Information

Visit Tampere (☑03-5656-6800; www. visittampere.fi; Hämeenkatu 14B; ⊘9am-5pm Mon-Fri Sep-May, 9am-6pm Mon-Fri, 10am-3pm Sat & Sun Jun-Aug; 🛜) On the main street in the centre of town. Can book activities and events.

ℹ Getting There & Away

There are left-luggage lockers at the bus and train stations.

AIR

Airlines flying to/from Tampere:

Finnair/Flybe Flies to Helsinki (though it's more convenient on the train) with connections to other Finnish cities.

Ryanair Daily services to several European destinations including London Stansted, Frankfurt, Milan and Girona.

SAS Flies direct to Stockholm.

BOAT

Lakeboats from Tampere can take you south to Hämeenlinna via Visavuori, or north to Virrat via Ruovesi.

BUS

Regular express buses run from Helsinki (€27, 2¾ hours) and Turku (€25.60, two to three hours), and most other major towns in Finland are served from here.

TRAIN

The train station is central. Express trains run hourly to/from Helsinki (€39, 1¾ hours), and there are direct trains to Turku (€33.30, 1¾ hours) and other cities.

Getting Around

TO/FROM THE AIRPORT

Tampere-Pirkkala airport is 15km southwest; arriving flights are met by a **bus** (✆ 0100-29400; www.paunu.fi; €4.70) to the city centre (€4.70, 30 minutes). **Tokee** (✆ 0200-39000; www.airpro.fi) serves Ryanair flights, leaving from the train station forecourt about 2½ hours before take-off (€6).

Shared **airport taxis** (✆ 0100-4131; www.taksitampere.fi; per person €19) must be booked in advance from the city to the airport. A regular cab will cost around €35.

BUS

The local bus service is extensive. A one- /24-hour ticket costs €2.60/6.50. Check route maps online at joukkoliikenne.tampere.fi

CAR

Several car-hire companies operate at the airport and in town. **Bikes** can be hired from about €15 a day from several places, including **Holiday Inn Tampere** (✆ 03-245-5111; Yliopistonkatu 44; per 24hr €15). The **Citybike** (www.tamperecitybike.fi; ⊘ mid-Jun–mid-Oct) scheme requires a €10 fee and €40 deposit – do this online. Get the key from the tourist office and you have access to a whole network.

ROUTE 66

✆ 03

Route 66, starting northeast of Tampere and winding 75km north to Virrat, is one of Finland's oldest roads. When the famous song was translated into Finnish, popular rock star Jussi Raittinen adapted the lyrics to this highway in his song 'Valtatie 66'. It's a good drive, through young pine forest and lakescapes; the route is parallelled by the Poet's Way lake cruise. Good hiking and fishing opportunities exist; Ruovesi is the best-equipped base. Outside the June to August high season, there's little going on.

Kallenaution Kievari

Dating from 1757, this charismatic wooden roadhouse (www.kallenautio.fi; ⊘10am-6pm mid-May–mid-Aug) is the oldest building along Route 66. The complex has a beautiful cafe; sit at old long wooden tables and imagine winter travellers huddled around the blazing fire. There are handicraft exhibitions, including on *päre,* thin wooden sheeting used for shingle roofs and also burned to provide light in houses. Historically this was often the cause of blazes that destroyed entire towns.

Siikaneva

This large protected **marshland** accommodates some unusual bird species, including owls. It's a great place to walk, with duckboard paths across the peat bog alternating with stretches in peaceful pine forests. There are two loops: one of 3km, and one of about 10km. The entrance is signposted 20km south of Ruovesi; you pass some sinister-looking military buildings on the way.

Ruovesi

Peaceful and pretty, Ruovesi's the main town on the Route 66 stretch and has the most accommodation choices. Apart from enjoying the nearby lakeside, there is not a huge amount to see or do, but it makes a good base for exploring the area's attractions by car.

⊙ Sights & Activities

The lakes around Ruovesi are prime fishing country; various fishing guides can take you out on trips in the area: the website www.zanderland.fi is a good resource.

Ruoveden Kotiseutumuseo　　　MUSEUM
(✆ 044-526-2118; www.ruovesi.fi; Museotie 2; adult/child €2/1; ⊘11am-5pm Tue-Sat late Jun–mid-Aug) The local open-air museum has a collection of 18th-century farm buildings including a picturesque wooden windmill.

🛏 Sleeping & Eating

Haapasaaren Lomakylä　　　CAMPGROUND €
(✆ 044-080-0290; www.haapasaari.fi; Haapasaarentie 5; tents €16 plus adult/child €5/2, cabins €40-70, 4-/8-person cottages €155/225; P 🛜) This is a great place to stay on an islet north of the town, connected to town by a causeway. There's water all around, and fabulous self-contained cottage with sauna, barbecue and kitchen. The cabins are simpler, but also have basic cooking facilities. It's great for kids, with a large play area. It discounts heavily when things are quiet.

★ **Ylä-Tuuhosen Maatila**　　　B&B €€
(✆ 03-472-6426; www.yla-tuuhonen.fi; Tanhuantie 105; s/d €60/80, cabins s €45, d €60-80; P 🛜)

A rustic, historic organic farm run by generous-hearted owners, who offer three pretty rooms (sharing bathrooms) and an excellent kitchen and lounge. There's a variety of cabins available too, plus evening meals. Head 9km north from Ruovesi on Route 66, then right onto Rd 3481 (signposted to Haapamäki). Continue 9km; the farmhouse is 1km up a turn-off on the left.

Hotelli Liera HOTEL €€
(☑ 050-442-4600; www.hotelli-liera.fi; Ruovedentie 11; s/d €65/95) One of two hotels in the town centre, this looks like a dive outside but is a friendly spot operated out of a bar. Rooms are surprisingly good, with heaps of space, sofas and peaceful pastoral views to the lake, plus a long shared balcony divided by privacy screens. You get breakfast on a tray in the morning, and the pub does no-nonsense pizzas, fish and steaks until 10pm.

ℹ Information

Tourist Information (Wiljamakasiini; ☑ 044-787-1388; www.ruovesi.fi; Ruovedentie 5; ⊘ 11am-6pm Jun-Aug) Summer tourist information in this old wooden building on the road through town.

ℹ Getting There & Away

Several daily buses connect Ruovesi with Tampere and other places in the region. The S/S *Tarjanne*, travelling along the Poet's Way between Tampere and Virrat, stops at Ruovesi.

Helvetinjärvi National Park

Northwest of Ruovesi, this park's main attraction is narrow **Helvetinkolu Gorge**, gouged out by retreating glaciers at the end of the last Ice Age. The numerous trails include a walk to **Haukanhieta**, a sandy beach and popular camping spot on Haukkajärvi. There are designated campsites through the park and a free hut at Helvetinkolu, a couple of kilometres from the parking area. Signposted 8km west off Route 66 about 9km north of Ruovesi.

Virrat

Virrat is the end point of Route 66 and the Poet's Way cruise from Tampere, though itself not an especially romantic place. There's little accommodation, but **Domus Virrat** (☑ 03-475-5600; www.domusvirrat.fi; Sipiläntie 3;

s/d €48/72; ⊘ early-Jun–mid-Aug; P 🤶) is a reliable summer hotel not far up from the harbour. Smart rooms have kitchens (though not utensils) and plenty of space; there's also a tennis court, bookable sauna and bikes for hire. Breakfast is available.

There's **tourist information** (☑ 03-485-1276; www.virrat.org; Mäkitie 2; ⊘ 10am-7pm Mon-Fri) in the libary and limited information is also available in the bar by the harbour, 1km from town. Several daily buses head from Virrat to Tampere and other towns in the region.

KEURUU
☑ 014

Sweet Keuruu sits in a lovely location on the northern shore of Keurusselkä. Its major drawcard is its fascinating **wooden church** (adult/child €2/free; ⊘ 11am-5pm Jun–mid-Aug, ask at museum rest of year), built in 1758, with superb portraits of Bible characters (although the artist didn't complete the set, due to a pay dispute), and a firmament peopled by scattered beasts, angels and devils. There are also photos of the mummified corpses buried below the chancel, and a set of stocks for miscreants.

Across the road (and railway), **Kamana** (☑ 040-572-5640; www.keuruu.fi; Kangasmannilantie 4; ⊘ 11am-5pm daily Jun-Aug, Mon-Fri Sep-May) serves as local museum and tourist office. It's one of a clutch of historic buildings here (Vanha Keuruu), housing craft shops and the like. The cafe serves tasty buffet lunches.

Lake cruises on historic **M/S Elias Lönnrot** (☑ 010-422-5600; www.eliaksenristeilyt.fi; ⊘ early-Jun–mid-Aug) run Wednesday to Sunday in summer. It also sails to Mänttä on Saturdays in July (one way/return €26/39, 2¾ hours each way).

Another magnificent wooden church is 28km east of here at Petäjävesi (p160).

Buses run to Keuruu from Tampere and Jyväskylä. Trains between Jyväskylä and Seinäjoki also stop here.

MÄNTTÄ
☑ 03

Mänttä, set on a narrow isthmus between fast-flowing rapids, grew around its paper mill, founded in the mid-19th century by the Serlachius dynasty. Progressive in outlook, the family endeavoured to build a model industrial community and endowed the town with noble buildings and art.

◉ Sights

★ Gösta
GALLERY

(www.serlachius.fi; Joenniementie 47; adult/child incl Gustaf €8/free; ☉10am-6pm daily Jun-Aug, noon-5pm Wed-Sun Sep-May) Mänttä's principal attraction was once the private home of Gösta Serlachius and is now among Finland's premier galleries. Situated 2km east of the town centre in elegant grounds, it comprises two buildings: a spectacular new wooden gallery houses high-quality exhibitions of contemporary art, while the original home houses an excellent collection of Finnish golden-age works.

All the big names are here, including seemingly two dozens of Gallen-Kallelas, plenty of Edelfelts and Schjerfbecks, as well as Wickström sculptures. Look out for a mischievous painting of Gallen-Kallela getting pissed with his mate Sibelius, and Hugo Simberg's whimsical *Entrance to Hades*. There's also a sizeable European collection, including a fine Deposition by Van der Weyden.

Gustaf
MUSEUM

(www.serlachius.fi; Erik Serlachiuksenkatu 2; adult/child incl Gösta €8/free; ☉10am-6pm daily Jun-Aug, noon-5pm Wed-Sun Sep-May) In the town centre, an elegant white 1930s modernist mansion, formerly company HQ of the Serlachius family that founded the town, is now a museum. There's a most comprehensive display on the history of the paperworks and family, with audio exhibits on every conceivable aspect: you'd be here a week listening to them all. The attractive building also has two to three reliably excellent temporary exhibitions. Borrow a bike here to explore the town.

⌷ Sleeping

Hotelli Alexander
HOTEL €

(☑03-474-9232; www.hotellialexander.fi; Kauppakatu 23; s/d €59/82; P☞) In the centre of town is a welcoming and very decent option with compact rooms above a pleasant modern cafe. It also runs a nearby summer hotel; prices are similar but rooms have kitchens.

❶ Getting There & Away

On Saturdays in July, you can catch the M/S *Elias Lönnrot* from Keuruu. Several weekday buses and a couple on weekends run to Jyväskylä (€20.60, 1½ hours) via Keuruu, and Tampere (€20.60, 1½ to 1¾ hours). The town appears as Mänttä-Vilppula on timetables.

TAMPERE TO HÄMEENLINNA

Several interesting sights lie just off the main Tampere–Hämeenlinna motorway.

Visavuori

Once the studio of renowned sculptor Emil Wickström (1864–1942), **Visavuori** (☑03-543-6528; www.visavuori.com; adult/child €8/2; ☉10am-6pm daily Jun-Aug, 10am-4pm Tue-Sun Sep-Nov & Feb-May, 10am-4pm Tue-Fri Dec-Jan) has a stunning situation on a ridge with water on both sides. It consists of three houses, the oldest of which was the home of Wickström, built in 1902 in Karelian and Finnish Romantic styles, and containing fantastic art nouveau furniture; it really brings the man to life and is worth visiting first. The beautiful studio next door, with dozens of models and sculptures, was built in 1903.

Pervasive smells of baking oblige stopping for a *pulla* (cardamom-flavoured bun) in the brick-vaulted cafe. Kari Paviljonki is dedicated to Kari Suomalainen, Emil Wickström's grandson, whose long career as a political cartoonist spanned several decades. His cartoons are excellent; even more amusing is the 1959 award from the US National Cartoonist Society for 'exposing the deceit of communism'.

Visavuori is 4km (signposted) off the motorway. Summer boats between Hämeenlinna and Tampere stop here.

Iittala

Little Iittala, 23km northwest of Hämeenlinna, is world-famous for the glass produced in its factory, and has been at the forefront of Finnish design for decades.

Behind the large **shop** (www.iittala.com; ☉10am-6pm Sep–mid-May, 10am-8pm mid-May–Aug) and restaurant, a craft village includes the **Lasimuseo** (Glass Museum; www.designmuseum.fi; adult/child €4/2; ☉11am-5pm May-Aug, weekends only rest of year), whose two levels cover the history of the glassworks and glass-making process, with pieces from most of the firm's famous ranges on display. Free tours of the nearby factory leave from here at noon and 3pm Monday to Friday; otherwise you can watch a glass-blower at work in an adjacent shop.

Trains between Hämeenlinna (15 minutes) and Tampere (45 minutes) stop in Iittala, and buses also run here weekdays from Hämeen-linna. Tampere–Hämeenlinna express buses stop on the highway 2km from town.

Hattula & Parola

Nine kilometres north of Hämeenlinna, Hattula has one of Finland's oldest and most memorable churches. **Pyhän Ristin Kirk-ko** (www.hattula-evl.fi; guided tour €6; ⊙11am-5pm mid-May–mid-Aug) `FREE` dates from the early 1400s and has an interior filled with fabulous naive frescoes from the early 16th century. They tell key Bible stories as you go around the nave; the Tree of Jesse in the sacristy is particularly fine. It must have been an awe-inspiring place for illiterate pa-rishioners; it still is. Grab the interpretative booklet as you go in, or take the free guided tour. The nearby **old grain store** houses the information office and sells handicrafts. The church is easy to reach from Hämeenlinna by public transport; take bus 5, 6 or 16.

Four kilometres away, on the edge of the village of Parola, and easily accessed off the Tampere–Hämeenlinna motorway, **Pans-sarimuseo** (www.panssarimuseo.fi; Hattulantie 334, Parola; adult/child €7/4, joint ticket with Mili-taria museum in Hämeenlinna €10; ⊙10am-6pm May-Sep, 10am-3pm Oct-Apr) is an imposing exhibition of tanks and armour on a hillside above a museum that puts them in context and has an exhibition of anti-tank weapon-ry and Finnish war memorabilia. You can climb into some tanks; it's a good one for vehicle-obsessed kids.

HÄME

This region of southern central Finland, also known as Tavastia, has historically been an important one. The castle at Hämeenlinna was the middle of the line of three imposing Swedish fortifications across the breadth of Finland. Today this ancient stronghold con-trasts with the modernity of Lahti, the re-gion's other main city.

Hämeenlinna

☑ 03 / POP 67,800

Dominated by its namesake, majestic Häme Castle, Hämeenlinna (Swedish: Tavastehus) is Finland's oldest inland town, founded in 1649, though a trading post had existed here since the 9th century. The Swedes built the castle in the 13th century, and Hämeenlin-na developed into an administrative, edu-cational and garrison town around it. The town is quiet but picturesque, and its wealth of museums will keep you busy for a day or two. It makes a good stop between Helsinki and Tampere; you could head on to the lat-ter by lakeboat.

◉ Sights & Activities

Despite its small size, Hämeenlinna has a wealth of museums and other attractions. Combined entry to Hämeenlinna, the Vankilamuseo and Museo Militaria is €14.

★**Hämeenlinna** CASTLE
(Häme Castle; www.nba.fi; adult/child €8/4; ⊙10am-4pm Mon-Fri, 11am-4pm Sat & Sun) Hämeenlinna means Häme Castle, so it's no surprise that this bulky twin-towered red-brick fortress is the town's pride and most significant attraction. Construction was be-gun in the 1260s by the Swedes, who wanted to establish a military redoubt against the power of Novgorod. It was originally built on an island, but, the lake receded and ne-cessitated the building of new walls. It nev-er saw serious military action and, after the Russian takeover of 1809, was converted into a jail. The interior has a modern exhibition annexe, displaying period costumes and fur-niture, tacked on to the original bare-roomed building. Multilingual guided tours are on of-fer – book them ahead outside of summer.

Vankilamuseo MUSEUM
(☑03-621-2977; www.hameenlinna.fi; adult/child €6/2; ⊙11am-5pm Tue-Sun) Häme Castle's old cellblock, last used in 1993, has been convert-ed into a prison museum where you can visit a solitary confinement cell or see graffiti left by former inmates. Most interesting are three cells left more or less as they were when the inmates departed, along with a brief descrip-tion of their occupants' crime and lifestyle. There's also a sauna, where prisoners would sometimes violently settle disputes.

Museo Militaria MUSEUM
(Tykistömuseo; www.museomilitaria.fi; adult/child €8/3; ⊙11am-5pm Sep-May, 10am-6pm Jun-Aug) There are numerous museums devoted to Finnish involvement in WWII, but this takes the cake. There are three floors packed with war memorabilia, including good informa-tion in English on the beginnings of the Winter War. Outside, and in a separate hall, is a collection of phallic heavy artillery big enough to start a war on several fronts.

Hämeenlinna

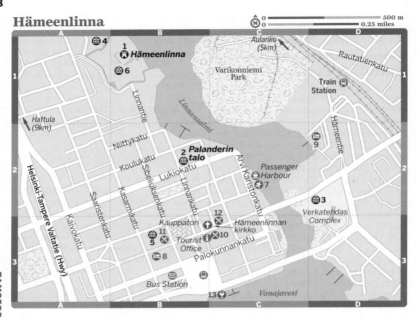

Hämeenlinna

Hämeenlinnan Taidemuseo   GALLERY
(www.hameenlinna.fi; Viipurintie 2; adult/child €6/
free; ⊙11am-6pm Tue-Thu, 11am-5pm Fri-Sun)
Housed in a former granary designed by CL
Engel, the town gallery has an interesting collection of Finnish art from the 19th and 20th
centuries. Notable is Gallen-Kallela's painting
of the *Kalevala*'s final scene, with the shaman Väinämöinen leaving Finland, representing the conquest of Christianity. A couple
of Schjerfbecks include a *Rigoletto* painted
when she was just 19. The building opposite
houses excellent temporary exhibitions.

★**Palanderin talo**   MUSEUM
(www.hameenlinna.fi; Linnankatu 16; adult/child
€5/2, incl Sibeliuksen syntymäkoti €8; ⊙noon-
4pm Tue-Sun May-Aug, Sat & Sun Sep-Apr) Finland
loves its house-museums and this is among
the best, offering a wonderful insight into
well-off 19th-century Finnish life, thanks
to excellent English-speaking guided tours.
There's splendid imperial and art nouveau
furniture as well as delicate little touches
like a double-sided mirror to spy on street
fashion, and a set of authentic children's
drawings from the period.

Sibeliuksen syntymäkoti   MUSEUM
(www.hameenlinna.fi; Hallituskatu 11; adult/child
€5/2, incl Palanderin talo €8; ⊙10am-4pm May-Aug,
noon-4pm Tue-Sun Sep-Apr) Johan Julius Christian (Jean) Sibelius was born in Hämeenlinna in 1865 and was schooled here, but the
town makes surprisingly little fuss about
it. His childhood home is a small museum
containing photographs, letters, his upright

piano and some family furniture. It's a likeable place, although uninformative about his later life. Concert performances on summer Sundays are free with an entry ticket.

Aulanko PARK

(www.aulanko.fi) North of the town centre, this was created early in the 20th century by Hugo Standertskjöld, who spent a fortune creating a beautiful central-European-style park with ponds, swans, pavilions, a granite fortress and exotic trees. Although the best way to explore it is on foot, the sealed one-way road loop is accessible by private car. Bus 2, 13 or 17 will take you to Aulanko from central Hämeenlinna, or it's a pleasant 5km bike ride.

Suomen Hopealinja CRUISE

(Finnish Silverline; ☑ 010-422-5600; www.hopeal inja.fi) Cruises to Visavuori (one way/return €48/72, 2¾ hours) at 11.30am, Wednesday to Saturday between early June and mid-August. You can continue to Tampere (one way/return €58/87, 8½ hours).

🛏 Sleeping

Aulanko Camping CAMPGROUND, COTTAGES €

(☑ 03-675-9772; www.aulankocamping.fi; Aulangonheikkiläntie 168; tent/van site incl 4 people €20/29, cottages €90-100; P ⚙) By the main entrance to Aulanko park, this offers good cottages and great grassy campsites on a spectacular lakeshore. There's a cafe, restaurant and sauna.

Hotelli Emilia HOTEL €€

(☑ 03-612-2106; www.hotelliemilia.fi; Raatihuoneenkatu 23; s/d €99/119; P ⚙) Located on the pedestrian street, this privately owned hotel is a good deal. Sizeable modern rooms, some of which can be connected for families, offer large windows, crisp white sheets and air-conditioning. There's a bar with terrace seating, a sauna, weekend nightclub and worthwhile buffet breakfast. Weekend prices (single/double €86/98) are also in place from June to August.

Sokos Hotel Vaakuna HOTEL €€

(☑ 020-123-4636; www.sokoshotels.fi; Possentie 7; s/d €125/145; P @ ⚙) Across the river from the town centre and very near the train station, this attractive hotel has been designed to echo Häme Castle. Many of the rooms, all recently renovated, have great water views, as does the rounded restaurant, and the sunny bar terrace is particularly pleasant on a summer evening.

🍴 Eating & Drinking

In summer two adjacent **boat bars** (Paasikiventie; ⊙ 11am-2am mid-May–mid-Sep) offer lakeside drinking on floating wooden decks.

A MUSICAL GHOST

Leaving racing drivers out, Jean Sibelius, born in 1865 in Hämeenlinna, probably still takes the garland of most famous Finn. Apart from his towering musical legacy, the role he played in the cultural flowering that inspired Finnish independence makes him a legend in his homeland.

Like many artists of the time, Sibelius was fascinated by mythology and forests at the heart of Finnishness. His first major works (*Kullervo*, *En Saga* and the *Karelia Suite*) were based on the *Kalevala* epic, but his overtly political 1899 *Finlandia* symphony became a powerful symbol of the Finnish independence struggle and is still his best-known work. His genius lay in his ability to distill the essence of traditional forms into a tight modern product. The best example, his masterful seventh symphony, shoehorns a powerful feeling of Finnish landscape and an epic Nordic quality into a very compact package.

Before his death in 1957, at the age of 92, he had produced very little in three decades. His missing eighth symphony is an El Dorado legend, but evidence suggests that he consigned it to the fire in the 1940s.

A Sibelius trail could lead from his Helsinki monument to Ainola, where he lived with wife Aino Järnefelt (sister of the painter Eero), and their six daughters, his birthplace in Hämeenlinna and the excellent Sibelius Museum in Turku. Festivals devoted to Sibelius include at Loviisa, where he had a summer home, and Lahti, whose symphony orchestra is famed for its expertise in his works.

While Finland's current musical pre-eminence owes much to his legacy, younger musicians also sometimes feel that it can be difficult to escape the shadow of Sibelius, whose lofty ghost still paces the forests and lakeshores of his beloved land.

Laurell CAFE €
(☑03-467-7722; www.laurell.fi; Sibeliuksenkatu 7; pastries €2-3; ⊘8.30am-6pm Mon-Fri, 8.30am-8pm Wed, 8.30am-5pm Sat, 11am-5pm Sun; ☎) This cafe on the market square is a Hämeenlinna stalwart and popular meeting place. There's an appetising selection of squishy cakes, rolls, pastries and pasties, both savoury and sweet and including many options for special diets. A more sandwich-y **branch** (www.laurell.fi; Raatihuoneenkatu 11; lunches €5.50-9.50; ⊘7am-5pm Mon-Fri, 9am-2pm Sat; ☎) is in the same building as the tourist office.

★**Piparkakkutalo** FINNISH €€
(☑03-648-040; www.ravintolapiparkakkutalo.fi; Kirkkorinne 2; mains €16-28; ⊘11am-10pm Tue-Thu, 11am-11pm Fri, noon-11pm Sat) Pleasing for both eye and stomach, the 'gingerbread house' occupies a 1906 shingled house once home to artist Albert Edelfeldt; the interior still has a warm, domestic feel. Food includes Finnish classics as well as more adventurous fare, all served in generous portions. There's a cosy pub downstairs.

ℹ Information

Tourist Office (☑03-621-3373; www.hameenlinna.fi; Raatihuoneenkatu 11; ⊘9am-4pm Mon-Fri; ☎) In the Kastelli information centre.

ℹ Getting There & Away

Boats (p139) cruise to Tampere via Visavuori in summer.

Hourly buses between Helsinki (€17, 1½ hours) and Tampere (€12.60, one hour) stop in Hämeenlinna. From Turku, there are several buses daily (€29.90, two hours).

The train station is 1km from the town centre, across the bridge. Hourly trains between Helsinki (€21 to €26, one hour) and Tampere (€19 to €22, 40 minutes) stop here. From Turku, change in Toijala.

Lahti

☑03 / POP 103,400
The region is steeped in history – indeed, some of Finland's oldest prehistoric sites are to be found not far away – but Lahti itself is basically a modern town, with an important technology sector. Its name is famous for winter sports – the frighteningly high ski jumps here have hosted several world championships – and classical music, with the city's symphony orchestra having gained worldwide recognition under former conductor Osmo Vänskä.

Lahti

◎ Sights

Lahden Urheilukeskus SPORTS CENTRE
At Lahti's Sports Centre, a 10-minute walk west of town, things are dominated by three imposing ski jumps, the biggest standing 73m high and stretching 116m. You'll often see high-level jumpers training in summer. There's a whole complex here, including the football stadium, a summer swimming pool, ski tracks and the delightful ski museum.

➡ **Hiihtomuseo**
(Ski Museum; www.lahdenmuseot.fi; adult/child €7/3; ⊘9am-4pm Tue-Fri, 11am-5pm Sat & Sun Sep–mid-Jun, 10am-5pm Tue-Fri, 11am-5pm Sat & Sun mid-Jun–Aug) A history of skis includes excavated examples from 2000 years ago. The fun starts in the next room: frustrate yourself on the ski-jump simulator, then try the biathlon: skiing on Velcro before nailing five bulls-eyes. In summer take the chairlift up to the **observation terrace** (adult/child €6/3, incl Hiihtomuseo €10/5; ⊘10am-5pm Mon-Fri, 11am-5pm Sat-Sun Jun-Aug) at the top of the ski jump; great if there's someone practising, and good for the views in any event.

Lahden Historiallinen Museo MUSEUM
(www.lahdenmuseot.fi; Lahdenkatu 4; adult/child €7/3; ⊘9am-4pm Tue-Fri, 11am-5pm Sat & Sun Sep–mid-Jun, 10am-5pm Tue-Fri, 11am-5pm Sat & Sun mid-Jun–Aug) Lahti's historical museum is in a beautiful old manor house by the bus station. Changing exhibitions illustrate

Lahti

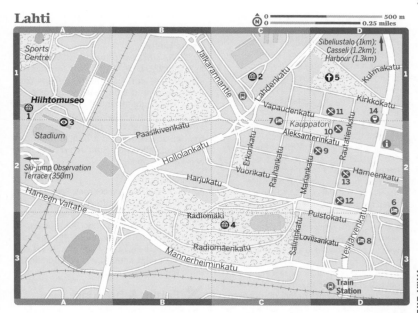

aspects of Lahti's history, while the middle floor is mostly devoted to the collection of former diplomat Klaus Holma. It's a treasury of French and Italian religious art, rococo furniture and fine porcelain; excellent interactive screens allow you to access detailed information on every piece.

Radio- Ja Tv-Museo MUSEUM
(www.lahdenmuseot.fi; Radiomäki; adult/child €7/3; ⊘9am-4pm Tue-Fri, 11am-5pm Sat & Sun Sep–mid-Jun, 10am-5pm Tue-Fri, 11am-5pm Sat & Sun mid-Jun–Aug) This radio and television museum, on a hill by the radio mast just south of the centre, has an interesting history of those appliances in the basement. The entrance level has a feast of interactive exhibits. Some, like classic '60s Finnish TV hits, won't keep you long, but the kids will love the chance to record their own radio show, or to find out why weather reporters can't wear blue.

Ristinkirkko CHURCH
(Church of the Cross; www.lahdenseurakuntayhtyma. fi; Kirkkokatu 4; ⊘10am-3pm) This striking church was designed by Alvar Aalto and finished in 1978. The brick exterior and concrete steeple give little clue as to the interior, a white and airy triangular space with wooden benches echoing the organ's pipes. Structural lines angle towards the simple wooden

cross behind the altar or perhaps emanate from it like rays.

Sibeliustalo CONCERT HALL
(Sibelius Hall; www.sibeliustalo.fi; Ankkurikatu 7) By the harbour on Vesijärvi, this spectacular concert hall in glass and wood is the home of the top-notch Lahti Symphony Orchestra, which is responsible for some of the best Sibelius recordings of recent years (there's a good selection in the shop here). The hall is wonderfully lit at night and has excellent acoustics.

🏃 Activities

At the sports centre, Lahden Urheilukeskus, there's a winter ice-skating hall and 145km of cross-country ski tracks (great for summer biking too), some illuminated. Skiing and skating gear can be rented.

Cruises

In summer there are several daily one- to two-hour **cruises** (€6.50 to €12) from the passenger harbour.

Päijänne Risteilyt Hildén CRUISE
(☑014-263-447; www.paijanne-risteilythilden.fi; ⊘Jun-Aug) Offers a large variety of lake cruises from Lahti, including day-long voyages to Jyväskylä (€76, 10½ hours, Tuesday) and

SKI-JUMPING

Finland takes the apparently suicidal sport of ski-jumping seriously, and Lahti is a major centre. You'll see competitors practising even in summer, with the 'whoosh' as they descend the ramp sounding like fighter aircraft on manouevres.

Technical innovations over the years have added significant distance to the sport, which started in 19th-century Norway. Ski-jumpers lean forward, keeping skis in a 'V' as they sail towards, and hopefully beyond, the target line, usually set at 90m or 120m. Points are given for style as well as distance, so a slick, controlled flight and landing is preferable to a messy, longer jump. The 'extreme' version is ski-flying, where special pistes produce extraordinary leaps of nearly 240m.

You can't really try it as a visitor: you have to join a local ski-jumping club, and start on gentle slopes before graduating to the serious jumps, but it's certainly worth watching these gravity-defying athletes perform.

shorter jaunts, including trips to the Vääksy canal, some with optional lunch buffet.

✨ Festivals & Events

Ski Games SKIING
(www.lahtiskigames.com) Lahti hosts several annual winter sports events including the Ski Games in early March.

★ Sibelius Festival MUSIC
(www.sinfonialahti.fi) This festival in mid-September has performances by Sinfonia Lahti, the city's famous symphony orchestra.

🛏 Sleeping

There are central chain hotels; the closest characterful hotel is at Messilä (p143).

Lahden Kansanopisto HOSTEL €
(✆03-87810; www.lahdenkansanopisto.fi; Harjukatu 46; dm €28, s/d €55/80, without bathroom €45/70, all incl breakfast; ☺Jun–mid-Aug; 🅿🛜) A standout budget option, this college offers excellent summer accommodation in an enormous art nouveau building. Rooms feature comfortable beds, desks and bedside lamps, and there's a good kitchen on each

floor. Shared facilities are spotless. HI discount; dorm rates only available to members.

Patria Hostel GUESTHOUSE €
(✆03-782-3783; www.patriahostel.fi; Vesijärvenkatu 3; s/d €37/54; 🛜) Very handy for the train station, this curious guesthouse has compact singles and twins with washbasin, TV and cheery aquamarine sheets on the beds. Some rooms have bunks; front rooms are airier but the street's pretty noisy. There's free tea and coffee and a bun in the morning. Phone ahead for Sunday arrivals as reception isn't open.

Omenahotelli HOTEL €€
(✆0600-18018; www.omena.com; Rauhankatu 14; r €50-80; 🛜) With a great location on the central square, this staffless hotel makes a value-packed place to stay. Book online or via the terminal in the lobby. Rooms have a double bed and two fold-outs. If it's full, there's a similar hotel run by Forenom in the same building.

🍴 Eating & Drinking

The place to enjoy the summer sunshine is down at the harbour where a number of beer terraces, boat bars, cute cafes in wooden warehouses and the old station building, and an historic lake-ship-turned-ice-cream kiosk draw the crowds.

Café Sinuhe CAFE, BAKERY €
(www.sinuhe.fi; Mariankatu 21; light meals €5-10; ☺6.30am-7pm Mon-Fri, 9am-4pm Sat, 10am-4pm Sun; 🛜) Half a block from the kauppatori, this is Lahti's best central cafe, with folk streaming in at all hours to sip mellow coffee, fork-up salads bursting with fresh things or buy a loaf of crusty bread.

Mamma Maria ITALIAN €
(✆03-751-6716; www.mammamaria.fi; Vapaudenkatu 10; mains €9-25; ☺11am-10pm Mon-Thu, 11am-11pm Fri, noon-11pm Sat, noon-9pm Sun) With a range of risottos, chicken, pastas and pizzas as well as horse steaks, this Italian eatery on the kauppatori is a firm Lahti favourite. Quantities are generous and the food's tasty enough, particularly the homemade gelati.

Kauppahalli MARKET €
(☺8am-5pm Mon-Fri, 8am-2.30pm Sat) 🍴 The kauppahalli is a cosy spot for a coffee or snack; in fact it seems to have more cafes than stalls.

Ravintola Roux   FINNISH €€
([☎] 010-279-2930; www.roux.fi; Rautatienkatu 7;
mains €23-28; ⊙ 4-9pm Mon-Fri, 1-9pm Sat) In
an atmosphere of quiet elegance, with well-
spaced tables, this corner restaurant has
brought a touch of culinary sophistication
to the city. Local lakefish and crustaceans
appear alongside hearty meat dishes, and
the odd vegetarian option. The food's not
as gourmet as it thinks it is, but it's easily
Lahti's best.

Casseli   FUSION €€
([☎] 010-422-5950; www.casseli.fi; Borupinraitti 4;
mains €21-27; ⊙ 11am-3pm Mon, 11am-10pm Tue-
Fri, 1-10pm Sat) Look for the brick chimney
by Sibeliustalo to find this appealing harbourside restaurant, boasting a summertime deck with great water views. Dishes
combine a few Spanish and Asian influences
with typically Finnish ingredients with some
success; it's refreshingly original.

Taivaanranta   FINNISH €€
([☎] 042-492-5230; www.taivaanranta.com; Rautatienkatu 13; mains €18-25; ⊙ 11am-11pm Mon-Tue,
11am-midnight Wed-Fri, noon-midnight Sat; 🛜)
This good-natured place sits above the stills
that produce Teerenpeli's single malt, so it's
no surprise that whisky crops up in various
sauces. It specialises in steaks and sausages,
but also does fine Finnish favourites such as
liver and salmon.

Teerenpeli   PUB
(www.teerenpeli.com; Vapaudenkatu 20; ⊙ noon-
2am Sun-Thu, noon-3am Fri & Sat) A real Lahti
success story, this pub sells its own beers
and ciders (try the blueberry one) and
distils a single-malt whisky. It's got an upmarket interior, plush stools and is always
humming with chatter or live jazz. There's
a summer **branch** (www.teerenpeli.com; Vesijär-
ven satama; ⊙ 11am-11pm or later May-late Sep) on
a boat at the harbour.

☆ Entertainment

FC Lahti play their home games at the stadium at Lahden Urheilukeskus (p140), while
the Pelicans, the local ice-hockey team, appear at nearby Isku Areena.

❶ Information

Lahti has free wi-fi through its town centre.
Lahti Info ([☎] 020-728-1750; www.lahtiregion.
fi; Aleksanterinkatu 18; ⊙ 9am-5pm Mon-Fri,
10am-4pm Sat; 🛜) In a central shopping
centre. Can book cruises and hotels.

❶ Getting There & Away

BOAT
Boats (p141) travel from Lahti to Jyväskylä on
Tuesday.

BUS
There are regular buses from Helsinki (€24, 1½
hours), and frequent services from other large
cities. There are also hourly buses to Helsinki
airport.

TRAIN
Numerous direct trains run daily to/from Helsinki (€26.90, one hour) and Riihimäki, where
you can change for Tampere. It's substantially
cheaper from Helsinki if you don't catch an
Intercity train.

Around Lahti

Hollola
[☑] 03
Hollola was the area's major settlement until Lahti's rapid growth left the venerable
parish a pleasant rural backwater. There
are two Hollolas – the modern centre is on
the highway 7km west of Lahti, but the old
village is 18km northwest of Lahti on the
southern shores of Vesijärvi. Either head
north from modern Hollola, or take Rd 2956
from Lahti. It's close enough to cycle.

Heading west along the lake from Lahti, the first place you'll reach, after 8km, is
Messilä ([☎] 03-86011; www.messila.fi; Messiläntie
208; s/d €115/125, 3-/4-person cottages €175/250;
[P] 🛜 ⛷), a fine old estate with manor house
accomodation, golf course and ski resort.
There's also a busy lakeshore **campground**
([☎] 03-876-290; www.campingmessila.fi; tent sites
€17 plus per adult/child €5/2, cabins/apt €60/95;
[P] 🛜) here.

Nine kilometres further, on Vesijärvi's
shores, large Hollola **church** (www.hollolans
eurakunta.fi; ⊙ 11am-6pm May-Aug, 11am-4pm Sun
Sep-Apr) [FREE] is an elegant late-15th-century
structure with steep gables; the bell tower
was designed CL Engel in the 19th century.
Above the double nave are painted wooden
sculptures of saints; also noteworthy are
the elaborate coats of arms, plus the 14th-
century baptismal font and Pietà from the
earlier, wooden church. The church and village are signposted 'Hollola kk'.

Nearby you'll find the local museum, with
an indoor and outdoor sections.

The Lakeland

Best Places to Stay

➡ Lossiranta Lodge (p148)

➡ Mannila (p151)

➡ Valamo monastery (p155)

➡ Hotel Yöpuu (p157)

➡ Oravi Outdoor Centre (p152)

Best Places to Eat

➡ Musta Lammas (p164)

➡ Pöllöwaari (p159)

➡ Huvila (p149)

➡ Figaro (p157)

➡ Kummisetä (p164)

Why Go?

Most of Finland could be dubbed lakeland, but around here it seems there's more water than terra firma. And what water: sublime, sparkling and clean. Reflecting sky and forests as clearly as a mirror, it leaves an indelible impression.

Get outdoors here, whether you rent a cottage and try your hand at kindling the perfect blaze in the sauna stove, grab a canoe and paddle the family-friendly Squirrel Route or go in search of rare freshwater seals.

Towns, too, have much to offer. Savonlinna hosts opera in the wonderful setting of its island castle. Jyväskylä's lively feel and architectural portfolio have obvious appeal, while Kuopio offers lake trips and a great smoke sauna.

Lakeland's people – the *savolaiset* – are among the most outspoken and friendly of Finns. They are often lampooned due to their distinctive Savo dialect, accent and humour. But they have the last laugh thanks to the unparalleled beauty of their region.

When to Go
The Lakeland

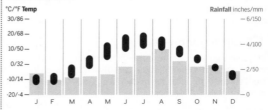

Feb Check out the ice sculptures in Savonlinna, and explore Linnansaari National Park on skates.

Jul Great weather for water activities, and the best festivals, including opera in Savonlinna's castle.

Aug See all the highlights in decent weather but without the July crowds.

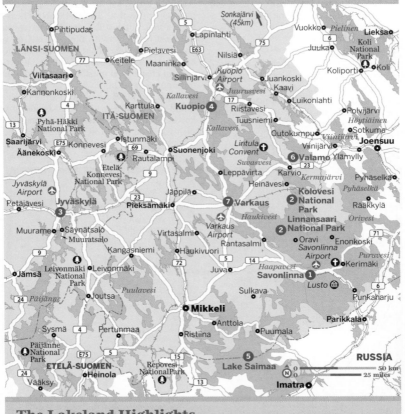

The Lakeland Highlights

1 Soaring on the wing of an aria in the memorable castle setting of the **Savonlinna Opera Festival** (p147)

2 Paddling around the **Linnansaari and Kolovesi National Parks** (p152) seeking a glimpse of the rare Saimaa ringed seal

3 Peering at the visionary buildings of **Alvar Aalto** (p156) in the lively university town of Jyväskylä

4 Sweating it out in Kuopio's sociable **smoke sauna** (p161)

5 Relaxing in a cottage by one of the region's thousands of lakes, including

its largest, **Lake Saimaa** (p152)

6 Cruising the picturesque lakeland en route to a visit to the Orthodox monastery at **Valamo** (p155)

7 Entering a fantasy land at the seriously offbeat **mechanical music museum** (p154) in Varkaus

Savonlinna

015 / POP 27,420

One of Finland's prettiest towns, Savonlinna shimmers on a sunny day as the water ripples around its centre. Set on islands between Haapavesi and Pihlajavesi lakes, it's a classic Lakeland settlement with a major attraction: perched on a rocky islet

is one of Europe's most visually dramatic castles, Olavinlinna. The castle hosts July's world-famous opera festival in a spectacular setting.

Even if you're no ariaholic, the buzz of the festival makes this the most rewarding time to visit, with more restaurants and cafes open and animated post-show debriefs over dinner or bubbly going deep into the darkless night.

But Savonlinna rewards a visit any time, with lots to see in the surrounding area.

◉ Sights

★ **Olavinlinna** CASTLE
(www.olavinlinna.fi; adult/child €8/4; ⊙11am-6pm Jun–mid-Aug, 10am-4pm Mon-Fri, 11am-4pm Sat & Sun mid-Aug–mid-Dec & Jan-May) Standing immense and haughty, 15th-century Olavinlinna is one of the most spectacularly situated castles in northern Europe and, as well as being an imposing fortification, is also the stunning venue for the month-long Savonlinna Opera Festival. The castle's been heavily restored, but is still seriously impressive, not least in the way it's built directly on a rock in the middle of the lake. To visit the upper part of the interior, including the towers and chapel, you must join a guided tour (around 45 minutes).

Tours are multilingual depending on demand and depart on the hour. Guides are good at bringing the castle to life and furnish you with some interesting stories: the

Savonlinna

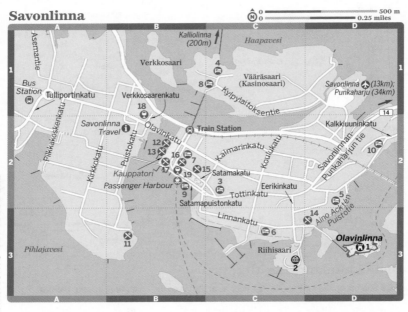

Savonlinna

SAVONLINNA OPERA FESTIVAL

The **Savonlinna Opera Festival** (☑015-476-750; www.operafestival.fi; Olavinkatu 27) enjoys an enviably dramatic setting: the covered courtyard of Olavinlinna Castle. It offers four weeks of top-class opera performances in July. The atmosphere in town during the festival is reason enough to come; it's buzzing, with restaurants serving post-show midnight feasts, and animated discussions and impromptu arias on all sides.

The festival's excellent website details the program: there are rotating performances of four or five operas by the Savonlinna company, as well as an international guest company performing, and a couple of concert and ballet performances. The muscular castle walls are a magnificent backdrop to the set and add great atmosphere. There are tickets in various price bands. The top grades (€115 plus) are fine, but the penultimate grades (€85 to €120) put you in untiered seats, so it helps to be tall. The few cheap seats (€50) have a severely restricted view. Buy tickets up to a year in advance online.

soldiers, for instance, were partly paid in beer – 5L a day and 7L on Sundays, which makes the castle's frequent changes of hands more understandable.

Savonlinna Maakuntamuseo　　MUSEUM
(www.savonlinna.fi/museo; Riihisaari; adult/child €5/3, incl Olavinlinna €9/4; ⊙10am-5pm daily, closed Mon Sep-May) The town's provincial museum, in an old Russian warehouse near Olavinlinna Castle, tells of local history and the importance of water transport. There are old photographs, models and a changing art exhibition. Here also is **Nestori**, a national parks information centre, and a selection of **museum ships**, open from mid-May to mid-September during the same hours as the museum (included in ticket or €3 alone).

🏃 Activities

From June to August, Savonlinna **passenger harbour** is buzzing with dozens of daily scenic cruises that last an hour to 90 minutes and cost around €12 to €20. Boats anchor alongside the kauppatori (market square) and you can soon see which is the next departure. There are also many boats available for charter.

S/S Heinävesi　　CRUISE
(☑0500-653-774; www.savonlinnanlaivat.fi) This centenarian steamship runs daily to Punkaharju, giving you 2½ hours there. It didn't run the last summer we visited, so check if service has resumed.

M/S Puijo　　CRUISE
(☑015-250-250; www.mspuijo.fi; ⊙late Jun-early Aug) A standout lake trip, century-old M/S *Puijo* travels from Savonlinna to Kuopio on Monday, Wednesday and Friday at 9am (one

way €90, 10½ hours), returning on Tuesday, Thursday and Saturday. The boat passes through scenic waterways, canals and locks, stopping en route at Oravi among others. You can book a return with overnight cabin accommodation for €175 or get a same-day bus back (€130 return).

Meals are available. Look for the English PDF on the Finnish-language website.

M/S Brahe　　CRUISE
(☑05-541-0100; www.saimaatravel.fi) Heads to/from Lappeenranta (€69, 8½ hours) roughly twice weekly from early June to mid-August; the fare includes return bus transfer to Savonlinna. The *Brahe* also sails from Helsinki to Lappeenranta, so you could combine all these routes into a Helsinki–Kotka–Lappeenranta–Savonlinna–Kuopio extravaganza.

✺ Festivals & Events

Mobile Phone Throwing World Championships　　SPORT
(www.mobilephonethrowing.fi) One of Finland's bizarre festivals, keenly contested in late August some years, is the Mobile Phone Throwing World Championships.

Jäälinna　　ICE
(www.jaalinna.fi) In February Olavinlinna Castle hosts Jäälinna, an ice-sculpture contest.

🛏 Sleeping

Prices rise sharply during the opera festival, when several student residences are converted to summer hotels. Book July accommodation well in advance.

Kesähotelli Vuorilinna　　SUMMER HOTEL €
(☑015-73950; www.spahotelcasino.fi; Kylpylaitoksentie; s/d €70/90, dm/hostel s €30/40; ⊙Jun-Aug;

THE LAKELAND SAVONLINNA

P) Set in several buildings used by students in term time, this is run by the Spahotel Casino and has an appealing location across a beautiful footbridge from the town centre. Rooms are clean and comfortable; cheaper ones share bathroom and kitchen (no utensils) between two. Happily, dorm rates get you the same deal, and there's a HI discount.

SKO
HOSTEL €

(☎015-572-910; www.sko.fi; Opistokatu 1; dm/s/d €25/70/90, s/d without bathroom €45/70; P@☎) Six kilometres southwest of Savonlinna, this Christian college offers rooms in a variety of buildings in a peaceful location near a lake. Each building has a kitchen; some have good common areas. There's a big range: some cheaper rooms in Villa Tupala are brighter than pricier ensuite rooms in Wanha Pappila, for example. Facilities include bikes and meals. HI discount. Bus 3 stops nearby. Signposted 'Kristillinen Opisto'.

S/S Heinävesi
BOAT €

(☎0500-653-774; www.savonlinnanlaivat.fi; d upper/lower deck €75/65; ☉Jun-late Aug) After 5pm during high summer, this steamer offers cramped but cute two-bunk cabins. There's a good chance of getting a bed here, even during the opera festival, and it's moored right in the centre of things.

Vuohimäki
CAMPGROUND €

(☎015-537-353; www.suncamping.fi; tent sites €15 plus per person €5.50, 4-person r €75-80, cabins €65-90; ☉early Jun-late Aug; P@☎) Located 7km southwest of town, this campground has good facilities but fills quickly during July. You can hire canoes, bikes and rowing boats. Rooms and cabins are cheaper in June and August.

Perhehotelli Hospitz
HOTEL €€

(☎015-515-661; www.hospitz.com; Linnankatu 20; s/d €88/98; ☉Apr-Dec; P☎) This cosy Savonlinna classic was built in the 1930s and maintains that period's elegance. The rooms are stylish, although beds are narrow and bathrooms small; larger family rooms are available. Balconies cost a little extra. There's a pleasant terrace and orchard-garden with access to a small beach. Opera atmosphere is great with a midnight buffet, but rates rise (single/double €130/155): book eons in advance.

Lomamokkila
B&B, COTTAGES €€

(☎015-523-117; www.lomamokkila.fi; Mikonkiventie 209; s €40-100, d €45-105, cabins €50-65, cottages €110-120; P☎) ✐ Readers love this handsome old farmhouse 13km north of Savonlinna. It's run by a genial Finnish family and has large grounds, a wood and lake to explore. Accommodation runs across a variety of buildings and ranges from simple rustic summer rooms, to elegant ensuite chambers with period features; cabins and cottages are also available. An excellent rural Finnish experience. Meals available in summer.

Spa Hotel Casino
HOTEL €€

(☎015-73950; www.spahotelcasino.fi; Vääräsaari (Kasinosaari); s/d €99/114, superior d €154; P@☎☰) On an island across a footbridge from the kauppatori, this is old-fashioned in parts but a good option. Nearly all rooms have a balcony; those that don't have their own sauna. Some have dreamy outlooks west over water. Try for a recently renovated room. Guests have access to the spa facilities; nonguests can use them for €10 in the afternoons. The terrace bar is lively in summer.

Sokos Hotel Seurahuone
HOTEL €€

(☎015-20202; www.sokoshotels.fi; Kauppatori 4-6; s/d €105/121; P☎) Towering over the kauppatori, this friendly hotel offers a bit of everything; its rooms have views, big flatscreen TVs, sofas, sober but updated decor and decent little bathrooms. The top-floor bar has great views and fries up *muikku* (vendace, or whitefish, a small lake fish); however, the restaurant has disappointing food. Weekend prices are good but opera prices are substantially higher.

Kesähotelli Tott
SUMMER HOTEL €€

(☎015-206-3630; reception.tott.savonlinna@sok.fi; Satamakatu 1; s/d/f €80/100/140; ☉early Jun–mid-Aug; P☎) Not far from the kauppatori, this university residence will have you envying the Finnish student. Decent rooms feature comfortable beds and furniture and a fridge; some have great views. Apartment-style rooms are larger, a little more downmarket (lino floors) but have fully equipped kitchens. Rates rise during July.

Huvila
B&B €€

(☎015-555-0555; www.panimoravintolahuvila.fi; Puistokatu 4; tw €85; P☎) Above this microbrewery and restaurant are two cosy, compact attic rooms (€125 during the opera festival).

★Lossiranta Lodge
BOUTIQUE GUESTHOUSE €€€

(☎044-511-2323; www.lossiranta.net; Aino Acktén Puistotie; d €160-200; P☎) To get up close and personal with Olavinlinna Castle, this lakeside spot is the place to be: the impressive castle looms just opposite. Offering five snug little nests in an outbuilding, this is one of Finland's most charming hotels. All are very different but decorated with love and style; they come with a small kitchen (yes, that's it in the cupboard) and numerous personal touches.

The best has a wood sauna and Jacuzzi – a honeymoon special. Breakfast is served on the lawn if weather allows; when the snow falls an outdoor spa bath will keep the chills out. This is like a rural retreat but in the middle of town; warm personal service seals the experience. If it's full, the same people run nearby Tavis Inn

Tavis Inn   BOUTIQUE GUESTHOUSE €€€
(☑ 044-511 2323; www.lossiranta.net; Kalkkiuuninkatu; d €160-200; P ⓢ) In a secluded end-of-the-road spot, but a short lakeside stroll from Olavinlinna Castle, this annexe of Lossiranta Lodge (where you check-in) offers peace in its spacious, attractive rooms and suites. Summer art exhibitions give it its own discrete ambience.

✕ Eating & Drinking

The lakeside **kauppatori** is the place for casual snacking. A traditional *lörtsy* (turnover) comes savoury with meat *(lihalörtsy)* or sweet with apple *(omenalörtsy)* or cloudberry *(lakkalörtsy)*. Savonlinna is also famous for fried *muikku*; try these in summer at **Kalastajan Koju** (www.kalastajankoju.com; Kauppatori; ⓢ 10.30am-9pm Mon-Thu, 10.30am-10pm Fri-Sat, 11am-6pm Sun Jun-Aug) on the kauppatori, or the **Muikkubaari** (www.sokoshotels.fi; Kauppatori 4-6; vendace €8-11; ⓢ noon-10pm Mon-Thu, noon-midnight Fri-Sat, noon-8pm Sun May-Aug) on the top floor of the Sokos Hotel Seurahuone. Restaurants open later during the opera festival.

Kalliolinna   CAFE €
(http://kalliolinna.blogspot.com; Sulosaari; pancakes €3.50-5; ⓢ 10am-7pm late May–mid-Aug) Savonlinna's nicest cafe is this lovely spot, tucked away on a wooden island north of the town centre. It's a very pleasant stroll over bridges to get there; when you do, relax with a book and a cup of coffee or try the tasty choose-your-own-filling pancakes.

Sirkan Torikahvio   CAFE €
(www.torikahvio.fi; Kauppatori; snacks €3-6; ⓢ 9am-7pm summer, 9am-3pm rest of year) Run by a stout grandmotherly figure, this is a worthwhile option on the square to try the local speciality, *lörtsy*, available here with all sorts of fillings. Delicious!

★ Huvila   FINNISH €€
(☑ 015-555-0555; www.panimoravintolahuvila. fi; Puistokatu 4; mains €20-28; ⓢ 4-11pm Mon-Fri, 2-11pm Sat Jun & Aug, noon-midnight Mon-Sat, noon-10pm Sun Jul; ⓢ) This noble wooden building was formerly a fever hospital then asylum, but writes happier stories now as an excellent microbrewery and restaurant across the harbour from the town centre. Food focuses on fresh local ingredients with some unusual meats sometimes featuring, all expertly prepared and served. Home-brewed beers are exquisite and the terrace is a wonderful place on a sunny afternoon, with occasional live music.

Majakka   FINNISH €€
(☑ 015-206-2825; www.kattaasavon.fi; Satamakatu 11; mains €16-27; ⓢ 11am-11pm Mon-Thu, 11am-midnight Fri & Sat, noon-9pm or 10pm Sun; ⓢ) This restaurant has a deck-like terrace, fitting the nautical theme (the name means 'lighthouse'). Local meat and fish specialities are tasty, generously sized and fairly priced, and the select-your-own appetiser plate is a nice touch. It's child-friendly too.

Linnakrouvi   FINNISH €€
(☑ 015-576-9124; www.linnakrouvi.fi; Linnankatu 7; mains €17-32; ⓢ noon-10pm or later Mon-Sat, 3-10pm or later Sun late Jun–mid-Aug) Closest to Olavinlinna Castle, this is the best of the summertime food options that cater to the pre- and post-opera crowd. This offers tiered outdoor seating, an attractive interior and a range of fare, running from upmarket, tasty sandwiches and burgers to more elaborate fish and meat dishes prepared with a gourmet flourish.

Liekkilohi   FISH €€€
(www.liekkilohi.fi; buffet €39; ⓢ 11am-9pm Mon-Sat, noon-9pm Sun Jun-Aug) This bright-red pontoon, anchored just off the kauppatori, specialises in 'flamed' salmon, a delicious plate that you can have on its own (€20) or as part of a fish buffet.

Olutravintola Sillansuu   PUB
(Verkkosaarenkatu 1; ⓢ 2pm-2am Tue-Sat, 2pm-midnight Sun & Mon) Savonlinna's best pub is compact and cosy, offering an excellent variety of international bottled beers, a decent whisky selection and friendly service. There's a downstairs area with a pool table;

during the opera festival amateur (and sometimes professional) arias are sung as the beer kegs empty.

Waahto BAR
(www.savonmafia.fi; Satamapuistonkatu 5; ⊙ 11am-10pm Mon-Thu, 11am-11pm Fri, noon-11pm Sat, noon-10pm Sun) By the kauppatori and harbour, this has a great summer terrace, perfect for a sundowner, and a cosy lounge area. It's better for drinks than food.

ℹ Information

Savonlinna Travel (☑ 0600-30007; www.savonlinna.travel; Puistokatu 1; ⊙ 9am-4pm Mon-Fri Aug-Jun, 10am-6pm Mon-Sat, 10am-2pm Sun Jul) Tourist information including accommodation reservations, cottage booking, farmstays, opera festival tickets and tours. The Sokos Hotel Seurahuone can help with tourist information when this is closed.

ℹ Getting There & Away

AIR
Finnair/FlyBe fly daily between Helsinki and Savonlinna in summer (except late June and early August), weekdays in winter.

BOAT
Lake boats (p147) connect Savonlinna with other towns.

BUS
Savonlinna is not on major bus routes, but there are several express buses a day from Helsinki (€49.90, five to 5½ hours), and buses run regularly from Mikkeli (€24, 1½ hours). There are also direct services to Joensuu(€26.30, 2¾ hours) and Jyväskylä (€43.90, 3½ hours).

TRAIN
Trains from Helsinki (€65.70, 4¼ hours) and Joensuu (€34, 2¼ hours) both require a change in Parikkala. The train station is right in the centre of things, near the kauppatori.

ℹ Getting Around

Savonlinna airport is 13km northeast; shared **taxis** (☑ 0500-250-099; www.jsturvataksit.fi) meet flights.

There are car-hire agencies at the airport, and **Sixt** (☑ 020-112-2557; www.sixt.fi; Olavinkatu 15) and **Hertz** (☑ 020-555-2750; www.hertz.fi; Rantakatu 2) in town. Book well ahead.

Several places hire bikes in summer, including **InterSport** (Olavinkatu 52; per day/week €20/50; ⊙ 9.30am-6pm Mon-Fri, 9.30am-3pm Sat).

Punkaharju
☑ 015

Punkaharju, the famous pine-covered esker (sand or gravel ridge) east of Savonlinna, is touted as 'Finland's national landscape'. The region was first declared a protected area by Tsar Alexander in 1803 and became a favoured summering spot for St Petersburg gentry. The area is very picturesque and great for walking or cycling. It's an easy day trip from Savonlinna on the train but also an appealing place to stay. Punkaharju village has services including a guesthouse and a large supermarket.

⊙ Sights & Activities

The underground Retretti gallery, a fabulous attraction, was closed at the time of writing through lack of funding. Its future was uncertain.

You can hire boats, kayaks and bikes from the **service station** (☑ 044-755-0382; www.harjunportti.fi; Tuunaansaarentie 2; bike per day/24hr €10/15, kayak per day €30-45) by Retretti train station.

Punkaharju NATURAL FEATURE
During the Ice Age, formations similar to this 7km-long sand ridge were created all over the country. Because it crosses a large lake, it's always been an important travel route. Short sections of the original unsealed road along the ridgetop remain – once part of a route to Russia connecting the Olavinlinna and Vyborg (Viipuri) castles. To stroll on the ridge, get off at Retretti train station and walk east towards Punkaharju village, either shadowing the main road, or along the quieter byroad signposted 'Harjualue'. It is a spectacular walk, particularly on a sunny day, with water on both sides. Other labelled trails explore the forested areas from the Arboretum car park, between Lusto and Retretti.

Lusto MUSEUM
(www.lusto.fi; adult/child €10/5; ⊙ 10am-5pm Tue-Sun Oct-Apr, 10am-5pm daily May & Sep, 10am-7pm Jun-Aug) Dedicated to Finnish forests and forestry, Lusto is a good visit, with plenty of English information. Displays cover hunting, cottage culture and global forest resources; another section has a kid-pleasing range of machinery and chainsaws. More peaceable is the lakescape from the Expo 2000 pavilion – a spot to relax for five minutes. The building itself is an interesting timber struc-

KERIMÄKI'S GIANT CHURCH

Finland has many notable churches, but few impose like Kerimäki's – the largest **wooden church** (Kerimäki Church; www.kerimaenseurakunta.fi; ⊙ 10am-6pm Jun & early Aug, to 7pm Jul, to 4pm late Aug) **FREE** in the world. Built in 1847, it was designed to accommodate 5000. The oversized church was no mistake, but deliberately inflated from plans by overexcited locals. At the time, the population of Kerimäki parish was around 12,000, and the reverend felt that half should be attending church on any given Sunday. Worshippers arrived by water, crossing the lakes in a *kirkkovene* (church longboat).

As stunning as the yellow-and-white church appears from outside (dominating the tiny township), the scale isn't apparent until you survey the massive interior – the height of the nave is 27m. Eight stoves couldn't heat it, so a smaller winter chapel was built at the rear. The main church is still used for services in summer. It's largely unadorned apart from an altarpiece by Aleksandra Såltin. A cafe and shop occupy the separate bell tower (proceeds go to maintenance, an onerous burden for this small parish). For a small donation you can climb the steep wooden steps for a different perspective.

Hourly buses run Monday to Friday between Savonlinna and Kerimäki (€6.10, 30 minutes). Don't catch a train: Kerimäki train station is miles away from the village.

ture with the main display hall designed to represent a tree's trunk. The attractive cafe does a summer lunch buffet (€18).

🛏 Sleeping & Eating

Punkaharjun Lomakeskus   CAMPGROUND €
(☑ 029-007-4050; www.punkaharjunlomakesk-us.fi; tent sites €14 plus per adult/child €5/2.50, 2-/4-person cabins €42/63, self-contained cottages €135-205; P 🛜) Near Retretti train station, this enormous lakeside campground has a whole town's worth of solid cabins and cottages, and a raft of facilities. Good for kids, who'll soon find a posse of Finnish playmates; there's also a reindeer to feed and a popular waterpark next door.

★ Mannila   HOTEL, FARMSTAY €€
(☑ 015-644400; www.maatilamatkailumannila. com; Koskelonniementie 127, Vaahersalo; d main/outbuilding €110/90, tent site €6 plus per person €3, farm d €60-80; ⊙ May-Sep plus winter if prebooked; P 🛜) This farm complex is remote enough for a great retreat but handy enough for a base. The highlight is the wonderful lakeside, where there's the campground and welcoming Rantakatti hotel, offering attractive rooms, some with an enormous balcony. Rooms in a secondary building are smaller but share a large common area. Cheaper rooms occupy converted barns. There are also self-contained family apartments, bikes, saunas, ponies and a restaurant.

Punkaharjun Valtionhotelli   HOTEL €€
(☑ 020-752-9100; www.punkaharjunvaltionhotelli. fi; Tuunaansaarentie 4; s/d €95/140, tw without

bathroom €95; ⊙ Jun-late Aug; P @ 🛜) Right on the old ridge-road between Lusto and Retretti, this romantic 19th-century wooden hotel was once the gamekeeper's lodge for the Russian royal hunting estates, and includes a majestic separate villa built for the tsarina. There's a variety of room types and prices, including cabins. Doubles are old-fashioned with cramped sleeping space but an extra sitting area; superiors are huge and beautiful, with views.

It's wonderfully peaceful up here among the pines, and there's also a fine restaurant (buffet lunch €21 to €25).

❶ Getting There & Away

Trains between Savonlinna and Parikkala stop at Retretti, Lusto and Punkaharju train stations (€4.30, 30 minutes, five to six daily).

Seal Lakes

📷 015

Two primarily watery national parks in the Savonlinna area offer fabulous lakescapes dotted with islands, best explored by hiring a canoe or rowboat. Several outfitters offer these services, and free camping spots dot the lakes' shores. This is perhaps the best part of the Lakeland to really get up close and personal with this region's natural beauty.

This is the habitat of the freshwater Saimaa ringed seal. Separated from its Baltic cousins at the end of the last Ice Age, it was in imminent danger of extinction during the 20th century due to hunting and human

A COTTAGE BY A LAKE

The Lakeland is a particularly enticing place to search out a waterside cottage retreat or cosy rural farmstay for a true Finnish holiday. Around 100,000 rental cabins and cottages are dotted around the myriad lakes.

A good first point of investigation is the nationwide operators – Lomarengas (p288) has heaps of options and also links to farmstays and rural B&Bs. A local operator with a decent portfolio is **Saimaa Tours** (www.saimaatours.fi). Savonlinna's travel website, www.savonlinna.travel, and Mikkeli's, www.visitmikkeli.fi, both link to farmstay and cottage-rental providers.

interference. Though there remain only a precarious 300-odd of the greyish beasts, population levels are on the increase. Late May is the most likely time to see seals, as they are moulting and spend much time on rocks. Nestori (p147) in Savonlinna has national park information.

Linnansaari National Park

This scenic **national park** (www.outdoors.fi) consists of Haukivesi lake and hundreds of uninhabited islands; the main activity centres around the largest island, Linnansaari, which has marked trails. As well as seals, rare birds, including ospreys, can also be seen.

The best way to experience the park is renting a kayak and spending a few days exploring. Rowboats, motorboats, kayaks, canoes and camping equipment can be hired from **Saimaaholiday** (🖉Oravi 015-647-290, Porosalmi 020-729-1760; www.saimaaholiday.net), an excellent co-operative with a comprehensive range of services and advice, as well as great accommodation options at the two main park access points. It can book the huts on Linnansaari island and organise activities; this region is tops in winter too, with a skating track right across the lake, ice-fishing and snowshoe walks.

🛏 Sleeping & Eating

Sammakkoniemi   CAMPGROUND, CABIN €
(🖉050-027-5458; www.outdoors.fi; tent sites €7, cabins €49) On Linnansaari island in Linnansaari National Park, this campground offers a sauna, cooking places and (from late June to mid-August) a kiosk-cafe. Cabins sleep up to four; you can take a bed on a dorm basis (€20). Camping is free outside of high summer. Several smaller islands also have designated campgrounds.

★**Oravi Outdoor Centre**   HOTEL €€
(🖉015-647-290; www.saimaaholiday.net/oravi; Kiramontie 15, Oravi; s/d €90/109; 🅿@🛜) Beautifully set by the river in Oravi, the eastern access point for Linnansaari National Park, this excellent facility, as well as providing everything necessary to get on the water (or ice), offers comfortable accommodation. As well as upmarket holiday villas, it has a cracking modern hotel. The rooms have kitchen, drying cabinet and free sauna use; it's cheaper outside July.

There's an attractive waterside restaurant in summer and a year-round cafe-shop. Canoe hire costs €32/149 per day/week, all included. It also runs guided trips.

Lomakeskus Järvisydän   COTTAGE, HOTEL €€
(🖉020-729-1760; www.jarvisydan.com; Porosalmentie 313, Porosalmi; s/d/ste €85/110/200, cottages from €190, villas from €260; 🅿@🛜) At Porosalmi, an embarkation point for Linnansaari National Park, this impressive medieval-themed holiday village offers a big variety of accommodation, mostly in log cottages which, despite the old-time look, feature plenty of modern comforts. It runs activities and rents out all sorts of equipment. Good meals are available in the atmospheric restaurant: don't miss the unusual wine cellar.

A lake spa was being built at last visit.

❶ Information

Oskari (🖉020-564-5916; www.outdoors.fi; Rantasalmi; ⊗9am-4pm Mon-Fri mid-Feb–mid-Jun & mid-Aug–Oct, 9am-5pm mid-Jun–mid-Aug) in Rantasalmi is the visitor information centre for the park and village, and also has an environmental display and a film about a Saimaa seal pup (adult/child €3/1.50). It rents canoes too. Nestori (p147) in Savonlinna is another good spot for information.

❶ Getting There & Around

Buses run to Oravi and Rantasalmi from Savonlinna. From Rantasalmi, it's 7km to the turn-off for Porosalmi (Varkaus-bound buses can drop you here), and a further 3km walk down to the accommodation complex. The Savonlinna–Kuopio cruise stops at Oravi.

Scheduled boat services run to Linnansaari island from Oravi (adult/child €9.50/4.50, four daily mid-June to mid-August, 15 minutes), as well as on-demand water-taxi services from Oravi and Porosalmi, run by Saimaaholiday.

Kolovesi National Park

Northeast of Linnansaari, less-trafficked **Kolovesi** (www.outdoors.fi) covers several pine-forested islands. There are high hills, rocky cliffs and caves, and prehistoric rock paintings. Saimaa seals, as well as otters and eagle owls, call Kolovesi home.

The park's a paradise for canoeing, the best way to explore the fantastic scenery. Motorboats are prohibited. There are several restricted areas, and the islands are out of bounds all winter to protect the seals, whose pups are born in February.

The gateway town is pleasant Enonkoski, with a bright stream and rapids dividing it in two. There's a **park information cabin** (Enonkoski; ⊙ 10am-4pm Mon-Fri, 10am-3pm Sun Jun & early Aug, 10am-5pm Mon-Fri, 10am-3pm Sat-Sun Jul) here. The park starts a further 12km north. A free ferry north of Enonkoski crosses the narrows between two lakes on Rd 471.

Kolovesi Retkeily (☑ 040-558-9163; www.sealtrail.com) specialises in canoe rental, outfitting and multiday journeys for all abilities. Simple campgrounds dot the park. You can head from Kolovesi to Oravi and thence Linnansaari National Park by canoe; Saimaaholiday will deliver canoes to Kolovesi for you if you want to do this.

CANOEING THE SQUIRREL ROUTE

The **Oravareitti** (Squirrel Route; www.oravareitti.fi) canoeing route is a Lakeland highlight. The 57km beginner- and family-friendly journey starts at Juva and traverses lakes, rivers and gentle rapids on the way to Sulkava. It's a very pretty journey: you feel miles away from the stresses of everyday life; information boards along the route describe local nature.

You can do the trip in two strenuous days; there's a good campsite midway. But this means around six to nine hours of paddling each day, so you may want to do it in three, or even four days. This would mean taking a tent, which you can hire at Juva Camping. Another option is a drop-off further along the route, making for an easier first day.

Late spring and early summer see the best water levels.

Getting Started

Hospitable **Juva Camping** (☑ 015-451-930; www.juvacamping.com; tent €17, cabins €35-90; ⊙ May-Sep; [P] 🐾) provides everything you need: it hires two-person Canadian canoes (per day €40) or single kayaks (per day €30), supplies a good waterproof route map, hires tents and camping gear, and can arrange to pick you (or just the canoe) up at Sulkava (€20/60 for canoes/canoes plus passengers). It's just off the north–south highway between Mikkeli and Varkaus, 3km west of Juva and 63km from Savonlinna. Buses stop nearby.

The Route

There are regular rest stops with fireplaces and toilets. From Juva Camping it's an easy 8km paddle across Jukajärvi to the beginning of the river section, Polvijoki, where you must carry your canoe around the dam to the right. Passing through the small lakes Riemiö and Souru, you come to gentle 200m Voikoski rapids. Continue along the canal, carrying the canoe across the road at the end, before negotiating the Karijoki.

On Kaitajärvi, **Sulkavan Oravanpesät** (☑ 040-093-8076; www.oravanpesat.fi; Kalajärventie 13; tent sites €12 plus per person €3, cabins €60-110; ⊙ May-Sep; [P]) is a really friendly campground with tent sites, cabins and a much-appreciated smoke sauna. These folk also hire canoes and kayaks, and arrange transport along the route. A kiosk sells drinks; they can organise food with notice. This is approximately the halfway point. Next comes a series of rapids including Kissakoski and the strong currents of the Kyrsyänjoki. Continue through Rasakanjoki and Tikanjoki before coming to large Halmejärvi. The route continues on the western shore of Lohnajärvi to Lohnankoski. From here it's a leisurely paddle down Kuhajärvi, past a final set of rapids and into Sulkava. Pull in at Kulkemus Boat Centre on the right after the bridge. There's a summer cafe here and you can camp.

MARVELS OF MECHANICAL MUSIC

It's worth visiting the timber-pulp town of Varkaus for the **Mekaanisen Musiikin Museo** (☎050-590-9297; www.mekaanisenmusiikinmuseo.fi; Pelimanninkatu 8; adult/child €14/7; ⊙11am-6pm Tue-Sat, to 5pm Sun Mar–mid-Dec, to 6pm daily Jul). 'You must understand', says the personable owner, 'it's not a normal museum; more a madhouse'. A truly astonishing collection of mechanical musical instruments ranges from a ghostly keyboard-tinkling Steinway to a robotic violinist to a full-scale orchestra emanating from a large cabinet. This is just the beginning; political cabaret in several languages and an overwhelming sense of good humour and imagination make it a cross between a Victorian theatre and Willy Wonka's chocolate factory. It's an extraordinary place.

Entry is by guided tour that lasts around 75 minutes. Having a coffee outside under the steely gaze of a sizeable macaw seems like a return to normality. The museum is signposted 1km west of the main north–south highway.

Sulkava

☑ 015

Sedate, scenic Sulkava, 39km southwest of Savonlinna, is the finishing point for the Squirrel Route (p153). There's tourist info in **Alina** (☎044-417-5215; www.sulkava.fi; Alanteentie 28; ⊙9am-4pm Mon-Fri, 9am-2pm Sat Aug-Jun, 9am-5pm Mon-Fri, 10am-4pm Sat, 11am-3pm Sun Jul), a friendly cafe that can provide details of the numerous rental cottages in the area.

Sulkavan Suursoudut (www.suursoudut. fi) is a massive rowing festival that attracts big crowds and some 7000 competitors over its four days in mid-July. Competitors row wooden boats around Partalansaari over a 70km two-day course or a 60km one-day course, then get thoroughly hammered. The highlights are races between *kirkkovenettä* (large longboats) traditionally used to get to church across the lakes. There are competitions for all abilities, and you might be able to find an oar for yourself in one of the teams.

Right in the town centre, **Ollinpolun Matkakoti** (☎050-593-9688; www.ollinpolun-matkakoti.fi; Ollinpolku 2; s/d €55/100; [P][⊗]) has simple, comfortable, typically Finnish rooms. A good breakfast is served at the owner's nearby cafe.

There are daily buses from Savonlinna and weekday ones from Mikkeli. Two buses run weekdays from Sulkava to Juva.

Mikkeli

☑ 015 / POP 49,000

Mikkeli is a sizeable provincial town on the shores of Saimaa, Finland's largest lake. It's an important transport hub and military base and was the headquarters of the Finnish army during WWII; museums relating to those years are the main sights. It's a friendly place that can make a convenient stopover.

◉ Sights & Activities

Päämajamuseo (Headquarters Museum; www. mikkeli.fi/museot; Päämajankatu 1-3; adult/child €5/free; ⊙10am-5pm Fri-Sun Sep-Apr, 10am-5pm daily May-Aug) was Gustav Mannerheim's command centre during WWII; and **Jalkaväkimuseo** (Infantry Museum; ☎015-369-666; www.jalkavakimuseo.fi; Jääkärinkatu 6; adult/child €8/free; ⊙10am-5pm May–mid-Sep, 11am-4pm Wed-Sun mid-Sep–Apr) is one of the largest military museums in Finland. You can also visit Mannerheim's wartime railway carriage at the train station. The Mikkeli area is excellent for **fishing** – the lakes teem with perch, salmon and trout, and ice-fishing is popular in winter. The tourist office can help with permits, guides and equipment rental.

★ Festivals & Events

Mikkeli Music Festival (Mikkeli Music Festival; www.mikkelinmusiikkijuhlat.fi) in late June/early July is a week-long classical music event featuring top Finnish and Russian conductors. Balancing it out is **Jurassic Rock** (www.jurassicrock.fi), a two-day festival in early August featuring plenty of Nordic bands.

⌂ Sleeping & Eating

Hotelli Uusikuu   HOTEL €

(☎015-221-5420; www.uusikuu.fi; Raviradantie 13; r €59-69; [P][⊗]) This staffless hotel is quite a bargain. Rooms are clean, comfortable, modern and spacious; some have a fold-out bed so they can sleep up to four. Book online. It's about 15 minutes' walk from the town centre; turn right out of the train or bus station, then left on Savilahdenkatu; Raviradantie is on your right after crossing the small river.

Huoneistohotelli Marja   APARTMENT €€

(☑044-777-0676; www.marjanmatkakoti.fi; Jääkärinkatu 8; s €78, d €98-122; [P]🛜) In a characterful wooden 19th-century barracks building right by the infantry museum, Jalkaväkimuseo, friendly Marja offers very pleasant, quirky apartment-style rooms, handicrafts for sale and a genuine welcome. She also has a nearby guesthouse with slightly cheaper chambers.

Pruuvi   MEDITERRANEAN €€

(www.oxa.fi/pruuvi; Raatihuoneenkatu 4; mains €14-27; ⊙11am-10pm Mon-Thu, 11am-11pm Fri, 2-11pm Sat; 🛜) With a cellar-like ambience just off the kauppatori, this is welcoming and turns out decent dishes with Finnish and Mediterranean influences: a slab of salmon in bouillabaisse, for example. Lunch is buffet-style. Upstairs is Päämaja, a pretty good pub with a range of home-brewed beers.

❶ Information

Tourist Office (☑044-794-5669; www. visitmikkeli.fi; Savilahdenkatu 8; ⊙9am-5pm Mon-Fri, plus 9am-3pm Sat Jun-Aug) Upstairs in Stella shopping centre on the kauppatori.

❶ Getting There & Away

The train and bus stations are adjacent, a block east (downhill) from the kauppatori. Bus destinations include Helsinki (€40.80, 3½ hours) and Savonlinna (€24, 1½ hours). Trains run to Helsinki (€48.90, 2¾ hours), Kuopio (€28.90, 1½ hours) and further north. For other cities, change at Pieksämäki or Kouvola.

Valamo

Finland's only Orthodox **monastery** (☑017-570-111; www.valamo.fi; Valamontie 42, Uusi-Valamo) is a great visit. One of the ancient Russian monasteries, old Valamo, set on an island in gigantic Lake Ladoga, survived the Russian Revolution's aftermath as it fell just within newly independent Finland, but was endangered during the 1939 Winter War. Ladoga froze (a rare occurrence), allowing a hurried evacuation of monks, icons and treasures. Those that survived the journey resettled here in a beautiful lakeside estate. Monks and novices, almost a thousand strong a century ago, can now be counted on one hand, but the complex in general is thriving.

Visitors are free to roam and enter the churches. The first was made by connecting two sheds; the rustic architecture contrasts curiously with the fine gilded icons. The new church, completed in 1977, has an onion-shaped dome and icons, and is redolent with incense.

From June to August there's a **service** at 1pm. **Guided tours** (€5) are recommended for insight. Take time to stroll to the peaceful **cemetery**, with a *tsasouna* (chapel) dedicated to a Valamo missionary monk who took Christianity to Alaska. There's also a museum and summer boat cruises to fill out the day, or you could take a walk to the Pilgrims' Cross.

The community encourages visitors, whether just for coffee or chant CDs, or the opportunity to engage further in Orthodox culture by attending a service or doing a course in philosophy or icon-painting.

Valamo makes an excellent place to **stay** (☑017-570-1810; www.valamo.fi; s/d without bathroom €45/66, hotel s/d from €70/110; [P]🛜), especially peaceful once evening descends. Guesthouses in picturesque wooden buildings provide comfortable, no-frills sleeping with shared bathroom; there are also two grades of hotel room offering a higher standard. Prices drop midweek and outside summer. The complex's eatery, **Trapesa,** (www. valamo.fi; Valamon Luostari; buffet lunch €14, high tea €10; ⊙7am-6pm Mon-Thu, to 9pm Fri-Sat) has high-quality buffet lunches and, in summer, Russian-style high tea (€10). There's no monastic frugality: try its own range of berry wines.

❶ Getting There & Away

Valamo is clearly signposted 4km north of the main Varkaus–Joensuu road. A couple of daily buses run here from Joensuu and from Helsinki via Mikkeli and Varkaus.

The most pleasant way to arrive in summer is on a Monastery Cruise (p147) from Kuopio. The cruise uses a combination of the regular Kuopio to Savonlinna boat and road transport (adult return €80).

Jyväskylä

☑014 / POP 134,800

Vivacious and young at heart, western Lakeland's main town has a wonderful waterside location and an optimistic feel. Jyväskylä (*yoo*-vah-skoo-lah), thanks to the work of Alvar Aalto, is of global architectural interest,

OFF THE BEATEN TRACK

LINTULA

An 18km walk or short drive from Valamo, the nation's only Orthodox **convent** (www.lintulanluostari.fi; Honkasalontie 3, Palokki; ⊘9am-6pm Jun-Aug) is much quieter. It's a serene contrast that is worth the short detour. Lintula was founded in Karelia in 1895 and transferred west during WWII. A souvenir shop on the premises sells wool and hand-made candles (the nuns supply all the Orthodox churches in Finland), and there's a pleasant cafe. The lovely grounds are perfect for strolling. In the garden is a beautifully simple log chapel, whose icons glint in the candlelight.

Lintulan Vierasmaja (☑020-610-0500; www.lintulanluostari.fi; s/d €27/46; ⊘Jun-Aug; ℗) is a small red house at the back. There are simple but clean rooms, with separate bathrooms; it's open to men and women.

and petrolheads know it as a legendary World Rally Championships venue. The big student population and lively arts scenes give the town plenty of energy and nightlife.

◎ Sights

For architecture buffs the best visiting days are Tuesday to Friday, as many buildings are closed on weekends and the Alvar Aalto Museum is closed on Monday.

Jyväskylä's museums are all free on Fridays outside of the summer season.

Alvar Aalto Museo   MUSEUM
(www.alvaraalto.fi; Alvar Aallonkatu 7; adult/child €6/free; ⊘11am-6pm Tue-Sun, 10am-6pm Tue-Fri Jul-Aug) Alvar Aalto, a giant of 20th-century architecture, was schooled in Jyväskylä, opened his first offices here and spent his summers in nearby Muuratsalo. The city has dozens of Aalto buildings, but stop first at one of his last creations, this museum in the university area. It chronicles his life and work, with detailed focus on his major buildings, as well as sections on his furniture design and glassware. It's very engaging; you get a real feel for the man and his philosophy.

The cafe does decent lunches. The museum stocks *Alvar Aalto's Jyväskylä* (€1), a pamphlet plotting some of his significant buildings in and around Jyväskylä. It

also has simple bikes for hire (per 1/2 days €10/15) to help you explore them.

➡ Alvar Aalto Buildings

Aalto's list includes the university's main buildings and the **City Theatre** (Vapaudenkatu 36). On the corner of Kauppakatu and Väinönkatu, the **Workers' Club Building** (1925) is an early work with Renaissance-inspired features such as columns and a Palladian balcony; downstairs is a karaoke pub.

Keski-Suomen Museo   MUSEUM
(Museum of Central Finland; www.jyvaskyla.fi/keskisuomenmuseo; Alvar Aallonkatu 7; adult/child €6/free; ⊘11am-6pm Tue-Sun) Adjacent to the Alvar Aalto Museo and designed by him, this worthwhile attraction's main exhibition is an overview of rural life from prehistoric times onwards. There's an ancient sledge-runner dated to 4000 BC, and displays on hunting, fishing and logging, giving a good feel for traditional Finnish life and finishing in a typical old grocery. Upstairs is a history of Jyväskylä itself, with great scale models; the top floor holds temporary art exhibitions.

Suomen Käsityön Museo   MUSEUM
(www.craftmuseum.fi; Kauppakatu 25; adult/child €6/free; ⊘11am-6pm Tue-Sun) This is all about Finnish handicrafts and their history, and incorporates the National Costume Centre, displaying regional dress from around Finland. The permanent collection is small; most space is taken up with temporary exhibitions. It's an enjoyable insight into activities that, partly due to the long winters, have always been an important part of life here. There's a good shop.

🏃 Activities

It's a nice walk or cycle around the lake of about 12km, which you can cut in half using the road bridge. There are numerous boating options – check visit.jyvaskyla.fi for more choices, or wander along the pleasant harbour area, where there's everything: boat bars, jet-ski hire, houseboats (www.houseboat.fi) and floating saunas for rent.

Päijänne Risteilyt Hilden   CRUISE
(☑014-263-447; www.paijanne-risteilythilden.fi; ⊘early Jun–mid-Aug) The main cruise operator runs several vessels, including the *Suomi*, one of the oldest steamers plying the Finnish lakes. Short cruises depart daily from the passenger harbour (some are lunch or dinner cruises) and cost €18 to €24, half-price for kids. Longer trips include trips

northwards to the Keitele canal or south to Lahti. Boats leave Lahti on Tuesdays, returning from Jyväskylä on Wednesdays (one way €76, 10½ hours).

Laajavuori
SNOW SPORTS

(www.laajis.fi; Laajavuorentie) This winter sport centre has 12 modest slopes, some for kids, two terrain parks, ski-cross and cross-country trails, as well as a number of scary ski jumps. There's a good ski area for children and the resort is popular with families; there's a spa hotel and guesthouse accommodation. It's 4km from Jyväskylä centre; catch bus 25.

✪ Festivals & Events

Jyväskylän Kesä
ARTS

(Jyväskylä Arts Festival; www.jyvaskylankesa.fi) In mid-July this festival has an international program of concerts, exhibitions, theatre and dance. It has a strong liberal and radical tradition and is one of Finland's most important arts festivals.

Neste Oil Rally Finland
MOTORSPORTS

(www.nesteoilrallyfinland.fi) In early August Jyväskylä hosts what many Finns regard as summer's most important event, the Finnish leg of the World Rally Championship. Perhaps the most spectacular of all the stages, it draws half a million spectators. The event goes for four days, with big concerts and parties. Book tickets (€65) online. **Jyväskylä Booking** (☎014-339-8144; www.jklpaviljonki.fi) can help find private accommodation.

🛏 Sleeping

Kesähotelli Harju
SUMMER HOTEL €

(☎010-279-2004; www.hotelharju.fi; Sepänkatu 3; s/d/tr incl breakfast €60/70/87; ☺early Jun-early Aug; P@🛜) Five minutes uphill from the city centre, this summer hotel has modern, light, spacious student rooms each with a kitchenette (no utensils) and good bathrooms. It's great value.

★Hotel Yöpuu
BOUTIQUE HOTEL €€

(☎014-333-900; www.hotelliyopuu.fi; Yliopistonkatu 23; s/d/ste €108/135/195; P@🛜) Among Finland's most enchanting boutique hotels, this exquisite spot has lavishly decorated rooms, all individually designed in markedly different styles. Service is warm and welcoming with an assured personal touch – including a welcome drink – that makes for a delightful stay. Renovating and improving is always going on here so standards are kept high. Suites offer excellent value.

Hotelli Milton
HOTEL €€

(☎014-337-7900; www.hotellimilton.com; Hannikaisenkatu 29; s/d €85/120; P@🛜) Right in the thick of things, this family-run hotel has an old-fashioned dark foyer, but modern rooms offer plenty of natural light, space and attractive wooden floors; most have a balcony. An evening sauna on weekdays is included and it's very handy for the bus and train stations. Weekend prices are great (s/d €65/85).

Hotelli Alba
HOTEL €€

(☎014-636-311; www.hotellialba.fi; Ahlmaninkatu 4; s/d/ste €101/124/178; P@🛜) Within the university campus, this hotel is right by the water, and the terrace of its bar-restaurant takes full advantage. Telescopic corridors lead onto unremarkable compact rooms, but the view from those facing the water compensates; you could fish out of the windows. Junior suites are much more spacious, and come with a sauna. Summer and weekend prices are good.

Omenahotelli
HOTEL €€

(☎010-470-5550; www.omena.com; Vapaudenkatu 57; r €65-90; P🛜) A central, reception-less hotel. It's one of the better of the chain, with comfortable beds and endless corridors. Book online or via the lobby terminal.

🍴 Eating

Soppabaari
SOUP BAR €

(www.soppabaari.fi; Asemakatu 11B; soup, pasta €8.80; ☺11am-8pm Mon-Thu, 11am-10pm Fri & Sat) This friendly licensed soup bar makes a great stop at any time but especially in low temperatures. It does three daily soups and pasta specials, pretty much guaranteed to be delicious. There are also salads and tapas-sized portions of Finnish treats such as meatballs.

Katriinan Kasvisravintola
VEGETARIAN €

(www.maijasilvennoinen.fi; Kauppakatu 11; lunch €6-9; ☺11am-2.30pm Mon-Fri; 🍴) A couple of blocks west of the pedestrian zone, this vegetarian lunch restaurant is an excellent bet. Six euros gets you soup and salad bar, seven buys a hot dish instead of the soup, and nine gets you the lot. It changes daily – you might get pasta, ratatouille or curry – but it's always tasty.

★Figaro
FINNISH €€

(☎020-766-9810; www.figaro-restaurant.com; Asemakatu 4; mains €24-29; ☺11am-3pm Mon, 11am-11pm Tue-Fri, noon-11pm Sat) With a warm drawing-room feel and cordial service, this place backs up the atmosphere with excellent food served in generous portions. The fish is especially good, served with creamy sauces and inventive garnishes. Sizeable steaks are a given, and reindeer and bear make occasional appearances. There are good vegetarian mains too, and it's youngster-friendly

Next door, in the 'Winebistro', a number of interesting drops are served by the glass, and Spanishy tapas plus good-value bistro plates (€18 to €24; open 11am to 11pm Monday, 2pm to 10pm Sunday) are available.

Kissanviikset FINNISH €€
(☑010-666-5150; www.kissanviikset.fi; Puistokatu 3; mains €20-30; ◷11am-10pm Mon-Thu, 11am-10.30pm Fri, 1-10.30pm Sat, 1-8.30pm Sun) Quiet, romantic and welcoming, the 'cat's whiskers' is an enticing choice. The genteel upstairs dining room is complemented by an atmospheric cellar space when busy. Dishes are thoughtfully prepared and feature delicious combinations of hearty flavours such as salmon with baked fennel, or well-proportioned meat dishes with sinfully creamy wild mushroom sauces.

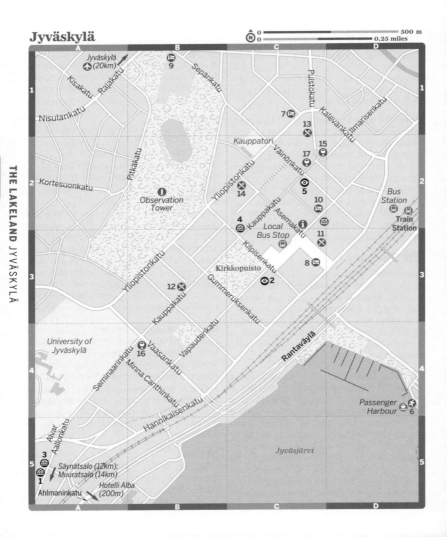

Jyväskylä

★ Pöllöwaari FINNISH €€€
(☑014-333-900; www.hotelliyopuu.fi; Yliopistonka-tu 23; mains €27-30; ⊘11am-10.30pm Mon-Fri, 1-10.30pm Sat; 🛜) The Hotel Yöpuu's fine-dining restaurant makes a tempting meal stop. There are various set menus, including an eight-course degustation special, but the à la carte dining is rewarding here too, with main courses fairly priced for the excep-tional quality on offer. Wines are pricey, but there's a good selection including some great Burgundy, and the welcoming staff are keen to explain the matching possibilities.

🍷 Drinking & Nightlife

Jyväskylä's students ensure a lively nightlife when they're not on holidays. Head down to the harbour for relaxed decktop drinking on one of a clutch of boat bars.

★ Sohwi PUB
(www.sohwi.fi; Vaasankatu 21; ⊘2pm-midnight Tue-Thu, 2pm-2am Fri, noon-2am Sat, 2-10pm Sun-Mon; 🛜) A short walk from the city centre is this excellent bar with a spacious wooden terrace, a good menu of snacks and soak-it-all-up bar meals with decent veggie options, and plenty of lively student and academic discussion lubricated by a range of good bot-tled and draught beers. A great place.

Ye Old Brick's Inn PUB
(www.oldbricksinn.fi; Kauppakatu 41; ⊘11am-2am Mon-Thu, 11am-3am Fri, noon-3am Sat, noon-2am Sun; 🛜) In the liveliest part of the pedes-trian zone, this warm and welcoming pub has several excellent beers on tap, a cosy interior and an outdoor terrace screened by plastic plants – the place to be on a summer evening. It also has a good upmarket bar menu (mains €16 to €27).

London CLUB
(www.london.fi; Puistokatu 2; admission €5-8; ⊘10pm-4am Sun-Thu, 9pm-4am Fri & Sat) This massive space has several areas with live music, disco, Suomi-pop and rock.

☆ Entertainment

Poppari JAZZ
(www.jazz-bar.com; Puistokatu 2; ⊘3pm-3am Mon-Thu, 3am-4am Fri, 7pm-4am Sat, 4pm-3am Sun) This downstairs venue is the place for relaxing live music, with regular jazz slots and jam sessions, particularly on weekends (admission usually €3 to €8).

ℹ Information

Tourist Office (☑014-266-0113; visit.jyvaskyla.fi; Asemakatu 6; ⊘9am-4pm Mon-Fri, also 10am-2pm Sat Jul) Information and ticket sales.

ℹ Getting There & Away

Finnair operates flights Sunday to Friday (except July) from Helsinki to Jyväskylä.

Boats (p156) travel between Jyväskylä and Lahti.

The bus and train stations share the Mat-kakeskus building. Daily express buses connect Jyväskylä to southern Finnish towns, including hourly departures to Helsinki (€50.20, four to five hours). Some services require a change.

There are regular trains from Helsinki (€56.10, four hours) via Tampere, and some quicker direct trains.

ℹ Getting Around

TO/FROM THE AIRPORT
The airport is 23km north of the city centre; a few buses between Jyväskylä and other towns stop in here (€6 to €10; check www.matkahuolto.fi for times). A taxi is around €40.

THE LAKELAND JYVÄSKYLÄ

BICYCLE

Jyväskylä is great to explore by bike. The tourist office has a list of bike-hire operators and maps of three-to-five-day Lakeland circular routes. **Polkupyörä Tori** (✆ 040-535-2010; www.polkupyoratori.fi; Minna Canthinkatu 22B; per day/week €10/40; ☉ 9.30am-6pm Mon-Fri)

BUS

Local buses all leave from Vapaudenkatu, near the tourist office. Tickets cost €3.30 to €6.80 depending on distance. Day tickets can be bought at the tourist office – value if you'll be making three or more journeys.

Around Jyväskylä

Säynätsalo

Säynätsalon Kunnantalo   NOTABLE BUILDING
(✆ 014-266-1526;   www.jyvaskyla.fi/saynatsalo; Parviaisentie 9, Säynätsalo; ☉ 8.30am-3.30pm Mon-Fri) **FREE** Säynätsalo town hall, one of Aalto's most famous works, is on an island southeast of Jyväskylä. The sturdy brick tower of this 'fortress of democracy' recalls a castle, but the grassy patio bathes the interior with light and reflects a relationship with nature that is present in much of Aalto's work. The classroom-like council chamber is on the top floor.

Reach Säynätsalo from Jyväskylä on bus 16 or 21 (€5.50, 30 minutes); get off at the S/S-Kunnantalo stop.

THE WIFE-CARRYING WORLD CHAMPIONSHIPS

What began as a heathenish medieval habit of pillaging neighbouring villages in search of nubile women has become one of Finland's oddest – and most publicised – events. Get to Sonkajärvi, in the northern Lakeland, for the **Wife-Carrying World Championships** (www.eukonkanto.fi) in early July.

It's a race over a 253.5m obstacle course, where competitors must carry their 'wives' through water traps and over hurdles to achieve the fastest time. The winner gets the wife's weight in beer and the prestigious title of World Wife-Carrying Champion. To enter, men need only €50 and a consenting female. There's also a 40-plus and team competition, all accompanied by a weekend of drinking, dancing and typical Finnish frivolity.

Two rooms (€50) are available, named after the man and his second wife, who often slept here while supervising construction. They are singles (although extra beds can be put in), share a bathroom and have simple kitchen facilities.

Muuratsalo

Muuratsalon Koetalo   ARCHITECTURE
(✆ 014-266-7113;   www.alvaraalto.fi;   adult/student/child €17/8/free; ☉ 1.30-3.30pm Mon, Wed & Fri Jun–mid-Sep, plus Tue & Thu Aug) Peaceful Muuratsalo islet, connected to Säynätsalo by bridges, was Aalto's summer retreat. On Päijänne's shores he built his **Experimental House**, a must-see for Aalto lovers, but pricey if you're not. Entrance is by guided tour pre-arranged by phone or email (the Alvar Aalto Museo or Jyväskylä tourist office can do this). Take bus 16 (€5.50, 40 minutes) from central Jyväskylä to the end of the route; the house is 500m further.

You first see his beloved boat, *Nemo Propheta in Patria* ('Nobody is a Prophet in their Homeland') on terra firma: it was never very seaworthy. Then it's the lakeside sauna and house itself. Aalto used the charming patio to try out various types and patterns of bricks and tiles to see how they looked in different seasons and how they weathered.

The interior is surprisingly small; it's cool and colourful. A guest wing is perched on timber and stones (another playful experiment). You can well imagine Aalto looking out over the beautiful, peaceful lake and pondering his designs.

Petäjävesi

Thirty-five kilometres west of Jyväskylä, Petäjävesi has a wonderfully gnarled Unesco-listed wooden **church** (✆ 040-582-2461; www.petajavesi.fi/kirkko; Vanhankirkontie; adult/child €5/3.50; ☉ 10am-6pm Jun-Aug, call for low-season visits). Finished in 1765, it's a marvellous example of 18th-century rustic Finnish architecture with endearingly crooked wooden pews, a pulpit held up by a rosy-cheeked St Christopher, and a fairytale shingle roof. Burials took place under the floorboards, and there's also a spooky wine cellar under the nave – ask the guide to show you.

Buses from Jyväskylä to Keuruu stop in Petäjävesi. If coming by car, walk across a road bridge to the church from the car park.

Kuopio

📞 017 / POP 106.450

Most things a reasonable person could desire from a summery lakeside town are in Kuopio, with pleasure cruises on the azure water, spruce forests to stroll in, wooden waterside pubs, and local fish specialities to taste. And what better than a traditional smoke sauna to give necessary impetus to jump into the chilly waters?

◎ Sights

Puijo   HILL

Even small hills have cachet in flat Finland, and Kuopio was so proud of Puijo that it was crowned with a tower. Views from the top of **Puijon Torni** (Puijo Tower; www.puijo.com; adult/child €6/3; ⊙ 10am-9pm Mon-Sat, 10am-7pm Sun Jun-Aug, 11am-7pm Mon-Thu, 11am-9pm Fri-Sat, 11am-4pm Sun Sep-May) are very impressive; the vast perspectives of lakes and forests represent a sort of idealised Finnish vista. Atop is a revolving restaurant, cafe and open-air viewing deck. Surrounding it is one of the region's best-preserved spruce forests, with trails for walking, biking and cross-country skiing.

Also here is a ski jump and chairlift. In high summer there's a public bus to Puijo, but it's a nice walk through the trees, or a short drive or cab ride.

Kuopion Museo   MUSEUM

(www.kuopionmuseo.fi; Kauppakatu 23; adult/child €7.50/free; ⊙ 10am-5pm Tue-Sat) In a castle-like art nouveau mansion, this museum has a wide scope. The top two floors are devoted to cultural history, but the real highlight is the natural history display, with a wide variety of beautifully presented Finnish wildlife, including a mammoth and an ostrich wearing snowboots. The ground floor has temporary exhibitions. Pick up English explanations at the ticket desk.

Kuopion Korttelimuseo   MUSEUM

(Old Kuopio Museum; www.korttelimuseo.kuopio. fi; Kirkkokatu 22; adult/child €5.50/free; ⊙ 10am-5pm Tue-Sat mid-May–Aug, 10am-3pm Sep–mid-May) This block of old town houses forms one of Kuopio's delightful museums. Several homes – all with period furniture and decor – are very detailed and thorough and the level of information (in English) is excellent. **Apteekkimuseo** in building 11 contains old pharmacy paraphernalia, while in another building it's fascinating to compare photos of Kuopio from different decades. There's also a cafe serving a delicious *rahkapiirakka* (a local sweet pastry).

Suomen Ortodoksinen Kirkkomuseo   MUSEUM

(Orthodox Church Museum; www.ortodoksinenkirkko museo.fi; Karjalankatu 1) This museum holds an excellent collection of items brought here from monasteries and churches now in Russian-occupied Karelia. It was being renovated at last visit, but reopens in 2015.

Kuopion Taidemuseo   GALLERY

(www.taidemuseo.kuopio.fi; Kauppakatu 35; adult/child €5.50/free; ⊙ 10am-5pm Tue-Sat) This features mostly modern art in temporary exhibitions, but also displays permanent works. Look out for paintings by local Juho Rissanen (1873–1950), whose realistic portraits of working Finns contrasted with the prevalent Romanticism.

VB Valokuvakeskus   MUSEUM, GALLERY

(www.vb.kuopio.fi; Kuninkaankatu 14; adult/child under 12yr €7/free; ⊙ 11am-6pm Tue-Fri, 11am-4pm Sat & Sun Jun-Aug, closes one hour earlier Sep-May) Excellent summer exhibitions grace this photographic centre, devoted to Victor Barsokevitsch, a pioneer of Finnish photography.

🏃 Activities

★ Jätkänkämppä   SAUNA

(📞 030-60830; www.rauhalahti.fi; adult/child €12/6; ⊙ 4-10pm Tue, also Thu Jun-Aug & Nov-Dec, 4-11pm Jun-Aug) This giant *savusauna* (smoke sauna) is a memorable, sociable experience that draws locals and visitors. It seats 60 and is mixed: you're given towels to wear. Bring a swimsuit for lake dipping – devoted locals and brave tourists do so even when it's covered with ice. Repeat the process several times. Then buy a beer and relax, looking over the lake in Nordic peace.

The **restaurant** (adult/child buffet plus hot plate €21/10.50; ⊙ 4-8pm) in the adjacent loggers' cabin serves traditional Finnish dinners when the sauna's on, with accordion entertainment and a lumberjack show. Buses 7 and 9 head to Rauhalahti hotel, from where it's a 600m walk, or take a summertime cruise from the harbour.

Rauhalahti   OUTDOORS

(www.rauhalahti.com; Katiskaniementie 8) This estate is full of activities for families, including boating, cycling, tennis and minigolf in summer, and skating, ice-fishing and snowmobiling in winter. You can hire bikes, rowboats, canoes, in-line skates and Icelandic ponies for gentle rides. Take bus 7/9 or 20 from the town centre or a boat trip in summer. There's also accommodation here.

Cruises

Several different cruises depart from the town's passenger harbour daily during summer. Tickets for all cruises are available at the tourist office or directly on the boat. M/S *Puijo* (p147) offers lake trips to Savonlinna.

Roll Cruises   CRUISE
(Kuopion Roll Risteilyt; ☎017-277-2466; www.roll. fi; adult/child €15/8; ☺mid-May–late Aug) Runs regular 90-minute scenic cruises from Kuopio's harbour, as well as trips to a local berry wine farm.

Koski-Laiva Oy   CRUISE
(☎0400-207-245; www.koskilaiva.com; adult/child €15/8; ☺mid-May–Aug) Offers 90-minute scenic cruises, lunch trips and trips to Rauhalahti, a nice way of reaching the smoke sauna.

☞ Tours

Vesilento Taksi   SCENIC FLIGHTS
(☎050-572-6552; www.vesilentotaksi.fi; Kuopion satama) Runs quick jaunts over the town and lakes in a Cessna floatplane. There's a minimum of three passengers for the standard 15-minute flight, which costs €65 per person.

✷ Festivals & Events

Kuopion Tanssii ja Soi   DANCE
(www.kuopiodancefestival.fi) In mid-June this is the most interesting of Kuopio's annual events. There are open-air classical and modern dance performances, comedy and theatre gigs, and the town is buzzing.

⌕ Sleeping

Matkailukeskus Rauhalahti   CAMPGROUND €
(☎017-473-000; www.visitrauhalahti.fi; Rauhankatu 3; tent sites €15-16 plus per person €6, cabins €33-60, cottages €120; ☺mid-May–late Aug; P☎) Near the Rauhalahti hotel complex,

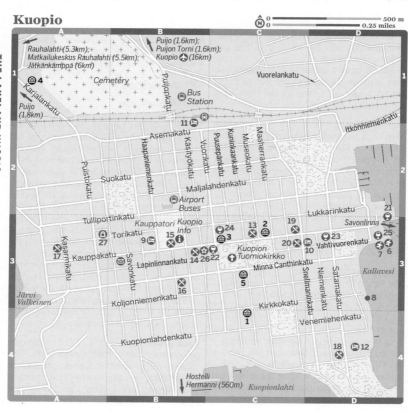

Kuopio

this place has a great location, plenty of facilities and is well set up for families. Bus 20 will get you here. The upmarket cottages are open year-round.

Hostelli Hermanni HOSTEL €
(☑040-910-9083; www.hostellihermanni.fi; Hermanninaukio 3D; dm/s/d €35/55/65; P@⊜) Tucked away in a quiet area 1.5km south of the kauppatori (follow Haapaniemenkatu and bear left when you can: the hostel's in the Metsähallitus building), this is a decent hostel with comfy wooden bunks and beds, bright bedspreads, high ceilings and reasonable shared bathrooms and kitchen. Bus 3 from the town centre makes occasional appearances nearby. No breakfast.

Check-in is between 2pm and 9pm; if you are going to arrive later, call ahead.

Hotel Atlas HOTEL €€
(☑020-789-6101; www.hotelatlas.fi; Haapaniemenkatu 22; s/d €130/150; P@⊜) An historic Kuopio hotel that reopened in 2012 after complete remodelling, the Atlas is now the town's most appealing option, not least for its prime location on the kauppatori. The commodious modern rooms are of good size, with a sofa, are well soundproofed and offer perspectives over the square, or, more unusually, the interior of a department store.

Prices are variable and there are three grades of room (superiors are €25 to €40 more than standards) plus suites.

Spa Hotel Rauhalahti SPA HOTEL €€
(☑030-60830; www.rauhalahti.fi; Katiskaniementie 8; s/d €114/146; P@⊜☒) Though it feels faded in parts, this spa hotel 6km south of town still makes a great place to stay, largely because of the huge scope for activities. The pool complex is good (available to nonguests for €12.50), and the modernised rooms are spacious and attractive. Excellent family packages are offered on its website. Take bus 7/9, or it's €25 in a cab. In the same complex is **Hostelli Rauhalahti** (s/d €77/92), with simple Nordic rooms sharing kitchens and with full use of the hotel's facilities, plus **Apartment Hotel Rauhalahti** (2-/4-person apt from €146/224) which has excellent modern pads with all the trimmings, including (for very little extra) a sauna.

Hotelli Jahtihovi HOTEL €€
(☑017-264-4400; www.jahtihovi.fi; Snellmaninkatu 23; s/d €94/114; P@⊜) Well located near the harbour on a quiet street, this cordial independent hotel makes a good address. Regular rooms are good-sized and pleasant (twins are a fair bit larger than doubles); the superiors (s/d €104/124), in a modern wing, add big windows, extra mod-cons and a stylish look. A session in the smart sauna is included, and parking's free. Prices drop €20 on weekends.

Kuopion Asemagrilli GUESTHOUSE €€
(Hostal Asema; ☑017-580-0569; www.kuopionasemagrilli.com; Asemakatu 1; s/d €55/79; P⊜) Let's get one thing straight: sleeping as close

THE LAKELAND KUOPIO

as you can to transport terminals isn't lazy, it's practical. True. This friendly place, operating out of the grilli (fast-food outlet) in the train station, actually offers ensuite rooms in the building itself – very comfortable, exceedingly spacious and surprisingly peaceful. It's a good deal. Decent rooms for groups available.

Scandic Hotel Kuopio · · · · · · · · · · · HOTEL €€€
(☎ 017-195-111; www.scandichotels.fi; Satamakatu 1; s/d €144/164; P @ 🖥 🕸) 🏊 This unobtrusive but large hotel has an appealing, quiet lakeside location and fine facilities that include a gym, sauna and Jacuzzi, as well as bikes for hire. Rooms have plenty of natural light and criss-cross parquet floors. Superior rooms are worth the extra €20, as they have king-sized beds and balconies with lake views. Supply-and-demand pricing operates; there can be good summer rates.

🍴 Eating

Kaneli · CAFE €
(www.kahvilakaneli.net; Kauppakatu 22; cakes €4-5; ⊙ 11am-5pm Mon-Fri, 11am-4pm Sat, 11am-3pm Sun) This cracking cafe just off the kauppatori evokes a bygone age with much of its decor, but offers modern comfort in its shiny espresso machine, as well as many other flavoured coffees to accompany your toothsome, sticky *pulla* (cardamom-flavoured bun). It opens earlier in winter.

Lounas-Salonki · · · · · · · · · · · · · · · FINNISH €
(www.lounassalonki.fi; Kasarmikatu 12; lunches €7.50-9.50; ⊙ 9am-9pm Mon-Sat, noon-9pm Sun; ☑) This charming wooden building west of the town centre is warm and friendly, with little rooms sporting elegant imperial furniture. It serves a salad buffet and daily hot lunch (11am to 3pm) featuring traditional Finnish fare. It's reliably delicious and offers excellent value, including dessert, soft drinks and coffee. There are also à la carte options including vegetarian choices. On Sundays the expanded lunch buffet costs €16.70.

Kauppahalli · · · · · · · · · · · · · · · · · · MARKET €
(⊙ 8am-5pm Mon-Fri, 8am-3pm Sat; ☑) 🏊 At the southern end of the kauppatori is a classic Finnish indoor market hall, beautifully restored. Here stalls sell local speciality *kalakukko*, a large rye loaf stuffed with whitefish and then baked. It's delicious hot or cold. A whole one – a substantial thing – costs around €25, but you can buy halves.

Sorrento · ITALIAN €
(www.trattoriasorrento.fi; Snellmaninkatu 22; mains €10-15; ⊙ 10.30am-8.30pm Mon-Fri, noon-8.30pm Sat) Finland is obsessed with Italian restaurants, but this neighbourhood trattoria has a far more authentic feel than most. Tasty fresh pasta, decent pizzas, a couple of outdoor tables and a genuine welcome make this a welcome addition to the Kuopio scene. Lunch specials are very worthwhile.

★ Kummisetä · · · · · · · · · · · · · · · · FINNISH €€
(www.kummiseta.com; Minna Canthinkatu 44; mains €17-30; ⊙ kitchen 3-9.30pm Mon-Sat) The sober brown colours of the 'Godfather' give it a traditional feel replicated on the menu, with sauces featuring fennel, berries and morel mushrooms garnishing prime cuts of beef, tender-as-young-love lamb and succulent pike-perch. Food is hearty rather than gourmet; it and the service are both excellent. In summer eating on the spacious two-level back terrace is an absolute pleasure. Hours change slightly every week; these are an approximation.

Sampo · FINNISH €€
(www.wanhamestari.fi; Kauppakatu 13; dishes €14-18; ⊙ 11am-10pm Mon-Thu, 11am-midnight Fri & Sat, noon-10pm Sun) Have it stewed, fried, smoked or in a soup, but it's all about *muikku* here. This is one of Finland's most famous spots to try the small lakefish that drives Savo stomachs. The 70-year-old restaurant is cosy, and classically Finnish.

Isä Camillo · · · · · · · · · · · · · MEDITERRANEAN €€
(☎ 017-581-0450; www.isacamillo.net; Kauppakatu 25; mains €21-29; ⊙ 11am-9.30pm Mon-Thu, 11am-10.30pm Fri, noon-10.30pm Sat) Set in a beautifully renovated former bank – look out for the old strongroom – this is an elegant but informal spot for a meal, with Mediterranean-inspired dishes from a variety of countries as well as some Finnish specialities. There's a good enclosed terrace at the side and a decent pub downstairs.

★ Musta Lammas · · · · · · · · · · · · · FINNISH €€€
(☎ 017-581-0458; www.mustalammas.net; Satamakatu 4; mains €28-33, degustation menu €59; ⊙ 5-9pm Mon-Thu, 5-11pm Fri & Sat; ☑) One of Finland's best restaurants, the Black Sheep has a golden fleece. Set in an enchantingly romantic brick-vaulted space, it offers a short menu of delicious gourmet mains using top-quality Finnish meat and fish, with complex sauces that complement but never overpower the natural flavours. Wines

include a fabulous selection of generously priced special bottles (healthy credit card required). There's also a roof terrace.

🍸 Drinking & Nightlife

Kuopio's nightlife is conveniently strung along Kauppakatu, running east from the market square to the harbour. Here, grungy, popular and likeable **Ale Pupi** (www.alepupi.fi; Kauppakatu 16; ⊙ 9am-1am Mon, 9am-2am Tue-Sat, 9am-midnight Sun) has a huge interior, surprisingly classy decor and big drawcards of cheap beer and karaoke, but there are many other options in this block, some with summer terraces.

Wanha Satama   PUB
(www.wanhasatama.net; ⊙ 11am-11pm Mon-Thu, 11am-4am Fri & Sat, noon-9pm Sun May-Aug) In a noble blue building by the harbour, this has one of Lakeland's best terraces, definitely the place to be on a sunny day to watch the boats come and go. There's decent Finnish fish and meat dishes, and regular live music. Hours reduce at the beginning and end of the season.

Albatrossi   PUB
(www.ravintolaalbatrossi.fi;   Makasiininkatu   1;
⊙ 2pm-late Mon-Thu, noon-late Fri-Sun May–mid-Sep) This old wooden warehouse conversion is an atmospheric place to see some live music or grab a drink, particularly when you can sit outside and look at the lake. Drinks are served in plastic, but the atmosphere's great. Opening hours vary week by week: check its Facebook page.

Helmi   PUB
(www.satamanhelmi.fi;   Kauppakatu 2;   ⊙ 11am-11pm Mon-Thu, 11am-2am Fri, noon-2am Sat, noon-8pm Sun) This historic 19th-century sailors' hang-out by the harbour has recently been remodelled and is a cosy, comfortable spot with a range of local characters. There's a decent pool table, tasty pizzas (€8 to €10) and a sociable enclosed terrace.

Ilona   CLUB
(www.ilonacity.fi;   Vuorikatu 19;   ⊙ 10pm-4am) The city's best nightclub has an attractive London-themed bar with a smoking cabin done out like a red bus, and a separate karaoke bar where enthusiastic punters belt out Suomi hits. There's a fat list of English-language songs if you don't fancy trying out your Finnish vowels. There's a 22-year-old minimum age on weekends.

☆ Entertainment

Henry's Pub   LIVE MUSIC
(www.henryspub.net; Käsityökatu 17; ⊙ 9pm-4am Tue-Sat, from 11pm Sun & Mon; ☎) An atmospheric underworld with bands playing several times a week, usually free, and usually at the heavier end of the rock/metal spectrum.

🛍 Shopping

Pikku-Pietarin Torikuja   CRAFTS
(www.pikkupietarintorikuja.fi;   ⊙ 10am-5pm Mon-Fri, 10am-3pm Sat Jun-Aug) An atmospheric narrow lane of renovated red wooden houses converted into quirky shops stocking jewellery, clothing, handicrafts and other items. Halfway along is an excellent cafe (open from 8am) with cosy upstairs seating and a great little back deck for the summer sun.

ℹ Information

Kuopio Info (☎ 0800-182-050; www.visitkuopio.fi; Apaja Shopping Centre, Kauppakatu 45; ⊙ 8am-3pm Mon-Fri) Underneath the kauppatori. Information on regional attractions and accommodation. May open on Saturday in the future.

ℹ Getting There & Away

Finnair flies daily to Helsinki.

Boats (p162) travel between Kuopio and Savonlinna.

Express bus services to/from Kuopio (change in Varkaus for Savonlinna) include the following:
Helsinki (€66.30, 6½ hours)
Jyväskylä (€25.60, 2¼ hours)

Daily trains services include the following:
Helsinki (€68, 4½ to five hours)
Kajaani (€30.70, 1¾ hours)
Oulu (€53.70, four hours)

Change at Pieksämäki or Kouvola for other destinations.

ℹ Getting Around

TO/FROM THE AIRPORT
Kuopio airport is 16km north of town. **Bus 40** (joukkoliikenne.kuopio.fi) runs there roughly hourly Monday to Friday.

BICYCLE & CAR
You can hire bikes for €12 to €15 a day at **Hertz** (☎ 020-555-2670; www.hertz.fi; Asemakatu 1) and Kuopion Asemagrilli (p163), both in the train station building. Both also offer car hire.

Karelia

Best Places to Eat

➡ Wolkoff Restaurant & Wine Bar (p171)

➡ Teatteri (p176)

➡ Parppeinpirtti (p178)

➡ Alamaja (p180)

➡ Säräpirtti Kippurasarvi (p171)

Best Places to Stay

➡ Kestikievari Herranniemi (p181)

➡ Imatran Valtionhotelli (p173)

➡ Lappeenrannan Kylpylä (p170)

➡ Timitraniemi Camping (p182)

➡ Ruunaa Hiking Centre (p184)

Why Go?

If you're looking for wilderness, powerful history and even the Finnish soul, your search starts here. Densely forested and gloriously remote, the region is a paradise for nature lovers. Bears, wolverines and wolves roam freely across the Russian frontier, and animal hides allow visitors a close encounter. Opportunities to get active abound: the landscape is threaded by hiking routes, whitewater rapids and waterways navigable by canoe, and lakes offer idyllic kayaking and boating. In winter outdoor pursuits include fantastic skiing, dog-sledding, snowshoeing and ice-fishing.

Karelia straddles both sides of the Finnish–Russian border, with a distinct culture, language, religion, cuisine, music and architecture. In Finland's Karelian regions, lakeside Lappeenranta is still strongly connected to its sister cities that have been part of Russia since WWII. Once-battle-scarred Joensuu is now a vibrant university town, and Imatra still recalls its 18th-century golden age as a Russian aristocracy playground.

When to Go

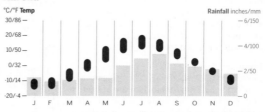

Karelia

Mid-Apr The bear-watching season begins, when brown bears wake from their winter sleep.

Jul Joensuu's party atmosphere amps up during the international Ilosaari Rock Festival.

Dec Koli National Park's ski resort opens for business.

Karelia Highlights

1 Swooshing down the ski slopes or swooping above the tree line aboard the summer chairlift at **Koli National Park** (p179)

2 Shooting Ruunaa's rapids on a rubber **raft** (p183)

3 Cruising from Lappeenranta to the Karelian town of Vyborg on a 'visa-free' **trip to Russia** (p170)

4 Ticking another 'superlative place' off your list beyond Hattuvaara at the far-flung **easternmost point of the EU** (p178)

5 Walking with a **reindeer** (p180) in its natural habitat in the pristine Lake Pielinen region's Haapalahti

6 Dangling upside down over torrents of water on a flying fox across the **Imatra Rapids** (p172)

7 Falling in love with the woodland chapel at **Paateri** (p181), carved by artist Eva Ryynänen

8 Spending the night in an **animal hide** (p182) near Lieksa, awaiting wolverines, lynx and bears

9 Hiking the poignant **Karhunpolku** (Bear's Trail; p183), scattered with WWII remains

SOUTH KARELIA

Over the centuries the border has shuttled backward and forward and the South Karelian trade town of Vyborg (Finnish: Viipuri) and the Karelian Isthmus reaching to St Petersburg are now part of Russia, accessible from former garrison town Lappeenranta.

Lappeenranta

📞 05 / POP 72,700

On the banks of Lake Saimaa – Finland's largest lake – Lappeenranta has encountered wild swings of fortune. Once famous for its scarlet-clad garrison, the 17th-century 'Cavalry City' was a humming trade port at the edge of the Swedish empire. In 1743 it came under Russian control, where it remained for the next 68 years, becoming an exclusive spa town. Much of the town was destroyed during the Winter and Continuation Wars, but its massive fortress and spa endure.

Russia still owns half of the 43km Saimaa Canal, which links Lappeenranta to the Gulf of Finland. It's currently 'leased' to Finland until 2063 – popular day trips run through its eight locks and across the Russian border.

Lappeenranta

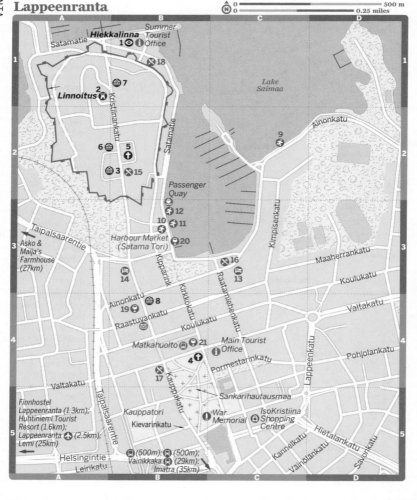

⊙ Sights

★ Linnoitus
FORTRESS, MUSEUM

(www.lappeenranta.fi/linnoitus; fortress free, adult/child combined museum ticket €9/free; ⊙10am-6pm Mon-Fri, 11am-5pm Sat & Sun Jun-late Aug, 11am-5pm Tue-Sun late Aug-May) Standing guard above the harbour, this hulking hilltop fortification was begun by the Swedes and finished by the Russians in the late 18th century. Today it contains galleries, craft workshops and fascinating museums, including the history-focused **South Karelian Museum** (Etelä-Karjalan Museo; adult/child €6.50/free), **Cavalry Museum** (Ratsuväkimuseo; adult/child €3/free; ⊙10am-6pm Mon-Fri, 11am-5pm Sat & Sun) and **South Karelia Art Museum** (Etelä-Karjalan Taidemuseo; adult/child €6.50/free). Its **Orthodox Church** (⊙10am-5pm Tue-Sun Jun–mid-Aug), Finland's oldest church, was completed in 1785 by Russian soldiers. Pick up the tourist office's free walking guide *The Fortress of Lappeenranta*.

★ Hiekkalinna
SANDCASTLE

(http://hiekkalinna.lappeenranta.fi; ⊙10am-8pm early Jun-Aug) **FREE** Every summer around 30 sand artists from Finland and abroad gather to build the Hiekkalinna, a giant themed 'sandcastle' made from some three million kilograms of sand. Themes have included dinosaurs, a Wild West scene incorporating a gigantic steam train, and 'outer space' featuring ET and Darth Vader. Kids' entertainment here includes small carousel-style rides.

Wolkoff Home Museum
MUSEUM

(Wolkoffin Talomuseo; ☎05-616-2258; Kauppakatu 26; adult/child €6.50/free; ⊙10am-4pm Mon-Fri, 11am-5pm Sat & Sun early Jun-late Aug, 11am-5pm Sat & Sun Mar-early Jun & late Aug-early Dec) Built in 1826, this lovingly preserved Russian home was owned by the merchant Wolkoff family from 1872 to 1986, and its 10 rooms have been maintained as they were in the late 1800s. The house is visitable only by 40-minute guided tours. From early June to late August, English tours depart at quarter to the hour. The rest of the season, tours in Finnish depart at quarter past the hour, with English-language audio guides available.

Lappee Church
CHURCH

(Kirkkokatu 11; ⊙10am-6pm Jun–mid-Aug) Diagonally across the park from its bell tower, the adorable wooden Lappee Church was built in 1794 to an unusual 'double cruciform' floor plan, the only one of its kind in Finland. South of the church stretches the graveyard, with an evocative **war memorial**, which features poignant cubist and modernist sculptures commemorating Finns who died in the Winter and Continuation Wars.

🏃 Activities

Myllysaari
BEACH

On the lakeshore this sandy beach has an outdoor swimming pool, beach volleyball and the Myllysaari **beach sauna** (admission €6, heated dressing rooms €7.65; ⊙women 4-8pm Wed & Fri, men 4-8pm Tue & Thu). Hardy souls can swim here in winter when two pools are cut into the ice.

Saimaan Risteilyt
CRUISE

(☎020-787-0620; www.saimaanristeilyt.fi; adult/child €16/2; ⊙departs 11am, 3pm & 6pm late May-Oct) Offers popular two-hour trips on Lake Saimaa and the Saimaa Canal aboard the M/S *El Faro*.

TRAVELLING TO RUSSIA

A boat cruise along the Saimaa Canal to Vyborg, 60km southeast, in Russia, is something of a spiritual journey to reunite Karelia.

Saimaan Matkaverkko runs quick-and-easy 'visa-free' day cruises for all nationalities from Lappeenranta to Vyborg aboard the M/S *Carelia* (from €65, departs 7.45am four to six times weekly from late May to mid-September) that allow you around 3½ hours to sightsee and shop. It's also possible to stay overnight in Vyborg, with prices varying by season and usually costing more on weekends. You must provide the company with a copy of your passport at least three days before departure (and passports must be valid for at least a further six months from the end date of your trip). Book well in advance, as these cruises are heavily subscribed. The company can also organise a package (from €278, single supplement €175, meals and excursions extra, departing July to August) to St Petersburg that includes the cruise to Vyborg and a bus on to St Petersburg, with two nights' accommodation in Russia.

If you want to travel independently (and you have a visa), several train and bus services pass through Lappeenranta on the way to St Petersburg and Moscow. For non-EU citizens who haven't organised a Russian tourist visa before leaving their country of residence, independent travel is difficult to impossible. If you can endure a long wait and complex bureaucracy you could try the embassy in Helsinki or the **Russian consulate** (☑05-872-0722; Kievarinkatu 1A; ☺9am-noon Mon, Wed & Fri) in Lappeenranta. For more on applying for a Russian visa see p69.

Saimaan Matkaverkko CRUISE
(☑05-541-0100; www.saimaatravel.fi; Kipparinkatu 1; ☺9am-5pm Mon-Fri) Day cruises (Thursday and Saturday, June to August; from €59) cross Lake Saimaa to Savonlinna aboard M/S *Brahe* (returning by bus). Also runs 'visa-free' trips along the canal to Vyborg and St Petersburg in Russia.

Salpasafarit CRUISE
(☑044-553-6384; www.salpasafarit.fi; hovercraft trips per 15min from €15; ☺hovercraft trips noon & 5pm Wed, Fri & Sat) Activities outfit Salpasafarit runs a range of trips on and around Lake Saimaa including zippy hovercraft trips.

☆ Festivals & Events

Lemin Musiikkijuhlat MUSIC
(www.leminmusiikkijuhlat.fi; tickets free-€20) This four-day chamber-music festival takes place in late July or early August, mainly in churches throughout Lappeenranta, Imatra and Lemi.

🛏 Sleeping

Chain hotels such as Sokos are plentiful.

Huhtiniemi Tourist Resort HOSTEL, CAMPGROUND €
(☑05-451-5555; www.huhtiniemi.com; Kuusimäenkatu 18; tent sites €14 plus per person €5, 2-/4-person cottages €40/50, apt €80-98; ☺mid-May–Sep; ☎) Situated 2km west of the city centre, this large lakeside campground has waterside sites, neat cottages and self-contained apartments that fill to the gills in summer – reservations are a must. Also here are two HI hostels, the simple **Huhtiniemi Hostel** (☑05-451-5555; www.huhtiniemi.com; dm €15; ☺Jun-Aug) and hotel-style **Finnhostel Lappeenranta** (☑05-451-5555; www.huhtiniemi.com; s/d/tr €75/95/115). Bus 5 from the city stops here, as do most intercity buses.

★ Lappeenrannan Kylpylä SPA HOTEL €€
(☑020-761-3761; www.kylpyla.info; Ainonkatu 17; s €80-110, d €120-160; @ ☎ ⊠) Bronze- and gold-toned, minibar-equipped rooms – some opening to balconies overlooking the park and water – range over the revamped 1970s spa hotel housing reception and the upper floors of the lakefront art nouveau Wanha Kylpylä (Old Spa) building across the street. Facilities include a gym, a couple of pools and a waterfall that delivers a pounding shoulder massage.

Scandic Hotel Patria HOTEL €€
(☑05-677-511; www.scandichotels.com; Kauppakatu 21; s €95-141, d €103-161; @) ✿ Definitely one of the best places to stay in Lappeenranta, the Patria is close to the harbour and fortress. The pick of its Scandi-chic rooms feature balconies with park views. Satff are super helpful.

Eating

Kahvila Majurska
CAFE €

(www.majurska.com; Kristiinankatu 1; dishes €3-5; ◷10am-5pm Mon-Sat, 11am-5pm Sun) If you can't border-hop to a genuine Russian tea-house, this is as close as you'll get in Finland. A former officer's club (check out the vintage furniture and august portrait of Mannerheim), it still serves tea from the samovar and does a range of homemade pastries.

Wanha Makasiini
BISTRO €€

(☑010-666-8611; www.ravintolawanhamakasiini.fi; Satamatie 4; pizzas €13-15, mains €19-31.50; ◷noon-10pm Mon, noon-11.30pm Tue-Sat, noon-6pm Sun; ✍) High-quality dishes at this cosy spot range from fresh fish to horse steaks and seasonal delicacies like chanterelle soup. Thin, crispy pizzas come with traditional toppings as well as local specialities like smoked *muikku* (vendace, or whitefish, a small lake fish) and pickled cucumber.

Tassos
GREEK €€

(☑010-762-1452; www.tassos.fi; Valtakatu 33; meze dish/platter €2.80/10.80, mains €19.50-38; ◷11am-10pm Mon-Sat, 1-7pm Sun; ☎) Start with a plateful of meze dishes at this long-standing family restaurant in the stately old Nordea bank building, followed by Greek favourites like *soutsoukakia* (lamb meatballs in tomato sauce), *garides* (king prawn skewers with garlic yoghurt) and *stifado* (beef, onion and tomato stew served with rice).

Kasino
RUSSIAN, INTERNATIONAL €€

(☑020-729-6738; Ainonkatu 10; lunch buffets €12.60-14.80, mains €17-32; ◷11am-3pm & 5-10pm Tue-Sat, 11am-3pm & 5-9pm Sun & Mon) Salmon blini (pancakes) and *zakuska* (light buffet) are among the Russian options served at this venerable century-old wooden building but the rest of the menu travels the globe, from steak with cognac cream sauce to pulled-pork burgers and courgette and artichoke lasagne. In summer the best seats are on the floating terrace moored on the lake.

★Wolkoff Restaurant & Wine Bar
FINNISH €€€

(☑05-415-0320; www.wolkoff.fi; Kauppakatu 26; lunch buffet €15, mains €21-30, 3-course menu €46; ◷11am-11pm Mon-Fri, 4.30-11pm Sat) This grand old-world restaurant utilises organic produce and seasonal ingredients to create gourmet Finnish cuisine with adventurous flavour combinations like reindeer tartare with Dijon mustard ice cream, and duck

---

LEMI

The tiny village of Lemi, 25km west of Lappeenranta, is synonymous with its signature dish *lemin särä* (roast mutton). Hailed as one of the seven wonders of Finland, it's cooked in a birch trough to infuse the meat with a sweet, woody flavour and takes nine hours to prepare so you'll need to book at least two days in advance.

The best place to sample it is the lakeshore restaurant **Säräpirtti Kippurasarvi** (☑05-414-6470; www.sarapirtti.fi; Rantatie 1; adult/child €32/16; ◷see website for serving times), which serves nothing but *lemin särä*, accompanied by thick rye bread and homemade *kalja* (beer).

KARELIA LAPPEENRANTA

---

breast with plum, sweet potato and dark wheatbeer sauce. The laden lunch buffet is a veritable bargain.

⚱ Drinking & Nightlife

The harbour's **boat bars** are great for a summertime drink above deck in the sunshine.

Birra
BAR

(Kauppakatu 27; ◷2pm-2am Tue-Sat, 2pm-1am Sun & Mon; ☎) One of the swankier bars in town, Birra has a shaded terrace, cosy booths, and a great beer and cider selection.

Old Park
IRISH PUB

(Valtakatu 36; ◷9am-1am Mon & Tue, 9am-2am Wed-Fri, noon-2am Sat, noon-1am Sun; ☎) Gently Irish-themed (no shamrocks!), this lively hang-out opens to a busy terrace.

① Information

Main Tourist Office (☑05-667-788; www.visitlappeenranta.fi; Valtakatu 37; ◷10am-5pm Mon-Fri, 10am-2pm Sat) Has an accommodation booking service for €3.50.

Summer Tourist Office (☑040-352-2178; www.visitlappeenranta.fi; ◷10am-8pm late Jun-early Aug, 10am-6pm early Aug-late Aug) Located at the sandcastle Hiekkalinna (p169).

① Getting There & Away

Bus and train tickets can be booked at the town-centre office of **Matkahuolto** (☑0200-4000; www.matkahuolto.fi; Valtakatu 36B; ◷9am-5pm Mon-Fri).

❶ FARMSTAYS

If you're looking to get off the beaten track, meet locals and experience rural life, try a farmstay in the countryside around Lappeenranta. Your double room, costing around €70, could be in a traditional 19th-century farmhouse, a former granary or perhaps a cosy log cabin in the grounds. Some places have animals for children to pet, and almost all offer outdoor activities, such as smoke saunas, rowing, fishing, snow-shoeing, snowmobiling or horse-drawn sleigh-riding.

A great option is the lakeside **Asko & Maija's Farmhouse** (☑ 040-507-5842; www.rantatupa.net; Suolahdentie 461, Tai-palsaari; homestay per person €30, cottages per week from €430; ⊙ mid-May–late Sep; 🅿), 30km northwest of Lappeenranta off Rd 408. Homestay accommodation is in a traditional log cabin built in 1843; there are also three charming timber cottages. Contact Lappeenranta's main tourist office (p171) to find others.

AIR

From Lappeenranta airport, 3km west of the city centre, Ryanair flies to Bergamo (Italy), Girona (Spain) and Weeze (Germany).

BUS

Lappeenranta's bus station is 1.2km south of the city centre; most intercity buses also stop on Valtakatu in the middle of town. Bus 9 (€3) runs between the bus station and the city centre.

Regular services include the following:
Helsinki (€40.50, 4¼ hours, 16 daily)
Imatra (€12, one hour, 11 daily)
Joensuu (€43.90, 4½ hours, two daily)
Mikkeli (€24, 1¾ hours, eight daily)
Savonlinna (€27.80, four hours, four daily)

TRAIN

Intercity trains use Lappeenranta train station, next to the bus station 1.2km south of town. Services include Helsinki (€47.20, two hours, eight daily), Imatra (€8.60, 25 minutes, five daily) and Joensuu (€41.20, two hours, four daily).

International trains to/from Russia use Vainikkala train station, 29.5km south of Lappeenranta, linked by bus (€6.80, 40 minutes, up to 10 daily) from the bus station and Valtakatu in town. Trains run to Vyborg (€31.80, 25 minutes, five daily) and St Petersburg (€47.80, 1½ hours), as well as Moscow (€76.40, 10¼ hours, one overnight service daily).

Book through **VR** (Finnish Railways; ☑ 060-041-902; www.vr.fi).

❶ Getting Around

TO/FROM THE AIRPORT
Bus 4 (€3.30) links the city centre and the airport.

BICYCLE
The best way to explore this large town is to hire a bike from **Pyörä-Expert** (☑ 05-411-8710; www.pyoraexpert.com; Valtakatu 64; bike hire per day €9; ⊙ 10.30am-5pm Mon-Fri, 10.30am-2pm Sat Jun-Aug, 9am-6pm Mon-Fri, 9am-2pm Sat Sep-May).

PUBLIC TRANSPORT
In summer you can rest your feet aboard the **street train** (per ride adult/child €4/2; ⊙ hourly noon-5pm Mon, 10am-5pm Tue-Sun early Jun-Aug), which links the market square, IsoKristiina shopping centre, Linnoitus, Hiekkalinna and Myllysaari beach.

Imatra

☑ 05 / POP 28,320

Imatra was once the darling of Russian aristocracy – one of the first tourists to the area was Catherine the Great who in 1772 gathered her entourage to view Imatra's thundering rapids. Although the rapids were harnessed for hydroelectricity in 1929, the water pours forth again during dramatic daily summer shows. The town has a number of dispersed 'centres', mostly brassy and modern and all separated by kilometres of highway. Imatrankoski, the site of the rapids, is of most interest to visitors and has the majority of services. Boaties, beach goers and spa babes may prefer the Imatran leisure area, 7km northwest of Imatrankoski.

◉ Sights & Activities

Imatra Rapids RIVER
(⊙ Rapids Show 6pm Jun-late Aug) The 1929 construction of Imatra's hydroelectric complex (Finland's largest) dammed the river, but the watery wonder lives on with the spectacular 20-minute **Rapids Show**, when the dam is opened to a rousing *son et lumière*.

If your inner daredevil wants to get involved, **Imatra Express** (☑ 044-016-1096; www.imatraexpress.fi; basic/inverted €35/50, cheaper options when no rapids; ⊙ 5-7pm Mon-Fri & Sun, noon-7pm Sat Jun-late Aug, or by arrangement) runs a flying fox over the gushing waters with a death-defying upside-down option.

Imatran Taidemuseo GALLERY
(Virastokatu 1; ⊙10am-7pm Mon-Thu, 10am-4pm Fri Jun-Aug, 10am-7pm Mon-Fri, 11am-3pm Sat Sep-May) **FREE** Attached to the public library, this bright white space has temporary exhibitions and a strong collection of Finnish modernism, including works by Wäinö Aaltonen and a Gallen-Kallela watercolour of the rapids during their heyday in 1893.

Vuoksen Kalastuspuisto FISHING
(✍05-432-3123; www.vuoksenkalastuspuisto.com; Kotipolku 4; fishing €5, plus €14-22 per kg of fish caught; ⊙9.30am-6pm May, 9am-10pm Jun-Sep) You can fish for salmon and trout in these stocked ponds in Mansikkala, use the on-site smoker and purchase licences (€12/24 per day/week) for the surrounding waters. There's a seafood restaurant; it also rents bikes, rowboats and kayaks (€20 per day), and offers comfy camping (tent sites €15 plus €4 per person) and good-sized fishing cabins (€45).

Saimaa Adventures OUTDOOR ACTIVITIES
(✍05-230-2555; www.saimma-adventures.fi; Purjekuja 2) Summer activities include quad-bike safaris (two people €180 per hour) and jet-ski rental (€99 per hour); winter options include ski or snowshoe rental (€10/25 per two hours/day), ice-fishing (equipment rental €10/20 per two hours/day), and for the truly fearless, 90-minute tours floating in a drysuit along an icy stream (€48).

⚑ Festivals & Events

Imatra Big Band Festival MUSIC
(✍050-441-2461; www.ibbf.fi; tickets €18.50-80) Since 1982, jazz, swing and blues players have been blowing their trumpets around Imatrankoski in late June to early July.

⛏ Sleeping

Ukonlinna Hostel HOSTEL €
(✍010-322-7711; ukonlinna@elisanet.fi; Leiritie 8; dm €30, f €140-160) With a prime position on the beach this endearing little HI hostel is popular with families and books out quickly. There are three saunas (€50 per hour); staff are delightful.

Vuoksenhovi Hotelli HOTEL €€
(✍05-687-8000; www.vuoksenhovi.com; Siitolankatu 1; s/d/tr/ste €99/140/165/250; 🛜) Don't be dissuaded by the dated concrete-block facade: this well-run hotel has 94 spotless rooms, most with a private balcony or patio, and four saunas (suites also have their own sauna in-room), as well as a large restaurant and bar, and lightning-fast wi-fi. It's handy for the train and bus stations.

Imatran Kylpylä Spa SPA HOTEL €€
(✍020-710-0500; www.imatrankylpyla.fi; Purjekuja 1; s €102, d €129-190, apt €220; **P**@🛜) The whopping flagship of Imatra's leisure area incorporates the family-oriented Promenade Hotel (with lake views), newly renovated Spa Hotel, and gorgeous two- to four-person luxury apartments set on their own little hill. There are cafes, bars, a bowling alley (€23 per lane), bike hire, a badminton court and of course the spa itself, with several pools, Jacuzzis and treatments galore.

★**Imatran Valtionhotelli** CASTLE HOTEL €€€
(✍05-625-2000; www.rantasipi.fi; Torkkelinkatu 2; s/d from €118/138; @🛜🛜) Topped by flamboyant turrets, this fairy-tale Jugend-style castle was built in 1903 to replace the buildings that had hosted Russian aristocracy after the original wooden structures burnt down. Some of the castle's art nouveau–furnished rooms overlook the rapids. The adjacent modern spa centre's contemporary chocolate- and cream-coloured rooms are stylish and spacious but lack their neighbour's grandeur.

✗ Eating & Drinking

Caffe Prego CAFE €
(Napinkuja 2; dishes €3-8, lunch buffet €7; ⊙9am-5pm Mon-Fri, 9am-4pm Sat) This excellent Italian coffee spot also does good salads and sandwiches, and has a lovely little terrace.

Buttenhoff FRENCH, RUSSIAN €€
(✍05-476-1433; www.buttenhoff.fi; Koskenparras 4; lunch mains €12.50-20, dinner mains €19-36; ⊙11am-9.30pm Mon-Fri, noon-9.30pm Sat) Cooking up specialities from France (Burgundy escargot) and Russia (blini with caviar), this 1st-floor restaurant also creates hybrid

> ### ℹ KARELIA SELF-CATERING ACCOMMODATION
>
> In South Karelia, **GoSaimaa** (www.gosaimaa.com) has a good selection of lakeside cottages around Imatra and Lappeenranta.
>
> For North Karelia, the tourist service **Karelia Expert** (✍0400-239-549; www.visitkarelia.fi) has a dedicated accommodation booking service for cottage, cabin and apartment rental.

French-Russian dishes such as pan-fried perch *à la Russe*. On the ground floor and run by the same operator, casual **Café Julia** (dishes €3-7; ⊘8am-5pm Mon-Fri, 9am-5pm Sat) has fabulous cakes.

LinnaSali   REGIONAL CUISINE €€€
(☑05-625-2100; www.rantasipi.fi; Torkkelinkatu 2; mains €17-39; ⊘5-10pm Sun-Tue, 4-11pm Wed-Fri, 2-11pm Sat) Inside the landmark Imatran Valtionhotelli (p173), with a front-row view of the rapids from the stone terrace, Imatra's most romantic restaurant serves artfully prepared local cuisine (beef liver with fig jam and crushed lingonberries; elk hotpot; pike-perch fried in horseradish butter with boletus mushroom sauce) accompanied by outstanding wines.

Kuohu   BAR
(Imatran Kaskentie 1; ⊘noon-11pm Mon-Thu, noon-midnight Fri & Sat, noon-10pm Sun; 🐾) Set in a leafy park close to the rapids, this stylish Arctic-white bar opens to an umbrella-shaded terrace (heated in winter) and hosts live music on weekends.

ℹ **Information**

Tourist Office (☑05-235-2330; www.go-saimaa.com; Lappeentie 12; ⊘9am-5.30pm Mon-Fri Jun–mid-Aug, plus noon-4pm Sat mid-Jul–Aug, 9am-4.30pm Mon-Fri mid-Aug–May) Helpful and friendly; extended opening hours for the Imatra Big Band Festival.

ℹ **Getting There & Around**

The bus and train stations are 3km north of Imatrankoski in Mansikkala, linked by frequent local buses (€3.30). Otherwise you'll need a **taxi** (☑020-016-464).

Trains offer the speediest (and often cheapest) connections:

Helsinki (€50.30, 2¾ hours, seven daily)
Joensuu (€30.40, two hours, five daily)
Lappeenranta (€8.60, 25 minutes, five daily)

NORTH KARELIA

Criss-crossed by dusty gravel roads, Finland's sparsely populated frontier has some of Finland's best wildlife. Its strong Russian influence is evident in striking Orthodox churches: North Karelia was fought over for centuries by Sweden and Russia, with fierce fighting during the Winter and Continuation Wars. You'll often stumble across trenches, old battlegrounds and memorials to the fallen inside the quiet forests.

Just beyond North Karelia, Kuhmo (p217) also has a Karelian heritage, though it's not strictly part of this province.

Joensuu
🌐 013 / POP 74,480

At the egress of the Pielisjoki (Joensuu means 'river mouth' in Finnish), North Karelia's capital is a spirited university town, with students making up almost a third of the population. Joensuu was founded by Tsar Nikolai I and became an important trading port following the 1850s completion of the Saimaa Canal. During the Winter and Continuation Wars, 23 bombing raids flattened many of its older buildings, and today most of its architecture is modern. It's a lively place to spend some time before heading into the Karelian wilderness.

⊙ Sights

★**Carelicum**   MUSEUM
(Koskikatu 5; adult/child €5/3; ⊘9am-5pm Mon-Fri, 10am-3pm Sat year-round plus 10am-3pm Sun Jul) Themed displays – on the region's prehistory, its war-torn past, the Karelian evacuation, the importance of the sauna etc – cover both sides of the present-day border at this excellent museum.

Taitokortteli   ARTS CENTRE
(☑013-220-140; www.taitokortteli.fi; Koskikatu 1; ⊘10am-5pm Mon-Fri, 10am-3pm Sat year-round, plus noon-4pm Sun Jul) You can see weavers at work, browse contemporary art and purchase local designers' clothing, toys and homewares at this cluster of wooden buildings. There's a sweet cafe and gallery space.

Joensuun Taidemuseo   GALLERY
(☑013-267-5388; Kirkkokatu 23; adult/child €5/3; ⊘10am-4pm Tue & Thu-Sun, 10am-8pm Wed) The impressive collection at Joensuu's art museum spans Chinese pieces, examples of

Joensuu

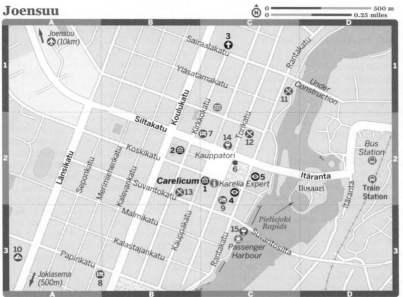

Joensuu

Finnish modernism and an intriguing selection of Orthodox icons.

Town Hall NOTABLE BUILDING

(Rantakatu 20) Dominating the town centre, the art deco town hall was designed by Eliel Saarinen – the architect most famous for Helsinki's train station – and completed in 1914. It now houses the local theatre and terrific Teatteri restaurant.

Orthodox Church of St Nicholas CHURCH

(Kirkkokatu; ⊙10am-4pm Mon-Fri early Jun-late Aug) Joensuu's most intriguing church is the wooden Orthodox church, built in 1887 with icons painted in St Petersburg during the late 1880s.

🏃 Activities

Pielisjoki Cruise CRUISE

(📞050-566-0815; www.satumaaristeilyt.fi; adult/child from €15/7) From June to mid-August, the M/S *Vinkeri II* and M/S *Satumaa* run two-hour scenic cruises on the Pielisjoki, departing from the passenger harbour south of Suvantosilta bridge. Sailing schedules are posted online; buy tickets on board.

☞ Tours

Carriage Ride TOUR

(Koskikatu 5; tours from €20) From the park by the kauppatori you can take a carriage tour in a 19th-century Victorian buggy from

June to mid-August. In winter the operator switches to sled tours.

✹ Festivals & Events

Ilosaari Rock Festival `MUSIC`
(www.ilosaarirock.fi; 2-day ticket €95) Held over a weekend in mid-July, this massive rock festival attracts Finnish and international acts. It has received awards for its environmental record.

⌂ Sleeping

Hotel GreenStar `HOTEL €`
(☏010-423-9390; www.greenstar.fi; Torikatu 16; r €59-69; ⊘reception 8am-8pm Mon-Fri, 9am-8pm Sat, 9am-1pm & 3-7pm Sun; 🖼) 🕭 Eco-initiatives at this contemporary hotel include water heating rather than air-con and small communal areas to reduce heating. Clean, comfortable rooms sleep up to three for the same price (a pull-out armchair converts into a single bed). Breakfast (€7) is optional. Try to arrive when reception is staffed as the lobby's automatic check-in kiosk can be temperamental.

Finnhostel Joensuu `HOSTEL €`
(☏013-267-5076; www.islo.fi; Kalevankatu 8; s €54, without bathroom €44, tw €64, 4-person apt €84, all incl breakfast; ⊘reception 3-8pm; 🖼) Great-value, sizeable rooms come with mini-kitchens and small balconies; some share bathroom and kitchen facilities with one other room. Prices include access to a private sauna session and a gym in the sports institute across the road that handles reception. HI discount.

Linnunlahti `CAMPGROUND €`
(☏010-666-5520; www.linnunlahti.fi; Linnunlahdentie 1; tent sites €7 plus per person €2, cottages €119-160; 🖼) This bargain almost-lakeside campground is mobbed during the rock festival, but otherwise has sites to spare. Cottages sleeping two to six people have free wi-fi.

Cumulus Joensuu `HOTEL €€`
(☏013-511-2100; www.cumulus.fi; Kirkkokatu 20; d €117-132; 🖼) The pick of Joensuu's central chain hotels has primary-coloured, squeaky-clean rooms with ultrapowerful showers, free parking, friendly staff and fast wi-fi.

✗ Eating

At the busy kauppatori food stalls look for Karelian specialities such as the classic *karjalanpiirakka* (rice-filled savoury pastry) and *kotiruoka* (homemade) soups.

Kahvila & Konditoria
Houkutus `CAFE, BAKERY €`
(www.houkutus.fi; Torikatu 24; dishes €1.50-5.50, mains €8-16; ⊘7.30am-7pm Mon-Fri, 8.30am-5pm Sat) Houkutus does great coffee and even better cakes (the mint blackcurrant cake is a treat), along with meal-sized salads and filled bread rolls.

★Teatteri `KARELIAN €€`
(☏010-231-4250; www.teatteriravintola.fi; Rantakatu 20; lunch buffet €8.60-10.50, mains €16.50-26.50; ⊘11am-10pm Mon & Tue, 11am-11pm Wed & Thu, 11am-midnight Fri, 11.30am-midnight Sat) Locally sourced ingredients prepared in innovative ways are served in the town hall's art deco surrounds and on its beautiful summer terrace. Dishes span braised, smoked pork neck with wild boar sausage and rhubarb compote to thyme-crusted chicken with blackcurrant sauce; lush desserts such as liquorice jelly, vanilla-infused strawberries and liquorice meringue are the icing on the cake.

Astoria `HUNGARIAN €€`
(☏013-229-766; www.astoria.fi; Rantakatu 32; mains €18-30; ⊘4-10pm Mon, 4-11pm Tue-Fri, noon-midnight Sat, noon-8pm Sun) In a former girls' school built in brick-Gothic style, this wood-panelled restaurant is a stylish affair with a Hungarian menu of paprika- and garlic-laced goulashes and hefty steaks complemented by Hungarian wines. Finish with a chilled *slivovitz* (plum brandy).

Ravintola Kielo `KARELIAN €€€`
(☏013-227-874; www.ravintolakielo.fi; Suvantokatu 12; mains €22-29, tasting menu €46; ⊘4-10pm Mon-Fri, noon-10pm Sat) 🕭 At the high end of Karelian cuisine, artfully presented miniature starters such as whitefish escabeche with ratatouille and sour cream set the stage for mains like ravioli and pan-fried pike-perch in fish broth, and horsebean risotto with overnight-braised pork. Wine pairings are available.

🍶 Drinking & Nightlife

The pedestrianised area of Kauppakatu has several late-night bars that pump up the volume on weekends.

Jokiasema `BAR`
(www.jokiasema.fi; Hasanniementie 3; ⊘8am-midnight Jun-Aug) Sunsets are spectacular from this bar perched on the edge of Lake Pyhäselkä, with a resident peg-leg pirate statue and seating on the terrace and pier.

Romeo 1914 BAR
(Matkustajasatama; ☺2-9pm Sun-Tue, 2-10pm Wed & Thu, 2pm-midnight Fri, noon-midnight Sat May-Sep) Live music plays most nights aboard this former timber transporter built in 1914, now moored on the Pielisjoki. Several other boat bars are located nearby.

Muru CLUB
(www.barmuru.fi; Siltakatu 10; ☺10pm-2am Mon-Thu, 10pm-4am Fri & Sat, 6pm-2am Sun) Joensuu's students hit the dance floor of this epicentral club with beat-spinning DJs. Dress to impress.

ℹ Information

Karelia Expert (🖉0400-239-549; www.visitkarelia.fi; Koskikatu 5; ☺9am-5pm Mon-Fri year-round plus 10am-3pm Sat & Sun Jun-Aug) In the Carelicum, enthusiastic staff handle tourism information and bookings for the region.

ℹ Getting There & Around

Joensuu is a transport hub for North Karelia.

TO/FROM THE AIRPORT
The airport is 11km west of central Joensuu. A bus service (one way €5) departs from the bus station (50 minutes before plane departures) and the corner of Koskikatu and Kauppakatu (45 minutes before departures). A **taxi** (🖉060-110-100) costs €20.

AIR
Finnair (www.finnair.com) operates several flights a day between Helsinki and Joensuu.

BUS
Major bus services:
Helsinki (€60.10, 7½ hours, up to 14 daily)
Ilomantsi (€15.50, 1¼ hours, nine daily)
Jyväskylä (€43.90, four hours, six daily)
Kuhmo (€53.50, six hours, one daily); change at Sotkamo
Kuopio (€29.90, 2½ hours, up to two hourly)
Lappeenranta (€43.90, 4½ hours, two daily)
Nurmes (€28.80, two hours, up to 12 daily)
Oulu (€72.90, seven hours, up to seven daily)

SHARED TAXI
A **shared taxi** (🖉040-104-4687) route runs from Joensuu to Koli at 8.30am, noon and 5.50pm daily year-round. Prices cost €15 to €45 per person depending on the time/day of travel. Also has an airport service (€5) on demand.

TRAIN
Services include the following:
Helsinki (€78.90, 4½ hours, seven daily)

Lieksa (€15.10, 1¼ hours, two daily)
Nurmes (€22.50, two hours, two daily)
Savonlinna (€31.80, two hours, five daily); change at Parikkala

Ilomantsi

🖉013 / POP 5700

The closest town to the Russian border, Ilomantsi has an Orthodox religion and its own dialect. There are a handful of interesting sights here, but with little worthwhile accommodation (the main 'hotel', Pääskynpesä, is primarily a rehabilitation centre, which does not make for a holiday atmosphere) and few eating options, you're better off visiting for just a day and then heading for the national parks and scenic areas beyond.

⊙ Sights

Parppeinvaara MUSEUM
(www.parppeinvaara.fi; Parppeintie; adult/child €7/5; ☺10am-4pm Jun & Aug, 10am-6pm Jul) Karelian traditions are celebrated at this little Bardic village, 2km south of Ilomantsi. It's named for bard and *kantele* player Jaakko Parppei (1792–1885), whose songs inspired the *Kalevala* epic. Listen to the harpsichord-like sounds of this local stringed instrument at the small **cultural museum** on the hour from noon. Parppeinpirtti (p178) does a wonderfully authentic Karelian buffet. The **Mesikkä Animal Museum** explores the relationship between Karelians and nature, and there's a fascinating exhibition on the war years in the **Border General's Cabin**. The cabin served as headquarters for Major General Erkki Raappana, a local hero who was decorated by Mannerheim for his achievements; it contains many of his personal effects, plus a case of Finnish and Russian weaponry from Uzis to homemade bombs.

Hermanni Wine Tower TOWER
(Viintorni; 🖉0207-789-230; www.hermanninviinitila.fi; Kappalaisentie; ☺10am-10pm Jun–mid-Aug) Blackcurrants, crowberries and white currants from the fields and bogs around Ilomantsi are blended by **Hermanni Winery** (🖉0207-789-230; www.hermanninviinitila.fi; Käymiskuja 1; ☺9am-5pm Mon-Fri, 10am-5pm Sat Jun-Aug plus noon-5pm Sun Jul, 9am-4pm Mon-Fri Sep-May) – Finland's oldest, established in 1989. At the top of the local water tower, you can sample its local berry wines and liqueurs by the glass or tasting tray (€12 for five wines

OFF THE BEATEN TRACK

EASTERNMOST POINT OF THE EU

If you've got your own wheels, you can take a trip to the EU's easternmost point. From the northern end of Hattuvaara, turn east on Polvikoskentie (initially sealed but quickly becoming rough gravel), from where it's a twisting, bumpy 19km drive through the forest to the end of the road. Park here and stay within the cobalt-coloured ropes marking the Finnish–Russian frontier zone as you walk for 100m, the last 40m of which are along a boardwalk, to the blue waters of Virmajärvi. By the lakeshore, a rustic 'monument' (made from a tree trunk and topped with a birdhouse-style wooden roof) marks the most easterly point in the EU that it's possible to reach.

The actual easternmost point is on a small island in the lake, where posts painted in the colours of the Finnish (blue-and-white) and Russian (red-and-green) flags sit either side of the shorter, plain-white border post. Border restrictions mean swimming and boating in the lake are forbidden, but it's a unique photo op.

and one liqueur). The balcony's panoramas are fabulous.

Pyhän Elian Kirkko
CHURCH
(Kirkkotie 15; ⊙11.30am-5.30pm late Jun–mid-Aug) This beautiful wooden Orthodox church has a striking Russian influence. Follow the *kalmisto* (graveyard) sign to the waterfront **Kokonniemi Cemetery**, where trees shade the graves of those lost in the many conflicts the town has endured.

Lutheran Church
CHURCH
(Henrikintie 1; ⊙11.30am-5.30pm late Jun–mid-Aug) When the Swedes took the area they sought to convert the Orthodox population by building this gigantic Lutheran church in 1796. It's also known as the Church of a Hundred Angels for its colourful and comprehensive wall paintings, completed in 1832 by Samuel Elmgren.

✦ Festivals & Events

Ilomantsi celebrates the Orthodox **Petru Praasniekka** on 28 and 29 June and **Ilja Praasniekka** on 19 and 20 July every year. Once strictly religious events, these days they welcome the public, with dancing afterwards.

⌂ Sleeping & Eating

Hotelli Ilomantsi
HOTEL €€
(⌨046-623-7551; www.hotelliilomantsi.com; Kalevalantie 12; s/d/f €61/79/99; 📶) If you need to stay in Ilomantsi, this simple but clean and friendly hotel with en suite bathrooms is your best bet. There's no in-house kitchen (so no breakfast).

★ Parppeinpirtti
KARELIAN €€
(⌨010-239-9950; www.parppeinpirtti.fi; lunch €22; ⊙10am-6pm Jul, to 5pm Jun & Aug, to 3pm

Mon-Fri, 11am-3pm Sat & Sun Sep) Ilomantsi's one foodie highlight is this traditional house in the Parppeinvaara (p177) village, which does a real-deal *pitopöytä* (Karelian buffet) complete with a *kantele* soundtrack. Heap your plate high with *vatruskoita* (salmon-stuffed pastry), swill down nonalcoholic *kotikalja* (which tastes like home-brewed beer) and finish with sticky berry soup.

ℹ Information

Karelia Expert (⌨0400-240-072; www.visitkarelia.fi; Kalevalantie 13; ⊙9am-5pm Mon-Fri Jun-Aug, 8am-4pm Mon-Fri Sep-May) Reservations and information.

ℹ Getting There & Away

Buses to/from Joensuu (€15.90, 1½ hours, nine daily Monday to Friday, fewer on weekends) stop in the town centre. During the school term there are weekday buses to surrounding villages, but in summer you'll have to rely on **taxis** (⌨040-088-1001).

Hattuvaara
📷 013

About 40km northeast of Ilomantsi, Finland's most easterly settlement was famous for poem-singers, such as Arhippa Buruskainen who is thought to have inspired tales in the *Kalevala*. The Runon ja Rajan tie (Poem and Border Rte) runs through Hattuvaara as a tribute.

⊙ Sights

Taistelijan Talo
HISTORIC BUILDING
(Heroes' House; ⌨0400-273-671; www.taistelijantalo.fi; ⊙10am-6pm Sun-Tue, to 8pm Wed-Sat Jun-Aug) The striking wooden Taistelijan Talo was de-

signed by Joensuu architect Erkki Helasvuo in 1988 to symbolise the meeting of East and West. On the ground floor, the **restaurant** (buffet €17) offers an excellent all-day Karelian buffet. The **WWII museum** downstairs has multimedia exhibits, photo exhibitions and weaponry displays relating chiefly to the Winter and Continuation Wars fought along the nearby border. Outside are artillery and vehicles as well as a **Big Hat sculpture** (the town's name translates as 'Hat Mountain').

Orthodox Tsasouna   CHURCH
(⊙ noon-5pm Tue-Sun Jul) Hattuvaara has Finland's oldest Orthodox *tsasouna*, a sweet white wooden chapel by the side of the main road. Built in 1790, it has several original Russian icons and its small tower became a watchtower during WWII. On 29 June each year the colourful Praasniekka festival takes place here, complete with a *ristinsaatto* (Orthodox procession).

❶ Getting There & Away

A **shared taxi** (✆ 0500-675-542; one way €6) runs here from Lieksa, twice daily on Mondays and Thursdays only.

LAKE PIELINEN REGION

At the heart of northern Karelia is Pielinen, Finland's fourth-largest lake. On its shores, precipitous Koli National Park has epic views and winter skiing.

Bring your hiking boots because this is a place to be active; towns here are really just bases for getting into the great outdoors.

Koli National Park

The magnificent 347m-high Koli inspired Finland's artistic National Romantic era with artists including Pekka Halonen and Eero Järnefelt setting up their easels here. Koli was declared a national park in 1991 after intense debate between environmentalists and landowners, mainly about the placement of the Sokos Hotel Koli on the hill. The area remains relatively pristine with over 90km of marked walking tracks and superb skiing.

⊙ Sights & Activities

From the Luontokeskus Ukko nature centre, it's a brief walk to **Ukko-Koli**, the hill's highest point; 200m further is **Akka-Koli**.

On Akka-Koli's western slope is a 'Temple of Silence', an open space for contemplation, with a stone altar and wooden cross mounted in the rock. For a slightly longer walk, it's 2.6km from Ukko to Koli village or a steep 1.9km walk to Satama.

Luontokeskus Ukko   NATURE CENTRE
(✆ 020-564-5654; www.outdoors.fi; exhibition adult/child €5/2; ⊙ 9am-7pm mid-Jun–early Aug, shorter hours rest of year) By the Sokos Hotel Koli's upper car park, this modern nature centre has exhibitions on the history, flora, fauna and geology of the park, and info on hiking.

Koli Ski Resort   SNOW SPORTS
(✆ 045-138-7429; www.koli.fi; ski/snowboard hire per day €32, lift ticket all areas per hour/day €22/37; ⊙ 10am-5pm early Dec-Easter) Koli is one of the closest ski resorts to Helsinki and southern Finland, with two skiing areas: **Loma-Koli** (✆ 010-762-3631), with four slopes, is suitable for snowboarders and families; **Ukko-Koli** (✆ 010-762-3630) has six steeper, more challenging slopes. There are more than 60km of cross-country trails, including 22km of lit track.

Summer Chair Lift   CHAIR LIFT
(one way/return €4/6; ⊙ 11am-5.45pm mid-Jun–late Jun & early Aug, 10am-5.45pm Jul) Across from the Sokos Hotel Koli's upper car park, a summer chair lift sweeps you down the east side of Koli Hill to the shore of Lake Pielinen and back. Definitely not for the vertigo prone!

Koli Husky   DOG-SLEDDING
(✆ 040-876-6587; www.kolihusky.com; trips from €45) Winter husky trips.

Matkailutila Paimentupa   HORSE RIDING
(✆ 040-080-2709; www.paimentupa.fi; Kotaniemntie 1; 1/4hr rides €30/80, 15-/45-min lessons €7/20) Treks and lessons (including in English) on Icelandic horses.

☞ Tours

Koli Activ   WALKING TOUR
(✆ 040-085-7557; www.koliactiv.fi; 2hr guided walks from €17) Offers guided walks as well as mountain-bike rental (€15/35 three hours/day), canoe and kayak hire (€10 per hour) and rowboats (€15 per day) plus wintertime ice-fishing (equipment €35 per four hours).

🛏 Sleeping & Eating

Koli National Park has eight basic cabins that can be booked through the Luontokeskus

WORTH A TRIP

REINDEER ENCOUNTERS

Santa's Reindeers (☑050-592-4252; www.santasreindeers.fi; Haapalahdentie 171, Haapalahti; 2-/4-/10-person cottages €60/95/200; ☉10am-9pm, activities by reservation) At this delightful farm you can pet a reindeer (€7), take one for a 90-minute forest walk (€40), be led by reindeer aboard a 20-minute winter sleigh ride (€20), or (Rudolph fans: look away now) dine on reindeer (in dishes from soup to sautéed steak; mains €15 to €20) or buy it vacuum packed.

Other activities include a 2½-hour foraging walk (€40) for mushrooms or berries (followed by pie baking), and ice-fishing (€20 per two hours). Cottage accommodation is available.

Ukko (p179) nature centre. To rent other holiday cottages in the area, use Karelia Expert's **Koli accommodation service** (☑045-138-7429; www.visitkarelia.fi).

Future Freetime RESORT €€
(☑010-322-3040; www.futurefreetime.fi; Kopravaarantie 27; tent site €16 plus per person €4, hostel s/d €40/60, guesthouse s/d €40/70, apt €80, cottages €90-170) Situated 14km southwest of Koli village, just off Hwy 6 on Lake Valkealampi, this multipurpose place has a huge range of accommodation options – from camping through to fully kitted-out timber cottages (the biggest sleeps up to 10 people) – plus four saunas (three are traditional smoke saunas), a barbecue and smoker, and handy laundry and drying room.

Vanhan Koulun Majatalo GUESTHOUSE €€
(☑050-343-7881; www.vanhankoulunmajatalo.fi; Niinilahdentie 47; s/d/tr/q from €36/52//72/88, 2-person apt €80-120; @☎) ✦ An old schoolhouse in the countryside 6km from Koli village now houses this environmentally conscious hostel. Its eight rooms and two apartments are all simply decorated; linen is an extra €8 per person. Facilities include a self-catering kitchen and smoke sauna.

Sokos Hotel Koli HOTEL €€
(☑020-123-4662; www.sokoshotels.fi; Ylä-Kolintie 39; s/d €122/137; ☎) Yep, this is the controversial place at the top of Koli Hill that infamously sparked fierce environmental debate. But it has some of Finland's finest views, four saunas and a hot tub, and you can hit the ski slopes from the front door. Book well ahead for winter.

★**Alamaja** CAFE €
(Ranatatie 12; lunch buffet €12, mains €15-18; ☉10am-8pm mid-Jun–mid-Aug, 10am-6pm mid-Aug–mid-Jun) Right on the lakeshore at Koli harbour, this rust-red, double-storey timber building has two terraces overlooking the water (or, in winter, ice) and some of the best food for miles around: reindeer steaks with lingonberry jam, butter-fried vendace with sour cream and dill potatoes, delicious haloumi burgers and a different soup each day (plus, this being Finland, two saunas).

Kahvila Kolin Ryynänen CAFE €
(Kolintie 1C; mains €9-16.50; ☉10am-5pm Mon-Thu, 10am-7pm Fri, 11am-9pm Sat) In Koli village, this charming cafe serves as an exhibition space and has an artist-in-residence. There's often live music.

ⓘ Information

Koli village has a post office and a supermarket (with limited fuel), but the last stop for ATMs is Kolinportti.

Karelia Expert (☑045-138-7429; www.visit karelia.fi; Ylä-Kolintie 4; ☉10.30am-6pm Jun-Aug, 9am-5pm Sep-May) Tourist office with a comprehensive range of information and maps.

ⓘ Getting There & Away

Koli Hill has road access with a short **funicular** (☉7am-10pm) ride from the lower car park up to the Sokos Hotel Koli (you can also drive to the hotel's upper car park).

In winter, when the ice is thick enough, an ice road (Finland's longest at 7km) crosses the lake from Vuonislahti to Loma-Koli, 8.5km east of Koli village, providing a shortcut of 60km.

BOAT

In summer the best way to arrive is by **lake ferry** (MF Pielinen; ☑0400-228-435; www. pielis-laivat.fi; one way adult/child/car/bicycle €18/10/12/5) from Lieksa.

BUS

Buses run to Koli *kylä* (village) from Joensuu (€13.70, 1½ hours, five daily), some via a change in Ahmovaara, 9km west of Koli.

SHARED TAXI

A **shared taxi** (☑040-104-4687) service operates year-round between Joensuu and Koli, with three taxis per day (€15 to €45 depending on time/day of travel).

Paalasmaa

☑ 013

Panoramic Paalasmaa is the largest island in Lake Pielinen and the highest in Finland at 225m above sea level. It's linked to the mainland by a free ferry in summer and an ice road in winter; bridges continue the journey through two smaller islands tucked behind it.

The best view is from the 18m-high wooden **observation tower**, 3km along a marked trail from the island's campground **Paalasmaan Lomamajat** (☑ 040-088-2008; www.paalasmaancamping.fi; tent sites €20, cabins €40-50; ☉ Jun–mid-Aug), a gorgeous waterside spot on the island's eastern tip that rents rowboats (€10 per day) and canoes (€5 per hour).

The ferry terminal is 15km east of the main road; the turn-off is about 2km north of Juuka.

Vuonislahti

☑ 013

Little more than a train station in a field, this rural lakeside hamlet is a peaceful place to break your journey.

There are two daily trains to Vuonislahti from Joensuu (€12.10, one hour) and Lieksa (€3.70, 20 minutes).

⌂ Sleeping

★**Kestikievari Herranniemi** GUESTHOUSE €€
(☑ 013-542-110; www.herranniemi.com; Vuonislahdentie 185; dm €16, s/d from €59/84, cabins €30-84, cottage €145) In an idyllic lakeside setting 2km south of Vuonislahti's train station, comfortable accommodation at this quaint 200-year-old farm includes dorms in a recently refurbished cottage. There are home-cooked local dishes (lunch/dinner buffet €10/25), two lakeside saunas, rowboats, and bike hire (€3/15 per hour/day). Treatment therapies span herbal baths (€12) to *turvesauna* (a sauna/mud bath; €25 per hour).

Hotelli Pielinen HOTEL €€
(☑ 045-264-0303; www.hotellipielinen.com; Läpikäytäväntie 54; s/d €60/88, without bathroom €40/64; ☎ ❄) Peacefully set near (but not on) the lake in Vuonislahti, Hotelli Pielinen has modern, good-value rooms – ask for one with a balcony overlooking the hares loping about the garden. In winter the ice road across to Koli's slopes makes this a handy base for skiers.

WORTH A TRIP

WOODLAND WOODCARVINGS

Paateri (☑ 040-104-4055; Paateri 21, Vuonisjärvi; adult/child €4/2.50; ☉ 10am-6pm mid-May–mid-Sep) Between Vuonislahti and Vuonisjärvi, Paateri was the home and workshop of Eva Ryynänen (1915–2001), Finland's most respected wood sculptor – as well as her greatest work, Paateri Wilderness Church (1991). Carved flowers and animals adorn the beams; the great tree-root altar is framed by a glass window that draws the living pine trees outside into the building. Every surface of wood in Eva's home is embellished, and some beautiful sculptures are displayed in her workshop.

Lieksa

☑ 013 / POP 12.570

On the banks of Lake Pielinen, Lieksa is unlovely in itself, but from here you can easily explore Koli or go whitewater-rafting, horse riding, canoeing and bear-watching.

⊙ Sights

Pielisen Museo MUSEUM
(☑ 040-104-4151; www.lieksa.fi/museo; Pappilantie 2; adult/child €6/1.50; ☉ 10am-6pm mid-May–mid-Sep) Over 70 Karelian buildings and open-air exhibits at this outdoor museum are organised by century or trade (such as farming, milling, fire-fighting). A fascinating insight into the forestry industry includes a look at a logging camp and floating rafts and machinery used for harvest and transport.

In winter the only section open is the **indoor museum** (admission winter adult/child €3/1; ☉ 10am-3pm Tue-Fri mid-Sep–mid-May) featuring photographs and displays on Karelian history.

🏃 Activities

Karelia Expert (p182) can book most trips and activities and provides detailed driving instructions for out-of-the-way operators; pick-ups from Lieksa for whitewater rafting trips in the Ruunaa Recreation Area can be arranged.

Lake Pielinen, Pudasjoki River and the Ruunaa and Änäkäinen have great recreational fishing areas. Each requires a separate permit, available from local sports shops, such as **Lieksan Retkiaitta** (📞040-017-2226; Pielisentie 33), or Karelia Expert.

★**Erä Eero**   BEAR-WATCHING
(📞040-015-9452; www.eraeero.com; trips per person €175; ⊙4pm-6am) Erä Eero runs awesome overnight trips to its observation cabin, where you may see bears, wolves and beavers between April and October, as well as birds of prey, wolverines and lynx.

Ratsastustalli Ahaa   HORSE RIDING
(📞040-525-7742; www.ahaatalli.fi; 30-/45-min lessons €25/38, cross-country treks €25 per hour) Offers lessons and cross-country treks.

Bear Hill Husky   DOG-SLEDDING
(📞040-779-0898; www.bearhillhusky.com; expeditions from €139) Wintertime husky-dog-sled expeditions along the Russian border, starting from 2½ hours.

⚡ Festivals & Events

Lieksa Brass Week   MUSIC
(📞045-132-4000; www.lieksabrass.com; Koski-Jaakonkatu 4; tickets free to €20) During the last week of July, Lieksa Brass Week attracts international musicians.

🛏 Sleeping & Eating

Lieksa has a handful of places to stay but for more atmosphere consider options in nearby Vuonislahti, Koli and Ruunaa.

Decent places to eat and drink are limited but you'll find supermarkets on Lieksa's main street, Pielisentie.

Timitranlinna   HOSTEL €
(📞044-333-4044; www.timitra.fi; Timitrantie 3; dm from €22, d €52; 🅿) Once the national training centre for the Finnish border guard, this HI-affiliated hostel is peacefully situated about 800m south of the main street. Its 1st-floor rooms are standard fare, but kayaks are available for exploring the nearby river.

Timitraniemi Camping   CAMPGROUND €
(📞045-123-7166; www.timitra.com; Timitrantie 25; tent sites €15 plus per person €4, cabins €48-110; ⊙mid-May–mid-Sep) At the mouth of the river, well-equipped Timitraniemi has 45 log cabins of varying sizes and plushness and plenty of grassy pitches. Facilities include a lakeside cafe, saunas, and bikes and boats for hire; rafting and fishing trips can be arranged.

Lieksan Leipomo   BAKERY €
(📞013-521-777; www.liekasnleipomo.fi; Pielisentie 31; dishes €1.80-6.50, lunch buffet €8; ⊙6am-5pm Mon-Fri, 9am-2pm Sat) In a beautiful wooden building, this endearing bakery is a local favourite for filling lunch buffets and fantastic cakes.

ℹ Information

Karelia Expert (📞0400-175-323; www.visitkarelia.fi; Pielisentie 22; ⊙9am-5pm Mon-Fri Jun & Aug, to 5pm Mon-Fri, to 2pm Sat Jul, 8am-4pm Mon-Fri Sep-May) Books tours and accommodation.

ℹ Getting There & Away

BOAT
The car ferry M/F *Pielinen* (p180) makes the 1¾-hour trip from Lieksa to Koli twice daily from mid-June to mid-August, departing from Lieksa at 10am and 3pm, and returning from Koli at 11.40am and 4.40pm.

BUS
There are 10 weekday buses (€18.70, 1¾ hours) from Joensuu, with fewer on weekends.

SHARED TAXI
There's a **shared taxi** (📞0500-675-542) service to Ruuna (€6, one per day Monday and Friday) and another **shared taxi** (📞0500-599-3998) to Jongunjoki/Nurmijärvi (€6, two daily Monday and Friday).

TRAIN
There are daily trains from Helsinki to Lieksa (€72.60, 6½ hours, four daily), via Joensuu (€15.10, 1¼ hours, two daily).

Patvinsuo National Park
📞013

This large marshland area between Lieksa and Ilomantsi is a habitat for swans and cranes, and if you're exceedingly lucky you might see bears. Using the *pitkospuu* (boardwalk) network, you can easily hike around; there are 80km of marked trails in total.

It's an easy 3.5km stroll through forests and wetlands to the southern shore of Suomunjärvi from the main road, where you'll find a **birdwatching tower** at Teretinniemi.

There are three marked nature trails (between 3km and 4.5km long), and several challenging hiking routes (mostly half-day walks). In winter cross-country skiing is possible on the unmaintained **Mäntypolku** and

Nämänpuro Trails, which both start from Suomu car park.

Suomu Information Hut (☎013-548-506; ⊙10am-5pm daily Jun-Aug, 10am-5pm Wed-Sun May & Sep) has a summer warden who can help with advice, fishing permits and maps, and point you towards the eight camping areas. You can hire canoes and rowboats here (€8/30 per hour/day; cash only), and make bookings for accommodation: there are nine beds (€12 per night) in the information hut itself and 20 beds in the old forest ranger's house (€12 per night).

WildNordic(☑030-502-502;www.villipohjola. fi) can also book cabins in and around the park.

⊙ Getting There & Away

The only way to get to the national park is to drive. Or walk – if you're trekking, the Susitaival (Wolf's Trail) and Karhunpolku (Bear's Trail) meet at the park.

Ruunaa Recreation Area

☑013
Just 30km northeast of Lieksa, Ruunaa is an outdoor activities hub with 38km of waterways. Designated campsites (with fire rings) are also provided and maintained. Keep your eyes peeled as the area is home to otters, deer and sometimes bears.

A hilltop **observation tower** at Huuhka-javaara offers a magnificent panorama over Neitijärvi.

🏃 Activities

Ruunaa is busy all year, hosting snow sports in winter and rafting in summer.

Rafting & Canoeing

Above all, Ruunaa is synonymous with rafting. There are six rapids (class II–III) that you can shoot in wooden or rubber boats, the latter being more thrilling (and sometimes more spilling). From May to October several launches depart daily from the Ruunaa Visitor Centre area or the rafting operators' wilderness camps. Prices are around €45/30 with/without lunch for a three-hour trip. Advance reservations are definitely recommended. Transport can also be arranged from Lieksa if you book a tour, and packages that include camp meals, smoke saunas or overnight accommodation are available.

Koski-Jaakko RAFTING
(☑050-036-6033; www.koski-jaakko.fi; Yläviekintie 50; trips €30) This place is a smidge cheaper than Ruunaa's other rafting operators. Rubber rafts leave from the Koski-Jaakko HQ around 7km along Siikakoskentie (turn right immediately after the Naarajoki bridge). Trips in wooden boats (made by Jaakko himself) leave from the car park at Naarajoki.

Ruunaan Matkailu RAFTING
(☑013-533-130; www.ruunaanmatkailu.fi; Ruunaantie 129) Offers rafting (wooden/rubber rafts €43/45) and can organise cottages in the area, plus skiing, snowmobile safaris (from €120 for two hours) and rental (€50 for two hours), and ice-fishing during winter. Trips depart from Cafe Ruunaan Tupa, opposite the Ruunaa Visitor Centre.

Lieksan Matkakaverit RAFTING
(☑040-708-5726; www.ruunaa.eu; Siikakoskentie 65; adult/child trips €32/16, lunch €17/8.50) Offers rafting and canoeing trips, as well as a smoke sauna.

Erästely CANOEING
(☑040-027-1581; www.erastely.fi) Organises guided trips down the rapids (from €50 per person), and gentler canoeing expeditions on the surrounding lakes and rivers. Equipment hire and excellent information on self-guided routes are available.

Fishing

Ruunaa is a prized fly-fishing area. Trout and salmon fishing is exhilarating in the numerous rapids, with quieter areas accessible along a long wooden walkway.

One-day/week fishing permits (€15/75) are available in Lieksa and at the Ruunaa Visitor Centre; there's also a fishing-permit machine near the Neitikoski rapids. Fishing is permitted from June to early September and again from mid-November to late December.

Trekking

The **Karhunpolku (Bear's Trail)** passes through Ruunaa. You can pick it up just 50m north of the Naarajoki bridge – the path is marked with round orange symbols on trees.

Around the river system and over two beautiful suspension bridges runs **Ruunaan Koskikierros**, a marked 29km loop along good *pitkospuu* (boardwalk) paths. If you have more time, there are another 20km of side trips you can take. Starting at the Naarajoki bridge, walk 5km along Karhunpolku

KARELIAN TREKS

North Karelia's best trekking routes form the **Karjalan Kierros** (Karelian Circuit; www. vaellus.info), a loop of 14 marked hiking trails (plus some canoe and cycling variants) with a total length of more than 1000km between Ilomantsi and Lake Pielinen. The best known are the Bear's Trail (not to be confused with the more famous Bear's Ring in Oulanka National Park) and Wolf's Trail, which link up in Patvinsuo National Park. They're described here from south to north but you can walk in either direction. On school days only, a bus connects Ilomantsi and Möhkö village (€4.10, 25 minutes, one daily); otherwise you'll need to arrange transport to the trailheads in advance.

Wilderness huts and lean-to shelters are scattered along the way, but it's advisable to carry a tent. Equipment hire can be arranged with Karelia Expert. Much of the terrain is boggy marshland, so waterproof footwear is essential. Contact the Lieksa (p182) or Ilomantsi (p178) offices of Karelia Expert, or **Metsähallitus** (☑020-564-100; www.metsa.fi), the information office for the Forest and Park Service, for information. Wild Nordic (p183) can book huts and cabins along the trail.

See also www.outdoors.fi for extensive info on hiking in Finland.

Susitaival (Wolf's Trail)

The 97km Wolf's Trail is a marked four- to six-day trek running north from Möhkö village to the marshlands of Patvinsuo National Park. The terrain consists mostly of dry heath, pine forest and swampy marshland, which can be wet underfoot – in places, you'll need to haul yourself over water courses on a pulley-operated raft. This trail skirts the Russian border in areas where many of the battles in the Winter and Continuation Wars were fought. Early in the trek, at Lake Sysmä, you'll see a memorial and antitank gun. There are five lean-to shelters and three wilderness cabins along the route, and farm or camping accommodation is available in the village of Naarva. Around 100 bears and 50 wolves inhabit the area – the

---

to reach the trail. Another 3.3km brings you to the Ruunaa Hiking Centre.

🛏 Sleeping

There are 12 free *laavu* (basic lean-to sleeping shelters) in the hiking area. Campers are encouraged to pitch tents by the shelters, or at one of the 19 dedicated campfire sites. Book national park accommodation at Wild Nordic (p183), Karelia Expert and the Ruunaa Visitor Centre.

Ruunaa Hiking Centre CAMPGROUND €
(☑013-533-170; www.ruunaa.fi; tent sites €12 plus per person €3, cabins/cottages €35/100; ℗) Near the *pitkospuu* (boardwalk) to the Neitikoski rapids, this excellent hiking centre incorporates a large cafe, camping area, kitchen, sauna, luxurious four- to six-bed cottages and simple cabins. Mountain bikes, canoes and rowboats are available for hire.

Ruunaan Matkailu COTTAGES €€
(☑013-533-130; www.ruunaanmatkailu.fi; Siikakoskentie 47; d from €30, cabins €40-150; ℗) These self-contained cabins (plus basic accommodation upstairs from the cafe) are situated 5km east of the Naarajoki bridge. A traditional smoke sauna, boats and various

snowmobile, rafting and boating tours are available.

ℹ Information

Ruunaa Visitor Centre (☑020-564-5757; ☺10am-6pm May-Sep) Near the Naarajoki bridge, this friendly visitor centre has exhibitions, maps, a library and a short film about the area, and also sells fishing permits. It's a great place to read up on Ruunaa's wildlife, and to research hiking trails.

ℹ Getting There & Away

A **shared taxi** (☑0500-675-542; one way €6) between Lieksa and Ruunaa runs twice daily on Mondays and Fridays only.

Nurmijärvi District

☑013

Renowned for its canoeing routes on the Jongunjoki, the Nurmijärvi area is wild and remote. Nurmijärvi village (www.nurmijarvi. fi) has enough services to get you to the Jongunjoki or Lieksajoki, or to the Änäkäinen area for fishing and trekking.

chances of running into one are slim but not impossible. If you do happen to meet a bear or wolf in the wild, back away slowly in the direction you came from.

Karhunpolku (Bear's Trail)

The Bear's Trail is a 133km marked trail of medium difficulty leading north from Patvinsuo National Park near Lieksa, through a string of national parks and nature reserves along the Russian border, including through the Ruunaa Recreation Area. This accessibility means the trail can be walked, or even mountain-biked, in relatively short stages. The trail ends at Teljo, about 50km south of Kuhmo. You'll need to arrange transport from either end.

From Patvinsuo, the trail crosses heathland and boardwalks for 17km to the first lean-to shelter at Ahokoski, then runs another 9km to a wilderness hut at Pitkäjärvi. Four kilometres further, a short trail detours to the WWII battleline of Kitsi. The trail then heads northwest to the Ruunaa Recreation Area.

Beyond Ruunaa it's around 30km to Änäkäinen, once a WWII battlefield but today a tranquil recreational fishing area. The trail follows the Jongunjoki through a peatland nature reserve on its final leg to the Ostroskoski wilderness hut, about 6km from Teljo. If you still have energy to burn, it's possible to canoe back to Nurmijärvi: contact canoe-rental outfit Erästely in advance.

Tapion Taival (Fighter's Trail)

The easternmost trekking route in Finland, Tapion Taival gives you the choice of a 13km wilderness track along the Koitajoki, an 8km northern extension across the Koivusuo Nature Park, or another extension north of Koivusuo to Kivivaara. The Koitajoki section through epic Karelian wilderness is a highlight. The path is marked by orange paint on tree trunks. You'll need your own transport and a good local map to reach the trekking area.

🏃 Activities

Canoeing

Canoe experts at **Erästely** (☎ 040-027-1581; www.erastely.fi) offer all manner of guided trips (from €40). If you want to go it alone, you can hire canoes and kayaks (from €10/40/110 per hour/day/week) and arrange transport to and from the beginning or end of a route.

The circular **Pankasaari Route** from Nurmijärvi village can easily be done with a free route guide, available from Karelia Expert. It follows the Lieksajoki downstream to Pankajärvi, then rounds Pankasaari before returning to Nurmijärvi. There's almost no gradient and it's suitable for beginners – only the Käpykoski might present a challenge.

The beautiful wilderness river **Jongunjoki** has nearly 40 small rapids, none of them very tricky. Karelia Expert has a free route guide. You can start at either Jonkeri up north (in the municipality of Kuhmo), further south at Teljo bridge, at Aittokoski, or even at Lake Kaksinkantaja. Allow four days if you start at Jonkeri and one day from Lake Kaksinkantaja.

Fishing

The Forest and Park Service controls fish quantities in three lakes in the Änäkäinen fishing area, 8km northeast of Nurmijärvi village, including some stocking of the waters. Fishing is allowed year-round, except in the first three weeks of May. **Kahvila Annukka** (☎ 040-964-1083; Nurmijärventie 154) has fishing permits (€8/30 per day/week in summer). Permits are also available from the Lieksan Retkiaitta (p182) outdoor shop in Lieksa.

🛏 Sleeping

Erästelyn Melontakeskus   HOSTEL **€**
(☎ 040-027-1581; www.erastely.fi; Kivivaarantie 1, Jongunjoki; dm/d incl breakfast €35/50) Canoe-rental company Erästely offers bed and breakfast at its headquarters – a former schoolhouse – with rooms sleeping four to 25 people. There's an on-site cafe.

Jongunjoen Matkailu   B&B **€€**
(☎ 040-094-9215; www.jongunjoenmatkailu.com; Kivivaarantie 21, Jongunjoki; s/d/f without bathroom €45/90/125; 🖥) This exuberantly run, spick-and-span place is 2km east of the main road towards Änäkäinen. Three of its six

sparingly decorated but comfortable rooms have lake views; all share bathrooms. You can hire canoes and boats, as well as fishing or skiing equipment.

Nurmes

🖉 013 / POP 8360

On the northern shores of Lake Pielinen, Nurmes is a great base for activities such as snowmobiling, ice-fishing, dog-sledding and cross-country skiing tours in winter, and wildlife-watching, canoeing, hiking and more come summer. Karelia Expert takes bookings (at least 24 hours in advance) for most services; Hyvärilä and Sokos Hotel Bomba also offer a huge range of high-energy activities.

Founded in 1876 by Tsar Alexander II, the town is pleasant in its own right, with an Old Town area (Puu-Nurmes) of historical wooden buildings along Kirkkokatu.

◉ Sights

Bomba Village   VILLAGE
(🖉 020-123-4908; Tuulentie 10) The centrepiece of this re-created Karelian 'village' at Sokos Hotel Bomba is the imposing **Bomba Talo**, with its high roof and ornate wooden trim. It's a replica of a typical 19th-century Karelian family house and was completed in 1978. It now houses the Bomban Talo (p186) restaurant and eating here is the only way to see inside. Outside are craft studios and a summertime market.

🛏 Sleeping & Eating

The best places to stay are around the lake, about 3.5km east of the town centre.

Hyvärilä   HOTEL, CAMPGROUND €
(🖉 040-104-5960; www.hyvarila.com; Lomatie 12; campsites €10 plus per person €5, cabins €48-63, hostel dm €22, hotel s/d/f €81/98/118; ☺ camping Jun–mid-Sep; 🅿) Next door to a golf club, this lakeside resort incorporates a campground, hostel accommodation, a 14-room hotel and a restaurant, all managed by cheerful staff. Golf aside, activities include a small swimming beach, tennis courts, and canoe and boat hire. Wi-fi is available in the main building.

Sokos Hotel Bomba   SPA HOTEL €€
(🖉 020-123-4908; www.sokoshotels.fi; Tuulentie 10; s €105-119, d €111-131, Karelian cabins €160, spa

for nonguests from €12.50; ☺ spa 10am-10pm May-Aug, to 9pm Sep-Apr; @ 🛜 🖾) This sprawling complex has an enormous indoor pool and spa area overlooking the lake and stylish modern rooms. There are also comfortable Karelian-style cabins (all with private bathrooms and several with their own saunas) within the replica Karelian Bomba Village. On-site adventure company **Bomba Action** (🖉 040-087-9890; www.bomba-action.fi; ☺ 10am-2pm Mon-Fri, by appt Sat & Sun) can arrange no end of outdoor activities. Options include quad bike trips, canoeing expeditions, snowmobile safaris, fishing, hiking, jet-skiing and waterskiing.

Loma Sirmakka   APARTMENT €€
(🖉 013-480-455; www.lomasirmakka.com; Tavintie 6; apt €112) Each of these lakeside apartments has a full kitchen and laundry, making them ideal for larger families. Rates are cheaper for longer stays, and you can hire bikes, boats and canoes.

Bomban Talo   KARELIAN €€
(🖉 020-123-4908; www.sokoshotels.fi; Tuulentie 10; Karelian buffet €17, mains €15-28.50; ☺ 11am-10.30pm, buffet until 7pm) The mammoth wood cabin at Bomba Village contains the Sokos Bomba Hotel's restaurant serving a Karelian buffet to the masses, with *karjalanpiirakka* (rice-filled savoury pastry) designed to swab up *karjalanpaisti* (stew), and *sultsina* (semolina porridge pie) with *puolukkahillo* (lingonberry jam). À la carte options include rainbow trout and rosehips.

❶ Information

Karelia Expert (🖉 050-336-0707; www.visitkarelia.fi; Kauppatori 3; ☺ 9am-5pm Mon-Fri Jun-Aug, to 4pm Mon-Fri Sep-May) Local information and bookings.

❶ Getting There & Away

Buses and trains depart from just by the main square.

Buses run regularly to/from Joensuu (€28.80, two hours, 12 daily), Kajaani (€23.50, two hours, six daily) and Lieksa (€11.80, one hour, five daily).

Trains run to Joensuu (€22.50, two hours, twice daily) via Lieksa (€8.70, 45 minutes). The train station is unmanned; buy tickets online before you travel or on the train.

West Coast

Best Places to Eat

➜ Juurella (p199)
➜ Linds Kök (p198)
➜ Pavis (p197)
➜ Café Fäboda (p205)
➜ Gustav Wasa (p202)

Best Places to Stay

➜ Kylmäpihlajan Majakka (p192)
➜ Hotel Kantarellis (p201)
➜ Hotel Alma (p199)
➜ City Hovi (p192)
➜ Yyterin Kylpylähotelli (p194)

Why Go?

Stretching for 500km along the sandy shoreline, Finland's west coast harbours a cache of historic old wooden towns such as Uusikaupunki, Kristinestad and Unesco-listed Rauma, founded at the height of the Swedish empire. The area still retains strong links with neighbouring Sverige (Sweden), with Swedish spoken almost everywhere.

Fantastic summer festivals held in the region include the Nordic countries' biggest folk-music gathering in tiny Kaustinen, huge rock and tango festivals in Seinäjoki, and world-renowned jazz in Pori.

But the coastline itself is the biggest attraction. Some of the best beaches are in and around the arty, seaside city of Vaasa, with kids' amusement parks, waterparks and spas on its adjacent island. Stunning beaches also extend south of Kalajoki at Hiekkasärkät, where holiday cottages hide among the dunes and forests, and the horizon turns a fiery kaleidoscope of crimson, orange and magenta hues during spectacular sunsets.

When to Go
West Coast

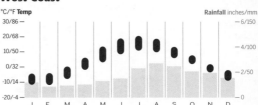

May Windsurfing season starts at the beautiful 6km-long beach, Yyteri.

Jun Outdoor waterparks open their slides and turn on the wave machines.

Jul Some big festivals: Pori Jazz, Seinäjoki's Tango-markkinat and Vaasa's Hietsku Rock.

West Coast Highlights

1 Wandering the colourful Unesco World Heritage–listed wooden Old Town of **Rauma** (p190)

2 Pondering outlandish retro-futuristic inventions at Uusikaupunki's humorous **Bonk Museum** (p189)

3 **Cruising** (p203) the rapidly rising islands of the scattered Kvarken Archipelago

4 **Nordic walking** (p206) through the white-sand dunes of the sport's birthplace, Hiekkasärkät

5 Zipping to the top of modernist architect Alvar Aalto's **Lakeuden Risti Church** (p198) to view his harmonious town centre in Seinäjoki

6 Taking in natural history exhibits and artworks by Finnish and international masters at Vaasa's diverse **Pohjanmaan Museo** (p199)

7 Surveying the stone burial cairns scattered through the forest at the Bronze Age **Sammallahdenmäki** (p194) burial site

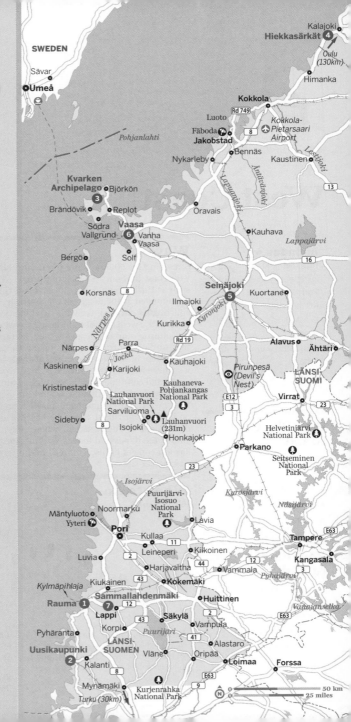

Uusikaupunki

📞 02 / POP 15,700

Ironically, for a town founded in 1617 and filled with historic wooden buildings, Uusikaupunki translates as 'New Town'. It's famous for the treaty of 1721, which quelled hostilities between Sweden and Russia after the gruelling Great Northern War.

Straddling an inlet, the town's port was once a popular destination for smugglers... until the customs house was built in 1760. Today it draws a buzzing yachtie crowd in summer.

☉ Sights

★ **Bonk Museum**   MUSEUM
(📞 02-841-8404; www.bonkcentre.fi; Siltakatu 2; adult/child €8/3; ☉ 10am-6pm daily late Jun-early Aug, 11am-3pm Tue-Sat early Jun-late Jun & mid-Aug–late Aug) The creation of local artist Alvar Gullichsen, this spoof museum-art installation is a classic display of oddball Finnish humour. It traces the rise of the Bonk dynasty, who rose from humble beginnings to become the owners of a multiglobal industrial empire producing 'fully defunctioned machinery'. Kids can construct their own Bonk machines in the lethal-looking workshop – they don't receive wages, 'but neither are they charged for swallowed nuts and bolts'.

Vanha Kirkko   CHURCH
(Old Church; www.ukisrk.fi; Kirkkokatu 2; ☉ 11am-5pm Mon-Sat, noon-4pm Sun Jun–mid-Aug) The lovely 17th-century Vanha Kirkko is one of Uusikaupunki's highlights. Its star-speckled, barrel-vaulted roof was built to resemble a ship's hull and its interior has retained the original rustic furniture. The new church was built when architects suspected the original was unstable, and its construction practically bankrupted both the parish and the widow who commissioned RW Ekman's vast altarpieces. Outside are the neatly tended graves of young Finns who died during the Winter War.

Wahlberg House   MUSEUM
(📞 044-351-5447; Ylinenkatu 11; adult/child €4/free; ☉ 10am-5pm Mon-Fri, noon-3pm Sat & Sun early Jun-Aug, noon-3pm Tue-Fri Sep-early Jun) Ground-floor rooms in this delightful house built by a shipping magnate are furnished in wealthy 19th-century style, while the attic is given over to the story of Uusikaupunki's maritime history.

🏃 Activities

Isokari Lighthouse Cruises   CRUISE
In July and early August, two boats run day cruises from Uusikaupunki to the brown-and-white-striped Isokari Lighthouse, Finland's second-oldest, dating from 1833. The waterbus **Diana** (📞 044-515-2502; adult/child €45/20) heads across at 10am on Tuesday, Wednesday, Friday and Saturday, and the brigantine **Mary Ann** (📞 040-010-2111; www.maryann.fi; adult/child €46/23) sets sail at 11am on Thursday and Sunday and 2pm Friday.

Katanpää Fort Island Cruises   CRUISE
During July and early August, a popular weekend cruise runs to Katanpää Fort Island (adult/child €46/23). The *Mary Ann* sails at 11am on Saturday and *Diana* at 11am on Sunday.

🛏 Sleeping

Santtioranta Camping   CAMPGROUND €
(📞 02-842-3862; www.santtionranta-camping.fi; Kalalokkikuja 14; tent sites €14 plus per person €4, 2-/4-person cabins €45/60; ☉ Jun-early Sep) This peaceful beachside campground is 1.5km northwest of the town centre. Simple cabins (linen extra €8) have kitchens with hotplates and fridge. You can hire bikes, rowboats and canoes (each €3/20 per hour/day) to explore the area.

Hotelli Aquarius   HOTEL €€
(📞 02-841-3123; www.hotelliaquarius.fi; Kullervontie 11; s/d/ste incl breakfast & sauna €115/135/205; @ 📶 🏊) Set in a park on the edge of town, this large hotel caters to business travellers, so there are bargains on weekends when prices drop. Most rooms have sea views; facilities include tennis courts and a pool.

🍴 Eating

The converted red shop-houses just south of the bridge contain appealing riverside bar-restaurants to enjoy a beer when the sun's out.

Pakkahuone Café   CAFE €
(📞 044-712-3500; www.vierasvenesatama.fi; Pakkahuoneentori 2; dishes €2.50-8, mains €12-14.50; ☉ 8.30am-8pm Mon-Sat, 9am-8pm Sun May, 8.30am-10pm daily Jun-early Aug, 8.30am-8pm daily early Aug-Sep) The guest-harbour cafe serves coffee, homemade doughnuts, salads and fish and chips to customers gazing at the traditional and gleaming-new yachts. Around the corner, the quayside terraced

bar opens until late and occasionally hosts
live music.

Gasthaus Pooki INTERNATIONAL €€
(☑02-847-7100; www.gasthauspooki.com; Ylinenkatu 21; lunch buffet €6-9, mains €15-30; ⊙11am-
10pm Mon-Fri, noon-10pm Sat, noon-6pm Sun) ✍
This multilevel courtyard and indoor dining room has an award-winning Slow Food
menu of seasonal dishes like pork cheek
braised in local Prykmestar Savu beer, fried
pike-perch with fennel, and spinach-filled
ravioli, and desserts such as meringue with
butterscotch sauce and locally picked summer berries. If you don't want to move far,
there are four guest rooms (single/double
€85/120).

ⓘ Information

Tourist Office (☑02-8451-5443; www.
uusikaupunki.fi; Rauhankatu 10; ⊙9am-5pm
Mon-Fri, 9am-3pm Sat late Jun-early Aug, 9am-
4pm Mon-Fri Sep-late Jun) Offers bikes for hire
(€3/15/45 per hour/day/week).

ⓘ Getting There & Away

The bus station is behind the kauppatori (market
square). Services include the following:
Rauma (€10.10, one hour, seven daily Monday to Friday, some with a change in Laitila;
reduced services Saturday and Sunday, all
require a change in Laitila)
Turku (€13.70, 1½ hours, hourly Monday to
Friday, reduced services Saturday and Sunday)

WORTH A TRIP

SWEDISH ROOTS

The first sizeable party of Swedish
crusaders arrived in 1155 at the village
of **Kalanti**, about 9km east of Uusikaupunki. Led by King Erik, the party also
contained Henry, bishop of Uppsala,
who spread Christianity in Finland.

Kalanti's **St Olaf's Church** (www.
ukisrk.fi; Pyhän Olavintie; ⊙11am-5pm
Mon-Sat, noon-4pm Sun Jun–mid-Aug)
dates from the late 14th century and
has exquisite frescoes, one of which
records the historic occasion of Bishop
Henry meeting a devilish pagan on the
Finnish coast.

Buses to Kalanti are limited; it's best
reached using your own wheels.

Rauma

☑02 / POP 39,870

Centred on its lively kauppatori, Rauma's
Unesco World Heritage–listed Old Town district, Vanha Rauma, is the largest preserved
wooden town in the Nordic countries, and
the main pleasure here is simply meander-
ing its quaint streets.

In the Middle Ages Rauma's lace-makers
ignored King Gustav Vasa's order to move to
Helsinki to boost the capital's industry. By
the 18th century Rauma (Swedish: Raumo)
was a thriving trade centre, thanks to the
European fashion for lace-trimmed bonnets.
Locals still turn out the delicate material,
and celebrate their lace-making heritage
with an annual festival.

You might hear snatches of Rauman
giäl, the local dialect that mixes English,
Estonian, German and other languages
that worked their way into the lingo from
Rauma's intrepid sailors. Rauma remains
an important shipping centre, transporting
Finnish paper around the world.

⊙ Sights

In the heart of modern Rauma, the Old Town
remains a living centre, with cosy cafes,
shops and a few artisans working in small
studios; try to visit between Tuesday and
Friday when everything's open and the town
hums with life. There are over 600 18th- and
19th-century wooden buildings here, each
with its own name – look for the small oval
nameplate near the door. For a detailed history, pick up a free copy of *A Walking Tour
in the Old Town* from the tourist office.

Rauma Museum MUSEUM
(☑02-567-9183; adult/child combined entry to 4
museums €7/free, single entry €4/free) Rauma
Museum encompasses four sites. The impressive 1776-built **Vanha Raatihuone** (Old Town
Hall; ☑02-834-3532; Kauppakatu 13; ⊙10am-5pm
daily Jul, 10am-5pm Tue-Sun mid-May–Jun & Aug,
noon-5pm Tue-Fri, 10am-2pm Sat, 11am-5pm Sun
Jan–mid-May & Sep-Dec) has lace and changing local history displays. **Marela** (☑02-
834-3528; Kauppakatu 24; ⊙10am-5pm daily Jul,
10am-5pm Tue-Sun mid-May–Jun & Aug, noon-5pm
Tue-Fri, 10am-2pm Sat, 11am-5pm Sun Jan–mid-
May & Sep-Dec) is the period-furnished home
of a wealthy 19th-century merchant family.
At the other end of the social scale, **Kirsti**
(☑02-834-3529; Pohjankatu 3; ⊙10am-5pm daily
Jul, 10am-5pm Tue-Sun mid-May–Jun & Aug), a lov-

able collection of lopsided wooden buildings, represents home life through to the 1970s. Outside the Old Town (due to the fire risk), **Savenvalajan Verstas** (Potter's Workshop; ☑044-793-3529; Nummenkatu 2; ☺11am-4pm Jul) once made distinctive stove tiles.

Pyhän Ristin Kirkko   CHURCH
(www.rauma.seurakunta.net; Luostarinkatu 1; ☺10am-6pm Mon-Fri, to 3pm Sat, to 4pm Sun May-Sep) This 15th-century Franciscan monastery church has early 16th-century frescoes and several beautiful painted panels, a Prussian triptych from the 15th century and an ornate pulpit.

Rauman Taidemuseo   GALLERY
(☑02-822-4346; www.raumantaidemuseo.fi; Kuninkaankatu 37; adult/child €5/free; ☺11am-5pm Mon-Thu, to 4pm Fri-Sun Jun-Aug, closed Mon Sep-May) Changing exhibitions of traditional and modern art stretch over two sides of a courtyard and two storeys.

Rauma Maritime Museum   MUSEUM
(☑02-822-4911; www.rmm.fi; Kalliokatu 34; adult/child €9/3; ☺11am-5pm daily Jun–mid-Aug, noon-4pm Mon-Fri & Sun May, noon-4pm Tue-Fri & Sun mid-Aug–late Aug, noon-4pm Sun Sep-Apr) Wandering around the Old Town it's easy to forget that Rauma is a port, but its maritime museum is an engaging reminder of the town's seafaring livelihood. As well as old photos and displays, there's a thrilling navigation simulator of the M/S *Jenny,* which you can 'steer' into New York and San Francisco's harbours. Kids love it.

Torni   TOWER
(Vesitorni; ☑02-822-0550; www.taidekahvilatorni.fi; adult/child €2/1; ☺tower 10am-8pm May–mid-Sep) A spectacular 360-degree panorama of Rauma radiates from this 70m-high water tower accessible by lift (elevator). At its summit is a new restaurant, **Torni Kahvila** (www.ravintolatorni.varaa.com; lunch buffet €23, 3-course dinner menus €30-37; ☺9am-9pm), serving Finnish cuisine; tower admission is free if you're dining.

⚜ Festivals & Events

Rauma Rock   MUSIC
(www.raumarock.fi) A predominantly Finnish rock festival held in March.

Rauma Blues Festival   MUSIC
(www.raumablues.com; tickets €58) Finland's best blues musicians and international visitors perform over a weekend in mid-July.

ⓘ FINNISH OR SWEDISH?

Just when you thought you'd got the hang of Finnish double vowels, you're in a part of the country where Swedish is often spoken as a first language. In addition to large parts of the west coast, officially bilingual or unilingual Swedish-speaking areas include much of the south coast as well as Åland.

By Finnish law, if there's a majority Swedophone population, the Swedish name comes first. But you'll generally need to know both place names. Jakobstad, for example, generally sticks to its Swedish name. If you look on the VR railway website (www.vr.fi), however, you'll have to know its Finnish alias, Pietarsaari.

As elsewhere in Finland, English is widely spoken but a few basic Swedish phrases will make your trip more rewarding:

Hello. Hej. (hey)

Goodbye. Hej då. (*hey* daw)

Please. Tack. (tak)

Thank you. Tack. (tak)

Cheers! Skål! (skawl)

Pitsiviikko   CULTURAL
(Rauma Lace Week; www.pitsiviikko.fi) Beginning in the last week in July, Rauma's biggest event celebrates the town's lace-making history. From the turning of the first bobbin to the crowning of Miss Lace, the whole town comes to life, particularly for Mustan Pitsin Yö (Black Lace Night), when everyone wears in black lace.

Festivo   CLASSICAL
(www.raumanfestivo.fi; tickets free-€25) Chamber music plays at venues throughout the Old Town over five days in early August.

⌒ Sleeping

Good chain hotels near the Old Town include Cumulus.

Poroholma   CAMPGROUND €
(☑02-533-5522; www.poroholma.fi; Poroholmantie; tent sites €10 plus per person €5, cottages €80-100; ☺May-Aug) On beautiful Otanlahti bay, 2km northwest of Rauma, this five-star seaside holiday resort bursts at the seams with sun-browned families. Great facilities include a

Rauma

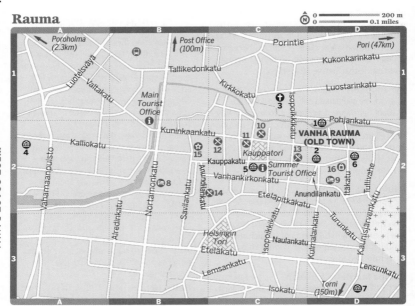

sauna, laundry, kitchen, on-site restaurant, and bike and canoe hire, even sailing ship cruises. Cottages are spick and span; the higher-priced ones are just a few years old.

★ Kylmäpihlajan
Majakka
LIGHTHOUSE HOTEL €€

(☑045-175-0619; www.kylmapihlaja.com; s €99-119, d €135-155, q €185, ste €235; ⊘early Jun-Aug) To get right away from it all, take a 30-minute boat ride (adult/child return €18/10) from Poroholma campground to this 1952-built lighthouse rising 36m above the sea surrounding the island of Kylmäpihlaja. Nautical-styled rooms are simple (all bathrooms are shared, even the suite with four-way views and a kitchenette) but atmospherically furnished with wrought-iron beds. On-site restaurant.

City Hovi
BOUTIQUE HOTEL €€

(☑02-8376-9200; www.cityhovi.com; Nortamonkatu 18; s/d/tr €89/99/120; 🛜) Enter via Pakkahuoneenkatu to reach this freshly renovated 18-room boutique hotel near the Old Town. Small but chic rooms done out in dove-greys, charcoals and Arctic whites have patterned wallpaper. Breakfast, sauna and parking included in the rate make it the best all-round bargain in town.

Hotelli Vanha Rauma
HOTEL €€

(☑02-8376-2200; www.hotelvanharauma.fi; Vanhankirkonkatu 26; s/d €130/160; 🛜) Once a warehouse in the old fish market, this is now the Old Town's only hotel. Its 20 rooms embrace modern Scandinavian design with lino flooring, leatherette chairs, flatscreen TV and views of the park or courtyard. Service is attentive, and the restaurant, SJ Nyyper, is well respected.

✗ Eating

Look out in restaurants and bars for Rauma's signature drink, Puksprööt – a juniper-rowan liqueur mixed with white wine and served with tar-infused rope!

Café Sali
CAFE, BISTRO €

(www.cafesali.fi; Kuninkaankatu 22; lunch mains €8.20-12.80, dinner mains €11-16.50; ⊘8am-10pm Jun-Aug, 9am-9pm Sep-May; 🛜) Once you get over the shock of stepping from the Old Town's 18th-century surroundings into a stark white space filled with giant photos of New York skyscrapers, Sali is a real buzz, with great lunch buffets (€9.50), a fine bistro menu in the adjoining lounge and a bustling terrace on the square.

Rauma

Kontion Leipomo CAFE €
(www.kontion.fi; Kuninkaankatu 9; dishes €4-8, mains €8-14; ⊙7.30am-5.30pm Mon-Fri, 8am-3pm Sat, 11am-4pm Sun) A 50-year-old bakery bakes all the breads, cakes and pastries for this old-school local icon (it even has its own cookbook). Light lunches – soups, stews – are also available. Enjoy them in the secluded summer courtyard or wrestle a resident teddy bear for a seat inside.

Osteria da Filippo ITALIAN €
(www.osteriafilippo.com; Kauppakatu 20; gelato €3.50, pizza €8.50-13, pasta €9-10.50; ⊙11.30am-7.30pm Mon, Tue & Thu, to 10pm Wed, to 11pm Fri & Sat) Authentic Italian pizzas, pastas and exceptional gelato – look for the queues.

⭐**Wanhan Rauman Kellari** FINNISH €€
(☏02-866-6700; www.wrk.fi; Anundilankatu 8; mains €14.50-34; ⊙11am-10pm Mon, to 11pm Tue-Thu, to midnight Fri & Sat, noon-10pm Sun) A Rauma institution, this atmospheric former potato cellar and air-raid shelter has a sun-drenched rooftop summer terrace. Starters such as salmon salad or smoked reindeer and wild mushroom soup are followed by a huge choice of fresh fish, poultry and meat dishes (plus a solitary vegetarian option),

and desserts like seabuckthorn parfait or fried brie and cloudberry compote.

Goto INTERNATIONAL €€
(☏02-822-2750; www.ravintolagoto.fi; Kuninkaankatu 17; lunch mains €10.50-13, dinner mains €22-29, 3-course menu €45; ⊙kitchen 11am-2pm & 5-10pm Mon-Fri, noon-3pm Sat) Watch chefs prepare inventive dishes like Gulf of Bothnia whitefish with cucumber and dill, barbecued Iberico pork with new potatoes, red sole meunière (floured, fried and served in brown butter and lemon sauce) and retro desserts like an 'ode to Dr Pepper' (cherry-cola sorbet, with plums and cherries) in this minimalist-chic restaurant's open kitchen. Great courtyard and all-day bar.

⭐ **Entertainment**

Iso Hannu CINEMA
(☏050-555-6644; www.isohannu.fi; Savilankatu 4; tickets Mon-Thu €10, Fri-Sun €11) This delightful independent cinema hosts its own mini film festival (www.blueseafilmfestival.net; tickets €8) in August.

🛍 **Shopping**

Pits-Priia CRAFTS
(Kauppakatu 29; ⊙10am-6pm Mon-Fri, to 4pm Sat & Sun Jun-Aug, 10am-3pm Mon-Fri, to 2pm Sat Sep-May) You can watch the town's distinctive bobbin lace being made at this venerable workshop and buy handmade lace too.

Lumo FOOD & DRINK
(www.ruokapuotilumo.fi; Kuninkaankatu 26; ⊙10am-6pm Mon-Fri, to 2pm Sat) 🌿 Browse shelves laden with local and/or organic Finnish produce and products: fruit, vegetables, cured and fresh meat, cheeses, jams, preserves, vinegars, chocolate, beer and cider, as well as handmade soaps, herbal shampoos and all-important insect repellent.

ℹ **Information**

Main Tourist Office (www.visitrauma.fi; Valtakatu 2; ⊙9am-6pm) Open year-round.
Summer Tourist Office (☏02-834-3512; www.visitrauma.fi; Kauppakatu 13; ⊙9am-6pm Jun-Aug) In Vanha Raatihuone (the Old Town Hall) on the kauppatori.

ℹ **Getting There & Away**

Major bus services:
Helsinki (€42.80, four hours, up to four hourly Monday to Friday, fewer on Saturday and Sunday)

Pori (€11.80, one hour, two to three hourly Monday to Saturday, fewer on Sunday)

Tampere (€28, 2½ hours, up to two hourly Monday to Friday, fewer on Saturday and Sunday)

Turku (€22, 1½ hours, two to three hourly Monday to Saturday, fewer on Sunday)

Uusikaupunki (€10.10, one hour, every two hours Monday to Friday, fewer on Saturday and Sunday)

Around Rauma

Sammallahdenmäki

The Unesco World Heritage–listed Bronze Age burial complex Sammallahdenmäki dates back more than 3500 years. Thirty-six stone burial cairns of different shapes and sizes are spread over a kilometre of forest. The two biggest are **kirkonlattia** (church floor), a monumental quadrangle measuring 16m by 19m, and the **huilun pitkä raunio** (long cairn of Huilu).

Sammallahdenmäki is close to Lappi village, 20km east of Rauma, signposted from Hwy 12. Buses run on school days only (€6.10, 30 minutes, eight daily).

Pori

🖉 02 / POP 83,500

Try to get to Pori (Swedish: Björneborg) during its renowned jazz festival, which attracts 150,000 visitors and has the streets scatting for a week in July. The whole town buzzes; even the local football team changed its name a couple of decades ago to FC Jazz.

After the festival, Pori settles back down to business as one of the most important deep-water harbours in Finland.

◉ Sights & Activities

Although Pori is one of Finland's oldest towns, devastating fires (the last in 1852) mean there are few historic buildings. The most distinctive are the neo-Renaissance **Old Town Hall** (Hallituskatu 9), designed by CL Engel in 1831, and neo-Gothic **Keski-Pori church** (Hallituskatu 4; ⊙10am-1pm Mon-Fri) with its cast-iron steeple.

Situated 17km northwest of Pori, **Yyteri** is a fabulous 6km-long powdery-sand beach backed by dunes and forest, with family swimming areas, some of Finland's best windsurfing and a naturist beach.

Satakunta Museum MUSEUM
(🖉02-621-1063; Hallituskatu 11; adult/child €4/1.50; ⊙11am-6pm Tue & Thu-Sun, 11am-8pm Wed) Fascinating exhibits at this well laid-out museum range from intact Viking skis to a display showing how a handbag's contents have changed over the centuries, as well as regional customs and traditions traced through a poignant journey from birth to death.

Yyteri Surfclub WATER SPORTS
(www.purjelautaliitto.fi/yyteri; Sipintie 1; ⊙10am-6pm Jun–mid-Aug, 10am-6pm Sat & Sun mid-Aug–late Aug) Rents windsurfing equipment (€35/140 per hour/six hours) and stand-up paddleboards (SUPs; €25 per hour).

🛌 Sleeping

Some of the best options are by the beach at nearby Yyteri. In town, reliable chain hotels include Sokos and Scandic.

Jazz festival accommodation in and around Pori books out up to a year in advance and prices skyrocket.

Hostel River HOSTEL €
(🖉02-534-0500; www.hostelriver.fi; Karjapaiha 2; dm/s/d/tr/q €30/42/60/85/110; @🛜) Right across from the river (but lacking views due to newly built apartments across the street), the lemon-yellow wooden building housing this superb HI-affiliated hostel has a slew of facilities including a self-catering kitchen, sauna (private/shared €10/5 per hour), laundry, bike hire (€10 per day) and optional breakfast (€6.50). Colourful dorms and private rooms all share bathrooms.

Top Camping Yyteri CAMPGROUND €
(🖉02-634-5700; www.topcampingyyteri.fi; Yyterinsantojentie, Yyteri; tent sites €16 plus per adult €4, cottages €73-130) Surrounded by forest just footsteps from the beach, this large family campground has an on-site restaurant, a new Angry Birds–themed playground, minigolf, tennis, bike hire (€12 per day) and a laundry. Year-round cottages sleep up to six people (linen €9 per person).

Yyterin Kylpylähotelli SPA HOTEL €€
(🖉02-628-5300; www.yyterinkylpyla.fi; Sipintie 1, Yyteri; s/d €115/153; 🛜🕭) Spa facilities at this beachfront complex are top-notch and free for guests. Nordic walking sticks and wintertime sledges and toboggans are also free; there's a handy laundry and drying room. Many rooms overlook overlook the dunes and sea beyond.

Pori

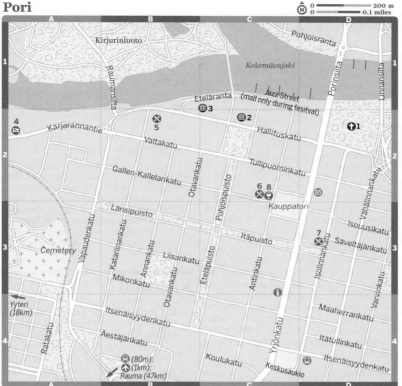

Eating & Drinking

Kauppahalli   MARKET €

(Isolinnankatu; ⊙9am-5pm Mon-Fri, 8am-2pm Sat) At Pori's kauppahalli (covered market), look out for the local speciality smoked river lamprey, an eel-like fish that killed England's Henry I when he gorged too many.

Elba Cafè   MEDITERRANEAN €€

(☑040-908-300; www.elba.fi; Gallen-Kallelankatu 5; tapas €6.50-11.50, mains €16-26.50; ⊙11am-6pm Tue, 11am-10pm Wed-Sat, noon-4pm Sun) Fronted by a terrace that gets jam-packed in summer, this classy yet cosy cafe-wine bar has light tapas dishes, substantial mains and luscious desserts like tiramisu, but the showstopper is the fantastic selection of wines with by-the-glass options. Service is spot on.

Bucco   MEDITERRANEAN €€€

(☑02-622-6185; www.bucco.fi; Hallituskatu 22; mains €29-36, 3-/4-/6-course set menus

Pori

◉ **Sights**
1 Keski-Pori Church D2
2 Old Town Hall C2
3 Satakunta Museum C1

⬤ **Sleeping**
4 Hostel River A2

⊗ **Eating**
5 Bucco B2
6 Elba Cafè C2
7 Kauppahalli D3
Raatihuoneen Kellari .... (see 2)

◉ **Drinking & Nightlife**
8 Beer Hunter's C2

€46/54/68; ⊙11am-3pm & 5-11pm Tue-Fri, 4-11pm Sat) Once an old brewery workers' canteen and now Pori's top restaurant, this stylish spot gives Mediterranean dishes a Finnish twist, such as grilled whitefish served on

DON'T MISS

ALL THAT JAZZ

Pori Jazz Festival (☑010-522-3200; www.porijazz.fi; tickets free–€70) Held over nine days in mid-July, the Pori Jazz Festival, established in 1966, is one of Finland's biggest summer events. Over 100 concerts take place in diverse indoor and outdoor venues, along with free jam sessions. Much of the action is along Jazz Street, the closed-off section of Eteläranta along the riverfront, with stalls, makeshift bars and street dancing.

risotto with sautéed tomatoes and spinach, reindeer fillet with caramelised fennel and potato purée, and blueberry sorbet with prosecco.

Raatihuoneen Kellari   FINNISH €€€
(☑02-633-4804; Hallituskatu 9; lunch buffet €12-15, mains €19-37.50; ☺11am-11pm Mon-Thu, 11am-midnight Fri, 1pm-midnight Sat, by appt Sun) Atmospherically set in the vaulted cellar of the Old Town Hall, Raatihuoneen Kellari has mighty weekday lunch buffets and inventive evening dishes like duck confit with blackberry sauce, accompanied by a discerning wine list.

Beer Hunter's   BREWPUB
(www.beerhunters.fi; Antinkatu 11; ☺11am-2am) An ale-lovers' paradise, this distillery and microbrewery sells its own beers, cider and whisky along with a vast array of international brews.

❶ Information

Tourist Office (☑02-621-7900; www.maisa.fi; Yrjönkatu 17; ☺9am-6pm Mon-Fri, 9am-3pm Sat Jun–mid-Aug, 9am-4.30pm Mon-Fri mid-Aug–May) Sells concert tickets and can book cabins in the area.

❶ Getting There & Away

There are 24-hour coin-operated left-luggage lockers at the train and bus stations (€3 to €5).

AIR

Pori's small airport, 2km south of the town centre, has some charter flights but few-to-no domestic services outside the jazz festival.

BUS

Frequent direct daily services:
Helsinki (€42.80, four hours)

Rauma (€11.80, one hour)
Tampere (€20.60, 2½ hours); some services require a change at Huittinen and take considerably longer
Turku (€28.80, 2¼ hours)
Vaasa (€38.10, 3¼ hours)

TRAIN

Frequent services include Tampere (€19.20, 1½ hours, six daily), which has good connections to/from Helsinki (€38.30, three to four hours, 10 daily).

❶ Getting Around

Local buses run from the kauppatori to the beach at Yyteri (€5.50, 40 minutes, hourly Monday to Friday, four daily Saturday and Sunday).

The tourist office's excellent *Pori Pyöräilykartta* details cycling paths around town. Hire bikes from **Porin Kaupungin Vapaa-aikavirastosta** (☑044-701-1421; www.pori.fi; Isolinnankatu 12; per day €7; ☺8.30am-6.30pm Jun-Aug, 8.30am-4.30pm Mon-Fri Sep-May).

Kristinestad

☑06 / POP 7080

Named for Queen Kristina of Sweden, seaside Kristinestad (Finnish: Kristiinankaupunki) was founded in the mid-17th century by maverick count Per Brahe. It was once a booming shipbuilding centre and a port for shipping tar and timber out of Pohjanmaa, but these days it's a sleepy little spot sustained by potato farming. In 2011 Kristinestad became Finland's first 'Cittaslow' town, an extension of the Slow Food movement, which aims to rebalance the hectic pace of modern life not only with 'ecogastronomy' but also local arts, crafts, nature, cultural traditions and heritage.

◉ Sights

The town itself, with its rows of colourful wooden houses, is Kristinestad's key draw.

Old Customs House   HISTORIC BUILDING
(Staketgatan) In the port's heyday, travellers entering Kristinestad had to pay customs duty, collected at the Old Customs House, a smallish rust-wood building dating from 1720, just along from the imposing town hall.

Ulrika Eleonora Kyrkan   CHURCH
(Old Church; ☺9am-4pm Mon-Sat mid-May–Aug) Behind Kristinestad's Old Customs House is the charming red-wood Ulrika Eleonora Kyrkan, with a crooked shingled steeple. Built in 1700, it retains much of its original detail.

Nya Kirka CHURCH
(New Church; Parmansgatan; ⊘ 9am-4pm Mon-Sat mid-May–Aug) The red-brick New Church has a high wooden ceiling and an archetypal church-ship dedicated by mariners.

Sjöfartsmuseum MUSEUM
(☑ 06-221-2859; Salutorget 1; adult/child €4/1; ⊘ noon-4pm Tue-Sun mid-Jun–mid-Aug) Sjöfartsmuseum was originally built in 1837 as a merchant's home to dominate the market square. Today it showcases Kristinestad's maritime heritage, especially shipbuilding, with reconstructions of a captain's cabin and a ship's helm.

🛏 Sleeping & Eating

Bockholmens Camping CAMPGROUND €
(☑ 050-527-3356; Salavägen 32; tent sites €15, cabins €40-85; ⊘ mid-May–early Sep) Just 1.5km southwest of the town centre, this small, friendly campground has its own beach, and bikes for hire. Cabins share bathrooms but all come with kitchenettes. Linen costs €5 per person.

Hotel Leila HOTEL €€
(☑ 040-418-5185; www.hotelleila.fi; Västra Långgatan 39; s/d €98/130; 🛜) Hotel Leila hosts the reception for both its own attractive rooms and the atmospheric, pistachio-painted **Hotel Alma** (www.hotelleila.fi; Parmansgatan; 🛜), whose crowning glory is a splendid crow's-nest-like tower suite (€170) with four-way views across the wooden rooftops and water. Basic breakfast provisions are supplied in-room.

Huoneistomajoitus Krepelin B&B €€
(☑ 040-066-1434; www.krepelin.fi; Östra Långgatan 47; d €80, incl breakfast & sheets €100; 🛜) If you're curious about what it would be like to live in one of Kristinestad's little wooden houses, this former sailor's residence will give you a taster. Refurbished double rooms are tiny but ever so sweet and include kitchenettes.

★ Pavis FINNISH €€
(☑ 050-554-1570; www.pavis.fi; Korkeasaarentie 16; lunch buffet €12, mains €17-34; ⊘ 11am-11pm Tue-Sat, noon-9pm Sun Jun-Aug) 🥢 From Kristinestad's centre, it's a 3km drive south to the tiny island of Högholmen where, beyond a picturesque patch of woodland, you'll find this fairy-tale eggshell-blue wooden summer pavilion with a terrace overlooking an idyllic little boat-filled harbour. Exquisite dishes include forest mushroom soup, baked perch with blueberry Dijon mustard, blackcurrant-marinaded chicken with liquorice sauce, and seabuckthorn and cranberry parfait.

ℹ Information

Tourist Office (☑ 06-221-2311; www.visitkristinestad.fi; Östralånggatan 53; ⊘ 10am-5pm Mon-Fri year-round, plus 11am-2pm Sat & Sun Jun & Jul) Rents bikes (€10 per day).

ℹ Getting There & Away

Kristinestad is on Rd 662 off Hwy 8, 100km south of Vaasa. Buses between Pori (€22, 1½ hours) and Vaasa (€24, 1¾ hours) stop at Kristinestad five times daily Monday to Friday, four on Saturday and Sunday.

Närpes & Around
☑ 06 / POP 9390

Surrounded by greenhouses, Finland's tomato capital, Närpes (Finnish: Närpiö), has one of the country's highest populations of Swedish speakers (93% Swedophone), with a local accent that has evolved into a distinct dialect.

⊙ Sights

Närpes Church CHURCH
(Kyrkvägen 21; ⊘ 10am-5pm Jun-Aug) Medieval Närpes Church, 1km south of Närpes' town centre, is surrounded by over 150 *kyrkstallar* (church stables), built in the 15th century for parishioners who rode in from rural farms to worship. Its altar dates from 1803 and was painted by the Swedish court painter Pehr Hörberg; the crucifix that lies upon it is from the 1400s.

Öjskogparken MUSEUM
(☑ 040-505-5377; Kyrkvägen 23; admission by €2 donation, theatre tickets adult/child €20/10; ⊘ 11am-4pm Mon-Fri Jun–mid-Aug) Just 100m southwest of Närpes Church, Öjskogparken is a collection of historic buildings, the marooned locomotive Kasköbässin, and an incredible outdoor **revolving theatre**, which hosts summer performances in the local dialect.

★ Festivals & Events

Siirrettävien Saunojen CULTURAL
(Mobile Sauna Festival; www.sauna-ajot.com; admission free, parking €5) An only-in-Finland experience, the two-day Siirrettävien Saunojen festival held in early August at lakeside

Parra, 34km west of Närpes, sees entrants vie for the most unique homemade mobile sauna (the only rules: it must be mobilised, and fit one person). There are also *vihta* (bunch of fragrant, leafy birch twigs) making and throwing competitions, best sauna outfit prizes and live music.

🛏 Sleeping & Eating

Närpes' shiny-new town-centre hotel and restaurant **Red & Green** (www.hotelredgreen. fi) opened as this book went to print. Check its website for details.

★**Linds Kök**   FINNISH €€
(📞 040-510-8124; www.lindskok.fi; Bäcklidvägen 476; mains €24-32; ⊗ noon-3pm & 8-11pm Tue-Fri, noon-3pm Sat-Mon Jun-early Aug, by appt rest of year) 🍴 Dine amid mandarin and lime trees, strawberries, herbs and tomatoes growing inside this extraordinary greenhouse 10km southeast of Närpes. Fresh-as-it-gets Finnish specialities include pork with liquorice sauce, grilled salmon with cloudberry sauce, and tomato pannacotta. Serious tomato fans should go for the seven-course tomato menu (€59), starting with creamy tomato soup and ending with tomato ice cream.

❶ Getting There & Away

Buses link Närpes with Kristinestad (€9.40, 30 minutes) and Vaasa (€15.50, 1¼ hours) up to 11 times daily Monday to Friday, and four times on Saturday and Sunday.

OFF THE BEATEN TRACK

DEVIL'S NEST

Pirunpesä (Devil's Nest; www.jalasjarven kylat.fi/ylivalli_pirunpesa; Pirunpesäntie, Jalasjärvi; adult/child €5/3; ⊗ noon-8pm Sat & Sun May–mid-Jun, noon-8pm daily mid-Jun–mid-Aug, 10am-6pm Sat & Sun mid-Aug–Sep) OK, so it's a hole in the ground, but it's Europe's deepest, at 23m, with a diameter of 14m, and mystery surrounds its origins (glacial erosion or a natural-gas blow-out are the most plausible theories). You can descend a metal staircase into the cavity or view it from the 21m-high observation tower. Pirunpesä is 52km south of Seinäjoki (there's no public transport). Take Rd 19 to the Jalasjärvi exit then head southeast for 16km; it's on your right.

Seinäjoki
📞 06 / POP 60,480

Seinäjoki (Swedish: Östermyra) is often overlooked by visitors hugging the coast, but anyone interested in Finnish architecture shouldn't miss its striking Alvar Aalto–designed town centre.

Huge festivals, especially Tangomarkkinat (Tango Fair) and Provinssirock, draw crowds in their thousands each summer.

⊙ Sights

In 1951 Alvar Aalto won a competition to design Seinäjoki's civic and cultural heart from scratch, down to the last light fitting and door handle. The **Aalto Centre**, completed in the 1960s, is one of his most important works – a collection of icy white structures and green spaces that exemplify his modernist style. The fan-shaped **public library** is characteristic of Aalto's multilevel approach; the **theatre** foyer contains a series of his famous wooden reliefs; and the glittering blue-tiled, wave-like crest of the **town hall** incorporates the architect's 'signature' ('aalto' is Finnish for wave).

Lakeuden Risti Church   CHURCH
(lift admission €1; ⊗ 10am-8pm mid-May–mid-Aug, noon-6pm Mon-Fri mid-Aug–mid-May, lift noon-6pm mid-May–mid-Aug, 2-6pm Mon-Fri mid-Aug–mid-May) Alvar Aalto's crowning achievement, Lakeuden Risti Church, is recognisable by its oddly secular steeple-clock tower. You'll get a great perspective of the buildings making up the Aalto Centre by taking the **lift** to the top.

Civil Guard & Lotta Svärd Museum MUSEUM
(📞 06-416-2734; Kauppakatu 17; adult/child €4/2; ⊗ noon-7pm Wed, to 5pm Thu-Sun May-Aug, noon-6pm Wed, to 4pm Thu, Fri & Sun Sep-Apr) This Alvar Aalto–designed museum houses a collection based around the Lotta Svärd women's voluntary (and unarmed) defence force, which took on military service during WWII and became one of the world's largest auxiliaries.

✪ Festivals & Events

Provinssirock   MUSIC
(📞 06-421-2700; www.provinssirock.fi; 1-/2-day pass €69/95) Held 4km south of town, near Törnävä, over two days in late June, this open-air rock concert sees international acts duel with top Finnish bands from across

the musical spectrum (David Bowie and the Black Eyed Peas have held the same stage as HIM and The Rasmus). Festival buses run from Seinäjoki's train station (€3; cash only).

Tangomarkkinat DANCE
(206-420-1111; www.tangomarkkinat.fi; 1-/5-day pass €30/100) Seinäjoki is the undisputed tango capital of a country that is certifiably tango-mad, and enormous crowds descend on this international festival in early July. The first heels are kicked up at a huge open-air dance party in 'Tango Street', followed by five days of dance competitions, tango classes and other festivities.

🛏 Sleeping & Eating

Book accommodation well in advance for Seinäjoki's summer festivals. Central chain hotels include Cumulus and Sokos.

Aside from reliable hotel restaurants, Seinäjoki has limited dining options but a gastronomic standout.

Hotel Alma BOUTIQUE HOTEL €€
(206-421-5200; www.hotelalma.fi; Ruukintie 4; s/d €108/128; @🤶) Next to the train station, this central wooden charmer has 20 generously sized art-nouveau-furnished rooms named after steam trains, a quality restaurant and a terrace area for a tipple.

Hotel Sorsanpesa HOTEL €€
(2020-741-8181; www.sorsanpesa.fi; Törnäväntie 27; s/d €78/98; @🤶🐕) You're welcomed with a drink and tapas snack at this riverside hotel 4.5km south of Seinäjoki's town centre. Spacious rooms have chocolate tones and staff keep things running smoothly. The restaurant and bar open to a vast terrace overlooking the river.

★ Juurella MODERN FINNISH €€
(206-414-0720; www.juurella.fi; Keskustori 1; mains €14-28; ⊙4-10pm Tue-Fri, 2-10pm Sat) 🍴 Seasonal local organic produce is utilised by Juurella's award-winning chefs to create masterpieces like beef with juniper-berry sausage, forest-mushroom pancakes, and perch with cauliflower and peas. Don't by fooled by the descriptions' simplicity: 'carrot cake', for example, is a symphony of spiced cake in warm carrot soup with a crispy deep-fried carrot wafer and cool carrot sorbet. Seriously, wow.

ℹ Information

Tourist Office (206-420-9090; www.epmatkailu.fi; ⊙9am-5pm Mon-Fri May-Aug, 9am-4pm Sep-Apr) In the bus and train station complex; can book accommodation in private homes during the festivals.

ℹ Getting There & Away

The adjacent bus and train stations are in the town centre.

Buses serve towns and villages throughout Western Finland.

Seinäjoki is a rail hub; services include Helsinki (€53.70, three hours, up to two hourly), Jyväskylä (€27.40, three hours, up to two hourly) and Vaasa (€13.40, one hour, every two hours).

Vaasa
206 / POP 66.450

Vaasa (Swedish: Vasa) sits above the 63rd parallel and southern Finns consider it 'The North'. Just 45 nautical miles from Sweden, the city has a significant Swedophone population, with a quarter of residents speaking Swedish as a first language.

The 17th-century town was named after Swedish royalty, the noble Vasa family, but 200 years later it was in Russian hands. The Old Town burned down in Vaasa's Great Fire of 1852 – caused by a careless visitor who fell asleep and dropped his pipe – and the new city was built from scratch, 7km away from the cinders.

Long a family holiday playground, Vasa also has three universities and a thriving arts scene.

◉ Sights & Activities

Look out for public art as you wander the streets.

★ Pohjanmaan Museo MUSEUM
(Ostrobothnian Museum; www.pohjanmaanmuseo.fi; Museokatu 3; adult/child €7/free, Fri free; ⊙noon-6pm Tue-Thu, noon-4pm Fri-Sun late May-late Aug, noon-5pm Tue, Thu & Sun, noon-8pm Wed late Aug-late May) Vaasa's dynamic, modern museum is divided into three sections. Downstairs, **Terranova** has a brilliant evocation of the region's natural history – complete with dioramas and storm-and-lightning effects – that includes information on the Kvarken Archipelago. On the ground floor, yesteryear Vaasa is brought to life in the **Pohjanmaan Museo**. Upstairs, the **Hedman collection** contains some 300 works of art, including a

Tintoretto, a Botticelli Madonna, works from all the Finnish masters and a huge number of ceramics.

Wasalandia
AMUSEMENT PARK

(☑020-796-1200; www.wasalandia.fi; Vaskiluoto; day pass €18, incl Tropiclandia €36; ⊘11am-7pm late Jun–mid-Aug, 11am-5pm early-Jun–mid-Jun, 11am-6pm mid-Jun–late Jun) Great for preteens, Wasalandia is the centrepiece of the island of Vaskiluoto, with lots of pirate-themed rides and a 'traffic park' for junior drivers. Across the road, the outdoor **Tropiclandia** (☑020-796-1300; www.tropiclandia.fi; Sommarstigen 1, Vaskiluoto; spa & waterpark €23, incl Wasalandia €36, spa only €17; ⊘waterpark 10am-7pm Jun-early Aug, spa 8am-9pm Mon-Fri, 9am-9pm Sat, 10am-9pm Sun early Oct-late Aug) has enough water slides, wave machines, Jacuzzis, saunas and spa treatments to keep both kids and adults happy. Packages can be arranged with the **spa hotel** here. The **Lilliputtila** (per person/family €5/15; ⊘10.30am-5.30pm late Jun-early Aug) street train runs hourly from

Vaasa's kauppatori to Vaskiluoto during summer.

Kuntsi
GALLERY

(☑06-325-3920; http://kuntsi.vaasa.fi; Sisäsatama; adult/child €5/free; ⊘11am-5pm Tue-Sun) The beautiful former customs house now hosts changing exhibitions of pop art, kinetic art, surrealism and postmodernism. At its core is the collection of Simo Kuntsi, who gathered almost a thousand modern Finnish works from the 1950s onwards.

Tikanojan Taidekoti
GALLERY

(☑06-325-3916; www.tikanojantaidekoti.fi; Hovioikeudenpuistikko 4; adult/child €5/free; ⊘10am-4pm Tue-Sun) Works by Degas, Gauguin, Matisse and Picasso are among this gallery's strong international collection.

Stundars Handicraft Village
MUSEUM

(☑06-344-2200; www.stundars.fi; adult/child €7/free; ⊘11am-5pm Jul–mid-Aug) In the attractive village of Solf (Finnish: Sulva), about 15km

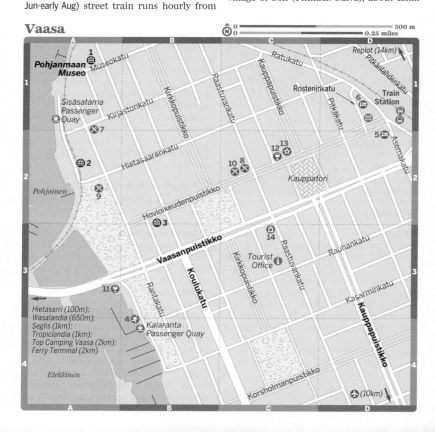

Vaasa

south of Vaasa, is this fine open-air museum and crafts centre. Its 60 traditional wooden buildings were moved here from surrounding villages and include crofts, cottages and cowsheds, a pottery, windmills and a schoolhouse. There's a humming calendar of events in summer, from markets to craft demonstrations. The entrance fee includes a guided tour. Buses are a pain: you really need your own transport.

M/S Tiira   CRUISE
(☑050-553-1236;   www.jannensaluuna.com; adult/child €18/8; ☺up to 2 departures daily late Jun–mid-Aug) M/S *Tiira* cruises the Vaasa archipelago to Kuusisaari, departing from the Kalaranta passenger quay. Cruises lasts about 3½ hours, with a lunch stop (food not included) at **Janne's Saloon** (light lunch €10-12, mains €23.50-29), a restaurant owned by the same outfit.

⚔ Festivals & Events
Hietsku Rock   MUSIC
(www.hietskurock.fi; 1-/2-day pass €30/52.50) The tiny island of Hietasarri, between Vaasa and Vaskiluoto, reverberates during this two-day festival held in mid-July with mostly Finnish and Swedish bands.

⊨ Sleeping
Decent central chain hotels include Radisson Blu and Sokos.

Top Camping Vaasa   CAMPGROUND €
(☑020-796-1255; www.topcamping.fi; tent sites €12 plus per person €8, 4-person cabins €70; ☺mid-May–mid-Aug) This popular family getaway is 2km from town on Vaskiluoto. It hires bicycles (€3/6 per two/six hours) and rowboats (€4 per hour). A minimum two-night stay is required for cabins. Ask about discount packages with the nearby Wasalandia amusement park and Tropiclandia.

★Hotel Kantarellis   BOUTIQUE HOTEL €€
(☑06-357-8100; www.hotelkantarellis.fi; Rosteninkatu 6; s/d €134/157; @⊚) Every room at this independent boutique gem has a private sauna, and most have air Jacuzzis and air-conditioning. The decor is dramatically dark, with spotlit wilderness-themed photos. Solid soundproofing means you won't hear your neighbours' giant flatscreen TV set.

Hotel Astor   HOTEL €€
(☑06-326-9111; www.astorvaasa.fi; Asemakatu 4; s €124, d €130-144; @⊚) Handy for the bus or train station, this great little hotel has a historic interior and personal feel, down to the fresh-baked cakes at breakfast. Rooms in the older wing feature polished floors and dark-wood furnishings. Higher-priced doubles have their own sauna. Wi-fi can be patchy.

✗ Eating
Sweet Vaasa   CAFE €
(www.sweetvaasa.fi; Hovioikeudenpuistikko 11; mains €9-12; ☺9am-6pm Mon-Fri, 10am-5pm Sat; ⊚) Huge, healthy salads, such as a 'protein monster' (bell pepper, bacon, egg, chicken, tuna, salmon, seeds and nuts), and a daily special (anything from pesto chicken pasta to haloumi with chickpea salsa or smoked-salmon cheesecake) are the mainstays of this buzzing post-industrial-style cafe; prices include gluten-free crispbread plus coffee or tea.

Bacchus   FINNISH €€
(☑010-470-6200; www.bacchus.fi; Rantakatu 4; mains €15-21; ☺6-10pm Tue-Fri, 4-10pm Sat) In a rustic brickwork interior warmed by animal skins, seasonally changing dishes might include fried whitefish with champagne sauce, roast reindeer with juniper sauce and mushroom croquettes, or polenta with truffles

and spiced vegetables. As you'd expect from a place named for the Greek god of boozing, the wine cellar is exceptional.

Strampen FINNISH €€
(☑041-451-4512; www.strampen.com; Rantakatu 6; lunch buffet €8.50-12, mains €18.50-29; ☺11am-10pm Mon-Fri, noon-10pm Sat & Sun) Right on the water, this perennial favourite in a 19th-century pavilion serves top-end meals inside and affordable burgers et al on its terrace. In summer staff keep the outdoor bar pumping until late.

Seglis FINNISH €€
(☑010-320-3779; www.seglis.fi; Uddnäsvägen 14; lunch buffet €12, mains €14-31; ☺11am-2pm Mon-Fri May, 11am-2pm Mon, 11am-10pm Tue-Fri Jun-Aug) On the island of Vaskiluoto near Wasalandia you can dine on Finnish classics (smoked herring, hare, reindeer) on this wooden pavilion's waterside terrace overlooking the city.

★ Gustav Wasa MODERN FINNISH €€€
(☑050-466-3208; www.gustavwasa.com; Raastuvankatu 24; mains €18-36, 7-course tasting menu €69, with wine pairings €50; ☺gastropub 5-10pm Mon-Fri, 3-10pm Sat, fine dining 6-10pm Mon-Fri, 4-10pm Sat) A former coal cellar is home to one of Finland's best restaurants, newly split into a casual gastropub with by-the-glass wines and on-tap Finnish beers, and an intimate candlelit fine-dining space serving sublime seven-course tasting menus. Cooking courses are available; you can also order food for its adjacent sauna (sauna €250, plus €6 per person; sauna buffets €25 to €36).

🍸 Drinking & Nightlife

Faros BAR
(☑045-151-3007; www.faros.fi; Kalaranta; ☺noon-11.30pm Mon-Sat, noon-9pm Sun late May-Aug) Moored in Kalaranta Harbour south of the bridge, this wooden ship has frequent live music and dancing on the pier.

Fontana CLUB
(www.fontanaclub.com; Hovioikeudenpuistikko 15; ☺10pm-4am Wed-Sat) With six bars, two dance floors and a huge heated terrace, this dressy place is one of the biggest clubs in town.

☆ Entertainment

Doo-bop Club LIVE MUSIC
(www.doobop.fi; Kauppapuistikko 12; admission €8; ☺9pm-2am Fri & Sat) Jazz, funk and soul play amid suitably darkened surrounds, along with occasional jam sessions.

🛍 Shopping

Loftet ARTS & CRAFTS
(☑06-318-5315; www.loftet.fi; Raastuvankatu 28; ☺10am-5pm Mon-Fri, 10am-3pm Sat) Great jewellery, linen and traditional regional gifts made from rush, tin plate and wood, plus a cute adjoining cafe.

ℹ Information

There are coin-operated left-luggage lockers (€3 to €5) at the bus and train station.

Tourist Office (☑06-325-1145; www.visit vaasa.fi; Raastuvankatu 30; ☺9am-5pm daily Jul, 9am-5pm Mon-Fri Jun & Aug, 10am-4pm Mon-Fri Sep-May) Books accommodation and has bikes for hire (€10 per day).

ℹ Getting There & Away

AIR
Finnair (www.finnair.com) flies several times daily to Helsinki and Stockholm.

BOAT
From late June to early August daily ferries (adult/car/bicycle €35/50/5, 4½ hours) run between Vaasa and the Swedish town of Umeå (Finnish: Uumaja) with **Wasaline** (☑020-771-6810; www.wasaline.com). The ferry terminal is on the western side of Vaskiluoto.

BUS
Up to four buses an hour serve Helsinki (€50.20, 7½ hours) and Turku (€60.10, six hours), most with a change in Pori or Huittinen. Buses run up and down the west coast pretty much hourly from Monday to Friday.

TRAIN
Vaasa trains connect via Seinäjoki (€11.70, one hour, up to 10 daily) to main-line destinations such as Tampere (€40.80, 2½ hours) and Helsinki (€61.10, four to five hours).

ℹ Getting Around

The airport is situated 12km southeast of the town centre; local buses pass by Monday to Friday (one way €3). A **taxi** (☑06-100-411) costs about €25.

Major car-hire companies have offices at the airport and train station.

Rent bicycles from the tourist office, Top Camping Vaasa (p201) or **Bikes A Viertola** (☑06-317-1423; Kauppapuistikko 28; per day €10; ☺10am-5pm Mon-Fri, to 1pm Sat).

> **WORTH A TRIP**
>
> ## KVARKEN ARCHIPELAGO
>
> Listed as a Unesco World Heritage site in 2006, Kvarken stretches across to the Umeå region of Sweden and includes the sea and islands between the two countries. The land here is rising at an astonishing rate – around 8mm per year. During the last ice age, the weight of the ice covering Kvarken depressed the earth's crust by up to 1km. Since the ice melted, the pressure has been released and new islands are emerging – it's estimated that by the year 4500, a land bridge will join Sweden and Finland. Vaasa's Terranova (p199) is a great place to learn more; information is also available online at www.kvarken worldheritage.fi.
>
> Kvarken's most accessible point is **Replot** (Finnish: Raippaluoto), a large island just off the Vaasa coast, linked by Finland's longest bridge (1.045km), which opened in 1997. By the bridge, **Havets Hus** (☑050-378-5988; www.havetshus.fi; ⊙10am-5pm Jun, 10am-7pm Mon-Fri, 10am-5pm Sat & Sun Jul, 10am-7pm early–mid-Aug) has maps and information on activities including fishing, kayaking and canoeing. Alongside it, the **M/S Corina** (☑050-026-0751; www.berny.fi; adult/child €16/8; ⊙2pm Mon, Wed, Fri & Sat late Jun–mid-Aug) runs two-hour cruises of the archipelago. It's a great cycle out here with bridges connecting smaller islands.
>
> There are a handful of accommodation options on the archipelago, including the beautifully situated **Björkö Camping** (☑050-526-2300; www.bjorkocamping.com; Raippaluodontie 1089; 4-/6-person cabins €100/120). Its timber cabins come with en suite bathrooms, kitchenettes equipped with fridges, microwaves and coffee makers, and covered terraces overlooking the private beach. Great facilities include a beach sauna, rowboats and fishing equipment.
>
> The only really decent place to dine on Kvarken is **Cafe Arken** (☑06-352-0329; www.cafearken.fi; Byhamnvägen 194; dishes €9-13, lunch buffet €13, mains €17-29; ⊙noon-10pm Mon-Thu, to midnight Fri & Sat, to 4pm Sun Jun–mid-Aug), a delightful summer pavilion with a terrace overlooking a small harbour. The menu ranges from light bites like burgers to mains such as schnitzels, steaks, fish and filling veggie casseroles. You can just stop by for a drink at the bar, which has occasional live music.

Jakobstad

☑06 / POP 19,670

Stretching for several blocks north of the new town, Jakobstad's mainly residential Old Town, Skata, has around 300 of the best-preserved wooden houses in Finland.

Over half the population are Swedophone in Jakobstad (Finnish: Pietarsaari). The town's name comes from Swedish war hero Jacob de la Gardie, whose widow Ebba Braha founded Jakobstad in 1652 in her husband's memory. It's the birthplace of Finland's national poet, JL Runeberg (1804–77), who wrote in Swedish.

◉ Sights

Most of the houses in Skata were originally occupied by sailors. While the 18th-century houses along Hamngatan are the oldest, the prettiest street is Norrmalmsgatan, which has a stunning clock tower bridging the street.

The Gamla Hamn (Old Harbour) has a child-friendly swimming beach.

Aspegrens Trädgård Rosenlund GARDENS (Aspegren's Gardens; ☑06-724-3101; www.rosenlund.fi; Masaholmsvägen 1; admission €3; ⊙noon-4pm Tue-Sat, noon-3pm Sun Jul–mid-Aug) A little walled oasis lies 1km southeast of the kauppatori. Aspegren's Gardens was created by priest Gabriel Aspegren in the 1700s. Butterflies flit around the formal flower beds and a tiny, scented rose garden. The rectory outbuildings hold the **Hembygdsmuseum** (☑050-378-4242; ⊙noon-6pm Tue-Sat, noon-3pm Sun Jul-Aug) FREE, crammed with sleighs, agricultural equipment and hunting traps. In the orangery, the cafe uses produce from the gardens.

Jakobstads Museum MUSEUM (☑06-786-3373; Storgatan 2; admission €3; ⊙noon-4pm Jun & Aug, noon-6pm Jul) Finland's richest man, shipping magnate Otto Malm, was the last person to live in Malm House. On his death in 1898, the house became

Jakobstad

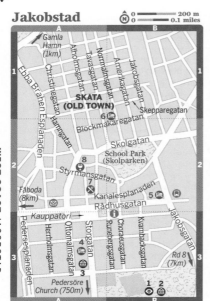

Jakobstad

Jakobstads Museum, with displays on the shipping industry and local history.

Pedersöre Church　　　　　　　CHURCH
(☏ 040-310-0447; Vasavägen 118; ◷ 9am-4pm mid-May–mid-Aug) Dating from the 1400s, this is one of the region's oldest churches. King Gustav III of Sweden personally signed off on the plans to expand the church into the cruciform, though builders ignored his instruction to demolish the towering spire, which was later destroyed by fire, before being restored to its original form.

🛏 Sleeping

Hostel Lilja　　　　　　　　　　HOSTEL €
(☏ 06-781-6500; www.aftereight.fi; Storgatan 6; s/d/tr/ste €45/55/65/75; ⊚) Eight restored rooms range over two storeys of a 19th-century barn at this friendly hostel. Most share bathrooms but the 'honeymoon suite' has a small en suite. Extras include laundry facilities, bike hire (€5 per day) and a sauna. Breakfast is €6.50.

Westerlunds Inn　　　　　　GUESTHOUSE €
(☏ 06-723-0440; www.multi.fi/westerlund; Norrmalmsgatan 8; s/d/tr without bathroom €30/50/60) You'll forgive this charming inn's minuscule rooms (and shared bathrooms) given its peaceful location in Jakobstad's Skata (Old Town). Rooms still manage to cram in a tiny table and washbasin and there is, of course, a sauna. Breakfast is €6.

Hotel Epoque　　　　　　　　　HOTEL €€
(☏ 06-788-7100; www.hotelepoque.fi; Jakobsgatan 10; s/d €116/136; ◷ reception 7am-10pm Mon-Fri, 8am-10pm Sat, 8am-4pm Sun; @⊚) This restored customs house is the best place in town – service is great (although reception hours are limited), and with just 16 rooms, it feels quiet, private and exclusive.

🍴 Eating & Drinking

Jakobstad has a couple of lovely daytime cafes, but a dearth of decent evening options. Out by the beach, Café Fäboda is well worth the trip.

After Eight　　　　　　　　　　　CAFE €
(www.aftereight.fi; Storgatan 6; lunch €9.20; ◷ 10am-7pm Mon-Fri) This smashing cafe-cultural centre is the best hang-out in town, with a relaxed atmosphere, well-spaced tables, chilled-out music and a grassy courtyard garden. Lunch (served from 10am to 1pm – don't be late!) offers simple but tasty dishes such as salmon soup, roast beef stew, Swedish meatballs and vegetable gratin. Homemade cakes are available throughout the day.

Café Konditori Frederika　　　　CAFE €
(☏ 06-723-3533; www.nylundsbageri.fi; Storgatan 13; dishes €2.50-5.50, lunch buffet €9; ◷ 9am-9pm Mon-Thu, to 7pm Fri, to 5pm Sat, noon-6pm Sun) Everyone crowds into this central cafe for indulgent cakes and well-priced lunches. The terrace is irresistible when the sun's shining.

Black Sheep　　　　　　　　　　　PUB
(Storgatan 20; ◷ 4pm-2am Mon-Sat) Live music performs most weekends at this sociable

pub opening to a huge beer garden. Bonus: pinball machine.

❶ Information

Tourist Office (✆ 06-723-1796; www.jakob-stad.fi; Salutorget 1; ⊙ 8am-6pm Mon-Fri, 9am-3pm Sat Jun-Aug, 8am-4pm Mon-Fri Sep-May) Next to the town square.

❶ Getting There & Around

There are regular buses to Jakobstad from Vaasa (€22, 1¾ hours), Kokkola (€8.20, 45 minutes) and other west coast towns.

Bennäs (Finnish: Pännäinen), 11km away, is the closest train station. A shuttle bus (€3.90, 15 minutes) meets arriving trains.

Kokkola-Pietarsaari airport is 30km northeast of Jakobstad; buses (€9.40, 25 minutes) meet arriving flights.

Fäboda

About 8km west of Jakobstad, Fäboda's small sandy beaches framed by rocky inlets and thick forests offer idyllic swimming, sunbathing, surfing and windsurfing. Take care cycling here as the country road is narrow and winding.

◉ Sights

Nanoq Arctic Museum   MUSEUM
(✆ 06-726-3679; www.nanoq.fi; Pörkenäsvägen 60; adult/child €10/4; ⊙ 11am-6pm mid-May–Aug) Nanoq Arctic Museum is a surprisingly good museum housed in a model of a Greenlandic peat house. The collection is the private achievement of Pentti Kronqvist, who has made several expeditions to the Arctic. There are Inuit tools, fossils, authentic Arctic huts from Greenland and elsewhere, and various other Arctic souvenirs.

✖ Eating

★ Café Fäboda   FINNISH €€
(✆ 06-723-4533; www.faboda.fi; Lillsandvägen 263; mains €18.50-32; ⊙ noon-9pm May-Aug) Right on the beach, this breezy, beach-house-style spot is the best place to dine for miles around. Everything is made on the premises, condiments and breads included. Specialities include gourmet cheese and bacon burgers, fried whitefish with lemon-butter sauce and steaks such as rib-eye fillet with red-wine jus. Live music plays on the terrace on summer evenings.

Kokkola

✆ 06 / POP 46,720

The biggest attraction in Kokkola (Swedish: Karleby) is its charming Old Town, Neristan, where the town's sailors and fisherfolk once lived. Until the 1960s fishing boats could sail up the coffee-coloured river to sell fish in the kauppatori, but you wouldn't believe it to look at the shallow water today. As with the Kvarken archipelago (p203), the land around Kokkola is rising, which means Kokkola is chasing its port as the sea gets further from the town.

◉ Sights & Activities

Once the working-class area of Kokkola, Neristan ('Lower Town') has a collection of 19th-century wooden houses and makes for a pleasant wander. Pick up the free *Neristan/Oppistan Step by Step* brochure at the tourist office.

Following the Suntti stream beyond Neristan brings you to the retreating harbour-turned-beach **Halkokari**. A British attack was repelled here during the Crimean War. The captured gunboat at the **English Park** just north of Neristan is one of the few ever taken from the British navy, and the only vessel to never have been returned (despite requests from British officials since 1914).

Mineraalikokoelma   MUSEUM
(Pitkänsillankatu 28; ⊙ 11am-4pm Tue, Wed & Fri-Sun, to 6pm Thu Jun-Aug, noon-3pm Tue-Fri, to 5pm Sat & Sun Sep-May) **FREE** Dazzling exhibits at the Mineral Collection include fragile crystals and meteorite fragments. In the same

---

WORTH A TRIP

FINLAND'S WOODSTOCK

Kaustinen Folk Music Festival (✆ 040-170-1966; www.kaustinen.net; Jyväskyläntie 3; 1-/6-day pass €35/160) Kicking off in early July, this 1968-established folk gathering in the village of Kaustinen, 53km southeast of Kokkola, sees more than 3000 Finnish and international musicians perform over six days at concerts, bar gigs and endless impromptu jam sessions. The festival's **accommodation office** (✆ 068-229-811) can assist with reservations. Check the website for details of festival express buses.

building, the **Luontomuseo** (adult/child €4/free) natural history collection includes stuffed mammals and birds, as well as traps and other hunting devices.

Tankar Island ISLAND
(www.tankar.fi) This lighthouse island, 18km northwest of Kokkola, once offered safe passage through tangled waters. Now it makes a popular day trip (adult/child €18/8; lighthouse €3/free) for birdwatching, nature walks and salmon soup at the pierside **Café Tankar** (☑044-780-9139; mains €15; ⊙9am-10pm mid-May–Aug). M/S *Jenny* makes the 1½-hour sailing in summer up to eight times weekly in June and August and 12 times weekly during July, departing from Kokkola Camping: book with the tourist office.

🛏 Sleeping

Town-centre accommodation is dominated by chain hotels of varying standards.

Kokkola Camping CAMPGROUND €
(☑06-831-4006; www.kokkola-camping.fi; Mentie 10; tents €13 plus per person €4, cabins €90, apt €170) This small, super-friendly riverside campground is 2km north of the town centre at the harbour. Cabins and amenities have been recently refitted and the brand-new apartments have terraces looking onto the water.

Sokos Hotel Kaarle HOTEL €€
(☑06-111-8256; www.hotelkaarle.fi; Kauppatori 4; s/d €125/150; @ 🕏 🖈) Right on the central square, this is Kokkola's best hotel (admittedly competition is minimal). Staff are immensely helpful, and facilities are good; light sleepers should ask for a room away from the restaurant-nightclub.

🍴 Eating

Vanhankaupungin Ravintola INTERNATIONAL €€
(☑06-834-9030; www.vanhankaupunginravintola. fi; Isokatu 28; mains €23-33; ⊙4-10pm Tue-Thu, to 11pm Fri & Sat) Inside a timber town house dating from 1831, this elegant affair often serves dishes with a French accent such as fresh asparagus and lime hollandaise, sirloin with port jus and *frites,* and cheese boards for dessert.

Kaavya Kitchen INDIAN €€
(☑06-822-0900; www.kaavyakitchen.com; Pitkänsillankatu 23; lunch €9, mains €14-22; ⊙11am-9pm Mon-Thu, to 10pm Fri, 11.30am-10pm Sat) Contemporary and stylish Kaavya, Kokkola's first (and only) Indian restaurant, is a town favourite for tandoori dishes cooked in a proper clay oven.

ℹ Information

Tourist Office (☑040-806-5075; www. kokkola.fi; kauppatori 3; ⊙8am-5pm Mon-Tue & Thu-Fri, to 8pm Wed, 9am-1pm Sat Jun-Aug, 8am-4pm Mon-Fri Sep-May) In the main square.

ℹ Getting There & Around

Kokkola-Pietarsaari airport is 20km southeast of Kokkola and served by a regional bus service (€10.60, 15 minutes). Flybe has several flights daily to/from Helsinki.

Regular buses run to/from all coastal towns, especially Vaasa (€28.80, 2½ hours) and Jakobstad (€8.20, 45 minutes). The bus station is one block northwest of the train station.

Kokkola's train station is a main western-line stop to/from Helsinki (€69.60, four to five hours, up to nine daily).

Kalajoki & Hiekkasärkät
☑08 / POP 12,600

Families flock here for summer holidays in reddish-brown timber cottages snuggled in the white sand dunes and gleaming beachside resorts. Swimming, golf and Nordic walking, which was invented here, keep visitors active in summer, while winter offers great cross-country skiing.

Kalajoki village is just off the highway, with most of the facilities (bus station, banks et al); the resort area, with the beach, airfield and most accommodation, is 6km south of the village along Hwy 8 in Hiekkasärkät.

🏃 Activities

Nordic walking was born here in the 1930s when world-championship skier Jussi Kurikkala decided to keep up his form in summer by working out on the dunes. A 44km network of walking routes was marked out around Hiekkasärkät in his honour in 2011. **Fontana Hotelli Rantakalla** (☑08-466-642; www.rantakalla.fi; Matkailutie 150) rents Nordic walking sticks (€15 per day).

Lohilaakso restaurant has salmon fishing.

Kylpylä SaniFani SPA
(☑08-469-2500; www.kalajokiresort.fi; Jukupolku 3; adult/child €15/9; ⊙2-9pm Mon-Fri, 11am-8pm Sat, 11am-7pm Sun) SaniFani offers slippery slides and a flowing 'river' for kids, massag-

es, beauty treatments and a bowling alley. The spa also owns **JukuPark** (⊘08-469-2308; www.jukupark.fi; Hiekkasärkät; admission €21; ☺11am-5pm late Jun, 11am-7pm Jul–mid-Aug), an outdoor waterpark with loads of water slides, rides and paddle boats. A combination ticket (€28) covers both. Hotel guests get free spa and pool entry.

Kalajoki Golf GOLF
(⊘08-466-666; www.kalajokigolf.fi; Hiekkasärkät; admission & green fee €45; ☺8am-10pm Mon-Sat, to 9pm Sun year-round, snow permitting) This 18-hole golf course meanders between the forest and beach. Prices include sauna and towel.

🛏 Sleeping

Hiekkasärkät is the ideal place for beachside accommodation.

Tapion Tupa RESORT, HOSTEL €
(⊘08-466-622; www.tapiontupa.fi; Hiekkasärkät; s/d/q €45/70/87, cabins €78-108, cabins without bathroom €53-85, apt €148-215; 🛜🌊) Just off the main road near the beach, this rambling HI-affiliated mini-village has a range of red cottages amid the forest. Options include rooms in an Ostrobothnian house, basic log cabins and brand-new self-contained holiday apartments. Wi-fi available in common areas.

Spa Hotel SaniFani SPA HOTEL €€
(⊘08-466-2500; www.kalajokiresort.fi; Jukupolku 3-5; s/d/f standard €121.50/167/198, superior €137.50/199/230; 🛜🌊) SaniFani's modern rooms, although conventional, have huge windows and amazing sea views. Entrance to the spa and pools is included in the price.

🍴 Eating & Drinking

Lohilaakso SEAFOOD €
(⊘08-466-645; www.lohilaakso.fi; Tahkkorvantie 39; mains €9-16; ☺10am-9pm Jun-Aug) Smoked salmon – served whole with potato gratin, in salads, and in creamy smoked salmon soup – is the speciality of this stocked salmon-fishing pond and smokery's waterside restaurant. If you want to catch your own, rod-and-reel rental is €15. Any fish you land costs €16 per kg; smoking is €3 per fish and takes an hour.

Hotelli-Ravintola Lokkilinna PIZZA €€
(⊘08-469-6700; www.lokkilinna.fi; lunch buffet €14.50, pizzas €10.50-13, mains €16-29; ☺11am-8pm Mon-Sat, noon-4pm Sun) Overlooking the dunes, Lokkilinna has a fantastic summer terrace perfect for a beer and pizza (toppings range from smoked reindeer to snails), accompanied by regular live music. It's a large place with an attached hotel (some rooms with balconies and ocean views; doubles €120 to €140) but retains a charming family feel.

Sandy Kelt PUB
(www.sandykelt.fi; Kalakuja 7; ☺11am-1am Sun-Thu, to 2am Fri & Sat) You'll spot the crowds long before you make it inside this lively – and then some – 'traditional' Irish pub. There's regular live music and a huge menu of hearty pub grub including Full Irish fry-up breakfasts served all day.

ℹ Information

Tourist Office (⊘08-469-2500; www.visit kalajoki.fi; Jukupolku 3; ☺8am-4pm Mon-Thu, to 3pm Fri) Inside the SaniFani spa complex at Hiekkasärkät.

ℹ Getting There & Away

Several daily buses between Oulu (€28.80, two hours) and Kokkola (€17, one hour) stop at Kalajoki village and Hiekkasärkät.

Oulu, Kainuu & Koillismaa

Best Places to Eat

➜ Hella (p212)

➜ Ravintola Hugo (p213)

➜ Riipisen Riistaravintola (p222)

Best Places to Stay

➜ Hotel Lasaretti (p212)

➜ Luotsihotelli (p215)

➜ Kartanohotelli Karolineburg (p216)

➜ Royal Hotel Ruka (p222)

➜ Hotelli Kalevala (p219)

➜ Basecamp Oulanka (p226)

Why Go?

Stretching across Finland's waist from the Gulf of Bothnia to the long Russian border, this broad swath of territory takes in Oulu's technology boffins and brown bears raising their shaggy heads as they patrol the eastern forests. It offers some of the nation's most memorable outdoor experiences, from birdwatching and beachcombing in the west to skiing, canoeing and trekking in the east.

The further you get from Oulu, the more remote things become. Kainuu is a heavily wooded wilderness and important animal habitat traversed by the famed UKK trekking route. Koillismaa, near the Russian border, is the transitional region between the south and Lapland, and includes Oulanka National Park, one of Finland's natural highlights. It is an area of tumbling rivers, isolated lakes and dense forests. This is perhaps Finland's best destination for getting active in the great outdoors, whether in summer or winter.

When to Go

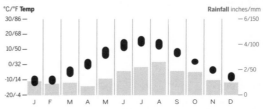

Oulu

Apr Still good snow cover for skiing, but acceptable temperatures and plenty of light.

Jul Bear-watching in Kuusamo, canoeing in Oulanka National Park and chamber music in Kuhmo.

Sep The most beautiful time for hiking, with autumn *ruska* colours filling the forests.

Oulu, Kainuu & Koillismaa Highlights

1 **Canoeing** river routes or **trekking** the Karhunkierros trail in Oulanka National Park (p223), through some of Finland's finest wilderness scenery

2 Creeping into the evening forests to **spot brown bears** (p221) or meet their boisterous

orphaned cousins (p220) near Kuusamo

3 Chilling out in the evening sunshine that kisses the **kauppatori** (market squares; p210) in Oulu

4 Getting back to Finland's Stone Age at the informative **Kierikkikeskus** (p215) museum

5 Braving the Bothnian waters on relaxing **Hailuoto** (p214) island

6 Letting the young musicians string you along at Kuhmo's excellent **chamber music festival** (p218)

History

The region reflects its tar-producing history. In the 19th century the remote Kainuu and Koillismaa areas began producing tar from the numerous pines, and sent it on the precarious journey downriver to Oulu, whence it was shipped to the boat-building nations of Europe. The merchants prospered, and Oulu still has a sleek, cosmopolitan vibe

compared with the backwoodsy feel of the rest of its province.

Oulu

☑ 08 / POP 141,670

Prosperous Oulu (Swedish: Uleåborg) is one of Finland's most enjoyable cities to visit. In summer angled sunshine bathes the

Oulu

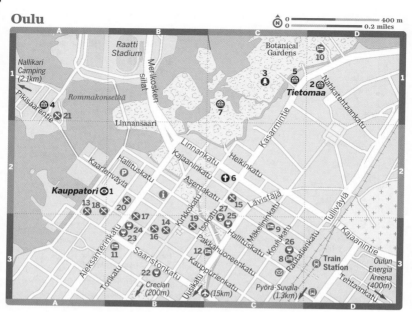

kauppatori (market square) in light and all seems well with the world. Locals, who appreciate daylight when they get it, crowd the terraces, and stalls groan under the weight of Arctic berries.

The city centre is spread across several islands, elegantly connected by pedestrian bridges and cycleways: Oulu's network of bike paths is one of Europe's best. Oulu is also a significant technology city; the university turns out top-notch IT graduates and the corporate parks on the city's outskirts employ people from all over the globe.

⊙ Sights

★ Kauppatori   SQUARE

Oulu has the liveliest market square of all Finnish towns, and its position at the waterfront makes it all the more appealing. The square is bordered by several old wooden storehouses now serving as restaurants, bars and craft shops. The squat *Toripolliisi* statue, a humorous representation of the local police, is a local landmark.

★ Tietomaa   MUSEUM

(www.tietomaa.fi; Nahkatehtaankatu 6; adult/child €15/11; ⊙10am-5pm, 6pm or 8pm) This huge, excellent science museum can occupy kids for the best part of a day with a giant IMAX

screen, hands-on interactive exhibits on planets and the human body, and an observation tower. Each year there is a mega-exhibition that's the focal point.

Pohjois Pohjanmaan Museo   MUSEUM

(☑08-5584-7150; www.ouka.fi/ppm; Ainolanpuisto; adult/child €6/free; ⊙10am-5pm Tue-Sun) The Museum of Northern Ostrobothnia in the city park has almost too much information to take in at first bite. It covers the earliest habitation of the region through to the 20th century, including plenty of information on the tar trade. Cameras allow you to zoom in on the impressive scale model of 1938 Oulu; a traditional pharmacy, paintings of the 1822 Great Fire, and a schoolroom are included in the wide-ranging display.

Oulun Tuomiokirkko   CHURCH

(Kirkkokatu 36; ⊙11am-8pm Jun & Aug, to 9pm Jul, noon-1pm Sep-May) Oulu's imposing cathedral was built in 1777 but then came the great fire of 1822, which severely damaged the structure. Tireless architect CL Engel rebuilt it in Empire style, adding a dome and Renaissance-style vaulting, which impart a powerful airiness to the fairly unadorned interior.

Oulu

Oulun Taidemuseo GALLERY
(www.ouka.fi/taidemuseo; Kasarmintie 7; adult/child €6/free; ⊙10am-5pm Tue-Thu, Sat & Sun, noon-7pm Fri) Oulu's art museum is a bright spacious gallery with excellent temporary exhibitions of both international and Finnish contemporary art, and a cafe.

Ainola & Huupisaaret PARK
Just north of the city centre and connected by small bridges, this great park has bike paths, museums, greenhouses and a summer cafe, as well as a fishway built so that salmon can bypass the hydroelectric dam to get to the spawning grounds.

Merimiehen Kotimuseo MUSEUM
(Matila; www.ouka.fi/ppm; Pikisarentie 6; ⊙11am-5pm late May-early Sep) FREE This house-museum on Pikisaari belonged to a local sailor. Built in 1737, it is the oldest house in Oulu and was transferred here from the city

centre in 1983. The wallpaper and extendable bed are typical of 19th-century Finnish homes.

🏃 Activities

One of Oulu's best features is the extensive network of **bicycle paths** crossing bridges, waterways and islands all the way out to surrounding villages. Grab a cycle map from the tourist office.

A good 3km walk or ride is from the kauppatori, across the bridge to Pikisaari and across another bridge to Nallikari, where there's a lovely beach facing the Gulf of Bothnia.

👉 Tours

From late June to late August, bus tours and free walking tours in English leave from the town hall: check www.oulunseudunoppaat.fi for times.

Go Arctic! SUMMER, WINTER
(☎044-022-4060; www.goarctic.fi) Runs a weekly program of activities in summer (and winter), including tar-boat cruises to Turkansaari, cycling tours, sea canoeing, guided walks, and excursions to Kierikki.

🎉 Festivals & Events

In a country that wrote the book on oddball festivals, Oulu has one of the weirdest.

Tervahiihto SKIING
(Oulu Tar Ski Race; www.tervahiihto.fi) Held in early March. This 70km skiing race (40km for women) has been running since 1889.

Air Guitar World Championships MUSIC
(www.airguitarworldchampionships.com) Part of the Oulu Music Video Festival in late August. Contestants from all over the world take the stage to show what they can do with their imaginary instruments.

🛏 Sleeping

There's little budget accommodation in Oulu.

Forenom House HOTEL €
(☎020-198-3420; www.forenom.fi; Rautatienkatu 9; r €54-70; 🅿🛜) You can't beat this spot for convenience: it's bang opposite the train station. There's a range of rooms, sleeping up to five, with plenty of space as well as fridge and microwave; they could do with better curtains. Book online or via the lobby terminal. Rates can be excellent value. It also

offers apartments elsewhere in Oulu. Reception is staffed Monday to Friday during working hours.

Nallikari Camping
CAMPGROUND €

(☎ 044-703-1353; www.nallikari.fi; Hietasaari; tent site €13 plus per adult/child €4/2, cabins €40-45, cottages €105-145; P @ 🛜) This excellent campground offers all sorts of options in a location close to the beach on Hietasaari, a 40-minute walk to the city centre via pedestrian bridges. Both summer and winter activities are on offer, plus a large variety of cabins and cottages, substantially cheaper outside of high season. It's very child-friendly. Take bus 15 from the city centre, or the summer tourist train.

★ Hotel Lasaretti
HOTEL €€

(☎ 020-757-4700; www.lasaretti.com; Kasarmintie 13; s/d €148/169, Sat & Sun €82/98; P @ 🛜 ⊠) Bright, modern and optimistic, this inviting hotel sits in a group of renovated brick buildings, once a hospital. It's close to town but the parkside location by the bubbling-bright stream makes it feel rural. The artistically modern rooms are great: ask for one with a water view. Facilities and staff are excellent, and there's also a busy bar-restaurant with sun-kissed terrace spaces.

Sokos Hotel Eden
SPA HOTEL €€

(☎ 020-123-4603; www.sokoshotels.fi; Holstinsalmentie 29, Nallikari; s/d €122/142, superior €142/162; P @ 🛜 ⊠) This excellent spa hotel by the beach on Hietasaari offers great watery facilities – slides, intricate indoor pools, saunas – and massage treatments. Superior rooms on the new side of the building are bigger and have air-conditioning (handier than you may think) as well as a sea-view balcony. Nonguests can use the spa facilities for €15 per day (€9 for kids).

It's a 3km walk or cycle west of the city centre. Take bus 15 from the centre, or the summer tourist train.

Hotel Apollo
HOTEL €€

(☎ 08-52211; www.hotelapollo.fi; Asemakatu 31; s/d €115/140, Sat, Sun & summer r €82; P @ 🛜) Handy for the train station, this spot boasts warm and efficient service and three types of room. Standard rooms are compact, with ultracompact bathrooms; the top-floor rooms have sloping ceiling windows and more space; while the sauna rooms are classier, with dark furniture and coffee machines. Check for good-value packages on the website.

Omenahotelli
HOTEL €€

(☎ 0600-555-222; www.omenahotels.com; Uusikatu 26; r €60-90; 🛜) This no-staff hotel is in a good central location and features comfortable plasticky rooms with giant TV, spacious double bed and fold-out chairs sleeping two more. Book online or via the terminal in the lobby.

Hotel Scandic Oulu
HOTEL €€€

(☎ 08-543-1000; www.scandichotels.com; Saaristonkatu 4; s/d €145/165; P @ 🛜) 🌊 This sleek hotel occupies half a city block right in the middle of town. From the space-opera lights in its spacious foyer to the high-ceilinged rooms with clean Nordic decor and flatscreen TV, it's a temple to efficiency, hygiene and modern design (art, individuality: look elsewhere).

✖ Eating

Local specialities can be found in and around the kauppatori.

Café Bisketti
CAFE €

(www.cafebisketti.fi; Kirkkokatu 8; lunches €6-10; ☉ 7.30am-9.30pm Mon-Sat, 10am-8pm Sun; 🛜) This top double-sided spot transforms itself throughout the day. Think twice before getting that pastry with your morning coffee; they're enormous and might not leave room for lunch, with cheap deals on soup, salad, coffee and a pastry, and hot dishes for not much extra. In the evenings, the terrace is a decent spot for a people-watching beer.

Oulun Kauppahalli
MARKET €

(www.oulunliikekeskus.fi/kauppahalli; ☉ 8am-5pm Mon-Thu, 8am-6pm Fri, 8am-3pm Sat; 🍴) 🌊 On the square, the kauppahalli (covered market) has freshly filleted salmon glistening in the market stalls and plenty of spots to snack on anything from cloudberries to sushi.

Kauppuri 5
BURGERS €

(www.kauppuri5.fi; Kauppurienkatu 5; burgers €8-12; ☉ 11am-1.30am) With a cosy, almost claustrophobic interior and a great sunny terrace on the pedestrian strip, this is very popular for its delicious handmade burgers. They're very tasty and pretty good value.

★ Hella
BISTRO €€

(☎ 08-371-180; www.hellaravintola.fi; Isokatu 13; mains €20-27; ☉ 10.30am-10pm Mon-Thu, 10.30am-11pm Fri, 3-11pm Sat) This sweet little corner spot is a welcoming two-person show that offers excellent Italian-inspired fare. Attentive service is backed up by the food, which changes seasonally but features great salads, cannelloni stuffed with goat's cheese, and tender, well-treated meat dishes. Opens shorter hours in July.

Puistola
BISTRO €€

(☏020-792-8210; www.ravintolapuistola.fi; Pakkahuoneenkatu 15; mains €16-26; ☺bistro 10.45am-10pm Mon-Thu, 10.30am-11pm Fri, 3-11pm Sat; 🐾) This handsome place offers a deli-cafe that does great breakfasts, plus a bistro. This is a comfortable space that turns out tasty, sizeable dishes – think pastas, ribs, burgers, fish, salads, steaks – from its open kitchen with plenty of flair, and also does good-value lunches. –Try for a seat out on the terrace. Service throughout is excellent. Check out the toilets – highly original.

Crecian
GREEK €€

(www.crecian.fi; Kirkkokatu 55; mains €17-30; ☺11am-10pm Mon-Thu, 11am-11pm Fri, noon-11pm Sat, noon-8pm Sun) It's worth the short stroll from the town centre to this popular neighbourhood restaurant, predictably decked out in blue and white, though the owner's actually Cypriot. Dishes are tasty and generously proportioned, and the service is welcoming.

Sokeri-Jussin Kievari
FINNISH €€

(☏08-376-628; www.sokerijussi.fi; Pikisaarentie 2; mains €20-33; ☺11am-10pm Mon-Sat, noon-9pm Sun) An Oulu classic, this timbered inn on Pikisaari was once a sugar warehouse and has outdoor tables that have good views of the centre. It's an attractive spot to eat, with no-frills traditional dishes, including reindeer, and a selection of more upmarket plates. It's also a nice place for a few beers away from the bustle of the city but just a few steps from it.

★ Ravintola Hugo
SCANDINAVIAN €€€

(☏020-143-2200; www.ravintolahugo.fi; Rantakatu 4; set menus €38-70; ☺11am-1.30pm Mon, 11am-1.30pm & 5-10pm Tue-Fri, 5-10pm Sat) Innovative gourmet dining generally using locally available products makes this a real Oulu highlight. There are some outstanding flavour combinations and a variety of degustation menu options with matched wines.

1881 Uleåborg
FINNISH €€€

(☏08-881-1188; www.uleaborg.fi; Aittatori 4; mains €31-35; ☺5-11pm Mon-Thu, 5pm-midnight Fri & Sat) In an old warehouse near the kauppatori, this classy spot combines chic Finnish style with a traditional setting. The terrace

by the water is one of Oulu's loveliest summer spots.

Istanbul Oriental
TURKISH €€€

(☏08-311-2922; www.istanbuloriental.fi; Kauppurienkatu 11; mains €26-37; ☺5-11pm Tue-Fri, 3pm-midnight Sat) This stylishly decorated place in the heart of things is a rather good Turkish restaurant with plenty of vegetarian options, great meze selections and succulent chargrilled meat. Service is excellent, though the food's somewhat overpriced.

🍷 Drinking & Nightlife

There's plenty going on at night. The kauppatori is the spot to start in summer: bars set in traditional wooden warehouses have terraces that lick up every last drop of the evening sun.

★ St Michael
IRISH PUB

(www.stmichael.fi; Hallituskatu 13; ☺2pm-2am; 🐾) This convivial Irish pub has a brilliant selection of craft beer, including excellent guest ales, and a fine array of whisky. The large terrace makes it a top spot when the sun's shining.

Never Grow Old
BAR

(www.ngo.fi; Hallituskatu 17; ☺8pm-2am Sun-Tue, 6pm-2am Wed-Thu, 6pm-3am Fri & Sat) Enduringly popular, NGO hits its stride after 10pm, with dancing, DJs and revelry in the tightly packed interior. The goofy decor includes some seriously comfortable and extremely uncomfortable places to sit, and a log palisade bar that seems designed to get you to wear your drink. It opens earlier in summer.

Jumpru
PUB, CLUB

(www.jumpru.fi; Kauppurienkatu 6; ☺11am-2am Mon & Tue, 11am-4am Wed-Sat, noon-2am Sun) This Oulu institution is a great place for meeting locals and its enclosed outdoor area always seems to be humming with cheerfully sauced-up folk. There's a warren of cosy rooms inside, as well as an upstairs nightclub, **Kaarlenholvi** (☺from 10pm Wed-Sat).

Snooker Time
BAR

(Asemakatu 28; ☺4pm-1am Sun-Thu, 4pm-2am Fri & Sat) With a bohemian clientele and dive-bar feel, this characterful place is an Oulu favourite: locals describe it as the city's living room. Streetside seating, downstairs pool and snooker tables, and a graffiti-splashed smoking chamber are the highlights.

Graali PUB

(www.graali.fi; Saaristonkatu 5; ☺2pm-2am) When it's cold and snowy outside, there's nowhere cosier than this pub, decorated with suits of armour and sporting trophies. Sink into a leather armchair by the open fire and feel the warmth return to your bones. A good whisky selection will help you along.

45 Special CLUB

(www.45special.com; Saaristonkatu 12; ☺4pm-4am) This grungy three-level club pulls a good mix of people for its downstairs rock and chartier top floor. There's a €7.50 admission on selected nights and regular live gigs. It serves food until 3am.

☆ Entertainment

Oulu loves its ice-hockey team, the Kärpät (Stoats), who have been successful in recent years. They play at **Oulun Energia Areena** (☑0600-10800; www.oulunkarpat.fi; tickets €8-26) in Raksila east of the city centre.

ℹ Information

Wi-fi is available throughout the city centre on the PanOulu network.

Tourist Office (☑08-5584-1330; www.visit oulu.fi; Torikatu 10; ☺9am-5pm Mon-Fri, plus 10am-4pm Sat Jun-Aug) Good range of information on Oulu and other Finnish destinations. Closes 4pm Fridays in winter.

ℹ Getting There & Away

AIR

There are daily direct flights from Helsinki with Finnair and Norwegian. SAS flies direct to Stockholm, and Norwegian has a direct Alicante service.

BUS

Bus services include the following:
Helsinki €98.30, 10 to 11½ hours
Kajaani €31.40, 2¾ hours
Rovaniemi €30 to €44, 3½ hours
Tornio €25.20, two to 2½ hours

TRAIN

Several direct trains run daily to Helsinki (€77 to €94, six to eight hours). There are also trains via Kajaani and trains north to Rovaniemi.

ℹ Getting Around

There's a good network of local buses (www.oulunjoukkoliikenne.fi). Each ride costs €3.30; check route maps online and at bus stops. Bus 9 goes to the airport every 30 minutes (€4.70, 25 minutes).

Bicycles can be hired from **Pyörä-Suvala** (☑08-338-175; www.pyorasuvala.fi; Lekatie 2; per hour/day/24hr/week €5/12/15/42; ☺9am-6pm Mon-Fri, 10am-2pm Sat) – ask for a better one if you don't like the yellow hire ones – and from the Nallikari campground, which also hires out skis in winter.

The various car-hire operators in town, including **Sixt** (☑02-112-2590; www.sixt.com) at the airport and **Budget** (☑020-746-6640; www.budget.fi; Kaarnatie 10), do cheap weekend deals.

Around Oulu

The zoo at Ranua (p236) is an easy day trip from Oulu.

Turkansaari

Set across two river islands on the scenic Oulujoki, this **open-air museum** (www.ouka.fi/ppm; Turkansaarentie 165; adult/child €4/2; ☺10am-6pm late May–mid-Aug, to 4pm mid-Aug–mid-Sep) is a collection of wooden buildings of various traditional types, from loggers' cabins to stables, and includes a handsome traditional farmhouse. The 1694 church is an original from this former trading settlement. A working tar pit comes to the fore during **Tar-Burning Week**, a festival in late June.

Turkansaari is 14km east of Oulu off Rd 22; catch bus 41. You can also get there by boat from town in summer. Entry is free with the Pohjois Pohjanmaan Museo ticket.

Hailuoto

☑08 / POP 990

A favourite Oulu beach escape, Hailuoto is a sizeable island of traditional red farmhouses, venerable wooden windmills, modern wind farms, and pines growing tall from the sandy soil.

The road winds 30km from the ferry slip to the beach at **Marjaniemi** at the island's opposite end.

In the middle, Hailuoto village has services, a striking A-frame church and **Kniivilä** (Marjaniementie 20; adult/child €2/1; ☺11am-5pm late Jun-late Aug), an open-air museum of old wooden buildings.

At Marjaniemi, there's a shallow-water beach perfect for kids, looked over by a **lighthouse** (adult/child €5/3; ☺noon-2pm Jul). At the base is Luototalo, which contains a free **nature exhibition** (☺11am-5pm) on the dune ecosystem.

🛌 Sleeping & Eating

Sinisen Pyörän Kievari　　　　　B&B €

(📞 045-312-3990; www.sinisenpyorankievari.fi; Viinikantie 32; r €60; 🅿 🛜) In Hailuoto, the 'Blue Bike Inn' is a handsome complex of wooden farm buildings in a tranquil setting. Three pretty rooms share a bathroom above a cafe, while summer-only rooms are also available in the barn. Breakfast costs €8.

RantaSumppu　　　　　　　CAMPGROUND €

(📞 029-170-8360; Sumpuntie 103; tent sites €20, small/large cabins €85/100; ⊙May-Oct; 🅿) At Marjaniemi beach, with cabins within striking distance of the sea and sand-gravel tent pitches. Check in at the Luotsihotelli, a 10-minute walk along the strand.

★Luotsihotelli　　　　　　　HOTEL €€

(📞 029-170-8360; http://wildnordic.fi/wild-nordic-luotsihotelli; Marjaniementie 783; small d/d/atelier/ste €90/109/129/149; ⊙Mar-Nov; 🅿 🛜) Right by the water, this is an upbeat place with rooms airily kitted out in light wood. The 'small' rooms live up to their name: it's worth upgrading to the spacious other categories, some of which have marvellous views. The suites are wonderful spaces with curving picture windows. The restaurant-cafe has a summer lunch buffet and great sea views.

ℹ Information

Tourist Office (📞 044-497-1991; www.hailuoto tourism.fi; Marjaniemi; ⊙10am-6pm Mon-Fri) This main office is at Marjaniemi, but you can get a map and information in nearly all the island's cafes and spots of interest.

ℹ Getting There & Around

Bus 59 travels one to three times daily from Oulu, running the length of the island to Marjaniemi (€7.40, 1½ hours). Free **ferries** (www.finferries.fi) make the half-hour journey half-hourly to hourly. The ferry is 28km southwest of Oulu via Rd 816. In winter there's an ice road to the island.

Liminganlahti

The bird sanctuary at Liminka Bay attracts numerous avian species, with several rare waders nesting here during summer, and many species of waterfowl and birds of prey also visible. Prominent species include the yellow-breasted bunting, black-tailed godwit, Ural owl, bittern, marsh harrier and tern. There are several observation towers, boardwalks and a couple of designated campsites.

Head first for **Liminganlahden Luontokeskus** (📞 040-832-1781; www.liminganlahti. fi; Rantakurvi 6; ⊙10am-6pm Mon-Fri, 10am-4pm Sat & Sun Apr-May, weekdays only Jun-early Aug), a well-equipped nature centre 6km west of Liminka village. Accommodation is available: call 📞 0400-565-040 outside of centre opening hours.

Several daily Raahe-bound buses make the 30km trip from Oulu to Liminka and on to Lumijoki, and will stop at the turn-off to the nature centre.

WORTH A TRIP

MUSEUM OF THE STONE AGE

Kierikkikeskus (www.ouka.fi; Pahkalantie 447, Yli-Ii; adult/child €8/4; ⊙10am-5pm Mon-Sat, noon-6pm Sun late Jun–mid-Aug, 10am-5pm Mon-Sat late Aug, 10am-4pm Mon-Fri May-late Jun & Sep-Oct) This excellent museum is by the Iijoki, whose banks are riddled with important Stone Age settlements. The informative display sensibly only includes a handful of artefacts, including fortunately preserved wooden fences to trap fish. A ponderous video gives excavation histories, and a boardwalk leads to the picturesque riverbank, with re-created period buildings. In summer you can take potshots using a primitive bow and arrow, or send the kids paddling in a Stone Age canoe.

Settlements in the Kierikki area date from about 4000 BC to 2000 BC and were coastal, moving gradually west as the land rose. Communities made a comfortable living fishing and sealing.

There's also a **hotel** (📞 040-159-9580; www.arctichotelkierikki.fi; d €84; ⊙year-round; 🅿) here, consisting of wooden buildings surrounding a little pond; the attractive, spacious rooms have balconies.

Kierikki is 5km south of Yli-Ii, itself 27km east of Ii, on the Oulu–Kemi road.

WORTH A TRIP

SKIING AT SYÖTE

Syöte, the southernmost fell in Finland, is a popular winter-sports escape from Oulu, with both downhill and cross-country skiing available. **Syöte National Park** (www.outdoors.fi) covers discrete areas of old-growth spruce forest and is great for ski-trekking or hiking. There's a visitors centre and plenty of accommodation, including a couple of good hotels with great views, and rentals managed by **Pudasjärven Matkailu** (☑08-823-400; www.syote.net; Romekievarintie 1, Syöte; ⊙9am-5pm Mon-Fri); you can book online. A bus from Oulu to Syöte (€26.30, 2¼ hours) leaves once daily Monday to Friday. Another option is changing in Pudasjärvi.

Haukipudas

Haukipudas, 21km north of Oulu at a scenic spot along the Kiiminkijoki, is known for its beige church (www.oulunseurakunnat. fi; ⊙10am-6pm Mon-Fri early Jun-late Aug), one of Finland's most notable 'picture churches'. The interior is decorated with striking naive scenes painted in the 18th century and depicting biblical events, including a scary Day of Judgement. Outside, by the separate belfry, stands a wooden moustachioed *vaivaisukko* (pauper statue).

From Oulu, buses 20 and 23 run to Haukipudas.

Kajaani

☑08 / POP 38,010

Essentially a one-street town, Kajaani, capital of the Kainuu region, is nevertheless the major settlement in these parts. Apart from its pretty riverside and church at nearby Paltaniemi, it's more a stopover than a destination.

Kajaani was a tar town; until the 19th century, the Kainuu region produced more than anywhere in the world. Other claims to fame are that Elias Lönnrot, creator of the *Kalevala,* worked here for a period, using it as a base for his travels, and long-reigning president Urho Kekkonen lived here as a student (at Kalliokatu 7).

◉ Sights

In the pedestrian zone, the old **town hall** was designed by CL Engel. The wooden **church** is also worth a look.

Kajaanin Linna CASTLE
(www.kajaaninlinna.fi) **FREE** Picturesquely set on a river island in the town centre, these ruins show all the signs of damage by war, time and more-recent mischief. It's a fine spot to bask on the grass on a sunny day, but there isn't much more to it than what you can see. Nearby there's a **tar-boat channel** with a lock built to enable boats laden with tar barrels to pass the Ämmäkoski rapids.

Kainuun Museo MUSEUM
(www.kainuunmuseo.fi; Asemakatu 4; adult/child €4/free; ⊙noon-4pm Sun-Fri, noon-7pm Wed, also noon-4pm Sat late Jun-early Aug) The town museum, near the train station, has a good permanent exhibition on Kajaani's history, including info on the castle, tar boats and Elias Lönnrot. There are also regular temporary exhibitions.

⌂ Sleeping & Eating

As you head north, Finland's restaurant scene starts to worsen somewhere around Kajaani.

Kartanohotelli Karolineburg HOTEL €€
(☑050-346-4737; www.karolineburg.fi; Karoliinantie 8; s/d from €95/105, d with sauna from €115, ste from €185; P🐾) Set in a wooden manor house and various outbuildings, this makes an intriguing place to stay, offering a wide range of chambers, from suites with their own sauna and terrace to simpler modern rooms. Elegant furnishings, bosky grounds and friendly staff make it a romantic choice. Cross the bridge past the castle and you'll see it signposted to your left.

Sirius FINNISH €
(☑08-612-2087; www.ravintolasirius.fi; Brahenkatu 5; lunches €7-14; ⊙10.30am-2pm Mon-Fri) Located above the rapids, this restaurant is set in a striking 1940s villa built as a residence for the local paper company. There are good daily lunch specials and a great terrace out the back.

Ranch TEX-MEX €€
(www.ranch.fi; Kauppakatu 26; mains €15-30; ⊙10.30am-2pm Mon, 10.30am-8pm Tue, 10.30am-10pm Wed-Thu, 10.30am-11pm Fri, noon-11pm Sat, 2-8pm Sun) In an alley off the main street, the

painted windows here defy casual sticky-beaking but conceal a pleasant interior. The food's for meat-eating people with an appetite; big burgers and choose-your-weight steaks smothered in sauce, alongside some Mexican options. Good service and free corn chips add points.

❶ Information

Kajaani Info (☑ 08-6155-2555; www.visit-kajaani.fi; Pohjolankatu 13; ⊘9am-4.30pm Mon-Fri) Helpful tourist office in the town hall building.

❶ Getting There & Around

Finnair/Flybe flies daily from Helsinki. The airport is 8km northwest; a **bus** (www.akyllonen.fi; ticket €5.50) runs from the kauppatori via the Kajanus hotel to coincide with flights. It's about €20 in a cab.

Kajaani is Kainuu's travel hub. There are daily trains from Helsinki (€84.30, 6½ hours), via Kuopio, and services on to Oulu.

Paltaniemi

The enchantingly weathered wooden **church** (Paltamon Vanha Kirkko; www.paltamonsrk.fi; Paltaniementie 851; ⊘10am-6pm mid-May–mid-Aug) in this village 9km northwest of Kajaani was built in 1726, and has some of Finland's most interesting church paintings: rustic 18th-century works full of life and colour that enliven the roof and walls. Above the entrance, symbolically representing the dangers of life outside the church's protective bosom, is a vivid scene of hell, covered for years to avoid offending parish sensibilities.

Alongside the church, what looks like a woodshed is the **Keisarintalli**, the best available local accommodation (moved from Vuolijoki) for Tsar Alexander I when he toured Finland in 1819.

Nearby, **Eino Leino-Talo** (www.einoleino talo.fi; Sutelantie 28; ⊘10am-6pm Sun-Fri mid-Jun–mid-Aug) FREE re-creates where one of Finland's foremost independence-era poets was born in 1878. It's a lovely lakeside spot, with a cafe plus photos and memorabilia.

Bus 4 from Pohjolankatu in Kajaani runs to Paltaniemi hourly on weekdays only.

Kuhmo

☑ 08 / POP 9270

Surrounded by wilderness, Kuhmo makes a natural base for hiking and wildlife-watching. Vast taiga forests run from here right across Siberia and harbour 'respect' animals like wolves, bears and lynx. Kuhmo is also the unofficial capital of Vienan Karjala, the Karelian heartland now in Russia, explored by artists in the movement that was crucial to the development of Finnish national identity. Most of their expeditions set off from Kuhmo, as did one of Elias Lönnrot's, when he headed into 'Songland' to record the verses of bards that he later wove into the *Kalevala* epic. There's a fine *Kalevala* resource centre in town.

This likeable little town also has a great chamber music festival in July.

WORTH A TRIP

SOTKAMO

The Sotkamo area, 30km to 40km east of Kajaani, offers a typically beautiful Finnish land- and lakescape that's great fun to explore year-round, with plenty of family-friendly outdoor activities on offer. It's known as a winter-sports centre, and there are ski runs as well as extensive cross-country tracks. There's even a **ski tunnel** (www.vuokattisport.fi; Vuokatinhovintie 1, Vuokatti; adult/child €15/7.50; ⊘9am-6pm Jun-early Oct), with 1.3km of snow to practise on when it's melted outside. Sotkamo is also famous for *pesäpallo*, the super-tactical Finnish version of baseball: the successful local team plays in the stadium in the centre of Sotkamo town, next to the attractive lake beach. There's plenty of accommodation both here and around the **ski resort** (www.vuokatti.fi; Veikontie 5, Vuokatti; lift pass per day/week €38/163; ⊘Dec–mid-Apr) at Vuokatti, 9km west, ranging from no-frills guesthouses to enormous spa resorts. Make sure you check out Sotkamo's enormous 19th-century wooden **church** (www.sotkamonseurakunta.fi; Ristijärventie 1; ⊘10am-4pm Jun-Aug). The pretty gorge at **Hiidenportti National Park** (www.outdoors.fi) is also within striking distance.

◎ Sights

★ Juminkeko   CULTURAL CENTRE
(www.juminkeko.fi; Kontionkatu 25; adult/child
€4/2; ☉noon-6pm Mon-Fri, daily in Jul) If you
are interested in the *Kalevala* or Karelian
culture, pay a visit to this excellent resource
centre, a beautiful building made using traditional methods and modern styling. The
fantastic staff can tell you anything you wish
to know; there are also three to four detailed
exhibitions here yearly.

Tuupalan Museo   MUSEUM
(www.kuhmo.fi; Tervatie 1; adult/child €4/2; ☉10am-
4pm Mon-Fri Jun-late Aug) This house-museum
consists of various traditional Karelian
red-painted wooden farm buildings that
have been fitted out to depict traditional
Kuhmo life at the turn of the 20th century
for wealthy families and their servants. It's
a gentle, charming display of everyday objects from the past. The optional guided visit
(English available) is worthwhile.

Petola Luontokeskus   NATURE CENTRE
(www.outdoors.fi; Lentiirantie 342; ☉9am-4pm
Mon-Fri May–mid-Jun & mid-Aug–Oct, 9am-5pm
daily mid-Jun–mid-Aug) On the main road 3km
from the town centre, this has an informative exhibition in various languages on Finland's quartet of large carnivores, known
hereabouts as *karhu* (bear), *ilves* (lynx),

ahma (wolverine) and *susi* (wolf), as well as
wild reindeer, locally present in small numbers, and golden eagles. There's a summer
cafe, national park information and a cute
gift shop.

Kuhmon Talvisotamuseo   MUSEUM
(☑08-6155-5395; www.kuhmo.fi/talvisotamuseo;
Väinämöinen 11; adult/child €5/3; ☉9am-6pm Mon-
Fri, 11am-4pm Sat & Sun Jun–mid-Aug) By Hotelli
Kalevala, this Winter War museum covers
that bitter conflict in the Kuhmo area, mostly through maps and excellent photographs
(descriptions available in English). The Finns
were very successful on this front, inflicting
enormous casualties on Russian divisions
in frighteningly low temperatures. It sometimes opens for reduced hours in winter.

✦ Activities

Hiking is the big drawcard in Kuhmo – the
eastern 'branch line' of the UKK route passes through here – but there are plenty of
other ways to get active.

The website www.wildtaiga.fi has details
of wildlife-watching and other outdoor activities offered in the region. There are bears,
elk, flying squirrels, beavers, wolverines and
wild reindeer around here; excursions cost
from €80 to €150.

Erämatkailu Piirainen   CANOEING
(☑0400-219-197; www.erapiira.fi) Offers canoeing and wildlife-watching.

Taiga Spirit   WILDLIFE-WATCHING
(☑040-746-8243; www.taigaspirit.com) Organises wildlife safaris and bear- and wolverine-
viewing from hides.

Wild Brown Bear   WILDLIFE-WATCHING
(☑040-546-9008; www.wildbrownbear.fi; ☉Mar-
Sep) Runs bear-watching excursions (€120),
with chances to view wolverines, wolves and
other creatures. Accommodation available.

✦ Festivals & Events

★ Kuhmon Kamarimusiikki   MUSIC
(Kuhmo Chamber Music Festival; www.kuhmo
festival.fi; tickets €17-24) This two-week festival
in late July has a full program performed
by a variety of Finnish and international
musicians, many youthful. Most concerts,
usually five or six short pieces bound by a
tenuous theme, are held in the Kuhmo-Talo,
a beautiful, comfortable hall that looks like a
matchstick hobby model. Tickets are a steal
at around €17 for most events.

OFF THE BEATEN TRACK

TREKKING THE UKK

Pockets of pristine Finnish wilderness
exist along the eastern border, best
experienced along the **UKK route**. This
240km trail is the nation's longest and
greatest trekking route, starting at Koli
in Karelia, and ending in Syöte.

There are numerous possible access
points, and alternative branches of the
route, but the Kuhmo area offers some
excellent portions of it: the Kuhmo
to Hiidenportti leg and the Kuhmo to
Lentiira leg. The trek east from Kuhmo
to Lentiira via Iso-Palonen park takes
at least four days and offers superb
scenery. It's well marked and has simple
laavu shelters at regular intervals, with
campfire, firewood and pit toilet. Carry
a sleeping bag and *plenty* of insect
repellent. Pick up route maps at Petola
Luontokeskus in Kuhmo.

EXPLORING NORTHERN KAINUU

Kainuu is a sizeable swath of little-visited territory. As you head north, rivers and lakes become steelier, you'll see traditional haystacks and farmsteads in the middle of no-where, and might spot your first reindeer or hear the howling of sled-dogs impatient for snow.

There are buses to Suomussalmi from Kajaani. Minibuses run between Suomussalmi and Kuusamo via Hossa.

Suomussalmi & Around

Suomussalmi, set on a pretty lakeside, is northern Kainuu's hub. Some of the bitterest fighting of the Winter War, and Finland's greatest triumph, was around here, along the Raate road. Rusted ordnance and memorials commemorate it, as does **Raatteen Port-ti** (www.raatteenportti.fi; adult/child €8.50/5; ⊙10am-5pm May–mid-Jun & Sep, 10am-7pm mid-Jun–Aug), 20km east of town, a museum of memorabilia with a good audiovisual display. Alongside, the moving **Avara Syli** monument is endowed with 105 bells, one for each day of the war, and surrounded by a field of stones, one for each dead soldier.

Thirty kilometres north of Suomussalmi, on Rd 5 to Kuusamo, another unearthly field confronts travellers; **Hiljainen Kansa** is a thousand scarecrow-like figures with heads of peat and straw standing like mute witnesses to the triumphs and failures of humanity. A creation of local choreographer Reijo Kela, they are given a biannual change of look by locals donating clothes: you are welcome to swap shirts with one. A summer cafe along-side does rustic coffee and pancakes on a wood stove.

Hossa

This remote, strung-out settlement is wonderfully set up for fishing, hiking, snow-mobiling and cross-country skiing: there are many marked trails and numerous lakes. A **reindeer park** (Hossa Reindeer Park; www.hossanporopuisto.fi; boat trips adult/child €12/7; ⊙9am-8pm mid-Jun–Sep) offers meetings with these gentle antlered beasts and boat trips to a lake island.

The **Luontokeskus** (☑040-751-7221; www.outdoors.fi; ⊙9am-5pm mid-Feb–mid-Jun, 9am-9pm mid-Jun–mid-Aug, 9am-8pm mid-Aug–Sep, 9am-4pm Oct) is a nature centre and cafe arranging fishing permits and hiring equipment. It books the trail huts scattered around the area and runs adjacent **Karhunkainalo** (www.suomussalmi.fi; tent sites €14 plus per adult/child €4/1; ⊙mid-Feb–Oct; P) with tent sites and cottages. Trails run from here deep into the forest; the 3km nature trail is a good introduction with informative signboards. At Värikallio are rock paintings depicting shamans and elk.

Four kilometres south, **Hossan Lomakeskus** (☑08-732-322; www.hossanlomakeskus. com; s/d €55/70, cottages €65-80, cabins per person €20; P ♠) has lake frontage and cab-ins, as well as a long hotel, whose rooms have decent bathrooms and exterior entrances. Sauna and breakfast are included, and there's a bar and mediocre restaurant. Staff will organise transfers from Kuusamo or Kajaani.

🛏 Sleeping & Eating

Book well ahead during the festival, when prices rise a little. The **town hall** (☑08-6155-5291; neuvonta@kuhmo.fi) can help you find ac-commodation in private homes at this time.

Matkakoti Parkki　　　　　GUESTHOUSE €
(☑08-655-0271;　matkakoti.parkki@elisanet.fi; Vienantie 3; s/d €35/60; P ♠) Run in a kindly manner, this quiet and handsome little fam-ily guesthouse offers excellent value near the centre of town. Rooms share bathrooms,

which are spotless. There's a kitchen you can use, and a tasty breakfast is included.

Hotelli Kalevala　　　　　HOTEL €€
(☑08-655-4100; www.hotellikalevala.fi; Väinämöi-nen 9; s/d €98/132; P @ ♠) Four kilometres from central Kuhmo, this striking building of wood and concrete is the area's best place to stay. Pretty rooms in pastel colours mostly have tantalising lake views: the situation is gorgeous, and the hotel takes full advantage, with a relaxing Jacuzzi and sauna area with

vistas and plenty of activity options in winter and summer.

It tends to close on off-season days when there are no bookings. Restaurant opening depends on bookings too.

Hotelli Kainuu HOTEL €€
(☏08-655-1711; www.hotellikainuu.com; Kainuuntie 84; s/d €70/86; P@☎) Right in the slow-beating heart of Kuhmo, this family-run hotel offers rooms that are comfortable without being flashy; there's also a gym and sauna, a bar with a terrace, and a restaurant, Eskobar, serving uninspiring food. It's cheaper on weekends; a little extra cash gets you a room with private sauna.

Neljä Kaesaa CAFE €
(www.neljakaesaa.fi; Koulukatu 3; lunches €7-10; ⊙9am-4.30pm Mon-Fri, 9.30am-2pm Sat, lunch 10.30am-2.30pm Mon-Fri) The best central option at lunchtimes, when it doles out portions of warming and traditional Finnish comfort food like stews (sometimes with elk) or fried *muikku* (vendace, or whitefish, a small lake fish). Opens extended hours during the festival.

ℹ️ Information

There's no tourist office. The town hall, sights and hotels give out info.

ℹ️ Getting There & Around

Several daily buses head to/from Kajaani (€20.40, 1¾ hours), and a couple to Nurmes, changing at Sotkamo. There's a bus Monday and Friday on schoolday mornings to Suomussalmi. For other destinations, go via Kajaani.

Kuusamo & Ruka

📱 08 / POP 16,180
Kuusamo is a remote frontier town 200km northeast of Oulu and close to the Russian border, while Ruka is its buzzy ski resort 30km to the north. Both make great activity bases: wonderful canoeing, hiking and wildlife-watching is available in the surrounding area. In winter it's packed; in summer it makes a useful base for hiking the Karhunkierros.

⊙ Sights

In Kuusamo, the factory shops of Bjarmia ceramics and Kuusamo fishing lures are popular stops, while sleek Kuusamotalo

concert hall, designed by Arto Sipinen, is the town's pride.

★Kuusamon Suurpetokeskus ZOO
(www.kuusamon-suurpetokeskus.fi; Keronrannantie 31; adult/child €10/5; ⊙10am-5pm Apr-Sep) 🖉 There's a great backstory to this bear sanctuary 33km south of Kuusamo on the Kajaani road. Rescued as helpless orphans, the bears were nursed by their 'father' Sulo Karjalainen, who then refused to have them put down (they can't return to the wild) when government funding dried up. He casually takes them fishing and walking in the forest, but you'll meet them in their cages here; it's thrilling to see these impressive, intelligent animals up close and appreciate their different personalities. There are also lynx, foxes and reindeer.

Hannun Luontokuvakeskus GALLERY
(www.hannuhautala.fi; adult/child €5/2; ⊙9am-5pm Mon-Fri, 10am-2pm Sat, plus noon-4pm Sun Jul-Sep) In the tourist-office building, this rotating exhibition displays the work of famous Finnish nature photographer Hannu Hautala with great information. There are some stunning shots; equally impressive is the patience that it required to get them.

🏃 Activities

There's plenty to do around Ruka in summer, with great walking and birdwatching on your doorstep and good mountain-biking trails. There are lots of free activities organised throughout summer, including some for kids if you fancy an afternoon off. In winter it's a centre for skiing, husky-sledding, snowmobiling and more.

There are many tour operators offering a full range of winter and summer activities. The Ruka webpage, www.ruka.fi, is a good place to look for ideas.

In the centre of Ruka, RukaStore is open daily year-round and has mountain bikes for hire (€25 per day). RukaPalvelu does too, as well as fishing equipment and canoes.

Rukatunturi SNOW SPORTS
(www.ruka.fi; day/week €38/189) Busy Ruka fell boasts 34 ski slopes, dedicated snowboard areas, a vertical drop of 201m and a longest run of 1300m. The 200-day-plus season normally runs from November to May. Ruka also boasts cross-country trails totalling an impressive 500km, with 40km illuminated. Lift passes allow you to ski at Pyhä in Lapland too.

🛏 Sleeping

Ruka's very busy in winter; in summer it's great value. There are numerous apartments in Ruka itself, and hundreds of cabins and cottages throughout the surrounding area. For cottages, contact the Kuusamo tourist office (p223), **Lomarengas** (☑030-650-2502; www.lomarengas.fi) or **ProLoma** (☑020-792-9700; www.proloma.fi). For apartments and chalets in Ruka, contact **Ski-Inn** (☑08-860-0300; www.ski-inn.fi; apt €75-200) or **Ruka-ko** (☑020-734-4790; www.rukako.fi; Rukanriutta 7). There are links to more cabin and cottage providers on www.ruka.fi.

If you stay in Ruka in summer, you get a 'Summer Wristband', which gets you plenty of decent discounts on meals and activities in the area.

Kuusamo-opisto   GUESTHOUSE **€** (☑050-444-1157; www.kuusamo-opisto.fi; Kitkantie 35, Kuusamo; s/d €36/60, without bathroom €30/52; ℗) Around the corner from Kuusamo's bus station, this college offers great budget accommodation in comfortable spacious rooms with en suites (some share shower facilities) in a variety of buildings; there are kitchen and laundry facilities. The bad news is that you have to arrive during office hours (8am to 3.45pm Monday to Friday), though you may be able to arrange a key drop by calling ahead.

GETTING ACTIVE AROUND KUUSAMO & RUKA

The Kuusamo and Ruka area is probably Finland's best equipped for outdoor activities. There are numerous operators offering year-round excursions:

Karhu-Kuusamo (☑0400-210-681; www.karhukuusamo.com; trips €120-140) Recommended bear-watching trips. You spend the evening at a comfortable hide overlooking a meadow where bears regularly stop by for a feed: most of the summer you have a very high chance of seeing a honeypaw. You get back to town around midnight or the next morning. The guide Tuomo is very knowledgeable and can also arrange birdwatching.

NorthTrek (☑040-418-2832; www.northtrek.net; Erkkorannantie 1, Ruka) Offers family-friendly rafting, canoeing and hiking trips. In winter it's snowshoeing, cross-country skiing, huskies and snow ponies.

Ruka Safaris (☑08-852-1610; www.rukasafaris.fi; Rukarinteentie 1, Ruka) Located at the hairpin on the way up to Ruka fell. Wide range of summer and winter activities including reindeer safaris, fishing and canoeing, and it has its own accommodation and restaurant.

Rukapalvelu (Tailored Adventures; ☑010-271-0500; www.rukapalvelu.fi; Rukakyläntie 13, Ruka) Comprehensive range of trips from husky and snowmobile safaris to winter and summer fishing, canoeing and river-rafting. It also arranges trips to Russia to see breathtakingly pretty Karelian villages (visa required).

Ruka Adventures (☑08-852-2007; www.rukaadventures.fi; Rukanriutta 7, Ruka) At the main-road turn-off. Canoeing, fishing, ATV trips and winter activities.

Basecamp Oulanka (☑0400-509-741; www.basecampoulanka.fi; Myllykoskentie 30, Juuma) These guys are great for rafting trips on the Kitkajoki. The family-friendly Käylä–Juuma trip lasts three hours (adults €36). The Wild Route (€49) lasts two hours and is for those aged 18 and over, as is the longer trip to the border zone (€89). Winter activities include snowshoeing and ice climbing. Conservation fee included.

Stella Polaris (☑040-843-3425; www.stellapolaris.fi; Sompatie 2, Ruka) Covers all the local rafting trips as well as fishing classes, canoeing and snowmobiling.

Kota-Husky (☑040-718-7287; www.kota-husky.fi; Jaksamontie 58, Karjalaisenniemi) Excellent small-group husky excursions and picturesque kennels in an old barn. Based north of Posio.

Erä-Susi (☑canoes 040-913-6652, huskies 040-570-0279; www.erasusi.com; canoe/kayak hire from €75/50) Hire canoes and kayaks from the Oulanka Visitor Centre (p225) in the middle of Oulanka National Park. Prices include pick up or drop off. It also does guided trips. In winter there are husky safaris from Ruka; in summer you can hike with huskies or visit their farm.

EXPLORING RIISITUNTURI

A worthwhile national park is Riisitunturi, 54km northwest of Kuusamo, not far from the town of Posio. Consisting of fells and hillside bogs, it offers spectacular views and rewarding hiking: a 29km trail crosses the park from one side to the other. See www.outdoors.fi for details of huts and trails.

Willi's West
MOTEL €

(☑0400-242-992; www.williswest.com; Rukanriutta 13, Ruka; apt s/d summer €49/59, winter €66/99; P☎) At the Ruka turn-off on the main road is this friendly motel-style set-up offering good value. Rooms are small apartments sleeping up to five, and have spacious bathroom and a small, equipped kitchen. It's a steal in summer. The owners will take groups of walkers to the Karhunkierros trailheads.

Royal Hotel Ruka
HOTEL €€

(☑040-081-9840; www.royalruka.fi; Mestantie 1, Ruka; s/d €110/149, r Jul-Oct €100; ⊙Jul-Apr; P☎) Down at the foot of the fell at the turn-off to Rukajärvi, this small and intimate hotel looks like a children's fort to be populated with toy soldiers. It's the closest to a boutique hotel in the Kuusamo area; service is excellent here, and the classy restaurant offers delicacies such as roast hare. From July to November it only opens for bookings.

Hotelli Kuusanka
HOTEL €€

(☑08-852-2240; www.kuusanka.fi; Ouluntie 2, Kuusamo; s/d €67/80; P) A cordial welcome is guaranteed at this sweet main-street hotel, whose blue-shaded rooms are so clean you can smell them. They vary widely in size and sleep up to four; some have tables, chairs and a sofa, so if it's not busy ask for one with extra space. Good breakfast is included; it also has big, well-equipped cottages 6km up the Ruka road.

Rantasipi Rukahovi
HOTEL €€

(☑08-85910; www.rantasipi.fi; Rukankyläntie 15, Ruka; s/d/superior d €110/135/165, summer r €89; P@☎) Right by the major slopes in the centre of town, this huge complex aims to please everyone from conferencing execs to snowball-lobbing families, and largely succeeds, thanks to plenty of facilities and a wide variety of rooms. Standard rooms are fine, though a long hike from reception. Superiors have balconies and are much more spacious. Both have drying cupboards. Down the road are capacious duplex apartments. Its restaurant, bars and nightclub are the heart of Ruka nightlife in the ski and autumn *ruska* seasons.

✗ Eating & Drinking

Near the tourist office in Kuusamo are several giant supermarkets where you can stock up on trekking or cottage supplies.

Martai
FINNISH €

(Airotie, Kuusamo; lunches €7-10; ⊙10am-3pm Mon-Fri) In an unattractive industrial area not far from the tourist office (look behind the ABC service station), this place keeps lunching workers happy with excellent, very authentic hot dishes. Sautéed reindeer and fried vendace (whitefish) are typical choices; there's also a plate for kids.

Riipisen Riistaravintola
GAME €€

(☑08-868-1219; www.ruka.fi; Kelo, Ruka; mains €16-45; ⊙1-9pm Mon-Sat) At the Kelo ski-lift area, a five-minute walk from Ruka's main square, this friendly log cabin has an attractively rustic interior. It specialises in game dishes, and you'll find Rudolf, Bullwinkle and, yes, poor Yogi (€61) on the menu here in various guises, depending on availability and season. Arctic hare also features, while capercaillie in a creamy sauce will get bird lovers twitching too.

Piste
FINNISH €€

(www.ruka.fi; Ruka; mains €14-25; ⊙11am-midnight daily Sep-May, noon-9pm Jun-Aug; ☎) At the base of the lifts on Ruka's main square, this cavernous wooden hall has several attractive dining areas and good service. Dishes range from burgers to well-prepared meat dishes. Service is helpful. Things get pretty lively at the bar with regular bands during ski season.

Zone
BAR

(www.ravintolazone.fi; Ruka; ⊙noon-4am; ☎) This year-round central bar's big glassed-in terrace packs out at night in the ski season and has its own fast-food kiosk. There's karaoke nightly, regular live music and a general vibe of pissed-up goodwill.

ℹ Information

Ruka has a free wi-fi network.

Karhuntassu (☑ 040-860-8365; www.ruka.
fi; Torangintaival 2, Kuusamo; ⊙9am-5pm
Mon-Fri, 10am-2pm Sat, plus noon-4pm Sun
Jun-Aug) This large visitor centre is at the
highway junction, 2km from central Kuusamo.
There's comprehensive tourist information,
rental cottage booking and a cafe-shop. Hours
vary through the year; there's also a wildlife
photography exhibition and national park
information desk here.

Ruka Info (☑ 08-860-0250; www.ruka.fi; Ruka;
⊙9am-5pm early Jun & late Aug, 9.30am-7pm
Sep & late Jun–mid-Aug, 10am-8pm daily Oct-
May) In the Kumpare building in the main village. Tourist information and accommodation
booking. In the same building is a self-service
laundry, supermarket, gym and more.

❶ Getting There & Around

Finnair hits Kuusamo airport, 6km northeast
of town, from Helsinki. Buses meet flights (€7
to Kuusamo, €10 to Ruka). Call ☑ 0100-84200
for a taxi.

Buses run daily from Kajaani (€43.60,
3½ hours), Oulu (€40.80, three hours) and
Rovaniemi (€34.50, three hours).

Buses run between Kuusamo and Ruka a few
times daily (€6.80, 30 minutes). During the ski
season there's a shuttle bus, stopping at major
hotels.

Karhunkierros Trek & Oulanka National Park

The Karhunkierros (Bear's Ring), one of the
oldest and best-established trekking routes
in Finland, offers some of the country's most
breathtaking scenery. It is extremely popular
in summer but it can be walked practically
any time between late May and October.

Despite the name, it's not a circuit, rather a point-to-point walk of anything from
52km (Ristikallio to Juuma) to 82km (Hautajärvi to Ruka). There are four trailheads:
the northern access point is from Hautajärvi
Visitor Centre on the road to Salla; further

south on Rd 950 the Ristikallio parking area
is another access point; in the south you can
start the walk at Ruka ski resort; or further
northeast at Juuma village. Juuma also has
a spectacular loop trail, the 12km Pieni Karhunkierros (Little Bear's Ring; p226).

Most people choose to walk north to
south for transport-connection reasons.

Much of the walk is through the Oulanka
National Park, also a great destination for
canoeing and rafting.

Trekking

The track is very well marked. Prior to mid-
June the ground is too soggy to make hiking enjoyable. Even if you don't intend to
walk the whole route, a day walk can take
you from Ristikallio to Oulanka Canyon and
back, for example. It's also possible to drive
to within 1km of Oulanka Canyon along a
signposted dirt road about 12km north of
Ristikallio.

There are plenty of wilderness huts, so
you can divide the route up according to
your own pace. People tend to do Ristikallio
to Juuma in two or three days, with a further
long day to Ruka.

🏃 From Ristikallio

Start at the parking area at Ristikallio;
you'll soon enter the national park. There's
a wilderness hut (of use if you're coming the
other way) about an hour in. Less than an
hour further gets you to Puikkokämppä hut
at a small lake. Continue another kilometre
and a bit past the lake to Taivalköngäs (9km
from the start, near the wilderness hut of
the same name), with two sets of rapids and
three suspension bridges.

🏃 From Hautajärvi

Another starting point is further north at
the Hautajärvi Visitor Centre – this adds
an extra 10km to the hike. The landscape is

unimpressive until the path reaches the Savinajoki. The deep Oulanka Canyon is a highlight of this part of the trek. A wilderness hut is at the Oulanka riverfront near Savilampi, a lake 15km south of Hautajärvi. The distance from Savilampi to Taivalköngäs – where you'll join the Ristikallio trail – is 4km.

Taivalköngäs to Juuma

From Taivalköngäs the first stretch is through typical forest scenery enlivened by beautiful lakes. After 4km, you can camp at Lake Runsulampi; there's dry wood availa-

ble. About 3.5km further east, there's Oulanka Camping; another kilometre brings you to the Oulanka Visitor Centre and its welcome cafe. The rugged cliffs and muscular waters of the Kiutaköngäs rapids are a short way further on. From Oulanka it's 7km to Ansakämppä cabin, and a further 8km to Jussinkämppä wilderness hut on Kulmakkajärvi.

From here the trail is a little tougher. A hike through ridges and forests takes you to the Kitkajoki in another deep gorge. When you meet the Pieni Karhunkierros trail, you can turn right to head directly to Juuma via the bridge at Myllykoski, or turn left for the more scenic route via the Jyrävä waterfall (where you'll find Siilastupa hut, 16km beyond Jussinkämppä). Three and a half kilometres beyond here is Juuma, where there are campsites, and the Basecamp Oulanka lodge on the trail just outside it.

Juuma to Ruka

Juuma is one possible endpoint, but you can also walk 24km further to Ruka, which has a big choice of accommodation and better road connections to Kuusamo. There is one wilderness hut, Porontimajoki (often full), 9km down this trail, and several lean-to shelters. The first 15km are easy going, but then a series of ascents and descents mean that post-hike beer in Ruka will be very well earned.

Sleeping

There is a good network of wilderness huts along the Karhunkierros. All are pretty similar and tend to be crowded in high season. Although tradition says there's always room for the last to arrive, a tent will come in handy, as someone often ends up sleeping outside. Dry firewood is generally available, and there's a gas cooker in most, but carry a lightweight mattress. See www.outdoors.fi for hut details.

Oulanka Camping CAMPGROUND €
(☑ 0400-188-049; www.outdoors.fi; Liikasenvaarantie 137; tent sites for 1 person/more €7.50/15, 4-person cabins €48; ☉ Jun-Aug; ℗) The trail runs right through this place, 1km from the Oulanka Visitor Centre. It rents canoes and rowboats to use on the Oulankajoki, and has a kiosk and sauna. It will open in early September if you book ahead. A 5km circular walk leaves from here.

❶ Information

The website www.outdoors.fi has comprehensive route information. The 1:50,000 *Rukatunturi-Oulanka* map (€19.90) is sold at park visitor centres and tourist offices. A map guide to the Karhunkierros costs €25. The trail is so well signposted that you can easily make do with the free map.

Rukapalvelu in Ruka rents tents, packs and other hiking equipment.

Hautajärvi Visitor Centre (☑ 040-834-6814; www.outdoors.fi; ☉ 9am-4pm Tue-Fri mid-Feb–May & Oct, 8.30am-5pm Mon-Fri, 9am-5pm Sat & Sun Jun-Sep) Helpful, at the northern

trailhead, right on the Arctic Circle on the Kuusamo–Salla road, 1km north of Hautajärvi village. There's a cafe and exhibition on the ecosystem of the mires, dotted with apposite literary quotes.

Oulanka Visitor Centre (☑ 040-732-5615; www.outdoors.fi; Liikasenvaarantie 132; ☉ 10am-4pm Oct-May, 10am-6pm Jun-Sep; ☎) In the middle of Oulanka National Park, accessible along a 13km unsealed road from Käylä. There's an exhibition, trekking supplies, cafe, maps and fishing licences. An 8km round walk takes you along the Oulankajoki to the Kiutaköngäs rapids. You can also rent kayaks and canoes here (p221); the price includes pick up or drop off and a safety lesson.

❶ Getting There & Around

From early June to early August, a handy early-morning **bus** (☑ 040-722-2022; www.rukacharter.fi; Kuusamo to trailheads €11.80-13.70, Ruka to trailheads €6.80-10.10) runs from Kuusamo to Salla via Ruka, Juuma, Ristikallio and Hautajärvi from Monday to Friday, and returns. There's a connection from Käylä to Oulanka Visitor Centre on Monday, Wednesday and Friday.

Outside these dates, there's a less convenient afternoon service, with no weekend buses.

A **taxi** (☑ 08-868-1222; www.rukataksi.fi) from Ruka costs a fixed €42 to €48 to Juuma, and €77 to €90 to Hautajärvi.

River Routes Around Kuusamo

The Oulankajoki and Kitkajoki, which meet close to the Russian border, offer wonderful canoeing and rafting opportunities in wilderness areas. You can do these trips as organised, guided adventures, or hire canoes or kayaks from one of many outfitters, who can arrange transport at either end.

Oulankajoki

Shadowing the Karhunkierros much of the way, the Oulankajoki gives you a chance to see mighty canyons from a canoe or kayak. The first leg, a 20km trip, starts from Rd 950, north of Ristikallio. The first 7km or so is relatively calm paddling, until you reach the impressive Oulanka Canyon. The safe section extends for about 1km, after which pull aside and carry your canoe twice past dangerous rapids. You can overnight at Savilampi hut, also a popular starting point.

Some 3km after Savilampi are Taivalköngäs rapids (carry), where there's a hut. The next 9km are quiet, passing a couple of campgrounds before reaching Oulanka Visitor Centre, which rents canoes for this trip. Not far downstream are Kiutaköngäs rapids (carry). Below them the Lower Oulankajoki stretch is 25km of easy paddling, suitable for beginners, ending at Jäkälämutka parking area just short of the Russian border.

Kitkajoki

The spectacular Kitkajoki offers some of Finland's best canoeing and rafting. There are two main sections: the family-friendly section from Käylä, on the Kuusamo–Salla road, to Juuma, and the challenging 'wild' section beyond Juuma, which includes plenty of tricky rapids.

KÄYLÄ TO JUUMA

The first 14km leg is suitable for families, involving no carrying. Start at the Käylänkoski, continue 3km to the easy Kiehtäjänniva, and a further kilometre to the Vähä-Käylänkoski: also class I. Next come three class II rapids spaced every 400m. A kilometre further is the trickiest: 300m class III Harjakoski. The remaining 7km is mostly lakes.

JUUMA TO THE RUSSIAN BORDER

This 20km journey is one of Finland's most challenging river routes: you should be an expert paddler, and *must* carry your canoe at least once – around the 12m, class VI Jyrävä waterfall. Ask for local advice and inspect the tricky rapids before you let go. There's a minimum age of 18.

The thrill starts just 300m after Juuma, with the class II Niskakoski. From here on, it's busy. Myllykoski, with a watermill, is a tricky class IV waterfall. Right after Myllykoski, the 900m class IV Aallokkokoski rapids mean quick paddling for quite some time. The Jyrävä waterfall comes right after this long section. Pull aside and carry your canoe; you might want to carry it from Myllykoski to beyond Jyrävä, skipping Aallokkokoski altogether.

After Jyrävä things cool down considerably, although there are some class III rapids. When you meet the Oulankajoki, 13km further downriver, paddle upriver to Jäkälämutka or downriver to Kuusinkiniemi, by the border zone. Arrange return transport from these remote points in advance.

Juuma
🎵 08

Juuma is a popular base for Karhunkierros treks and canoeing on the Kitkajoki. The **Pieni Karhunkierros** (Little Bear's Ring) is an easy-to-moderate 12km loop trail taking in some fantastic scenery as it follows the river valley far below. It leaves from by the Retki-Etappi cafe and traverses varying terrain. It's one of the most scenic short routes in Finland. There's a wilderness hut on this trail – Siilastupa – and a day hut at Myllykoski. It's well signposted, and busy. You can do it with snowshoes in winter.

🛏 Sleeping & Eating

Juuman Leirintäalue   CAMPGROUND €
(✆ 044-272-7872; www.juumanleirintaalue.fi; Riekamontie 1; tent sites per 1/4 person €10/17, cabins €30-40, cottages €70; ☺ Jun-Sep; 🅿) This place has a lovely lakeside location at the beginning of the Käylä road. There's a sauna, a laundry and a cafe that can do evening meals if you book the day before. It also arranges fishing licences and hires boats. The heated cottages are open year-round.

Lomakylä Retki-Etappi   CAMPGROUND €
(✆ 040-565-3474; www.retkietappi.fi; Juumantie 134; tent sites per 1 person €12, plus €5 per additional person, cabins €35-80; ☺ Jun-Sep; 🅿) This place, at the start of the Little Bear's Ring and a Karhunkierros trailhead, is a convenient spot to stay. There are several cabins, a couple of them available in winter, and a cafe serving snacks and meals. There's also a sauna, and boats and bikes to hire.

★ Basecamp Oulanka   LODGE €€
(✆ 0400-509-741; www.basecampoulanka.fi; Myllykoskentie 30; s/d/tw €99/140/150, summer €69/100/110; 🅿) 🖊 This excellent wilderness lodge is right on the Karhunkierros trail itself about 1km from Juuma (but 5.5km by car). Snug rustic rooms smell of pine: larger ones are great for families and groups, with extra sleeping space in the roof, and a charming balcony overlooking forest. There's a convivial bar and restaurant (lunch always on, dinner by prior arrangement), sauna and Jacuzzi. Friendly staff organise all sorts of daily activities: rafting, fishing and snowshoeing among others. It gets cheaper if you stay more than one night; in low season it's worth asking for discounted rates. There's no internet and no kitchen facilities, but you can hire skis, canoes, kayaks and more.

Lapland

Best Places to Trek

➡ Urho Kekkonen National Park (p253)

➡ Kevo Strict Nature Reserve (p260)

➡ Pallas-Yllästunturi National Park (p243)

Best Places to Stay

➡ Lumihotelli (p237)

➡ Porotila Toini Sanila (p262)

➡ City Hotel (p233)

➡ Levi Panorama (p241)

Why Go?

Lapland casts a powerful spell and irresistibly haunts the imagination and memory. There is something lonely and intangible here that makes it magic.

The midnight sun, the Sámi peoples, the aurora borealis (Northern Lights) and wandering reindeer are all components of this, as is good old ho-ho-ho himself, who 'officially' resides here. Another part of the spell is in the awesome latitudes – at Nuorgam, the northernmost point, you have passed Iceland and nearly all of Canada and Alaska.

Lapland, which occupies 30% of Finland's land area but houses just 3% of its population, has vast and awesome wildernesses, ripe for exploring on foot, skis or sledge. The sense of space, pure air and big skies are what is memorable here, more than the towns.

Lapland's far north is known as Sápmi, home of the Sámi people, whose main communities are around Inari, Utsjoki and Hetta. Rovaniemi is the most popular gateway to the north.

When to Go

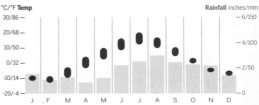

Lapland

Apr The best month for sled treks and skiing, with plenty of light and reasonable temperatures.

Aug Lots of light and sunshine, trails are less crowded, and biting insects fewer.

Dec Reindeer, snow and Santa Claus himself are guaranteed to inject Christmas spirit.

Lapland Highlights

1 Trekking the lonely wildernesses around **Saariselkä** (p249) or Finland's highlands at **Kilpisjärvi** (p244)

2 Dashing through the snow pulled by a team of **reindeer** (p250) or **huskies** (p242) in Muonio or Saariselkä

3 Sailing on an **ice-breaker** (p237) in Kemi, then sleeping in the ethereally beautiful **snow castle** (p237)

4 Panning for gold in beautiful **Lemmenjoki** (p258) and walking in the national park

5 Learning about northern environments at Rovaniemi's **Arktikum** (p231)

6 Taking your first steps at exploring Sámi culture at **Siida** (p255) in Inari

7 Skiing at Lapland's best-equipped resort at **Levi** (p240)

8 Gazing in awe at the **aurora borealis** (p249)

9 Fishing the **Tenojoki** (p261), Lapland's most beautiful stretch of river

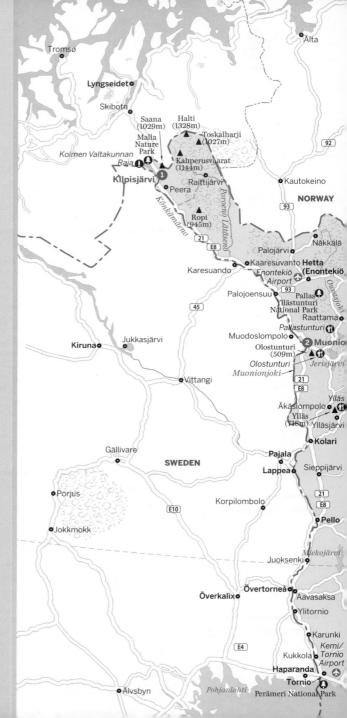

History

Sámi were spread throughout Lapland, but during the 1600s Swedes increased their presence and in 1670 various cult sites and religious objects were destroyed by the Lutheran Church's Gabriel Tuderus (1638–1703). In the following centuries, more Finns came, adopted reindeer-herding and were assimilated into Sámi communities (or vice versa).

The Petsamo area, northeast of Inari, was ceded to Finland in 1920 by the Treaty of Tartu. The Soviet Union attacked the mineral-rich area during the Winter War (1939–40), annexed it in 1944, and has kept it. Skolt Sámi from Petsamo were resettled in Sevettijärvi, Nellim and Virtaniemi.

The German army's retreat in 1944–45 was a scorched-earth affair; they burned all buildings in their path to hold off pursuit. Only a few churches, villages and houses in Lapland date from the prewar period.

Activities

Lapland's joy is the range of exciting outdoor activities year-round. There's good downhill skiing for six months of the year at several spots; Levi is the biggest resort, while smaller Pyhä-Luosto and Ylläs are more family- than party-oriented. All have extensive cross-country trails.

Most memorable are sleigh safaris. Pulled by a team of huskies or reindeer, you cross the snowy wilderness, overnighting in log cabins with a relaxing wood sauna and eating meals cooked over a fire. You can organise trips of up to a week or more, or just head out for a jaunt of a couple of hours. Similar trips can be arranged on snowmobiles.

Once the snow melts, there are fabulous multiday treks and shorter walks. The national parks network offers everything from wheelchair-accessible nature trails to demanding wilderness routes for experienced hikers, but there are good walks almost everywhere.

Lapland's frisky rivers offer several excellent canoeing routes and spots for whitewater rafting. Fishing is popular year-round: ice-fishing is a memorable experience, and the beautiful Teno Valley offers superb salmon fishing.

Major settlements have plenty of tour operators offering all these activities. Rovaniemi, Lapland's capital, is a popular base, but Saariselkä, Levi and Muonio are closer to genuine wilderness.

Self-Catering Accommodation

There is a huge quantity of self-catering apartments, cottages and cabins throughout the region. Ski resorts are particularly fertile ground; fully furnished places with their own sauna can be great value in summer. Local tourist offices often double as booking agents for these accommodation options. **Lomarengas** (☑ 030-650-2505; www.lomarengas.com) has a large selection of cabins throughout the region.

Language

Three Sámi languages are spoken in Finnish Lapland; signs in Sámi areas are bilingual.

ⓘ Dangers & Annoyances

From mid-June to early August, Lapland is home to millions of biting insects, and during this räkkä season, you'll need heavy-duty repellent. By early August most squadrons have dispersed.

Parts of Lapland are real wildernesses; always consult national park centres before attempting unmarked routes.

Winter temperatures are seriously low: don't head outdoors without being properly equipped.

Driving in Lapland calls for particular caution due to reindeer (see p296).

ⓘ Getting Around

Considering the remoteness, bus connections are good, although there may only be one service a day, and none on Sundays. Hiring a car from Rovaniemi, Levi or Saariselkä/Ivalo is a good option.

LAPLAND SEASONS

It's important to pick your time in Lapland carefully. In the far north there's no sun for 50 days of the year, and no night for 70-odd days. In June it's very muddy, and in July insects can be hard to deal with. If you're here to walk, August is great and in September the *ruska* (autumn leaves) can be seen. There's thick snow cover from mid-October to May; December draws charter flights looking for Santa, real reindeer and guaranteed snow, but the best time for skiing and husky/reindeer/snowmobile safaris is March and April, when you get a decent amount of daylight and less-extreme temperatures.

ROVANIEMI & AROUND

Rovaniemi

016 / POP 60,900

A tourism boomtown, the 'official' terrestrial residence of Santa Claus is the capital of Finnish Lapland and a more-or-less obligatory northern stop. Its wonderful Arktikum museum is the perfect introduction to the mysteries of these latitudes, and Rovaniemi is a good place to organise activities from. It's also Lapland's transport hub. Thoroughly destroyed by the retreating German army in 1944, the town was rebuilt to a plan by Alvar Aalto, with the major streets in the shape of a reindeer's head and antlers (hint: the stadium near the bus station is the eye). Its unattractive buildings are compensated for by its marvellous riverside location.

◉ Sights

Combination tickets are available for the three major sights: Arktikum, Pilke Tiedekeskus and Rovaniemen Taidemuseo.

★ Arktikum   MUSEUM

(www.arktikum.fi; Pohjoisranta 4; adult/child/family €12/5/28; ⊙9am-6pm Jun-Aug & Dec–mid-Jan, 10am-6pm Tue-Sun mid-Jan–May & Sep-Nov) With its beautifully designed glass tunnel stretching out to the Ounasjoki, this is one of Finland's best museums. One side deals with Lapland, with information on Sámi culture and the history of Rovaniemi. The other side offers a wide-ranging display on the Arctic, with superb static and interactive displays focusing on flora and fauna, as well as on the peoples of Arctic Europe, Asia and North America. There's a research library here if you want to learn more. There's an audiovisual – basically a pretty slide show – downstairs on constant loop. There's a good-value cafe, too.

★ Pilke Tiedekeskus   MUSEUM

(www.sciencecentrepilke.fi; Ounasjoentie 6; adult/child €7/5; ⊙9am-6pm Mon-Fri, 10am-6pm Sat & Sun, closed Mon mid-Jan–May & Sep-Nov) Downstairs in the Metsähallitus (Finnish Forest and Park Service) building next to the Arktikum, this is a highly entertaining exhibition on Finnish forestry. It has dozens of interactive displays that are great for kids of all ages, who can clamber up into a logging vehicle or play games about forest man-

agement. Multilingual touchscreens provide interesting background information. Sustainable forestry is the focus, though a bear-hunting simulation breaks the PC mould.

Rovaniemen Taidemuseo   GALLERY

(Korundi; www.korundi.fi; Lapinkävijäntie 4; adult/child €8/4, Sat free; ⊙11am-6pm Tue-Sun, plus Mon Dec-early Jan & Jun-Aug) This gallery in an old brick truck depot has a wide collection of contemporary Finnish art that it rotates in its clean white exhibition space. A concert hall here has regular events.

Lappia-talo   NOTABLE BUILDING

(www.rovaniementeatteri.fi; Hallituskatu 11) Rovaniemi's concert hall is one of several buildings in Rovaniemi designed by Alvar Aalto (others include the adjacent library and town hall).

Rovaniemen Kirkko   CHURCH

(Rauhankatu 79; ⊙9am-9pm mid-May–Aug) Completed in 1950, this church replaced the one destroyed during WWII. The impressively large fresco behind the altar depicts a Christ figure emerging from Lappish scenery. A work of Lennart Segerstråle, it has two sides, one populated by the faithful, the other by brawling drunkards and ravening wolves.

☆ Activities

Hire bicycles from **Europcar** (040-306-2870; www.europcar.fi; Pohjanpuistikko 2; per 3/24hr €10/20).

Ounasvaara   SNOW SPORTS

(www.ounasvaara.fi; ⊙mountain-biking & toboggan run 11am-5pm late Jun–mid-Aug) This long fell across the river to the east of town is a place to get active. In winter there's a

LAPLAND ROVANIEMI

Rovaniemi

Rovaniemi

◎ Top Sights
1 Arktikum	C1
2 Pilke Tiedekeskus	C1

◎ Sights
3 Lappia-talo	B4
4 Rovaniemen Kirkko	C4
5 Rovaniemen Taidemuseo	B3

⊕ Activities, Courses & Tours
6 Europcar	D2
7 Lapland Safaris	D3
8 Lapland Welcome	C2
9 Safartica	C2

🛏 Sleeping
10 City Hotel	C3
11 Guesthouse Borealis	A3
12 Hostel Rudolf	B2
13 Hotel Santa Claus	C2

14 Hotelli Aakenus	B2
15 Ounaskoski Camping	D3

⊗ Eating
Arktikum Cafe	(see 1)
16 Cafe & Bar 21	C3
17 Mariza	C3
Monte Rosa	(see 10)
18 Nili	C2
19 ZoomUp/Gaissa	C2

⊖ Drinking & Nightlife
20 Kauppayhtiö	C2
Paha Kurki	(see 18)
21 Roy Club	C2
ZoomIt	(see 13)

🛍 Shopping
22 Marttiini	C1

ROVANIEMI ADVENTURES

Rovaniemi is great for winter and summer activities, offering frequent departures with multilingual guides.

In summer, activities include guided walks, mountain biking (€55 to €70), river cruises (€30), visiting reindeer or huskies (€50 to €90), rafting, canoeing, moose-watching and wilderness camping.

Winter activities include snowmobiling (€100 to €170 for a two- to six-hour trip), snowshoeing (€55), reindeer-sledding (€100 to €130), husky-sledding (€75 to €250), cross-country skiing (€50 to €60), ice-fishing, aurora-watching, overnighting in a wilderness hut or a combination. All prices are based on two people sharing a snowmobile/sled; you'll pay up to 50% more if you want one all to yourself. You need a driving licence to operate a snowmobile.

Some recommended operators (most offices are unstaffed in summer so call, or book via the tourist office):

Lapland Safaris (☑016-331-1200; www.laplandsafaris.com; Koskikatu 1) Reliable and well-established outfit for most of the above activities.

Lapland Welcome (☑016-439-148; www.laplandwelcome.fi; Rovakatu 26) Winter and summer excursions with good customer service.

Husky Point (☑0400-790-096; www.huskypoint.fi; Kittiläntie 1638, Sinettä) From short rides to multiday treks. It also does summer dog trips and reindeer visits.

Safartica (☑016-311-485; www.safartica.com; Koskikatu 9) One of the best for snowmobiling and river activities.

ski centre. There are ski jumps here, plus more than 100km of cross-country tracks. In summer there's a mountain-biking and toboggan run; walkers can take advantage of the cross-country skiing tracks. Bus 9 gets you here.

✫ Festivals & Events

Christmas is a big time of the year and there are plenty of festive activities in December.

Napapiirinhiihto SNOW SPORTS
(www.napapiirinhiihto.fi) In March Rovaniemi hosts skiing and ski-jumping competitions as well as a reindeer race in the centre of town.

Jutajaiset CULTURAL
(www.jutajaiset.fi) Jutajaiset, in late June, is a celebration of Lapland folklore by various youth ensembles.

🛏 Sleeping

Guesthouse Borealis GUESTHOUSE €
(☑016-342-0130; www.guesthouseborealis.com; Asemieskatu 1; s/d/tr €53/66/89; ▣@❧) Cordial hospitality and proximity to trains make this family-run spot a winner. Rooms are simple, bright and clean; some have a balcony. Guests have use of a kitchen (and sauna for a small charge), and there are two

self-contained apartments. Prices are higher in winter; substantially so over Christmas.

Hostel Rudolf HOSTEL €
(☑016-321-321; www.rudolf.fi; Koskikatu 41; dm/s/d mid-Jan–Mar €52/64/92, Apr-Nov €42/49/63, Christmas period €58/73/108; ▣❧) Run by Hotel Santa Claus, where you have to go to check in, this staffless hostel is Rovaniemi's only one and can fill up fast. Rooms are private and good for the price, with spotless bathrooms, solid desks and bedside lamps; dorm rates get you the same deal. There's also a kitchen available but don't expect a hostel atmosphere. HI discount.

Ounaskoski Camping CAMPGROUND €
(☑016-345-304; www.ounaskoski-camping-rovaniemi.com; Jäämerentie 1; tent sites €14 plus per adult/child €8/4; ☺late May-late Sep; ▣❧) Just across the elegant bridge from the town centre, this campground is perfectly situated on the riverbank. There are no cabins, but plenty of grassy tent and van sites, with great views over the Ounaskoski.

★ City Hotel HOTEL €€
(☑016-330-0111; www.cityhotel.fi; Pekankatu 9; s/d/superior d €129/149/177; ▣@❧) This very pleasing place retains an intimate feel, with excellent service and plenty of extras included free of charge. Rooms are very stylish

with large windows, arty silvery objects, good beds and plush fabrics. Luxe rooms offer a proper double bed, while smart suites have a sauna. Cheaper in summer.

Santasport   HOTEL €€
(☑ 020-798-4200; www.santasport.fi; Hiihtomajantie 2; s €74-99, d €96-150; P @ 🛜 🏊) A 15-minute stroll from the town centre at the base of Ounasvaara, this sports complex offers great value. Functional modern rooms – including excellent family suites – offer heaps of space, fridge, microwave and drying cupboard. On-site is a full-size swimming pool, spa facilities, bowling, gym, indoor playpark, and bike and cross-country ski hire. There are cheaper student-style rooms (summer single/double €54/72) and upmarket cottages sleeping six.

Hotelli Aakenus   HOTEL €€
(☑ 016-342-2051; www.hotelliaakenus.net; Koskikatu 47; s/d €77/89; P @ 🛜) Offering excellent summer value from mid-May to the end of August, this friendly, efficient little hotel is a short distance west of the town centre and a quick stroll from the Arktikum. The rooms are simple and spacious, with narrow beds. A sauna (switched on for several hours) and decent buffet breakfast are included. There are also some apartments out the back.

Aaria   B&B €€
(☑ 0400-238-235; www.bbaaria.com; Rannamukka 6; s/d May-Aug €50/85; P 🛜) Very handy for the ski lift, this cordially run guesthouse has compact, cosy modern rooms with red highlights and spotless parquet floors in a wooden building in a quiet suburban cul-de-sac. Rooms share sparkling bathrooms (one is en suite) and a kitchen/dining area where you prepare your own breakfast. Prices soar at Christmas.

Santa Claus Holiday Village   COTTAGES €€
(☑ 040-159-3811; www.schv.fi; Tähtikuja 2, Napapiiri; d €99-149; P 🛜) This cottage complex is right at Santa's Napapiiri home. It's run out of an enormous souvenir shop but staff bend over backwards to be helpful and can arrange all sorts of activities. Cottages are at a decent distance from tour groups and offer modern, spacious hotel-standard rooms with sauna and kitchenette. Staff will collect you from the airport, but a car can be a good idea so as not to be stuck out here. Prices are high in December and New Year, but include half-board.

Arctic Snow Hotel   ICE HOTEL €€€
(☑ 040-769-0395; www.arcticsnowhotel.fi; Lehtoahontie 27, Sinettä; s/d/ste €170/250/330, glass igloo tw €385; ⊘ mid-Dec–Mar; P) On the shore of a lake, the Arctic offers the complete snow hotel experience and also has a snow restaurant as well as warmer eating choices. Alongside the snow hotel is an array of glass igloos (available from the beginning of December), ideal for aurora-watching. It's 26km northwest of Rovaniemi, but staff will collect you for not much more. You can visit the complex (adult/child €12/6) even if you're not a guest.

Hotel Santa Claus   HOTEL €€€
(☑ 016-321-321; www.hotelsantaclaus.fi; Korkalonkatu 29; s/d €168/203; P @ 🛜) Thankfully this excellent hotel is devoid of sleighbells and 'ho-ho-ho' kitsch. It's right in the heart of town and very upbeat and busy, with helpful staff and a good bar and restaurant. Rooms have all the trimmings and are spacious, with a sofa and good-sized beds; a supplement gets you a slightly larger superior room. Unacceptably, wi-fi is charged. Prices can halve in summer.

🍴 Eating

Cafe & Bar 21   CAFE €
(www.cafebar21.fi; Rovakatu 21; dishes €8-11; ⊘ 11am-9pm Mon-Tue, 11am-midnight Wed-Thu, 11am-2am Fri, noon-2am Sat, noon-9pm Sun; 🛜) It's a surprise to find this artfully modern designer place here: a reindeer pelt collage on the grey concrete wall is the only concession to place. Modish black and white makes a stylish haunt for creative cocktails, espressos, hot chocolate and a very tasty selection of salads, tapas portions, and sweet and savoury waffles.

Mariza   FINNISH €
(www.ruokahuonemariza.fi; Ruokasenkatu 2; lunch €7.50-9.50; ⊘ 10am-2pm Mon-Fri; 🍴) A couple of blocks from the town centre in untouristed territory, this simple lunch place is a real fin. It offers a buffet of home-cooked Finnish food, including daily changing hot dishes, soup and salad. Authentic and excellent.

Nili   FINNISH €€
(☑ 0400-369-669; www.nili.fi; Valtakatu 20; mains €20-33; ⊘ 6-11pm Mon-Sat) There's much more English than Finnish heard at this popular central restaurant, with an attractive interior and a Lapland theme. The food's tasty rather than gourmet, but uses toothsome

local ingredients, with things like reindeer, lake fish, wild mushrooms and berries creating appealing northern flavours. The overpriced wine list needs work.

ZoomUp/Gaissa   FINNISH €€
(☑016-321-321; www.hotelsantaclaus.fi; Korkalonkatu 29; mains €14-28; ☉11am-1.30pm & 4-11pm Mon-Fri, 4-11pm Sat; ☎) The upstairs restaurant of the Hotel Santa Claus has a double identity. The Gaissa menu has petite, reindeer-heavy dishes aimed at visitors: there are some great creations. The ZoomUp bar menu has a lunch buffet and salads, pastas, steaks, ribs and snacks like potato wedges, aimed at pulling a local crowd.

Monte Rosa   FINNISH €€
(☑016-330-0400; www.monterosa.fi; Maakuntakatu 25; mains €25-35; ☉11am-10.30pm Mon-Fri, 3-10.30pm Sat, 5-9.30pm Sun; ☎) Attached to the City Hotel, this goes for the romance vote with a low candlelit interior and chummy booth seating. Good-sized portions of Finnish and Lapland fare are very tasty; there's plenty of reindeer and local fish. Downstairs, the Bull Bar serves ribs and huge burgers out of the same kitchen.

🍷 Drinking & Nightlife

Excluding ski resorts, Rovaniemi is the only place north of Oulu with decent nightlife.

★Kauppayhtiö   CAFE, BAR
(www.facebook.com/kauppayhtio; Valtakatu 24; ☉11am-8pm Mon-Thu, 11am-4am Fri & Sat; ☎) Rovaniemi's most personable cafe, this is an oddball collection of retro curios with a coffee and gasoline theme and colourful plastic tables. All the knick-knacks are purportedly for sale here, but it's the espresso machine, charismatic outdoor lounge and stage area, salads, rolls, burgers, Wednesday-to-Sunday sushi, sundaes and bohemian Lapland crowd that keep the place ticking There are often bands on weekends. The coffee is bottomless.

Roy Club   BAR, CLUB
(www.royclub.fi; Maakuntakatu 24; ☉10pm-4am) This friendly bar has a sedate, comfortable top half with cosy seating, cheap and long happy hours, and regular karaoke. There's also a downstairs nightclub that gets cheerily boisterous with students and stays open late.

ZoomIt   BAR
(www.hotelsantaclaus.fi; Koskikatu 14; ☉2pm-midnight Mon-Thu, 2pm-2am Fri, noon-2am Sat, noon-11pm Sun; ☎) Large, light, modern ZoomIt is a popular, buzzy central bar and cafe. Right in the heart of town, its terrace is the spot to be on a sunny afternoon and its spacious interior gives room to stretch out with a book if it's raining or snowing.

Paha Kurki   BAR
(www.pahakurki.com; Koskikatu 5; ☉4pm-3am; ☎) Dark but rather clean and modern, this rock bar has a fine variety of bottled beers, memorabilia on the walls and a good sound system. A Finnish rock bar is what other places might call a metal bar: expect more Pantera than Pixies.

🛍 Shopping

The widest souvenir selection can be found in shops at Napapiiri.

Marttiini   KNIVES
(www.marttiini.fi; Vartiokatu 32; ☉10am-6pm Mon-Fri, 10am-4pm Sat, plus noon-4pm Sun Jun-Aug) This former factory of Finland's famous knife manufacturer is now a shop open to visitors with a small knife exhibition – it has cheaper prices than you can get elsewhere. It's near the Arktikum.

ℹ Information

Metsähallitus (☑020-564-7820; www.outdoors.fi; Pilke, Ounasjoentie 6; ☉8am-6pm Mon-Fri, 10am-6pm Sat & Sun) Information centre for the national parks, sells maps and fishing permits.

Tourist Information (☑016-346-270; www.visitrovaniemi.fi; Maakuntakatu 29; ☉9am-6pm Mon-Fri, 9am-3pm Sat & Sun mid-Jun–mid-Aug & late Nov-early Jan, 9am-5pm Mon-Fri rest of year; ☎) On the square in the middle of town. Very helpful.

ℹ Getting There & Away

There are left-luggage lockers at the train and bus stations.

AIR

Rovaniemi's airport is a major winter destination for charter flights and it's the 'official airport of Santa Claus': he must hangar his sleigh here. Finnair and Norwegian fly daily from Helsinki.

BUS

Frequent express buses go south to Kemi (€20 to €27, 1½ to 2½ hours) and Oulu (€29 to €44, three to four hours), and there are night buses to Helsinki (€130.20, 12¾ hours). Daily connections serve just about everywhere else in Lapland. Some buses head on north into Norway.

LAPLAND ROVANIEMI

TRAIN

The train between Helsinki and Rovaniemi (€84 to €102, 10 to 12 hours) is quicker and cheaper than the bus. There are three daily direct services (via Oulu), including overnighters (various berth options available) with car transport. There's one train daily northeast to Kemijärvi (€15.50, 1½ hours).

ℹ️ Getting Around

Rovaniemi airport is 10km northeast. **Minibuses** (☏ 016-362-222; www.airporttaxirovaniemi. fi) meet arriving flights, dropping off at hotels in the town centre (€7, 15 minutes). They pick up along the same route about an hour before departures.

Major car-hire agencies have offices in the airport and in town.

Around Rovaniemi

Napapiiri

The southernmost line at which the sun doesn't set on at least one day a year, the Arctic Circle is called **Napapiiri** in Finnish and crosses the Sodankylä road 8km north of Rovaniemi (although the Arctic Circle can actually shift several metres daily). There's an **Arctic Circle marker** here; around it is

---

A DAY AT THE ZOO

Ranua Zoo (Ranuan Eläinpuisto; www. ranuazoo.com; Ranua; adult/child €16/13; ⏱ 9am-7pm Jun-Aug, 10am-4pm Sep-May) Little Ranua is famous for its excellent zoo, focused almost entirely on Finnish animals, although there are also polar bears and musk oxen. A boardwalk runs past all the creatures, which include minks and stoats, impressive owls and eagles, wild reindeer, elk, a big bear paddock (they hibernate from November to March), lynx and wolverines. There's plenty more for kids, with horse rides, mini-karts, pettable domestic animals and assault courses. Ice-cream stops dot the route, and there's a cafe and lunch restaurant.

Ranua, 82km south of Rovaniemi on Rd 78, has hotel, cottage and camping accommodation; there are three to six daily buses from Rovaniemi (€17.30, 1¼ hours) as well as connections from Kajaani and Oulu.

---

built the 'official' **Santa Claus Village** (www. santaclausvillage.info; ⏱ 10am-5pm mid-Jan–May & Sep-Nov, 9am-6pm Jun-Aug, 9am-7pm Dec–mid-Jan) **FREE**, a touristy complex of shops, winter activities and cottage accommodation.

The **Santa Claus Post Office** (www.santa claus.posti.fi) here receives over half a million letters yearly from children (and adults) all over the world. You can browse a selection of the letters, which range from rather mercenary requests for thousands of euros of electronic goods to heart-rending pleas for parents to recover from cancer. Santa answers as many as he can. Your postcard sent from here will bear an official Santa stamp, and you can arrange to have it delivered at Christmas. For €7.90, you can get Santa to send a Christmas card to you.

At the tourist information desk you can get your Arctic Circle certificate (€4.20) or stamp your passport (€0.50).

But the top attraction for most is, of course, **Santa** himself, who sees visitors year-round in a rather impressive **grotto** (www.santaclauslive.com) **FREE**, where a huge clock mechanism (it slows the earth's rotation so that Santa can visit the whole world's children on Christmas night) eerily surrounds those queuing for an audience. The portly saint is quite a linguist, and an old hand at chatting with kids and adults alike. A private chat (around two minutes) is absolutely free, but you can't photograph the moment, and official photos of your visit start at an outrageous €25.

Other things at the complex are Arctice/Snowman World with igloo accommodation, an ice bar and tyre tobogganing; Santamus, an atmospheric seasonal 'experience' restaurant; a husky park; reindeer rides; ice sculpture; and varying Christmassy exhibitions. There's also cottage accommodation and a cafe serving salmon smoked over a traditional fire.

Bus 8 heads here from the train station, passing through the centre (adult/child €6.60/3.80 return).

Santapark

Santapark   AMUSEMENT PARK
(www.santapark.com; Tarvantie 1; adult/child winter €33/27.50, summer €17.50/14.50; ⏱ 10am-6pm late Nov–mid-Jan, 10am-5pm Mon-Sat mid-Jun–mid-Aug) This Christmas-theme amusement park built inside a cavern in the mountain features an army of elves baking gingerbread, a magic sleigh ride, a carousel, an ice

bar, a theatre, a restaurant and, of course, Santa Claus himself. The most intriguing section is the gallery of ice sculpture. It's great fun for kids in winter but lacks a bit of atmosphere in the summer season (though it's cheaper). Tickets are valid for two days. Buses between Rovaniemi and Napapiiri stop here.

WESTERN LAPLAND

Kemi

▣ 016 / POP 22,290

Kemi is an industrial town and important deepwater harbour. Though only the gem museum and wide waterfront have much appeal in summer, it's home to two of Finland's blockbuster winter attractions.

◉ Sights & Activities

★**Lumilinna**   SNOW CASTLE
(Snow Castle; ▣ 016-258-878; www.visitkemi.fi; adult/child €15/7.50; ◔ 10am-6pm late Jan-early Apr) Of all the marvels under the big sky, few things conjure the fairy-tale romance of a snow castle. First built in 1996 as a Unicef project, the castle is a Lapland winter highlight and favoured destination for weddings, honeymoons, or general marvelling at the weird light and sumptuously realised decoration of the interior. The design changes every year but always includes an ethereally beautiful chapel, a **snow hotel**, an ice bar and a **restaurant** (menus €43 to €50; must be prebooked).

Jalokivigalleria   MUSEUM
(www.kemi.fi/gemstonegallery; Kauppakatu 29; adult/child €10/5; ◔ 9.30am-4pm Mon-Fri late Aug-late Jun, 9.30am-4pm Tue-Sat late Jun-late Aug) The Gemstone Gallery, in an old seaside customs house, has a notable collection of more than 3000 beautiful, rare stones and jewellery. Sheets in various languages guide you in an offbeat manner around the exhibits, which include replicas of famous diamonds and a solid dose of Finnish humour.

Sampo   CRUISE
(▣ 016-258-878; www.visitkemi.fi; 4hr cruises €270; ◔ mid-Dec–mid-Apr) This retired icebreaker runs memorable, though overpriced, excursions. The four-hour cruise includes a meal and ice-swimming in special drysuits. For extra cost you can choose to approach and leave the ship on snowmobiles (reindeer visit included). The best experience is when the ice is thickest, usually March. Book well in advance. Note that kids under 12 aren't allowed to do the ice-swimming part. Departures are from Ajos Harbour, 11km south of Kemi; transportation costs extra. The *Sampo* is out to pasture here in summer (late June to late August). You can visit the boat (€10; 10am to 2pm) but it's just not the same without the crunching of the ice.

🛏 Sleeping & Eating

In summer the best place for a drink and a snack is down by the water, where old wooden warehouses and a boat bar make lively and picturesque places to eat and drink.

Hotelli Palomestari   HOTEL €€
(▣ 016-257-117; www.hotellipalomestari.com; Valtakatu 12; s/d €94/129; ▣ 🛜) The 'fire chief' is a block south and one west of the train and bus stations on a pedestrian street, and offers friendly service and decent rooms with trademark Finnish furniture, including a desk and sofa. There's also a bar downstairs with outside seating. It's significantly better value on weekends and in summer.

★**Lumihotelli**   ICE HOTEL €€€
(▣ 016-258-878;   www.visitkemi.fi;   s/d/ste €190/320/350; ◔ late Jan-early Apr; ▣) The snow hotel's interior temperature is -5°C, but a woolly sheepskin and sturdy sleeping bag keep you warm(ish) atop the ice bed. There are also 'Olokolo' sleeping pods with a transparent ceiling for aurora-watching. In the morning you can thaw out in the sauna of a nearby hotel. It's cheaper midweek.

❶ Information

Tourist Office (▣ 040-680-3120; www.visit kemi.fi; Valtakatu 26; ◔ 8am-3.30pm Mon-Fri) In the town hall. Check out the views from the cafe upstairs in the same building.

❶ Getting There & Around

Kemi-Tornio airport is 6km northwest. Finnair/FlyBe has regular Helsinki flights. Airport taxis cost €20.

Buses run to Tornio (€6.80, 35 minutes) more than hourly (fewer on weekends), Rovaniemi (€20 to €26, 1½ to two hours) and Oulu (€20 to €26, 1¾ hours), among other places.

There are trains from Helsinki (€79 to €85, nine hours), Oulu (€22.50, one hour) and Rovaniemi (€22.30, 1½ hours).

Tornio

🗐 016 / POP 22,530

Right on the impressive Tornionjoki, northern Europe's longest free-flowing river, Tornio is joined to its Swedish counterpart Haparanda by short bridges. Cross-border shopping has boomed here in recent years, with new malls popping up like mushrooms. Note: Finland is an hour ahead of Sweden.

◉ Sights

Aineen Taidemuseo GALLERY
(www.tornio.fi/aine; Torikatu 2; adult/child €4/free; ⊙11am-6pm Tue-Thu, 11am-3pm Fri-Sun) The attractive modern Tornio gallery comprises the private collection of Veli Aine, a local business tycoon. It displays Finnish art from the 19th and 20th centuries, and has decent temporary exhibitions and a good cafe.

Tornionlaakson Maakuntamuseo MUSEUM
(www.tornio.fi/museo; Keskikatu 22; adult/child €5/3; ⊙11am-6pm Tue-Thu, 11am-3pm Fri-Sun) The local historical museum has an interesting, recently renovated collection of old artefacts and costumes.

Tornion Kirkko CHURCH
(www.tornio.seurakunta.net; Seminaarinkatu; ⊙10am-6pm Mon-Fri, 1.30-6pm Sat & Sun Jun-Jul, 10am-5pm Mon-Fri Aug) Completed in 1686, this is one of Finland's more beautiful wooden churches.

✻ Activities

The tourist office can book trips and handles fishing permits; there are several excellent spots along the Tornionjoki. River-rafting is popular in summer on the Kukkolankoski rapids north of town.

Pohjolan Safarit/Nordic Safaris RAFTING, WINTER
(☑0400-692-301; www.pohjolansafarit.fi) Rafting on the Tornionjoki, using inflatable rubber rafts or traditional wooden boats. In winter it runs snowmobile, husky and reindeer trips.

Green Zone Golf Course GOLF
(☑016-431-711; www.torniogolf.fi; Näräntie; green fee €45; ⊙9am-8pm May-Oct, 8am-10pm late Jun-late Jul) This course straddles Finland and Sweden, allowing you to fire shots into a different country and time zone. There are various group discounts; there's also a driving range and pitch 'n' putt course (adult/child €10/5).

OFF THE BEATEN TRACK

EXPLORING THE ARCHIPELAGO

Off the Kemi/Tornio coast, **Perämeri National Park** is an archipelago of small islands that's an important conservation area for seals and a richly populated bird habitat. You'll need a boat (or snowmobile) to explore; ask at the Kemi or Tornio tourist office about renting one.

⌁ Sleeping

There's a better choice of accommodation across the border in Haparanda, where the **Stadshotell** (☑0922-614 90; www.haparanda stadshotell.se; Torget 7; s/d Skr1375/1610; P🛜) and a couple of hostels offer good accommodation on the main square.

Camping Tornio CAMPGROUND €
(☑016-445-945; www.campingtornio.com; Matkailijantie 9; tent sites €12 plus per adult/child €4/2, cabins €38-52; ⊙May-Sep; P🛜) About 3km from the town centre, off the road to Kemi, in a very pleasant grassy riverside location. It offers boat and bike hire, tennis and a beach.

Kaupunginhotelli HOTEL €€
(☑0400-105-800; www.tch.fi; Itäranta 4; s/d €116/131; P@🛜▧) Tornio's only hotel could do with an injection of cash, optimism or both, but has decent facilities. Rooms are spacious with natural light but the furniture would benefit from a refit. In July and on weekends a room is €98.

E-City GUESTHOUSE €€
(☑044-509-0358; www.ecity.fi; Saarenpäänkatu 39; s/d €75/90, without bathroom €60/75; P🛜) This friendly, clean but no-frills guesthouse is a 15-minute walk from central Tornio near the river. Some things could do with a tweak, but the comfortable, colourful rooms are fine. Shared bathrooms have decent showers, and breakfast includes traditional Finnish porridge.

✕ Eating

There is little eating choice. In Haparanda, the Stadshotell has a quality restaurant.

Umpitunneli PUB FOOD €€
(www.umpitunneli.fi; Hallituskatu 15; mains €13-22; ⊙food 3-10pm Mon-Fri, 1-10pm Sat, 1-8pm Sun; 🛜) The 'Dead-End Tunnel' may be a road to nowhere but it's a most enjoyable one, with a huge terrace, and large plates of food, from

creamy pastas to steaks and Tex-Mex. There are often live bands.

ℹ Information

Tourist Office (☑ 050-590-0562; www.haparandatornio.com; Krannigatan 5; ☺ 9am-5pm Mon-Fri mid-Aug–May, 9am-7pm Mon-Fri, 10am-4pm Sat, 11am-5pm Sun Jun–mid-Aug; ☜) Tourist office for both towns in the Tornio-Haparanda bus station. These are the Finnish hours, though it's technically in Sweden.

ℹ Getting There & Away

Kemi-Tornio airport is 18km east of town, and there are regular flights to/from Helsinki. Buses drop off a kilometre away, or it's a €35 taxi.

From the shared Tornio-Haparanda bus station, there are a couple of direct services to Rovaniemi, but you usually must change (to bus or train) in Kemi (€6.80, 35 minutes, more than hourly, less on weekends). Swedish buses run to Luleå, from where buses and trains run to other Swedish destinations.

Ylläs

☑ 016

Thirty-five kilometres northeast of Kolari, **Ylläs** (www.yllas.fi) is Finland's highest skiable fell and Lapland's second-biggest ski resort. On either side of the mountain are the villages **Äkäslompolo**, prettily set by a lake, and smaller **Ylläsjärvi**. Both are typical ski-resort towns with top-end hotels, holiday cottages, charter flights and winter activities. They shut down substantially in summer, when reindeer roam with impunity. Both villages are about 5km from their respective slopes. The Ylläs area is enticing for hiking.

◉ Sights & Activities

Äkäslompolo's remarkable modern wooden church is worth a look.

Kellokas   NATURE CENTRE
(☑ 020-564-7039; www.outdoors.fi; Tunturintie 54; ☺ 9am-4pm Mon-Fri Nov-May, plus Sat & Sun at busy times, 9am-5pm daily Jun-Oct) At the foot of the fell's western slopes, 2.5km from Äkäslompolo, this has a good downstairs exhibition on the local environment and way of life, as well as a cafe, maps, tourist information and advice on hiking in the park.

Skiing & Snowboarding
Ylläs has 63 downhill slopes and 28 lifts, including special areas for snowboarders. The vertical drop is 463m and the longest

run is 3km. Cross-country skiing trails total 250km. **Lift passes** cost €40/194 per day/week; equipment hire and lessons available.

Mountain Biking
In summer Ylläs is popular with mountain bikers, and you can take your bike up in the **gondola lift** (www.yllas.fi; single/day €8/25; ☺ late Jun-Sep) to the top of the downhill trails (430m vertical descent). **Sport Shop** (www.sportresortyllas.com; ☺ 11am-5pm late Jun-Aug, 10am-4pm Sep & 10am-5pm late Nov-Apr), in the Taiga building at the base of the lifts on the Ylläsjärvi side, rents bikes of all types (€15 to €30 per day).

Hiking
There are excellent hiking possibilities in this underrated area. Check the Pallas-Yllästunturi pages on www.outdoors.fi for a list. A couple of long-distance treks head to Olos or Levi (54km and 50km); there are several shorter trails including the 12km **Kiirunankieppi (Ptarmigan Trail)** from the Kellokas nature centre. Longer routes lead all the way to Pallastunturi (72km) and from there to Hetta.

☞ Tours

Various tour operators cluster in Äkäslompolo along the road near the Ylläskaltio hotel. Most are open only in winter, and offer snowmobiling, reindeer safaris, snowshoeing and husky treks.

🛏 Sleeping & Eating

Most accommodation is shut in summer, but there are plenty of cottages around. **Destination Lapland** (☑ 016-510-3300; www.destinationlapland.com) is the major booker. A couple of the larger hotels stay open, offering summer rooms for around €85 a twin.

Hotel Ylläshumina   HOTEL €€€
(☑ 020-719-9820; www.yllashumina.com; Tiurajärventie; s/d €137/173, 2-/4-person apt €215/295; ☺ mid-Aug–Sep & early Nov–mid-Apr; P ☜) In Äkäslompolo, near the lake, this complex boasts flamboyant wooden architecture. There's full ski service, and the sauna and occasional outdoor hot tub are great after a day on the slopes. There are apartments, but even standard rooms, set in separate raised buildings, fit a whole family, with a loft sleeping area and kitchenette. It's considerably cheaper in low season. There's a pub and good restaurant serving buffet meals as well as upmarket set menus.

Lainio Snow Village ICE HOTEL €€€

(☑ 040-416-7227; www.snowvillage.fi; Lainiotie; s/d/ste €180/240/320; ☺ mid-Dec–mid-Apr; P) Between Ylläsjärvi and Kittilä, this ice hotel is built every winter. It's a spectacular complex of buildings including an ice bar in a huge igloo, and sumptuous rooms where you sleep in heavy-duty sleeping bags atop your icy bed. You can visit the complex for €10/5 per adult/child.

❶ Getting There & Away

During the ski season, a shuttle heads from Kittilä airport to Ylläsjärvi (€21) and Äkäslompolo (€24). Book at www.yllasexpress.fi. The nearest train station is in Kolari and there are connecting buses to Ylläsjärvi and Äkäslompolo in the ski season.

Levi (Sirkka)

☑ 016

One of Finland's most popular ski resorts, Levi's compact centre, top-shelf modern facilities and large accommodation capacity mean it hosts many high-profile winter events; it's also a very popular destination for *ruska* (autumn leaves) season hiking. There's enough going on here in summer that it's not moribund, and great deals on smart modern apartments make this a tempting base for exploring western Lapland, particularly for families. Levi is actually the name of the fell, while Sirkka is the village, but most people refer to the whole place as Levi. The ski season runs from November to May; in December overseas charter flights descend, bringing families in search of reindeer and a white Christmas.

⊙ Sights

Samiland MUSEUM

(www.samiland.fi; Tunturitie 205; adult/child €10/7; ☺ 10am-8pm) Attached to the Levi Panorama hotel at the top of the main ski lift, this museum gives plenty of good multilingual information on the Sámi, including details about their traditional beliefs and reindeer herding, accompanied by excellent past and present photographs. Outdoors on the hillside is a collection of traditional *kota* huts and storage platforms.

🏃 Activities

Skiing & Snowboarding

Levitunturi SNOW SPORTS

(www.levi.fi) The ski resort has 43 downhill slopes, many lit, and 27 lifts. The vertical drop is 325m, and the longest run 2.5km. There are two half-pipes and a superpipe for snowboarders, a snow park, and several runs and free lifts for children. High-season lift tickets cost €41/195 per day/week. Equipment hire and lessons are available. Cross-country skiing is also good, with hundreds of kilometres of trails, some illuminated. On longer ski-treks, you can overnight in wilderness huts.

Other Activities

In winter there's a full complement of snowy activities from husky, reindeer and snowmobile short trips or safaris to snowshoe-ing and ice-fishing. In summer canoeing on the Ounasjoki is deservedly popular, as is the mountain-biking park (www.levi.fi; ☺ mid-Jun–Sep) on the ski slopes: there are decent rigs available for hire and you can take your bike up in the gondola lift; the gravity trails have a drop of 310m. There's also a golf course and horse riding. The tourist office can book most activities. There's a free bike scheme in summer: sign up and ride away.

Lapland Safaris WINTER

(☑ 016-654-222; www.laplandsafaris.com; Keskuskuja 2) A full range of winter excursions. Closed summer.

PerheSafarit SUMMER, WINTER

(☑ 016-643-861; www.perhesafarit.fi; Leviraitti 1) Snowmobile and motor-sled excursions in winter and Ounasjoki canoeing in summer.

Polar Speed DOG-SLEDDING

(☑ 040-570-6572; www.polarspeed.fi) Single or multiday dog-sledding safaris with accommodation in wilderness huts. In summer visit the dogs in Köngäs, 10km northeast.

🛏 Sleeping

Levi is one of Finland's most popular winter holiday centres: prices go through the roof in the peak season of December, and from February to May. Virtually the whole town consists of holiday apartments and cottages. They typically sleep four to six, with a sauna, a fully equipped kitchen and many other mod cons. In summer they are a real bargain, costing €45 to €60 per night; in winter €1100 a week is average. Levin Matkailu Keskusvaraamo (☑ 0600-550-134; www.levi. fi; ☺ 9am-4.30pm Mon-Fri, 11am-4pm Sat & Sun Sep-May, 9am-7pm Mon-Fri, 11am-4pm Sat & Sun Jun-Aug), in the tourist office, is the place to book these.

Hullu Poro Hostel HOSTEL **€**

(☑016-651-0100; www.hulluporo.fi; Sivulantie 2; dm winter/summer €30/20; Ⓟ) A well-equipped budget option, this staffless choice occupies an apartment complex and offers rooms that have two single beds and a funky desk; they share a decent bathroom, pleasant lounge area and proper kitchen between two. It's a better option if you've got transport, as you must check in and out at Hullu Poro hotel, 2km down the road. HI discount.

Hullu Poro HOTEL **€€**

(☑016-651-0100; www.hulluporo.fi; Rakkavaarantie 5; d summer/winter from €78/120; Ⓟ@🛜) The friendly, informal 'Crazy Reindeer' is an enormous complex that has every kind of room you can imagine, with family suites, apartments and rooms with private sauna; there are various restaurants and a spa complex. It's a lot cheaper in summer.

★Levi Panorama HOTEL **€€€**

(☑016-336-3000; www.levipanorama.fi; Tunturitie 205; s/d winter €144/177, summer €80/89, superior d summer €97/105, winter €160/193; ⊗ Jun-Apr; Ⓟ@🛜) Halfway up the slopes, with a great ski-in-ski-out area downstairs, this stylish hotel has brilliant rooms with lots of space, modish furniture, big photos of Lapland wildlife and views over the pistes. Superiors add a balcony but most look the other way. The bar has a sensational outlook. You can nip up and down to town on the gondola. It's top value in summer.

K5 Levi HOTEL **€€€**

(☑016-639-1100; www.k5levi.fi; Kätkänrannantie 2; s/d €151/174, r summer €94; ⊗Nov–mid-Aug; Ⓟ@🛜) Right opposite the tourist office, this sleek, modern hotel has excellent rooms; most come with sauna and glassed-in balcony, or otherwise a Jacuzzi. There are also good family rooms and classy holiday apartments. Numerous facilities include drying cupboards in all the rooms and a gym.

Golden Crown IGLOO **€€€**

(☑044-056-6334; www.leviniglut.fi; igloos €325-550; Ⓟ🛜) These perspex igloos with kitchenette and bathroom are on the side of the fell. The beds are motorised so you move around while skywatching. Once you're paying these outrageous prices, you might as well upgrade to the premium ones in the front row. There's also a luxury house with large apartment suites.

❶ KITTILÄ

One of northwestern Lapland's main service centres, Kittilä is the gateway for the ski resorts of Ylläs and Levi. Although Kittilä is the regional centre, Levi is now, in fact, so popular, that their roles have been effectively reversed. Daily flights operate between Helsinki and Kittilä, as do winter charters from the UK and elsewhere. The airport is 4km north of Kittilä. Four to five daily buses run between Rovaniemi and Kittilä (€31.40, two hours). All continue to Levi.

✖ Eating & Drinking

Most eating and drinking options centre on the big hotels, which have multiple bars, restaurants and nightclubs. Most open only during the ski and autumn *ruska* seasons.

Panimo & Pub FINNISH **€€**

(www.levinpanimo.fi; Levinraitti 1; mains €15-27; ⊗food 1-11pm; 🛜) The atmospherically candlelit downstairs Kellari restaurant does very tasty Lappish meals; meat dishes are stronger than fish. The Lapland tapas plate has some standout flavours. Upstairs, pints of homebrew and a terrace that catches the evening sun are reasons to linger.

❶ Information

Tourist Office (☑0600-550-134; www.levi.fi; Myllyjoentie 2; ⊗9am-4.30pm Mon-Fri, 11am-4pm Sat & Sun Sep-May, 9am-7pm Mon-Fri, 11am-4pm Sat & Sun Jun-Aug; 🛜) Behind the tepee-like building on the roundabout in the centre of the resort. The main accommodation booking agency is also here, and staff can book activities such as snowmobile safaris, dog-sled treks and reindeer rides.

❶ Getting There & Around

Levi is on Rd 79, 170km north of Rovaniemi. All buses from Rovaniemi to Kittilä continue on to here, some continuing to Muonio. A bus meets all incoming flights at Kittilä airport, 15km to the south. Major car-hire franchises are at Kittilä airport; they will deliver to Levi free of charge.

Muonio

☑016

The last significant stop on Rd 21 before Kilpisjärvi and Norway, Muonio sits on the scenic Muonionjoki that forms the border between Finland and Sweden. It's a fine base for summer and winter activities, including low-key skiing at nearby Olos. Most of the town was razed during WWII, but the 1817 wooden church escaped that fate.

🏃 Activities

★Harriniva   OUTDOORS
(📞0400-155-100; www.harriniva.fi; Harrinivantie 35) Three kilometres south of town, this excellent set-up has a vast program of summer and winter activities, ranging from short jaunts to multiday adventures. In summer these include canoe and boat trips and fishing on the salmon-packed Muonionjoki. In winter wonderful dog-sledding safaris run from 1½ hours (€90) to two days (€580), or a week or more, perhaps adding reindeer-sledding and snowmobiling to the mix. Harriniva has the **Arktinen Rekikoirakeskus** (Arctic sled-dog centre) with around 450 lovable dogs, all with names. A great guided tour of their town costs €7/4 per adult/child. There are two departures daily. You can also hire bikes, boats and rods here.

🍴 Sleeping & Eating

Lomamaja Pekonen   GUESTHOUSE €
(📞040-550-8436; www.lomamajapekonen.fi; Lahenrannantie 10; s/d €45/60, cabins €40-50, cottages €75-95; 🅿🛜) In the centre of town, this appealing spot has wee red wooden cabins running up a slope just across from the Muonionjoki, and more upmarket apartments and cottages behind them. There's space for vans but not tents. It has canoes, fishing equipment and bikes for hire, and organises guided trips on the river in summer.

Harriniva   HOTEL, CAMPGROUND €€
(📞0400-155-100; www.harriniva.fi; Harrinivantie 35; s/d summer €80/90, winter €125/145, cabins d/q €38/50, tent sites €10 plus per adult/child €4/2; 🅿🍽🛜) Three kilometres south of town, this great place has a wide range of accommodation. The hotel rooms are simple but attractively done and have plenty of space – some come with their own sauna. There are also apartments, cottages, cabins by the river and camping space. The restaurant is the best place to eat in the area.

Swiss Cafe Konditoria   CAFE €
(www.swisscafemuonio.com; Puthaanrannantie 5; cakes €2-6; ⏱10am-5pm; 🛜) A top coffee stop, with delicious lattes and hot chocolate. It's also worth dropping in for the owner's excellent baking and his fantastic Lapland photographs on display.

ℹ Information

Kiela (📞0400-175-225; www.tunturi-lappi.fi; Valtatie 21; ⏱10am-6pm; 🛜) This nature centre has a gift shop, a Thai cafe, slow free internet, and a free 15-minute aurora borealis audiovisual.

ℹ Getting There & Away

Muonio is at the junction of western Lapland's main two roads: Rd 21, which runs from Tornio to Kilpisjärvi, and Rd 79, which runs northwest from Rovaniemi via Kittilä.

There are three daily buses from Rovaniemi (€43.90, 3½ hours) via Kittilä, and services from Kemi/Tornio changing at Kolari.

Hetta (Enontekiö)
🔲 016 / POP 1880

The village of Hetta, usually signposted as Enontekiö (the name of the municipal district) is an important Sámi town and a good place to start trekking and exploring the area. Though a bit spread out, it makes a good stop for a night or two. It's also the northern end of the popular Hetta–Pallastunturi Trek.

◎ Sights & Activities

Hetan Lumilinna   SNOW CASTLE
(📞040-127-1565; www.hettasafaris.com; visit per person incl sledge transport €20; ⏱Dec-Apr) This snow castle near the airport can be visited by appointment. There are various packages including a night's accommodation (single/double €149/220).

Skierri   NATURE CENTRE
(📞020-564-7950; www.outdoors.fi; Peuratie 15; ⏱9am-5pm Mar-Apr & Jun-late Sep, 9am-4pm Mon-Fri late-Sep–Feb & May) This nature centre at the eastern end of town provides information about Pallas-Yllästunturi National Park and the Enontekiö region. There's a smart exhibition on the Sámi and their nomadic history, and lots of audiovisuals, as well as nature displays on the park and a cafe.

Hetta Huskies   DOG-SLEDDING
(CAPE Lapland; 📞050-577-2762; www.hettahuskies.com; Hetantie 211; 2km/all-day safari €35/199) Based just west of town, these folk run reliably good husky-sledding excursions, from a 2km introduction to multiday explorations. You can meet the dogs any time of year (€8 to €10) and go hiking with a posse of them.

Hetta Hiihtomaa
SNOW SPORTS
(www.hettahiihtomaa.fi; Peuratie 23; 1-day lift pass €25) Hetta's small ski resort has two slopes as well as sledding, cross-country-skiing and snowshoe routes.

✦✦ Festivals & Events

Marianpäivät
RELIGIOUS
(www.marianpaivat.fi) Hetta's big festival is held over three days around the feast day of the Annunciation (late March); there are Sámi dances and parties, and the town buzzes with a lot of activity.

🛏 Sleeping & Eating

Hetan Majatalo
GUESTHOUSE €
(☑016-554-0400; www.hetan-majatalo.fi; Rie-kontie 8; s/d hotel €68/94, guesthouse €42/68; P@🗟) In the centre of town, but set back in its own garden away from the road, this welcoming pad offers two types of accommodation in facing buildings: clean and simple guesthouse rooms sharing bathrooms, and very handsome and spacious wood-clad hotel rooms, some sleeping six. It's an excellent deal that includes good breakfast and sauna.

Hetan Lomakylä
CAMPGROUND €
(☑0400-205-408; www.hetanlomakyla.fi; Ounastie 23; tent sites €13 plus per adult/child €4/2, cabins €30-50, cottages €65-100; ☉Mar-Oct; P🗟) Just near the junction of the westbound and northbound roads 2km from the town centre, this has grassy tent pitches and smart painted wooden cabins and cottages. The latter come with kitchen, sauna and a loft sleeping area. There are various discounts and activities on offer.

★ **Ounasloma**
COTTAGE €€
(☑016-521-055; www.ounasloma.fi; Ounastie 1; cottages €56 plus per person €12; P@🗟) This friendly family-run place has a series of excellent wooden cottages in a well-kept area with a river and a lake beach. The standard cottages are great for families, and there are bigger ones suitable for large groups. Some have an open fireplace. They are slightly more expensive in winter. Boats, bikes and sledges are free to use. In winter it runs snowmobile safaris, ice-fishing, and trips in an unusual heated sledge-bus.

Hotelli Hetta
HOTEL €€
(☑016-323-700; www.laplandhotels.com; Ounastie 281; hostel s/d winter €132/149, summer €70/85; P@🗟🏊) At the eastern end of town, Hetta feels old-fashioned but has good facilities and bland but spacious renovated rooms – the ones facing the lake have a much nicer outlook. There are also cheaper 'hostel' rooms that have their own toilet but shared shower. The restaurant opens for dinner and offers good, well-presented meals involving reindeer, char and other Lapland staples. The hotel is closed October, November and most of May.

🛍 Shopping

Hetta Silver
JEWELLERY
(www.hettasilver.com; Ruijantie 15; ☉10am-5pm Mon-Fri) ✎ At the junction of the westbound and northbound roads, this is a local silversmith's workshop.

ℹ Information

Head to Skierri nature centre for information on the national park and trekking routes.
Tourist Information (www.tosilappi.fi; Ounastie 165; ☉9am-4.45pm Mon-Fri) In the municipal building on the main road.

ℹ Getting There & Away

The airport, mainly used for winter charters, is 7km west.

Buses head out to the main road to Rovaniemi (€56.90, five hours) and Kilpisjärvi (€31.10, 3¼ hours) via a swap-over at Palojoensuu. There are also buses to Hetta from Muonio.

Pallas-Yllästunturi National Park

☑016

Finland's third-largest national park forms a long, thin area running from Hetta in the north to the Ylläs ski area in the south. The main attraction is the excellent 55km trekking route from the village of Hetta to Pallastunturi in the middle of the park, where there's a hotel, the Pallastunturi Luontokeskus nature centre and transport connections. You can continue from here to Ylläs, although there are few facilities on that section. In winter Pallastunturi fell is a small but popular place for both cross-country and downhill skiing.

🐾 Activities

Trekking
The 55km **trek/ski from Hetta to Pallastunturi** (or vice versa) is a Lapland classic and offers some of the best views in the country from the top of the fells. While

there's plenty of up and down, it's not a difficult route, though long stretches of it are quite exposed to wind and rain; pack weatherproof gear. The route is well marked, and there are several wilderness huts along the way. The popularity of the trek means huts get pretty crowded at peak times. See www.outdoors.fi for the route and wilderness huts.

The Hetta trailheads are separated from town by the lake. Various operators in town will run you across (around €10). Some can also drive your car to Pallastunturi while you are doing the trek (around €80). One such operator is **Paavontalo** (☑0405-765-721). If going the other way, there's a list of boat operators to phone when you reach the lake.

From Pallastunturi you can extend your trek a further 72km to the park's southernmost border, by the ski resorts at Ylläs.

⏨ Sleeping

Hotelli Pallas   HOTEL €€
(☑016-323-355; www.laplandhotels.com; Pallastunturi; s/d winter €104/131, summer €78/92; ☺Dec–late Sep; ℗☎) This old wooden place up in the fells is just what a weary trekker from Hetta wants to see. It's in need of a refit – rooms are plain with lino floors – but the natural setting is wonderful. Cheaper rooms have toilet but share a shower. There's skiing right alongside, a lakeside sauna (with winter ice-hole) and walks on the doorstep. Hikers can pay to shower here.

❶ Information

Pallastunturi Luontokeskus (☑020-564-7930; www.outdoors.fi; ☺9am-5pm Jun-Sep & mid-Feb–Apr, 9am-4pm Mon-Fri rest of year) This nature centre at Pallastunturi fell sells trekking maps, makes reservations for locked huts (€11 per person), and provides information and advice about the region. The Hetta route leaves from here; good shorter walks include a 9km loop across the tops of Taivaskero and Laukukero. Skierri nature centre (p242) in Hetta also has keys for the lockable huts.

❶ Getting There & Away

A morning bus runs Monday to Friday from Muonio (€9.30, 40 minutes) to Kittilä via Pallastunturi. In summer the return bus stops here in the afternoon. At other times, there are a couple of weekly Muonio services plus one on Thursday to Hetta. Otherwise, you'll have to hitch or call a local taxi on ☑016-538-582.

Kilpisjärvi
☑016

The remote village of Kilpisjärvi, the northernmost settlement in the 'arm' of Finland, has a memorable setting among lakes and snowy mountains on the doorstep of both Norway and Sweden. At 480m, this small border post, wedged between the lake of Kilpisjärvi and the magnificent surrounding fells, is also the highest village in Finland. Unless you're on your way to Norway, the main reason to venture out here is for brilliant summer trekking or spring cross-country skiing. Kilpisjärvi consists of two small settlements 5km apart – the main (southern) centre has most services, the northern knot, 2km shy of the Norwegian border, has the hiking centre and trailheads.

⚑ Activities

Hiking

The Kilpisjärvi area offers fantastic long and short hikes. All trekking routes and wilderness huts around the Kilpisjärvi area are clearly displayed on the 1:100,000 Halti Kilpisjärvi map. See also www.outdoors.fi.

Saana   HIKING
From the Retkeilykeskus, the ascent to slate-capped Saana Fell (1029m) begins with a gentle climb through woodland ending abruptly in a thigh-straining 742 wooden steps up the steeper part. From the top, it's an easier gradient up the angled slate cap to the highest point. When you come down, you can continue right around the base of the fell to make a long loop trail (10km plus the ascent/descent of 3km each way).

Kolmen Valtakunnan Raja   HIKING
(Treble Border Marker) This route heads through Malla Nature Park to a concrete block in a lake that marks the treble border of Finland, Sweden and Norway. From the carpark 2.5km north of the Retkeilykeskus, it is 11km, with a climb through birch forest rewarded with an easy but spectacular route along the hillside, with great lake views.

A summer **boat service** (☑0400-669-392; www.kilpisjarvi.org; single/return €20/25; ☺Jul-late Sep) leaves from below the Retkeilykeskus three times daily, dropping you a 3km stroll from the border marker. This allows an easy visit, or walking one way and cruising the other. Near the border marker is a free wilderness hut for overnighting.

Halti
HIKING

The 50km hike to Halti fell (1328m), the highest point in Finland, is a rewarding, reasonably well-marked trip. There are several wilderness cabins along the route with reservable sections. You can get close to it by road through Norway.

Scenic Flights

There's a heliport and float-plane dock at the southern end of Kilpisjärvi. Sightseeing flights cost €200 to €250 for a spin around Saana and the treble border, or €450 to €600 for flights around Halti. For information, call **Polar-Lento** (☑ 0400-396-087; www.harriniva.fi) for float-planes, or **Heliflite** (☑ 0400-155-111; www.heliflite.fi) for choppers.

🛏 Sleeping & Eating

Lining the main road are several campsites with cabins. Many places are only open during the trekking season, which is mid-June to September. As well as the hotel and Retkeilykeskus, several of the cabin complexes have their own cafe-restaurant, usually only open during the day.

Tundrea
COTTAGE €€

(Kilpisjärven Lomakeskus; ☑ 0400-396-684; www.tundrea.fi; Käsivarrentie 14188; 2-/4-person apt €89/108, cottage €109/138; P 🐾) This is the best of the clutch of cabin complexes in the centre of Kilpisjärvi. It has a decent restaurant (open June to September), and excellent wooden cottages and apartments with their own sauna, loft bedroom and a fully equipped kitchen. Prices rise in the April and September high seasons.

Kilpisjärven Retkeilykeskus
GUESTHOUSE, CABINS €€

(Kilpisjärvi Hiking Centre; ☑ 040-778-9445; www.kilpisjarvi.info; Käsivarrentie 14663; tent sites €12 plus €4/2 per adult/child, s/d €65/75, 2/4-person cottages €82/92; ⊘ mid-Mar–early May & early Jun-late Sep; P 🐾) Five kilometres north of the main village, this is conveniently close to the trekking routes and the Malla boat. You'll find a range of rooms and cottages here, all with bathroom. There's camping too. The no-frills restaurant dishes up a good all-you-can-eat buffet lunch daily in the high season (€14; open noon to 9pm) as well as breakfasts (€8) and à la carte dishes. It also hires bikes, hiking and skiing equipment.

Hotelli Kilpis
HOTEL €€

(☑ 016-323-300; www.laplandhotels.com; Käsivarrentie 14206; s/d €94/99, without bathroom €74/85, apt €140-280; ⊘ Mar-Sep; P 🐾) This ageing hotel is in the centre of town. Its rooms are simply appointed but comfortable enough; those that face the car park can be noisy. There's one suite that's worth the upgrade for the view alone. The 'hostel' rooms share bathrooms, and there are also apartments, more modern and stylish than the main hotel. The restaurant (mains €16 to €27; open 5pm to 11pm) is the best around, and serves decent Lapp-style food. The bar is the town's watering hole.

ℹ Information

The petrol station and Kilpisjärven Retkeilykeskus also sell trekking maps.

Kilpisjärven luontokeskus Visitor Centre
(☑ 020-564-7990; www.outdoors.fi; Käsivarrentie 14145; ⊘ 9am-5pm Tue-Sat Mar–mid-May & mid-Jun–Sep, plus 9am-6pm daily Jul; 🐾) At the southern end of the village, this national park centre is effectively the tourist information office. It has maps, advice on trekking and a nature display.

ℹ Getting There & Away

Two daily buses connect Rovaniemi and Kilpisjärvi (€72.90, six to eight hours) via Kittilä, Levi and Muonio, with connection to Hetta. In summer one heads on to Tromsø, Norway.

It's a spectacular drive from Muonio to Kilpisjärvi (196km). There are petrol stations at Kaaresuvanto (where there's a border crossing into Sweden) and Kilpisjärvi itself.

EASTERN LAPLAND

Kemijärvi
☑ 016 / POP 8150

Kemijärvi, situated on north–south Hwy 5, is many people's first glimpse of Lapland. Its location on a spectacular lake and the creations of its sculpture festival are the main attractions. It's a pleasant, quiet town that makes a good stop.

◉ Sights & Activities

Puustelli
GALLERY

(www.kemijarvi.fi; Pöyliöjärventie; admission €5; ⊘ noon-6pm Tue-Sun mid-Jun–Jul) On the western side of town (follow the path past the campsite and keep going), this noble old building displays many of the wooden sculptures from past years of the Kuvanveistoviikko festival. Follow signs for 'Taidekeskus'.

Off-Piste Adventures HORSE RIDING

(☑ 040-963-9807; www.offpisteadventures.com) Runs sleighing excursions pulled by well-loved reindeer or sturdy Finnhorses; you can also ride the latter year-round. Based at Kallela, a farm 10km from town on the Sodankylä road.

☞ Tours

Rautaparta FISHING

(☑ 050-414-1127; www.facebook.com/Rautapar taoy) This couple can take you out fishing on the lakes and organise permits and tackle. They also do longer trips to other parts of Lapland, including the Norwegian coast.

✪ Festivals & Events

Kuvanveistoviikko SCULPTURE

(www.kemijarven-kuvanveistoviikot.fi) This wood-sculpting festival is held in late June or early July every odd-numbered year. It attracts artists from many countries, whom you can watch as they create their works.

Ruska Swing MUSIC

(www.ruskaswing.fi) In early September Kemijärvi hosts this festival of swing music and dancing.

🛏 Sleeping & Eating

Lohen Lomakeskus HOSTEL, COTTAGE €

(☑ 040-581-6772, 040-581-2007; www.lohen lomakeskus.fi; Lohelankatu 1; dm/s/d €30/50/65, cottages €70-125; ℗) Just beyond Camping Kemijärvi, this complex offers various sleeping choices. Cheerful green-roofed wooden cottages come with bathroom, kitchen and sauna, while lakefront apartments are even fancier. In the reception building, wooden bunk rooms offer space and value, and simple private rooms share the same kitchen and bathroom facilities. HI discount. Reception closed between 10am and 5pm. You can hire canoes and bikes here.

Camping Kemijärvi CAMPGROUND €

(☑ 040-778-9106; www.facebook.com/camping-kemijarvi; Hietaniemenkatu 7; tent sites €14 plus per adult/child €5/2; ☉ late May-Aug; ℗@🛜) Very close to the town centre on Pöyliöjärvi, a secondary part of the main lake, this is a friendly grassy campground with not a great deal of privacy if it's full.

Mestarin Kievari HOTEL €€

(☑ 016-320-7700; www.mestarinkievari.fi; Kirkkokatu 9; s/d €88/105; ℗@🛜) Kemijärvi's eating and drinking scene pretty much begins and ends here, and it's also the better of the town's two hotels. It's a welcoming spot with comfortable, fairly unadorned rooms. Some are in a newer wing, while others have private sauna; spacious family rooms with sloping ceilings sit at the top. The restaurant features hearty fare (mains €13 to €28) with a popular lunch buffet (€11.50).

ⓘ Information

Tourist Office (☑ 040-189-2050; www.visit kemijarvi.fi; Vapaudenkatu 8; ☉ 9am-3.30pm Mon-Fri) In the town centre, this is a helpful information desk. It sometimes open weekends in summer.

ⓘ Getting There & Away

There are buses on weekdays to destinations including Pyhä (€11.80, one hour), Rovaniemi (€17.30, 1¼ hours, also some Sundays) and Sodankylä (€20.40, 1¾ hours). There's one daily train to Helsinki, via Rovaniemi (€15.50, 1½ hours).

Pyhä-Luosto

☑ 016

The area between the fells of Luosto (514m) and Pyhä (540m) forms a popular winter sports centre. Most forms part of Pyhä-Luosto National Park, excellent for trekking. Pyhä and Luosto both have ski slopes and are fully serviced resort 'villages'. They make value-packed, if quiet, places to stay in summer with bargain modern apartments and log cottages available. Pyhä is about 14km from the main Kemijärvi–Sodankylä road, while Luosto is the same distance east of the Rovaniemi–Sodankylä road. A good road connects the two resorts, 25km apart.

◉ Sights & Activities

Lampivaara MINE

(☑ 016-465-3530; www.amethystmine.fi; adult/child €14.50/8, in winter €25/10; ☉ 11am-5pm Jun–mid-Aug, 11am-4pm mid-Aug–Sep, 11am-3pm Tue-Sat Oct, 11am-2pm Mon-Sat Dec–mid-Apr) Five kilometres above Luosto, this amethyst mine focuses on small-scale production for jewellery, using low-impact mining methods. There are guided tours (English available) on the hour, and you get to have a dig around for your own piece of amethyst. The mine is a 30-minute walk from Ukko-Luosto parking; you're meant to get a cab there if you don't fancy the stroll. In winter go on skis, or use the snow train from Ukko-

Luosto parking (including admission adult/child €49/20, from Luosto €59/25).

Kopara REINDEER
(✆ 040-840-9199; www.kopara.fi; Luostontie 1160; ☺ 11am-3pm Mon-Fri early Jun-Sep, 11am-4pm Jan-Apr) More or less midway between Pyhä and Luosto, this is a good place to meet some reindeer. You can go on a short walk (€5 per person) that has information boards on the creatures, and tempt them closer with a feed bucket. In winter various sledge trips are on offer (from €30). The friendly cafe has good handicrafts for sale and specialises in blueberry pie in summer and, er, reindeer soup in winter.

Luontokeskus Naava NATURE CENTRE
(✆ 020-564-7302; www.outdoors.fi; Luontotie 1, Pyhä; ☺ 9.30am-5pm or 6pm) By the roundabout in Pyhä, this modern nature centre has a good exhibition on the geology and ecosystem of the area, information on Pyhä-Luosto National Park, and activities such as hiking and fishing. There's a decent cafe too.

Pyhä-Luosto National Park WALKING
(www.outdoors.fi) This park's core is the line of fells stretching 35km from Pyhä to beyond Luosto. It preserves old-growth forest with endangered plant species, the southern Lapland fell ecosystem, and *aapa* (open bog) areas harbouring snipe, bean geese, swans and golden eagles. There are several marked trails, which, together with the resorts' network of ski trails, mean that walkers are well provided for. There are several huts for overnighting.

Pyhätunturi & Luostotunturi SNOW SPORTS
(www.pyha.fi; lift tickets day/week €38/189) At Pyhä there are 14 ski runs and nine lifts. The longest run is 1.8km, with a vertical drop of 280m. At Luosto there are seven runs and three lifts, plus a half-pipe and snowboard slopes. Lift passes here are valid for Ruka too. Between them, Pyhä and Luosto have around 200km of trails for cross-country skiers, some 40km of which are lit. You can hire equipment and get lessons at either location.

⚐ Tours

Lapland Safaris SUMMER, WINTER
(✆ 016-624-336; www.laplandsafaris.com; Orresokantie 1, Luosto) In summer take trips on quad bikes to the amethyst mine or reindeer farm, or head to the river for canoeing and fishing. Winter has similar jaunts on snowmobiles; there are also husky- and reindeer-sledging excursions.

Pyhä Safaris SNOWMOBILE
(✆ 040-778-9106; www.pyhasafaris.com; Pyhäntie 2030, Pyhä) At the Pyhä roundabout, this outfit offers reindeer, husky and snowmobile trips.

🛏 Sleeping & Eating

Hundreds of cottages, cabins and apartments in the Pyhä-Luosto area make great places to stay. The three main agencies are excellent **Pyhähippu** (✆ 016-882-820; www.pyhahippu.fi; Kultakeronkatu 4, Pyhä; ☺ noon-8pm mid-Jun–Sep & Nov-Apr, noon-5pm at other times) by the Pyhä roundabout; **Pyhä Booking** (✆ 08-860-0400; www.booking.pyha.fi; Kultakeronkatu 21, Pyhä) in Hotel Pyhätunturi; and **Pyhä-Luosto Matkailu** (✆ 020-730-3020; www.pyha-luostomatkailu.fi; Laukotie 1, Luosto; ☺ 9am-5pm Mon-Fri) on the main road in Luosto. These offer hundreds of cabins, apartments and cottages that you can book online. For around €60 in summer, you can nab a luxury cottage or apartment for two. Rates increase sharply in winter.

Hotelli Pyhätunturi HOTEL €€
(✆ 040-010-1695; www.ski-inn.fi; Kultakeronkatu 21, Pyhä; r €85-125; ☺ mid-Jun–mid-Sep & mid-Nov–Apr; 🅿 @ 🛜) Pyhä's major hotel sits part-way up the chairlift at the top of the road: you can ski in and out. Rooms are decent value; some have great views, as does the restaurant, romantically candlelit at night. There are also self-contained chalets. A sauna, gym and Jacuzzi will ease those ski-tired muscles. The hotel also rents bikes.

★ Santa's Hotel Aurora HOTEL €€€
(Aurora Chalet; ✆ 0400-102-200; www.hotelaurora.fi; Luppokeino 1, Luosto; d €166-197; ☺ Aug–mid-Apr; 🅿 🛜) At the Luosto slope, this is one of Lapland's most original and stylish hotels and a great winter hideaway. All rooms have their own sauna, and many a wood fire; the wide floorboards, warm colours and romantic design create a whole ambience of great creativity, with an old-fashioned rustic air combined with modern comforts.

Reception will SMS you when the aurora borealis is visible, a nice touch that'll save a few shivers. Its activity company can arrange snowmobiling and more.

Hotelli Luostotunturi HOTEL €€€
(✆ 016-620-400; www.laplandhotels.com; Luostontie 1, Luosto; r summer/winter €97/165; 🅿 @ 🛜 🛍)

The rounded design of this curious hotel is supposed to resemble a reindeer's earmark. Most of the spacious rooms have a log-girt balcony, and some have an extra loft-style sleeping space, ideal for families. Excellent apartments come with kitchenette and sauna. There's a pretty indoor pool and various spa treatments; visitors can pay to use the facilities. Bikes for hire.

Kerttuli FINNISH €€
(016-624-385; www.luoston-kerttuli.fi; Hartsutie 1, Luosto; mains €14-26; 2-9pm Wed-Sat) In the centre of Luosto, this place offers pizzas as well as more intriguing fare such as elk stew, unusual cuts of reindeer, roast meats and risotto in its cosy interior. Portions are generous and the atmosphere excellent.

Getting There & Away
Two daily buses (four in winter) run to/from Rovaniemi to Luosto (€28, 1¾ hours) and Pyhä (€31, 2¼ hours); these are the only buses connecting Pyhä and Luosto (€6, 30 minutes). There are also buses to Pyhä from Kemijärvi and Sodankylä.

Sodankylä
016 / POP 5540
Likeable Sodankylä is the main service centre for one of Europe's least populated areas, with a density of just 0.8 people per sq km. It's at the junction of the main two highways and makes a decent staging post between Rovaniemi and the north; even if you're just passing through, stop to see the wooden church – humble but achingly beautiful. A contrast is provided by the high-tech observatory just outside town, an important collection point of data on the atmosphere and aurora.

Sights

Vanha Kirkko CHURCH
(0400-190-406; 9am-6pm early Jun–mid-Aug, 9am-6pm Fri-Mon late Aug) One of the few buildings in Lapland to survive the Germans' scorched-earth retreat in WWII is this, the region's oldest church, dating to 1689. It stands in a graveyard encircled by a low wooden fence and is noteworthy for its decorative shingles and prominent prong-like standards. The interior is simple and charming, with gnarled wooden benches and pulpit, and a simple altar made from leftover beams. For €20 it can be opened at other times. The stone church nearby was built in 1859.

Alariesto Galleria GALLERY
(www.visitsodankyla.fi; Jäämerentie 3; adult/child €5/3; 9am-5pm Mon-Fri, 10am-4pm Sat & Sun) Above the tourist office, this gallery displays paintings by the famous local artist Andreas Alariesto (1900–89), who depicted traditional Sámi life in an attractive naive style, and also has temporary exhibitions. There are good-value prints for sale.

Festivals & Events
Midnight Sun Film Festival FILM
(www.msff.fi) Dubbed the 'anti-Cannes', this festival in mid-June sees the village's population double with round-the-clock screenings in three venues, often with high-profile directors in attendance. If you can't find a bed, head for Luosto, less than 40km away.

Sleeping & Eating
Camping Sodankylä Nilimella CAMPGROUND €
(016-612-181; www.naturex-ventures.fi; tent sites €8 plus per adult/child €4/2, 2-/4-person cabins €38/54, apt €80-150; Jun-Aug;) Across the river from the town centre, this campground has a sauna and good showers as well as a riverside cafe-bar. Cabins, discreetly angled for privacy, are simple but spacious, with a fridge and camp stove; there are also cottage apartments with their own kitchen and sauna. You can hire bikes here.

Majatalo Kolme Veljestä GUESTHOUSE €
(0400-539-075; www.majatalokolmeveljesta.fi; Ivalontie 1; s/d/tr €48/68/80;) Five hundred metres north of the town centre, this family-run guesthouse has small but spotless rooms with wire storage units and other comfortable Ikea-type furniture. Guests share decent bathrooms and have use of a lounge and kitchen facilities (there's a big supermarket across the road). Price includes breakfast, sauna, tea and coffee.

Hotelli Karhu HOTEL €€
(Hotel Bear Inn; 040-122-8250; www.hotel-bear-inn.com; Lapintie 7; r €105-115;) This central hotel is Sodankylä's best option, offering decent rooms with grey-wood floors and modern bathrooms. Some single rooms come with a cute mini-sauna. The restaurant does OK lunches (€9) and dinners (€15).

THE AURORA BOREALIS

The aurora borealis (Northern Lights), an utterly haunting and exhilarating sight, is often visible to observers above the Arctic Circle, which includes a large portion of Lapland. It's particularly striking during the dark winter; in summer the sun more or less renders it invisible.

The aurora appears as curtains of greenish-white light stretching east to west across the sky for thousands of kilometres. At its lower edge, the aurora typically shades to a crimson-red glow. Hues of blue and violet can also be seen. The lights seem to dance and swirl in the night sky.

These auroral storms, however eerie, are quite natural. They're created when charged particles (protons and electrons) from the sun bombard the earth. These are deflected towards the North and South Poles by the earth's magnetic field. There they hit the earth's outer atmosphere, 100km to 1000km above ground, causing highly charged electrons to collide with molecules of nitrogen and oxygen. The excess energy from these collisions creates the colourful lights.

The ancient inhabitants of Lapland believed it was caused by a giant fox swishing its tail above the Arctic tundra. One of the Finnish words for the aurora is *revontulet* ('fires of the fox').

To see the lights, you'd best have a dark, clear night with high auroral activity. October, November and March are often optimal for this. Then it's a question of waiting patiently outside, preferably between the hours of 9pm and 2am, and seeing if things kick off. If you've got a vehicle, don't bother paying for an aurora-watching trip. There are several useful websites for predicting auroral activity:

Geophysical Institute (www.gi.alaska.edu/AuroraForecast) Change the view to Europe and away you go.

University of Oulu (www.cc.oulu.fi/~thu/Aurora/forecast.html) Finland-based page with links so you can make your own prediction.

Service Aurora (www.aurora-service.eu) Daily and hourly forecasts and text-message notification service.

Päivin Kammari
CAFE **€€**

(www.paivinkammari.fi; Jäämerentie 11; mains €15-29; ⊙10am-9pm Mon-Sat, noon-6pm Sun; 🛜) Cosy and homelike, this is the best eating spot in town with good coffee and streetside seating. It does cheap lunches and tasty à la carte meals with local *muikku* (vendace, or whitefish, a small lake fish) and reindeer.

Drinking & Nightlife

Rooperante
PUB

(www.facebook.com/Rooperante; Jäämerentie 19; ⊙6pm-midnight Sun-Thu, 6pm-2am Fri & Sat) This is Sodankylä's best pub, though, like in any Lapland bar, there are always a few shamblers about.

🛍 Shopping

Taiga Koru
JEWELLERY

(www.taigakoru.fi; Sompiontie 4; ⊙10am-5pm Mon-Fri, 10am-2pm Sat) In the centre of town, this jewellery shop is famous hereabouts for the gold and silver works of goldsmith Seppo Penttinen.

ℹ Information

Tourist Office (☑ 040-746-9776; www.visit sodankyla.fi; Jäämerentie 3; ⊙9am-5pm Mon-Fri 10am-4pm Sat & Sun) At the intersection of the Kemijärvi and Rovaniemi roads. Normally closes weekends in winter.

Getting There & Away

Sodankylä is on the main Rovaniemi–Ivalo road (Rd 4), and Rd 5 from Kemijärvi and Karelia ends here. There are regular buses from Rovaniemi, Ivalo and Kemijärvi. The bus station is on the main road.

Saariselkä
☑ 016

The bustling, touristy village of Saariselkä (Sámi: Suolocielgi), 250km north of the Arctic Circle, makes a great spot to get active from. It's a major winter destination for Christmassy experiences, sled safaris and skiing, and in summer serves as the main base for trekkers heading into the awesome

Saariselkä Wilderness. You could hike for weeks here; there's a good network of huts and marked trails. Saariselkä itself is basically a collection of enormous hotels and holiday cottages, more resort than community, but has plenty of accommodation and shops to stock up on trekking supplies and equipment, and high-quality souvenirs.

🏃 Activities & Tours

Saariselkä is bristling with things to do year-round. Things are most active in winter, with numerous snowy excursions organised by the many companies in town. Husky- and reindeer-sledding are popular, with trips of a couple of hours starting at around €120. Snowmobiling is a little cheaper, and there are combination excursions, as well as multi-day safaris. Snowshoeing, aurora-watching trips and ice-fishing are some other options.

In summer options include visits to Tankavaara (p252), reindeer farms, canoeing on the Tankajoki, fishing, whitewater rafting in Inari, whole-day rafting on the Ivalojoki, and various guided walks. All these can be booked at the tourist information desk within Kiehinen (p251) or via the hotels. The best hiking is in the Saariselkä Wilderness.

See www.saariselka.fi for a list of activities and operators. Most operators offer a complete winter and summer program and can also rent mountain bikes, skis and snowshoes.

Some recommended providers include **Husky & Co** (☑016-667-776; www.saariselka.fi/huskyco), **Lapland Safaris** (☑016-668-901; www.laplandsafaris.com; Riekonlinna hotel, Saariseläntie 13), which rents and sells camping gear, and **LuontoLoma/Pro Safaris** (☑016-668-706; www.luontoloma.fi; Tunturi hotel, Saariseläntie 14).

Skiing

Ski Saariselkä   SNOW SPORTS
(www.skisaariselka.fi; admission day/week €37/132; ⊗mid-Nov–early May) There are 15 downhill slopes served by five lifts; the longest run is 1300m and the vertical drop is 180m. There's also a freestyle park and some 240km of cross-country trails, some lit. Saariselkä is known for snow-kiting; lessons are available.

🛏 Sleeping

Prices in Saariselkä's hotels are highest during the ski season and *ruska* (late August to mid-September). Here, as in other parts of Finland, there are many rural cabins and cottages for rent. Ask at the Kiehinen nature centre, or browse **Lomarengas** (☑030-650-2502; www.lomarengas.fi) . **Saariselän Keskusvaraamo** (☑016-554-0500; www.saariselka.com; Honkapolku 2) is an accommodation service that can organise a wide range of cabins, cottages and apartments in and around the village.

Saariselän Panimo   INN €
(☑016-675-6500; www.saariselanpanimo.fi; Saariseläntie 10; s/d €53/63; P🐾) A friendly village pub offers good accommodation in a variety of buildings in the heart of Saariselkä. Rooms are spacious and warm, with bathroom and comfortable beds; they're an absolute steal in summer. There are also log cabins and apartments with sauna. A simple breakfast is served in winter only.

Santa's Hotel Tunturi   HOTEL €€
(☑016-681-501; www.tunturihotelli.fi; Lutontie 3; s/d standard €128/152, superior €193/229, 2-/4-person apt €204/260; ⊗Jun-Apr; P🐾🛜) Lapland's largest hotel, this complex sprawls across several buildings, including the very appealing Gielas, but hasn't lost sight of its roots as a solid old place with excellent service. There are numerous grades of rooms and apartments (all but the standards come with their own sauna); the most modern are the enticing superiors and junior suites. Prices drop in summer. It's right by the trailhead for the national park.

Holiday Club Saariselkä   SPA HOTEL €€
(☑030-686-6304; www.holidayclubresorts.com; Saariseläntie 7; d winter €150-190, summer €88-108; P@🛜🏊) In the centre of the village, this spa hotel is most family-friendly and a good choice in winter or summer. The rooms are gradually being renovated, so grab one of the new ones (same price), which have comfy chairs, trendy greys and magentas, and a backlit photo of old Lapland.

Nonguests can use the spa facilities (adult/child €18/12) or Angry Birds theme park. The pool's usually shut for a couple of weeks from May to June.

🍴 Eating & Drinking

Most restaurants close in summer, but hotels all keep one open. The Saariselän Panimo brews its own beer and is a cosy, welcoming spot for a drink.

Pirkon Pirtti   FINNISH €€
(☑016-668-060; www.pirkonpirtti.fi; Honkapolku 2; mains €17-26; ⊗3-11pm Tue-Sat late Jun-Apr) One of the few summer options, this has a

cosy wooden interior and welcoming service. It serves well-presented and generous portions of fish, reindeer and steaks, as well as tasty pizzas.

Laanilan Kievari   FINNISH €€
(☑040-023-9868; www.laanilankievari.fi; Rovaniementie 3410; lunch €7.90, dinner mains €25-36; ☺11am-4pm, dinner by reservation) Off the main road 2.5km south of Saariselkä, this cute wooden hut serves up good-value lunches. It's well worth booking in for dinner though, when the game-oriented mains might included woodpigeon or elk fillet.

Siberia   FINNISH €€€
(☑040-502-0409; www.ravintolasiberia.fi; Saariseläntie 3; degustation menu €105; ☺5-10pm Dec-Apr) This smart spot sits behind the rainbow screen on the main street and offers a sumptuous nine-course degustation menu with typical Lapland ingredients beautifully served, with the option of matching wines. It's quite modern molecular in style, and there's a minimalist, formal, designer feel. During the day it opens as a cafe and boutique, also open in the summer months.

Petronella   FINNISH €€€
(☑016-668-930; www.ravintolapetronella.fi; Honkapolku 5; mains €26-32; ☺6-11pm early Sep-late Sep & late Nov-Apr) Serves appetising portions of smart Lappish food in a wood-and-stone decorated dining room.

ℹ Information

Kiehinen (☑020-564-7200; www.outdoors.fi; Siula Centre; ☺9am-5pm Mon-Fri, plus 10am-4pm Sat & Sun high season) In the Siula building, just off the main road near the petrol station, this has hiking information, cabin reservations, fishing permits, maps and a small nature display. It also contains Saariselkä's **tourist information desk** (☑040-168-7838; www.saariselka.fi). The office opens weekends from high summer to late September and in peak skiing season.

ℹ Getting There & Away

There are three to five daily buses from Rovaniemi (€47.20, 3½ to 4¼ hours), continuing to Ivalo (€7.40, 30 minutes). Each incoming flight at Ivalo airport is met by a shuttle bus to Saariselkä.

ℹ Getting Around

From mid-November till early May a ski bus connects Ivalo, the major hotels, Saariselkä ski slopes, Kakslauttanen and Kiilopää several times daily (all-day ticket €5).

Around Saariselkä

Kiilopää

Kiilopää, 17km southeast of Saariselkä, is the best launchpad for hiking in the Saariselkä Wilderness; marked trails head directly into the wilderness from here. The Saariselkä-Kiilopää hiking map (€3) gives you a wealth of day-walk options. Short walks from here include the boardwalked ascent of Kiilopää fell (one hour return), with great views.

Right at the trailheads, **Suomen Latu Kiilopää** (Fell Centre Kiilopää; ☑016-670-0700; www.kiilopaa.fi; Kiilopääntie; dm €30, tent site €25, s/d summer €74/82, winter €96/128; ☺Nov-Apr & Jun-Sep; P@🏊) is an excellent facility. It has bikes, camping and skiing equipment (best to book) for hire, and can arrange guided treks. Outlying buildings hold simple, comfortable hotel rooms; a hostel with OK bunks (HI discount) and a small kitchen; and a variety of cottages and apartments starting at €74/114 for a two-/four-person apartment in summer. You can camp here too. There's a cafe-restaurant (packed lunch €8, dinner €23) and traditional **smoke sauna** that's fired up regularly (check times online); it costs €10 and is often free to those staying. Several daily buses do the one-hour trip between Ivalo and Kiilopää; a bus meets every incoming flight to Ivalo airport. If you are travelling by bus from Rovaniemi, check whether the bus runs to Kiilopää: some do, some don't.

Kakslauttanen

Kakslauttanen Arctic Resort   HOTEL, IGLOO
(☑016-667-100; www.kakslauttanen.fi; s/d cabins winter from €292/354, s/d snow igloos €285/380, s/d/f glass igloos €388/470/854; P@🏊) This large accommodation complex has a variety of comfortable log cabins, much cheaper in summer. In winter it's the site of an igloo village (November to April). The romance: you get the chance to watch the aurora borealis from the luxury of your own bed. The downside: you'd expect much more luxury and charm for the price, which seems to increase astronomically every year. There are traditional snow igloos (warm sleeping bag provided) as well as rows of glass igloos, which are by no means luxurious or spacious but are heated and have a tiny toilet cubicle. Family-sized ones include a shower. Don't expect even one-star service. You

are forced to eat in the hotel's worse-than-mediocre restaurant.

West of the hotel, Santa's Home, a wooden building, opens in winter, with reindeer, elves and the old man himself in attendance.

Kakslauttanen is on Rd 4, 11km south of Saariselkä. Kiilopää is 6km east of it. All north- and southbound buses will stop here on request.

Tankavaara

Back in 1868, a cry went up and started a gold rush to this remote area on the Ivalo-joki that saw a community of up to 500 pan-ners seeking their fortune after an arduous journey. Though people still work claims, today Tankavaara sees more income from the tourist trade than from the bottom of the goldpans.

◉ Sights & Activities

Kultamuseo MUSEUM
(www.kultamuseo.fi; Tankavaarantie 11C; adult/child €10/5; ⊙9am-5pm Jun-Sep, 10am-4pm Mon-Fri Oct-May) This gold museum has several parts. Nearest the entrance are replica buildings from American goldfields; the nearby smoke sauna and octagonal hut are less flashy but original. Rockhounds will

Saariselkä Wilderness & Urho Kekkonen National Park

enjoy the gemstone and mineral exhibition, but the highlight is the main museum, which covers the Finnish gold rush and gold production around the world. A cubic metre of sand is on display along with the sobering 2g of gold it normally contains here. In summer try your luck and pan for gold (€10/40 per hour/day).

Koilliskaira   NATURE CENTRE
(☑020-564-7251; www.outdoors.fi; Valtatie 4; ◷9am-5pm Mon-Fri, 10am-4pm Sat & Sun Jun-Sep, 10am-4pm Wed-Fri mid-Feb–May) At Tankavaara is this nature centre with advice on activities and trekking in Urho Kekkonen Nation-

al Park. It has good exhibitions on the local environment, including a display on raptors upstairs, as well as a half-hour audiovisual, an internet terminal, a shop and a selection of maps. Various circular **nature trails** arc out from the centre (1km to 6km).

✖ Eating

Wanha Waskoolimies   CAFE €
(☑016-626-158; www.tankavaara.fi; Valtatie 4; mains €12-19; ◷9am-11pm Sun-Thu, 9am-2am Fri & Sat, reduced hours winter) By the entrance to Kultamuseo, this atmospheric gold-panners' cafe-restaurant actually predates the museum and serves typical Lapland dishes. It has apartments (two/four people €80/98) and cabins (€55) and you can also camp here (€12). A gram of gold will buy you seven beers.

❶ Getting There & Away

Tankavaara is on the main Rovaniemi–Ivalo road 30km south of Saariselkä and 100km north of Sodankylä. All buses pass the village, stopping on request; nonexpress buses actually enter.

Saariselkä Wilderness & Urho Kekkonen National Park

Saariselkä Wilderness, including 2538-sq-km Urho Kekkonen National Park and large tracts of protected forest, extends to the Russian border. It's a fabulous slice of Finland, home to bears, wolverines and golden eagles, plus thousands of free-grazing reindeer. This is a brilliant trekking area, with a large network of wilderness huts amid the unspoilt beauty of this huge expanse of forest, marshland and low fells.

The park's divided into several zones, each with different rules. Check www.outdoors.fi for details. Although fires (using dead wood) are allowed in certain areas, take a camp stove, as fire bans are common in summer.

There are national park nature centres in Saariselkä, Tankavaara and Savukoski villages; you can also pick up information at Kiilopää. A map and compass are *essential* for the most remote areas of the park.

There are three Karttakeskus maps available for the area. The western part of the park is shown on the 1:50,000 *Saariselkä-Kiilopää* map; the 1:50,000 *Sokosti-Suomujoki* map will take you beyond Luirojärvi; the entire park is shown on the 1:100,000

Koilliskaira map. Visitor centres also sell a simpler map for day walks in the Saariselkä-Kiilopää area (€3).

◎ Sights

There are several natural attractions within the park boundaries, of which **Rumakuru Gorge**, near the hut of the same name, is closest to the main road. **Luirojärvi** is the most popular trekking destination, including a hike up the nearby **Sokosti summit** (718m), the highest in the park. **Paratiisikuru** (Paradise Gorge), a steep descent from the 698m **Ukselmapää summit**, and nearby **Lumikuru** (Snow Gorge), are popular day trips between Sarvioja and Muorravaarakka huts.

Two historical **Skolt Sámi settlements**, with restored old houses, lie 2km south of Raja-Jooseppi, and 2km west of Snelmanninmaja hut, respectively.

🏃 Activities

Hiking

There's some great hiking to be done on well-defined trails in the Saariselkä–Kakslauttanen–Kiilopää area. Grab a map and plan your own day hikes. For longer adventures, use wilderness huts as bases and destinations, and create your own itinerary according to your ability: an experienced, fit hiker can cover up to 4km per hour, and up to 28km per day. You will need to carry all food; water in rivers is drinkable.

The four- to six-day loop from the main road to Luirojärvi is the most popular, and can be extended beyond the lake. To reach areas where few have been, take a one-week walk from Kiilopää to Kemihaara.

The most remote route follows old roads and walking routes through the fells all the way from Raja-Jooseppi in the north to Kemihaara or Tulppio in the southeast.

🛏 Sleeping

Within the park are 200 designated free camping areas as well as some 40 free wilderness huts, some with locked bookable sections. Book these (€11 per bed; shared sleeping), and the few private cabins, at any of the park visitor centres.

You'll need a sleeping bag and mat for the wilderness huts; bookable ones have mattresses. Visitor centres supply maps and details of huts, as does the www.outdoors.fi website.

ℹ Getting There & Away

The easiest trailheads are Saariselkä or Kiilopää. From Savukoski contact the **post-taxi** (🗷 040-730-6484) for transport to Kemihaara, 1km from the park's boundary.

Raja-Jooseppi border station is another starting point for treks, as it takes you directly into real wilderness; you can get there on Murmansk-bound buses from Ivalo.

Ivalo

🗷 016 / POP 3130

A small town by most standards, Ivalo (Sámi: Avvil) is a metropolis in these latitudes. With plenty of services and an airport busy with Christmas charters, it's a useful place, though with few attractions. However, Inari's Sámi culture and Saariselkä's plentiful activities are close by.

🏃 Activities

Guesthouse Husky   DOG-SLEDDING
(🗷 040-510-7068; www.guesthousehusky.fi; Hirviniemientie 65; 1hr/4hr/day €100/177/276) Five kilometres from Ivalo, this outfit offers a big variety of trips, including overnight safaris. It has some guaranteed departure dates, meaning that couples can take advantage without having to pay for a minimum number of people. You get your own husky team on the longer excursions: this costs extra on shorter ones.

Kamisak   DOG-SLEDDING
(🗷 050-570-7871; www.kamisak.com; Rovaniementie 915) Kamisak is 8km south of Ivalo. From late June to mid-September, you can prebook a guided tour of the husky enclosures and meet the dogs (adult/child €30/15) or go riding on native Finnish horses. From November to April, it runs safaris that range from a half-day trip to multiday adventures.

🛏 Sleeping & Eating

★**Guesthouse Husky**   B&B €€
(🗷 016-663-377; www.guesthousehusky.fi; Hirviniemientie 65; s/d winter €80/115, summer €67/95; ⊙Nov-Apr & Jun-Sep; 🅿@🖥) Five kilometres from Ivalo, this friendly family husky farm offers great accommodation in a commodious wooden house. It's very well run, and the spotless rooms have a timber smell, splashes of arty colour, good modern showers, and use of a small kitchen area and sauna.

Breakfast is included and meals can be arranged. It has bikes for hire, and the highlight is meeting all the 140-odd dogs and playing with the puppies.

Hotel Kultahippu HOTEL €€
(☑016-320-8800; www.hotellikultahippu.fi; Petsamontie 1; s/d €85/110; [P][🛜]) In the friendly 'Speck of Gold' you might still see the odd gold panner stooped pensively over a beer. Rooms are simple but decent, with big windows. Some have their own sauna, and the riverside location appeals. The spacious restaurant does a €10.50 buffet lunch, and the pub and club are the main local nightspots. Try not to get a room above the club on weekends.

ℹ Information

Metsähallitus (☑020-564-7701; www.outdoors.fi; Ivalontie 10; ⊙9am-4pm Mon-Fri) On the main road, this has local and national park information.

ℹ Getting There & Around

There are numerous winter charter flights, and regular Finnair services from Helsinki. Norwegian also flies to/from Helsinki in winter. The airport is 12km south; a connecting bus meets flights.

There are a few daily buses from Rovaniemi (€53.50, 4½ hours) to Ivalo. Major car-hire companies are at the airport.

Three weekly buses travel the 300km east to Murmansk, Russia.

Nellim

This tucked-away village with a population of under 200 is one of the major Skolt settlements and worth a visit for anyone interested in Sámi culture. There's also a significant Inari Sámi and Finnish population, and Nellim likes to dub itself as the meeting point of three peoples. Situated on the shores of Inarijärvi 42km northeast of Ivalo (no bus service), it has a beautiful wooden Orthodox church amid the forest, built in 1987. You can head out in a boat on Inarijärvi with **Safari Service** (☑040-773-9142; www.safariservice.fi).

🛏 Sleeping & Eating

★Erähotelli Nellim HOTEL
(☑040-041-5989; www.nellim.fi; Nellimintie 4230; s/d winter €110/140, summer €80/98; ⊙ Jun-Apr; [P]) A great place to stay in a remote corner of Lapland, with lovely modern rooms

smelling of wood and beds with Sámi blankets in old timber buildings surrounding a courtyard. There are also excellent cabins and apartments sleeping up to eight and meals served in a rustic wooden dining room. There are a couple of wilderness lodge options. In winter it does packages with activities like aurora-watching, huskies and snowmobiles.

Inari

☑016 / POP 550
The tiny village of Inari (Sámi: Anár) is Finland's most significant Sámi centre and is *the* place to begin to learn something of their culture. It boasts the wonderful Siida museum and Sajos, cultural centre and seat of the Finnish Sámi parliament, as well as excellent handicrafts shops. It's also a great base for locations like Lemmenjoki National Park and the Kevo Strict Nature Reserve.

The village sits on Lapland's largest lake, Inarijärvi, a spectacular body of water with more than 3000 islands in its 1153-sq-km area.

◉ Sights

★Siida MUSEUM
(www.siida.fi; adult/child €10/5; ⊙9am-8pm Jun–mid-Sep, 10am-5pm Tue-Sun mid-Sep–May) One of Finland's finest museums, Siida, a comprehensive overview of the Sámi and their environment, should not be missed. The main exhibition hall consists of a fabulous nature exhibition around the edge, detailing northern Lapland's ecology by season, with wonderful photos and information panels. In the centre of the room is detailed information on the Sámi, from their former seminomadic existence to modern times. In an adjacent hall is a timeline framing Sámi prehistory and history alongside other world events. Other halls have excellent temporary exhibitions. Outside is what was the first Siida museum, a complex of mostly original buildings including farmhouses, storage huts and a courthouse, where miscreants scratched their names on the wooden walls while awaiting a likely flogging. Back inside, a theatrette shows pretty visuals of the aurora and Inarijärvi a few times daily; there's also a fine craft shop and a good lunch cafe.

Siida's website is itself worth a mention: via the 'web exhibitions' page you can access a series of excellent pages on the Inari and Skolt Sámi cultures.

Sajos   CULTURAL CENTRE
(www.sajos.fi; Siljotie; ⊙9am-5pm Mon-Fri) FREE
The spectacular wood-and-glass Sámi cultural centre stands proud in the middle of town. It holds the Sámi parliament as well as a library and music archive, restaurant, exhibitions and craft shop. In summer there are tours of the building, and Sámi handicraft workshops.

Pielpajärven Kirkko   CHURCH
(⊙24hr) This *erämaakirkko* (wilderness church) is accessible by a marked walking track (7.5km one way) from the parking area at Siida. If you have a vehicle there's another trailhead beyond here from where it's 4.3km. In winter you'll need snowshoes. The area has for centuries been an important marketplace for the Sámi; the first church was erected in 1646. The present church was built in 1760, and restored in the 1970s. Open the shutters to get the full benefit, but close them again after your visit.

🏃 Activities

As well as the walk to the wilderness church, there are other worthwhile trails, including one that leads 9km from Siida to the top of Otsamo fell.

Ivalon Lentopalvelu   SCENIC FLIGHTS
(☑040-570-8369; www.lentopalvelu.fi; ⊙Jun-Sep) The seaplanes parked in the lake do scenic flights and chartered trips (one to three people €200) around Inarijärvi.

LuontoLoma/Pro Safaris   RAFTING
(☑016-668-706; www.luontoloma.fi) Organises three-hour rafting jaunts on the rapids as well as other watery trips in the region.

Tuula Airamo   REINDEER
(☑043-200-1898; Tulvalahdentie 235, near Riutula; 1/2/3hr visit €28/39/60) Friendly Tuula offers a great experience here, 17km northwest of Inari off the Angeli road. The one-hour visit lets you meet and feed reindeer, the two-hour visit adds a Sámi handicrafts workshop, and the three-hour visit adds a visit to Tuala's typical Lapland home. Book in advance.

🧭 Tours

Visit Inari   SUMMER, WINTER
(Lake & Snow; ☑040-179-6069; www.visitinari.fi; Inarintie 38) This outifit organises summer and winter excursions, including fishing, visits to reindeer farms, snowshoe walks, husky and snowmobile safaris, and aurora borealis hunting. It also operates cruises (adult/child €22/11) on Inarijärvi from June (as soon as the ice melts) to late September, with one or two daily departures from Siida car park. The destination is **Ukko Island** (Sámi: Äjjih), sacred to the Sámi. During the brief (20-minute) stop, most people climb to the top of the island, but there are also cave formations at the island's northern end.

RideNorth   HORSES, HUSKIES
(Arctic Hysteria; ☑0400-814-424; www.ridenorth.fi; Kotiniemi, Inari; horse riding €55, husky-sledding from €100) This welcoming set-up offers sled excursions with well-cared-for huskies, and year-round trips with beautiful, hardy Norwegian fjording horses. You can even go hiking in summer with the huskies pulling you along.

Petri Mattus   REINDEER
(☑0400-193-950; www.petrimattus.com; Kittiläntie 3070) Offers the chance to head out in snowmobiles to feed the reindeer (one/two people €140/240, two to four hours) or, in May, to head out to watch calving and earmarking – depending on conditions, this could be an overnight trip.

🎉 Festivals & Events

Skábmagovat   FILM
(www.skabmagovat.fi) This indigenous-themed film festival in late January sees collaborations with groups from other nations. There's enough English content to make it worthwhile.

King's Cup   REINDEER RACING
(www.paliskunnat.fi) Held over the last weekend of March or first weekend of April, this is the grand finale of Lapland's reindeer-racing season and a great spectacle as the beasts race around the frozen lake, jockeys sliding like water-skiers behind them. The semifinals are on Saturday, the final on Sunday, and plenty of betting livens things up. There's also a race for visitors, which degenerates into comedy, as driving a reindeer is harder than it looks.

Inari Viikot   CULTURAL
(www.inariviikot.fi) Two weeks of cultural events in the second half of July.

Ijahis Idja
MUSIC

(www.ijahisidja.fi) Over a weekend usually in August is this excellent music festival that features groups from all spectra of Sámi music. Ijahis Idja means 'Nightless Night'.

🛏 Sleeping & Eating

Lomakylä Inari
CAMPGROUND €

(☎016-671-108; www.saariselka.fi/lomakylainari; tent sites for 1/2/4 people €10/15/20, 2-/4-person cabins €67/79, without bathroom €40/50, cottages €85-170; P🐾) The closest cabin accommodation to Inari, this is 500m south of the town centre and a good option. There's a range of cabins and facilities that include a cafe. Lakeside cabins cost a little more but are worth it for the memorable sunsets. Camping and nonheated cabins are June to September only.

Uruniemi Camping
CABIN, CAMPGROUND €

(☎050-371-8826; www.uruniemi.fi; Uruniementie; tent sites €16, r from €23, cabins €26-120; ⊙Jun-mid-Sep; P🐾) This place, 2km south of town, is a well-equipped lakeside campground with rooms, cottages, a cafe, sauna, and kayaks, boats and bikes for hire. It's the most pleasant place to pitch a tent hereabouts. Heated cottages are available year-round.

★Tradition Hotel Kultahovi
HOTEL €€

(☎016-511-7100; www.hotelkultahovi.fi; Saarikoskentie 2; s/d €78/102, annexe s/d €112/128; P@🐾) This cosy place run by a Sámi family overlooks the Alakoski rapids and has spruce rooms, some with a great river view. The standard rooms have been recently renovated, while chambers in the annexe have appealing Nordic decor, drying cupboard, riverside balcony/terrace and (most) a sauna. The restaurant (open 11am to 10.30pm) serves delicious Lappish specialities (mains €20 to €31) with relaxing views. There's a riverside sauna that's a great experience. In summer an underwater camera beams trouty goings-on to your room TV, while in winter it's an aurora borealis cam.

Hotelli Inari
HOTEL €€

(☎016-671-026; www.hotelliinari.fi; Inarintie 40; s/d €88/106, incl sauna €116/136; P🐾) In the heart of Inari, this has modernised, spacious rooms with good showers. Slightly cheaper 'small doubles' have two beds end-to-end. A modern annexe behind has top rooms, all modish greys and blacks with sauna and lovely lake views. The restaurant serves pizzas and reasonable local fish and reindeer

FINLAND'S COLDEST COFFEE-STOP

Tieva-Baari (☎0500-673-838; Inarintie 6595, Pokka; light meals €3-6; ⊙9am-10pm Mon-Fri, 10am-10pm Sat & Sun) A great coffee-and-petrol stop between eastern and western Lapland, 105km from Inari on the road to Kittilä, this curious cafe sits in the hamlet of Pokka, proud to be Finland's coldest place, having registered a chilly -51.5°C a few years back. The interior features stuffed birds, tropical plants, great doughnuts and a charismatic owner who isn't happy until the needle hits -30°C. It's got cabins, camping and can organise winter excursions.

dishes (mains €10 to €20). Watch the amazing sun at these latitudes out the windows.

Villa Lanca
GUESTHOUSE €€

(☎040-748-0984; www.villalanca.com; s/d €63/85, incl kitchen €80/105; P🐾) On the main road through town, this is a very characterful lodging, with original rooms that are full of atmosphere and decorated with Asian fabrics, feather charms and real artistic flair. The cute attic rooms are spacious and cheaper but lack a bit of headroom. An excellent breakfast with delicious homemade bread is included. It's a great place to learn about Sámi culture and stories.

🛍 Shopping

Inari is the main centre for Sámi handicrafts and there are several studios and boutiques in the village.

Sámi Duodji Ry
HANDICRAFTS

(wwwsamiduodji.com; Siljotie; ⊙10am-5pm Mon-Fri) 🖉 In the Sajos building, this is the main shop of the Finnish association of Sámi craftspeople. It has a good range of Sámi books and CDs, as well as beautifully crafted silverware and handmade clothing.

Samekki
JEWELLERY, HANDICRAFTS

(☎016-671-086; www.saariselka.fi/samekki; Lehtolantie; ⊙10am-4pm Mon-Fri, also Sat & Sun mid-Jun–Aug) 🖉 Down a small lane behind the library is the studio of Petteri Laiti, a famous Sámi artisan. The silverwork and handicrafts are very highly regarded; you'll often see the artist at work here.

Nativa   HANDICRAFTS
(www.natureco.info; ⊙noon-6pm Mon-Sat) 🚲
Original and excellent Sámi handicrafts next
to Villa Lanca. It also hires bikes (€10/20 per
half-day/24 hours).

ℹ Information

Tourist Office (☑ 020-564-7740; www.inari.fi;
Inarintie 46; ⊙9am-8pm Jun–mid-Sep, 10am-
5pm Tue-Sun mid-Sep–May; 🛜) Located in the
Siida museum. There's also a nature information point here and internet access.

ℹ Getting There & Away

Inari is 38km north of Ivalo on Rd 4. Buses run
here from Ivalo (€8.20, 30 minutes). Two daily
buses hit Inari from Rovaniemi (€60.10, five
hours) and continue to Norway, one to Karasjok
and on to Nordkapp in summer, another to Tana
bru (four weekly in winter).

Lemmenjoki National Park

At 2855 sq km, Lemmenjoki (Sámi: Leam-
mi) is Finland's largest national park, covering a remote wilderness area between Inari
and Norway. It is prime hiking territory,
with desolate wilderness rivers, rough landscapes and the mystique of gold, with solitary prospectors sloshing away with their
pans in the middle of nowhere. Boat trips
on the river allow more leisurely exploration of the park.

The launchpad is Njurgulahti, an Inari
Sámi community by the river; it's often
simply referred to as Lemmenjoki. It's 11km
down a turn-off signposted 34km southwest
of Inari on the Kittilä road.

◉ Sights

Lemmenjoki Nature Centre   NATURE CENTRE
(www.outdoors.fi; ⊙9am-5pm mid-Jun–late Sep) A
small nature centre with displays on the river, maps, walking information, fishing permits and a powerful set of binoculars trained
on a nearby fell. The entrance to Lemmenjoki National Park itself is 1.5km away.

Sallivaara   HISTORIC SITE
Accessed off the Inari–Kittilä road, 70km
southwest of Inari, this reindeer round-
up site was used by Sámi reindeer herders
twice yearly until 1964. Round-ups were
an important social event, lasting several
weeks and involving hundreds of people
and animals. The corrals and cabins have

been reconstructed, and you can overnight
in one of the huts. There's top-quality birdwatching on nearby wetlands. From the
parking area it's a 6km signposted walk.

Kaapin Jouni   MUSEUM
This historic farm on the other side of the
river from Njurgulahti was once the home
of the 'reindeer king' Jouni Aikio. You can
visit it by organising boat trips from places
to stay such as Ahkun Tupa.

Paltto   GALLERY
(☑ 0400-287-544; www.lemmenjoki.org; ⊙10am-
6pm Jun-late Sep or by appointment) 🚲 Felt
artworks and handicrafts of extraordinary
quality in this artist's studio a kilometre
from Njurgulahti.

Kammigalleria   GALLERY
(www.kammigalleria.fi; Lemmenjoentie 650;
⊙noon-6pm Tue-Sat Jun-Sep) 🚲 Male reindeer
drop their heavy antlers in November: see
beautiful jewellery and handicrafts that
Kikka Laakso makes from them here on the
Lemmenjoki road.

🏃 Activities

Hiking
Most trails start from Njurgulahti, including a family-friendly 4.5km marked nature
trail. Marked trekking routes are in the relatively small 'basic area' between the rivers
Lemmenjoki and Vaskojoki; a 20km loop
between Kultahamina and Ravadasjärvi
huts takes you to some of the most interesting gold-panning areas. Another route
heads over Látnjoaivi fell to Vaskojoki hut
and back, taking you into the 'wilderness
area', which has less restrictions on where
to camp but no trail markings. For any serious trekking, you will need the 1:100,000
Lemmenjoki map (€19.90), available at the
Lemmenjoki Nature Centre.

From Kultahamina, it's a 21.5km walk
back to Njurgulahti along the river, via Ravadas, 6.5km closer. You can get the boat
one-way and walk the other.

Boat Trips
In summer a scheduled boat service runs
from Njurgulahti village to the Kultahamina wilderness hut at Kultasatama (Gold
Harbour) via the Ravadas falls. There are
departures at 10am and 5pm from mid-
June to mid-August; in early June and from
mid-August to mid-September, only the
evening one goes (one way €20, 1½ hours
to Kultasatama).

MODERN SÁMI LIFE

The reindeer year starts at the beginning of June because the calves that are born around May have to be earmarked. After that marking they are free in the fells for the summer. In autumn we start herding them and decide which are to be killed for meat. To herd them I use an ATV and after the snow falls, a snowmobile. It takes over two months to herd the reindeer and it's hopefully done by Christmas. During the winter we move the reindeer from one area to another because there's not enough food to last them in one place.

You should never ask a Sámi how many reindeer they have; it's like asking someone's salary. I wouldn't even tell a close friend. Some people have hundreds, some only have a few.

Our traditions are still important, even to young Sámi. We describe by yoiking (chanting) nature, people, all sorts of happenings, but one never yoiks about oneself. Traditional clothes are still important to us; we do wear them, mainly on special occasions. The locations of *seita* (holy site) places are still remembered by people, but they don't visit them. And if they do visit them, it's a secret that you wouldn't tell to anybody else.

The Sámi parliament deals with all aspects of Sámi life. We meet four times a year in Inari and are elected by the Sámi people. Our government does listen to us, though that doesn't mean that they do anything. If we want something, it is our only channel so in that way it is important. The government asks our advice a lot if they want to know something. That is our main power I suppose. Of course, we'd like to have more!

Though some areas are protected, in parts of Lapland we have big battles with the forestry industry. Some are solved, and some are not. I think the question will never go away; there will always be people wanting to make money from the forest.

Tourism is a good thing for the Sámi people if Sámi people get the results, the benefits from it. That isn't always the case. Where I live, in Lemmenjoki, tourism directly benefits the Sámi community, but in other parts the money flows straight out to other places.

Heikki Paltto, reindeer herder and member of the Sámi parliament

☞ Tours

All the accommodation options in the area can organise river trips, including gold panning and insights into Sámi culture.

🛏 Sleeping & Eating

Several places offer camping and/or cabin accommodation, food and boat trips. Inside Lemmenjoki National Park, a dozen wilderness huts provide free accommodation (another three can be booked in advance for a fee).

Paltto　　　　　　　　　　CABIN **€**
(☏016-673-413; www.lemmenjoki.org; cabins €55-75; ⊙Jun–mid-Oct; **P**) A kilometre from the centre of Njurgulahti, this home of an active Sámi family has a felt studio selling some extraordinary works of art, as well as comfortable cabin accommodation with sauna and boat. Excellent boat trips are on offer (€45 to €65): from half-day to full-day trips that can include reindeer-meeting, Sámi yoiks (chants), gold panning and traditional lunch. The heated cottage is available year-round.

Valkeaporo　　　　COTTAGE, CAMPGROUND **€**
(☏0400-394-682; www.valkeaporo.fi; Lemmenjoentie 134; tent sites 1 person/2 person or family €10/20, cottages €50-120; ⊙Mar-Sep) A kilometre down the Lemmenjoki turn-off from the main Inari–Kittilä road, with splendid water frontage on spectacular Menesjärvi, this place has smart cottages, good facilities, and boat and canoe hire. You can also camp here. It offers good boat trips on the Lemmenjoki.

Ahkun Tupa　　　　CABIN, CAMPGROUND **€**
(☏040-755-4306; www.ahkuntupa.fi; 2-/4-person cottages €40/50-80, d/q €30/40; ⊙Jun-late Sep; **P**) By the water in Njurgulahti, this has rooms, cottages and some further-flung log cabins. You can also pitch a tent for pennies. It offers English-speaking river cruises (from €10 for a runabout to €45 for a seven-hour day including gold panning) and rents canoes. The restaurant does lunch specials and salmon and reindeer mains (€13 to €22), including reindeer tongue.

Hotel Korpikartano
HOTEL €€

(☑040-777-4339; www.menesjarvi.fi; Menesjärvi; s/d €77/91, lake d €106, apt €117-159; P @ 🛜) Three kilometres short of the Lemmenjoki turn-off, this wilderness hotel has a superb position on the shores of one of the region's most beautiful lakes. Spruce, colourful rooms, some with kitchenette, are complemented by excellent activities and a flexible attitude that makes staying here a delight. Skis, canoes and kayaks are available. There's a great wood-burning sauna with outdoor hot tub that's the place to be in winter.

❶ Getting There & Away

In school holidays (early June to early August) there's a **taxi-bus** (☑0400-295-588) service once daily Monday to Friday between Inari and Lemmenjoki (€10).

During the school year, you may be able to squeeze onto the school taxi service, but it's far from guaranteed. Ask at the Inari tourist office.

Inari to Norway
☑016

Norway stretches right across the top of Finland, and there are three main routes north from Inari: to the west via Karigasniemi (the most common Nordkapp route); north to Utsjoki; and east to Sevettijärvi. From Utsjoki, you can turn east along the fabulous Tenojoki to Nuorgam, the EU's northernmost village. The Kevo Strict Nature Reserve stretches between the western route and the northern one.

Kaamanen

Kaamanen, 25km north of Inari, is the crossing point of the three northern roads. There's petrol, food and drink at the Kaamasen Kievari roadhouse, where buses stop.

🛏 Sleeping

Jokitörmä
CAMPGROUND, HOSTEL €

(☑016-672-725; www.jokitorma.net; tent site €14 plus per adult/child €3/1, s/d €38/49, cabin/hostel dm €25/28, 2-/4-person cabins €38/59; P) On the highway about 24km north of Inari, this is a great campground and hostel. Cabins are small, cosy and look over the river (pack repellent in summer). They have a simple stove but no fridge. Adjacent campsites are grassy, there are good two- and four-person rooms in the main building, and a separate set of full-facility cottages. The friendly owners can sort out transport to trailheads.

Karigasniemi

The border village of Karigasniemi (Sámi: Gáregasnjárga) thrives on Norwegian trade, and has seven-day supermarkets, bars and restaurants, petrol stations, as well as plenty of accommodation catering to fishermen beating the Tenojoki. Locals speak Fell Sámi, the main Sámi language of northern Norway.

A few accommodation choices are in the centre of town, by the border crossing, while others are strung out along the Tenojoki north and south of town. The 100km drive northeast to Utsjoki is stunningly beautiful.

Kalastajan Majatalo (☑040-484-8171; www.hansabar.fi; d €70, apt €85-110, cabins €50) is in the village centre, and offers comfortable rooms and apartments, and simple cabins. The restaurant (mains €15 to €24) serves tasty salmon and is popular with Norwegians fleeing high beer prices.

Tenon Eräkievari (www.tenonerakievari.fi; Rovisuvannontie 59), in a great spot 8km up the Utsjoki road, is under ambitious new ownership and plans to offer accommodation, riding trips to a Sámi holy mountain, canoeing on the Teno, and reindeer- and husky-sledding with an interactive, get-involved attitude.

There's a daily bus from Ivalo to Karigasniemi via Inari. Another bus runs from Rovaniemi to Karasjok in Norway via here. In summer it continues to Nordkapp.

Kevo Strict Nature Reserve

The 712-sq-km Kevo Strict Nature Reserve, northwest of Inari, has within its boundaries some of the most breathtaking scenery in Finland along the splendid 40km gorge of the Kevojoki.

Rules for visiting the Kevo reserve are stricter than those concerning national parks: hikers cannot hunt, fish or collect plants and berries, and *must* stay on marked trails. The gorge area is off-limits from April to mid-June.

The main trail is 64km long and runs through the canyon, from the Sulaoja parking area 11km east of Karigasniemi on the road westbound from Kaamanen, to Kenesjärvi, on the Kaamanen–Utsjoki road. The trek is rough with several fords – ask about water levels before heading off – and takes about four days one way. The Guivi trail separates from the main trail and loops through fell scenery before rejoining further along: it's a 78km journey but has two extra huts en route. You can also walk a round-trip from Sulaoja. See www.outdoors.fi for more details and use the 1:100,000 *Utsjoki Kevo* outdoor map.

🛏 Sleeping

You will need a tent if you plan to hike the canyon, as there is only one wilderness hut on the main route (there are another two on the Guivi leg). Camping is permitted within the reserve at 20 designated sites.

Ruktajärvi wilderness hut is at the southern end of the gorge route near where the Guivi trail branches off, and Njávgoaivi and Kuivi are on the Guivi loop. There's also a simple turf hut between these two.

There are cabins on the main road 500m south of the eastern trailhead.

ℹ Getting There & Away

The preferred route is from the southwest; catch the Karigasniemi-bound bus from Inari and ask the driver to drop you off at the clearly marked Sulaoja trailhead. From Kenesjärvi you can catch buses to Inari or Utsjoki/Nuorgam. The early afternoon southbound bus that passes Kenesjärvi has a convenient changeover at Kaamasen Kievari (Monday to Friday) to the westbound bus for Sulaoja, allowing you to leave your car there.

Utsjoki

The border village of Utsjoki (Sámi: Ohcejohka) is strung out along the main road that crosses the Tenojoki into Norway over a handsome bridge. It's an important Sámi community. The river is the main attraction in these parts; head along its banks towards Nuorgam or Karigasniemi and you'll find several picturesque spots with cabins catering to families or groups of friends going fishing.

The **tourist office** (☑ parks info 020-564-7792, town info 040-181-0263; www.utsjoki.fi; ☺ 10am-6pm mid-Jun–mid-Sep) is in a hut on the left just before the bridge. It also serves as a Metsähallitus point; staff can give fishing information, as well as advice and maps for the Kevo trail and the various less-used trails that fan out from Utsjoki – the best is a 35km circular route with a wilderness hut at Koahpelásjärvi to overnight in. There's also a small exhibition that'll let you sort out a Silver Doctor from a Rusty Rat.

Kylätalo Giisá (☑ 040-822-8889; ☺ 8am-4pm Mon-Fri Sep–mid-Jun, 8am-6pm Mon-Fri, 10am-3pm Sat mid-Jun–Aug) ✐, the village hall, has an excellent handicraft shop, a cafe and internet access (per hour). It also sorts out bus tickets and fishing licences.

Opposite it is **Camping Lapinkylä** (☑ 040-559-1542; www.arctictravel.fi; tent sites per 2 people €13, cabins €55-80; ☺ Jun–mid-Sep; P ✈), which has a sauna, neat wooden cabins and plenty of grass underfoot to pitch your tent. It also does fishing trips and rents boats, and has heated apartments (two/four persons €110/130), which are available in winter.

Nuorgam & Teno Valley

The 44km road from Utsjoki northeast to Nuorgam (Sámi: Njuorggan), the northernmost village of Finland (N 70°04'), is one of Lapland's most spectacular. It follows the Tenojoki, one of Europe's best **salmonfishing** rivers, and a spectacular sight as its broad waters cut through the undulating dune-like landscape and across sandy spits and rocky banks. Most anglers gather near Boratbokcankoski and Alaköngäs Rapids (7km southwest of Nuorgam), but there are good spots right along this stretch, and the other way from Utsjoki, towards Karigasniemi, which is another beautiful drive following the Tenojoki and the Norwegian border.

Apart from fishing, there's not a great deal to do in Nuorgam, but it's a relaxing spot. Norwegians flock to the (comparatively) cheap supermarkets, Alko store and petrol stations in town, but the heart of village life is **Nuorgamin Lomakeskus** (☑ 0400-294-669; www.nuorgaminlomakeskus.fi; powered sites €20 plus per adult/child €5/3, cabins €60-95, apt €90-170; ☺ cafe & reception Mar–mid-May, mid-Jun–mid-Aug, Sep–mid-Oct; P @ ✈), which offers camping, cabins and cottage apartments with the works. It sells fishing permits, has a summer cafe-restaurant, and sells the *Nuorgam: Top of EU* T-shirt. Book ahead for cabins, as fishing groups fill them fast. You can stay here when reception isn't open by calling ahead.

There are many campsites and good-value cabin villages catering to fishing parties scattered by the river between Nuorgam and Utsjoki, and several more on the Karigasniemi road. The Utsjoki website (www.utsjoki.fi) has a full list: click on 'Majoituspalvelut' under the 'Matkailu' menu.

OFF THE BEATEN TRACK

TREKKING AROUND SEVETTIJÄRVI

There's excellent trekking in this remote lake-spangled wilderness. Though trails are easily followed, this is a remote area, so you'll need a compass and the 1:50,000 trekking maps for the area, available at tourist offices throughout the region. See www.outdoors.fi for more details of these routes.

The **Sevettijärvi to Pulmankijärvi** trek (60 to 70km) is the most popular. The better of two trailheads is just north of Sevettijärvi, at Saunaranta. There are several mountain huts along the route; after the last one, you emerge onto a road at Arola by Pulmankijärvi, along which you can walk 20km to Nuorgam, or call ☎0400-377-665 for a taxi.

Other marked routes from Sevettijärvi include the **Saamenpolku** (Sámi trail), a circular trail of 87km that loops around to Näätämö and the Norwegian border and back. Expect plenty of river crossings. The **Inarinpolku** is a 100km trek to the fjords of the Arctic Ocean in Norway.

There's a shop in Sevettijärvi, but if you have transport you might want to stock up on supplies at the supermarket by the Norwegian border at Näätämö, which is much larger and open daily.

Nuorgam is the northern end of a great trekking route from Sevettijärvi (p262).

There's a daily bus from Ivalo to Nuorgam via Inari and Utsjoki. A late-evening bus travels from Rovaniemi and on to Tana bru in Norway daily in summer and four times weekly in winter.

Sevettijärvi

The road east from Kaamanen heads along the shore of spectacularly beautiful Inarijärvi to the village of Sevettijärvi (Skolt Sámi: Ce'vetjäu'rr), in the far northeast of Finland. It's a remote area that merits exploration.

Sevettijärvi is a major village of the Skolt Sámi, who resettled here when Finland was forced to cede the Petsamo area to the USSR in 1944. About 300 Skolt live in and around Sevettijärvi, which has a church (Orthodox, as the Skolt were evangelised by the Russians back in the 15th century), a shop and bar (Sevetin Baari), and a school, whose dozen-odd pupils are taught in the Skolt language. There's also **Kolttien Perinnetalo** (⌚10am-6pm Jun-late Sep) FREE, a delightful little museum with photos, crafts and explanations of the poignant Skolt history.

Sevettijärvi's namesake lake offers good fishing, as does the Näätämöjoki and, of course, Inarijärvi. Sevettijärvi also has some excellent, remote, long-distance hiking trails.

The Orthodox **festival** of St Triphon is celebrated by the Skolt Sámi on the last weekend of August. It starts in Nellim on the Friday, then moves to Sevettijärvi, with celebrations and dances on the Saturday evening and Sunday morning. Visitors are welcome. As far as the Skolt are concerned, Lapp-dancing is the *katrilli* (quadrille).

There are a couple of good cabin options in and near town but **Porotila Toini Sanila** (☎016-672-509; www.sanila.fi; Sanilantie 36; r without bathroom €35-57, 2-/4-person cottages €160/200; P 📶) is the area's most inviting place to stay. The family has reindeer and taught at the local school: it's a good place to learn about the Skolt way of life. A series of rooms across a few central buildings offer simple, attractive comfort with shared bathrooms. Self-contained cottages sleeping up to eight are also available. The cafe does home baking and delicious reindeer and fish meals (three-course meals €18 to €28); the sauna is always on. It's 1km off the main road halfway between Sevettijärvi and the Norwegian border; the bus will drop you at the turn-off.

Between Sevettijärvi and Inari, at Partakko, friendly **Hietajoen Leirintä** (☎0400-434-411; www.hietajoenleirinta.net; Partakko; tent sites €16, cabins €38-50, cottages from €100; ⌚Jun–mid-Sep; P) has simple cabins and more upmarket cottages in a wonderful position on Inarijärvi. There's a sauna on the lakeshore and boats for hire.

There is a bus connection between Ivalo and Sevettijärvi on weekdays. There is no petrol station in Sevettijärvi; the nearest is in the border village of Näätämö, 30km northeast.

Understand
Finland

Finland Today

Though Finland was affected by the global downturn, overall this hundred-year-old nation is in good health, always scoring highly on indexes measuring quality of life, education, democracy and equality. Bailouts and increased immigration have led some to question involvement in the euro and EU, but in general the country is focused on tackling challenges like climate change together with the rest of Europe.

Best on Film

Man Without a Past (2002) One of Aki Kaurismäki's best.
Miesten Vuoro (Steam of Life; 2010) Brilliant documentary of men sharing the stories of their lives in the sauna.
Tuntematon Sotilas (The Unknown Soldier; 1955) Considered Finland's greatest film about the Winter War.

Best in Print

Kalevala (Elias Lönnrot) Readable 'national epic' compiled from the songs of bards.
The Year of the Hare (Arto Paasilinna) Offbeat tale of hare-y travels.
Seven Brothers (Aleksis Kivi) A 19th-century Finnish classic.

Century of Success

Since independence from Russia in 1917, remote, forested, cold, sparsely populated Finland has had a hell of a last century. It has propelled itself from agricultural backwater of the Russian Empire to one of the world's most prosperous nations, with great standards of living and education, low crime, a practical, deep-rooted sense of environmentalism, strong cultural output and a muscular technology industry. On the centenary in 2017 Finns can toast a remarkable success story.

Russia

The enormous eastern neighbour has been one of the main talking points in Finland since the 12th century, when Russian power began to loom over the land. Long experience with the Bear has stood Suomi in good stead, and the two countries have a strong relationship, with much exchange of commerce and tourism. It's a very important market for import and export of goods and services, and any Russian counter-sanctions against the EU could cost Finland dear. Nevertheless, Finns on the street are understandably nervous of a nationalistic Moscow, exacerbated by events in Ukraine in 2014. Memories of bitter fights for freedom are too painful for national service and the army not to be taken seriously here.

External Relations

The 2011 parliamentary elections in Finland sent a shockwave through Europe as the nationalistic, populist True Finns party came from nowhere to seize 19% of the vote. Their absolute rejection of bailouts of other EU economies meant that rather than compromise their principles by entering a coalition government, they opted to become the major opposition party instead, establishing them as a serious political force. Meanwhile, the other MPs finally formed a six-party coalition under the prime ministership of centre-right Jyrki Katainen.

Katainen was succeeded as prime minister in 2014 by the charismatic Alexander Stubb.

The success of what is now just called the Finns Party (Perussuomalaiset) reflected concerns about rising immigration and a feeling of frustration that Finnish taxpayers were being forced to pay for other countries' problems. It evoked a stereotype of the lonely Finn sitting at home and not caring much about the rest of the world. It remains to be seen if their influence is extended or diminished in the 2015 elections.

Climate Change

Southern Finland has already noticed dramatically changed weather patterns, with much milder winters. The once unthinkable prospect of a non-white Christmas in Helsinki is now a reality. Scientists in the Arctic are producing increasingly worrying data and it seems that northern nations like Finland may be some of the earliest to be seriously affected. Though Finland will reap corn sown by bigger nations, its people and government are very environmentally conscious. Finland's own commitment to combating climate change is strong, having set a legally binding target in 2014 of 80% emissions reduction by 2050. A large nuclear power sector is backed by an increasing percentage of renewable energy.

Society & Culture

Finns are rightly proud of the strong foundations of their society. Famously high tax rates means the nation is well equipped to look after its citizenry with some of the world's best healthcare and education. Though Finns grumble about the high excise on alcohol, they appreciate the reliable public transport and world-class universities, libraries and other infrastructure these same taxes afford. Like much of the world, the country is holding its breath as ageing baby boomers retire and it attempts to maintain high pensions.

Finland's superior education system manifests itself in an extraordinary cultural output, particularly in the sphere of classical music. Finland produces a constant stream of brilliant composers, conductors and musicians, while music-school graduates have also gone on to form some of the country's huge variety of heavier rock and metal bands.

Economy

Finland's economy, once dominated by forestry, is now as much or more about technology and services. Like most European economies, Finland's has had a hard time of it in recent years and at the time of writing was still struggling to emerge from recession. Apart from the worldwide malaise, two principal factors have been Nokia's failure to crack the smartphone market and declining demand for paper due to increasingly digital reading habits. Nevertheless, the long-term outlook is positive, with a well-balanced economy built on strong foundations with a highly skilled workforce.

POPULATION: **5.5 MILLION**

AREA: **338,145 SQ KM**

PERCENTAGE OF WATER: **10%**

GDP PER CAPITA: **€27,833**

UNEMPLOYMENT: **8.7%**

AVERAGE CUPS OF COFFEE PER DAY: **4**

if Finland were 100 people

90 would speak Finnish as their first language
5 would speak Swedish as their first language
1 would speak Russian as their first language
1 would speak Estonian as their first language
3 would speak other languages

electricity generation
(% of power sources)

Nuclear — 33   Hydro — 22

Fossil Fuels — 21   Renewable Wood — 19   Peat — 5

population per sq km

FINLAND   UK   DENMARK

♂ ≈ 17 people

History

Finland's history is the story of a cold country which for centuries was used as a wrestling mat between two heavyweights, Sweden and Russia, and the nation's eventful emergence from their grip to become one of the world's most progressive and prosperous nations.

Early Days

One of the best places to learn about the Stone Age in Finland is the Kierikkikeskus museum near Oulu.

What is now Finland was inhabited way back: pre-ice-age remains have been found dating from some 120,000 years ago. But the big chill erased most traces and sent folk scurrying south to warmer climes. Only at the retreat of the formidable glaciers, which had blanketed the country 3km deep, was human presence re-established.

The first post-thaw inhabitants had spread over most of Finland by about 9000 BC. The people used stone tools and hunted elk and beaver.

Pottery in the archaeological record shows that a new influence arrived from the east to southern Finland about 5000 years ago. Because Finland was the furthest point west that this culture reached, it's suggested that these new people brought a Finnic language with them from Russia. If so, those who lived in Finland at this time were the ancestors of the Finns and the Sámi.

In the 1st century AD, the Roman historian Tacitus mentioned a tribe called the Fenni, whom he described as wild savages who had neither homes nor horses. He might have been referring to the Sámi or their forebears, whose nomadic existence better fits this description. Studies indicate that today's Sámi are descended mostly from a small original group, and some claim that a divergence of pre-Finnish and Sámi cultures can be seen as far back as 700 BC. Nomadic cultures leave little archaeological evidence, but it seems the Sámi gradually migrated northwards, probably displaced by the southerners and the advance of agriculture into former hunting lands. Verses of the *Kalevala,* which is derived from ancient oral tradition, seem to refer to this conflictive relationship.

TIMELINE	120,000 BC	10,000 BC	3000 BC
	Present-day Finland is inhabited, as finds at Susiluola cave, near Kristinestad, indicate, but its residents, of whom we know little, are eventually evicted by the last ice age.	The retreat of the ice age's glaciers reopens the northern lands to human habitation. The forests and lakes that replace the ice provide tempting hunting and fishing grounds.	The appearance of distinctive 'Comb Ware' pottery indicates the presence of a new culture that seems to come from the Volga region to the east, perhaps bringing a pre-Finnish language with it.

Swedish Rule

The nascent kingdom of Sweden saw Finland as a natural direction for extending its influence in the Baltic and countering the growing power of Novgorod (later to become Russia) in the east. Missionary activity began in the 12th century, and legend tells of an Englishman, Bishop Henry, leading an expedition of baptism that ended stickily when he was murdered by Lalli, a disgruntled peasant.

Things started to heat up in the 13th century. The Pope called a crusade against the Häme tribe, which was increasingly influenced both religiously and politically from Novgorod, and Russian and Swedish forces clashed several times in the first battles of an ongoing saga.

Swedish settlement began in earnest around the middle of the century when Birger Jarl established fortifications at Häme and Turku, among other places. The cathedral at Turku was also under construction and this city was to be Finland's pre-eminent centre for most of its history. The Swedish knights and nobles in charge of these operations set a pattern for a Swedish-speaking bourgeoisie in Finland, which lasted well into the 20th century. Other Swedes, including farmers and fishers, gradually settled, mainly along Finland's Baltic coast. A number of incentives such as land grants and tax concessions were given to encourage new settlers, many of whom were veterans of the Swedish army.

Sweden's squabbles with Novgorod continued for two centuries. Treaties drawn up by the two powers defined the spheres of influence, with Sweden gaining control of southwest Finland and much of the west coast, while Novgorod controlled Karelia, spreading the Orthodox faith and Byzantine culture in the region.

In 1527 King Gustav Vasa of Sweden adopted the Lutheran faith and confiscated much of the property of the Catholic Church. The Finnish Reformation was ushered in by Mikael Agricola, who studied with Luther in Germany, and returned to Finland in 1539 to translate parts of the Bible into Finnish. His hard-line Protestant attitudes meant that most of the frescoes in medieval churches were whitewashed (to be rediscovered some 400 years later in relatively good condition).

Sweden started another chess game with Russia in Savo and Kainuu, using its Finnish subjects as pawns to settle areas well beyond the agreed boundaries. Russia retaliated, and most of the new settlements were razed in the bloody Kainuu War of the late 16th century.

The 17th century was Sweden's golden age, when it controlled much of the Baltic. Finland was put under the control of various governors.

During the Thirty Years' War in Europe, political power in Finland was exercised by Count Per Brahe, who travelled around the country and founded many towns. He was a larger-than-life figure who made his own

Duke Karl, regent of Finland, didn't care much for the family business. Campaigning against his nephew the king, he encouraged a peasant mutiny in 1596 and finally deposed him, exacting brutal revenge on his opponents.

As well as being the biggest landowner in Sweden, Per Brahe was a gourmet and wrote his own cookbook, which he took with him on his travels and insisted was followed to the letter.

AD 100	1155	1323	1527
The Roman historian Tacitus refers to the 'Fenni', most likely the Sámi, in the first known historical mention of the area. He isn't complimentary about their lack of permanent housing.	The first Christianising expedition is launched from Sweden against the pagan Finns. Further expeditions follow, and Finland is effectively under Swedish dominion for the next six centuries.	The Peace of Oreshek, signed by Sweden and Novgorod at Pähkinäsaari, establishes a frontier in the Karelian Isthmus, and delineates permitted spheres of influence still evident in present-day Finland.	King Gustav Vasa of Sweden adopts the Lutheran faith and confiscates much of the property of the Catholic Church. Finland's main Reformation figure, Mikael Agricola, returns from Germany in 1539.

rules: once censured for having illegally bagged an elk, he responded curtly that it had been on its last legs and he had killed it out of mercy.

Although Finland never experienced feudal serfdom to the extent seen in Russia, ethnic Finns were largely peasant farmers forced to lease land from Swedish landlords.

In 1697 the Swede Karl XII ascended the throne. Within three years he was drawn into the Great Northern War (1700–21), between Sweden and allied forces of Russia, Denmark and other Baltic powers, which marked the beginning of the end of the Swedish empire.

From Sweden to Russia

Peter the Great took advantage of Sweden's troubles and, though losing early engagements, soon stormed through Finland, which had been recently decimated by famine. From 1714 to 1721 Russia occupied Finland, a time still referred to as the Great Wrath, when several thousand Finns were killed and many more taken into slavery. The 1721 Treaty of Uusikaupunki brought peace at a cost – Sweden lost south Karelia to Russia.

Finland again paid the price for thwarted Swedish ambitions in the war of 1741–43; Russia again occupied the country, a period called the Lesser Wrath.

Tsar Alexander I signed a treaty with Napoleon and then attacked Finland in 1808. Following a bloody war, Sweden ceded Finland to Russia in 1809. Alexander pledged to respect Finnish customs and institutions; Finland kept its legal system and its Lutheran faith, and became a semi-autonomous grand duchy. At first, Russia encouraged development, and Finland benefited from the annexation. The capital was transferred from Turku to Helsinki in 1812.

Finland was still very much an impoverished rural society in the 19th century, and travel to the interior, especially in Lapland, could be an arduous journey of weeks by riverboat and overland. The tar and paper industries produced revenue from the vast forests, but were controlled by magnates in Baltic and Bothnian ports such as Oulu, which flourished while the hinterland remained poor.

Tar, used to caulk sailing ships, was a major 19th-century Finnish export, produced by burning pine trees in a tar pit; bark was removed from the trees four years earlier to stimulate resin production.

A Nation Born

Early stirrings of Finnish nationalism could be heard in the 19th century. Dissatisfaction with the Swedish administration came to a head with a letter written from officers of the Finnish army to the queen of Sweden questioning the legality of the war they were pursuing against Russia. Meanwhile, academic studies of Finnish cultural traditions were creating a base on which future nationalistic feelings could be founded.

The famous phrase 'Swedes we are not, Russians we will not become, so let us be Finns', though of uncertain origin, encapsulated the growing

1637	1640	1700	1714
Per Brahe becomes governor of Finland and goes on to found many towns. Meanwhile, Finnish cavalry earn a fearsome reputation in the Thirty Years' War.	Finland's first university is founded in Turku, which is the country's principal city until Helsinki is made capital in 1812.	Karl XII of Sweden is drawn into the Great Northern War, which is to mark the beginning of the end for the Swedish empire.	Russia occupies Finland, marking the beginning of the seven years known as the Great Wrath. When peace is made, Russia retains southern Karelia.

sense of Finnishness. Artistic achievements like Elias Lönnrot's *Kalevala* and Johan Ludvig Runeberg's poem 'Our Land', which became the national anthem, acted as standards to rally around. As Russia tightened its grip with a policy of Russification, workers, and artists such as Jean Sibelius, began to be inspired against the growing oppression, and the nation became emotionally ripe for independence.

In 1906 the Eduskunta parliament was introduced in Finland with universal and equal suffrage (Finland was the first country in Europe to grant women full political rights); however, Russian political oppression continued and poverty was endemic. In search of work and a better life, many Finns moved south to Helsinki or emigrated to North America in the first decades of the 20th century.

The Russian Revolution of October 1917 enabled the Finnish parliament to declare independence on 6 December of that year. Although Russia recognised the new nation, it hoped for a parallel workers' uprising; it fomented dissent and supplied arms to that end.

Following an attack by Russian-armed Finnish Reds on the civil guards in Vyborg, the Finnish Civil War flared in late January 1918. During 108 days of heavy fighting, approximately 30,000 Finns were killed. The Reds, comprising the rising working class, aspired to a Russian-style socialist revolution while retaining independence. The nationalist Whites, led by CGE Mannerheim, dreamed of monarchy and sought to emulate Germany.

In the first elections in 1907, 19 female members were elected to the Eduskunta, the first woman MPs in the world. Finland has been a trailblazer for equality in politics ever since.

LENIN IN FINLAND

One man who spent plenty of time in Finland was Vladimir Ilyich Lenin, father of the Russian Revolution. Having had a Finnish cellmate during his exile in Siberia, he then regularly visited the country for conferences of the Social Democratic Party, meeting Stalin for the first time at one of them. Lenin lived near Helsinki in 1907 before he was forced to flee the Russian Empire. In a Hollywood-style escape, he jumped off a moving train to avoid tsarist agents, and was then sheltered in Turku, before being moved to remote island communities in the southwest. Lenin found shelter on Parainen, but fearing capture, he walked across thin ice with a local guide to Nauvo (there's a famous painting of this in the Hermitage in St Petersburg), from where he finally jumped on a steamer to Stockholm.

Lenin entered Finland again via Tornio in 1917. After the abortive first revolution, he lived in a tent for a while in Iljitsevo, before going back to Russia and his date with destiny.

Lenin, even before having visited Finland, had agitated for Finnish independence, a conviction which he maintained. In December 1917, he signed the declaration of Finnish independence; without his support, it is doubtful that the nation would have been born at that time.

You can learn more about Lenin in Finland at the Lenin-Museo (p129) in Tampere.

1741–43	1808	1812	1827
Russia again occupies Finland. The Treaty of Turku ends what becomes known as the Lesser Wrath, but cedes parts of the Savo region of Finland to Russia.	Finland is invaded and occupied by Russia, becoming a grand duchy of the Russian Empire in 1809; Tsar Alexander I promises to respect its autonomy at the Diet of Porvoo.	Helsinki becomes the capital replacing the old, and more Swedish-oriented capital, Turku.	Elias Lönnrot makes the first of his song-collecting journeys into remote Karelian forests, which culminate in the publication of *Kalevala*, the national epic.

THE WINTER WAR & ITS CONTINUATION

Diplomatic manoeuvrings in Europe in the 1930s meant that Finland, inexperienced in the sinuous negotiations of Great Power politics, had a few difficult choices to make. The security threat posed by the Soviet Union meant that some factions were in favour of developing closer ties with Nazi Germany, while others favoured rapprochement with Moscow. On 23 August 1939, the Soviet and German foreign ministers, Molotov and Ribbentrop, signed a nonaggression pact, which gave the Soviet Union a free hand in Finland. The USSR argued that its security required a slice of southeastern Karelia and the right to build bases on Finnish soil. Finland refused, and on 30 November 1939 the Winter War between Finland and the Soviet Union began.

This was a harsh winter – temperatures reached -40°C and soldiers died in their thousands. Despite a lack of artillery and planes, Finland resisted the Red Army, with mobile skiing troops conducting successful guerrilla-style assaults in small groups. Stalin was forced to send more and more divisions to the front, with some 600,000 soldiers eventually being committed. Several Russian divisions were destroyed, with an estimated 130,000 dead as the Finns stopped the Russian advance by early January. But this was an unwinnable war; after 105 days of fighting in the harshest imaginable conditions, Finland conceded. In the Treaty of Moscow (March 1940), Finland was forced to cede the Karelian Isthmus, together with the eastern Salla and Kuusamo regions and some islands: in total nearly one-tenth of its territory. Over 400,000 Karelian refugees flooded across the new border into Finland.

In the following months, the Soviet Union attempted to persuade Finland to cede more territory. Isolated from the Western Allies, Finland turned to Germany for help and allowed the transit of German troops. When hostilities broke out between Germany and the Soviets in June 1941, German troops were already on Finnish soil, and the Continuation War between Finland and the Red Army followed. In the subsequent fighting, the Finns advanced, reaching their old borderline in December. Finns began to resettle Karelia. When Soviet forces staged a huge comeback in the summer of 1944, Finnish president Risto Ryti, who had promised Ribbentrop that Finland would not negotiate peace with Russia without German agreement, resigned, with CGE Mannerheim taking his place. Mannerheim negotiated an armistice with the Russians, ceding Finland's 'other arm', the Petsamo area of the Kola Peninsula, and ordered the evacuation of German troops. Finland waged a bitter war in Lapland to oust the Germans, who staged a 'scorched earth' retreat from the country until the general peace in the spring of 1945.

Against the odds, Finland had remained independent, but at a heavy price: the territorial losses of 1940 and 1944 were ratified at the Peace of Paris in February 1947, and heavy war reparations were ordered to be paid to the Soviet Union. Many in Finland are still bitter about the loss of these territories. Nevertheless, the resistance against the might of the Red Army is something of which Finns are still proud.

1853	1865	1899	1917
As part of the Russian Empire, Finland is involved in the Crimean War, with British troops destroying fortifications at Loviisa, Helsinki and Bomarsund.	Jean Sibelius, Finland's most famous composer, is born in Hämeenlinna. His 1899 *Finlandia* symphony becomes a symbol of the Finnish independence movement.	The Tsar implements a policy of Russification in Finland, and attempts to impose the Russian language on the country. Widespread protests result and campaigns for independence gain strength.	Finland declares independence from the Soviet Union. Shortly afterwards the Finnish Civil War breaks out between the communist Reds and the establishment Whites.

The Whites, with substantial German help, eventually gained victory and the war ended in May 1918. Friedrich Karl, Prince of Hessen, was elected king of Finland by the Eduskunta on 9 October 1918, but the defeat of imperial Germany a month later made Finland choose a republican state model, under its first president, KJ Ståhlberg.

Though internal struggles continued, and despite the crushing blows of WWII, Finland gained fame internationally as a brave new nation. Significant events included Finland's Winter War heroics, Paavo Nurmi's distinguished career as a long-distance runner, Ester Toivonen's Miss Europe title in 1933, Artturi Virtanen's Nobel Prize for Chemistry in 1945, the Helsinki Olympics of 1952, and plaudits won by Finnish designers in international expositions. These achievements fostered national confidence, helped Finland to feel that it belonged at the table of nations, and gave it strength to survive the difficult Cold War period that followed.

Mannerheim had a fascinating life divided into several distinct phases. Check out www.mannerheim.fi for an extremely comprehensive online biography.

HISTORY THE COLD WAR

The Cold War

The year of the Helsinki Olympics, 1952, was also the year that Finland completed paying its heavy war reparations to the Soviet Union. Mostly paid in machinery and ships, they in fact had a positive effect, as they established the heavy engineering industry that eventually stabilised the Finnish postwar economy.

Finnish society changed profoundly during this period. In the 1940s the population was still predominantly agricultural, but the privations of the war, which sent people to the towns and cities in search of work, as well as the influx of nearly half a million Karelian refugees, sparked an acute housing crisis. Old wooden town centres were demolished to make way for apartment blocks, and new suburbs appeared almost overnight around Helsinki; conversely, areas in the north and east lost most of their young people (often half their population) to domestic emigration.

From the end of the war until the early 1990s, the overriding political issue was a familiar one: balance between East and West. Stalin's 'friendship and cooperation' treaty of 1948 was used by the USSR throughout the Cold War as coercion in an attempt to limit Finland's interaction with the West.

A savvy political head was needed to negotiate these choppy waters, and Finland found it in the astute if controversial figure of Urho K Kekkonen, president from 1956 to 1981 and a master of diplomacy.

Canny and unorthodox, Kekkonen realised that he was the devil the Kremlin knew, and he used this to his advantage. Similarly, he did so with the West's fear that Finland would fall completely under the sway of the USSR. He signed a free-trade agreement with the European Free Trade Association (EFTA) in 1961 which brought Finland closer to a European orbit, but also signed a parallel agreement for preferential trade with the Soviets.

Though still part of Russia, Finland issued its first postage stamps in 1856 and its own currency, the markka, in 1860.

1920	1939	1948	1950
Relations with the Soviets are normalised by the Treaty of Tartu, which sees Finnish territory expand to its largest point ever, including the Petsamo region in the far northeast.	The Winter War sees the Soviet Union invade Finland. After 15 weeks of fighting in subzero conditions, Finland is forced to cede a substantial amount of territory.	The 'friendship and cooperation' treaty is signed between Finland and the Soviet Union.	Urho K Kekkonen becomes prime minister for the first time. In 1956 he is elected to the position of president, which he holds for 25 years.

Kekkonen and his government had a close relationship with many of the KGB's big men in Finland, and political nominations were submitted to Moscow for approval within a framework of 'friendly coexistence'. Many Finns regard his era with embarrassment, believing that Kekkonen abased the country by such close contact with the Bear, and that his grip on power and web of behind-the-scenes manoeuvrings were uncomfortably reminiscent of the Kremlin itself. Nevertheless, Kekkonen presided over a period in which the nation moved from an impoverished agricultural state to a modern European democracy with a watertight welfare system and healthy economy, all in the shadow of a great power whose actions in Eastern Europe had given ample reason for Finland to tread with extreme caution.

After Kekkonen's resignation due to ill health at 81, the Soviets continued to dabble in Finnish politics, mostly with the aim of reducing US influence and preventing Finland joining what is now the EU. That particular chapter of Finland's long and complicated relationship with its eastern neighbour came to a close with the collapse of the USSR.

A *kotiryssä* (Russian contact) was crucial for politicians of ambition in Cold War Finland, when much career advancement was under Moscow's control. But those friendly dinners on the Kremlin's tab could look a little treasonous if the vodka loosened your tongue...

Modern Finland

Following the collapse of the Soviet Union, a load was lifted from Finland, but the early 1990s were not the easiest of times. The bubble of the 1980s had burst, the Soviet Union disappeared with debts unpaid, the markka was devalued, and unemployment jumped from 3% to 20%.

However, Finland could finally integrate itself fully with Europe. Since joining the EU in January 1995, Finland has largely prospered, and was a founder member of the euro in 2002.

Balancing power between the president and the parliament had long been on the agenda since Kekkonen's monarch-like presidency, and in 1999 a new constitution was approved limiting certain presidential powers. The first to take the wheel under the new order was Tarja Halonen of the Social Democratic Party, elected in 2000. Referred to affectionately as Muumimamma (Moominmamma), she was well loved by many Finns, and was re-elected for a second (and, by law, final) six-year term in 2006 before being succeeded in 2012 by the National Coalition Party's Sauli Niinistö.

In the new millennium, Finland has boomed on the back of the technology sector – which, despite the plunge of Nokia, continues to be strong – the traditionally important forestry industry, design and manufacturing, and, increasingly, tourism. Despite suffering economically along with most of the rest of the world in recent years, it's nevertheless a major success story of the new Europe with a strong economy, robust social values, and super-low crime and corruption. Finland consistently

1952	1971	1973	1995
Helsinki hosts the summer Olympic Games. Finland completes war reparation payments of US$300 million to the USSR as decreed by the Peace of Paris in 1947.	For the first time, urban dwellers outnumber rural dwellers in Finland.	The Delegation for Sámi affairs, the beginnings of the Sámi parliament, convenes for the first time. Finland signs a trade agreement with the EEC despite Soviet pressure not to.	After a referendum with a 57% 'yes' vote in October 1994, Finland joins the EU.

ranks highly in quality-of-life indices and has in recent years outperformed its traditionally superior neighbour Sweden in many areas.

Russia is, as ever, still high on the agenda. Finland's geographical proximity and close historical relationship with its neighbour gave it a head start in dealing with post-Soviet Moscow, and the trade relationship remains close between the two countries. Many Finnish companies contract much of their business to Russia, where wages and overheads are lower, while Russian labour and tourism both make important contributions to the Finnish economy. Nevertheless, many Finns are still suspicious of Russia and the Putin brand of nationalism. The Winter War has not been forgotten: national service and border patrols are taken seriously.

Though Finland has experienced far less immigration than most European countries, immigration has increased in recent years and is an issue that has raised headlines.

Finland's own indigenous people, the Sámi, have been afforded greater recognition in the last 50 years, with the establishment of a Finnish Sámi parliament and the enshrinement of their languages in regional laws. However, disputes between reindeer herders and forestry firms in the north have ignited debate as to whether Sámi interests continue to come second to those of the country's timber industry.

Despite the challenges ahead, Finland can feel just a wee bit pleased with itself. For a cold and remote, sparsely populated forest nation, it's done rather well.

For more on Finnish history, head to www.finland.fi, which has excellent essays written by experts on various periods.

HISTORY MODERN FINLAND

2000	2002	2007–08	2011
Finland elects Tarja Halonen as its first female president. She proves a popular figure and holds the post for the maximum 12 years.	Along with several other European countries, Finland adopts the euro, bidding farewell to the markka after 142 years.	Two similar shooting sprees prompt nationwide mourning and a bout of self-examination in this usually peaceful nation.	The rise of the anti-immigration True Finns party reflects increasingly ambivalent attitudes towards Finland's role in the EU.

The Sámi

Sámi are the indigenous inhabitants of Lapland and are today spread across four countries from the Kola Peninsula in Russia to the southern Norwegian mountains. The Sámi region is called Sápmi, and about half of Finnish Sámi live in it. According to archaeological evidence, this region was first settled soon after the last ice age around 10,000 years ago, but it wasn't until the beginning of the Christian era – the early Iron Age – that Finns and Sámi had become two distinct groups with diverging languages.

Traditions & Beliefs

For more information, visit the excellent Siida museum in Inari, Samiland in Levi or the Arktikum in Rovaniemi. Hidden away via the 'web exhibitions' page on the Siida website (www.siida.fi) you can access a series of excellent pages on the Inari and Skolt Sámi cultures.

The early inhabitants were nomadic people – hunters, fishers and food-gatherers – who migrated with the seasons. Early Sámi society was based on the *siida*, small groups comprising a number of families who controlled particular hunting, herding and fishing grounds. Families lived in a *kota*, a traditional dwelling resembling the tepee or wigwam of native North Americans. Smaller tents served as temporary shelters while following the migrating reindeer herds; a 'winter village' system also developed, where groups came together to help survive the harsh winter months. Mechanisation in the 1950s meant reindeer herders could go out on snowmobiles and return home every night. This ended the need for nomadism and the Sámi became a settled people.

The natural environment was essential to Sámi existence: they worshipped the sun (father), earth (mother) and wind, and believed all things in nature had a soul. There were many gods, who dwelled in *seita* (holy sites): fells, lakes or sacred stones. The link with the gods was through the *noaidi* (shaman), the most important member of the community.

Traditional legends, rules of society and fairy tales were handed down through the generations by storytelling. A unique form of storytelling was the yoik, a chant in which the singer would use words or imitate the sounds of animals and nature to describe experiences or people. It's still used by the Sámi today, sometimes accompanied by instruments.

Groups

More than half of the 70,000 Sámi population are in Norway, while around 9000 reside in Finland; there are close cross-border cultural ties. Five distinct Sámi groups with distinct cultural traditions live in Finland. Vuotso Sámi live around Saariselkä and are the southernmost group. Enontekiö Sámi dwell around Hetta in the west and, with Utsjoki Sámi, who settled from Finland's northernmost tip along the Norwegian border to Karigasniemi, have the strongest reindeer-herding heritage. Inari Sámi live around the shores of Inarijärvi and have a strong fishing tradition. Skolt Sámi originally inhabited the Kola Peninsula around Petsamo, and fled to Finland when the Soviet Union took back control of that area. They number around 600, live around Sevettijärvi and Nellim, and are of Orthodox religion.

LOCAL KNOWLEDGE

SÁMI CULTURE TO ME MEANS...

'Sámi culture to me means the very act of staying and being alive – it's a life source. It's been my roots; what has bound me to something. When I was a child, I spent a lot of time in my grandmother's house in Karigasniemi. My grandfather showed me the flowers, nature, told me things. Later I understood how valuable it had been to have heard even short parts of the stories. I asked to tape them but he said no, there must be a possibility for mistakes. I fill the missing parts in. That's how these tales have always developed and grown.

'Do parents still maintain the oral tradition? Unfortunately not so much, but there's still something like that going on. Mostly you see it in attitude, the way of behaving in nature, respect for animals. Stories and beliefs have disappeared more, partly because of Christianity, partly because of the school system. People don't explain things in the same way these days.

'There'll never be a united Sámi people, but self-confidence is stronger all the time. Sámi people are respecting their roots more and are finding positives from their own culture. But we are somehow in danger of being hugged into destruction. So many subsidies are sort of destroying the culture. We have no real political power but at least you can study Sámi in school these days.

'Sámi women have always been strong women. They needed to run the home – the men were always somewhere else, away with the reindeer and so on. It's been quite a maternal culture and still is in most ways.'

Satu Natunen, Sámi Artist

Role of the Reindeer

Reindeer have always been central to the Sámi existence. Sámi consumed the meat and milk, used the fur for clothing and bedding, and made fish hooks and harpoons from the bones and antlers. Today a significant percentage of Sámi living in Sápmi are involved in reindeer husbandry; tourism is another big employer.

Originally the Sámi hunted wild reindeer, usually trapping them in pitfalls. Hunting continued until around the 16th century, when the Sámi began to domesticate entire herds and migrate with them. Towards the end of the 19th century, Finland's reindeer herders were organised into *paliskunta* cooperatives, of which there are now 56 in northern Finland. Reindeer wander free around the large natural areas within each *paliskunta,* which are bordered by enormous fences that cross the Lapland wilderness. Each herder is responsible for his stock and identifies them by earmarks – a series of distinctive notches cut into the ear of each animal. GPS collars now help owners to track their animals.

Handicrafts

The colourful Sámi costumes, featuring jackets, pants or skirts embroidered with bright red, blue and yellow patterns, are now mostly worn on special occasions and during Sámi festivals.

Sámi handicrafts (including bags and boots made from reindeer hide, knitted gloves and socks, textiles, shawls, strikingly colourful Sámi hats, jewellery and silverware) are recognised as indigenous art. Genuine handicrafts carry the name 'Sámi duodji'. Inari is one of the best places to buy them.

Languages

Sámi languages are related to Finnish and other Finno-Ugric languages. There are three Sámi languages, not very mutually intelligible, used in Finland today. There are another seven Sámi languages in Norway, Sweden and Russia.

Never ask a Sámi how many reindeer he or she owns. It's a very personal matter, like someone's bank balance. It's something they wouldn't even necessarily reveal to their closest friends.

Finnish Lifestyle & Culture

Despite the magnificent lakescapes and outdoor activities, Finland's greatest highlight is the Finns. Isolated in this corner of Europe, they do their own thing and have developed a strongly independent, self-reliant streak, coloured by a seriously offbeat sense of humour.

Love of Nature

Finns have a deep and abiding love of their country's forests and lakes. In July Finland is one of the world's most relaxing, joyful places to be – a reason Finns traditionally have not been big travellers. After the long winter, why miss the best their country has to offer? Finns head en-masse for the *mökki* from Midsummer until the end of the July holidays. Most Finns of any age could forage in a forest for an hour at the right time of year and emerge with a feast of fresh berries, wild mushrooms and probably a fish or two. City-dwelling Finns are far more in touch with nature than most of their European equivalents.

Despite its proximity, Finland is generally considered not to be part of Scandinavia, either culturally or geographically. Many Finnish-speaking Finns are insistent on this point, and prefer the less specific term 'Nordic countries' to describe Finland and its western neighbours.

Sisu

Finland is not Scandinavia, nor is it Russia; nevertheless, Finnish tradition owes something to both cultures. But the modern Finn is staunchly independent. The long struggle for emancipation, together with the battle to survive in a harsh environment, has engendered an ordered society which solves its own problems in its own way. They have also given birth to the Finnish trait of *sisu*, often translated as 'guts', or the resilience to survive prolonged hardship. Even if all looks lost, until the final defeat, a Finn with *sisu* will fight – or swim, or run, or work – valiantly. This trait is valued highly, with the country's heroic resistance against the Red Army in the Winter War usually thought of as the ultimate example.

DRIVIN' WHEELS

Few countries have such an obsession with cars as Finland. The interest goes right down the scale, from watching Formula One to changing the oil in the old Datsun parked outside.

You won't be in Finland for long before you'll hear a baritone bellow and see a glint of fins and whitewall tyres as some American classic car rolls by, immaculately polished and tuned. You probably never knew that so many Mustangs, Chargers or Firebirds existed this side of the Atlantic. Even non-classics long since dead elsewhere are kept alive here with loyal home maintenance.

Rally driving sends Finns wild; the exploits of legends like Tommi Mäkinen and Marcus Grönholm are the latest of a long line in a sport in which Finland has excelled. In Formula One, too, Suomi punches well above its weight, with Keke Rosberg, Mika Häkkinen and Kimi Räikkönen all former world champions. In small towns, often the only entertainment for the local young is trying to emulate them by doing blockies around the kauppatori...

THE MÖKKI

Tucked away in Finland's forests and lakelands are half a million *kesämökkejä* (summer cottages). Part holiday house, part sacred place, the *mökki* is the spiritual home of the Finn and you don't know the country until you've spent time in one. The average Finn spends less than two days in a hotel per year, but several weeks in a cottage.

These are places where people get back to nature. Amenities are often basic – the gloriously genuine ones have no electricity or running water – but even the highest-flying Euro-techno-executives are in their element, chopping wood, DIY-ing, picking chanterelles and blueberries, rowing, and selecting young birch twigs for the *vihta* (sauna whisk). There's no better sauna than a *mökki* one: the soft steam of the wood stove caresses rather than burns, and the nude dash for an invigorating spring into the chilly lake is a Finnish summer icon. As is the post-sauna can of beer, new potatoes with fresh dill, and sausages grilled over pine cones on the barbecue. It's hard not to feel at peace when gazing out at the silent lake, trees perfectly reflected in it by the midnight sun, and anything of consequence miles away.

The best way to experience a *mökki* is to be invited to one by a Finnish friend, but failing that, there are numerous ones that you can rent, particularly in the Lakeland area.

Saunas

No matter where you are in Finland, you'll never be far from a sauna (pronounced *sah*-oo-nah, not *saw*-nuh). With over two million in homes, hotels, summer cottages, campsites and numerous other unlikely places, saunas are prescribed to cure almost every ailment, and are used to seal business deals or just socialise over a few beers.

Traditionally, saunas were used as a family bathhouse as well as a place to smoke meat and even give birth. The earliest references to the Finnish sauna date from chronicles of 1113, and there are numerous mentions of their use in the *Kalevala*.

Most saunas are private, in Finnish homes, but public saunas are common and most hotels have one. An invitation to a family's sauna is an honour, as it is to be invited to a person's home for a meal. The sauna is taken naked. While a Finnish family will often take the sauna together, in mixed gatherings it is usual for the men and women to go separately.

Public saunas are usually separated by gender and if there is just one sauna, the hours are different for men and women. In unisex saunas you will be given some sort of wrap or covering to wear. Finns strictly observe the nonsexual character of the sauna and this point should be respected. The sauna was originally a place to bathe and meditate.

The most common sauna is the electric sauna stove, which produces a fairly dry, harsh heat compared with the much-loved chimney sauna, driven by a log fire and the staple of life at summer cottages. Even rarer is the true *savusauna* (smoke sauna), without a chimney. The smoke is let out just before entry and the soot-blackened walls are part of the experience. Although the top of a sauna can reach over 120°C, many Finns consider the most satisfying temperature for a sauna to be around 80°C. At this temperature you'll sweat and, some Finns claim, feel the wood smoke in your lungs.

Proper sauna etiquette dictates that you use a *kauha* (ladle) to throw water on the *kiuas* (sauna stove), which then gives off the *löyly* (sauna steam). At this point, at least in summer in the countryside, you might take the *vihta* or *vasta* (a bunch of fresh, leafy birch twigs) and lightly strike yourself. This improves circulation, has cleansing properties and gives your skin a pleasant smell. When you are sufficiently warmed, you'll jump in the sea, a lake, river or pool, then return to the sauna

Traditional ballroom-style dancing is big in Finland in dedicated dance bar/restaurants or in summer dance pavilions. The website www.tanssi.net encourages visitors to participate in a night of Finnish dancing (no Finnish required) and has a detailed English page explaining the etiquette.

Finland hits the headlines every now and then for the fact that its speeding fines are based on income. You're a multimillionaire doing 80km/h in a 50km/h zone? Expect a fine of €100,000 or more...

to warm up and repeat the cycle several times. If you're indoors, a cold shower will do. The swim and hot-cold aspect is such an integral part of the sauna experience that in the dead of winter Finns cut a hole in the ice and jump right in.

Sadness

There's a definite depressive streak in Finns, more so than in their western neighbours. While they aren't among Europe's biggest drinkers per capita, the incidence of alcoholism is high. The winter darkness can strain even the most optimistic soul – seasonal affective disorder (SAD) is significant here and suicide levels are higher than the comfortable standard of living would predict. The melancholic trend is reflected in Finns' love of darkly themed music and lyrics of lost love; even the cheeriest summer Suomi-pop hits sound like the singer's just backed over their dog, and Finnish tango takes lugubriousness off the chart.

> While suicide rates are a problem, it's a myth that Finns have the highest rate of it in the world. Actually, it only comes in ninth in Europe, between Serbia and Belgium.

Silence

While the 'silent Finn' concept has been exaggerated over the years, it's certainly true that Finns believe in comfortable silences, so if a conversation dies off naturally there's no need to jump-start it with small talk. Finns quip that they invented text messaging so they didn't have to talk to each other, and sitting in the sauna for 20 minutes with your best friend, saying nothing, is perfectly normal. Finns generally have a quirky, dark, self-deprecating sense of humour and may just be saving their words for a well-timed jibe.

Not to say Finns don't talk. They do, and once they get a couple of pints of lager in them, they really do, as that reserve goes out the window to be replaced by boisterous bonhomie.

> Finns love the weekend, when they head to the summer cottage, play sport or party in the evening. But the working week also has a high point. On Wednesday nights restaurants are busy, music is playing at all the nightspots, bars are full – Finns are celebrating *pikku lauantai*: 'little Saturday'.

Religion

The Lutheran church dominates the religious scene here, with some 78% describing themselves as such on a census form; the next religious group, Finnish Orthodox, makes up only 1.5% of the population. Nevertheless, Finns have one of the lowest rates of church attendance in the Christian world.

Various Lutheran revivalist movements are seeking to combat this and are often in the news. The ultra-conservative Laestadian movement – many of whose members frown on such evils as dancing and earrings – has many adherents, as does the charismatic church Nokia-Missio. Almost one in 10 Finns belongs to a revivalist movement.

Finnish Design

The rustle of the birch or waterbird's splash on a lake are never far below the surface of a Finn's soul and they have taken this closeness to nature and melded it to a solid Nordic practicality to create a unique design tradition. World leaders in the field for nigh on a century, Finnish designers evoke both the colourful optimism of summer and the minimalist austerity of winter in their work, which ranges from traditional Suomi design icons to avant-garde modern creations that test the limits of 3D printing.

The Roots of Creativity

Its inhabitants' almost mystical closeness to nature has always underpinned design in Finland, and it's rarely been a self-conscious art. However high Finland may climb on the lifestyle indexes these days, its design still has its roots in practicality. Indeed, it is a practicality originally born of poverty: the inventiveness of a hand-to-mouth rural population made life easier in very small steps.

Finland's location, and its historical role as a pawn in a long-running Russia–Sweden chess game, have given it a variety of influences and a certain flexibility. As a meeting point between east and west, Finland has traditionally been a place of trade, a point of tension and, therefore, a point of change and innovation. Its climate, too, is a key factor, as it has meant that efficiency has always been the primary requisite for design of everyday objects. In bald terms, if that axe didn't chop enough wood for the winter, you wouldn't survive.

The forest is ever-present in Finnish life, so it's no surprise to find that nature is the dominant and enduring motif in the country's designs, from Lapland's sheath knives to the seasonal flower-and-forest colours of Marimekko's palette. Timber remains an important material, and reassuringly chunky wooden objects adorn almost every Finnish home and summer cottage.

The website www.finnishdesign.com mostly sticks to the well-established names but it's a good introduction. Design Forum Finland's webpage (www.designforum.fi) has useful links; its awards are another good way to keep tabs on the scene.

NEW THINGS THAT'LL FIT IN YOUR CASE

➡ One of Sami Rinne's engagingly quirky ceramics – maybe that mug with a handle like a reindeer's antlers?

➡ A set of Verso's colourful, original felt mats and coasters to brighten up your dinner table.

➡ A pair of Minna Parikka's shoes – 21st-century style straight from a smoky 1930s nightclub.

➡ One of Jani Martikainen's birch trivets (pot-plant bases) from his Majamoo company. The only trouble is that the plant hides it.

➡ Whatever the versatile Harri Koskinen has just designed – from lighting to glassware.

➡ Some baggy, edgy but humorous streetwear from Daniel Palillo.

Alvar Aalto

Alvar Aalto was for many the 20th century's number one architect. In an era of increasing urbanisation, postwar rebuilding and immense housing pressure, Aalto found elegant solutions for public and private edifices that embraced functionalism but never at the expense of humanity. Viewed from the next century, his work still more than holds its own, and his huge contributions in other areas of art and design make him a mighty figure indeed.

Top Aalto Buildings

Finlandia Talo, Helsinki

Otaniemi University, Espoo

Workers' Club Building, Jyväskylä

Aalto Centre, Seinäjoki

Kolmen Ristin Kirkko, Imatra

Aalto had a democratic, practical view of his field: he saw his task as 'a question of making architecture serve the wellbeing and prosperity of millions of citizens' where it had previously been the preserve of a wealthy few. But he was no utilitarian; beauty was always a concern, and he was adamant that a proper studio environment was essential for the creativity of the architect to flower.

Born in 1898 in Kuortane near Seinäjoki, Aalto worked in Jyväskylä, Turku and Helsinki before gaining an international reputation for his pavilions at the World Fairs of the late 1930s. His 1925 marriage to Aino Marsio created a dynamic team that pushed boundaries in several fields, including glassware and furniture design. Their work on bending and laminating wood revolutionised the furniture industry, and the classic forms they produced for their company, Artek, are still Finnish staples. Aalto's use of rod-shaped ceramic tiles, undulated wood, woven cane, brick and marble was particularly distinctive.

Aalto's notable buildings are dotted throughout Finland. A comparison of the Aalto Centre in Seinäjoki with the Ristinkirkko in Lahti highlights the range of his work. Charmingly, Aalto's favourite design was his own wooden boat (on show at his summer house near Jyväskylä), which he planned and built with great love, but little knowledge of boatbuilding. It was barely seaworthy at the best of times, and regularly capsized and sank.

The Classics

If the early 21st century is a new golden age for Finnish design, the original one was in the 1950s and 1960s. The freelance designers producing marvels in glass for Iittala, ceramics for Arabia, cookware for Hackman and furniture for Artek won international recognition and numerous prestigious awards, particularly at the Triennale di Milano shows. Though times were still tough after the war, and the country was struggling to house refugees from occupied Karelia, the successes of these firms, together with the Helsinki Olympic Games of 1952, helped put a still-young nation on the map and build confidence and national pride, which had been weakened after the gruelling battles with Russia and Germany.

FINNISH DESIGN CLASSICS

➡ Artek's Aalto chairs. To think that we take bent wood for granted in our furniture these days.

➡ The Iittala vase. Yes, Aalto again. Whether or not it actually resembles an Inuit woman's leather pants, it's undeniably a classic.

➡ An Unikko bed sheet from Marimekko. Who doesn't dream better under those upbeat red poppies?

➡ 1930s ringed tumblers designed by Aino Aalto – you'll drink your breakfast juice out of one of them within a couple of days of your arrival.

➡ Marttiini knives, which are made way up north at Rovaniemi and are still first choice for outdoors folk 80 years after they were first produced.

The story of the Iittala glass company could be a metaphor for the story of Finnish design. Still producing to models imported from Sweden in the early 20th century, the company began to explore more home-grown options. Glass design competitions were an outward-looking source of ideas: from one of these came Alvar Aalto's famous Iittala vase, which he described as 'an Eskimo woman's leather trousers'. Then two giants of postwar design, Tapio Wirkkala (1915–85) and Timo Sarpaneva (1926–2006), began to explore textures and forms gleaned from Finnish lakescapes. Coloured glass fell from use and the classic Iittala ranges were born, with sand-scouring creating the appearance of cut ice, and Wirkkala's impossibly fluid forms seemingly melting away. The opaque look, which resembled ceramics, was a later creation as a new generation took to the field. Harri Koskinen (b 1970) and Annaleena Hakatie (b 1965) were among the leading lights, though the company has never been afraid to commission foreign designers. Iittala is today under the same ownership as Hackman, the long-established cutlery and cookware producers, and Arabia, who roughly paralleled Iittala's glassware trajectory with ceramics.

One of the biggest and most versatile names on the Finnish design scene is Stefan Lindfors, whose reptile- and insect-inspired work has been described as a warped update of Aalto's own nature-influenced work.

Clothing has been another area of success. Finland, unlike its Nordic neighbours, has tended to beat its own fashion path. It's traditionally been a place where teenagers can wear a jumper knitted by granny to school, and though new and exciting ideas are constantly created here, they tend to be built on solid, traditional foundations.

The godfather of Finnish design, Kaj Franck (1911–89) took ideas from traditional rustic clothing for his pared-back creations, but it was the birth and rapid rise to prominence of Marimekko, founded in 1951, that made an international impact. Optimistic, colourful and well-made, it bucked contemporary trends, focusing on a simple and unashamed beauty. Though the company went through a difficult period, it's back at the top these days, as the retro appeal of its classic shirts, bags, curtains and fabrics fills wardrobes with flowers once again.

Other well-established Finnish names include Aarikka, whose wooden jewellery and other accessories have always had a cheerily reassuring solidity and honesty, and Kalevala Koru, a byword for quality silver and gold jewellery. Pentik's wide range of interior design and homeware products includes the recent Saaga range, inspired by the designs of Sámi shaman drums.

The Newcomers

A strong design tradition tends to produce good young designers and Finland's education system is strong on fostering creativity, so Suomi is churning them out at a fair rate. New names, ranges and shops crop up in Helsinki's design district like mushrooms overnight, and exciting contemporary design is being produced on all fronts. Fennofolk is the name for one broad movement that seeks, like the original giants of Finnish design, to take inspiration from Suomi's natural and cultural heritage, adding a typically Finnish injection of weirdness along the way.

There are exciting things continuing to happen across all fields of design. Paola Suhonen's IvanaHelsinki clothing label combines innovation with practicality and sustainability, while Hanna Sarén's clothing shot to fame after being referenced in *Sex and the City*. Julia Lundsten and Minna Parikka are head-turning young stars of the footwear world. In industrial design, Harri Koskinen is a giant; his clean-lined minimalism produces objects that are always reassuringly practical but quite unlike anything you've ever seen before. Helsinki bristles with high-quality graphic design studios that are leading lights in their field.

The Arts

Finland has a flourishing cultural scene and puts a high priority on the arts, especially music, in its education system. Writers and artists looking to the Finnish wilderness for their inspiration evoked a pride in Finland that became an important part of the movement that eventually led to Finnish independence in 1917.

Literature

There's an excellent, detailed, though somewhat out-of-date, index of Finnish and other Nordic authors in English at www.kirjasto.sci.fi.

Finland had a rich oral tradition of folklore, but written Finnish was created by the Reformation figure Mikael Agricola (1510–57), who wrote the first alphabet. Although written Finnish was emerging in schools, the earliest fiction was written in Swedish.

All that changed in the early 19th century with the penning of the *Kalevala* and the beginning of a nationalistic renaissance. Poet JL Runeberg wrote *Tales of the Ensign Stål,* capturing Finland at war with Russia, while Aleksis Kivi wrote *Seven Brothers,* the nation's first novel, about brothers escaping conventional life in the forest, allegorising the birth of Finnish national consciousness.

This theme continued in the 1970s with *The Year of the Hare,* looking at a journalist's escape into the wilds by the prolific, popular and bizarre Arto Paasilinna. Other 20th-century novelists include Mika Waltari who gained international fame with *The Egyptian,* and FE Sillanpää who re-

FINLAND'S NATIONAL EPIC

It's hard to overestimate the influence on Finland of the *Kalevala,* an epic tale compiled from the songs of bards that tells everything from the history of the world to how to make decent homebrew. Intrepid country doctor Elias Lönnrot trekked eastern Finland during the first half of the 19th century in order to collect traditional poems, oral runes, legends, lore and folk stories. Over 11 long tours, he compiled this material with his own writing to form what came to be regarded as the national epic of Finland.

The mythology of the book blends creation stories, wedding poems and classic struggles between good and evil. Although there are heroes and villains, there are also more nuanced characters that are not so simply described. The main storyline concentrates on the events in two imaginary countries, Kalevala (characterised as 'our country') and Pohjola ('the other place', or the north). Many commentators feel that the epic echoes ancient territorial conflicts between the Finns and the Sámi. Although impossible to accurately reproduce the Finnish original, the memorable characters are particularly well brought to life in poet Keith Bosley's English translation of the *Kalevala,* which is a fantastic, lyrical read.

The first version of *Kalevala* appeared in 1833, with another following in 1835 and yet another, the final version, *Uusi-Kalevala* (New Kalevala), in 1849. Its influence on generations of Finnish artists, writers and composers was and is immense, particularly on painter Akseli Gallen-Kallela and composer Jean Sibelius, who repeatedly returned to the work for inspiration. Beyond Finland the epic has influenced the Estonian epic *Kalevipoeg* and American poet Henry Wadsworth Longfellow. Indeed, JRR Tolkien based significant parts of his mythos on the *Kalevala.*

MODERN SÁMI MUSIC

Several Finnish Sámi groups and artists have created excellent modern music with the traditional yoik (chant; also *joiks* or *juoiggus*) form. The yoik is traditionally sung a capella, often invoking a person or place with immense spiritual importance in Sámi culture. Wimme is a big name in this sphere, and Angelit produce popular, dancefloor-style Sámi music. One of their former members, Ulla Pirttijärvi, releases particularly haunting solo albums, while Vilddas are on the trance-y side of Sámi music, combining it with other influences. Look out too for rockier offerings from SomBy and Tiina Sanila.

ceived the Nobel Prize for Literature in 1939. The national bestseller during the postwar period was *The Unknown Soldier* by Väinö Linna. The seemingly endless series of autobiographical novels by Kalle Päätalo and the witty short stories by Veikko Huovinen are also very popular. Finland's most internationally famous author is Tove Jansson, whose books about the fantastic Moomin family have long captured the imagination. Notable living writers (apart from Paasilinna) include the versatile Leena Krohn and Mikko Rimminen, who has attracted attention for both novels and poetry.

As well as compiling and writing the *Kalevala*, Elias Lönnrot's work in creating a standard Finnish grammar and vocabulary was of great importance. Finnish has remained very much the same ever since, at least in written form.

Music

Finland's music scene is one of the world's richest and the output of quality musicians per capita is amazingly high, whether we're talking another polished symphony orchestra violinist or a headbanging bassist for the next big death-metal band. Summer here is all about music festivals of every conceivable type.

Classical Music

Composer Jean Sibelius' work dominates Finland's music but some contemporary composers are also turning heads. Partly thanks to Helsinki's Sibelius Academy, Finnish musical education is among the best in the world, with Finnish conductors, singers and musicians performing with some of the world's top orchestras. There are some excellent classical music festivals in Finland.

Popular Music

In recent years Finnish bands, mostly from the heavier side of the spectrum, have taken the world by storm, and indeed Finland has one of the liveliest metal scenes around. The biggest exports are HIM with their 'love metal' and darkly atmospheric Nightwish, whose former vocalist Tarja Turunen is also pursuing a solo career. Catchy light-metal rockers the Rasmus continue to be successful. All genres of metal, as well as a few made-up ones, are represented, including Finntroll's folk metal (blending metal and humppa), the 69 Eyes' gothic metal, Apocalyptica's classical metal, Children of Bodom's melodic death metal, Sonata Arctica's and Stratovarius' power metal, Eternal Tears of Sorrow's symphonic metal, and Impaled Nazarene's black metal. All great stuff.

Increasingly though, young people in Finland are listening to local hip-hop, known as Suomirap. Artists like Elastinen and Pyhimys have taken the airwaves by storm in recent years, and there's always some new underground project.

But there is lighter music, such as surf-rockers French Films, poprockers Sunrise Avenue, the Von Hertzen Brothers, indie band Disco Ensemble, emo-punks Poets of the Fall and melodic Husky Rescue. Past legends (still going in some cases) include Hanoi Rocks, the Hurriganes and, of course, the unicorn-quiffed Leningrad Cowboys. While singing in English appeals to an international audience, several groups sing in

Best Rock Festivals
Ruisrock, Turku

Provinssirock, Seinäjoki

Ilosaari Rock Festival, Joensuu

Tammerfest, Tampere

Finnish, including Eppu Normaali, Zen Café, Kotiteollisuus, Apulanta and mellow folk rockers Scandinavian Music Group. There's also a huge number of staggeringly popular solo artists; you'll hear their lovelorn tunes at karaoke sessions in bars and pubs around the country.

Jazz is also very big in Finland, with huge festivals at Pori and Espoo among other places. Finns have created humppa, a jazz-based music that's synonymous with social dances. One of the biggest names in humppa is the Eläkeläiset, whose regular albums are dotted with tongue-in-cheek covers of famous rock songs.

Painting & Sculpture

Modern Finnish art and sculpture explores disaffection with technological society (think warped Nokias) and reinterprets the 'Finnishness' (expect parodies of sauna, birches and blonde stereotypes). It's a long way from the pagan prehistoric rock paintings found across Finland in places such as Hossa. Medieval churches in Åland and southern Finland have enchanting frescoes that are well worth seeking out.

Although contemporary art enjoys a high profile in Finland, it is the work produced by painters and sculptors active during the National Romantic era that is thought of as Finland's 'golden age' of art. The main features of these artworks are virgin forests and pastoral landscapes. Following is a list of the most well-known artists of this era. The most comprehensive collections are displayed by the Ateneum and Kansallismuseo in Helsinki, and the Turun Taidemuseo in Turku.

Fanny Churberg (1845–92) One of the most famous female painters in Finland, created landscapes, self-portraits and still lifes using ahead-of-her-time techniques.

Albert Edelfelt (1854–1905) Among the most appreciated of Finnish artists. Was educated in Paris, and a number of his paintings date from this period. Many paintings are photo-like depictions of rural life.

Akseli Gallen-Kallela (1865–1931) An important figure in the National Romantic movement, drinking companion of composer Jean Sibelius and perhaps Finland's most famous painter. Had a distinguished and prolific career as creator of *Kalevala*-inspired paintings.

Pekka Halonen (1865–1933) A popular artist of the National Romantic era. Thought of as a 'nature mystic', his work, mostly devoted to ethereal winter landscapes, is largely privately owned.

Eero Järnefelt (1863–1937) A keen visitor to Koli, where he created more than 50 paintings of the 'national landscape'. His sister married Sibelius.

Juho Rissanen (1873–1950) Depicted life among ordinary Finns, and his much-loved paintings are displayed at the Ateneum and at Turun Taidemuseo.

Tyko Sallinen (1879–1955) The greatest of the Finnish expressionists, Sallinen is often considered the last of the golden age artists.

Helene Schjerfbeck (1862–1946) Probably the most famous female painter of her age, she is known for her self-portraits, which reflect the situation of Finnish women more than 100 years ago. Considered Finland's greatest artist by many contemporary observers.

Hugo Simberg (1873–1917) Most famous for his haunting work in Tampere's cathedral, which employs his characteristic folk symbolism. Unusual and well worth investigating. Also well represented in Helsinki's Ateneum.

von Wright, Magnus (1805–68), Wilhelm (1810–87) and Ferdinand (1822–1902) The brothers von Wright are considered the first Finnish painters of the golden age, most famous for their paintings of birds. They worked in their home near Kuopio and in Porvoo.

Emil Wickström (1864–1942) Was to sculpture what Gallen-Kallela was to painting, and sculpted the memorial to Elias Lönnrot in Helsinki. Many of his works are at his studio in Visavuori.

Best Painted Churches

Pyhän Ristin Kirkko, Hattula

Keuruu church, Keuruu

Pyhän Laurin Kirkko, Lohja

Sankta Maria Kyrka, Kvarnbo

Sankt Mikael Kyrka, Finström

Haukipudas church, Haukipudas

Paltamon Vanha Kirkko, Paltaniemi

Food & Drink

Finland's eating scene has perked up dramatically in the last few years as a wave of gourmet restaurants in the major cities has added gastronomic innovation to the always-excellent fresh local produce.

Staples

Finnish cuisine has been influenced by both Sweden and Russia and draws on what was traditionally available: fish, game, meat, milk and potatoes, with dark rye used to make bread, and few spices employed.

Soups are a Finnish favourite. Heavy pea, meat or cabbage soups are traditional workers' fare, while fish soups have a more delicate flavour.

One light snack that you'll see everywhere is the rice-filled savoury pastry from Karelia, the *karjalanpiirakka*. These are tasty cold, heated, toasted or with egg butter, and have several variations.

Fish is a mainstay of the Finnish diet. Fresh or smoked *lohi* (salmon), marinated *silli* (herring), *siika* (lavaret, a lake whitefish), *kuha* (pike-perch or zander) and delicious *nieriä* or *rautu* (Arctic char) are common, and the tiny lake fish *muikku* (vendace, or whitefish, a small lake fish) are another treat.

Two much-loved favourites that you'll see in many places are grilled liver, served with mashed potatoes and bacon, and meatballs.

Reindeer has always been a staple food for the Sámi. The traditional way to eat it is sautéed with lingonberries, though many restaurants offer it on pizzas or as sausages. It also comes in fillet steaks, which, though expensive, is the tastiest. Elk is eaten, too, mostly in hunting season, and you can even get a bear steak – or more commonly, a potted or preserved meat – in some places, although the latter is very expensive, as only a small number are hunted every year.

Meals

Finns eat their biggest meal of the day at lunchtime, so many cafes and restaurants put on a *lounas* special from Monday to Friday. This usually consists of soup plus salad or hot meal or both, and includes a soft drink, coffee and sometimes dessert. Expect to pay around €8 to €14 for this deal.

Most hotels offer a free buffet breakfast, which includes bread, cheese, cold cuts, pastries, berries, cereals and lots of coffee, and may run to pickled or smoked fish, sausages and eggs.

Finns have dinner as early as 5pm, often just a light meal, but eat much later if it's an organised, 'going out for dinner' affair.

For a sweet snack at any time of day, hit a cafe for a *pulla* (cardamom-flavoured bun), *korvapuusti* (cinnamon whirl) or *munkki* (doughnut).

Weekend *brunssi* (brunch) has become a big deal in the cities (p61).

New Suomi Cuisine

Riding the wave of new Nordic cuisine is a new breed of Finnish chef experimenting with traditional ingredients such as lake fish, berries, wild mushrooms, reindeer and other seasonal produce in a decidedly

Late in the summer, it's a tradition to have crayfish parties, where the succulent little creatures are consumed by the dozen.

Finns love their sweets, although some of them make the unsuspecting visitor feel like the victim of a novelty shop joke. Salty liquorice, fiery 'Turkish peppers' and tar-flavoured gumdrops may sound like punishments rather than rewards, but are delicious after the first few times. Finnish chocolates, particularly those made by Fazer, are also excellent..

untraditional fashion. Especially in Helsinki, you'll find a number of gourmet restaurants offering exquisite multicourse tasting menus.

Foraging

The forage ethos is one of the principal drivers of new Nordic cuisine but it's not a new concept. Finns head out gleefully all summer to pick berries and mushrooms: blueberries, jewel-like wild strawberries, peppery chanterelles and the north's gloriously tart, creamy cloudberry, so esteemed that it features on the €2 coin. People here are enthusiastic kitchen gardeners too. The variety and quality of fresh produce means that summer is by far the best time to eat in Finland.

A Finnish institution is the *grilli*. These fast-food stalls sell burgers, sausages, chips and the like, and stay open late for the after-pub crowd.

Markets

Big towns all have a kauppahalli (covered market), the place to head for all sorts of Finnish specialities, breads, cheeses, deli produce, meat, and a super variety of fresh and smoked fish. It's also a top place for a cheap feed, with cafes and stalls selling sandwiches and snacks. The summer kauppatori (market square) also has food stalls, coffee stops and market produce.

Drinking

The Finns lead the world in coffee *(kahvi)* consumption, downing over 20 million cups per day – that's around four each for every man, woman and child. While the distinctive standard Finnish brew can be found everywhere, smarter cafes and restaurants will have espresso machines. Cafes are ubiquitous.

Finns drink plenty of beer *(olut)* and among the big local brews are Karhu, Koff, Olvi and Lapin Kulta. The big brands are all lagers, but there's quite a number of microbreweries in Finland (look for the word *panimo* or *panimo-ravintola*), and these make excellent light and dark beers. Cider is also popular, as is *lonkero,* a ready-made mix of gin and fruity soft drink, usually grapefruit. A half-litre of beer in a bar costs around €5 to €7. Finns don't tend to drink in rounds; everybody pays for their own.

Great Brewpubs

Panimoravintola Plevna, Tampere

....

Teerenpeli, Lahti and elsewhere

....

Huvila, Savonlinna

....

Beer Hunter's, Pori

....

Panimoravintola Koulu, Turku

Beer, wine and spirits are sold by the state network, Alko. There are stores in every town. The legal age for drinking is 18 for beer and wine, and 20 for spirits. Beer and cider with less than 4.8% alcohol can be bought at supermarkets, service stations and convenience stores. If you buy cans or bottles, you pay a small deposit (about €0.20). This can be reclaimed by returning them to the recycling section at a supermarket.

Wine is widely drunk, but very pricey in restaurants, where you might pay €45 for a bottle that would cost €10 in an Alko store. Sparkling wine is very popular in summer and keep an eye out for locally made berry wines.

Other uniquely Finnish drinks include *salmiakkikossu,* which combines dissolved liquorice sweets with the iconic Koskenkorva vodka (an acquired taste); *fisu,* which does the same but with Fisherman's Friend pastilles; *sahti,* a sweet, high-alcohol beer; and cloudberry or cranberry liqueurs.

VEGETARIANS IN FINLAND

Most medium-sized towns in Finland will have a vegetarian restaurant (*kasvisravintola*), usually open weekday lunchtimes only. It's easy to self-cater at markets, or take the salad/vegetable option at lunch buffets (which is usually cheaper). Many restaurants also have a salad buffet. The website www.vegaaniliitto.fi has a useful listing of vegetarian and vegan restaurants; follow 'ruoka' and 'kasvisravintoloita' (the Finnish list is more up-to-date than the English one).

Survival Guide

Directory A–Z

Accommodation

Finland's not generally a nation of quirky boutique hotels. Solid Nordic comfort in standard rooms dominates rather than whimsical conversions or new-agey decor. Many accommodation choices open only in summer, usually campsites or converted student residences.

➡ Budget: expect shared bathrooms.

➡ Midrange: private bathroom, good facilities and breakfast buffet included.

➡ Top end: business class or five-star facilities.

➡ The double bed is a rare beast; hotel rooms tend to have twin beds that can be pushed together.

➡ Family or group rooms are common, and extra beds can usually be added to a twin room at a low extra cost.

Camping

Finland's campgrounds are a delight, and have much to offer to all types of travellers.

Most campgrounds are open only from June to August; popular spots are crowded during July and the Midsummer weekend.

Sites usually cost around €14 plus €5/2 per adult/child.

Almost all campgrounds have cabins or cottages for rent, which are usually excellent value; from €40 for a basic double cabin to €120 for a cottage with kitchen, bathroom and sauna.

The **Camping Key Europe** (www.campingkeyeurope. com) offers useful discounts. You can buy it at most campgrounds for €16 or online at www.camping.fi, where you'll also find an extensive listing of campgrounds across the country.

Finland's *jokamiehenoikeus* (everyman's right) allows access to most land and means you can pitch a tent almost anywhere on public land or at designated free campsites in national parks.

Guesthouses

A Finnish *matkakoti* (guesthouse) is a no-frills spot offering simple but usually comfy accommodation with shared bathroom, typically for travelling salespeople. It can be pretty good value, usually includes breakfast, and sometimes rises well above the norm: check out places like Naantali and

FARMSTAYS

A growing, and often ecologically sound, accommodation sector in Finland is that of farmstays. Many rural farms, particularly in the south, offer B&B accommodation, a unique opportunity to meet local people and experience their way of life. Plenty of activities are also usually on offer. **ECEAT** (www.eceat.fi) lists a number of organic, sustainable farms in Finland that offer accommodation. Local tourist offices keep lists of farmstay options in the surrounding area; the website www. visitfinland.com links to a few, and **Lomarengas** (☎030-650-2502; www.lomarengas.fi) also has many listed on its website. In general, prices are good – from around €35 per person per night, country breakfast included. Evening meals are also usually available. Your hosts may not speak much English; if you have difficulties, the local tourist office will be happy to help arrange the booking.

HOSPITALITY WEBSITES

Organisations such as **Couchsurfing** (www.couchsurf ing.org) or **Hospitality Club** (www.hospitalityclub.org) put people in contact for informal free accommodation offers – a bit like blind-date couch surfing. Even if you're not comfortable crashing in a stranger's house, these sites are a great way to meet and socialise with locals. **Airbnb** (www.airbnb.com) is a community that has a whole range of options, from private rooms in people's flats to top-value holiday rentals and almost anything else you can think of.

Hanko for some exceptional sleeps in this class.

Hostels & Summer Hotels

For solo travellers, hostels generally offer the cheapest bed, and can be good value for twin rooms. Finnish hostels are invariably clean, comfortable and very well equipped, though most are in somewhat institutional buildings.

Some Finnish hostels are run by the Finnish Youth Hostel Association (SRM), and many more are affiliated. It's worth being a member of **Hostelling International** (HI; www.hihostels.com), as members save 10% per night at affiliated places. You'll save money with a sleep sheet or your own linen, as hostels tend to charge €4 to €8 for this.

From June to August, many student residences are made over as summer hostels and hotels. These are often great value, as you usually get your own room, with kitchen (bring your own utensils, though) and bathroom either to yourself or shared between two people.

Hotels

Most hotels in Finland cater to business travellers and the majority belong to one of a few major chains, including the following:

Cumulus (www.cumulus.fi)

Scandic (www.scandichotels .com)

Sokos (www.sokoshotels.fi)

Finlandia (www.finlandia hotels.fi) An association of independent hotels.

Omenahotelli (www.omena .com) Offers good-value un-staffed hotels booked online.

Hotels in Finland are designed with the business traveller in mind and tend to charge robustly. But on weekends and during the July summer holidays prices in three- and four-star hotels tend to drop by 40% or so.

Superior rooms vary in value. In many places they are identical to the standard and your extra cash gets you only a bathrobe and a fancier shampoo. In others, an extra €20 can get you 50% more space, views over the town and a private sauna. It's worth asking. The discount for singles is marginal at all times, so you may prefer to pay the little extra for a twin room, which is usually much larger.

Most hotel rooms have tiny Nordic bathrooms; if you want a bathtub, this can usually be arranged. Many hotels have 'allergy rooms', which have no carpet and minimal fabric.

Nearly all Finnish hotels have a plentiful buffet breakfast included in the rate and many include a sauna session.

Self-Catering Accommodation

One of Finland's joys is its plethora of cottages for rent, ranging from simple camping cabins to fully equipped bungalows with electric sauna and gleaming modern kitchen. These can be remarkably good value and are perfect for families.

There are tens of thousands of cabins and cottages available for rent in Finland, many in typical, romantic forest lakeside locations. Local booking agents are mentioned under individual destinations.

Local tourist offices and town websites also have lists. **Lomarengas** (⌮030-650-2502; www.lomarengas.fi) is by far the biggest national agent for cottage rentals.

Customs Regulations

Travellers arriving from outside of the EU can bring duty-free goods up to the value of €430 without declaration. You can also bring in up to 16L of beer, 4L of wine, 2L of liquors not exceeding 22% vol or 1L of spirits, 200 cigarettes or 250g of tobacco.

If you're coming from another EU country, there is no restriction on the value of gifts or purchases for personal use.

BOOK YOUR STAY ONLINE

For more accommodation reviews by Lonely Planet authors, check out http://lonelyplanet.com/hotels/. You'll find independent reviews, as well as recommendations on the best places to stay. Best of all, you can book online.

Although technically part of the EU, arriving on or from the Åland archipelago carries the same import restrictions as arriving from a non-EU country.

Electricity

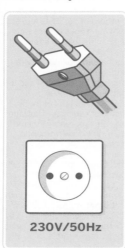

230V/50Hz

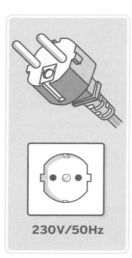

230V/50Hz

Food

See p285 for information on Finland's eating scene.

Eating choices are flagged with price indicators, based on the cost of an average main course from the dinner menu.

€	less than €17
€€	€17 to 27
€€€	more than €27

Gay & Lesbian Travellers

Finland's cities are open, tolerant places and Helsinki, though no Copenhagen or Stockholm, has a small but welcoming gay scene.

Health

Travel in Finland presents very few health problems. The standard of care is extremely high and English is widely spoken by doctors and medical clinic staff. Tap water is safe to drink, the level of hygiene is high and there are no endemic diseases.

The main health issues to be aware of are extreme climates (with the potential for nasties like hypothermia, frostbite or viral infections such as influenza) and biting insects such as horseflies and mosquitoes, though they're more of an annoyance than a real health risk.

Specific travel vaccinations are not required for visitors to Finland.

Citizens of the European Economic Area (EEA) are covered for emergency medical treatment on presentation of a European Health Insurance Card (EHIC), though they will be liable to pay a daily or per-appointment fee as a Finn would; see www.kela.fi for details. Enquire about EHICs at your health centre, travel agency or (in some countries) post office well in advance of travel. Citizens from other countries should find out if there is a reciprocal arrangement for free medical care between their country and Finland. If not, health insurance is recommended.

Insurance

A travel insurance policy to cover theft, personal liability, loss and medical problems is recommended. There's a variety of policies available. Travel insurance also usually covers cancellation or delays in travel arrangements; for example, if you fall seriously ill two days before departure.

Buy insurance as early as possible. If you buy it the week before you are due to fly, you may find that you're not covered for delays to your flight caused by strikes or other industrial actions that may have been in force before you took out the insurance.

Browse extensively online to find the best rates.

Paying for your airline ticket with a credit card often provides limited travel accident insurance, and you may be able to reclaim the payment if the operator doesn't deliver.

Certain bank accounts offer their holders automatic travel insurance.

Make sure you get a policy that covers you for the worst possible health scenario if you aren't already covered. Make sure it covers you for any activities you plan to do, like skiing. Be sure to check the small print. Also find out in advance if your insurance plan will make payments directly to providers or reimburse you later for overseas health expenditures.

Worldwide travel insurance is available at www.lonelyplanet.com/bookings. You can buy, extend and claim online anytime – even if you're already on the road.

Internet Access

Public libraries always have at least one free internet terminal; there's usually a time limit. Many tourist offices have an internet terminal that you can use for free (usually 15 minutes).

Wireless internet access is very widespread; several cities have extensive networks and nearly all hotels, as well as many restaurants, cafes and bars, offer free access to customers and guests.

Data is very cheap. If you've got an unlocked smartphone, you can pick up a local SIM card for a few euros and charge it with a month's worth of data at a decent speed for under €20. Ask at R-kioski shops for the latest deals.

Money

Finland adopted the euro (€) in 2002. Euro notes come in five, 10, 20, 50, 100, 200 and 500 denominations and coins in five, 10, 20, 50 cents and €1 and €2. The one- and two-cent coins used in other Eurozone nations are not accepted in Finland. See p17 for exchange rates.

Credit/Debit Cards

Credit cards are widely accepted and Finns are dedicated users of the plastic even to buy a beer or cup of coffee.

Using ATMs with a credit or debit card is by far the easiest way of getting cash in Finland. ATMs have a name, Otto, and can be found even in small villages.

Moneychangers

Travellers cheques and cash can be exchanged at banks and, in the big cities, at independent exchange facilities such as **Forex** (www.forex.fi).

Tipping

Service is considered to be included in bills, so there's no need to tip at all unless you

PRACTICALITIES

Newspapers & magazines *Helsingin Sanomat* (www.hs.fi/english) is the main daily paper in Finland. The *Helsinki Times* (www.helsinkitimes.fi) is an English-language weekly; and foreign newspapers and magazines are widely available.

Radio The national radio broadcaster is YLE (www.yle.fi), which has a number of stations offering news and various types of music.

TV National TV networks broadcast plenty of English-language programs, subtitled in Finnish.

Cinema Films are screened in the original language, with subtitles in Finnish and Swedish.

Weights & measures Finland uses the metric system. Decimals are indicated by commas.

want to reward exceptional service. Doormen in bars and restaurants expect a cloakroom tip if there's no mandatory coat charge.

Opening Hours

Many attractions in Finland, particularly outdoor ones, only open for a short summer season, typically mid-June to late August. Opening hours tend to shorten in winter in general.

Sample opening hours:

Alko (state alcohol store) 9am–8pm Monday to Friday, to 6pm Saturday

Banks 9am–4.15pm Monday to Friday

Businesses & shops 9am–6pm Monday to Friday, to 3pm Saturday

Nightclubs 10pm–4am Wednesday to Saturday

Pubs 11am–1am (often later on Friday and Saturday)

Restaurants 11am–10pm, lunch 11am–3pm. Last orders generally an hour before closing.

Public Holidays

Finland grinds to a halt twice a year: around Christmas and New Year, and during the Midsummer weekend. National public holidays:

New Year's Day 1 January

Epiphany 6 January

Good Friday March/April

Easter Sunday & Monday March/April

May Day 1 May

Ascension Day May

Whitsunday Late May or early June

Midsummer's Eve & Day Weekend in June closest to 24 June

All Saints Day First Saturday in November

Independence Day 6 December

Christmas Eve 24 December

Christmas Day 25 December

Boxing Day 26 December

Telephone

Public telephones basically no longer exist in Finland, so if you don't have a mobile you're reduced to making expensive calls from your hotel room or talking over the internet.

The cheapest and most practical solution is to purchase a Finnish SIM card and pop it in your own phone. First make sure your phone isn't blocked from doing this by your home network.

You can buy a prepaid SIM card at any R-kioski shop. There are always several deals on offer, and you might be able to pick up a card for as little as €5, including some call credit. Top the credit up at the same outlets, online or at ATMs.

Most Finnish mobile numbers start with ☑04 or ☑050.

At the R-kioski you can also buy cut-rate phone cards that substantially lower the cost of making international calls.

The country code for Finland is ☑358. To dial abroad it's ☑00.

Roaming charges within the EU are set to be abolished during the lifespan of this book.

Time

Finland is on Eastern European Time (EET), an hour ahead of Sweden and Norway. In winter it's two hours ahead of UTC/GMT; from late March to late October the clocks go forward an hour to three hours ahead of UTC/GMT.

Toilets

Public toilets are widespread in Finland but expensive – often €1 a time. On doors, 'M' is for men, while 'N' is for women.

Tourist Information

The main website of the Finnish Tourist Board is www.visitfinland.com.

Travellers with Disabilities

Finland may be the best-equipped country in the world for the disabled traveller. By law, most institutions must provide ramps, lifts and special toilets for disabled persons; all new hotels and restaurants must install disabled facilities. Trains and city buses are also accessible by wheelchair. Some national parks offer accessible nature trails, and Helsinki and other cities have ongoing projects in place designed to maximise disabled access in all aspects of urban life.

The website www.finland forall.fi has a searchable database of accessible attractions, accommodation and restaurants.

Before leaving home, get in touch with your national support organisation – preferably the 'travel officer' if there is one.

Visas

A valid passport or EU identity card is required to enter Finland. Most Western nationals don't need a tourist visa for stays of less than three months. South Africans, Indians and Chinese, however, are among those who need a Schengen visa. For more information contact the nearest Finnish embassy or consulate, or check the website www.formin.finland.fi.

Australian and New Zealand citizens aged between 18 and 30 can apply for a 12-month working holiday visa under a reciprocal agreement – contact the Finnish embassy in your home country.

Transport

GETTING THERE & AWAY

Finland is easily accessed from Europe and beyond. There are direct flights from numerous destinations, while Baltic ferries are another good option.

Flights, tours and rail tickets can be booked online at lonelyplanet.com/bookings.

Entering Finland

Entering Finland is a breeze and you'll experience no problems if your papers are in order. For visa requirements see p292. Finland has no issues with any previous visas or stamps you may have in your passport.

Air

Airports & Airlines

Most flights to Finland land at **Helsinki-Vantaa airport** (www.helsinki-vantaa.fi), 19km north of the capital. Winter charters hit **Rovaniemi**, Lapland's main airport, and other smaller regional airports. Other international airports include Tampere, Turku and Oulu. The Finavia website (www.finavia.fi) includes information for all Finnish airports.

Finland is easily reached by air, with direct flights to Helsinki from many European, American and Asian destinations. It's also served by budget carriers, especially Ryanair, from several European countries. Most other flights are with Finnair or Scandinavian Airlines (SAS).

Land

Border Crossings

There are several border crossings from northern Sweden and Norway to northern Finland, with no passport or customs formalities.

There are nine main border crossings between Finland and Russia, including several in the southeast and two in Lapland. They are more serious frontiers; you must already have a Russian visa.

For more on travel to Russia see p69 and p170.

Bus

SWEDEN

The linked towns of Tornio (Finland) and Haparanda (Sweden) share a bus station from where you can get onward transport into their respective countries. A possible, if remote, crossing point is the Lapland villages of Kaaresuvanto (Finland) and Karesuando (Sweden), separated by a bridge and both served sporadically by domestic buses.

NORWAY

Three routes link Finnish Lapland with northern Norway, some running only in summer. These are operated

---

CLIMATE CHANGE & TRAVEL

Every form of transport that relies on carbon-based fuel generates CO_2, the main cause of human-induced climate change. Modern travel is dependent on aeroplanes, which might use less fuel per kilometre per person than most cars but travel much greater distances. The altitude at which aircraft emit gases (including CO_2) and particles also contributes to their climate change impact. Many websites offer 'carbon calculators' that allow people to estimate the carbon emissions generated by their journey and, for those who wish to do so, to offset the impact of the greenhouse gases emitted with contributions to portfolios of climate-friendly initiatives throughout the world. Lonely Planet offsets the carbon footprint of all staff and author travel.

by **Eskelisen Lapin Linjat** (www.eskelisen.fi), whose website has detailed maps and timetables, as does the Finnish bus website **Matkahuolto** (www.matkahuolto.fi).

All routes originate or pass through Rovaniemi; the two northeastern routes continue via Inari to Tana Bru/Vadsø or Karasjok. The Karasjok bus continues in summer to Nordkapp (North Cape). On the western route, a Rovaniemi–Kilpisjärvi bus continues to Tromsø in summer.

RUSSIA

Daily express buses run to Vyborg and St Petersburg from Helsinki and Lappeenranta (one originates in Turku). These services appear on the website of **Matkahuolto** (www.matkahuolto.fi). Semi-official buses and minibuses can be cheaper options. **Goldline** (www.goldline.fi) runs three weekly buses from Rovaniemi via Ivalo to Murmansk.

Car & Motorcycle

Vehicles can easily be brought into Finland on ferries or overland, provided you have registration papers and valid insurance (Green Card).

Train

SWEDEN

There is no train between Finland and Sweden, but train passes give significant discounts on ferry and bus connections.

In the north, Swedish trains travel no closer than Boden/Luleå; from there take connecting buses to Haparanda/Tornio, and on to the train station at Kemi. International rail passes cover bus travel all the way from Boden to Kemi.

RUSSIA

Finland's only international trains are to/from Moscow and St Petersburg in Russia.

Three high-speed Allegro train services run daily

from Helsinki to the Finland Station in St Petersburg (2nd/1st class around €86/140, 3½ hours). The evening train is usually cheaper. The Tolstoi sleeper runs from Helsinki via St Petersburg (Ladozhki station) to Moscow (2nd/1st class €128/188, 13½ hours). The fare includes a sleeper berth. There are a number of more upmarket sleeper options.

All trains go via Lahti, Kouvola, Vainikkala (26km south of Lappeenranta) and the Russian city of Vyborg. At Helsinki station tickets are sold at the international ticket counter.

You must have a valid Russian visa; immigration procedures are carried out on board.

There are significant discounts for families and small groups. See www.vr.fi.

Sea

Arriving in Finland by ferry is a memorable way to begin your visit, especially if you dock in Helsinki. Baltic ferries are big floating hotels-cum-shopping plazas, with duty-free, restaurants, bars, karaoke, nightclubs and saunas. Many use them simply for boozy overnight cruises, so they can get pretty rowdy on Friday and Saturday nights.

Services are year-round between major cities: book ahead in summer, at weekends and if travelling with a vehicle. The boats are amazingly cheap if you travel deck class (without a cabin): they make their money from duty-free purchases. Many ferry lines offer 50% discounts for holders of train passes. Some offer discounts for seniors, and for ISIC and youth-card holders. There are usually discounts for families and small groups travelling together.

Ferry companies have detailed timetables and fares on their websites. Fares vary according to season.

Operators with their Finnish contact numbers:

Eckerö Line (☎0600-4300; www.eckeroline.fi) Finland–Sweden, Finland–Estonia.

Finnlines (☎010-343-4500; www.finnlines.com) Finland–Sweden, Finland–Germany.

Linda Line (☎0600-066-8970; www.lindaline.fi) Finland–Estonia.

St Peter Line (☎09-6187-2000; www.stpeterline.com) Finland–Russia.

Tallink/Silja Line (☎0600-15700; www.tallinksilja.com) Finland–Sweden, Finland–Estonia.

Viking Line (☎0600-41577; www.vikingline.fi) Finland–Sweden, Finland–Estonia.

Wasaline (☎020-771-6810; www.wasaline.com) Finland–Sweden.

SWEDEN

The daily Stockholm to Helsinki, Stockholm to Turku and Kapellskär to Mariehamn (Åland) routes are run by Tallink/Silja and Viking Line.

Viking offers a peak-season passenger ticket between Stockholm and Helsinki for around €50. You can doss down in chairs or on the floor; the cheapest berths in a shared cabin start at €35 in peak season. Cars cost from €60 but there are frequent discounts – check prices online.

Tallink/Silja doesn't offer deck tickets on the Helsinki run: berths in a shared cabin start at €45 for the crossing so this can be the cheapest option.

It's cheaper to cross to Turku (11 to 12 hours): tickets cost around €20 in summer on the day ferries. Note that Åbo is Swedish for Turku.

Eckerö Linjen sails from Grisslehamn, north of Stockholm, to Eckerö in Åland. It's by far the quickest option, at just two hours, and, with prices at €4/14 for an adult/car, it's an amazing bargain. There's a connecting bus from Stockholm and some other Swedish towns.

Finnlines runs a cargo ferry connecting Naantali, near Turku, with Kapellskär via Långnäs in Åland two to three times daily (adult/car €47/120, cabins from €120).

Wasaline sails almost daily from Vaasa in Finland to Umeå, Sweden (per person €35 plus €50 per car, 4½ hours).

RUSSIA

St Peter Line connects Helsinki with St Petersburg three to four times weekly. A significant added benefit of arriving in Russia this way is a visa-free stay of up to three days in St Petersburg. Canal cruises from Lappeenranta also allow you to do this.

ESTONIA

Several ferry companies zip between Helsinki and Tallinn in Estonia (p71). Car ferries cross in 3½ hours, catamarans and hydrofoils in about 1½ hours, although in winter there are fewer departures and traffic is slower due to the ice.

GERMANY

Finnlines runs six to seven ferries a week from Helsinki to Travemünde (peak one way adult/car €155/155, 27 hours) and less frequently to Rostock.

GETTING AROUND

A useful combined journey planner for Finland's public transport network is online at www.journey.fi.

Air

Airlines in Finland

Finnair runs a fairly comprehensive domestic service out of Helsinki. Standard prices are expensive, but check the website for offers. Some Lapland destinations are winter only.

Major airlines flying domestically include the following:

Finnair (www.finnair.com) Extensive domestic network.

Flybe (☑0600-94477; www.flybe.com) Runs several domestic routes in partnership with Finnair.

Norwegian (www.norwegian.com) High-quality budget provider with several routes between Helsinki and northern Finland.

Bicycle

Finland is as bicycle friendly as any country you'll find, with plenty of paths and low hills. Bikes can be taken on most trains, buses and ferries (see p32 for information about transporting bicycles on trains). Åland is particularly good for cycling. Helmets are required by law.

Hire

You can hire a bike in nearly every Finnish town. Most campsites and many urban hotels offer bikes for a small fee or for free, but these are made for cycling around town, not for ambitious road trips. Better bikes are available at dedicated outlets. Expect to pay around €20 per day or €100 per week for a good-quality road or mountain bike.

Boat

Lake boats were once important summer transport. These services are now largely kept on as cruises, and make a great, leisurely way to journey between towns. The most popular routes are Tampere–Hämeenlinna, Tampere-Virrat, Savonlinna–Kuopio and Lahti–Jyväskylä.

Coastal routes include Turku–Naantali, Helsinki–Porvoo and ferries to the Åland archipelago.

The site http://lautta.net is very handy for domestic lake-boat and ferry services.

Bus

Bus is the main form of long-distance transport in Finland, with a far more comprehensive network than the train. Buses run on time and are rarely full.

Intercity buses fall into two main categories: *vakiovuoro* (regular), stopping frequently at towns and villages; and slightly pricier *pikavuoro* (express). Because there are few motorways, even express buses aren't that fast, averaging about 60km/h.

Ticketing is handled by **Matkahuolto** (www.matkahuolto.fi), whose excellent website has all the timetables. Matkahuolto offices work normal business hours, but you can always just buy the ticket from the driver.

Towns have a *linja-autoasema* (bus terminal), with local timetables displayed (*lähtevät* is departures, *saapuvat* arrivals).

Separate from the normal system – though their timetables appear on the Matkahuolto website, **OnniBus** (www.onnibus.com) runs a variety of budget inter-city routes in comfortable double-decker buses. Most of these radiate from Helsinki and can be much cheaper than normal fares if booked in advance.

Departures between major towns are frequent, but reduce substantially at weekends. In more remote areas, there may be no weekend buses at all. Schedules change during the summer holidays; it can be much harder to move around isolated regions.

Costs

Prices refer to express services where available. Ticket prices are fixed – though there are some online advance-purchase offers – and depend on the number of kilometres travelled; return tickets are 10% cheaper than two one-way fares, provided the trip is at least 60km each way.

The one-way fare for a 100km trip is normal/express €18.70/22.

Discounts

Children aged four to 11 pay half, those aged 12 to 16 pay 70%. Student discounts require full-time study in Finland: buy a student coach discount card (€8) from any bus station. Proper student ID and a passport photo is required, and the card entitles you to a 50% discount on journeys more than 60km. If booking three or more adult tickets together, a 25% discount applies, meaning good news for groups.

Car & Motorcycle

Finland's road network is excellent, although there are few motorways. When approaching a town or city, *keskusta* indicates the town centre. There are no road tolls but lots of speed cameras.

Petrol is expensive in Finland, on a par with the UK. Many petrol stations are unstaffed, but machines take cash and cards. Change for cash is not given.

Hire

Car rental is expensive, but rates can work out reasonably with advance booking or with a group. A small car costs around €70/300 per day/week with 300km free per day. As ever, the cheapest deals are online.

Look out for weekend rates. These can cost little more than the rate for a single day, and you can pick up the car early afternoon on Friday and return it late Sunday or early Monday.

Car-rental franchises with offices in many Finnish cities include: **Budget** (www.budget.com), **Hertz** (www.hertz.com), **Europcar** (www.europcar.com) and **Avis** (www.avis.com). One of the cheapest is **Sixt** (www.sixt.com).

Road Conditions & Hazards

Beware of elk and reindeer, which don't respect vehicles and can dash onto the road unexpectedly. This sounds comical, but elks especially constitute a deadly danger. Notify the police if there is an accident involving these animals. Reindeer are very common in Lapland; slow right down if you see one, as there will be more nearby.

Snow and ice on the roads, potentially from September to April, and as late as June in Lapland, make driving a serious undertaking. Snow chains are illegal: people use either snow tyres, which have studs, or special all-weather tyres. The website http://liikennetilanne.liikennevirasto.fi has road webcams around Finland, good for checking conditions. Select 'kelikamerat' on the map.

Road Rules

➜ Finns drive on the right.

➜ The speed limit is 50km/h in built-up areas, from 80km/h to 100km/h on highways, and 120km/h on motorways.

➜ Use headlights at all times.

➜ Seatbelts are compulsory for all.

➜ Blood alcohol limit: 0.05%.

An important feature of Finland is that there are fewer give-way signs than most countries. Traffic entering an intersection from the right has right of way. While this doesn't apply to highways or main roads, in towns cars will often nip out from the right without looking: you must give way, so be careful at smaller intersections in towns.

Hitching

Hitching in Finland is possible but expect long waits. It's more common in remote areas where bus services are fewer, but still unusual. Your greatest friend will be your insect repellent. Mosquitoes can't believe their luck that such a large juicy mammal will stand in one place for such a very long time.

Local Transport

Helsinki has the only metro and trams. All Finnish cities and towns have a bus

ROAD DISTANCES (KM)

	Helsinki	Jyväskylä	Kuopio	Kuusamo	Lappeenranta	Oulu	Rovaniemi	Savonlinna	Tampere	Turku
Jyväskylä	272									
Kuopio	383	144								
Kuusamo	804	553	419							
Lappeenranta	223	219	264	684						
Oulu	612	339	286	215	551					
Rovaniemi	837	563	511	191	776	224				
Savonlinna	338	206	160	579	155	446	671			
Tampere	174	148	293	702	275	491	712	355		
Turku	166	304	448	848	361	633	858	446	155	
Vaasa	419	282	377	533	501	318	543	488	241	348

Train Routes

network, with departures every 10 to 15 minutes in large towns, every 30 to 60 minutes in smaller towns. Fares are around €2.50 to €3.50: pay the driver.

Taxi

The taxi (taksi) in Finland is an expensive creature, particularly for short rides. There's a flagfall of €5.90 in Helsinki (often more elsewhere) and a per-kilometre charge of €1.55. These increase if there are more than two passengers, and there's a surcharge for night and weekend service.

Hail taxis at bus and train stations or call. Shared taxis often cover airport routes, and are a common mode of transport in Karelia, Kainuu and, to a lesser extent, Lapland.

Train

State-owned **Valtion Rautatiet** (VR; www.vr.fi) runs Finnish trains: a fast, efficient service, with prices roughly equivalent to buses on the same route.

VR's website has comprehensive timetable information. Major stations have a VR office and ticket machines; tickets can be purchased online, where you'll also find discounted advance fares. You can board and pay the conductor, but if the station where you boarded had ticket-purchasing facilties, you'll be charged a small penalty fee (€2 to €5).

Types of Train

The main types of trains are the high-speed Pendolino (the fastest and most expensive class), fast Intercity (IC), Express and 2nd-class-only Regional trains (H on the timetable).

On longer routes there are two types of sleeping carriage. Traditional blue ones offer berths in one- /two- / three-bed cabins; newer sleeping cars offer single and double compartments in a double-decker carriage. There are cabins with bathroom, and one equipped for wheelchair use. Sleeper trains transport cars.

Costs

Fares vary slightly according to the type of train, with Pendolino the priciest. A one-way ticket for a 100km express train journey costs approximately €23 in 2nd ('eco') class. First-class ('extra') tickets cost around 35% more than a 2nd-class ticket. A return fare gives a 10% discount.

Children under 17 pay half; those under six years travel free (but without a seat). A child travels free with every adult on long-distance trips, and there are also discounts for seniors, local students and any group of three or more adults travelling together.

Train Passes

Various passes are available for rail travel within Finland, or in European countries including Finland. There are cheaper passes for students, people aged under 26, and seniors. Supplements (eg for high-speed services) and reservation costs are not covered, and terms and conditions change – check carefully before buying. Always carry your passport when using the pass.

EURAIL

Eurail (www.eurail.com) offers a good selection of passes available to residents of non-European countries, which should be purchased before arriving in Europe.

Most of the passes offer discounts of around 25% for under-26s, or 15% for two people travelling together.

The Eurail Scandinavia pass gives a number of days in a two-month period, and is valid for travel in Denmark, Sweden, Norway and Finland. It costs €261 for four days, and up to €403 for 10 days. A similar but cheaper pass includes just Sweden and Finland. The Finland Eurail Pass costs €137/182/245 for three/five/10 days' 2nd-class travel in a one-month period within Finland.

Eurail Global Passes offer travel in 24 European countries, either 10 or 15 days in a two-month period, or unlimited travel from 15 days up to three months. The Global Passes are much better value for under-26s, as those older have to buy a 1st-class pass.

On most Eurail passes, children aged between four and 11 get a 50% discount on the full adult fare.

Eurail passes give a 30% to 50% discount on several ferry lines in the region; check the website for details.

INTERRAIL

If you've lived in Europe for more than six months, you're eligible for an **InterRail** (www.interrail.eu) pass. The InterRail Finland pass offers travel only in Finland for three/four/six/eight days in a one-month period, costing €125/158/212/258 in 2nd class. The Global Pass offers travel in 30 European countries and costs from €281 for five days' travel in any 10-day period, to €668 for a month's unlimited train travel. On both passes, there's a 33% discount for under-26s.

InterRail passes give a 30% to 50% discount on several ferry lines in the region; check the website for details.

Language

Finnish is a distinct national icon that sets Finland apart from its Scandinavian neighbours. It belongs to the exclusive Finno-Ugric language family, which also counts Estonian and Hungarian as members. There are around six million Finnish speakers in Finland, Sweden, Norway and Russian Karelia. In Finnish, Finland is known as Suomi and the language itself as suomi.

If you read our coloured pronunciation guides as if they were English, you shouldn't have problems being understood. Note that a is pronounced as in 'act', ai as in 'aisle', eu as the 'u' in 'nurse', ew as the 'ee' in 'see' with rounded lips, oh as the 'o' in 'note', ow as in 'how', uh as the 'u' in 'run', and the r sound is rolled. The stressed syllables are indicated with italics in our pronunciation guides.

Basics

Hello.	Hei.	hayn
Goodbye.	Näkemiin.	na·ke·meen
Yes.	Kyllä.	kewl·la
No.	Ei.	ay
Please.	Ole hyvä.	o·le hew·va
Thank you (very much).	Kiitos (paljon).	kee·tos (puhl·yon)
You're welcome.	Ole hyvä.	o·le hew·va
Excuse me.	Anteeksi.	uhn·tayk·si
Sorry.	Anteeksi.	uhn·tayk·si

How are you?
Mitä kuuluu?   mi·ta koo·loo

Fine. And you?
Hyvää. Entä itsellesi?   hew·va en·ta it·sel·le·si

What's your name?
Mikä sinun nimesi on?   mi·ka si·nun ni·me·si on

My name is ...
Minun nimeni on ...   mi·nun ni·me·ni on ...

Do you speak English?
Puhutko englantia?   pu·hut·ko en·gluhn·ti·uh

I don't understand.
En ymmärrä.   en ewm·mar·ra

Accommodation

Where's a cheap/nearby hotel?
Missä olisi halpa/ lähin hotelli?   mis·sa o·li·si huhl·puh/ la·hin ho·tel·li

I'd like a single/double room.
Haluaisin yhden/ kahden hengen huoneen.   huh·lu·ai·sin ewh·den/ kuh·den hen·gen hu·o·nayn

How much is it per night/person?
Paljonko se on yöltä/hengeltä?   puhl·yon·ko se on ew·eul·ta/hen·gel·ta

I want a room with a ...	Minä haluan huoneen ...	mi·na huh·lu·uhn hu·o·nayn ...
bathroom	kylpy- huoneella	kewl·pew- hu·o·nayl·luh
window	jossa on ikkuna	yos·suh on ik·ku·nuh

Directions

Where's the ...?   *Missä on ...?*   mis·sa on ...
bank	pankki	puhnk·ki
market	kauppatori	kowp·pa·to·ri
post office	postitoi- misto	pos·ti·toy· mis·to

Can you show me (on the map)?
Voitko näyttää sen minulle (kartalta)?   voyt·ko na·ewt·ta sen mi·nul·le (kar·tuhl·tuh)

Eating & Drinking

I'd like ..., please.   *Saisinko ...*   sai·sin·ko ...

SIGNS

Sisään	Entrance
Ulos	Exit
Avoinna	Open
Suljettu	Closed
Kielletty	Prohibited
WC	Toilets

a table for (four)	pöydän (neljälle)	peu·ew·dan (nel·yal·le)
the non-smoking section	savutto-malta puolelta	suh·vut·to·muhl·tuh pu·o·lel·tuh

Do you have vegetarian food?
Onko teillä kasvisruokia? — on·ko teyl·la kuhs·vis·ru·o·ki·uh

What would you recommend?
Mitä voit suositella? — mi·ta voyt su·o·si·tel·luh

I'll have a ...
Tilaan ... — ti·laan ...

Cheers!
Kippis! — kip·pis

I'd like (the) ..., please.	Saisinko ...	sai·sin·ko ...
bill	laskun	luhs·kun
drink list	juoma-listan	yu·o·muh·lis·tuhn
menu	ruokalistan	ru·o·kuh·lis·tuhn
that dish	tuon ruokalajin	tu·on ru·o·kuh·luh·yin

breakfast	aamiaisen	aa·mi·ai·sen
lunch	lounaan	loh·naan
dinner	illallisen	il·luhl·li·sen

bottle of (beer)	pullon (olutta)	pul·lon (o·lut·tuh)
(cup of) coffee	(kupin) kahvia	(ku·pin) kuh·vi·uh
glass of (wine)	lasillisen (viiniä)	luh·sil·li·sen (vee·ni·a)
(cup of) tea	(kupin) teetä	(ku·pin) tay·ta
(mineral) water	(kivennäis-) vettä	(ki·ven·na·is·) vet·ta

Emergencies

Help!	Apua!	uh·pu·uh
Go away!	Mene pois!	me·ne poys
Call ...!	Soittakaa paikalle ...!	soyt·tuh·kaa pai·kuhl·le ...

a doctor	lääkäri	la·ka·ri
the police	poliisi	po·lee·si

I'm lost.
Olen eksynyt. — o·len ek·sew·newt

Where are the toilets?
Missä on vessa? — mis·sa on ves·suh

Shopping & Services

I'm looking for ...
Etsin ... — et·sin ...

How much is it?
Mitä se maksaa? — mi·ta se muhk·saa

Can you write down the price?
Voitko kirjoittaa hinnan lapulle? — voyt·ko kir·yoyt·taa hin·nuhn luh·pul·le

That's too expensive.
Se on liian kallis. — se on lee·uhn kuhl·lis

It's faulty.
Se on viallinen. — se on vi·uhl·li·nen

There's a mistake in the bill.
Laskussa on virhe. — luhs·kus·suh on vir·he

Do you accept ...?	Voinko maksaa ...?	voyn·ko muhk·saa ...
credit cards	luotto-kortilla	lu·ot·to·kor·til·luh
travellers cheques	matka-sekillä	muht·kuh·se·kil·la

I'd like ..., please.	Saisinko ...	sai·sin·ko ...
a receipt	kuitin	ku·i·tin
my change	vaihto-rahat	vaih·to·ruh·huht

I'd like ..., please.	Haluaisin ...	huh·lu·ai·sin ...
a refund	vaihtaa tämän	vaih·taa ta·man
to return this	palauttaa tämän	puh·lowt·taa ta·man

Time, Dates & Weather

What time is it?
Paljonko kello on? — puhl·yon·ko kel·lo on

It's in the ...	Kello on ...	kel·lo on ...
morning	aamulla	aa·mul·luh
afternoon	iltapäivällä	il·tuh·pa·i·val·la
evening	illalla	il·luhl·luh

Monday	maanantai	maa·nuhn·tai
Tuesday	tiistai	tees·tai
Wednesday	keskiviikko	kes·ki·veek·ko
Thursday	torstai	tors·tai
Friday	perjantai	per·yuhn·tai
Saturday	lauantai	low·uhn·tai
Sunday	sunnuntai	sun·nun·tai

What's the weather like?

Millainen ilma siellä on?	mil·lai·nen il·muh si·el·la on

It's ...	Siellä ...	si·el·la ...
cold	on kylmä	on kewl·ma
hot	on kuuma	on koo·ma
raining	sataa	suh·taa
snowing	sataa lunta	suh·taa lun·tuh

Transport

Can we get there by public transport?

Pääseekö sinne julkisella liikenteellä?	paa·see·keu sin·ne yul·ki·sel·luh lee·ken·teel·la

Where can I buy a ticket?

Mistä voin ostaa lipun?	mis·ta voyn os·taa li·pun

One ... ticket, please.	Saisinko yhden ... lipun.	sai·sin·ko ewh·den ... li·pun
one-way	yksi-suuntaisen	ewk·si·soon·tai·sen
return	meno-paluu	me·no·pa·loo

My luggage has been ...	Matkata-varani ...	muht·kuh·tuh·vuh·ruh·ni ...
lost	ovat kadonneet	o·vuht kuh·don·nayt
stolen	on varastettu	on vuh·ruhs·tet·tu

Where does this ... go?	Minne tämä ... menee?	min·ne ta·ma ... me·nay
boat	laiva	lai·vuh
bus	bussi	bus·si
plane	lentokone	len·to·ko·ne
train	juna	yu·nuh

What time's the ... bus?	Mihin aikaan lähtee ... bussi?	mi·hin ai·kaan lah·tay ... bus·si

NUMBERS

1	yksi	ewk·si
2	kaksi	kuhk·si
3	kolme	kol·me
4	neljä	nel·ya
5	viisi	vee·si
6	kuusi	koo·si
7	seitsemän	sayt·se·man
8	kahdeksan	kuhk·dek·suhn
9	yhdeksän	ewh·dek·san
10	kymmenen	kewm·me·nen
20	kaksi-kymmentä	kuhk·si·kewm·men·ta
30	kolme-kymmentä	kol·me·kewm·men·ta
40	neljäkymmentä	nel·ya·kewm·men·ta
50	viisikymmentä	vee·si·kewm·men·ta
60	kuusikymmentä	koo·si·kewm·men·ta
70	seitsemän-kymmentä	sayt·se·man·kewm·men·ta
80	kahdeksan-kymmentä	kuhk·dek·suhn·kewm·men·ta
90	yhdeksän-kymmentä	ewh·dek·san·kewm·men·ta
100	sata	suh·tuh
1000	tuhat	tu·huht

first	ensimmäinen	en·sim·mai·nen
last	viimeinen	vee·may·nen
next	seuraava	se·u·raa·vuh

I'd like a taxi ...	Haluaisin tilata taksin ...	huh·lu·ai·sin ti·luh·tuh tuhk·sin ...
at (9am)	kello (yhdeksäksi aamulla)	kel·lo (ewh·dek·sak·si aa·mul·luh)
tomorrow	huomiseksi	hu·o·mi·sek·si

How much is it to ...?

Miten paljon maksaa matka ...?	mi·ten puhl·yon muhk·saa muht·kuh ...

Please take me to (this address).

Voitko viedä minut (tähän osoitteeseen).	voyt·ko vi·e·da mi·nut (ta·han o·soyt·tay·sayn)

Please stop here.

Pysähdy tässä.	pew·sah·dew tas·sa

LANGUAGE TRANSPORT

Behind the Scenes

SEND US YOUR FEEDBACK

We love to hear from travellers– your comments keep us on our toes and help make our books better. Our well-travelled team reads every word on what you loved or loathed about this book. Although we cannot reply individually to postal submissions, we always guarantee that your feedback goes straight to the appropriate authors, in time for the next edition. Each person who sends us information is thanked in the next edition – the most useful submissions are rewarded with a selection of digital PDF chapters.

Visit **lonelyplanet.com/contact** to submit your updates and suggestions or to ask for help. Our award-winning website also features inspirational travel stories, news and discussions.

Note: We may edit, reproduce and incorporate your comments in Lonely Planet products such as guidebooks, websites and digital products, so let us know if you don't want your comments reproduced or your name acknowledged. For a copy of our privacy policy visit lonelyplanet.com/privacy.

OUR READERS

Many thanks to the travellers who used the last edition and wrote to us with helpful hints, useful advice and interesting anecdotes:

Markku Alho, Federico Buldrini, Daniel Griffin, Jana Kocjan, Hilkka Laikko, Manuela Linder, Chiara Manenti, Bethan McIlroy, Lakhraj Minhas, Eirik Olsen, Harold Poylio, Helen Strong.

AUTHOR THANKS

Andy Symington

I owe a large *kiitos* to many across the country, including Iain, Teija, Jonah and Alex Campbell, and the Schulman family for generous hospitality, Eira Torvinen for great company and an excellent dossier, Satu Natunen, Alexis Kouros and Heikki Paltto for various contributions, Ari-Matti Piippo and Tuomo Polo for sterling bar research and Laura Klefbohm for Suomenlinna help. Various much-appreciated friends keep things well-oiled at home during my frequent absences, particularly Eduardo Cuadrado Diogo, José Eliseo Vázquez González, Mike Burren and Richard Prowse. Excellent co-author Catherine Le Nevez and editor Gemma Graham have been an absolute pleasure to work with and my parents are a constant support.

Catherine Le Nevez

Kiitos paljon/tack så mycket first and foremost to Julian, and to all of the locals, tourism professionals and fellow travellers who provided insights, inspiration and good times. Thanks especially to Maria and family in Turku, Raisa in Uusikaupunki (and Newcastle), Mark for the language lessons and René for the beers. Huge thanks too to ace coordinating author Andy Symington and destination editor Gemma Graham, and all at LP. As ever, *merci encore* to my parents, brother, *belle-sœur* and *neveu*.

ACKNOWLEDGMENTS

Climate map data adapted from Peel MC, Finlayson BL & McMahon TA (2007) 'Updated World Map of the Köppen-Geiger Climate Classification', *Hydrology and Earth System Sciences*, 11, 163344.

Cover photograph: Aurora borealis over the Pyhä-Luosto National Park, Nicholas Roemmelt/Getty

THIS BOOK

This 8th edition of Lonely Planet's *Finland* guidebook was researched and written by Andy Symington and Catherine Le Nevez. The previous edition was written by Andy Symington and Fran Parnell. This guidebook was produced by the following:

Destination Editor
Gemma Graham

Product Editor
Tracy Whitmey

Coordinating Editor
Kristin Odijk

Book Designer Wibowo Rusli

Senior Cartographer
Valentina Kremenchutskaya

Cartographer James Leversha

Assisting Editors Kate James, Kate Mathews, Gabrielle Stefanos, Jeanette Wall

Cover Researcher Naomi Parker

Thanks to Sasha Baskett, Ryan Evans, Larissa Frost, Claire Naylor, Karyn Noble, Martine Power, Samantha Tyson, Lauren Wellicome

Index

Map Legend

Sights
- Beach
- Bird Sanctuary
- Buddhist
- Castle/Palace
- Christian
- Confucian
- Hindu
- Islamic
- Jain
- Jewish
- Monument
- Museum/Gallery/Historic Building
- Ruin
- Shinto
- Sikh
- Taoist
- Winery/Vineyard
- Zoo/Wildlife Sanctuary
- Other Sight

Activities, Courses & Tours
- Bodysurfing
- Diving
- Canoeing/Kayaking
- Course/Tour
- Sento Hot Baths/Onsen
- Skiing
- Snorkelling
- Surfing
- Swimming/Pool
- Walking
- Windsurfing
- Other Activity

Sleeping
- Sleeping
- Camping

Eating
- Eating

Drinking & Nightlife
- Drinking & Nightlife
- Cafe

Entertainment
- Entertainment

Shopping
- Shopping

Information
- Bank
- Embassy/Consulate
- Hospital/Medical
- Internet
- Police
- Post Office
- Telephone
- Toilet
- Tourist Information
- Other Information

Geographic
- Beach
- Hut/Shelter
- Lighthouse
- Lookout
- Mountain/Volcano
- Oasis
- Park
- Pass
- Picnic Area
- Waterfall

Population
- Capital (National)
- Capital (State/Province)
- City/Large Town
- Town/Village

Transport
- Airport
- Border crossing
- Bus
- Cable car/Funicular
- Cycling
- Ferry
- Metro/MRT/MTR station
- Monorail
- Parking
- Petrol station
- Skytrain/Subway station
- Taxi
- Train station/Railway
- Tram
- Underground station
- Other Transport

Note: Not all symbols displayed above appear on the maps in this book

Routes
- Tollway
- Freeway
- Primary
- Secondary
- Tertiary
- Lane
- Unsealed road
- Road under construction
- Plaza/Mall
- Steps
- Tunnel
- Pedestrian overpass
- Walking Tour
- Walking Tour detour
- Path/Walking Trail

Boundaries
- International
- State/Province
- Disputed
- Regional/Suburb
- Marine Park
- Cliff
- Wall

Hydrography
- River, Creek
- Intermittent River
- Canal
- Water
- Dry/Salt/Intermittent Lake
- Reef

Areas
- Airport/Runway
- Beach/Desert
- Cemetery (Christian)
- Cemetery (Other)
- Glacier
- Mudflat
- Park/Forest
- Sight (Building)
- Sportsground
- Swamp/Mangrove

OUR STORY

A beat-up old car, a few dollars in the pocket and a sense of adventure. In 1972 that's all Tony and Maureen Wheeler needed for the trip of a lifetime – across Europe and Asia overland to Australia. It took several months, and at the end – broke but inspired – they sat at their kitchen table writing and stapling together their first travel guide, *Across Asia on the Cheap*. Within a week they'd sold 1500 copies. Lonely Planet was born.

Today, Lonely Planet has offices in Franklin, London, Melbourne, Oakland, Beijing and Delhi, with more than 600 staff and writers. We share Tony's belief that 'a great guidebook should do three things: inform, educate and amuse'.

OUR WRITERS

Andy Symington

Coordinating author, Helsinki; Tampere & Häme; The Lakeland; Oulu, Kainuu & Koillismaa; Lapland Andy has covered Finland for Lonely Planet several times, having first visited Helsinki many years ago more or less by accident. Walking on frozen lakes with the midday sun low in the sky made a quick and deep impression on him, even as fingers froze in the -30°C temperatures. Since then they can't keep him away, fuelled by a love of wilderness hiking, the *Kalevala,* huskies, saunas, Finnish mustard, moody Suomi rock and metal, but above all of Finnish people and their beautiful country.

Catherine Le Nevez

Turku & the South Coast; Åland Archipelago; Karelia; West Coast Catherine's wanderlust kicked in when she roadtripped across Europe aged four, and she's been hitting the road at every opportunity since, completing her Doctorate of Creative Arts in Writing, Masters in Professional Writing, and postgrad qualifications in Editing and Publishing along the way – as well as scores of Lonely Planet guidebooks and articles covering destinations throughout Europe and beyond. Having experienced Finland's freezing mid-winter temperatures, this trip's highlights included hitting the country's fabulous summer festivals and blissfully warm beaches.

Published by Lonely Planet Publications Pty Ltd
ABN 36 005 607 983
8th edition – May 2015
ISBN 978 1 74220 717 9
© Lonely Planet 2015   Photographs © as indicated 2015
10 9 8 7 6 5 4 3 2 1
Printed in China